Learning
Microsoft®
Excel 2013

Catherine Skintik

Teri Watanabe

Prentice Hall

Boston • Columbus • Indianapolis • New York • San Francisco • Upper Saddle River
Amsterdam • Cape Town • Dubai • London • Madrid • Milan • Munich • Paris • Montreal • Toronto
Delhi • Mexico City • Sao Paulo • Sydney • Hong Kong • Seoul • Singapore • Taipei • Tokyo

Editor in Chief: Michael Payne
Product Development Manager: Laura Burgess
Director of Business & Technology Marketing:
  Maggie Moylan Leen
Marketing Manager: Brad Forrester
Marketing Coordinator: Susan Osterlitz
Marketing Assistant: Darshika Vyas
Production Project Manager: Kayla Smith-Tarbox
Operations Director: Alexis Heydt

Senior Operations Specialist: Maura Zaldivar-Garcia
Text and Cover Designer: Vanessa Moore
Media Project Manager, Production: Renata Butera
Editorial and Product Development: Emergent Learning, LLC
Composition: Vanessa Moore
Printer/Binder: Webcrafters, Inc.
Cover Printer: Lehigh-Pheonix Color
Text: 10/12 Helvetica

Credits and acknowledgements borrowed from other sources and reproduced, with permission, in this textbook are as follows: All photos courtesy of Shutterstock.com.

Microsoft® and Windows® are registered trademarks of the Microsoft Corporation in the U.S.A. and other countries. Screen shots and icons reprinted with permission from the Microsoft Corporation. This book is not sponsored or endorsed by or affiliated with the Microsoft Corporation.

ISBN 10: 0-13-314910-2

ISBN 13: 978-0-13-314910-4

1 2 3 4 5 6 7 8 9 10   V064   16 15 14 13

Table of Contents

Introduction

Microsoft Office 2013 is Microsoft's suite of application software. The Standard version includes Word, Excel, Outlook, and PowerPoint. Other editions may also include Access, Publisher, OneNote, and InfoPath. This book covers Excel (the spreadsheet tool). Because Microsoft Office is an integrated suite, the components can all be used separately or together to create professional-looking documents and to manage data.

How the Book Is Organized

Learning Microsoft Excel 2013 is made up of eleven chapters. Chapters are comprised of short lessons designed for using Microsoft Excel 2013 in real-life business settings. Each lesson is made up of six key elements:

- **What You Will Learn.** Each lesson starts with an overview of the learning objectives covered in the lesson.

- **Words to Know.** Key terms are included and defined at the start of each lesson, so you can quickly refer back to them. The terms are then highlighted in the text.

- **What You Can Do.** Concise notes for learning the computer concepts.

- **Try It.** Hands-on practice activities provide brief procedures to teach all necessary skills.

- **Practice.** These projects give students a chance to create documents, spreadsheets, database objects, and presentations by entering information. Steps provide all the how-to information needed to complete a project.

- **Apply.** Each lesson concludes with a project that challenges students to apply what they have learned through steps that tell them what to do, without all the how-to information. In the Apply projects, students must show they have mastered each skill set.

- Each chapter ends with two assessment projects: **Critical Thinking** and **Portfolio Builder**, which incorporate all the skills covered throughout the chapter.

Working with Data and Solution Files

As you work through the projects in this book, you'll be creating, opening, and saving files. You should keep the following instructions in mind:

- For many of the projects, you will use data files. The data files can be accessed from the Companion Web site (www.pearsonhighered.com/learningseries). Other projects will ask you to create new documents and files and then enter text and data into them, so you can master creating documents from scratch.

- The data files are used so that you can focus on the skills being introduced—not on keyboarding lengthy documents.

- When the project steps tell you to open a file name, you open the data file provided.

- All the projects instruct you to save the files created or to save the project files under a new name. This is to make the project file your own and to avoid overwriting the data file in the storage location. Throughout this book, when naming files and folders, replace *xx* with your name or initials as instructed by your teacher.

- Follow your instructor's directions for where to access and save the files on a network, local computer hard drive, or portable storage device such as a USB drive.

- Many of the projects also provide instructions for including your name in a header or footer. Again, this is to identify the project work as your own for grading and assessment purposes.

- Unless the book instructs otherwise, use the default settings for text size, margin size, and so on when creating a file. If someone has changed the default software settings for the computer you're using, your exercise files may not look the same as those shown in this book. In addition, the appearance of your files may look different if the system is set to a screen resolution other than 1024 × 768.

Companion Web Site (www.pearsonhighered.com/learningseries)

The Companion Web site includes additional resources to be used in conjunction with the book and to supplement the material in the book. The Companion Web site includes:

- Data files for many of the projects.
- Glossary of all the key terms from the book.
- Microsoft Office Specialist (MOS) correlations.
- Puzzles correlated to the chapters in the book.

Navigating the Textbook and Supplemental Print Resources

Lesson 39

Working with File Formats

> ### ➤ What You Will Learn
>
> Ensuring Backward-Compatibility in a Workbook
> Importing a File
> Saving Excel Data in CSV File Format
> Saving a Workbook As a PDF or an XPS File
> Sending a Workbook
> Sharing a Workbook

Software Skills
Each lesson begins with an introduction to the computer skills that will be covered in the lesson.

Words to Know
Vocabulary terms are listed at the start of each lesson for easy reference and appear in bold in the text on first use.

What You Can Do
The technology concepts are introduced and explained.

WORDS TO KNOW

CSV format
CSV stands for comma-separated value. A CSV file is a file format in which text is separated by commas. It is also known as a comma delimited file.

PDF format
PDF stands for Portable Document Format. It is a file format that preserves the original layout and formatting of most documents, so they can be viewed and shared.

XPS file
XPS stands for XML Paper Specification. This format retains the look and feel of an electronic document, much like electronic paper.

Software Skills   If you share Excel data, you can save that data in a format that's compatible with the program someone else is using, such as an older version of Excel. You can save your Excel data in many different formats, and use the Compatibility Checker to ensure that everything will work in the older program.

What You Can Do

Ensuring Backward-Compatibility in a Workbook

- Sometimes saving your workbook in a different format will result in a loss of some data—typically formatting changes.
- You can see which features might be lost before resaving a workbook in an older version of Excel by running Check Compatibility first.
- Check Compatibility scans the workbook, and lists any incompatibilities and the number of occurrences of an incompatibility.
  - Incompatibilities are grouped by severity.
  - You can copy this list of incompatibilities to a sheet in the workbook for further review.
- You can click the Find link in the Compatibility Checker to have Excel show you where the problem is.
- The Compatibility Checker will warn you if there are features or formatting that are not supported by the selected file format.
- For example, if you check the compatibility of an Excel 2003 worksheet and receive the formatting warning, in most cases, the worksheet will function properly in Excel 2003; it just might look a bit different.
  - ✓ It's always best to test a converted workbook to make sure that it looks and works as you want it to before you send it to anyone.

End-of-Chapter Activities

Topics include a variety of business, career, and college-readiness scenarios. Critical-thinking skills are required to complete the project.

Directions

Projects challenge students to apply what they have learned through steps that tell what needs to be done, without all the how-to information.

End-of-Chapter Activities

➤ Excel Chapter 10—Critical Thinking

Assessing Educational Outcomes

Your school has been working hard to raise test scores in Math and Science, and one of the projects your teachers have undertaken this year involves doing a series of assessments that track a series of results in Math and Science classes.

You have been given a workbook that someone else created, so you want to check the workbook for data integrity and accessibility. Because a variety of teachers will be adding values to the worksheet, you need to set up the file for track changes and sharing. You also want to use data validation rules to circle the failing scores and make them easier to identify. You will encrypt the file and save it to a Windows Live SkyDrive account so all teachers can access the file from home as well as school.

DIRECTIONS

1. Start Excel, if necessary, and open ECT10 from the data files for this chapter.
2. Save the file as ECT10_xx in the location where your teacher has instructed you to save files for this chapter.
3. Inspect the workbook for issues. Do not remove any of the document properties or personal information.
4. Check and correct any accessibility issues.
5. Click REVIEW, and turn on the sharing feature.
6. Set Track Changes to highlight all changes that are introduced. In the When box, select All.
7. Make changes to the values in column E.
8. Save the file, and use Highlight Changes to display the change history on a new sheet.
9. View the change history.
10. Remove sharing from the workbook.
11. In cell I22, add a digital signature line, and in the suggested signer box, type Approver for assessment scores.
12. For all cells with scores, add data validation for a whole number that is greater than or equal to 25. Circle the invalid data of failing percentages.
13. Save the file, and then save the file to your Windows Live SkyDrive account as ECT10_webapp_xx. Close the Excel workbook, and close Excel.
14. Open your Web browser, and go to https://skydrive.live.com.

    ✓ Check with your instructor before you access the Web. Depending on the security settings for your computer lab, you may be limited in the types of sites you can access and use.

15. Log in to your Windows Live SkyDrive account, and open the workbook.
16. Click OK to remove the data validation and digital signature objects from the file.
17. Edit the file in the browser by making changes to the values, and save the file. Your file should look similar to Illustration 10A on the next page.
18. **With your teacher's permission,** print the workbook, and write your name and today's date on the printout.
19. Close the browser to sign out of SkyDrive.

Teacher's Manual

The Teacher's Manual includes teaching strategies, tips, and supplemental material.

Lesson 70   Importing Data into Excel

What You Will Learn
- ✓ Importing Data from an Access Database
- ✓ Importing Data from a Web Page
- ✓ Importing Data from a Text File
- ✓ Importing Data from an XML File

Words to Know
Database	Markup language
Datasheet	Table
Delimited	Record
Delimiter character	XML
Field	

Tips, Hints, and Pointers
- Discuss each of the skills listed in the What You Will Learn section, and ask students if they have used any of these skills before.
- Inform students that they will use the skills covered in this lesson to complete the end-of-lesson Practice and Apply projects. Encourage them to ask questions if they are not sure about a topic covered or how to use a certain feature.
- **CUSTOMIZED INSTRUCTION: English Language Learners:** Have students make flashcards of the *Words to Know*, writing the term on one side and the definition on the other.

Importing Data from an Access Database
- Explain to students that because you can set up Excel ranges as tables, you can perform many of the same database tasks on worksheet data as you would on table data in a database.
- Point out the records (rows) and fields (columns) in the datasheet shown in Figure 70-1.
- **Try It! Importing Data from an Access Database, Step 1:** Point out to students that the workbook does not contain data yet, but they will import data from various sources to the designated worksheets.
- **Step 4:** If necessary, remind students where the data files for this lesson are stored. Point out the extension .accdb on Access database files.

Importing Data from a Web Page
- Discuss situations in which a user might want to copy data from a Web page into Excel. "Data" may consist of tabular data, text, hyperlinks, or even graphics.
- Caution students that Web page copyrights must be respected; no user should ever copy data from a Web page and pass it off as his or her own data. When data is copied for a report or other publication, proper permission should be secured and the source of the data should be indicated.
- Have students log in to their browser's start page and practice copying information from this page and pasting it in an Excel worksheet. Or, you might have students visit your school's home page from which they can copy information.
- **Try It! Importing Data from a Web Page:** Note that students will need Internet access in order to complete this exercise.
- **CURRICULUM CONNECTION:** When traveling abroad or conducting business internationally, it is important to know the exchange rate for converting American dollars to other currency. In some countries, the dollar will be worth more, and in others it will be less. Exchange rates change daily, but usually not by much.

  Have students look up the exchange rate of American dollars to Australian dollars. They should create a worksheet that lists the price of at least five items that they use on a regular basis and then use the conversion formula to list the equivalent cost of the same item in Australian dollars. Encourage them to expand the worksheet to include other foreign currency, such as the euro, or the Japanese yen.

Tips, Hints, and Pointers
These items help explain the content and provide additional information for instructors to use in the classroom.

Customized Instruction
Support for English Language Learners, Less Advanced Students, More Advanced Students, and Special Needs Students is provided throughout.

Skills Extension
These discussion topics relate directly and indirectly to the content on the current page.

Test Book with TestGen CD-ROM

Print tests include a pretest, posttest, and two application tests for each chapter in the student edition. Accompanying CD-ROM includes test-generator software so that instructors can create concept tests correlated to the chapters in the book.

Excel 2013	Chapter 5: Advanced Formatting and Workbook Features
Application Test 5A	• Use Paste Special Command Options • Transpose and Format Data
	• Switch Between Open Workbooks • Link Excel Files
	• Add a Footer • Set Print Options • Change Page Setup • Save as a PDF

✔ **Directions:**

Use Excel to complete the exercise below by carefully following all directions. Check all data after entry. (Time: 40 minutes. Point Scale: –2 for each formatting error; –5 per incorrect formula or transposition.)

The Stevens household wants to use its current Annual Budget to project the effects of a 5% or 7% increase in income and expenses. You will insert rows, format data, enter formulas, and transpose summary data. You will also add a graphic and save the worksheet in a different file format.

Directions

Steps tell students what to do, without all of the how-to detail, so critical-thinking skills must be used.

Open a Workbook and Add Rows
1. Start Excel, if necessary.
2. Open **XTEST5A** from the data files.
3. Enter **XTEST5A** in cell A1 and your name in cell A2. Apply bold to cell A1.
4. Save the workbook as **X5A1_xx** in the location where your teacher instructs you to store files.
5. Insert a blank row above and below the TOTAL INCOME line.
6. Insert a blank row above TOTAL EXPENSES.
7. Insert a blank row above NET SAVINGS.

Create Formulas to Project Increases
1. Enter a formula to find the 5% Projected Increase for Income from Salaries in cell E8.
   *Hint: =Current Year * 105% (1.05)*
2. Copy the formula for each budget item, but not the totals.
3. Enter a formula to find the 7% Projected Increase for Income from Salaries.
4. Copy the formula for each budget item, but not the totals.
5. Copy the formula for TOTAL INCOME from cell D13 to cells E13 and F13.
6. Copy the formula for TOTAL EXPENSES from cell D26 to cells E26 and F26.
7. Copy the formula for NET SAVINGS from cell D28 to cells E28 and F28.
8. Format all the values as currency with two decimal places and use the dollar sign symbol.
9. Adjust column widths, if necessary.
10. Right-align and bold column headings on the top and bottom tables.
11. Save the changes.

Transpose Copied Data
1. Transpose the Total Income data from cells D13:F13 in the Annual Budget to cells C34:C36 in the Summary of Projections table at the bottom of the worksheet using Transpose on the Paste drop-down list in the Clipboard group of the HOME tab.
2. Transpose the Total Expenses data from cells D26:F26 in the Annual Budget to cells D34:D36 in the Summary of Projections table at the bottom of the worksheet.
3. Transpose the Net Savings data from cells D28:F28 in the Annual Budget to cells E34:E36 in the Summary of Projections table at the bottom of the worksheet.
4. Format the transposed data as currency with two decimal places and use the dollar sign symbol if Excel doesn't apply the formatting for you automatically.
5. Adjust column widths, if necessary.
6. Save the changes.

Create a New Workbook and Link Data
1. Create a new, blank workbook file.
2. Save the workbook as **X5A2_xx** in the location where your teacher instructs you to store files.
3. Enter the following data in Sheet1 of the new workbook, starting from cell A1:

Card Name	Monthly Payment
MasterCharge	650
VEESA	350
Discova	115
Monthly Total	
Annual Total	

4. Adjust column widths as needed.

55

Solutions Manual   Contains final solution illustrations for all of the projects in the student textbook. Accompanying CD-ROM contains solution files in electronic format.

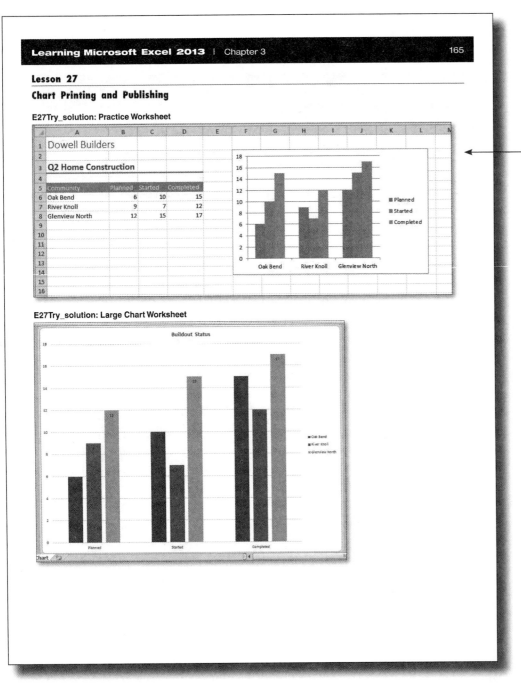

Solution Illustrations

Instructors can use the end-result illustrations to do a visual check of students' work.

Learning Microsoft® Excel 2013

(Courtesy Goodluz/Shutterstock)

Using the Common Features of Microsoft Office 2013

Lesson 1
Microsoft Office 2013 Basics

- Analyzing Information Technology
- Analyzing Microsoft Office 2013
- Using the Mouse
- Using Touch Mode
- Using the Keyboard
- Analyzing Data Storage
- Navigating with Windows Explorer
- Creating and Deleting a Folder
- Starting a Microsoft Office Program, Creating a Blank File, and Exiting the Program

Lesson 2
Saving, Printing, and Closing Microsoft Office Files

- Identifying Common Microsoft Office Screen Elements
- Entering and Editing Text
- Correcting Errors
- Saving a File
- Printing a File
- Closing a File

Lesson 3
Working with Existing Files

- Opening an Existing File
- Saving a File with a New Name
- Viewing File Properties
- Using the Ribbon
- Using Access Keys
- Selecting Text
- Formatting Text

Lesson 4
Using Command Options

- Using the Quick Access Toolbar
- Using the Mini Toolbar
- Using Shortcut Menus
- Using Dialog Box Options
- Using Task Panes
- Formatting Pages

Lesson 5
Managing Program Windows

- Changing the View
- Using Window Controls
- Zooming
- Scrolling
- Using Multiple Windows
- Using the Microsoft Office Clipboard

Lesson 6
Using Microsoft Office Help

- Using Microsoft Office Help
- Searching for Help
- Using the Help Table of Contents
- Viewing Application Options
- Customizing the Ribbon
- Using AutoRecover and Autosave

Lesson 7
Managing Information Technology

- Copying Files and Folders
- Moving Files and Folders
- Compressing Files
- Recognizing Types of Business Documents
- Determining the Risks and Rewards of Developing an IT Strategy
- Identifying Needed Equipment and Supplies
- Establishing, Scheduling, and Following Maintenance Procedures

End-of-Chapter Activities

Lesson 1

Microsoft Office 2013 Basics

➤ **What You Will Learn**

Analyzing Information Technology
Analyzing Microsoft Office 2013
Using the Mouse
Using the Keyboard
Navigating with Windows Explorer
Creating and Deleting a Folder
Starting and Exiting Microsoft Office Programs

Software Skills   Anyone trying to succeed in today's competitive business world benefits from an understanding of information technology. A good place to start is by learning how to use Microsoft® Office 2013, a suite of programs that may be used independently or together to create simple documents, such as letters and memos, as well as complex reports, data tables, and budget spreadsheets.

What You Can Do

Analyzing Information Technology

■ **Information technology,** or IT, refers to the use of computers to collect, store, and distribute information.

■ **Communications technology** is part of information technology. It refers to the use of technology to make communication easier and more efficient.

■ Businesses rely on technology of many types to make sure employees have the tools they need to complete assignments, tasks, and other responsibilities.

■ Technology purchases include **hardware** and **software**.

■ At the very least, almost all businesses require a computer, a printer, a connection to the Internet, and software such as Microsoft Office for basic business applications, such as word processing, data management, and spreadsheet functions.

■ Other IT needs depend on the type and size of business. Some common IT equipment includes **scanners** to convert printed material to digital format. Some businesses may use other input devices such as voice recognition software, digital cameras, touch screen monitors or tablet PCs, and microphones.

- Other technology a company might need includes projectors, bar code readers, cash registers, and video conferencing systems.
- Departments must evaluate the needs of each employee, research the available technologies and then purchase and install the appropriate systems. They must also be sure employees know how to use the new systems.
- Requirements vary from department to department and from company to company. For example, a large financial services company will have different technology needs than a small travel agency.
- When evaluating technology, consider the following:
  - Tasks you need to accomplish
  - Cost
  - Ease-of-use
  - Compatibility with existing systems
- You can learn more about hardware and software technology using the Internet, consulting a magazine or buyer's guide, or by visiting a retailer in your area to talk to a salesperson.

Analyzing Microsoft Office 2013

- Microsoft Office 2013 is a newest version of the popular Microsoft Office **software suite**.
- You use the Microsoft Office programs for many business tasks, including to create various types of documents, to communicate with co-workers and customers, and to store and manage information.
- The Microsoft Office 2013 software suite is available in different editions.
- Most editions include the following core Microsoft Office programs:
  - Microsoft® Word, a word processing program.
  - Microsoft® Excel®, a spreadsheet program.
  - Microsoft® PowerPoint®, a presentation graphics program.
  - Microsoft® Outlook®, a personal information manager and communications program.
- Some editions may include the following additional programs:
  - Microsoft® Access®, a database application.
  - Microsoft® Publisher, a desktop publishing program.
  - Microsoft® OneNote®, a note-taking and management program.
  - Microsoft® InfoPath™, an information gathering and management program.
- This book covers the most commonly used programs in the Microsoft Office 2013 suite: Word, Excel, Access, and PowerPoint.
- Microsoft Office 2013 runs with the Microsoft® Windows® 8 or Microsoft® Windows® 7 operating system.
- There may be slight differences in the programs depending on the operating system you are using.
- For example, features that involve browsing for storage locations are different depending on the operating system. This includes opening and saving a file, and selecting a file to insert.

Information technology (IT)
The use of computers to collect, store, and distribute information. Also the various technologies used in processing, storing, and communicating business and personal information.

Insertion point
The flashing vertical line that indicates where typed text will display.

Library
In Microsoft Windows 7 and above, a location where you can view files and folders that are actually stored in other locations on your computer system.

Menu
A list of commands or choices.

Mouse
A device that allows you to select items onscreen by pointing at them with the mouse pointer.

Mouse pad
A smooth, cushioned surface on which you slide a mouse.

Mouse pointer
A marker on your computer screen that shows you where the next mouse action will occur.

Object
Icon, menu, or other item that is part of an onscreen interface.

Random access memory (RAM)
Temporary memory a computer uses to store information while it is processing.

Read-only memory (ROM)
Fixed memory stored on a chip in a computer that provides startup and other system instructions.

Scanner
A device that converts printed documents into digital file formats.

Scroll
To page through a document in order to view contents that is not currently displayed.

Scroll wheel
A wheel on some mouse devices used to navigate through a document onscreen.

Software
Programs that provide the instructions for a computer or other hardware device.

- In addition, there may be some visual differences in the way the programs look onscreen.
- The procedures in this book assume you are using Microsoft Windows 8. Ask your teacher for information on procedures that may be different on systems using Windows 7.

Using the Mouse

- Use your **mouse** to point to and select commands and features of Microsoft Office 2013 programs.
- Most mouse devices work using light. Some older models work by sliding a tracking ball on your desk.
- Notebook computers may have a touchpad or trackball to move the pointer on the screen in place of a mouse.
- When you move the mouse on your desk, the **mouse pointer** moves onscreen. For example, when you move the mouse to the left, the mouse pointer moves to the left.
- Hovering the pointer over an **object** such as an **icon** or menu name usually displays a ScreenTip that identifies the object.
- When you click a mouse button, the program executes a command. For example, when you move the mouse pointer to the Save button and then click, the program saves the current document or file.
- Clicking a mouse button can also be used to move the **insertion point** to a new location.
- A mouse may have one, two, or three buttons. Unless otherwise noted, references in this book are to the use of the left mouse button.
- Your mouse might have a **scroll wheel**. Spin the scroll wheel to **scroll**—move—through the file open on your screen.

Table 1-1	Mouse Actions
Point to.	Move mouse pointer to touch specified element.
Click.	Point to element then press and release left mouse button.
Right-click	Point to element then press and release right mouse button.
Double-click.	Point to element then press and release left mouse button twice in rapid succession.
Drag.	Point to element, hold down left mouse button, then move mouse pointer to new location.
Drop.	Release the mouse button after dragging.
Scroll	Rotate center wheel backward to scroll down, or forward to scroll up.
Pan	Press center wheel and drag up or down.
Auto-Scroll.	Click center wheel to scroll down; move pointer up to scroll up.
Zoom	Hold down Ctrl and rotate center wheel.

- The mouse pointer changes shape depending on the program in use, the object being pointed to, and the action being performed. Common mouse pointer shapes include an arrow for selecting ☒, an I-beam ☒, and a hand with a pointing finger ☒ to indicate a **hyperlink**.
- You should use a mouse on a **mouse pad** that is designed specifically to make it easy to slide the mouse.
- You can move the mouse without moving the mouse pointer by picking it up. This is useful if you move the mouse too close to the edge of the mouse pad or desk.

Try It!   Using the Mouse

① Start your computer if it is not already on. Log in to your user account, if necessary.

  ✓ *Ask your teacher how to log in to your user account.*

② Click the Desktop tile on the Windows 8 Start screen.

  ✓ *If you are using Windows 7, skip step 2.*

③ Move the mouse pointer to point at the Recycle Bin icon.

④ Right-click the Recycle Bin icon. A shortcut menu displays (see picture at right).

⑤ On the shortcut menu, click Open. The Recycle Bin window opens and displays files and folders that have been deleted.

⑥ Click the Close button ☒ in the upper-right corner of the Recycle Bin window.

⑦ Double-click the Recycle Bin icon. This is another method of opening an object.

  ✓ *Some systems are set to open objects with a single click.*

⑧ Click the Close button ☒ in the upper-right corner of the Recycle Bin window.

Right-click to display a shortcut menu

Using a Touch Screen

- If you are using the Windows 8 operating system on a device with a touch screen, you can use touch mode.
- With touch mode, you use your fingers or a **stylus pen** instead of a mouse.
- The basic gestures for interacting with a touch screen are tap and swipe.
- Tap means to gently touch the screen and then lift straight up. A tap is similar to a mouse click.
- Swipe means to slide your finger or pen across the screen.
- See Table 1-2 on the next page for more information on touch screen gestures.

Software suite
A group of software programs sold as a single unit. Usually the programs have common features that make it easy to integrate and share data.

Storage
A computer device or component used to store data such as programs and files.

Stylus pen
A pen shaped device used to interact with a touch screen.

Subfolder
A folder stored within another folder.

Template
A document that contains formatting, styles, and sample text that you can use to create new documents.

Window
The area onscreen where a program or document is displayed.

Table 1-2	**Touch Gestures**
Tap.	Tap once on an item. This opens or selects the item that is tapped.
Press and hold.	Press down and hold for a few seconds. This selects an item (such as an icon), displays a ScreenTip, or opens a shortcut menu.
Pinch or stretch	Touch with two or more fingers and move the fingers closer (pinch) or apart (stretch). This displays different levels of information or zooms in or out.
Swipe to scroll	Drag across the screen. This scrolls in the direction you drag.
Swipe to select.	Quickly drag a short stroke in the opposite direction you would swipe to scroll. This selects an item.
Swipe from edge . . .	Start on an edge and swipe in. Results vary depending on the edge.

Try It!   **Using a Touch Screen**

❶ Start your computer if it is not already on. Log into your user account, if necessary.

   ✓ Ask your teacher how to log in to your user account.

❷ Swipe from right to left to scroll the Start screen.

❸ Swipe from left to right to scroll back.

❹ Tap the Desktop tile to display the desktop.

❺ Press and hold the Recycle Bin icon.

❻ Tap Open on the shortcut menu.

❼ Tap the Close button in the upper-right corner of the Recycle Bin window.

Using the Keyboard

- Use your keyboard to type characters, including letters, numbers, and symbols. The keyboard can also be used to access program commands and features.
- On a touch-enabled device, you can display a touch keyboard by tapping the Touch Keyboard button on the Taskbar.
- Function keys (F1–F12) often appear in a row above the numbers at the top of the keyboard. They can be used as shortcut keys to perform certain tasks.
- Modifier keys such as Shift, Alt, and Ctrl are used in combination with other keys or mouse actions to select certain commands or perform actions. In this book, key combinations are shown as: the modifier key followed by a plus sign followed by the other key or mouse action. For example, CTRL + S is the key combination for saving the **current file**.
- The 17-key keypad to the right of the main group of keyboard keys on an enhanced keyboard includes the numeric keys.

- Most notebook computers and portable devices integrate the numeric keys into the regular keyboard.
- When the Num Lock feature is on, the keypad can be used to enter numbers. When the feature is off, the keys can be used as directional keys to move the insertion point in the current file.
- The Escape key ESC is used to cancel a command.
- Use the Enter key ENTER to execute a command or to start a new paragraph when typing text.
- Directional keys are used to move the insertion point.
- Editing keys such as Insert INS, Delete DEL, and Backspace BACKSPACE are used to insert or delete text.
- The Windows key (sometimes called the Winkey or the Windows Logo key) is used alone to open the Windows Start **menu**, or in combination with other keys to execute certain Windows commands.
- The Application key is used alone to open a shortcut menu, or in combination with other keys to execute certain application commands.
- Some keyboards also have keys for opening shortcut menus, launching a Web browser, or opening an e-mail program.

| Try It! | **Using the Keyboard** |

1 Press ⌨ on your keyboard to open the Start screen.

✓ *On a touch-enabled device, tap the Touch Keyboard button on the Taskbar to display the keyboard.*

2 Press TAB twice to select the first tile.

3 Press the up- down-, left-, and right-arrow keys to select different tiles; stop when the Calendar tile is selected.

4 Press ENTER to open the Calendar app window.

5 Press ALT + F4 to close the window.

6 Press ESC to close the Start Screen and display the desktop.

Analyzing Data Storage

- Data **storage** is any device or component which can record and retain data, or information.

- Without storage, you would not be able to save files or access computer programs.

- Storage capacity is measured in bytes. One **byte** is equal to about one character.

- A typical hard disk drive today may have a capacity of 3 terabytes (TB) or more!

- The type of storage you have available depends on your computer system.

- Some common storage devices include the following:

  - Internal hard disk drive, which is a device mounted inside a computer, and used to store programs and data files.

  - External hard disk drive, which is similar to an internal hard disk drive except that it connects to the outside of the computer via a cable and a port, such as a Universal Serial Bus (USB).

  - Network drive, which is a hard disk drive attached to a network, Computers attached to the same network can access the information on the drive.

  - Flash drive, which is a small, portable device that can be attached to a USB port on the outside of a computer. A flash drive is convenient for transporting files from one computer to another.

  - Memory card, which is a small card that is usually inserted into a slot in a computer or other device, such as a digital camera or printer.

  - DVD, which is a disk that you insert into a DVD drive to record or read data. DVDs are often used for storing video, music, and pictures.

  - CD, which is an older form of storage disk.

  - Virtual drive, which is an area on a storage device that is identified as a separate drive.

  - Online storage, which allows you to save, access, and share data using storage space on the Internet. The data is protected from unauthorized access using a password. For example, SkyDrive, offered by Microsoft Corp., allows free access to up to 25 GB of online storage for saving and sharing files.

- Memory is also a type of storage. There are two types of computer memory:

  - **Read-only memory** (ROM) which is stored on a chip inside the computer. It provides the instructions your computer needs to start and begin operation, and it cannot be changed under normal circumstances,

  - **Random access memory** (RAM) is the temporary memory your computer uses to store information it is currently processing. Information stored in RAM is lost when then computer shuts down; you must save it on a storage device if you want to use it in the future.

Navigating with File Explorer

- You use File Explorer, a feature of the Windows 8 operating system, to navigate among your system components to find and use the information you need.

  ✓ *If you are using Windows 7, the navigation program is called Windows Explorer. The interface is slightly different. Ask your teacher for information on using Windows 7.*

- For example, you navigate to a storage device such as a disk drive to locate and open a file or program. You navigate to an output device such as a printer to perform maintenance, adjust settings, or use the device.

■ Windows comes with built-in **folders** that organize your computer components to make it easier to find the object you need. When you open a folder in File Explorer, its contents display in a **window** on your monitor.

■ For example, open the Computer folder window in File Explorer to display devices such as hard disk drives. Open the Libraries folder window to display **libraries** organized on your system. Open the Network window to display the devices connected to the same network as your system.

■ To select an item displayed in a window, click it. To open an item, double-click it.

  ✓ *This book assumes your system is set to open an object using a double click. If your system is set to open an object on a single click, you will use that method instead.*

  ✓ *This book assumes you are using a mouse. If you are using a touch-enabled device, you will use your finger or a pen instead.*

■ Every computer system has different components. For example, one system might have a DVD drive, and another system might not. One might connect to a networked printer, while another has a printer directly connected to a USB port. No matter what the system components might be, the methods for navigating are the same:

  ● Use the Back ⊕ and Forward ⊕ buttons to move through windows you have opened recently.

  ● Use the Recent Locations menu to go directly to a window you have opened recently.

  ● Click a location in the Address bar to open it.

  ● Click an arrow between locations in the Address bar to display a menu, then click a location on the menu to open it.

  ● Each window displays a navigation pane which provides links to common locations. Click a location in the Navigation pane to display its contents in the window.

Try It!   **Navigating with File Explorer**

1 If you have a removable storage device to use for storing your work in this class, connect it to your computer. For example, insert a removable disk in a drive, or connect a flash drive to a USB port.

2 If necessary, press ⌷ESC⌷ to switch from the Windows start screen to the desktop. Click the File Explorer icon 🗎 on the Taskbar.

3 Click Computer in the Navigation pane of the File Explorer window to open the Computer window to view the storage devices that are part of your computer system.

  OR

  If you are storing your work for this class on a network location, click Network in the Navigation pane to open the Network window to view the components that are part of your computer network.

  ✓ *The Computer and Network components are specific to your system and may be different from those shown in the illustration.*

4 In the Content pane of the open window, double-click the location where you are storing your work for this class. For example, double-click the icon for the removable device you connected in step 1.

5 Click the Back button ⊕ above the navigation pane to display the previous storage location.

6 Click the Forward button ⊕ to move forward to the last window you had opened.

7 Click the Close button ✖ to close the window. If other windows are open, close them as well.

(continued)

Try It!   Navigating with File Explorer *(continued)*

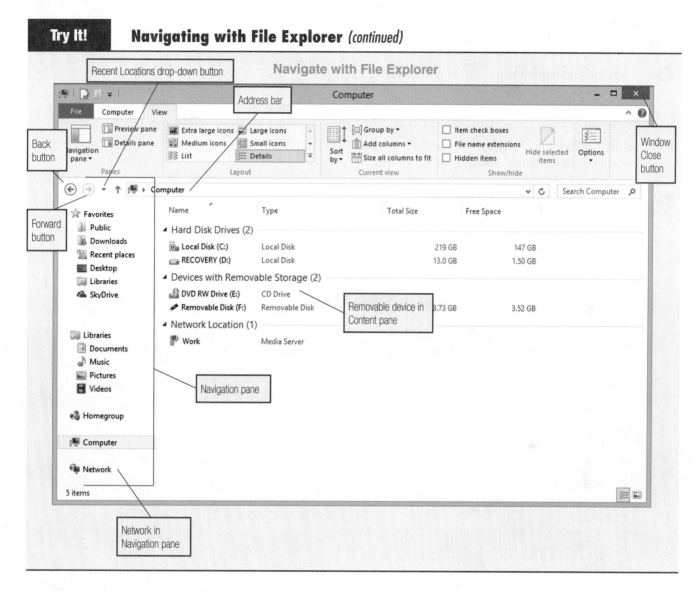

Navigate with File Explorer

Recent Locations drop-down button

Address bar

Back button

Window Close button

Forward button

Removable device in Content pane

Navigation pane

Network in Navigation pane

Creating and Deleting a Folder

■ A folder is a named location on a storage device that you create using the Windows operating system.

■ To create a folder, you specify where you want it on your computer system, and then give it a name.

■ Folders help you keep your data organized, and make it easier to find the files you need when you need them.

■ For example, you might store all the documents you use for planning a budget in a folder named Budget. You might store all the documents you use for a marketing project in a folder named Marketing Project.

■ You can create a folder within an existing folder to set up layers of organization. A folder within another folder may be called a **subfolder**.

■ You can delete a folder you no longer need. Deleting removes the folder from its current location and stores it in the Recycle Bin.

Try It!   **Creating a Folder**

1 Click the File Explorer icon 🖾 on the Taskbar, and then Computer in the Navigation pane. If you are storing files on a network location, click Network.

2 In the Content pane of the open window, double-click the location where you are storing your work for this class.

3 Click the Home tab on the Ribbon. In the New group, click the New Folder button 📁 .

OR

a. Right-click a blank area of the window.

b. Click New.

c. Click Folder.

OR

■ Click the New Folder button 📁 on the Quick Access Toolbar.

4 Type **B01Try**.

5 Press `ENTER` .

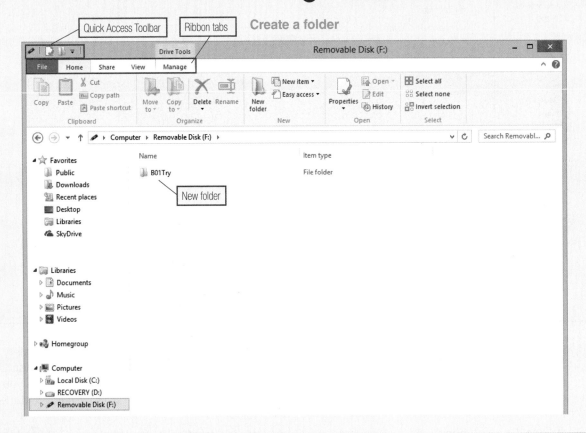

Create a folder

Try It!   **Deleting a Folder**

1 Right-click the **B01Try** folder.

2 Click Delete on the shortcut menu.

3 Click Yes to move the folder to the Recycle Bin.

4 Click the Close button █✕█ in the storage location window to close File Explorer.

Starting a Microsoft Office Program, Creating a Blank File, and Exiting the Program

- ■ To use a Microsoft Office 2013 program you must first start it so it is running on your computer.
- ■ Use Windows to start a Microsoft Office program.
- ■ The way you start a Microsoft Office program depends on your system configuration.
  - You will usually find the program's tile on your Windows Start screen. Click the tile to start the program.
  - If the program shortcut icon displays on your Windows desktop, you can click the Desktop tile on the Start screen, and then double-click the program icon.

- If the program icon has been added to the Taskbar, you can display the desktop and click the program icon on the Taskbar.
- If the program is not available on the Start screen or the desktop, you will find it on the Apps screen. The Apps screen lists all installed apps and programs alphabetically. Scroll to locate the Microsoft Office 2013 programs, then click the name of the program you want to open.

- ■ When you start a Microsoft Office 2013 program, it displays a list of recently-used files and a gallery of available **templates**.
- ■ Each program has a Blank template; click the Blank template to create a new blank file.
- ■ When you are done using a Microsoft Office program, close it to exit. If you have a file open, the program prompts you to save, or to exit without saving.

Try It! **Starting a Microsoft Office Program and Creating a Blank File**

1 From the Windows 8 Start screen, click the Word 2013 program tile:

✓ *Depending on the number of tiles displayed, you may have to scroll to the right to locate the tile.*

OR

a. From the Windows 8 Start screen, click the Desktop tile.

b. On the Windows desktop, double-click the Word 2013 shortcut icon.

OR

- ■ On the Taskbar, click the Word 2013 icon.

OR

a. Right-click a blank area of the Windows 8 Start screen.

b. Click the All apps button.

c. Scroll to the Microsoft Office 2013 programs.

d. Click Word 2013.

2 Click the Blank document template.

Try It! **Exiting a Microsoft Office Program**

1 In the Microsoft Word program window, click the Close button × at the right end of the program's title bar.

 If you have a file open, a dialog box displays. Click Save to save changes to the file and exit, or click Don't Save to exit without saving.

Lesson 1—Practice

You have just been hired as the office manager at Restoration Architecture, a growing firm that specializes in remodeling, redesign, and restoration of existing properties. In this project, you practice using your computer's operating system to create and name a folder. You also practice starting and exiting a Microsoft Office 2013 program.

DIRECTIONS

1. If you have a removable storage device to use for storing your work in this class, connect it to your computer. For example, insert a removable disk in a drive, or connect a flash drive to a USB port. (Close the AutoPlay dialog box without taking any action, if necessary.)

2. If necessary, press ESC to display the desktop. Click the **File Explorer** icon 🖿 on the Windows Taskbar.

3. Click **Computer** in the navigation pane. The computer window opens. It displays the storage devices that are part of your computer system.

4. Follow your teacher's directions to navigate to and open the specific location where you will store the files and folders for this book.

5. Click the **View** tab on the Ribbon to display the commands on the View tab of the Ribbon.

6. In the Layout group, click **Medium icons** to select the way the items in the window display.

7. Click the Home tab and then click the **New folder** button 🗐 to create a new folder.

8. Type **B01Practice_xx**.

   ✓ *Throughout this book, when naming files and folders, replace xx with your name or initials as instructed by your teacher.*

9. Press ENTER to name the new folder. The window should look similar to Figure 1-1 on the next page.

10. Double-click the new folder to open it.

11. Click the **Back** button ⬅ above the navigation pane to display the previous storage location.

12. Click the **Forward** button ➡ to move forward to the **B01Practice_xx** folder window.

13. Click the **Close** button ▬ ✕ to close the window.

14. Press ⊞ on your keyboard to display the Start screen.

15. Click the Excel 2013 tile:

    OR

    a. Right-click a blank area of the Start screen and click the **All apps** button ⊛.

    b. Scroll to locate the Microsoft Office 2013 programs.

    c. Click **Excel 2013**.

    ✓ *A quick way to locate a program from the Start screen is just to start typing its name. Windows displays a list of matching programs.*

16. Click the **Blank workbook** template.

17. Click the **Close** button ✕ to exit Excel. Click **Don't Save** if prompted, to exit without saving the file.

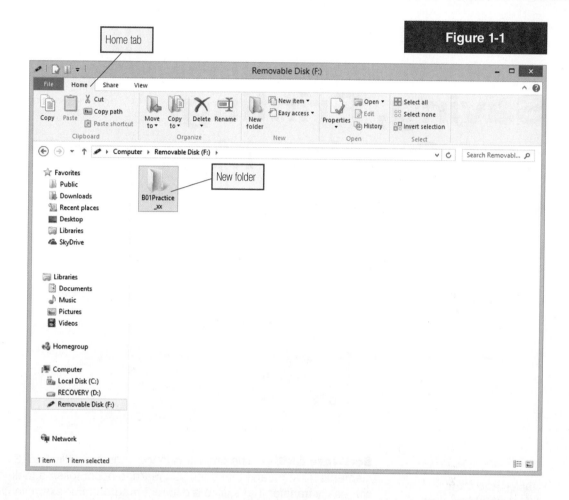

Figure 1-1

Home tab

New folder

Lesson 1—Apply

In this project, you use your computer's operating system to navigate to a storage location where you create a subfolder. You then delete a subfolder and a folder and, finally, you practice starting and exiting Microsoft Office 2013 programs.

DIRECTIONS

1. Use File Explorer to navigate to and open the **B01Practice_xx** folder you created in Lesson 1—Practice

2. Create a new folder named **B01Apply_xx**.

3. Open the **B01Apply_xx** folder, then navigate back to the **B01Practice_xx** folder.

4. Navigate forward to the **B01Apply_xx** folder.

5. Navigate back to the **B01Practice_xx** folder.

6. Delete the **B01Apply_xx** folder.

7. Navigate back to the storage location where the **B01Practice_xx** folder is stored, and then delete the **B01Practice_xx** folder.

8. Close the File Explorer window.

9. Start Word 2013 and create a blank document.

10. Exit Word.

11. Start PowerPoint 2013 and create a blank presentation.

12. Exit PowerPoint.

Lesson 2

Saving, Printing, and Closing Microsoft Office Files

➤ What You Will Learn

Identifying Common Microsoft Office Screen Elements
Entering and Editing Text
Correcting Errors
Saving a File
Printing a File
Closing a File

WORDS TO KNOW

Backstage view
A feature of Microsoft Office 2013 from which you access file and program management commands.

Toolbar
A row of command buttons.

Software Skills The programs in the Microsoft Office 2013 suite share common elements. That means that once you learn to accomplish a task in one program, you can easily transfer that skill to a different program. For example, the steps for saving a file are the same, no matter which program you are using.

What You Can Do

Identifying Common Microsoft Office Screen Elements

- When a program is running, it is displayed in a window on your screen.
- The program windows for each of the Microsoft Office applications contain many common elements.
- You will find more information about the individual program windows in the other sections of this book.
- Refer to Figure 2-1 on the next page to locate and identify these common window elements:
  - Ribbon. Displays buttons for accessing features and commands.
    - ✓ *Note that the way items display on the Ribbon may depend on the width of the program window. If your program window is wider than the one used in the figures, more or larger buttons may display. If your program window is narrower, fewer or smaller buttons may display. Refer to Lesson 3 for more information on using the Ribbon.*

- Ribbon tabs. Used to change the commands displayed on the Ribbon.
- Quick Access Toolbar. A **toolbar** that displays buttons for commonly used commands. You can customize the Quick Access Toolbar to display buttons you use frequently.
- Close button. Used to close the program window. It is one of three buttons used to control the size and position of the program window.
- Mouse pointer. Marks the location of the mouse on the screen.
- Scroll bar. Used with a mouse to shift the onscreen display up and down or left and right.
- Status bar. Displays information about the current document.

- Document area. The workspace where you enter text, graphics, and other data.

  ✓ *The appearance of the document area is different in each program.*

- ScreenTip. Displays information about the element on which the mouse pointer is resting.
- Title bar. Displays the program and file names.
- Zoom slider. Used to increase or decrease the size of the document onscreen.
- Help button. Used to start the program's Help system.
- View buttons. Used to change the document view.

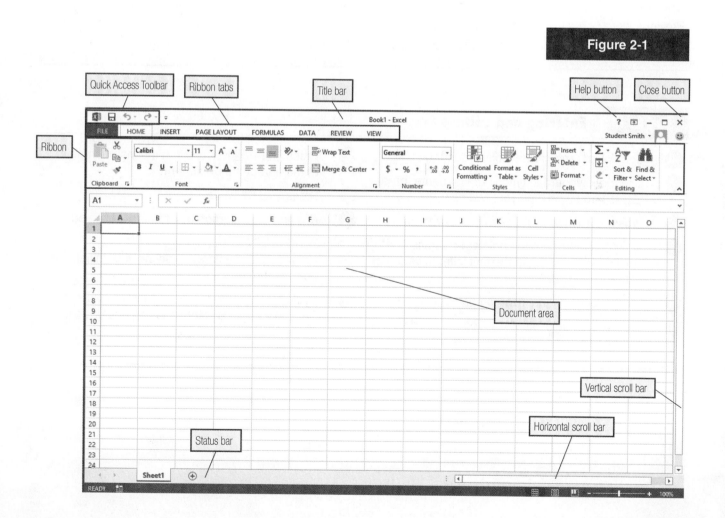

Figure 2-1

Entering and Editing Text

- Use your keyboard to enter or edit text in a file.
- Characters you type are inserted to the left of the insertion point.
- You position the insertion point using your mouse, touch device, or the directional keys on your keyboard.

- Press BACKSPACE to delete the character to the left of the insertion point.
- Press DEL to delete the character to the right of the insertion point.

  ✓ *When you are working in a program such as Access or Excel, text is entered into the selected cell. You learn about entering information in specific programs in each section of this book.*

Table 2-1	**Positioning the Insertion Point with the Keyboard**		
One character left	←	Up one paragraph	CTRL + ↑
One character right	→	Down one paragraph	CTRL + ↓
One line up	↑	Beginning of document	CTRL + HOME
One line down	↓	End of document	CTRL + END
Previous word	CTRL + ←	Beginning of line	HOME
Next word	CTRL + →	End of line	END

Try It!   Entering and Editing Text

1. Start Word, and create a blank document.
2. Use the keyboard to type your first name, press SPACEBAR and then type your last name.
3. Press ENTER twice to start two new paragraphs.
4. Move the mouse so the pointer I-beam is positioned to the left of the first letter in your last name.
5. Click to position the insertion point.
6. Type your middle initial followed by a period and a space.
7. Press CTRL + END to position the insertion point at the end of the document.
8. Press BACKSPACE twice.
9. Position the insertion point to the left of your middle initial.
10. Press DEL three times to delete your initial, the period, and the space.
11. Click the Close button × and then click Don't Save to exit Word without saving any changes.

Correcting Errors

- Press [ESC] to cancel a command or close a menu or dialog box before the command affects the current file.
- Use the Undo button ↺ on the Quick Access Toolbar to reverse a single action made in error, such as deleting the wrong word.
- Use the Undo drop-down list to reverse a series of actions. The most recent action is listed at the top of the list; click an action to undo it and all actions above it.

- Use the Redo button ↻ on the Quick Access Toolbar to reinstate any actions that you reversed with Undo.
- If the Undo button is dimmed, there are no actions that can be undone.
- If the Redo button is dimmed, there are no actions that can be redone.
- Sometimes when there are no actions to redo, the Repeat button ↻ is available in place of Redo. Use Repeat to repeat the most recent action.

Try It!   **Correcting Errors**

1 Start Excel, and create a blank workbook file.

2 Use the keyboard to type your first name in the first cell (the rectangular area in the upper-left corner) and then press [ENTER].

3 Click the Undo button ↺ on the Quick Access Toolbar. The previous action—typing your first name—is undone.

4 Click the Redo button ↻ on the Quick Access Toolbar. The undone action is redone.

5 Press the down arrow key [↓] three times to select the cell in the fourth row of column A.

6 Type today's date and press [ENTER].

7 Click the Undo drop-down arrow ↺▾ to display the Undo menu. It should list two actions you could undo.

8 Press [ESC]. The menu closes without any action taking place.

9 Click the Close button × and then click Don't Save to exit Excel without saving any changes.

Saving a File

- If you want to have a file available for future use, you must save it on a storage device.
- The first time you save a new file you must give it a name and select the location where you want to store it.
- Each Microsoft Office program is set to save files in a default storage location.

- You can select a different storage location on the Save As page in the program's Backstage view or in the Save As dialog box, or you can create and name a new folder using the New folder command on the menu bar in the Save As dialog box.
- After you save a file for the first time, you save changes to the file in order to make sure that you do not lose your work.
- Saving changes updates the previously saved version of the file with the most recent changes.

Try It!   Saving a File

1 Start Word, and create a blank document.

2 Click Save 🖫 on the Quick Access Toolbar.

OR

a. Click the FILE tab.

b. Click Save.

✓ *If the Save As dialog box displays, your computer was modified to skip the Backstage view. Skip step 3.*

3 On the Save As page in the Backstage view, click Computer, and then under Computer, click Browse 📁.

✓ *If the location where you want to store the file displays in the Backstage view, click it instead of clicking Browse.*

4 In the Save As dialog box, select the contents in the File name text box if it is not selected already.

✓ *To select the contents, drag across it with your mouse.*

5 Type **B02Try_xx**.

✓ *Remember to replace xx with your own name or initials, as instructed by your teacher. This will be the standard format for naming files throughout this book.*

6 Use the Navigation pane to navigate to the location where your teacher instructs you to store the files for this lesson. If necessary, click New folder on the menu bar to create and name a new folder.

✓ *If the Navigation pane is not displayed, click Browse Folders.*

7 Click Save or press ENTER .

8 Leave the **B02Try_xx** file open to use in the next Try It.

The Save As page in the Backstage view

Save As dialog box

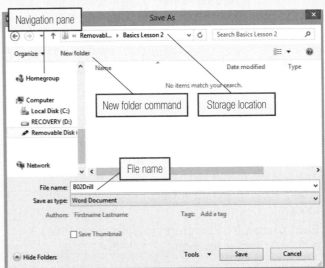

Try It!   **Saving Changes to a File**

1 In the **B02Try_xx** file, type your first name, press `SPACEBAR`, type your last name, and then press `ENTER`.

2 Type today's date.

3 Click Save 💾 on the Quick Access Toolbar.

OR

a. Click FILE.

b. Click Save.

✓ You can also press `CTRL` + `S` to save changes.

4 Leave the **B02Try_xx** file open to use in the next Try It.

Printing a File

- Printing creates a hard copy version of a file on paper.
- In Microsoft Office 2013 programs you use the Print page in the **Backstage view** to preview and print a file.
- You can also select printer settings such as the number of copies to print and which printer to use.

✓ Printer setting options vary depending on the system configuration.

- Your computer must be connected to a printer loaded with paper and ink in order to print.
- Ask your teacher for permission before printing.

✓ Steps for printing in Access are different from printing in the other Microsoft Office programs. You learn how to print in Access in the Access section of this book.

Try It!   **Printing the Current File**

1 In the **B02Try_xx** file, click FILE.

2 Click Print.

3 **With your teacher's permission,** click the Print button 🖨.

✓ You can select settings such as the printer and number of copies to print before printing.

4 Leave the **B02Try_xx** file open to use in the next Try It.

✓ To return to the current file from the Backstage view, click the Back button ⬅ in the upper-left of the page.

Closing a File

- A file remains open onscreen until you close it.
- If you try to close a file without saving, the program prompts you to save.
- You can close a file without saving it if you do not want to keep it for future use.

- You can use the Close button to close the file and exit the program; if there are multiple files open, the program remains running.
- You can also use the FILE > Close command

✓ In this book, the symbol > is used to indicate a series of steps. In this case, click the FILE tab and then click Close.

Try It!   **Closing a File**

1 With the **B02Try_xx** file open in Word, click the Close button ✕.

OR

a. Click FILE.

b. Click Close.

✓ If you have made changes since the last time you saved, click Save to save changes and close the file, or click Don't Save to close the file without saving. In Access, click Yes to save changes or click No to close without saving.

Lesson 2—Practice

In this project, you practice the skills you have learned in this lesson to create, save, and print a file in Microsoft Word 2013.

DIRECTIONS

1. If you have a removable storage device to use for storing your work in this class, connect it to your computer. For example, insert a removable disk in a drive, or connect a flash drive to a USB port.

2. Start Word, and click the **Blank document template**.

3. Move the mouse pointer so it is resting on the **Save** button 🖫 on the Quick Access Toolbar. The ScreenTip displays Save.

4. Point to the **Zoom** slider on the right end of the status bar.

5. Click the **INSERT** tab on the Ribbon.

6. Click the **FILE** tab.

7. Click **Save** > **Computer** > **Browse** 📂 to display the Save As dialog box.

8. Type **B02Practice_xx**.

9. Navigate to the location where your teacher instructs you to store the files for this lesson.

   ✓ *If necessary, create a new folder for storing the files.*

10. Click **Save** in the Save As dialog box to save the file.

11. In the new file, type your first name and your last name and press ENTER to start a new line.

12. Type today's date and press ENTER .

13. Type **Notes on using Microsoft Office 2013**.

14. Click the **Undo** button ↶ on the Quick Access Toolbar to undo the typing.

15. Click the **Redo** button ↷ to redo the action.

16. Click the **Save** button 🖫 on the Quick Access Toolbar to save the changes to the file.

17. Click the **FILE** tab.

18. Click **Print**. Your screen should look similar to Figure 2-2.

19. **With your teacher's permission,** click the **Print** button 🖶 to print the file.

    ✓ *If necessary, click the Printer drop-down arrow and select the printer your teacher wants you to use.*

20. Click the **FILE** tab, then click **Close** to close the file.

21. Exit Word.

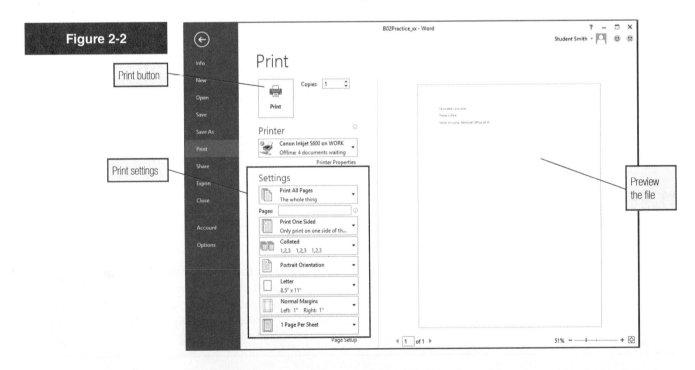

Figure 2-2

Lesson 2—Apply

As the new office manager at Restoration Architecture, you have been asked to analyze how the company might use Microsoft Office to achieve its business goals. In this project, you will use the skills you learned in this lesson to compare the Microsoft Office 2013 programs.

DIRECTIONS

1. Start Excel, and create a blank workbook.
2. Point to the following common elements in the Excel window: Zoom slider, Save button on the Quick Access Toolbar, View buttons, and the vertical scroll bar.
3. Click the **INSERT** tab on the Ribbon.
4. Click the **FILE** tab, and then click **Save**.
5. Click **Computer** > **Browse** 📁, and then type **B02ApplyA_xx**.
6. Navigate to the location where your teacher instructs you to store the files for this lesson, and then click **Save** to save the file.
7. In the new file, type your first name and your last name and press `ENTER`.

   ✓ *In Excel, typing displays in the current, or selected, cell. Pressing `ENTER` enters the data in the cell and usually moves to the next cell down. If it does not move to the next cell down, press the down arrow key.*

8. Type today's date and press `ENTER`

   ✓ *Excel might apply date formatting to the entry. You learn more about formatting in a worksheet in the Excel section of this book.*

9. Click **Undo** ↺ .
10. Click **Undo** ↺ again.
11. Click **Redo** ↻ twice.
12. Click the **Save** button 💾 on the Quick Access Toolbar to save the changes to the file.
13. Click the **FILE** tab, and then click **Print**.

14. **With your teacher's permission,** print the file.
15. Click the **Close** button × to close the file and exit Excel.
16. Start PowerPoint, and create a blank presentation.
17. Point to the following common elements in the PowerPoint window: Zoom slider, Save button on the Quick Access Toolbar, View buttons, and the Close button.
18. Click the **INSERT** tab on the Ribbon.
19. Click the **FILE** tab, and then click **Save**.
20. Click **Computer** > **Browse** 📁 and then type **B02ApplyB_xx**.
21. Navigate to the location where your teacher instructs you to store the files for this lesson, and then click **Save** to save the file.
22. In the new file, type your first name and your last name and press `ENTER`. Type today's date.

   ✓ *In PowerPoint, typing displays in the current, or selected, placeholder. Pressing `ENTER` starts a new line.*

23. Click **Undo** ↺ .
24. Click **Redo** ↻ .
25. Click the **Save** button 💾 on the Quick Access Toolbar to save the changes to the file.
26. Click the **FILE** tab, and then click **Print**.
27. **With your teacher's permission,** print the file.
28. Click the **Close** button × to close the file and exit PowerPoint.

Lesson 3

Working with Existing Files

WORDS TO KNOW

Access keys
Keys you can use to select or execute a command.

Command
Input that tells the computer which task to execute.

Contextual tab
A Ribbon tab that is only available in a certain context or situation.

Contiguous
Adjacent or in a row.

Dialog box launcher
A button you click to open a dialog box.

File properties
Information about a file.

Font
A complete set of characters in a specific face, style, and size.

Font color
The color of characters in a font set.

Font size
The height of an uppercase letter in a font set.

Font style
The slant and weight of characters in a font set.

Format
To change the appearance of text or other elements.

➤ What You Will Learn

Opening an Existing File
Saving a File with a New Name
Viewing File Properties
Using the Ribbon
Using Access Keys
Selecting Text
Formatting Text

Software Skills   You can open an existing file in the program used to create it. You can then use Microsoft Office program commands to save it with a new name so you can edit or format it, leaving the original file unchanged. Formatting improves the appearance and readability of text.

What You Can Do

Opening an Existing File

■ To view or edit a file that has been saved and closed, open it again.

■ Recently used files display when you first start a Microsoft Office program and on the Open page in the Backstage view; click a file to open it.

■ You can use the Open dialog box to locate and open any file.

Try It!	**Opening an Existing File**

 Start Excel.

 At the bottom of the Recent list on the left side of the page, click Open Other Workbooks.

 Click Computer, and then click the location you want to open, or click the Browse button 🖿 and navigate to the location where the data files for this lesson are stored.

(continued)

Try It!   **Opening an Existing File** *(continued)*

④ Double-click **B03TryA** to open it.

OR

a. Click **B03TryA**.
b. Click Open.

⑤ Click FILE > Close to close the file, but leave Excel open to use in the next Try It.

Open dialog box

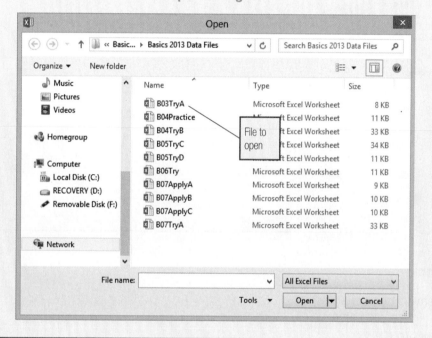

Try It!   **Opening a Recently Opened Document**

① In Excel, click FILE.

② In the list of Recent Workbooks, click **B03TryA**.

④ Leave the file open in Excel to use in the next Try It.

(continued)

Gallery
A menu that displays pictures instead of plain text options.

Highlighted
Marked with color to stand out from the surrounding text.

KeyTip
A pop-up letter that identifies the access key(s) for a command.

Live Preview
A feature of Microsoft Office that shows you how a command will affect the selection before you actually select the command.

Noncontiguous
Not adjacent.

Select
Mark text as the focus of the next action.

Selection bar
A narrow strip along the left margin of a page that automates selection of text. When the mouse pointer is in the selection area, the pointer changes to an arrow pointing up and to the right.

Toggle
A type of command that can be switched off or on.

Try It!	**Opening a Recently Opened Document** *(continued)*

Open a Recent Workbook

Excel

(←)

Info

New

Open

Open

Save

Save As

Print

Share

Export

Close

Account

Options

(L) Recent Workbooks

☁ Student Smith's SkyDrive

🖥 Computer

➕ Add a Place

Recent Workbooks

┌──────────┐
│ File to │
│ open   │
└──────────┘

📗 B03TryA
   F: » Basics 2013 Data Files

📗 B02ApplyA
   F: » Basics 2013 Data Files

Saving a File with a New Name

- Use the Save As command to save a copy of a file in a different location or with a different file name.
- The original file remains unchanged.

Try It!	**Saving a File with a New Name**

1. In Excel, with the **B03TryA** file open, click FILE.

2. Click Save As.

3. Click Computer and then click the location where you want to store the file, or click the Browse button 📂.

4. Type **B03TryB_xx** to rename the file.

5. Navigate to the location where your teacher instructs you to store the files for this lesson.

6. Click Save.

7. Close the file, and exit Excel.

Viewing File Properties

- You can view **file properties** on the Info tab in the Backstage view.
- File properties include information about the file, such as how big it is and when it was created or modified.

Try It!   **Viewing File Properties**

1 Start PowerPoint.

2 Click Open Other Presentations.

3 Click Computer, then click the location you want to open, or click Browse 📂 and navigate to the location where the data files for this lesson are stored.

4 Double-click **B03TryB** to open it.

5 Click FILE. The Info page displays, with the Properties listed on the right.

6 Close the file, and exit PowerPoint.

Properties display on the Info page

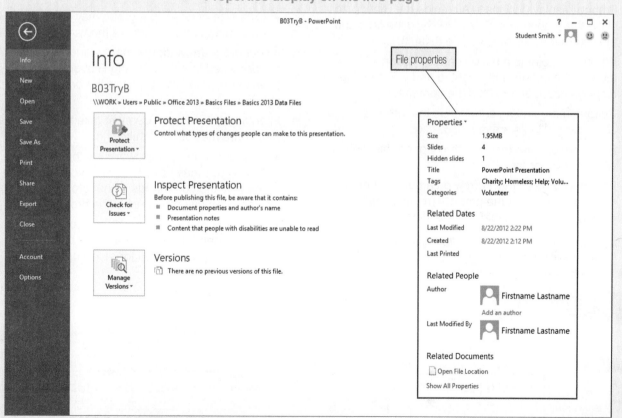

Using the Ribbon

- To accomplish a task in a Microsoft Office 2013 program, you execute **commands**. For example, Save is the command for saving a file.

- Most commands are available as buttons on the Ribbon. Refer to Figure 3-1 to identify parts of the HOME tab of the Ribbon.

- The Ribbon is organized into tabs based on activities, such as reviewing a file or inserting content. On each tab, commands are organized into groups.

- **Contextual tabs** are only available in certain situations. For example, if you select a picture, the PICTURE TOOLS tab becomes available. If you deselect the picture, the PICTURE TOOLS tab disappears.

- You can collapse the Ribbon to display only the tabs if you want to see more of a file, and expand it when you need to use the commands.

- In Word, Excel, and PowerPoint, you can change the Ribbon Display Options to Auto-hide the Ribbon, to show the Ribbon tabs only, or to show the tabs and the commands all the time (the default).

- When you point to a button on the Ribbon with the mouse, the button is highlighted and a ScreenTip displays information about the command.

- Buttons representing commands that are not currently available are dimmed.

- Some buttons are **toggles**; they appear highlighted when active, or "on."

- If there is a drop-down arrow on a button, it means that when you click the arrow, a menu or **gallery** displays so you can make a specific selection.

  ✓ *In this book, when it says "click the button" you should click the button; when it says "click the drop-down arrow" you should click the arrow on the button.*

- Sometimes, the entire first row of a gallery displays on the Ribbon.

- You can rest the mouse pointer on a gallery item to see a **Live Preview** of the way your document will look if you select that item.

- You can scroll a gallery on the Ribbon, or click the More button ⊽ to view the entire gallery.

- Some Ribbon groups have a **dialog box launcher** button ⌐ . Click the dialog box launcher to display a dialog box, task pane, or window where you can select additional options, or multiple options at the same time.

- Note that the way items display on the Ribbon may depend on the width of the program window.

  - If the window is wide enough, groups expand to display all items.

  - If the window is not wide enough, groups collapse to a single group button. Click the button to display a menu of commands in the group.

  - The size of icons in a group may vary depending on the width of the window.

- If your program window is narrower or wider than the one used in this book, the Ribbon on your screen may look different from the one in the figures.

- In addition, the steps you must take to complete a procedure may vary slightly.

  - If your screen is narrower than the one in this book, you may have to click a group button to display the commands in that group before you can complete the steps in the procedure.

  - If your screen is wider, you may be able to skip a step for selecting a group button and go directly to the step for selecting a specific command.

Figure 3-1

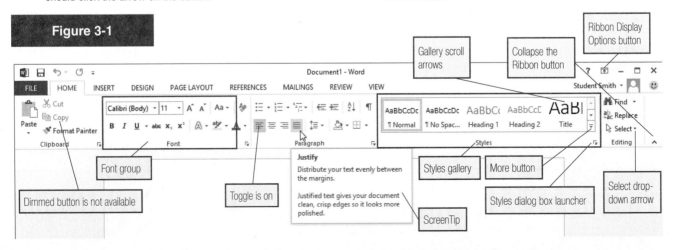

Try It! **Using the Ribbon**

1. Start Word, and create a blank document.

2. Save the file as **B03TryC_xx** in the location where your teacher instructs you to store files for this lesson.

3. Point to the Center button ≡ on the Ribbon. The ScreenTip displays the button name, shortcut keys, and a description.

4. Click the Center button ≡ . The insertion point moves to the center of the current line.

5. Type your first name, press ENTER , and then type your last name.

6. Press CTRL + ENTER , the shortcut key combination for starting a new page, and type today's date.

7. Click the VIEW tab on the Ribbon to make it active.

8. Click the Multiple Pages button ⊟⊟ . This command changes the view to display two pages at the same time.

9. Click the One Page button ⊟ . This command changes the view to display one page at a time.

10. Save the changes to **B03TryC_xx**, and keep it open to use in the next Try It.

Try It! **Setting Ribbon Display Options**

1. In **B03TryC_xx**, click the Collapse the Ribbon button ▲ . The Ribbon is hidden.

   ✓ CTRL + F1 *is the shortcut key combination for unpinning/ pinning the Ribbon.*

2. Click the INSERT tab. Clicking any tab expands the Ribbon temporarily so you can select a command.

3. Click the Pin the ribbon button ⊹ to keep the Ribbon displayed.

4. Double-click the VIEW tab. Double-clicking any tab is an alternative way to collapse/pin the Ribbon.

5. Click the Ribbon Display Options button ⊡ .

6. Click Show Tabs and Commands to expand the Ribbon and keep it displayed.

7. Save the changes to **B03TryC_xx**, and keep it open to use in the next Try It.

Using Access Keys

- Microsoft Office 2013 programs are designed primarily for use with a mouse or touch device.

- Some people prefer to select commands using the keyboard. In that case, you can press the Alt key to activate **access keys**.

- When access keys are active, **KeyTips** showing one or more keyboard letters display on the screen over any feature or command that can be selected using the keyboard.

- You press the letter(s) shown in the KeyTip to select the command or feature.

- If there is more than one access key for a command, you may press the keys in combination (at the same time) or consecutively (press the first key and then immediately press the next key).

- If a KeyTip is dimmed, the command is not available.

- The KeyTips remain active if you must press additional keys to complete a command.

- Once a command is executed, the KeyTips disappear.

- To continue using the keyboard, you must press the Alt key to activate the access keys again.

   ✓ *People accustomed to the shortcut key combinations in previous versions of Microsoft Office will be happy to know that they function in Microsoft Office 2013 programs as well. For example, you can still press CTRL + SHIFT + F to open the Font dialog box.*

Try It!   **Using Access Keys**

1 With the **B03TryC_xx** file still displayed, press [ALT]. The KeyTips for the Ribbon tabs display.

2 Press [W] to make the VIEW tab active. The KeyTips for the VIEW tab display.

3 Press [2] to change to Two Page view.

4 Press [ALT], [W], [1] to change to One Page view.

5 Press [ALT], [W], [J] to change the view to show the file at 100% magnification.

6 Press [ALT], [H] to make the HOME tab of the Ribbon active.

7 Press [ESC] twice to cancel the KeyTips.

8 Save the changes to **B03TryC_xx**, and keep it open to use in the next Try It.

KeyTips on the View tab

Selecting Text

- **Select** text in order to edit it or format it.
- You can select any amount of **contiguous** or **noncontiguous** text.
- You can also select non-text characters, such as symbols; nonprinting characters, such as paragraph marks; and graphics, such as pictures.
- By default, selected text appears **highlighted** onscreen.

- When you first select text, the Mini toolbar may display. Move the mouse pointer away from the selection to hide the Mini toolbar.
- When text is selected, any command or action affects the selection. For example, if text is selected and you press [DEL], the selection is deleted.
- To select text on a touch device, tap in the text and drag the selection handle. Refer to Table 3-1 for keyboard selection commands. Refer to Table 3-2 on the next page for mouse selection commands.

Table 3-1   **Keyboard Selection Commands**

To Select	Press
One character right	[SHIFT] + [→]
One character left	[SHIFT] + [←]
One line up	[SHIFT] + [↑]
One line down	[SHIFT] + [↓]
To end of line	[SHIFT] + [END]
To beginning of line	[SHIFT] + [HOME]
To end of document	[SHIFT] + [CTRL] + [END]
To beginning of document	[SHIFT] + [CTRL] + [HOME]
Entire document	[CTRL] + [A]

Table 3-2	Mouse Selection Commands
To Select	**Do This**
One word	Double-click word.
One sentence	CTRL + click in sentence.
One line	Click in **selection bar** to the left of the line.
One paragraph	Double-click in selection bar to the left of the paragraph.
Document	Triple-click in selection bar.
Noncontiguous text	Select first block, press and hold CTRL , then select additional block(s).

Try It!   Selecting Text

1. In **B03TryC_xx**, press CTRL + HOME , the shortcut key combination to move the insertion point to the beginning of a Word document.

2. Position the mouse pointer to the left of the first character in your first name.

3. Hold down the left mouse button.

4. Drag the mouse across your first name to select it.

5. Click anywhere outside the selection to cancel it.

6. Double-click your last name to select it.

7. Press DEL . The selected text is deleted.

8. Save the changes to **B03TryC_xx**, and keep it open to use in the next Try It.

Formatting Text

- You can **format** text to change its appearance.
- Formatting can enhance and emphasize text, and set a tone or mood for a file.
- Microsoft Office 2013 programs offer many options for formatting text; you will learn more in the other sections of this book.

- Some common formatting options include:
  - **Font**
  - **Font size**
  - **Font style**
  - **Font color**
- You can change the formatting of selected text, or you can select formatting before you type new text.
- You can preview the way selected text will look with formatting by resting the mouse pointer on the formatting command on the Ribbon.

Try It!　　　**Formatting Selected Text**

1 In **B03TryC_xx**, double-click your first name to select it.

2 On the HOME tab, in the Font group, click the Bold button **B** .

3 On the HOME tab, in the Font group, click the Font Size drop-down arrow [11 ▾] to display a list of font sizes, and rest the mouse pointer on the number 28 to preview the text with the formatting.

4 Click 16 on the Font size drop-down list to change the font size to 16 points.

5 On the HOME tab, in the Font group, click the Underline button **u** .

6 On the HOME tab, in the Font group click the Italic button **I** .

7 Click anywhere outside the selection in the document to deselect the text.

8 Save the changes to **B03TryC_xx**, and keep it open to use in the next Try It.

Try It!　　　**Formatting New Text**

1 In **B03TryC_xx**, move the insertion point to the end of your first name and press [ENTER] to start a new line.

2 Type your middle name. (If you do not have a middle name, type any name.) Notice that the current formatting carries forward to the new line.

3 Press [ENTER] to start a new line. Click the Bold **B** , Italic **I** , and Underline **u** buttons to toggle those commands off.

4 Click the Font drop-down arrow [Calibri (Body) ▾] and click Arial on the list of available fonts.

✓ *The list of fonts is alphabetical. Scroll down to find Arial.*

5 Click the Font Color drop-down arrow **A** ▾ and click Green.

6 Type your last name. The text displays in green 16-point Arial, without bold, italic, or underline formatting.

7 Close **B03TryC_xx**, saving the changes, and exit Word.

Select a font color

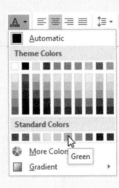

Lesson 3—Practice

As a public relations assistant at Voyager Travel Adventures, you are responsible for preparing press releases. In this project, you will open an existing press release file in Word and save it with a new name. You will then enter, edit, and format text to prepare it for distribution.

DIRECTIONS

1. If you have a removable storage device to use for storing your work in this class, connect it to your computer. For example, insert a removable disk in a drive, or connect a flash drive to a USB port.
2. Start Word.
3. Click **Open Other Documents**.
4. Click **Computer**, then click the location you want to open, or click **Browse** 📂, and navigate to the location where the data files for this lesson are stored.
5. Double-click the file **B03Practice** to open it.
6. Click the **FILE** tab, and then click **Save As**.
7. Click Computer, and then under **Computer**, click the **Browse** button 📂.
8. Type **B03Practice_xx** in the File name box.
9. Navigate to the location where your teacher instructs you to store the files for this lesson.
10. Click **Save**.
11. Select the headline: *Voyager Travel Adventures Announces Exciting Summer Tours*.
12. Click the **Bold** button ʙ.
13. Click the **Font Size** drop-down arrow 11 ▾ and click **14**.

14. Select the text *Denver, Colorado – Today's Date –* and then click the **Italic** button ɪ.
15. Select the text *Today's Date*, press DEL to delete it, and then type the actual date.
16. Press CTRL + END to move the insertion point to the end of the document, and press ENTER to start a new line.
17. Click the **Font** drop-down arrow Calibri (Body) ▾ and click **Arial**.
18. Click the **Font Size** drop-down arrow 11 ▾ and click **12**.
19. Type **For more information contact:** and press ENTER.
20. Click the **Bold** button ʙ.
21. Click the **Font Color** drop-down arrow A ▾ and click **Red**.
22. Type your full name. The file should look similar to Figure 3-2.
23. Save the changes to file.
24. Click the **FILE** tab. Click **Info**, if necessary, to view the file properties. Note the date and time the file was created and modified.
25. **With your teacher's permission**, print the file.
26. Close the file, saving changes, and exit Word.

Figure 3-2

FOR IMMEDIATE RELEASE:

Voyager Travel Adventures Announces Exciting Summer Tours

Denver, Colorado –Today's Actual Date– Voyager Travel Adventures, an adventure tour operator based in Denver, has announced three new travel opportunities for the coming summer months.

For more information contact:

Firstname Lastname

Lesson 3—Apply

In this project, you will open another press release and use the skills you have learned in this lesson to edit, format, and print the file.

DIRECTIONS

1. Start Word.
2. Open the file **B03Apply** from the location where the data files for this lesson are stored.
3. Save the file as **B03Apply_xx** in the location where your teacher instructs you to store the files for this lesson.
4. Change the font of the headline to Times New Roman and the font size to 16.
5. Replace the text *Today's Date* with the current date.
6. Position the insertion point at the end of the main paragraph and insert the paragraph shown in Figure 3-3, applying formatting as marked.

7. Move the insertion point to the end of the document, press ENTER , and type your full name in 12-point Times New Roman, bold, as shown in Figure 3-3.
8. Change the color of the first line of text to Light Blue and increase the font size to 12.

   ✓ *Use ScreenTips to identify the correct color.*

9. Save the changes.
10. **With your teacher's permission**, print the file.
11. Close the file, saving changes, and exit Word.

Figure 3-3

12-point Light Blue

Replace with today's date

16-point Times New Roman bold

FOR IMMEDIATE RELEASE:

Voyager Travel Adventures Announces Exciting Summer Tours

Denver, Colorado –Today's Date – Voyager Travel Adventures, an adventure tour operator based in Denver, has announced three new travel opportunities for the coming summer months.

The new tours include an **African safari**, **snorkeling in the Caribbean**, and **kayaking in Alaska**. Like all Voyager adventures. These tours include first-class meals and accommodations, small group sizes, and experienced guides.

For more information contact:

Firstname Lastname

Bold, underline

Your own name in 12-point Times New Roman bold

Lesson 4

Using Command Options

➤ What You Will Learn

Using the Quick Access Toolbar
Using the Mini Toolbar
Using Shortcut Menus
Using Dialog Box Options
Using Task Panes
Formatting Pages

Software Skills As you have learned, to accomplish a task in a Microsoft Office 2013 program, you must execute a command. Most commands are available on the Ribbon, but you may also use toolbars, menus, dialog boxes, or task panes. To prepare a file for printing or other types of distribution you may have to change the page formatting, such as adjusting the margin width, or selecting a page size.

What You Can Do

Using the Quick Access Toolbar

- The Quick Access Toolbar displays in the upper-left corner of the program window.
- To select a command from the Quick Access Toolbar, click its button.
- By default, there are three buttons on the Quick Access Toolbar: Save, Undo, and Repeat. The Repeat button changes to Redo once you use the Undo command.
- Use the Customize Quick Access Toolbar button ⌄ to add or remove buttons for common commands, or use the Customize the Quick Access Toolbar options in the Word Options dialog box.
- The buttons on the Quick Access Toolbar are not available in the Backstage view.

WORDS TO KNOW

Dialog box
A window in which you select options that affect the way the program executes a command.

Landscape orientation
Rotating document text so it displays and prints horizontally across the longer side of a page.

Margins
The amount of white space between the text and the edge of the page on each side.

Portrait orientation
The default position for displaying and printing text horizontally across the shorter side of a page.

Scale
Adjust the size proportionately.

Shortcut menu
A menu of relevant commands that displays when you right-click an item. Also called a context menu.

Task pane
A small window that displays options and commands for certain features in a Microsoft Office program.

Try It!   Adding and Removing Quick Access Toolbar Buttons

1 Start Word, create a blank document, and save it as **B04TryA_xx** in the location where your teacher instructs you to store the files for this lesson.

2 Click the Customize Quick Access Toolbar button ⁼ to display a menu of common commands.

✓ *A check mark next to a command indicates it is already on the Quick Access Toolbar.*

3 Click Print Preview and Print on the menu. The button for Print Preview and Print is added to the Quick Access Toolbar.

4 Right-click the Paste button 📋 on the HOME tab of the Ribbon.

5 Click Add to Quick Access Toolbar.

6 Click the Customize Quick Access Toolbar button ⁼ to display a menu of common commands.

7 Click Print Preview and Print. The button is removed from the Quick Access Toolbar.

8 Right-click the Paste button 📋 on the Quick Access Toolbar.

9 Click Customize Quick Access Toolbar.

10 In the list on the right side of the Word Options dialog box, click Paste to select it.

11 Click the Remove button ⌈ << Remove ⌉, and then click OK.

12 Save the changes to **B04TryA_xx**, and keep it open to use in the next Try It.

Using the Mini Toolbar

■ The Mini toolbar displays when the mouse pointer rests on selected text or data that can be formatted.

■ Select a command from the Mini toolbar the same way you select a command from the Ribbon.

Try It!   Using the Mini Toolbar

1 In the **B04TryA_xx** document, type your first name, and then select it. The Mini toolbar displays.

2 Click the Bold button **B** on the Mini toolbar.

3 Save the changes to **B04TryA_xx**, and leave it open to use in the next Try It.

Formatting with the Mini toolbar

Using Shortcut Menus

■ When you right-click almost any element on the screen in any Microsoft Office 2013 program, a **shortcut menu** displays.

■ Shortcut menus include options relevant to the current item.

✓ *Shortcut menus are sometimes called context menus.*

■ Click an option on the shortcut menu to select it.

■ Alternatively, press the access key—the key that is underlined in the command name.

✓ *Sometimes, selecting an option on a shortcut menu opens a submenu, which is simply one menu that opens off another menu.*

■ If you right-click selected data, the Mini toolbar may display in addition to the shortcut menu. The Mini toolbar disappears when you select an option on the menu.

Try It! Using a Shortcut Menu

1 In **B04TryA_xx**, click anywhere outside the selected text to deselect it.

2 Right-click the HOME tab of the Ribbon to display a shortcut menu.

3 Click Show Quick Access Toolbar Below the Ribbon on the shortcut menu. The Quick Access Toolbar moves below the Ribbon.

4 Right-click the status bar at the bottom of the Word window.

5 Click Zoom Slider on the shortcut menu to toggle the Zoom slider display off.

6 Click Zoom Slider on the shortcut menu again, to toggle the Zoom Slider display on.

7 Right-click the VIEW tab of the Ribbon to display a shortcut menu.

8 Click Show Quick Access Toolbar Above the Ribbon on the shortcut menu to move the toolbar back to its default position.

9 Leave the **B04TryA_xx** file open to use in the next Try It.

Use a shortcut menu to toggle screen elements off and on in Word

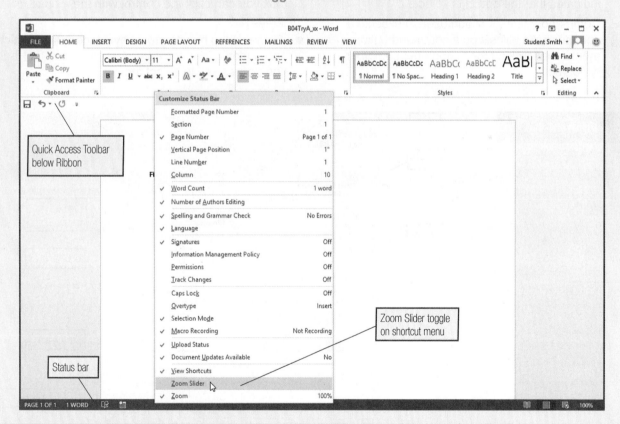

Using Dialog Box Options

- When you must provide additional information before executing a command, a **dialog box** displays.

- You enter information in a dialog box using a variety of controls (refer to Figures 4-1 and 4-2):

  - List box. A list of items from which selections can be made. If more items are available than can fit in the space, a scrollbar is displayed.

  - Palette. A display, such as colors or shapes, from which you can select an option.

  - Drop-down list box. A combination of text box and list box; type your selection in the box or click the drop-down arrow to display the list.

  - Check box. A square that you click to select or clear an option. A check mark in the box indicates that the option is selected.

  - Command button. A button used to execute a command. An ellipsis on a command button means that clicking the button opens another dialog box.

- Tabs. Markers across the top of the dialog box that, when clicked, display additional pages of options within the dialog box.

- Preview area. An area where you can preview the results of your selections before executing the commands.

- Increment box. A space where you type a value, such as inches or numbers, or use increment arrows beside the box to increase or decrease the value with a mouse. Sometimes called a spin box.

- Text box. A space where you type variable information, such as a file name.

- Option buttons. A series of circles, only one of which can be selected at a time. Click the circle you want to select it.

- To move from one control to another in a dialog box you can click the control with the mouse, or press TAB.

- Some dialog box controls have access keys which are underlined in the control name. Press ALT and the access key to select the control.

Figure 4-1

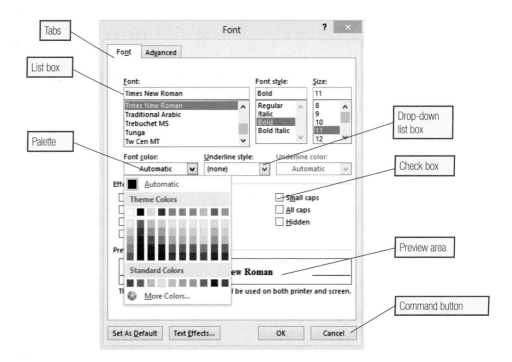

Learning Microsoft Excel 2013 | Basics

39

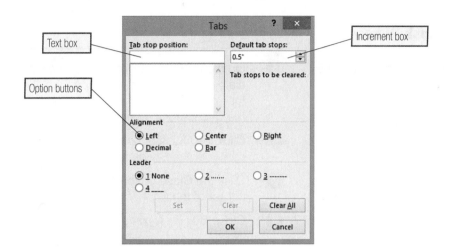

Figure 4-2

Text box

Option buttons

Increment box

Try It! Using Dialog Box Options

① In **B04TryA_xx**, select your first name.

② On the HOME tab, click the Font group dialog box launcher ⌐ to open the Font dialog box.

Font group on the Home tab

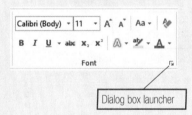

Dialog box launcher

③ In the Font style list box, click Italic.

④ In the Size box, select 11 and then type **8**.

⑤ Click the Underline style drop-down arrow, and click the double underline that is second from the top.

⑥ In the Effects section, click the Small caps check box to select it.

⑦ Click the OK command button to apply the formatting to the selected text.

⑧ Deselect the text, then save the changes to **B04TryA_xx**, and leave it open to use in the next Try It.

Displaying Task Panes

■ Some commands open a **task pane** instead of a dialog box. For example, if you click the Clipboard dialog box launcher, the Clipboard task pane displays.

■ Task panes have some features in common with dialog boxes. For example, some have text boxes in which you type text as well as drop-down list boxes, check boxes, and options buttons.

■ Unlike a dialog box, you can leave a task pane open while you work, move it, or close it to get it out of the way. You can also have more than one task pane open at the same time.

✓ *You learn how to accomplish tasks using task panes in the lesson in which that feature is covered. For example, in Basics Lesson 5 you learn how to use the Office Clipboard task pane to copy or move a selection.*

Try It!   Displaying Task Panes

1 In the **B04TryA_xx** document, on the HOME tab, click the Styles group dialog box launcher ⌐ to open the Styles task pane.

2 In the document window, click to position the insertion point at the end of your name.

3 In the Styles task pane, click Clear All. This clears the formatting from the text.

4 Press `ENTER` to start a new line, and then type your last name.

5 On the HOME tab, click the Clipboard group dialog box launcher ⌐ to open the Clipboard task pane. Now, both the Styles task pane and the Clipboard task pane are open.

6 Click the Close button × in the upper-right corner of the Styles task pane to close it.

7 Click the Close button × in the upper-right corner of the Clipboard task pane to close it.

8 Close **B04TryA_xx**, saving changes, and exit Word.

Open multiple task panes

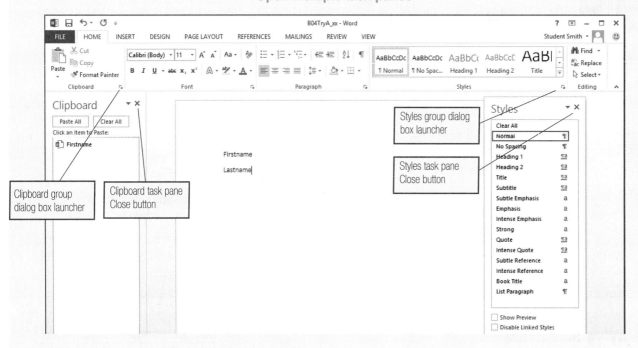

Formatting Pages

- Before you print or otherwise distribute a file, you may need to adjust the page formatting.
- Use the Print options in the Backstage view to select basic page formatting settings.
- In Access, use the options on the Print Preview tab.
- You can select an orientation, a paper size, and **margin** widths. You can also select to **scale** the file, if necessary, to fit on the selected paper size.
- Orientation is either portrait or landscape.

- Select **Portrait orientation**—the default—when you want data displayed across the shorter length of a page.
- Select **Landscape orientation** when you want data displayed across the wider length of a page.

✓ *You will learn about more advanced page formatting settings, such as setting custom margins and adjusting the alignment, in the program sections of this book.*

- You can select from a list of preset margins, including Normal, Wide, and Narrow. Margins are measured in inches.

Try It!   **Formatting Pages**

1 Start Excel, and open **B04TryB** from the data files for this lesson. Save the file as **B04TryB_xx** in the location where your teacher instructs you to store the files for this lesson.

2 Click the FILE tab, and then click Print. In the preview, you see that not all columns fit on the first page.

3 Click the Margins down arrow and click Narrow on the menu. This changes the width of the margins to 0.75" on the top and bottom and 0.25" on the left and right. Now, only the Total column is still on page 2.

4 Click the Scaling down arrow and click Fit Sheet on One Page. Now all columns fit, but they are quite small.

5 Click the Orientation down arrow and click Landscape Orientation to provide more room across the page.

6 Click the Margins down arrow and click Normal to increase the width of the margins.

7 Close **B04TryB_xx**, saving changes, and exit Excel.

Formatting pages before printing

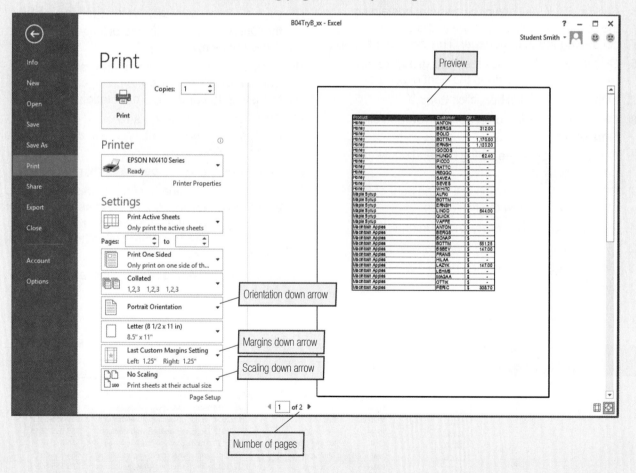

Lesson 4—Practice

As the store manager for Whole Grains Bread, a bakery, you must prepare a contact list of your employees for the franchise owner. In this project, you will use Excel to complete and format the contact list.

DIRECTIONS

1. Start Excel, open the file **B04Practice** from the data files for this lesson, and save it as **B04Practice_xx** in the location where your teacher instructs you to store the files for this lesson.
2. Double-click on the word *Position* (in cell A2). This positions the insertion point in the cell.
3. Select the word *Position*. The Mini toolbar displays.
4. Cick the **Bold** button в on the Mini-toolbar.
5. Click the next cell down the column, containing the text *Clerk*, and drag down to the cell in row 12, containing the text *Manager*. This selects the cells.
6. On the HOME tab, click the **Font group dialog box launcher** ⌐ to open the Font dialog box.
7. In the Font style list box, click **Italic**.
8. Click the **Underline** drop-down arrow and click **Double**.
9. Click **OK** to close the dialog box and apply the formatting.
10. Click cell **B12**—the blank cell to the right of the text *Manager* and below the text *Kevin*.
11. Type your own first name, and then press TAB.
12. Type your last name, and then press TAB.
13. Type today's date, and then press TAB.
14. Type your e-mail address, and then press TAB.
15. Right-click your e-mail address to display a shortcut menu
16. On the shortcut menu, click **Remove Hyperlink**. This removes the hyperlink formatting from your e-mail address. The data in your file should look similar to Figure 4-3.
17. Click the **Customize Quick Access Toolbar** button ⌐ and click **Print Preview and Print** to add the Print Preview and Print button to the Quick Access Toolbar.
18. Click the **Print Preview and Print** button ⌐ on the Quick Access Toolbar to display the Print tab in Backstage view.
19. Click the **Orientation** down arrow and click **Landscape Orientation** to change the page formatting to Landscape orientation.
20. Click the **Margins** down arrow and click **Normal** to change the page formatting to the default Normal margin widths.
21. **With your teacher's permission**, print the file.
22. Click the Back button to close Backstage view, click the **Customize Quick Access Toolbar** button ⌐, and click **Print Preview and Print** to remove the Print Preview and Print button from the Quick Access Toolbar
23. Close the file, saving all changes, and exit Excel.

Figure 4-3

	A	B	C	D	E	F	G
1							
2	**Position**	First Name	Last Name	Date Hired	Email	Telephone	
3	*Clerk*	Karen	Smith	5/8/2014	karen.smith@wgbreads.net	555-555-5551	
4	*Clerk*	William	Brown	1/17/2014	william.brown@wgbreads.net	555-555-5552	
5	*Baker*	Jorge	Hernandez	9/22/2013	jorge.hernandez@wgbreads.net	555-555-5553	
6	*Baker*	Lisa	McAnn-Dinardo	10/11/2013	lisa.mcann.dinardo@wgbreads.net	555-555-5554	
7	*Baker*	Amil	Muhammed	6/1/2012	amil.muhammed@wgbreads.net	555-555-5555	
8	*Baker*	Peter	Shepherd	5/22/2012	peter.j.shepherd@wgbreads.net	555-555-5556	
9	*Stock*	Jackson	Little	7/13/2014	jackson.little@wgbreads.net	555-555-5557	
10	*Assistant Manager*	Angela	Greene	8/23/2003	angela.greene@wgbreads.net	555-555-5558	
11	*Assistant Manager*	Kevin	Duchesne	9/22/2012	kevin.duchesne@wgbreads.net	555-555-5559	
12	*Manager*	Firstname	Lastname	9/18/2015	student@school.edu	555-555-5560	
13							

E12 fx student@school.edu

Lesson 4—Apply

The Whole Grains Bread franchise owner has asked for the employee list in a Word document. In this project, you will open an existing Word file and then revise, format, and print the document.

DIRECTIONS

1. Start Word.
2. Open the file **B04Apply** from the data files for this lesson, and save it as **B04Apply_xx** in the location where your teacher instructs you to store the files for this lesson.
3. Display the Print options in the Backstage view and change to Landscape Orientation.
4. Set the margins to Normal.
5. Close the Backstage view.
6. Select all data in the document, and use the Mini toolbar to increase the font size to **12** points.
7. Display the Quick Access Toolbar below the Ribbon.
8. Type your name, today's date, and your e-mail address into the appropriate cells in the document.
9. Use a shortcut menu to remove the hyperlink formatting from your e-mail address.
10. Select the line of text above the table, and use the Styles task pane to clear all formatting, then close the Styles task pane.
11. With the first line of text still selected, open the Font dialog box, and apply **Bold, Green, 14-point** formatting. When you deselect the text, your screen should look similar to Figure 4-4.
12. **With your teacher's permission**, print the file.
13. Return the Quick Access Toolbar to its position above the Ribbon.
14. Close the file, saving changes, and exit Word.

Figure 4-4

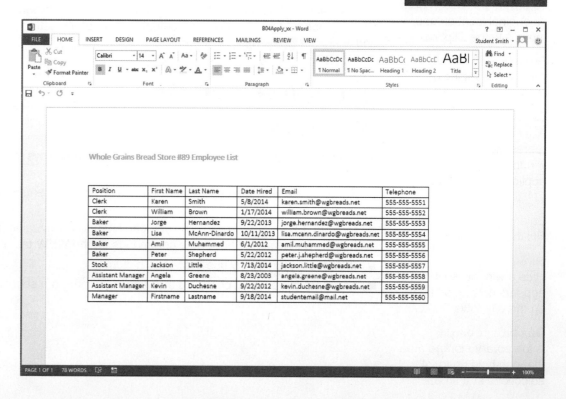

Lesson 5

Managing Program Windows

Active window
The window in which you are currently working.

Cascade
Arrange windows so they overlap, with the active window in front. Only the title bars of the nonactive windows are visible.

Copy
To duplicate a selection. The original remains unchanged.

Cut
To delete a selection from its original location and move it to the Clipboard.

Default
A standard setting or mode of operation.

Group button
A Taskbar button that represents all open windows for one application.

Maximize
Enlarge a window so it fills the entire screen.

Minimize
Hide a window so it appears only as a button on the Windows Taskbar.

Office Clipboard
A temporary storage area that can hold up to 24 selections at a time.

➤ What You Will Learn

Changing the View
Using Window Controls
Zooming
Scrolling
Using Multiple Windows
Using the Microsoft Office Clipboard

Software Skills   Controlling the way Microsoft Office 2013 programs and documents are displayed on your computer monitor is a vital part of using the programs successfully. For example, you can control the size and position of the program window onscreen, and you can control the size a document is displayed. In addition, you can open more than one window onscreen at the same time, so that you can work with multiple documents and even multiple programs at once. Use the Office Clipboard to copy or move a selection from one location in a file to another, and even to a location in a different file.

What You Can Do

Changing the View

- The Microsoft Office 2013 programs provide different ways to view your data in the program window.
- Although the view options vary depending on the program, most offer at least two different views.
- In Word, Excel, and PowerPoint, you can change views using the View shortcut buttons on the status bar or the commands on the VIEW tab of the Ribbon.
- In Access, you usually use the Views button.
- You learn more about changing the view in the program sections of this book.

...

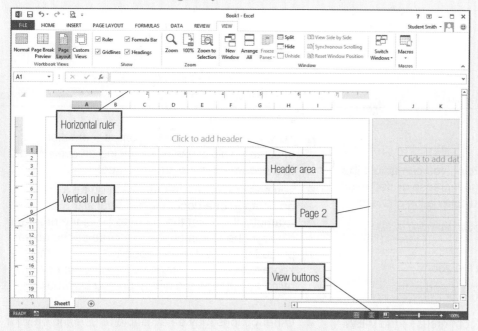

Try It!   Changing the View

1 Start Excel and create a blank workbook file.

2 Click the VIEW tab.

3 In the Workbook Views group, click the Page Layout button to change from Normal view to Page Layout view. In Excel, Page Layout view displays the header and footer areas and rulers.

4 On the status bar, click the Normal view button.

5 Leave the file open to use in the next Try It.

Page Layout view in Excel

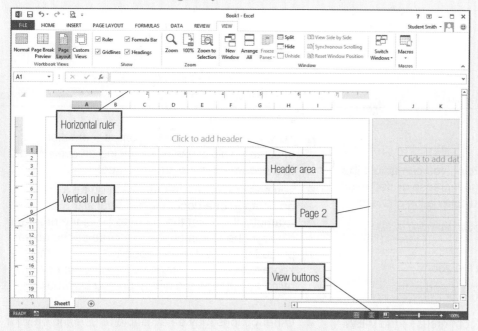

Using Window Controls

- When you start a Microsoft Office 2013 program, it opens in a program window using **default** settings.
- You can control the size and position of the program window.
  - You can **maximize** the window to fill the screen.
  - You can **minimize** the window to a Taskbar button.
  - You can **restore** a minimized window to its previous size and position.
  - You can **restore down** a maximized window to its previous size and position.
  - In Word, Excel, and PowerPoint, you can Auto-hide the Ribbon to display the window in Full Screen Mode.

Paste
To insert a selection from the Clipboard into a document.

Restore
Return a minimized window to its previous size and position on the screen.

Restore down
Return a maximized window to its previous size and position on the screen.

Scroll
Shift the displayed area of the document up, down, left, or right.

Tile
Arrange windows so they do not overlap.

Zoom
Adjust the magnification of the content displayed on the screen. This does not affect the actual size of the printed document.

Zoom in
Increase the size of the document as it is displayed onscreen.

Zoom out
Decrease the size of the document as it is displayed onscreen.

■ Use the Control buttons located on the right end of the title bar to control a program window.

  - Minimize

  ⬚ Maximize

  ⬚ Restore Down

  ✓ *Restore Down is only available in a maximized window.*

■ You can also use the program's control menu to Maximize, Minimize, or Restore the window.

Try It! **Using Window Controls**

1 In the Excel window, click the Minimize button – . When the program window is minimized, it displays as a button on the Windows Taskbar.

2 Click the Excel program icon on the Windows Taskbar to restore the window to its previous size and position.

3 In the Excel window, click the Maximize button ⬚ .

  ✓ *If the Maximize button is not displayed, the window is already maximized. Continue with step 4.*

4 Click the Restore Down button ⬚ to restore the window to its previous size and position.

5 Exit Excel without saving any changes.

Zooming

■ In Word, Excel, and PowerPoint, you can adjust the **zoom** magnification setting to increase or decrease the size a program uses to display a file onscreen.

  ✓ *The Zoom options may be different depending on the program you are using.*

■ There are three ways to set the zoom:

  • The Zoom slider on the right end of the program's status bar

  • The commands in the Zoom group of the VIEW tab on the Ribbon

  • The Zoom dialog box

■ **Zoom in** to make the data appear larger onscreen. This is useful for getting a close look at graphics, text, or data.

  ✓ *When you zoom in, only a small portion of the file will be visible onscreen at a time.*

■ **Zoom out** to make the data appear smaller onscreen. This is useful for getting an overall look at a document, slide, or worksheet.

■ You can set the zoom magnification as a percentage of a document's actual size. For example, if you set the zoom to 50%, the program displays the document half as large as the actual, printed document would appear. If you set the zoom to 200%, the program displays the document twice as large as the actual printed file would appear.

■ Other options may be available depending on your program.

  • In Word, you can select from the following preset sizes:

    ■ Page Width. Word automatically sizes the document so that the width of the page matches the width of the screen. You see the left and right margins of the page.

- Text width. Word automatically sizes the document so that the width of the text on the page matches the width of the screen. The left and right margins may be hidden.
- One Page (or Whole page). Word automatically sizes the document so that one page is visible on the screen.
- Multiple Pages. Word automatically sizes the document so that multiple pages are visible on the screen.
- Many pages. Word automatically sizes the document so that the number of pages you select can all be seen onscreen.

✓ Some options may not be available, depending on the current view. Options that are not available will appear dimmed.

- In Excel you can Zoom to Selection, which adjusts the size of selected cells to fill the entire window.
- In PowerPoint you can Fit to Window, which adjusts the size of the current slide to fill the entire window.

Try It!   **Zooming Using the Slider**

❶ Start Word, and open **B05TryA** from the data files for this lesson. Save the file as **B05TryA_xx** in the location where your teacher instructs you to store the files for this lesson.

❷ Drag the Zoom slider to the left to zoom out, or decrease the magnification. At 10% magnification, the document page is so small you cannot view the content.

❸ Drag the Zoom slider to the right to zoom in, or increase the magnification. At 500% magnification, the document page is so large you can only view a small portion of the content.

❹ Click the Zoom Out button at the left end of the Zoom slider. Each time you click, the magnification zooms out by 10%.

❺ Click the Zoom In button at the right end of the Zoom slider. Each time you click, the magnification zooms in by 10%.

❻ Leave the **B05TryA_xx** file open to use in the next Try It.

Zoom out to 10%

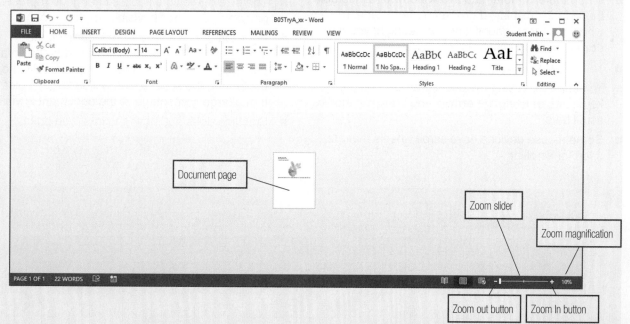

Try It!   Zooming Using the View Tab

1 With the **B05TryA_xx** file open, click the VIEW tab on the Ribbon and locate the Zoom group of commands.

2 Click the 100% button in the Zoom group. The magnification adjusts to display the document at its actual size.

3 Click the Zoom button in the Zoom group to open the Zoom dialog box.

4 Click the 75% option button and then click OK to apply the change and close the dialog box.

5 Click the Zoom button in the Zoom group again, and use the Percent increment arrows to set the zoom magnification to 150%.

✓ *In Excel, set the percentage in the Custom box.*

6 Click OK.

7 Save the changes to **B05TryA_xx**, and leave it open to use in the next Try It.

Zoom using the Zoom group on the View tab

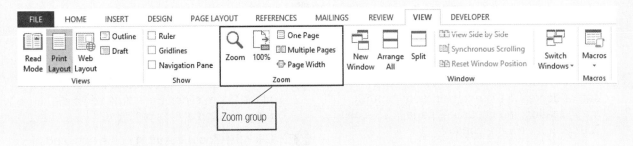

Zoom group

Scrolling

■ When there is more data in a window or dialog box than can be displayed onscreen at one time, or when the zoom magnification is set high, you must **scroll** to see the hidden parts.

■ You can scroll up, down, left, or right.

■ You can scroll using the directional keys on the keyboard, or using the arrows and boxes on the scroll bars.

■ Some mouse devices have scroll wheels that are used for scrolling.

■ If you are using a touch device, you scroll by swiping left, right, up, or down.

■ The size of the scroll boxes change to represent the percentage of the file visible on the screen.

■ For example, in a very long document, the scroll boxes will be small, indicating that a small percentage of the document is visible. In a short document, the scroll boxes will be large, indicating that a large percentage of the document is visible.

■ Scrolling does not move the insertion point.

Try It!   Scrolling

1 In the **B05TryA_xx** file, click the down scroll arrow ⊡ at the bottom of the vertical scroll bar on the right side of the window. The content in the window scrolls down.

✓ *If you have a wide screen, you may have to increase the zoom for the vertical scroll bar to display.*

2 Drag the vertical scroll box about halfway to the bottom of the scroll bar to scroll down in the file until you can see the line of text below the picture.

3 Click the right scroll arrow ▸ at the right end of the horizontal scroll bar above the status bar at the bottom of the window to scroll to the right so you can see the entire line of text.

4 Drag the vertical scroll box all the way to the top of the scroll bar to scroll to the top of the document page.

5 Save the changes to **B05TryA_xx**, and leave it open to use in the next Try It.

Tools for scrolling in a document

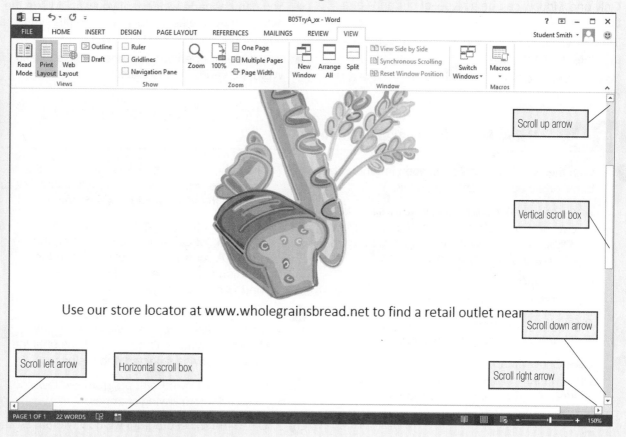

Using Multiple Windows

- You can open multiple program windows at the same time.
- You can also open multiple document windows in Word, PowerPoint, and Excel.
- Each open window is represented by a button on the Windows Taskbar.
- If there is not room on the Taskbar to display buttons for each open window, Windows displays a **group button**.

    ✓ *The Taskbar may not be visible onscreen if Windows is set to hide the Taskbar, or to display windows on top of the Taskbar. To see the Taskbar, move the mouse pointer to the edge of the screen where it usually displays.*

- Only one window can be active—or current—at a time.
- The **active window** is the one in which you are currently working.
- You can switch among open windows to make a different window active.

- You can **tile** windows if you want to see all of them at the same time. Tiled windows do not overlap; they are arranged side by side or stacked so you see the full width of each window across the screen. The active window has a brightly colored border.
- The more windows you have open, the smaller they display when tiled.
    - If necessary in smaller windows, the program may hide or condense common screen elements such as the Quick Access Toolbar and Ribbon and display only a program icon on the left end of the title bar.
    - You can click the program icon to display a shortcut menu of commands including Maximize, Minimize, and Close.
- You can **cascade** windows if you want to see the active window in its entirety, with the title bars of all open windows displayed behind it.
- You can also open and arrange multiple files in Word, PowerPoint, and Excel.

Try It! **Using Multiple Program Windows**

1 With the **B05TryA_xx** file still open in Word, start Excel and create a blank workbook.

   ✓ *To display the Windows desktop, move the mouse to the lower-right corner of the display, and click. To display the Windows 8 Start screen, move the mouse to the lower-left corner of the display and click.*

2 Start PowerPoint and create a blank presentation.

3 Right-click on a blank area of the Windows Taskbar to display a shortcut menu.

4 Click Show windows stacked to tile the three windows so you see the full width of each window; the window height is reduced.

5 Right-click on a blank area of the Windows Taskbar.

6 Click Cascade windows to overlap the three program windows; the active window displays on top.

7 Right-click on a blank area of the Windows Taskbar.

8 Click Show windows side by side to tile the three windows so you see the full height of each window; the window width is reduced.

9 Click at the beginning of the text in the **B05TryA_xx** document window. Now, the **B05TryA_xx** window is active. Notice the insertion point in the window, and that the window's border displays brighter.

10 Press and hold `ALT` and press `TAB`. A bar of icons representing open windows displays. Press `TAB` to move through the icons until the Excel window is selected, then release `ALT`.

11 Click in the PowerPoint program window and close it without saving changes.

12 Close the Excel program window without saving changes.

13 Maximize the Word program window.

14 Save the changes to **B05TryA_xx**, and leave it open to use in the next Try It.

(continued)

Try It! **Using Multiple Program Windows** (continued)

Arrange multiple windows side by side

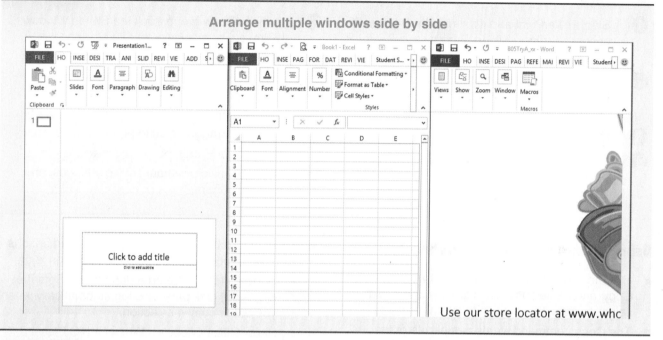

Try It! **Arranging Multiple Files in Word**

1 With the **B05TryA_xx** window open, click FILE > Open.

2 Open **B05TryB** from the data files for this lesson. Now, both files are open in Word at the same time.

3 Rest the mouse pointer on the Word icon on the Taskbar to view thumbnails of all open Word files.

4 Click the **B05TryA_xx** thumbnail to make that window active.

5 Click the VIEW tab on the Ribbon.

6 In the Window group, click the Arrange All button. The two open files are tiled in the program window.

✓ *If nothing happens when you click Arrange All, you may have to Restore Down the B05TryA_xx window.*

7 Close both files, without saving any changes, and exit Word.

Try It! **Arranging Multiple Files in Excel**

1 Start Excel and maximize the window, if necessary. Open **B05TryC** from the data files for this lesson.

2 Click FILE > Open, and then open **B05TryD** from the data files for this lesson. Both files are now open in Excel.

3 Click the VIEW tab on the Ribbon.

4 In the Window group, click the Arrange All button. The Arrange Windows dialog box opens.

5 Click the Horizontal option button and then click OK to tile the open files one above the other (stacked).

6 Click in the **B05TryC** window to make it active.

7 Click VIEW > Arrange All again to open the dialog box, click the Vertical option button, and then click OK. The files are tiles side by side.

8 Close both files, without saving any changes, and exit Excel.

Try It!   **Arranging Multiple Files in PowerPoint**

1 Start PowerPoint and maximize the window, if necessary. Open **B05TryE** from data files for this lesson.

2 Click FILE > Open, and then open **B05TryF** from the data files for this lesson. Both files are now open in PowerPoint.

3 Click the VIEW tab on the Ribbon.

4 In the Window group, click the Cascade button ⊟ to overlap the windows with the active window on top.

5 In the Window group, click the Switch Windows button ⊞ to display a list of open windows. A check mark displays beside the active window.

6 Click **B05TryE** on the Switch Windows drop-down list to make it active.

7 Click the VIEW tab, then, in the Window group, click the Arrange All button ⊟ to tile the windows side by side.

8 Close both files, without saving changes, and exit PowerPoint.

Using the Microsoft Office Clipboard

■ Use the Microsoft **Office Clipboard** with the Cut, Copy, and Paste commands to copy or move a selection from one location to another.

■ The **Copy** command stores a duplicate of the selection on the Office Clipboard, leaving the original selection unchanged.

■ The **Cut** command deletes the selection from its original location, and stores it on the Office Clipboard.

■ You can then use the **Paste** command to paste the selection from the Office Clipboard to the insertion point location in the same file or a different file.

■ By default, the last 24 items cut or copied display in the Office Clipboard task pane.

■ You can paste or delete one or all of the items.

■ You can turn the following Office Clipboard options off or on (a check mark indicates the option is on):

● Show Office Clipboard Automatically. Sets the Clipboard task pane to open automatically when you cut or copy a selection.

● Show Office Clipboard When Ctrl+C Pressed Twice. Sets Word to display the Clipboard task pane when you press and hold [CTRL] and then press [C] on the keyboard twice.

● Collect Without Showing Office Clipboard. Sets the Clipboard task pane so it does not open automatically when you cut or copy data.

● Show Office Clipboard Icon on Taskbar. Adds a Clipboard icon to the Show Hidden Icons group on the taskbar.

● Show Status Near Taskbar When Copying. Displays a ScreenTip with the number of items on the Clipboard when you cut or copy a selection.

Try It!   **Using the Microsoft Office Clipboard**

1 Start Word and maximize the window, if necessary. Open **B05TryG** from the location where the data files for this lesson are stored, and save it as **B05TryG_xx** in the location where your teacher instructs you to store the files for this lesson.

2 On the HOME tab click the Clipboard group dialog box launcher ⌐ to display the Clipboard task pane.

3 In the document, select the text *Whole Grains Bread*.

(continued)

Try It!   **Using the Office Clipboard** *(continued)*

4   Right-click the selection and click Copy. The selected text is copied to the Office Clipboard. Notice that it remains in its original location in the document, as well.

5   In the document window, click on the picture to select it. (A selection box displays around a selected picture.)

6   Right-click the selection and click Cut. The selection is deleted from the document, and displays in the Clipboard task pane.

7   In Word, open **B05TryH** from the location where the data files for this lesson are stored. The Clipboard task pane is still displayed.

8   Save the file as **B05TryH_xx** in the location where your teacher instructs you to store the files for this lesson. Make sure the insertion point is at the beginning of the document, and then press ENTER to insert a blank line. Press the up arrow key ↑ to move the insertion point to the blank line.

9   In the Clipboard task pane, click the picture of the bread. It is pasted into the document at the insertion point location. It also remains on the Clipboard so you can paste it again, if you want.

10   Right-click the picture of the runner in the document and click Copy to copy it to the Clipboard. Now, there are three selections stored on the Clipboard.

11   Save the changes to **B05TryH_xx**, and close it. **B05TryG_xx** is still open.

12   Position the insertion point at the end of the document and press ENTER to insert a new line.

13   Click the picture of the runner in the Clipboard task pane. It is pasted into the document. Even though the original file is closed, you can still paste a selection that is stored on the Clipboard. Save the changes to the file and leave it open to use in the next Try It.

Try It!   **Deleting Selections from the Office Clipboard**

1   With **B05TryG_xx** still open, click the Options button at the bottom of the Clipboard task pane. A menu of settings that affect the Clipboard displays. A check mark indicates that an option is selected.

2   In the Clipboard task pane, rest the mouse pointer on the picture of the runner, and click the down arrow that displays.

3   Click Delete on the drop-down menu. The selection is removed from the Clipboard, but it remains in place in the document.

4   Rest the mouse pointer on the picture of the bread in the Clipboard task pane, click the down arrow that displays, and click Delete.

5   Rest the mouse pointer on the text *Whole Grains Bread*, click the down arrow, and click Delete. Now, the Office Clipboard is empty.

   ✓ *Click Clear All at the top of the Clipboard task pane to quickly delete all selections.*

6   Close the Clipboard task pane.

7   Close **B05TryG_xx**, saving changes, and exit Word.

Lesson 5—Practice

You are a marketing assistant at Voyager Travel Adventures, a tour group operator. In this project, you will practice managing program windows and using the Office Clipboard to copy a picture of kayaking from a PowerPoint presentation to a Word document.

DIRECTIONS

1. Start Word, and create a blank document.

2. Save the file as **B05PracticeA_xx** in the location where your instructor tells you to store the files for this lesson.

3. Click the **VIEW** tab.

4. In the Zoom group, click the **100%** button to set the zoom to 100% magnification.

5. On the first line of the document, type the text **Kayak in the Land of the Midnight Sun** and then press ENTER .

6. Click the **HOME** tab.

7. Select the text, and then change the font to Times New Roman and the font size to 28 points.

8. Move the insertion point to the end of the document, set the font size to 12 points, and type: **Join Voyager Travel Adventures on a 10-day sea kayaking trip in one of the most beautiful and exciting places on earth! Experience the thrill of seeing whales, bears, and other wildlife up close, while enjoying a comfortable base camp and first-class dining.**

9. Press ENTER and then save the changes.

10. Click the **VIEW** tab on the Ribbon, and then, in the Document Views group, click the **Read Mode** button to change to Read Mode view.

11. Click the **Print Layout** button on the status bar to change back to Print Layout view.

12. Click the **Zoom In** button on the Zoom slider as many times as necessary to increase the zoom magnification to 150%.

13. Save the changes to the file, and then click the **Minimize** button – to minimize the Word program window.

14. Start PowerPoint and maximize the window if necessary. Open the file **B05PracticeB** from the location where the data files for this lesson are stored.

15. Click the **Word** button on the Windows Taskbar to restore the Word program window.

16. Right-click a blank area of the Windows Taskbar and click **Show windows Side by Side** to view both the Word and PowerPoint windows.

   ✓ *If you have other windows open, they will be arranged as well. Minimize them, and then repeat step 16.*

17. Click the **Maximize** button in the PowerPoint window.

18. Click the **HOME** tab, if necessary, and then click the **Clipboard group dialog box launcher** .

19. In the list of slides on the left side of the PowerPoint window, right-click **slide 2**—Kayaking in Alaska.

20. Click **Copy** on the shortcut menu to copy the selection to the Clipboard.

21. Close the PowerPoint window without saving any changes.

22. Click the **Maximize** button in the Word window.

23. Click the **HOME** tab and then click the **Clipboard group dialog box launcher** to open the Clipboard task pane. The picture copied from the presentation in step 20 should display.

24. Make sure the insertion point is at the end of the **B05PracticeA_xx** document, and then click **Kayaking in Alaska** in the Clipboard task pane to paste the selection into the Word document.

25. Click the **Zoom Out** button – on the Zoom slider until the magnification is set to 80%.

26. Rest the mouse pointer on the picture in the Clipboard task pane, click the **down arrow** that displays, and click **Delete**.

27. Click the **Close** button × in the Clipboard task pane.

28. **With your teacher's permission**, print the file.

29. Close the file, saving changes, and exit Word.

Lesson 5—Apply

In this project, you will use the skills you have learned in this lesson to cut a picture from a Word document and paste it into a PowerPoint presentation, and cut a picture from a PowerPoint presentation and paste it as an illustration in a Word document.

DIRECTIONS

1. Start Word, and open **B05ApplyA** from the data files for this lesson.
2. Save the file as **B05ApplyA_xx** in the location where your teacher instructs you to store the files for this lesson.
3. Zoom out to 80% so you can see all content in the document.
4. Display the Clipboard task pane.
5. Cut the picture from the document to the Clipboard.
6. Start PowerPoint and maximize the window, if necessary.
7. Open **B05ApplyB** from the location where the data files for this lesson are stored. Save it as **B05ApplyB_xx** in the location where your teacher instructs you to store the files for this lesson.
8. Display the Clipboard task pane, if necessary.
9. Click slide 3 in the list of slides to make that slide active. On the slide in the main area of the window, right-click the picture and click **Cut**.
10. Click the dotted line bordering the placeholder for content on the slide to select it, as shown in Figure 5-1 on the next page.
11. In the Clipboard task pane, click the picture you cut from the Word document to paste it on to the slide.
12. Close the Clipboard task pane and save the changes to the PowerPoint presentation.
13. Make the Word program window active, and then arrange the PowerPoint presentation and the Word document side by side.
14. Arrange them stacked.
15. Minimize the PowerPoint presentation window.
16. Maximize the Word window.
17. Paste the picture you copied from the PowerPoint presentation on to the last line of the Word document.
18. Close the Clipboard task pane and zoom out so you can see the entire document.
19. **With your teacher's permission**, print the file.
20. Close the file, saving all changes, and exit Word.
21. Maximize the PowerPoint window.
22. Close the file, saving changes, and exit PowerPoint.

Figure 5-1

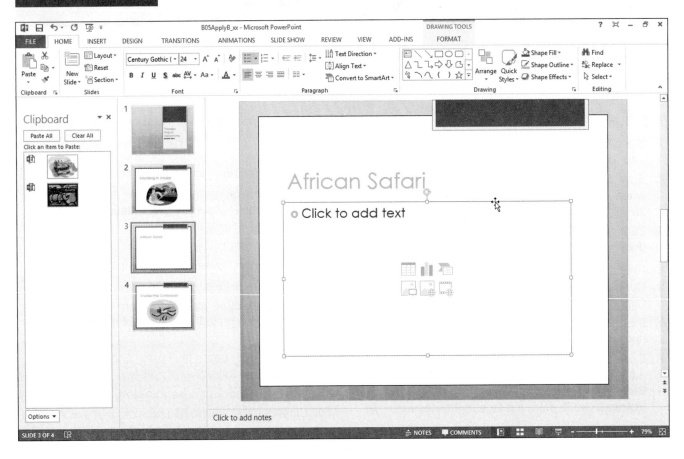

Lesson 6

Using Microsoft Office Help

➤ What You Will Learn

Using a Help Program
Searching for Help
Viewing Application Options
Customizing the Ribbon
Using AutoRecover and AutoSave

Software Skills   Each Microsoft Office 2013 program comes with Help information that you can access and display in a window while you work. Use the Help program to get help about using a specific command, search for help topics, or link to additional resources on the Microsoft Office Web site. Each program also has optional settings you use to control how the program operates. For example, you can specify how often the program should automatically save an open file.

What You Can Do

Using Microsoft Office Help

- Each Microsoft Office program has its own Help program.
- You can start Help by clicking the Help button **?** which displays in the upper-right corner of the program window, or in a dialog box.
- Help opens in a window that you can keep open while you work.
- By default, the Help Home page displays links to popular searches and program basics.
- When the mouse pointer touches a link, it changes to a hand with a pointing finger.
- Click a link to display a list of related articles or specific Help information.
- Links may be graphics, or text. Text links are formatted in blue so they stand out from the surrounding text.

WORDS TO KNOW

AutoRecover
A feature in some Microsoft Office 2013 programs that automatically saves files at a set interval so that in the event of a system failure the files may be recovered.

Read-only mode
A mode in which the open file can be viewed but not edited.

- Use the buttons on the Help window toolbar to control the Help display.
  - Back ⊖. Displays the previously viewed page.
  - Forward ⊕. Returns to a viewed page.
  - Home ⌂. Displays the Help Home page.
  - Print 🖶. Prints the current page.
  - Change Font Size A⁺. Displays an option to change the size of the characters in the Help window.
  - Keep Help on Top ⚹. Sets the Help window to always display on top of other windows.

- At the bottom of most Help pages there is a question asking if you found the information helpful. If you are connected to the Internet, click Yes, No, or I don't know to display a text box where you can type information that you want to submit to Microsoft.
- Most Microsoft Office Help information is available online. If you do not have Internet access, you may not be able to take full advantage of the Help program.

Try It!   Using Office Help

1. Start Access.
2. Click the Help button ? in the upper-right corner of the window
3. Click the first link under Popular searches.
4. Click the first link in the list that displays.
5. Click the Back button ⊖ on the toolbar to display the previously viewed page.
6. Click the Home button ⌂ on the toolbar to display the Help Home page.
7. Close the Help program window, and exit Access.

Searching for Help

- You can search for a Help topic from any Help page.
- Simply type the term or phrase for which you want to search in the Search box, and then click the Search button 🔍.

- A list of topics that contain the term or phrase displays in the Help window.
- Click a topic to display the Help information.

Try It!   Searching for Help

1. Start PowerPoint.
2. Click the Help button ? to to start the Help program.
3. Click in the Search box, and type **Print**.
4. Click the Search button 🔍. A list of topics related to the term *Print* displays.
5. Click the topic Create and print handouts to display that article.
6. Close the Help window, and exit PowerPoint.

Viewing Application Options

- Each of the Microsoft Office programs has options for controlling program settings.
- The settings depend on the program, although some are the same for all of Microsoft Office. For example, you can enter a user name, set a default storage location for files, and control the way the programs open read-only files.
- You view and set program options in the program's Options dialog box, which is accessed from the Backstage view.

Try It! Viewing Application Options

1. Start Excel and create a blank workbook. Maximize the window, if necessary.

2. Click FILE and then click Options to open the Excel Options dialog box. The General options display. Note the options under Personalize your copy of Microsoft Office.

3. Click Save in the list on the left side of the dialog box to display the Save options. Locate the default local file location, which is where Office files are saved by default.

4. Click Proofing to display the Proofing options. This is where you select options for spelling, including foreign languages.

5. Click Cancel to close the dialog box without making any changes.

6. Leave Excel open to use in the next Try It.

Customizing the Ribbon

- In Microsoft Office 2013 applications, you can customize the Ribbon by adding commands you use frequently or removing commands you rarely use.
- You can create new groups on a Ribbon tab, and you can even create a completely new tab with new groups.
- Commands for customizing the Ribbon are on the Customize Ribbon tab of the Options dialog box in each application.

Try It! Customizing the Ribbon

1. In Excel right-click anywhere on the Ribbon and click Customize the Ribbon.

2. On the right side of the dialog box, under Main Tabs, click to clear the check mark to the left of Insert, then click OK to apply the change and close the Excel Options dialog box. Notice on the Ribbon that the Insert tab no longer displays.

3. Click FILE > Options to open the Excel Options dialog box.

4. Click Customize the Ribbon.

5. Under Main tabs, click to select Home and then click the New Tab button. Excel creates a new tab with one new group.

6. Click to select New Tab (Custom), click the Rename button, and type WORKBOOK. Click OK.

7. Click to select New Group (Custom), click the Rename button, and type Management. Click OK.

8. In the upper-left of the dialog box, click the Choose commands from drop-down arrow and click File Tab.

(continued)

Try It!   **Customizing the Ribbon** *(continued)*

9 In the list of commands, click Close, and then click the Add button.

10 In the list of commands, click New, and then click the Add button.

11 In the list of commands, click Save As, and then click the Add button.

12 Click OK to close the Excel Options dialog box, then click the WORKBOOK tab on the Ribbon to view the new group of commands.

13 Right-click anywhere on the Ribbon and click Customize the Ribbon.

14 Click the Reset button and then click Reset all customizations.

15 Click Yes in the confirmation dialog box and then click OK. Leave Excel open to use in the next Try It.

Custom tab on the Ribbon

Using AutoRecover and AutoSave

■ By default the **AutoRecover** feature in Word, Excel, and PowerPoint is set to automatically save open files every ten minutes.

■ If you close a file that has been autosaved without saving changes, the autosaved version will be available on the Info tab in the Backstage view.

• If you were working in a new, unsaved file, click the Manage Versions button to recover a draft version from the UnsavedFiles folder.

• If you were working in a file that had been saved, but not since your most recent changes, it will be listed under Versions; click a version to open it.

■ An autosaved file opens in **read-only mode**, which means you must save it with a new name, or replace the existing file with the same name if you want to edit it.

■ AutoRecovered files are stored for up to four days or until you edit the file, and then deleted.

■ If a program closes unexpectedly due to a system failure or power outage, the Document Recovery task pane may display the next time you start the program.

■ Up to three autosaved versions of the file(s) you were working on before the program closed are listed in the task pane. You may select the version you want to save, and delete the others.

Try It!   **Setting AutoRecover and AutoSave Options**

1 In Excel, open **B06Try** from the location where the data files for this lesson are stored, and save it as **B06Try_xx** in the location where your teacher instructs you to store the files.

2 Click the FILE tab to display the Backstage view.

3 Click Options > Save to display the Save options in the Excel Options dialog box.

4 Use the Save AutoRecover information every increment arrows to set the time to 1 minute.

5 Verify that there is a check mark in the Keep the last autosaved version if I close without saving check box.

✓ *A check mark indicates the option is selected. If it is not, click the check box to select it.*

6 Verify that there is no check mark in the Disable AutoRecover for this workbook only check box.

7 Click OK to apply the changes and close the dialog box. Leave **B06Try_xx** open in Excel to use in the next Try It.

Try It!   Opening an Autosaved File

1 In the **B06Try_xx** file, click on cell B6, where the total sales figure displays, if it is not already selected.

2 Press DEL to delete the information.

3 Wait at least one minute without saving the file.

4 Click FILE > Close > Don't Save.

    ✓ *Notice the text in the file delete confirmation dialog box indicating that a recent copy of the file will be temporarily available.*

5 Open the **B06Try_xx** file in Excel.

6 Click FILE > Info. Under Versions, a list of autosaved versions of the file displays including versions closed without saving.

7 Under Versions, click the file that was automatically saved when you closed without saving. Notice the information bar that indicates that it is a recovered file that is temporarily stored on your computer. Notice also that the contents of cell B6 has been deleted.

8 Close both versions of the file without saving changes. Leave Excel open to use in the next Try It.

Open an autosaved file

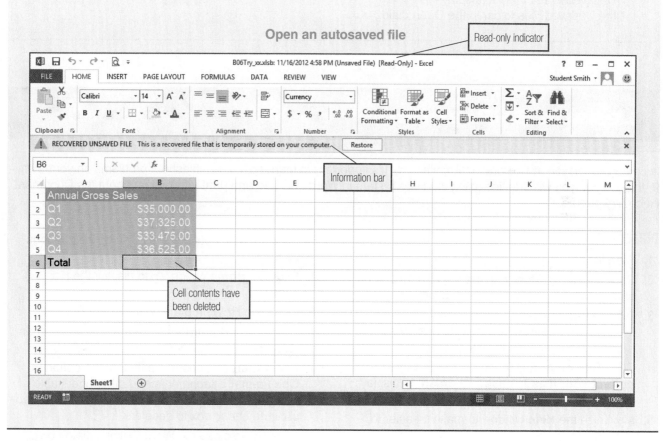

Read-only indicator

Information bar

Cell contents have been deleted

Try It! — Opening a Draft Version of an Unsaved File

1 In Excel, create a new blank workbook. Maximize the window, if necessary.

2 Type your first name, press `ENTER`, type your last name, and press `ENTER`.

3 Wait at least a minute without saving the file.

4 Close the file without saving.

5 Click FILE to display the Open page in the Backstage view.

6 At the bottom of the Recent Workbooks list on the right side of the window, click Recover Unsaved Workbooks to display the contents of the UnsavedFiles folder in the Open dialog box.

7 Click the unsaved file at the bottom of the list, and then click Open to open it in Excel.

8 Close the file without saving the changes.

9 Click FILE > Options > Save to display the Save tab of the Excel Options dialog box.

10 Change the Save AutoRecover information setting back to 10 minutes.

11 Click OK to apply the changes and close the dialog box. Exit Excel.

Lesson 6—Practice

As a new employee at Restoration Architecture, it's important to learn how to troubleshoot problems on your own. In this project, you will practice using the Help system in Word to locate and print information about the Document Recovery feature.

DIRECTIONS

1. Start Word.
2. Click the **Help** button **?** in the upper-right corner of the program window to start the Help program.
3. Type **autorecover** in the Search text box, and then click the **Search** button to display a list of articles about recovering files.
4. Click **Turn on AutoRecover and AutoSave to protect your files in case of a crash.** to display that article.
5. Maximize the **Help** window to make it easier to read the content.
6. Click the link to **My Office program did not open a recovered file** to display that article.
7. **With your teacher's permission**, click the **Print** button and print the article.
8. Click the **Back** button to display the previous page.
9. Click the **Home** button to display the Home page.
10. Close the Help program window.
11. Click **Blank document** to create a new document, and then click **FILE > Options**.
12. Under Start up options, verify that the option to Open e-mail attachments and other uneditable files in reading view is no selected. If it is selected, click the check box to deselect it.
13. Click **OK** to close the Word Options dialog box.
14. Exit Word.

Lesson 6—Apply

In this project, you will use the skills you have learned in this lesson to search the Help program in Word for information about formatting text with superscript and subscript.

DIRECTIONS

1. Start Word, and open the file **B06Apply** from the data files for this lesson.
2. Save the file as **B06Apply_xx** in the location where your teacher instructs you to store the files for this lesson.
3. Create a custom Ribbon tab named **DOCUMENT**, with a group named **Management**. Add the New, Close, Save As, and Print buttons to the group.
4. On the first line of the file, type your first name and last name. Press [ENTER] and type today's date, and then press [ENTER] to insert a blank line.
5. Start the Help program.
6. Search for information about how to format text with superscript and subscript.

7. Set the Help window to remain on top of other windows, and then use the information in the Help article to apply superscript to the *nd* and *rd* in the sentence.
8. Use the information in the Help article to apply subscript to the *2* in *H₂O*.
9. Close the Help program window. The **B06Apply_ xx** document should look similar to Figure 6-1.
10. Save the changes to the document.
11. **With your teacher's permission**, print the file.
12. Reset all Ribbon customizations.
13. Close the file, saving changes, and exit Word.

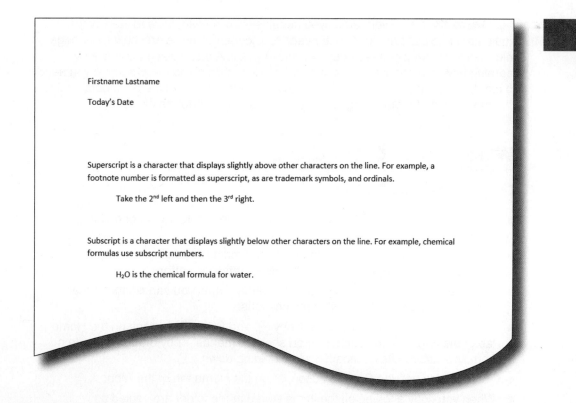

Figure 6-1

Firstname Lastname

Today's Date

Superscript is a character that displays slightly above other characters on the line. For example, a footnote number is formatted as superscript, as are trademark symbols, and ordinals.

    Take the 2nd left and then the 3rd right.

Subscript is a character that displays slightly below other characters on the line. For example, chemical formulas use subscript numbers.

    H_2O is the chemical formula for water.

Lesson 7

Managing Information Technology

WORDS TO KNOW

Business document
A professional document used to communicate information within a company, or between one company and another.

Compress
Minimize the size of something.

Destination location
The location where a folder or file is stored after it is moved.

Extract
Remove, or separate from.

IT strategy
A plan that identifies how information technology will be put in place over time to help an organization achieve its overall business goals.

Source location
The original location where a folder or file is stored.

Technology infrastructure
The computer systems, networking devices, software, and other technologies used to collect, store, and distribute information.

➤ What You Will Learn

Copying Files and Folders
Moving Files and Folders
Compressing Files
Recognizing Types of Business Documents
Determining the Risks and Rewards of Developing an IT Strategy
Identifying Needed Equipment and Supplies
Establishing, Scheduling, and Following Maintenance Procedures

Software Skills   Every employee benefits from knowing how to identify the equipment and supplies he or she needs to accomplish tasks and how to manage information technology resources to achieve goals. A basic place to start is by learning how to recognize types of business documents and the programs you need to create, view, and edit them. You can also save money and time by understanding the importance of maintaining IT equipment so that it performs efficiently.

What You Can Do

Copying Files and Folders

- You can use Windows File Explorer to copy a file or folder from one storage location to another.
- When you copy a file or folder, the original remains stored in it its **source location** and the copy is stored in the **destination location**.
- Both the original and the copy have the same name; you can tell them apart because they are stored in different locations.
- You copy a file or folder using the Copy 🗐 and Paste 📋 buttons on the Home tab of the File Explorer Ribbon or on shortcut menus, or by dragging the item from its source to its destination while holding down CTRL .
- You can also use the Copy to button 📋 on the Home tab of the Ribbon,
- When you copy a folder, all the items stored in the folder are copied as well.

- If you try to copy a folder or file to a location that already contains a folder or file with the same name, Windows offers three options:
  - Replace the file in the destination. Select this option to replace the existing file with the copy.

- Skip this file. Select this option to cancel the command.
- Compare info from both files. Select this option to display information about both files. You can choose to replace one file or to keep both.

Try It!   **Copying Files and Folders**

1 From the Windows desktop, click the File Explorer button 📁 on the Taskbar and navigate to the location where your teacher instructs you to store the files for this lesson.

2 Create a new folder named **B07Try_Copy_xx**, and open it.

3 Without closing the File Explorer window, right-click the **File Explorer** button 📁 on the Taskbar and click **File Explorer** on the shortcut menu to open a second File Explorer window. In the second window, navigate to the location where the data files for this lesson are stored.

4 Click a blank area of the Windows Taskbar and click Show windows side by side to arrange the two windows so you can see the contents of both.

5 In the location where the data files are stored, right-click the Excel file named **B07TryA** and click Copy on the shortcut menu.

6 Right-click a blank area in the **B07Try_Copy_xx** folder and click Paste on the shortcut menu.

7 Press and hold CTRL and drag the **B07TryB** Word file from the data files storage location to the **B07Try_Copy_xx** folder.

8 Drop the file and release CTRL when the ScreenTip displays *Copy to B07Try_Copy_xx*.

9 On your screen, you can see the two copied files in the **B07Try_Copy_xx** folder. The originals are still in the original location.

10 Maximize the **B07Try_Copy_xx** folder, and click the Back button ⬅ to return to the location where you are storing the files for this lesson.

11 Click the **B07Try_Copy_xx** folder to select it, and click Home > Copy to 📋 > Desktop.

12 Navigate to the desktop, locate the **B07Try_Copy_xx** folder, and open it.

13 Navigate back to the desktop and delete the **B07Try_Copy_xx** folder.

14 In File Explorer, navigate to the location where you are storing the files for this lesson. Notice that the original **B07Try_Copy_xx** folder is still there. Leave both File Explorer windows open to use in the next Try It.

(continued)

Try It!   Copying Files and Folders *(continued)*

Copy by dragging

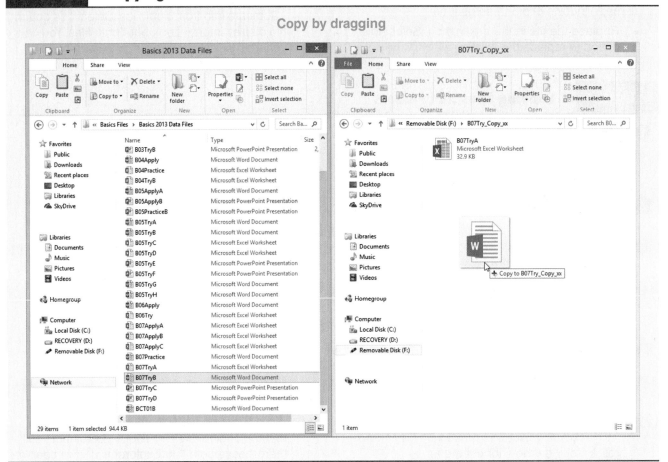

Moving Files and Folders

- You can move a file or folder from one storage location to another.
- When you move a file or folder, it is deleted from its source location and is stored in the destination location.
- You move a file or folder using the Cut ✂ and Paste 📋 buttons on the Home tab of the File Explorer Ribbon or on shortcut menus, or by dragging it to the destination.
- You can also use the Move to button 📁 on the Home tab of the Ribbon.

- When you move a folder, all the items stored in the folder are moved as well.
- If you try to move a folder or file to a location that already contains a folder or file with the same name, Windows offers three options:
  - Replace the file in the destination. Select this option to replace the existing file with the one you are moving.
  - Skip this file. Select this option to cancel the command.
  - Compare info for both files. Select this option to display information about both files. You can choose to replace one file or to keep both.

Try It!   Moving Files and Folders

1 In the File Explorer window open the **B07Try_Copy_xx** folder.

2 Right-click the **B07TryA** file, and click Cut on the shortcut menu.

3 Click the Back button ⊛ to display the location where you are storing the files for this lesson, right-click a blank area and click Paste on the shortcut menu. The file is deleted from its previous location and pasted into the new location.

4 In the current window, create a new folder named **B07Try_Move_xx**.

5 Drag the **B07TryA** file on to the **B07Try_Move_xx** folder.

6 Release the mouse button when the ScreenTip displays *Move to B07Try_Move_xx*. The file is deleted from its original location, and pasted into the **B07Try_Move_xx** folder.

7 Click the **B07Try_Move_xx** folder, and click Home > Move to 📁 > Desktop.

8 Navigate to the desktop and open the **B07Try_Move_xx** folder. Note that the file was moved as well.

9 Click the Back button ⊛, click to select the **B07Try_Move_xx** folder on the desktop, and click Home > Cut ✂ .

10 Navigate to the location where you are storing the files for this lesson, and click Home > Paste 📋 .

11 Open the **B07Try_Copy_xx** folder, and leave File Explorer open to use in the next Try It.

Compressing Files

- **Compress**, or zip, a file to minimize its size, making it easier to store or transmit.
- You use Windows to compress files.
- When you compress a file, you create a compressed, or zipped, folder in which the file is stored.
- By default, the compressed folder has the same name as the compressed file, but you can rename it, if you want.
- You can compress multiple files together into one folder.

- You can even compress entire folders.
- To use the compressed files, you must extract them from the folder.
- When you **extract** the files, you copy them from the compressed folder to a destination location. By default, the location is a new folder with the same name as the compressed folder, but you can select a different location.
- The Zip command is on on the Share tab of the File Explorer Ribbon and on shortcut menus; the Extract command is on the Compressed Folder Tools Extract tab of the Ribbon and on shortcut menus.

Try It!   Compressing Files

1 Arrange the **B07Try_Copy_xx** window and the window for the location where the data files for this lesson are stored side by side.

2 Press and hold `CTRL` and drag the **B07TryC** file to copy it from the location where the data files are stored to the **B07Try_Copy_xx** folder.

(continued)

Try It!   Compressing Files (continued)

3 In the **B07Try_Copy_xx** window, click to select the **B07TryC** file, then click Share > Zip 📁 on the Ribbon. Windows zips the file into a compressed folder. The new folder name is selected so you can type a new name.

4 Type **B07Try_compressed_xx**, and press ENTER . Notice that the compressed folder has fewer kilobytes (KB) than the original file. Kilobytes are a measurement of size.

5 In the location where the data files are stored, right-click the **B07TryD** file and click Copy on the shortcut menu.

6 Right-click the **B07Try_compressed_xx** folder and click Paste on the shortcut menu. This copies the **B07TryD** file into the compressed folder.

7 Double-click the **B07Try_compressed_xx** folder to open it and view its contents. It contains both the **B07TryC** and **B07TryD** files.

8 Click the Back button ⬅ and maximize the File Explorer window in which the **B07Try_compressed_xx** folder is stored. Leave it open to use in the next Try It.

A compressed file is smaller than the original

Extracting Compressed Files

1 In File Explorer, click to select the **B07Try_ compressed_xx** folder, and then click Extract all 📁 on the Extract tab of the Ribbon. Windows displays the name of the default folder where it will store the extracted files.

2 Select just the text *compressed* in the folder name and then type **extracted** to change the name to **B07Try_extracted_xx**.

3 Click Extract. Windows creates a new folder in the current location and copies the files to it. By default, it opens the new folder in a separate window. You can see the extracted files.

✓ *If the window does not open by default, double-click the B07Try_extracted_xx folder to open it.*

4 Close all open File Explorer windows.

Recognizing Types of Business Documents

- Some common **business documents** used by most companies include letters, memos, fax covers, marketing presentations, training slide shows, invoices, purchase orders, press releases, agendas, reports, and newsletters.

- Certain businesses—or departments within a larger company—may have specialized documents. For example, a law office or legal department produces legal documents such as wills, contracts, and bills of sale.

- In additional, individuals create personal business documents such as letters, research papers, and resumes.

- Each Microsoft Office program is designed for creating specific types of business documents.

  - Microsoft Word is used for text-based documents, such as letters, memos, and reports.

  - Microsoft Excel is used for numeric or financial documents, such as invoices, sales reports, and graphic analysis.

  - Microsoft PowerPoint is used for slide shows and presentation graphics.

  - Microsoft Access is used to store and search data and create forms, tables, and reports based on that data.

- Most business documents have standard formats, which means each type of document includes similar parts.

- You will learn about the standard formats for different types of documents throughout the lessons in this book.

Determining the Risks and Rewards of Developing an IT Strategy

- An **IT strategy** is a road map or plan that identifies how information technology will be put in place over time to help an organization achieve its overall business goals.

- A successful IT strategy prepares a business for future growth and puts the technology in place that a company needs to make the best use of available resources, solve problems, and compete.

- Companies that take the time and make the effort to include IT in their overall business plans are more likely to implement successful IT strategies.

  - Different businesses have different IT needs.

  - A small business might require only a desktop computer, an all-in-one printer/scanner device, and an Internet connection.

  - A large business might require hundreds of desktop PCs, notebook and tablet computers, one or more internal networks, corporate servers, a telephone system, printers, scanners, and copier machines, projection systems, and more.

- Some businesses might require specialized IT tools.

  - A construction company might require rugged portable devices that can withstand extreme weather or rough conditions.

  - A design firm might require high-end computer-aided design software, while an investment firm requires high-end financial applications.

- A successful IT strategy takes into consideration factors such as the current needs of the company, how to best use systems currently in place, and how to implement new technologies that support the business.

- It also takes into consideration the cost of new equipment, maintenance, and training, as well as the physical environment in which IT will be installed. For example, a small business must consider if there is space to install new computer systems. A large company might need to install a climate control system for a new data center.

- There are two primary risks of locking in to a particular IT strategy: a plan that is too advanced, and a plan that is not advanced enough.
  - If a company puts a plan in place that is more advanced than it can support, it wastes money on unnecessary technology that employees do not know how to use.
  - If a company puts a plan in place that is not advanced enough, the company may lose ground to its competition or find that it has to spend money to upgrade systems sooner than expected.

- When an IT strategy balances the needs, costs, and corporate goals, the risks are minimized and the rewards are achievable.

Identifying Needed Equipment and Supplies

- Almost every business has a **technology infrastructure**, which is the computer systems, networking devices, software, and other technologies used to collect, store, and distribute information.

- No matter how large or small a business may be, it is vital that someone monitor, manage, and maintain the technology infrastructure in order to keep the business running.
  - In a small organization, each employee might be responsible for his or her own technology. That might mean changing the ink in a desktop printer.
  - In larger organizations, the employees in the IT department are responsible for the IT systems.

- Performing an inventory of the current IT situation is a good first step in developing an IT strategy. Knowing what is already in place and how well it meets current needs helps define future needs.

- Researching and budgeting for an IT project is much like planning any project. You can check pricing online, get bids from various consultants and vendors, or use a combination of those techniques.

- When budgeting for IT systems, it is important to factor in the costs of ongoing support, maintenance, and training.

Establishing, Scheduling, and Following Maintenance Procedures

- Technology systems require maintenance to operate properly. In a large company, maintenance is a constant need. A dedicated staff of technicians responds to employee requests, services hardware, and upgrades software, or outside technicians are hired to provide service.

- In a small company, maintenance might be as basic as keeping a computer keyboard clean, installing a virus protection program, and changing the ink in the printer, when necessary.

- All systems will be more reliable and effective if maintenance is performed on a regular basis.

- Establishing maintenance schedules enables you to plan and perform maintenance appropriately, provide notice to users when maintenance is due, and budget for ongoing maintenance costs.

- Many maintenance tasks can be automated, including data backup, virus scans, and program updates.

- Manufacturers provide maintenance procedures for all equipment and programs. If the user does not follow the manufacturer's recommended maintenance procedures, warranties and service contracts become void, and the company becomes responsible for costs associated with damage and repair.

- In addition, qualified IT professionals are able to diagnose and solve problems individually and as a team to keep the systems running efficiently.

Lesson 7—Practice

You have been hired by the Michigan Avenue Athletic Club to set up policies for purchasing and maintaining information technology equipment and supplies. In this project, you use Word to create a memo to the office manager asking him to conduct an inventory of hardware currently owned by the club, the software programs currently in use, and the current maintenance schedules. You also ask him to provide you with a list of needed equipment and supplies. You will create a folder and a compressed folder where you can store the related files.

DIRECTIONS

1. Start Word.
2. Open the file **B07Practice** from the data files for this lesson, and save it as **B07Practice_xx** in the location where your teacher instructs you to store the files for this lesson.
3. Replace the text *Student's Name* with your own first and last name.
4. Replace the text *Today's Date* with the current date.
5. Press CTRL + END to move the insertion point to the last line of the document and type the following paragraph:

   Tom, as a first step in developing policies for purchasing and maintaining the club's IT equipment and supplies, I need to know what we have and what we need. Please take an inventory of the hardware we currently own, the software we currently use, and the maintenance schedule currently in place. I would also like a list of any equipment and supplies we need.

6. Press ENTER and type the following paragraph:

   I would like to receive this information by the end of the week. Thanks so much for your assistance. Let me know if you have any questions.

7. Save the document. It should look similar to Figure 7-1 on the next page.
8. **With your teacher's permission**, print the file.
9. Close the file and exit Word.
10. Open File Explorer and navigate to the desktop.

11. Create a folder named **B07Practice_xx** on the desktop.
12. Right-click the **B07Practice_xx** folder and click **Cut** on the shortcut menu. This cuts the folder from the desktop and stores it on the Clipboard.
13. Navigate to the location where your teacher instructs you to store the files for this lesson.
14. Right-click a blank area of the window, and click **Paste** on the shortcut menu to paste the folder from the Clipboard into the selected storage location.
15. Right-click the **B07Practice_xx** Word file, and click **Copy** on the shortcut menu.
16. Right-click the **B07Practice_xx** folder, and click **Paste** on the shortcut menu. This copies the file into the folder. The original file remains stored in its current location.
17. Right-click the original **B07Practice_xx** Word file, click Send to, and then click Compressed (zipped) folder. The file is sent to a compressed folder with the default name **B07Practice_xx**.
18. Type **B07Practice_xx_compressed** to rename the folder, and press ENTER to rename the compressed folder.
19. Right-click the original **B07Practice_xx** Word file, and click **Delete** on the shortcut menu.
20. Click **Yes** to delete the file. Now, you have a regular folder named **B07Practice_xx**, which contains the Word memo file, and a compressed folder named **B07Practice_xx_compressed**, which contains a compressed version of the Word memo file.
21. Leave File Explorer open to use in the Apply project.

Figure 7-1

Michigan Avenue Athletic Club
235 Michigan Avenue
Chicago, Illinois 60601

Memorandum

To: Office Manager
From: Firstname Lastname
Date: Today's Date
Re: Equipment Inventory

Tom, as a first step in developing policies for purchasing and maintaining the club's IT equipment and supplies, I need to know what we have and what we need. Please take an inventory of the hardware and software we currently use, and the maintenance schedule currently in place. Would also like a list of any equipment and supplies we need.

I would like to receive this information by the end of the week. Thanks so much for your assistance. Let me know if you have any questions.

Lesson 7—Apply

In this project, you use the skills you learned in this lesson to copy, move, and compress files.

DIRECTIONS

1. In File Explorer, in the location where your teacher instructs you to store the files for this lesson, create a new folder named **B07Apply_xx**.

2. Copy **B07ApplyA** from the location where the data files for this lesson are stored to the **B07Apply_xx** folder.

3. Copy **B07ApplyB** from the location where the data files for this lesson are stored to the **B07Apply_xx** folder.

4. Copy **B07ApplyC** from the location where the data files for this lesson are stored to the **B07Apply_xx** folder.

5. Compress the **B07Apply_xx** folder and its contents into a compressed folder named **B07Apply_xx_compressed**.

6. Move the **B07Practice_xx** regular folder into the **B07Apply_xx_compressed** compressed folder.

7. Open the **B07Apply_xx_compressed** compressed folder.

8. Extract all files from **B07Apply_xx_compressed** into a folder named **B07Apply_xx_extracted**.

9. Close all open File Explorer windows.

End-of-Chapter Activities

➤ Basics Chapter 1—Critical Thinking

Create an IT Strategy

You are responsible for developing a list of ways a group, organization, or business might use Microsoft Office 2013 as part of an IT strategy. Start by selecting the group. It might be a club, team, or organization to which you belong, the place where you work, or any business of your choice. Research its goals, current IT infrastructure, and requirements. You can do this by talking to the people responsible for the information technology and taking notes, and also by observing the information technology in use. Then, use Microsoft Office 2013 and the skills you have learned in this chapter to develop your list.

DIRECTIONS

1. Create a folder named **BCT01_xx** in the location where your teacher instructs you to store the files for this chapter.

2. Start the Microsoft Office 2013 program you want to use to create the list. For example, you might use Word or Excel.

3. Create a blank file and save the file as **BCT01A_xx** in the **BCT01_xx** folder.

4. Type your name in the file.

5. Type the date in the file.

6. Type a title for your list and format the title using fonts, font styles, and font color.

7. Type the list of ways the group, organization, or business might use Microsoft Office 2013 as part of an IT strategy.

8. Save the changes to the file.

9. Start Word, if necessary, and open **BCT01B**. Save it as **BCT01B_xx** in the **BCT01_xx** folder.

10. Type your name on the first line of the file and the date on the second line. Then, move the insertion point to the blank line above the picture, and type a paragraph explaining the list you typed in step 7.

11. Save the changes to the file.

12. **With your teacher's permission**, print the file. If necessary, adjust page formatting such as orientation, scale, and margins so its fits on a single page. It should look similar to Illustration 1A on the next page.

13. Copy the picture in the file to the Clipboard, and then close the file, saving all changes.

14. Make the **BCT01A_xx** file active, and paste the picture at either the beginning or end of the file.

15. Save the changes, and, **with your teacher's permission**, print the file. If necessary, adjust page formatting such as orientation, scale, and margins so it fits on a single page. It should look similar to Illustration 1B on the next page.

16. Close the file, saving changes, and exit all programs.

17. Compress the **BCT01_xx** folder into a compressed folder named **BCT01_xx_compressed**.

Illustration 1A

Firstname   Lastname

Today's Date

Ways the Marching Band Might Use Microsoft Office 2013

Use Microsoft Word to create memos to band members, letters to parents, and fundraising letters to send to neighborhood businesses.
Use Microsoft Excel to create worksheets tracking income and expenses, to create a budget, and to create graphs illustrating the data.
Use Microsoft Access to set up and maintain a database of members, parents, volunteers, and community supporters.
Use Microsoft Publisher to create postcard mailings, flyers, and even brochures.
Use Microsoft PowerPoint to create an informational presentation.
Use Microsoft Outlook for communication.

Illustration 1B

Firstname Lastname

Today's Date

Explanation of My List

I think the marching band could benefit from using all of the Microsoft Office 2013 programs. It will be faster to use Microsoft Word to create all text-based documents such as letters and memos. Old files can be reused and updated, and it is easier to make corrections. It also looks professional. Microsoft Excel automates calculations so it is easier to keep track of income and expenses and to identify ways to save and spend. It makes it easy to create charts that illustrate the data which might help the band convince the school committee to increase funding. By creating databases in Microsoft Access the band can easily keep track of the people and equipment it has. The databases can be used to generate mass mailings and reports. With Microsoft Publisher, the band can create professional quality publications. Microsoft Office makes it easy to create and store email messages, to schedule appointments and meetings, and to keep track of tasks that must be accomplished. With Microsoft PowerPoint, the band can create a presentation to use at back-to-school night and other times to provide information and even a little marketing.

➤ Basics Chapter 1—Portfolio Builder

Create a Memo

Voyager Travel Adventures is opening a new office. You have been asked to make a list of IT equipment and supplies needed to get the office up and running. In this project, you will create a folder for storing your work. You will start Microsoft Office 2013 programs and create, save, and print files. You will also open and save existing files, use the Office Clipboard to copy a selection from one file to another, and prepare a file for distribution. Finally, you will compress the files.

DIRECTIONS

1. On the Windows desktop, create a new folder named **BPB01_xx**.

2. Move the folder to the location where your teacher instructs you to store the files for this chapter.

3. Start Microsoft Word, and create a new blank document. Save the file in the **BPB01_xx** folder with the name **BPB01A_xx**.

4. On the first line of the document, type today's date. Press [ENTER] and type your full name. Press [ENTER] and type the following:

   I recommend the following IT equipment to get the new Voyager Travel Adventures office up and running:

5. Press [ENTER] and type the following list, pressing [ENTER] at the end of each line to start a new line.

   4 personal computers running Microsoft Windows 8, with Microsoft Office 2013

   2 notebook computers to be shared as necessary, also running Microsoft Windows 8, with Microsoft Office 2013

   2 tablet PCs

   Wireless network devices

   1 printer

   1 printer/fax/copier all-in-one

   1 external hard drive for backing up data

   Internet telephone system

6. Save the changes to the document.

7. Format the date in bold and increase the font size to 14, then format your name in bold italic, and increase the font size to 12.

8. Start the Help program and locate information about how to format a bulleted list.

9. Use the Help information to apply bullet list formatting to the list of equipment.

   If you cannot find information about bullet list formatting, select the items in the list, and then click the Bullets button :≡ ▾ in the Paragraph group on the HOME tab of the Ribbon.

10. Save the changes to the file.

11. Start Microsoft Excel and open the file **BPB01B** from the data files for this chapter. Save the file in the **BPB01_xx** folder as **BPB01B_xx**.

12. Copy the picture in the Excel file to the Clipboard.

13. Arrange the Excel and Word windows side by side.

14. Make the Word window active and display the Clipboard task pane.

15. Exit Excel without saving any changes, and maximize the Word window.

16. Paste the picture on to the last line of the document, and then delete it from the Clipboard.

17. Close the Clipboard task pane.

18. Save the changes to the Word document.

19. Change the margins for the document to Wide.

20. **With your teacher's permission**, print the document. It should look similar to Illustration 1C on the next page.

21. Close the file, saving changes, and exit Word.

22. Navigate to the location where you are saving the files for this lesson.

23. Compress the entire **BPB01_xx** folder into a compressed folder named **BPB01_xx_compressed**.

24. If you have completed your session, close all open windows and log off your computer account.

Today's Date

Firstname Lastname

I recommend the following IT equipment to get the new Voyager Travel Adventures office up and running:

- 4 personal computers running Microsoft Windows 8, with Microsoft Office 2013
- 2 notebook computers to be shared as necessary, also running Microsoft Windows 8 and Microsoft Office 2013
- 2 tablet PCs
- Wireless network devices
- 1 printer
- 1 printer/fax/copier all-in-one
- 1 external hard drive for backing up data
- Internet telephone system

(Courtesy Yuri Arcurs/Shutterstock)

Getting Started with Microsoft Excel 2013

Lesson 1
Touring Excel

- Starting Excel
- Naming and Saving a Workbook
- Exploring the Excel Window
- Exploring the Excel Interface
- Navigating the Worksheet
- Changing Worksheet Views
- Closing a Workbook and Exiting Excel

Lesson 2
Worksheet and Workbook Basics

- Creating a New (Blank) Workbook
- Entering Text and Labels
- Editing Text
- Using Undo and Redo
- Clearing Cell Contents
- Inserting a Built-In Header or Footer
- Previewing and Printing a Worksheet

Lesson 3
Adding Worksheet Contents

- Opening an Existing Workbook and Saving It with a New Name
- Entering and Editing Numeric Labels and Values
- Using AutoComplete
- Using Pick From List
- Using AutoCorrect
- Checking the Spelling in a Worksheet

Lesson 4
Worksheet Formatting

- Choosing a Theme
- Applying Cell Styles
- Applying Font Formats
- Merging and Centering Across Cells
- Applying Number Formats

Lesson 5
More on Cell Entries and Formatting

- Entering Dates
- Filling a Series
- Aligning Data in a Cell
- Wrapping Text in Cells
- Changing Column Width and Row Height
- Using Keyboard Shortcuts

Lesson 6
Working with Ranges

- Selecting Ranges
- Entering Data by Range
- Making a Range Entry Using a Collapse Button

Lesson 7
Creating Formulas

- Entering a Formula
- Using Arithmetic Operators
- Editing a Formula
- Copying a Formula Using the Fill Handle
- Using the SUM Function

Lesson 8
Copying and Pasting

- Copying and Pasting Data
- Copying Formats
- Copying Formulas Containing a Relative Reference
- Copying Formulas Containing an Absolute Reference

Lesson 9
Techniques for Moving Data

- Inserting and Deleting Cells
- Inserting, Deleting, Hiding, and Unhiding Columns and Rows
- Cutting and Pasting Data
- Using Drag-and-Drop Editing
- Transposing Columns and Rows

Lesson 10
Sheet, Display, and Print Operations

- Displaying, Printing, and Hiding Formulas
- Printing Titles
- Changing Orientation
- Scaling a Printout to Fit
- Previewing and Printing a Worksheet

End-of-Chapter Activities

Lesson 1

Touring Excel

➤ What You Will Learn

Starting Excel
Naming and Saving a Workbook
Exploring the Excel Window
Exploring the Excel Interface
Navigating the Worksheet
Changing Worksheet Views
Closing a Workbook and Exiting Excel

Software Skills   When you want to analyze business, personal, or financial data and create reports in a table format consisting of rows and columns, use the Microsoft Excel 2013 spreadsheet application in the Microsoft Office 2013 suite.

What You Can Do

Starting Excel

- Start Excel from the Windows 8 Start screen.
  - Click the Excel 2013 tile to start the program.
  - You can also find the program on the Apps screen. Scroll to the Excel 2013 tile and click to start.
- When you create a new blank worksheet, Excel displays a list of recently used files and a gallery of available **templates**.
- Click the Blank workbook tile to create a new Excel document.
- When Excel starts, it displays an empty **workbook** with one **worksheet**.
- A worksheet contains rows and columns that intersect to form **cells**.
- Gridlines mark the boundaries of each cell.

WORDS TO KNOW

Active cell
The active cell contains the cell pointer. There is a dark outline around the active cell.

The Backstage view
A feature of Microsoft Office 2013 from which you access file and program management commands.

Cell
A cell is the intersection of a column and a row on a worksheet. You enter data into cells to create a worksheet.

Cell address or cell reference
The location of a cell in a worksheet as identified by its column letter and row number.

Formula bar
As you enter data in a cell, it simultaneously appears in the formula bar, which is located above the worksheet.

Scroll
A way to view locations on the worksheet without changing the active cell.

Sheet tabs
Tabs that appear at the bottom of the workbook window, which display the name of each worksheet.

SkyDrive
A file hosting service that allows you to upload and sync files to a virtual, or cloud, storage environment. Files can then be accessed from a Web browser or a local device.

Tab scrolling buttons
Buttons that appear to the left of the sheet tabs, which allow you to scroll hidden tabs into view.

Template
A document that contains formatting, styles, and sample text that you can use to create new documents.

Workbook
An Excel file with one or more worksheets.

Worksheet
The work area for entering and calculating data made up of columns and rows separated by gridlines (light gray lines). Also called a spreadsheet.

Try It!   **Starting Excel**

① From the Windows Start screen, click the Excel 2013 program tile.

  ✓ *If your keyboard has a Windows key (a key with the Windows logo on it), you can press that key at any time to display the Start screen.*

  OR

  a. Right-click a blank area of the Windows Start screen.
  b. Click the All apps button .
  c. Scroll to the Excel 2013 tile.
  d. Click Excel 2013.

OR

  a. Move the mouse pointer to the lower-left corner of the screen.
  b. When you see the Windows Start screen icon, click to open the start screen.

② Click Blank workbook.

③ Explore the features of the Excel program window.

④ Leave the file open to use in the next Try It.

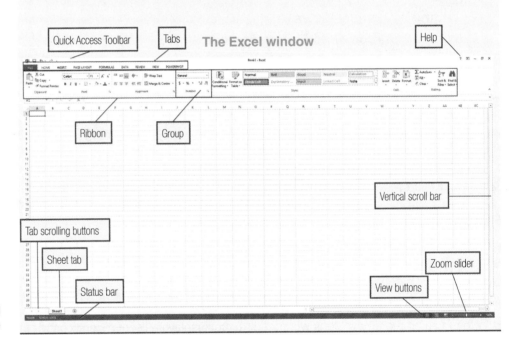

Naming and Saving a Workbook

■ After entering data in a workbook, you must save it, or that data will be lost when you exit Excel.

■ A saved workbook is referred to as a file.

■ A file may be saved on a hard disk, a removable disk, a shared group drive, or to the **SkyDrive**. Files saved to the SkyDrive are stored virtually on Microsoft's SkyDrive.com Web site.

■ You must provide a name for the file when you save it. File names should be descriptive, with a limit of 255 characters for the name, disk drive, and path.

■ A file name may contain letters, numbers, and spaces, but not \ / : * ? " < > or | .

■ Excel automatically adds a period and a file type extension (usually .xlsx) to the end of a file name when you save it.

- You must select a location in which to save your file, for example, the Documents folder. You can also create new folders in which to store your workbooks.

- The default Excel file format is .xlsx, or Strict Open XML Spreadsheet file format. This XML-based file format allows your workbooks to integrate more easily with outside data sources and results in smaller workbook file sizes than in earlier versions of Excel.

  ✓ *You can install updates to some older versions of Excel so they can read the new .xlsx format.*

- Data can also be saved in other formats, such as HTML, Excel Binary (a file format for very large workbooks), or older versions of Excel (.xls).

  ✓ *You might want to save data in a different format in order to share that data with someone who uses a different version of Excel or a Web browser to view your data.*

- **The Backstage view** shows the places in which you can save your file, such as the SkyDrive or Computer. The the Backstage view will display the first time you save a file.

  ✓ *You can exit the the Backstage view by clicking the Back button* ⊙.

- When you select Computer, the Recent Folders list provides the locations of folders you have recently opened.

- You can select a different storage location by double-clicking Computer or by clicking Browse.

- Once you've saved a workbook, you need only click the Save button 🖫 as you work to resave any changes made since the last save action. You will not need to reenter the file name.

- You can save a previously saved file with a different name by using the Save As tab in the the Backstage view.

- Click Browse to browse to a location and the Save As dialog box will open.

  ✓ *If the location where you want to store the file displays in the the Backstage view, click it instead of clicking Browse.*

- In the Save As dialog box, you can rename the file, browse to a location, and save the file.

Try It!   **Naming and Saving a Workbook**

① Click the FILE tab.

   OR

   Click the Save button 🖫 on the Quick Access Toolbar.

② Click Save As.

③ Click Computer and then click Browse 🗁.

   OR

   Double-click Computer.

④ In the File name text box, type **E01Try_xx**.

   ✓ *Replace xx with your own name or initials, as instructed by your teacher. For example, if your name is Mary Jones, type* **E01Try_MaryJones** *or* **E01Try_MJ**.

⑤ Use the Navigation pane to navigate to the location where your teacher instructs you to store the files for this lesson.

   ✓ *Use the drop-down lists at the top of the Save As dialog box or the locations in the Navigation pane at the left to select the folder to save to. Clicking the triangle beside any disk or folder in the Navigation pane displays or hides that location's contents. If saving to a USB drive, make sure it is inserted. Scroll down the Navigation pane at left, and click the USB drive under Computer. Refer to Lesson 1 of the Basics section of this book for more information on navigating.*

⑥ Click the Save button.

⑦ Leave the file open to use in the next Try It.

Exploring the Excel Window

- In the worksheet, a green border appears around the **active cell.**
- You can change the active cell using the mouse, touch device, or keyboard.
- Data is entered into the active cell.
- The Name box, located on the left side of the **formula bar,** displays the **cell reference** or **cell address** of the active cell (its column letter and row number). For example, A1 is the cell in the first row of the first column. B5 is the address for the cell in the fifth row of the second column.

- To help you identify the cell reference for the active cell, Excel surrounds the cell with a dark border and highlights its column letter (at the top of the worksheet) and row number (to the left of the worksheet). The column letters and row numbers are also known as the column and row headings.
- You can use the arrow keys ⬆⬇⬅➡ (alone or in combination with other keys), special key combinations, the mouse, a touch device, or Go To F5 to select a cell on the current worksheet.

Try It!   **Exploring the Excel Window**

1. In the **E01Try_xx** file, press ➡ twice.
2. Press ⬇ four times.
3. Click in the Name box, type **b3**, and press ENTER .
4. Press ⬇.
5. Click cell F13.
6. Press CTRL + HOME .
7. Save the **E01Try_xx** file, and leave it open to use in the next Try It.

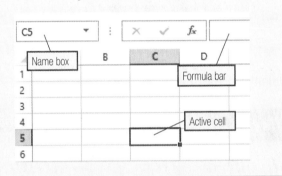

Key worksheet features

Exploring the Excel Interface

- In the Microsoft Office Basics section, you learned that you can access common commands such as Save and Undo through the buttons on the Quick Access Toolbar.
- Through the FILE tab, you can access commands for managing files such as New, Open, Save, and Print. Clicking the FILE tab displays the Backstage view.
- The Ribbon, located at the top of the Excel window, offers buttons for the most common Excel commands.

- The Ribbon offers several tabs, and on each tab, related command buttons are arranged in groups. Click a tab to display its contents, and then click a button to choose a command or display further choices.
- Some tabs, called contextual tabs, appear only when you've selected an item to which the tab's commands apply.
- To access Help, click the Help button **?** .

Try It! — Exploring the Excel Interface

1 In the **E01Try_xx** file, click the FILE tab.

2 In the list at the left of the Backstage view, click Print.

3 Click the Back button ⬅ in the upper-left corner of the window to go back to your document.

4 Click the FORMULAS tab.

5 On the FORMULAS tab, in the Function Library group, click the Date & Time button 📅.

6 Press [ESC].

7 Click the HOME tab.

8 Save the **E01Try_xx** file, and leave it open to use in the next Try It.

Navigating the Worksheet

- There are 16,384 columns and 1,048,576 rows available in a worksheet, but you don't need to fill the entire worksheet in order to use it—just type data in the cells you need.

- Since the workbook window displays only a part of a worksheet, you **scroll** through the worksheet to view another location.

- With the mouse or a touch device, you can scroll using the horizontal or vertical scroll bars.

  ✓ Using the mouse or touch device to scroll does not change the active cell.

- With the keyboard, you can scroll by pressing specific keys or key combinations.

  ✓ Scrolling with the keyboard does change the active cell.

- You can move to a specific cell that's not onscreen using Go To or the Name box.

  ✓ You can also use the Name box to go directly to a named cell or range. This is discussed in Lesson 13.

- The Go To function allows you to go to a specific cell and make that cell active.

- You can open the Go To dialog box by clicking HOME > Find & Select > Go To.

  ✓ In this book, the symbol > is used to indicate a series of steps.

- When you type the cell address into the Reference box and select OK, that cell will become the active cell.

Try It! — Navigating the Worksheet

1 In the **E01Try_xx** file, click the down scroll arrow on the vertical scroll bar to scroll one row down.

2 Click the right scroll arrow on the horizontal scroll bar to scroll one column right.

3 Roll the mouse wheel down until row 52 comes into view. (Do not press the wheel, just lightly roll it with your fingertip.)

  ✓ If you are using a touchpad, click the down arrow on the vertical scroll bar.

4 Click above the scroll box on the vertical scroll bar once or twice to redisplay row 1.

5 Drag the scroll box on the horizontal scroll bar all the way to the left to redisplay column A.

6 Click HOME > Find & Select > Go To.

7 In the Reference text box, type **ZZ88**.

8 Click OK.

9 Press [CTRL] + [HOME] to return to cell A1.

10 Save the **E01Try_xx** file, and leave it open to use in the next Try It.

Changing Worksheet Views

- To view or hide the formula bar, ruler, column and row headings, or gridlines, select or deselect them by checking or clearing the applicable check box in the Show group on the VIEW tab.

  ✓ *Hiding screen elements shows more rows onscreen.*

- To hide and redisplay the Ribbon, double-click any tab.
- Normal view is the default working view.
- Page Layout view is used to view data as it will look when printed and make adjustments.
- Page Break Preview is used before printing, to adjust where pages break.

  ✓ *You'll learn more about Page Layout view and Page Break Preview in later lessons.*

- You can use the view buttons on the status bar to change to the most common views.
- You also can use the buttons in the Workbook Views group on the VIEW tab to change views.
- Use Zoom to magnify cells in a worksheet by any amount up to 400%.
- Change the zoom using the Zoom slider on the status bar.
- You can also change the zoom using the mouse, touch device, or the buttons in the Zoom group on the VIEW tab.

Try It! Changing Worksheet Views

1. In the **E01Try_xx** file, click the VIEW tab on the Ribbon.
2. In the Show group, click one of the following:
   - Ruler
   - Gridlines
   - Formula Bar
   - Headings
3. Click the item you clicked in step 2 again to redisplay it.
4. Double-click the VIEW tab to hide the Ribbon.
5. Double-click the VIEW tab again to redisplay the Ribbon.
6. Click the Page Layout button 📄 in either the Workbook Views group or near the zoom slider to change to Page Layout view.
7. In the Zoom group, click the Zoom button 🔍. The Zoom dialog box offers the following magnifications:
   - 200%
   - 100%
   - 75%
   - 50%
   - 25%
   - Fit Selection
   - Custom

8. Click 50%, and then click OK.
9. On the status bar, click Zoom In ➕ once.
10. On the status bar, use the zoom slider to change the view to more than 100%.
11. On the status bar, drag the Zoom slider to the middle to change the view to 100%.
12. On the VIEW tab, in the Zoom group, click the Zoom to Selection button 🔍.
13. In the Zoom group, click the 100% button 📄.
14. In the Workbook Views group, click the Normal button ▦.
15. Save the **E01Try_xx** file, and leave it open to use in the next Try It.

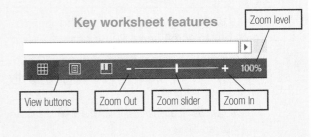

Key worksheet features — Zoom level — View buttons — Zoom Out — Zoom slider — Zoom In

Closing a Workbook and Exiting Excel

- When your worksheet is complete and you want to close the Excel workbook, use the Close command after clicking on the FILE tab.
- You can also click the File button ▣ on the Quick Access Toolbar, and then click Close.
- Closing a workbook file removes it from the screen without exiting Excel.
- Save a workbook before you close it or you will lose the current data or updated entries that you made.

- If you attempt to close a workbook or close Excel before saving, you will be prompted to save the changes.
- If you have more than one file open, Excel allows you to close and save all of the files before you exit the program.
- Exit the Excel application by clicking the Close button ✕ at the right end of the program's title bar.

Try It!   **Closing a Workbook and Exiting Excel**

1   In the **E01Try_xx** file, click the FILE tab on the Ribbon.

2   Click Close.

3   If necessary, click the Save button to save your changes to the file and close the workbook.

4   Click the **Close** button at the right end of the program's title bar to exit the Excel application.

Lesson 1—Practice

In this project, you will open an Excel worksheet, navigate the worksheet, change views, and close using the skills you learned in this lesson.

DIRECTIONS

1. Click **Excel 2013** and open a **Blank workbook** file.
2. Press → four times to select cell E1.
3. Press ↓ four times to select cell E5.
4. Click cell **H9** to make it the active cell, and then view its cell address in the Name box.
5. Click **HOME** > **Find & Select** 🔍 > **Go To**.
6. In the Reference text box, type **T98**.
7. Click **OK**. The active cell changes to T98.
8. Click in the Name box to change the active cell to the following, pressing ENTER after typing each new cell address:

    a. **B1492** (row 1492, column B)

    b. **XFD1048576** (bottom right of worksheet)

9. Press CTRL + HOME to move to cell A1.
10. Click cell **D4**.

11. Point to the horizontal scroll bar and click the right scroll arrow. The worksheet moves right by one column but the active cell does not change.
12. Point to the horizontal scroll bar and click to the left of the scroll box. The worksheet moves back left but the active cell does not change.
13. Point to the horizontal scroll bar, and then drag the scroll box all the way to the right. The view of the worksheet has changed again but the active cell does not change.
14. Click the down scroll arrow on the vertical scroll bar three times. The worksheet moves down three rows but the active cell does not change.
15. On the **VIEW** tab, in the Show group, deselect the **Formula Bar** check box to hide the formula bar.
16. Change to the **Page Layout** view by clicking its button on the status bar. Notice that the rulers have appeared just above the column headings and to the left of the row numbers.

17. On the **VIEW** tab, change to Normal view by clicking the **Normal** button ▦.

18. In the Show group, select the **Formula Bar** check box to redisplay the formula bar.

19. In the Zoom group, click the **Zoom** button 🔍 to display the Zoom dialog box.

20. Click in the Custom box, type **150**, and then click **OK**. The Zoom changes to 150%, so cells appear much larger.

21. Click the **Zoom Out** button ▬ on the Status bar twice. The Zoom changes to 130%.

22. Drag the **Zoom slider** to the left until the zoom is set to **70%**. The current zoom percentage shows on the Zoom button as you drag. If you have trouble setting the zoom to an exact percentage using the slider, drag the slider to roughly 70%, then click the Zoom Out or Zoom In button as needed to jump to exactly 70%.

23. Drag the **Zoom slider** to the middle to change the view to 100%.

24. Click the **FILE** tab and then click **Close** to close the workbook. If asked to save the workbook, click **Don't Save**.

25. Click the Close button ✕ at the right end of the program's title bar to exit Excel.

Lesson 1—Apply

You've recently been hired as a marketing specialist for Bike Tours and Adventures, and you've enrolled yourself in a class to learn to use Excel. In this project, you will start Excel, familiarize yourself with the Excel window, change your view of the worksheet, and practice moving around the worksheet using the mouse and the keyboard.

DIRECTIONS

1. Start Excel, if necessary, and open **E01Apply** from the data files for this lesson.

2. Save the file as **E01Apply_xx** in the location where your teacher instructs you to store the files for this lesson.

   ✓ *Replace the text xx with your own first name and last name or initials as directed by your teacher.*

3. Click cell **B1**, type your name, and press ⏎.

4. Increase the zoom to **150%**. Your document should appear as shown in Figure 1-1 on the next page. Scroll to the left and up, if necessary, to see your name.

5. Hide and redisplay these screen elements:

   a. Ribbon.

   b. Formula bar.

   c. Gridlines.

6. Change to **Page Layout** view, and then back to **Normal** view.

7. Click **HOME** > **Find & Select** 🔍 > **Go To**.

8. In the **Reference** text box, type **AL29**.

9. Click **OK**.

10. Click **HOME** > **Copy** 📋 to copy the contents of cell AL29.

11. Click **HOME** > **Find & Select** 🔍 > **Go To**.

12. In the **Reference** text box, type **F5**.

13. Click **OK**.

14. Click **HOME** > **Paste** 📋 to paste the contents of cell AL29 to cell F5.

15. Press ⌃ CTRL + HOME to return to cell A1.

16. Save and close the file, and exit Excel.

Figure 1-1

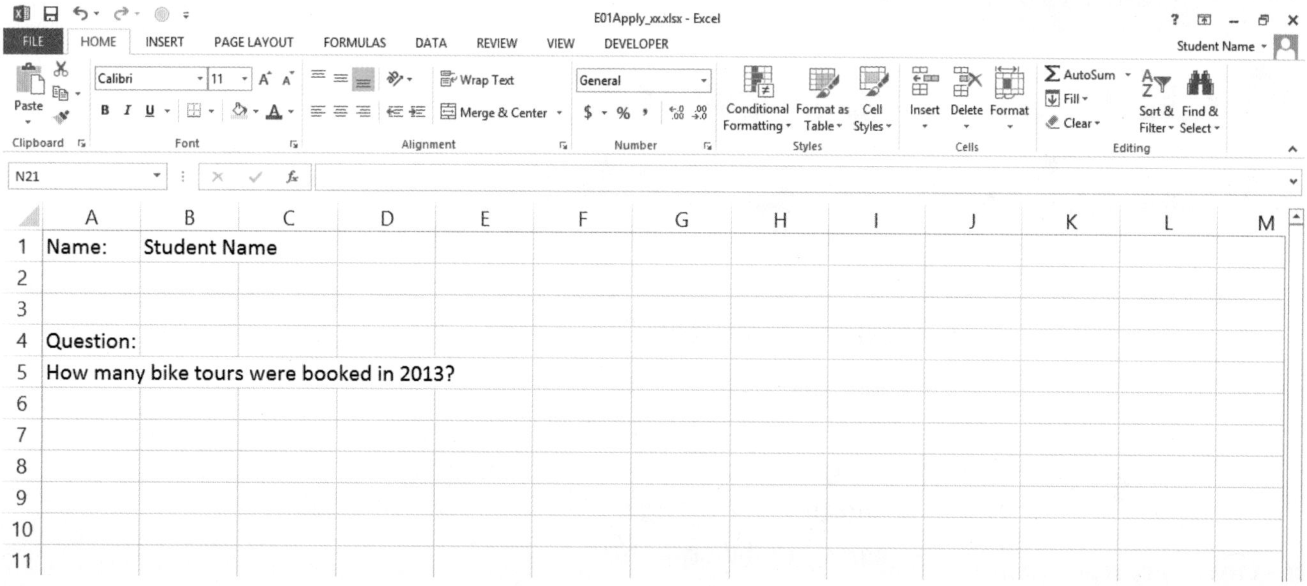
E01Apply_xx.xlsx - Excel
FILE
HOME
INSERT
PAGE LAYOUT
FORMULAS
DATA
REVIEW
VIEW
DEVELOPER
Student Name
Paste
Calibri
11
Wrap Text
Merge & Center
General
Conditional Formatting
Format as Table
Cell Styles
Insert
Delete
Format
AutoSum
Fill
Clear
Sort & Filter
Find & Select
Clipboard
Font
Alignment
Number
Styles
Cells
Editing
N21
Name:
Student Name
Question:
How many bike tours were booked in 2013?

Lesson 2

Worksheet and Workbook Basics

➤ **What You Will Learn**

Creating a New (Blank) Workbook

Entering Text and Labels

Editing Text

Using Undo and Redo

~~Clearing Cell Contents~~

Inserting a Built-In Header or Footer

Previewing and Printing a Worksheet

WORDS TO KNOW

Blank workbook
A new, empty workbook contains one worksheet (sheet).

Clear
To remove a cell's contents and/or formatting.

Default
The standard settings Excel uses in its software, such as column width or bottom alignment of text in a cell.

Footer
Descriptive text, such as page numbers, that appears at the bottom of every page of a printout.

Header
Descriptive text, such as page numbers, that appears at the top of every page of a printout.

Label
Text entered to identify the type of data contained in a row or column.

Software Skills   Building a workbook involves creating a new file, entering text to identify the data that will be calculated, making changes, and adding an identifying header and footer, among other information. You also can save and print a workbook before closing it. You'll learn these skills in this lesson.

What You Can Do

Creating a New (Blank) Workbook

- You can create a new workbook file any time after you begin working in Excel.

- A **blank workbook** file that you create has one worksheet by **default**, just like the blank workbook that appears when you start Excel.

- Use the Blank workbook choice in the Backstage view to create a blank file. Click the FILE tab > New > Blank workbook.

  ✓ *You can press* CTRL *+* N *at any time to create a blank file without displaying the Backstage view.*

- You can create a workbook using a template in the the Backstage view. You can choose from sample templates installed with Excel, or templates in a variety of categories on Office.com.

- During the current work session, Excel applies a temporary name to any new workbook you create. The first blank workbook that appears is named Book1 until you save it with a new name. Subsequent blank files you create are named Book2, Book3, and so on.

Try It!	**Creating a New Workbook in Excel**

① From the Windows Start screen, click the Excel 2013 program tile and then click Blank workbook. Excel starts and opens a blank workbook file.

  ✓ *If your keyboard has a Windows key (a key with the Windows logo on it), you can press that key at any time to display the Start menu.*

② Click FILE > New > Blank workbook.

  ✓ *Throughout this book, you will see instructions provided in a sequence format; for example, "Click FILE > New" means to click the FILE tab and then click New.*

③ Click Blank worksheet. A second new, blank workbook appears, with its sequentially numbered temporary name, *Book2*.

④ Save the file as **ETry02_xx** in the location where your teacher instructs you to store the files for this lesson.

⑤ Leave the file open for the next Try It.

The new file shown in title bar

Book2 - Excel

General ▾			Normal	Bad	Good	Neutral
$ ▾ % , .0 .00	Conditional Formatting ▾	Format as Table ▾	Check Cell	*Explanatory ...*	Input	Linked Cell
Number				Styles		

Preview
To see how a worksheet will look when printed.

Redo
The command used to redo an action you have undone.

Text
An alphanumeric entry in a worksheet that is not a cell or range address.

Undo
The command used to reverse one or a series of editing actions.

Entering Text and Labels

- The first character entered in a cell determines what type of cell entry it is—a label or **text**, number, or formula.

- If you enter an alphabetical character or a symbol (` ~ ! # % ^ & * ( ) _ \ | { } ; : ' " < > , ?) as the first character in a cell, you are entering a label.

- A **label** may be text data, such as the labels: Blue, Sally Smith, Ohio, or Above Average.

- Or, a label may be used to identify data in the row beside it or the column below it, such as the labels: Sales, Qtr 1, or January.

- As you type a label in a cell, it appears in the cell and in the formula bar.

- To enter the label in the cell, type the text and then do any of the following to finalize the entry: press the ENTER key, an arrow key, the TAB key, click another cell, or click the Enter button ✔ on the formula bar.

  ✓ *To enter multiple lines in a cell such as* Overtime *above and* Hours *below, type* Overtime, *press* ALT + ENTER . *Type* Hours *on the second line in the cell and press* ENTER *to finalize the entry.*

- You also can press [CTRL] + [ENTER] to finish a cell entry and leave the current cell selected. This is a good technique to use if you later need to copy the cell's contents.
- The default width of each cell is 8.43 characters in the standard font (Calibri, 11 point).
- A label longer than the cell width displays the complete text only if the cell to the right is blank, or if you make the column wide enough to fit the entry.

- If you enter a lot of text in a cell, that text may not fully display in the formula bar. You can expand the formula bar (make it taller) by clicking the Expand Formula Bar button ˅ at the right end of the formula bar.
- A label automatically aligns to the left of the cell, making it a left-justified entry.

Try It!   **Entering Labels (Text)**

1 In the **E02Try_xx** file, click cell A1, type **Client Survey**, and press [ENTER] twice.

2 Type **Client ID**, and press [ENTER] twice.

3 Type the following entries, pressing [ENTER] after each one:

Was the room temperature appropriate?

Were the staff members cordial?

Was your appointment administered on time?

Were your treatments explained in advance?

Were your treatments explained in advance?

Were you offered a beverage?

4 Click cell E4. Type **A Rating**, and press [→].

5 Type **B Rating** and **C Rating** in the next two cells to the right, pressing [TAB] to complete each entry.

6 Click the Save button ⊟ on the Quick Access Toolbar to save the file, and leave it open for the next Try It.

The file with label entries

⁄	A	B	C	D	E	F	G	H	I
1	Client Survey								
2									
3	Client ID:								
4					A Rating	B Rating	C Rating		
5	Was the room comfortable?								
6	Were the staff members cordial?								
7	Did your appointment start on time?								
8	Were your treatments explained in advance?								
9	Were your treatments explained in advance?								
10	Were you offered a beverage?								

Editing Text

- As you type data in a cell, if you notice a mistake before you press `ENTER` (or any of the other keys that finalize an entry), you can press the `BACKSPACE` key to erase characters to the left of the insertion point.

- Before you finalize an entry, you can press the `ESC` key or click the Cancel button ✕ on the formula bar to cancel it.

- After you enter data, you can make the cell active again (by clicking it, pressing an arrow key, etc.) and then type a new entry to replace the old one.

- You can double-click a cell in which the entry has been finalized to enable in-cell editing (also called Edit mode) and then make changes to only part of the entry.

- When in Edit mode, in a cell with data, the word *EDIT* displays at the left end of the status bar.

- Use the `BACKSPACE`, `DEL`, and other keys and selection techniques (as in Word) as needed to select and replace data.

Try It! Editing Text

1. In the **E02Try_xx** file, click cell A9. This cell has a repeated entry that you want to replace.

2. Type **Were you relaxed during the process?**, and press `CTRL` + `ENTER` to finish the entry.

3. Click cell A5 and press `F2`. Drag over *temperature appropriate* to select those words, type **comfortable**, and press `ENTER`.

4. Double-click cell A7, and press `HOME` to make sure the insertion point is at the beginning of the cell entry. Press and hold `SHIFT` while pressing `→` three times to select *Was*. Type **Did**.

5. With the cell still in Edit mode, double-click *administered* to select it.

6. Type **start**, and press `ENTER`.

7. With cell A8 selected, click in the formula bar to the right of the word *explained*, press `SHIFT` and click to the right of the word *advance*, press `DEL`, and then press `ENTER`. This finishes the current edits.

8. Press `CTRL` + `S` to save your changes to the **E02Try_xx** file, and leave it open to use in the next Try It.

Editing a text entry

The edited text

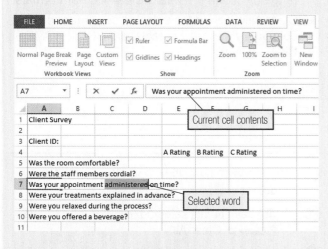

Using Undo and Redo

- Use the **Undo** button � on the Quick Access Toolbar to reverse any editing action.
- Some actions can't be undone (such as saving a workbook); in such cases, the Undo button will not be available and will be grayed out.
- You can reverse up to 100 previous editing actions with Undo.

✓ *The default number of Undo actions is 25.*

- The Undo button's name changes to reflect the most recent editing action.
- You can also redo (reinstate any action you've undone in error) up to 100 reversed actions using the **Redo** button ↻.
- Both the Undo and Redo buttons include a drop-down list that enables you to undo or redo multiple edits at once.

Try It!   Using Undo and Redo

1. In the **E02Try_xx** file, click cell E4.
2. Type **Yes**, and press TAB.
3. In cell F4, type **No** and press CTRL + ENTER to finish the entry.
4. On the HOME tab, in the Font group, click the Bold button **B**.
5. Click the Undo button � on the Quick Access Toolbar.
6. Click the Redo button ↻ on the Quick Access Toolbar.
7. Click the Undo drop-down arrow on the Quick Access Toolbar, and click the third choice in the menu, which should be **Typing 'Yes' in E4**.
8. Click the **Redo** button ↻ on the Quick Access Toolbar twice.
9. Save the **E02Try_xx** file, and leave it open to use in the next Try It.

Clearing Cell Contents

- Press ESC or click the Cancel button ✗ on the formula bar to clear a cell's contents before finalizing any cell entry.
- To erase a finished cell entry, select the cell and then press DEL.
- You also can use the **Clear** button ✐ Clear ▾ in the Editing group of the HOME tab to delete the cell's contents or to selectively delete its formatting or contents only.

- Right-click a selected cell or range and click Clear Contents on the shortcut menu to remove the contents of the selected cell or range.
- You can clear the formatting of a selected cell or range by clicking HOME > Clear > Clear Formats.
- Clear All will clear the selected cell or range completely (format, contents, etc.). Click HOME > Clear > Clear All.

Try It!   Clearing Cell Contents

1. In the **E02Try_xx** file, drag over the range E4:G4 to select it.

   ✓ *The above instruction means to drag the mouse from cell E4 across to cell G4. The shorthand E4:G4 is the address for the range of cells. Lesson 6 provides more detail about selecting and working with ranges.*

2. In the Font group of the HOME tab, click the **Bold** button **B**.
3. Click cell G4, and press DEL.
4. Click the Undo button �

 on the Quick Access Toolbar.
5. With cell G4 still selected, click HOME > Clear ✐ Clear ▾ > Clear All.
6. Drag over the range E4:F4 to select it.
7. Click HOME > Clear ✐ Clear ▾ > Clear Formats.
8. Save the **E02Try_xx** file, and leave it open to use in the next Try It.

Inserting a Built-In Header or Footer

- When you want to repeat the same information at the top of each printed page, create a **header**.

- When you want to repeat the same information at the bottom of each printed page, create a **footer.**

- Header and footer information only appears in the Page Layout view or the printed worksheet.

- You can select a predesigned header or footer or create customized ones.

- To create a predesigned header or footer, click the INSERT tab, go to the Text group, and the Header & Footer button ▯ to display the HEADER & FOOTER TOOLS DESIGN tab. Then click either the Header ▯ or Footer ▯ buttons, and choose one of the predefined headers or footers.

- To customize the header/footer from there, type text in the appropriate section of the header or footer area: left, center, or right.

✓ From here on, you will need to add a header with your name, the current date, and a page number print code to all the project workbooks.

- You can also click buttons in the Header & Footer Elements group to insert print codes for the page number, total pages, current date, current time, file path, file name, or sheet name.

✓ A print code is a set of characters that represent an element. For example, &[Page] is the print code for a page number.

- You can also insert a graphic or picture (such as a company logo) in a header or footer.

- You can change the font, font style, and font size of the header or footer using the tools on the HOME tab.

- Press ESC to finish editing a custom header or footer and close the HEADER & FOOTER TOOLS DESIGN tab.

Try It! Inserting a Built-In Header or Footer

① In the **E02Try_xx** file, click cell A1.

② On the INSERT tab, in the Text group, click the Header & Footer button ▯.

③ On the HEADER & FOOTER TOOLS DESIGN tab, in the Header & Footer group, click the Header button ▯, and then click **E02Try_xx, Page 1** on the menu. The header appears in PAGE LAYOUT view.

✓ If you've entered your name as the user name in Excel's options, you can choose a predefined header or footer that includes your name.

④ Click INSERT > Header & Footer ▯.

⑤ On the HEADER & FOOTER TOOLS DESIGN tab in the Navigation group, click the Go to Footer button ▯.

⑥ With the insertion point in the center box of the footer, type your name, and then press TAB to move the insertion point to the right box.

⑦ On the HEADER & FOOTER TOOLS DESIGN tab in the Header & Footer Elements group, click the Current Date button ▯ to insert a code that will display and print the current date.

⑧ Press TAB to finish the entry in the right box.

⑨ Press ESC to finish working with the header and footer.

⑩ Review the footer you created, then scroll up and view the header.

⑪ Click VIEW > Normal ▦ to return to Normal view.

⑫ Save the **E02Try_xx** file, and leave it open to use in the next Try It.

Previewing and Printing a Worksheet

■ You may print the selected worksheet(s), an entire workbook, or a selected data range.

■ You can **preview** a worksheet before you print it. Previewing enables you to see a more accurate representation of how the worksheet will look when printed, so you don't waste paper printing a sheet with the wrong settings.

  ✓ *In Lesson 20, you learn how to print an entire workbook and a selected range.*

■ Before you print a worksheet, you have the opportunity to review its appearance in the Backstage view.

■ You also can specify print options in the Backstage view.

■ If you decide not to print, click the HOME tab to leave the Backstage view.

Try It!   **Previewing and Printing a Worksheet**

❶ In the **E02Try_xx** file, click FILE > Print.

❷ Review the document preview at the right side of the Backstage view. The preview shows the placement of headers and footers and all entries on the page.

  ✓ *If the worksheet you were printing consisted of multiple pages, you could use the buttons at the lower left to move between them.*

❸ The various print settings appear in the Print pane area of the Backstage view.

❹ Make sure that Print Active Sheets is selected under Settings.

❺ **With your teacher's permission**, click the Print button. Otherwise, click the HOME tab.

❻ Save and close the file, and exit Excel.

Print Preview

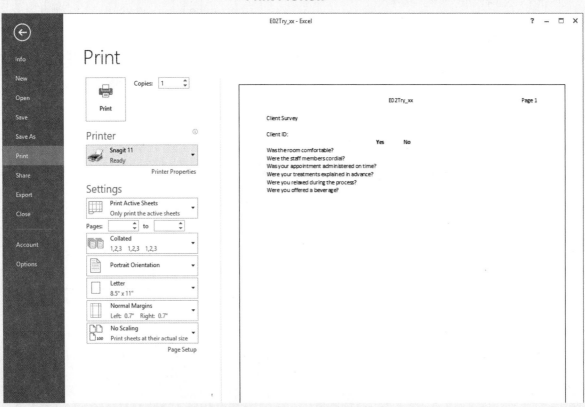

Lesson 2—Practice

In this project, you will create a new Excel worksheet, insert a built-in header, and undo and redo editing actions using the skills you learned in this lesson.

DIRECTIONS

1. Start Excel, if necessary.
2. Click **Blank workbook**.
3. Save the blank file that appears as **E02Practice_xx** in the location where your teacher instructs you to store the files for this lesson.
4. Click **INSERT** > **Header & Footer** 📄.
5. In the HEADER & FOOTER TOOLS DESIGN tab, click **Header** 📄, and click the **Page 1** choice.
6. Click **INSERT** > **Header & Footer** 📄.
7. Type **your name** in the left header box, and press TAB twice to move to the right header box.
8. In the HEADER & FOOTER TOOLS DESIGN tab, click **Current Date** 🗓 to insert a date printing code.
9. Press TAB and then ESC to finish creating the header.
10. Click **VIEW** > **Normal** ⊞ to return to Normal view.
11. Type **Invoice** in cell **A1**, and press ENTER twice.
12. Type **Remit To:** and press TAB.
13. Type **Serenity Health Club**, press ENTER, and press ➡ if needed to select cell B4.
14. Type **200 W. Michigan Ave.** and press ENTER.
15. In cell **B5**, type **Chicago, IL 60614**, and press ENTER.
16. In cell **B6**, type **606-555-1200**, and press ENTER.
17. Click cell **A8**, and type the following three entries, pressing ENTER after each:
    a. Time:
    b. Number:
    c. Due Date:
18. Press ENTER again to select cell **A12**, and make the following two entries, pressing ENTER after each:
    a. **Client ID:**
    b. **Client:**
19. Click the **Undo** button ↺ on the Quick Access Toolbar twice to undo the previous two entries.
20. Click the **Redo** button ↻ on the Quick Access Toolbar twice to redo your entries.
21. Scroll up and drag over the range **B3:B6** to select it.
22. Click **HOME** > **Clear** ✐ Clear▾ > **Clear Contents**.
23. Click the **Undo** button ↺ on the Quick Access Toolbar.
24. Click cell **A8**, type **Date:**, and press ENTER to replace that cell's entry.
25. With cell **A9** selected, press F2, press CTRL + ⬅ to move the insertion point to the beginning of the cell, type **Invoice**, press SPACE, and press ENTER.
26. Drag over cell A10's entry in the formula bar, type **Terms:**, and click the **Enter** button ✔ on the formula bar to replace the entry. The finished worksheet appears as shown in Figure 2-1 on the next page.
27. Click **FILE** > **Print**.
28. **With your teacher's permission**, click the **Print** button. Otherwise, click the Back button ⬅ to exit the Backstage view.
29. Click the **Save** button 💾 on the Quick Access Toolbar, and then click the Close button ✕ at the end of the program's menu bar to exit Excel.

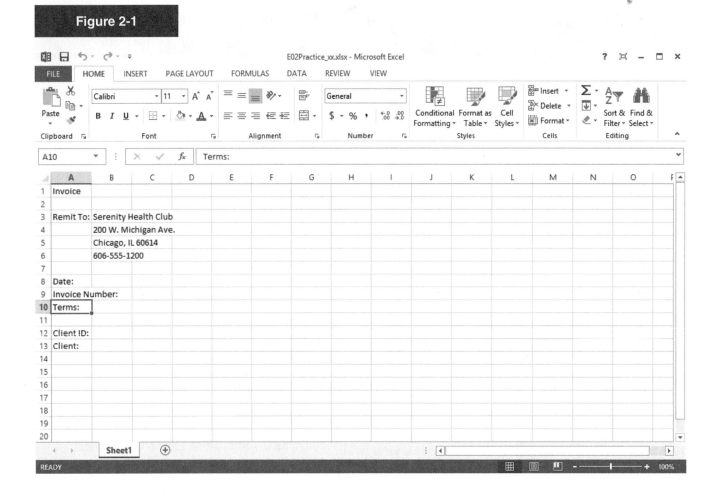

Figure 2-1

Lesson 2—Apply

You are the Accounts Receivable Supervisor at the Serenity Health Club. A member has charged several services but has not yet paid for them. You need to create an invoice detailing the charges.

DIRECTIONS

1. Start Excel, if necessary, and open **E02Apply** from the data files for this lesson.
2. Save the file as **E02Apply_xx** in the location where your teacher instructs you to store the files for this lesson.
3. Add a header that has your name at the left, the date code in the center, and the page number at the right.
4. Change back to **Normal** view.

5. Enter the following data in cells **B8:B10**:
   a. 1/3/14
   b. 546
   c. **Due on receipt**
6. Click cell **A9** and replace **Number** with **No.**.
7. Click cell **B10**, and then click **HOME > Align Right** ≡ in the Alignment group.
8. Clear the formatting you just applied in cell B10.
9. Click the **Undo** button ↶ on the Quick Access Toolbar to undo the formatting change.

10. Change the entries in cells **A12:A13** to the following:
    a. **Member ID:**
    b. **Member:**
11. Click cell **B12**, and enter **A1054**.
12. Enter the following data in cells **B13:B15**:
    a. **Joy Wen**
    b. **12 W. 21st St.**
    c. **Chicago, IL 60602**
13. Make entries in the portion of the invoice that calculates the invoice charges, as follows:
    a. cell **A18: 2**
    b. cell **B18: Massage Hours**
    c. cell **C18: 45**
    d. cell **A19: 1**
    e. cell **B19: Facial**
    f. cell **C19: 75**
    g. cell **A20: 3**
    h. cell **B20: Personal Trainer Hours**
    i. cell **C20: 50**

14. Scroll down. Notice that the worksheet already has calculations built in, so it calculates values in the Amount column and Total cell for you.
15. You have been informed that the rate for personal training has changed. Click the **Undo** button ↶ on the Quick Access Toolbar, and then enter a rate of **55** in cell C20.
16. Click **FILE** > **Print** to preview the file in the Backstage view.
17. **With your teacher's permission**, click the **Print** button. Otherwise, click the Back button ⊙ to exit the Backstage view. Submit the printout or the file for grading as required.
18. Save and close the file, and exit Excel.

Lesson 3

Adding Worksheet Contents

➤ What You Will Learn

Opening an Existing Workbook and Saving It with a New Name
Entering and Editing Numeric Labels and Values
Using AutoComplete
Using Pick From List
Using AutoCorrect
Checking the Spelling in a Worksheet

WORDS TO KNOW

AutoComplete
A feature used to complete an entry based on previous entries made in the column containing the active cell.

AutoCorrect
A feature used to automate the correction of common typing errors.

Numeric label
A number entered in the worksheet as a label, not as a value—such as the year 2014 used as a column label.

Pick From List
A shortcut used to insert repeated information.

Spelling checker
A tool used to assist you in finding and correcting typographical or spelling errors.

Value
A cell entry that consists of a number and numeric formatting only.

Software Skills Save a copy of a workbook with a new name to use it as the basis for another workbook. You also need to know how to enter numeric values, which are the basis for calculations. When entering data, take advantage of the many time-saving features Excel offers. Excel's AutoComplete feature, for example, automatically completes certain entries based on previous entries that you've made. AutoCorrect automatically corrects common spelling errors as you type, while the spelling checker checks your worksheet for any additional errors.

What You Can Do

Opening an Existing Workbook and Saving It with a New Name

- When you have saved and closed a workbook file, you can open it from the same disk drive, folder, and file name you used during the save process.

- When Excel starts, you can access a recently used file from the Recent list on the left. Click a file to open it.

  ✓ *You can also click Open Other Workbooks to go to the Backstage view and select a file from a specific location.*

- Click FILE > Open to display the Backstage view and access recently opened workbooks, the Skydrive, and Computer. The Recent Workbooks window is displayed by default. Click a workbook or location to open it.

- Click SkyDrive to access files from Microsoft's virtual storage location.

- Click Computer to access files from a specific location on your computer. Click Browse 🗀 to open the Open dialog box.

- In the Open dialog box, use the arrows in the text box at the top to navigate the disks, libraries, and folders on your computer.

- You also can use the Navigation pane at the left to go to the location of the workbook. Clicking the triangle beside any location displays the location's contents, and clicking again hides its contents.

- The default file location, the Documents library in Windows 8, appears in the Navigation pane by default. You can navigate to other libraries, favorite locations (under Favorites), locations on your computer, locations on the network, and locations on the Skydrive. You can also navigate to Homegroup (local network) locations if that feature is enabled.

- Click the Change your view button in the Open dialog box to preview a file, change the list to display file details, or display the properties of a file.

- You can pin a recently used workbook or location to the Recent lists so it is always easily accessible.

- A newly opened workbook becomes the active workbook and hides any other open workbook.

Try It!   **Opening an Existing Workbook and Saving It with a New Name**

1. Start Excel.

2. Click FILE > Open.

3. Navigate to and select the folder containing the data files for this lesson.

4. Click the **E03Try** file. The file appears onscreen.

5. Add a header that has your name at the left, the date code in the center, and the page number code at the right, and change back to Normal view.

6. Click FILE > Save As.

7. Navigate to the folder where your teacher instructs you to store the files for this lesson.

8. Click in the File name text box, and edit the file name to read **E03Try_xx**.

9. Click the Save button to finish saving the file, and leave it open to use in the next Try It.

Renaming the file

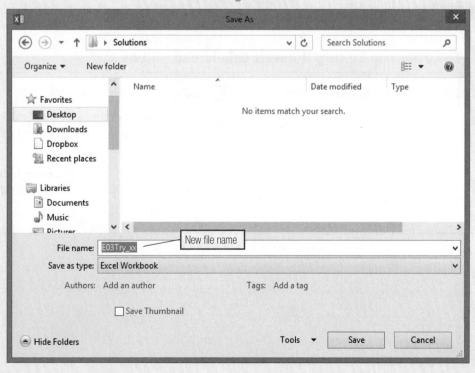

Entering and Editing Numeric Labels and Values

- A cell contains a **value** when its first character begins with either a number or one of the following symbols (+, −, =, $).
- Type the value, and then do one of the following to enter it in the cell:
  - Press [ENTER].
  - Press an arrow key.
  - Click the Enter button ✔ on the formula bar.
  - Click another cell.
- The default cell format in Excel is General.
- To display any number in a different format, apply the number format you want to use, as explained in Lesson 4.
- If you see pound signs displayed in a cell instead of a number, widen the column to display the value.
- You can enter some numbers with their formatting and Excel will recognize them as numbers, including:
  - Thousands: You can enter numbers with thousands separators, as in 1,543,009.24
  - Currency values: You can enter values with currency formatting, as in $1,299.60.
  - Percentages: You can enter a percent symbol to specify a percentage, as in 54%.

- When you enter numbers that contain hyphen formatting—such as Social Security numbers, phone numbers, and Zip codes—Excel treats the entries as text, and they cannot be used in calculations.
- A **numeric label**, such as a year number above a column of data that identifies the data's timing, is a number that typically will not be used in calculations.
- Begin the entry of a numeric label with an apostrophe (') as a label prefix to indicate that the number should be treated as a label (text) and not as a value. The entry will align at the left of the cell, unlike other value entries, which align right.
- Although the label prefix (') is shown on the formula bar, it is not displayed on the worksheet or printed.
- When you enter a value with an apostrophe, Excel displays a green triangle in the upper left-hand corner of the cell. Select the cell again, and an error button appears. You can:
  - Click the button and click Ignore Error to confirm that the number is really a label.
  - Click the button and click Convert to Number if the apostrophe was entered in error and the entry should be treated as a number.
- Edit a cell with a value or numeric label using the same techniques as editing a cell with a text entry.

Try It!   Entering and Editing Numeric Labels and Values

1 In the **E03Try_xx** file, click cell A12, type **Roll**, and press [TAB].

2 Type **Spelt** and press [TAB].

3 Type **8** and press [TAB].

4 Type **.35** and press [ENTER].

5 In cell A13 type **Mini Roll**, and press [TAB].

6 Type **Oat** and press [TAB].

7 Type **'24** and press [TAB]. Notice that the number left aligns in the cell and a green triangle appears.

8 Click cell C13, click the Error button, and click Convert to Number. The entry right aligns in the cell.

(continued)

| **Try It!** | **Entering and Editing Numeric Labels and Values** *(continued)* |

⑨ Press TAB, type **$.20**, and press CTRL + ENTER .

⑩ Click cell D8, type **$1.15**, and press ENTER to replace the current entry.

⑪ Click cell C10, press F2, press BACKSPACE, type **8**, and press ENTER .

⑫ Save the **E03Try_xx** file, and leave it open to use in the next Try It.

Converting a numeric label to text

	Flour	Quantty	Price	Value
	Wheat		$0.25	$3.00
tte	White	*Values entered with formatting*	$0.95	$2.85
i	White		$0.65	$5.20
nt	White	24	$0.30	$7.20
Mie	Wheat	24	$0.20	$4.80
	Spelt	8	$0.35	$2.80
ll	Oat	⬦ ▾ 24		$0.00
				$0.00
				$0.00
				$0.00

Error button

- Number Stored as Text
- Convert to Number
- Help on this error
- Ignore Error
- Edit in Formula Bar

Using AutoComplete

- When you need to repeat a label that has already been typed in the same column, the **AutoComplete** feature allows you to enter the label automatically.

- Type part of the label. If an entry with the same characters has already been entered in the column above, a suggestion for completing the entry appears in black.

- To accept the AutoComplete suggestion, press TAB or ENTER . Otherwise, continue typing the rest of the entry.

| **Try It!** | **Using AutoComplete** |

① In the **E03Try_xx** file, click cell A14.

② Type **Pan**. An AutoComplete suggestion appears in the cell.

③ Press TAB to accept the AutoComplete entry and move to cell B14.

④ Type **Whe**, and press TAB to accept the AutoComplete entry and move to cell C14.

⑤ Type **8**, and press TAB.

⑥ Type **$.70**, and press ENTER .

⑦ Save the **E03Try_xx** file, and leave it open to use in the next Try It.

An AutoComplete suggestion

11	Pain de Mie	Wheat
12	Roll	Spelt
13	Mini Roll	Oat
14	Pannini	
15		

Using Pick From List

- If several labels are entered in a list and the next items to be typed are repeated information, you also can use the **Pick From List** feature to make entries. Right-click a cell and then click the Pick From Drop-down List command on the shortcut menu.

✓ *The cells in the list and the cell to be typed must be next to each other and in the same column. Use the Undo button ↺ on the Quick Access Toolbar to reverse any editing action.*

- Click the desired choice in the list of entries that appears to enter it in the cell, and then press TAB or ENTER to move to the next cell, if needed.

Try It!   **Using Pick From List**

1 In the **E03Try_xx** file, right-click cell A15, and click Pick From Drop-down List.

2 In the list that appears, click Roll.

3 Right-click cell B15, and click Pick From Drop-down List.

4 In the list that appears, click White, and then press TAB.

5 Type **36**, and then press TAB.

6 Type **$.23**, and then press TAB.

7 Save the **E03Try_xx** file, and leave it open to use in the next Try It.

Using AutoCorrect

- If you type a word incorrectly and it is in the **AutoCorrect** list, Excel automatically changes the word as you type.

- AutoCorrect automatically capitalizes the names of days of the week; corrects incorrectly capitalized letters in the first two positions in a word; and undoes accidental use of the Caps Lock key.

- When certain changes are made with AutoCorrect, you're given an option to remove the corrections by clicking the arrow on the AutoCorrect Options button that appears, and selecting the action you want.

- You can add words to the AutoCorrect list that you often type incorrectly. Click FILE > Options. In the Excel Options dialog box, click Proofing in the list at the left. Click the AutoCorrect Options button. Type entries in the Replace and With text boxes, and then click the Add button. Repeat as needed, and then click OK to close both dialog boxes.

Try It!   **Using AutoCorrect**

1 In the **E03Try_xx** file, click cell A16.

2 Type **Cafe Biscotti**, and press TAB. Notice that when you press SPACE to finish the first word, Excel adds the accent to correct its spelling.

3 Type **O**, and then press TAB. AutoComplete fills in the word *Oat* for you.

4 Type **92**, and then press TAB.

5 Type **$.28**, and then press TAB.

6 Click FILE > Options.

7 In the Excel Options dialog box, click Proofing in the list at the left.

8 Click the AutoCorrect Options button.

9 Type **quantty** in the Replace text box, and **quantity** in the With text box.

10 Click the Add button.

11 Click the OK button twice.

✓ *If your teacher asks you to, reopen the AutoCorrect Options dialog box, select the quantty correction, and click Delete.*

12 Click cell A18 to select it.

13 Type **quantty**, and then press ENTER . Notice that AutoCorrect corrects the text you typed.

14 Click Undo.

15 Save the **E03Try_xx** file, and leave it open to use in the next Try It.

Checking the Spelling in a Worksheet

- To check the spelling of text in a worksheet and obtain replacement word suggestions, use the **spelling checker** feature.

- Start the spelling check from cell A1 to ensure it checks all sheet contents.

✓ *If you don't start the spell check from the beginning of the worksheet, Excel completes the spell check and then displays "Do you want to continue checking at the beginning of the sheet?"*

✓ *Press CTRL + HOME to go to the beginning of the worksheet.*

- To start the spelling checker, click the REVIEW tab and in the Proofing group, click the Spelling button ✓.

✓ Pressing F7 also starts a spelling check.

✓ Checking spelling in Excel works much as it does in Word.

Try It!   **Checking the Spelling in a Worksheet**

1. In the **E03Try_xx** file, click cell A1.

2. Click REVIEW > Spelling ✓.

3. At the first misspelling, Quantty, make sure the proper spelling is selected in the Suggestions list, and click the Change button.

4. At the next misspelling, Pannini, make sure the proper spelling is selected in the Suggestions list, and click the Change All button.

5. Save and close the file, and exit Excel.

Lesson 3—Practice

In this project, you will enter and edit text, undo and redo editing actions, and check the spelling in a worksheet.

DIRECTIONS

1. Start Excel, if necessary.

2. Click **Blank workbook** to open a new file.

3. Save the file as **E03Practice_xx** in the location where your teacher instructs you to store the files for this lesson.

4. Add a header that has your name at the left, the date code in the center, and the page number code at the right, and change back to **Normal** view.

5. Type **Whole Garins Bread (r)** in cell A1, and press SPACE . (Type the entry exactly as shown; errors will be corrected later.) Notice that the AutoCorrect feature changes the (r) entry to a register mark: ®.

6. Press ENTER three times.

7. Type **Bakery Schedule**, and press ENTER .

8. Type **10/10/14**, and press ENTER twice.

9. Type the following cell entries, pressing TAB after each:
   a. **Customer**
   b. **Item**
   c. **Qty Needed**
   d. **Qty Shipped**
   e. **Qty to Bake**

10. Click cell **A8**, and type the following cell entries exactly as shown, pressing ENTER after each (note AutoCorrect in action again):
    a. **Cafe Latte**
    b. **Java Cafe**
    c. **Villige Green**

11. Click cell **B8**, and type the following cell entries exactly as shown, pressing ENTER after each:
    a. **Bagels**
    b. **Croissants**
    c. **Wheat Bread**

12. Click cell **C8**, and type the following cell entries exactly as shown, pressing ENTER after each:
    a. **325**
    b. **100**
    c. **25**

13. Click cell **D8**, and type the following cell entries exactly as shown, pressing ENTER after each:
    a. **300**
    b. **100**
    c. **25**

14. Click cell **A11**, type **J**, and press TAB to complete the cell entry using AutoComplete.

15. Type the following cell entries, pressing TAB after each:

   a. **Pastries**

   b. **150**

   c. **125**

16. Click cell **A1**.

17. Click **REVIEW > Spelling** ✓.

18. At the first misspelling, *Garins*, make sure that **Grains** is selected in the Suggestions list, and then click the **Change** button.

19. At the next misspelling, *Qty*, click the **Ignore All** button.

20. At the next misspelling, *Villige*, make sure that **Village** is selected in the Suggestions list, and then click the **Change** button.

21. In the message box that informs you that the spelling check is complete, click the **OK** button. The finished spreadsheet appears as shown in Figure 3-1.

22. **With your teacher's permission**, print the worksheet. Submit the printout or the file for grading as required.

23. Save and close the file, and exit Excel.

Figure 3-1

	A	B	C	D	E	F	G	H	I
1	Whole Grains Bread ®								
2									
3									
4	Bakery Schedule								
5	10/10/2014								
6									
7	Customer	Item	Qty Needed	Qty Shipped	Qty to Bake				
8	Café Latte	Bagels	325	300					
9	Java Café	Croissants	100	100					
10	Village Green	Wheat Bread	25	25					
11	Java Café	Pastries	150	125					
12									
13									
14									

Lesson 3—Apply

You're the team leader at Whole Grains Bread, and you need to complete the baking schedule for today so the other chefs will know what needs to be done for delivery tomorrow. You want to compare today's schedule with yesterday's, in order to compile a list of any items that were not completed on time. Those items will be given the highest priority.

DIRECTIONS

1. Start Excel, if necessary, and open the **E03Apply** file from the data files for this lesson.

2. Save the file as **E03Apply_xx** in the location where your teacher instructs you to store the files for this lesson.

3. Add a header that has your name at the left, the date code in the center, and the page number code at the right, and change back to **Normal** view.

4. In cell **A12**, use **Pick From Drop-down List** to enter **Village Green**.

5. Click cell **A13**, and make the following entries, using AutoComplete where applicable and pressing [ENTER] after each:
   a. **Mike's Steak House**
   b. **Gribaldi's Risorante**
   c. **Java Café**
   d. **Café Latte**
   e. **Village Green**

6. Click cell **B12**, and make the following entries exactly as shown, using AutoComplete where applicable and pressing [ENTER] after each:
   a. **White Bread**
   b. **Pastry Assortment**
   c. **Garlic Bread**
   d. **Muffin Assotment**
   e. **Muffin Assortment**
   f. **Wheat Rolls**

7. Click cell **C12**, and make the following entries, pressing [ENTER] after each:
   a. 9
   b. 200
   c. 125
   d. 100
   e. 225
   f. 700

8. Click cell **D12**, and make the following entries, pressing [ENTER] after each:
   a. 9
   b. 200
   c. 125
   d. 100
   e. 175
   f. 650

9. Click cell **D10**, and change the entry to **0**.

10. Click cell **D13**, and change the entry to **160**.

11. Click cell **D15**, and change the entry to **48**.

12. Click cell **A1**.

13. Check the spelling in the worksheet.

14. At the first misspelling, *Qty*, click the **Ignore All** button.

15. At the next misspelling, *Gribaldi's*, click the **Ignore Once** button.

16. At the next misspelling, *Risorante*, edit the entry to read **Ristorante**, and then click the **Change** button. Click **Yes** to change the word even though it's not in the dictionary.

17. At the next misspelling, *Assotment*, make sure the right correction is selected in the Suggestions list, and click the **Change** button.

18. In the message box that informs you that the spelling check is complete, click **OK**.

19. **With your teacher's permission**, print the worksheet. Submit the printout or the file for grading as required.

20. Save and close the file, and exit Excel.

Figure 3-2

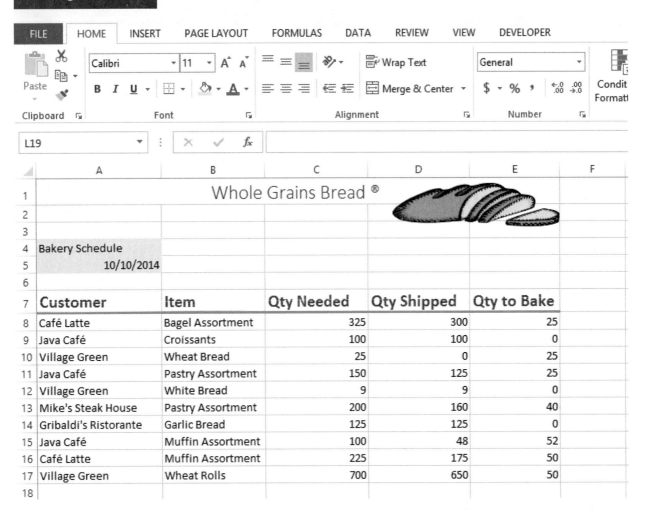

Lesson 4

Worksheet Formatting

➤ **What You Will Learn**

Choosing a Theme
Applying Cell Styles
Applying Font Formats
Merging and Centering Across Cells
Applying Number Formats

Software Skills   When you change the appearance of worksheet data by applying various formats, you also make that data more attractive and readable.

What You Can Do

Choosing a Theme

■ To make your worksheet readable and interesting, you can manually apply a set of formats.

■ You manually **format** data by selecting cells and then clicking options on the HOME tab, such as the Font [Calibri (Body) ▾] and Font Color ▲▾ buttons.

■ Using too many manual formats can make the worksheet seem disjointed and chaotic.

■ To make your worksheet more professional-looking, use a **theme** to apply a coordinated set of formats.

■ By default, the Office theme is applied to all new workbooks; if you select a different theme, the **fonts** and colors in your workbook will automatically change.

■ If you don't want to change the fonts in your worksheet, you can apply just the theme colors from a theme.

■ Likewise, you can change theme fonts and the theme effects applied to graphics without affecting the colors already in your worksheet.

■ You select a theme from the Themes gallery in the Themes group on the Page Layout tab.

■ As you move the mouse over the themes shown in the gallery, the worksheet automatically shows a **Live Preview** of the data.

■ When you type data in a cell, it's automatically formatted using the font in the current theme.

Format
To apply attributes to cell data to change the appearance of the worksheet.

Live Preview
A feature that shows you how a gallery formatting choice will appear in the worksheet when you move the mouse pointer over that choice.

Merge and Center
A feature that enables you to automatically combine cells and center the contents of the original far left cell in the new cell.

Number format
A format that controls how numerical data is displayed, including the use of commas, dollar signs (or other symbols), and the number of decimal places.

Percent format
A style that displays decimal numbers as a percentage.

Theme
A collection of coordinated fonts, colors, and effects for graphic elements, such as charts and images, that can be quickly applied to all sheets in a workbook.

■ You can apply a cell color (called a **fill**) or a text color. Click the down arrow on the Fill Color ◇▾ or Font Color ▲▾ buttons in the Font group of the HOME tab, and then click one of the choices under Theme Colors.

■ If you apply a theme color to text or as a fill and later switch themes, Excel updates the color according to the new theme.

■ If you choose one of the standard colors or use the More Colors option, the selected color will not change if you later change the theme.

Try It!   Choosing a Theme

① Start Excel.

② Open the **E04Try** file from the data files for this lesson.

③ Save the file as **E04Try_xx** in the location where your teacher instructs you to store the files for this lesson.

④ Add a header that has your name at the left, the date code in the center, and the page number code at the right, and change back to Normal view.

⑤ On the PAGE LAYOUT tab, click the Themes button [Aa].

Previewing a theme

⑥ Move the mouse pointer over the Integral choice in the Themes gallery. Notice how the fonts applied on the worksheet change.

⑦ Click the Slice theme.

⑧ Double-click the right column header border for columns C and E to make them wider to accommodate the text due to the theme font change. (Lesson 5 covers this technique in more detail.)

✓ *Move the mouse pointer over the right border of the column header you want to resize until you see the resizing pointer, which is a vertical bar with left and right arrows, then double-click to resize the column.*

⑨ Drag over the range B2:F2 to select it.

⑩ On the HOME tab in the Font group, click the Fill Color drop-down arrow ◇▾. Under Theme Colors, click the Red, Accent 6, Lighter 40% fill color in the tenth column. The selected range shows a Live Preview of the color. Click the color to apply it.

⑪ Click cell F13.

⑫ Click Fill Color drop-down arrow ◇▾. Under Standard Colors, click the Green color.

⑬ Save the **E04Try_xx** file, and leave it open to use in the next Try It.

(continued)

Try It!   **Choosing a Theme** *(continued)*

Applying a theme color

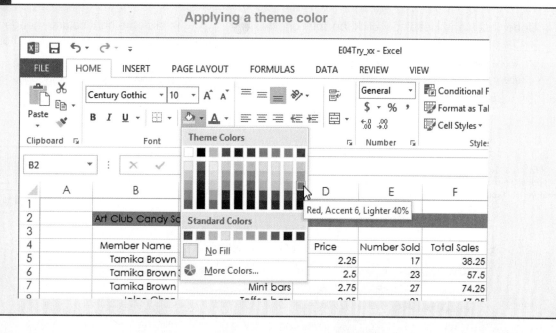

Applying Cell Styles

- Themes contain a coordinated set of colors, fonts, and other elements, such as **cell styles**.

- Cell styles in a theme include various styles you can apply to column headings or totals and title and heading styles.

- If you apply any of the title, headings, or themed cell styles, the cells using that style will update automatically if you change themes.

- You also can apply cell styles that aren't changed if you change themes, such as formats you might use to highlight good or bad values, a warning, or a note.

- There are also some number format cell styles available that won't change if you change themes.

  ✓ *Sometimes applying a cell style to a cell holding a label causes the label to be cut off rather than spilling over into the cell to the right as you might expect. If this happens and you don't want to change the column width, also apply the style to the next cell to the right.*

- If you have a widescreen monitor and display Excel using the full screen, the Cell Styles button will change to the Styles gallery.

- After you select a cell or ranges of cells, you can use the Cell Styles button or the Styles gallery to apply a style. Use the gallery scroll arrows to scroll through the styles. You can also use the More button to view the styles in one window.

Try It!   **Applying Cell Styles**

1. In the **E04Try_xx** file, drag over the range B4:F4 to select it.

2. On the HOME tab in the Styles group, click the Cell Styles button to display the gallery of cell styles.

   OR

   On the HOME tab, click the More button.

3. In the second column under Themed Cell Styles, move your mouse pointer over the 60% - Accent2 choice. The selected range shows a Live Preview of the cell style. Click the cell style to apply it.

4. Drag over the range E13:F13 to select it.

5. On the HOME tab, in the Styles group, click Cell Styles.

(continued)

Try It!   **Applying Cell Styles** *(continued)*

6 Under Titles and Headings, click the Total choice in the far right column.

✓ *Notice that the standard color you applied to cell F13 doesn't change when you apply the cell style.*

7 Double-click the right column header border for columns B, E, and F to adjust the column widths due to the new styles.

8 Save the **E04Try_xx** file, and leave it open to use in the next Try It.

Styles gallery preview

		Normal	Bad	Good	Neutral	Calculation	
Conditional Formatting ▾	Format as Table ▾	Check Cell	Explanatory ...	Input	Linked Cell	Note	

Styles

Gallery scroll arrows

More button

Styles gallery

Good, Bad and Neutral

Normal	Bad	Good	Neutral

Data and Model

Calculation	Check Cell	Explanatory ...	Input	Linked Cell	Note
Output	Warning Text				

Titles and Headings

Heading 1	Heading 2	Heading 3	Heading 4	Title	Total

Themed Cell Styles

20% - Accent1	20% - Accent2	20% - Accent3	20% - Accent4	20% - Accent5	20% - Accent6
40% - Accent1	40% - Accent2	40% - Accent3	40% - Accent4	40% - Accent5	40% - Accent6
60% - Accent1	60% - Accent2	60% - Accent3	60% - Accent4	60% - Accent5	60% - Accent6
Accent1	Accent2	Accent3	Accent4	Accent5	Accent6

Number Format

Comma	Comma [0]	Currency	Currency [0]	Percent

▦ New Cell Style...

▤ Merge Styles...

Applying Font Formats

- The Font group on the HOME tab of the Ribbon offers choices for formatting text, including font size, color, and attributes such as bold and italics.

  ✓ *This type of formatting is sometimes called direct formatting.*

- The Font group settings you apply override the formatting applied by the current theme.

- If a cell has formatting you applied directly using the Font group tools, such as bold or underlining, that formatting will NOT change if you change themes.

- Theme fonts, font colors, and cell colors appear at the top of the selection list when you click the appropriate button. For example, if you click the Font drop-down arrow, the theme fonts appear at the top of the list.

- Standard fill or text colors will not change if you select a different theme.

- The way in which your data appears after making font and font size changes is dependent on your monitor and printer.

- The available fonts depend on those installed in Windows.

- When you change **font size**, Excel automatically adjusts the row height but does not adjust the column width.

Try It!   **Applying Font Formats**

1 In the **E04Try_xx** file, click cell B2.

2 Click HOME > Font drop-down arrow.

3 Scroll down the list, and click Arial Black.

4 Click HOME > Font Size drop-down arrow.

5 Move the mouse pointer over the 24 size, view the Live Preview, and then click 24.

   ✓ *When you increase the font size, the row height increases automatically.*

6 Save the **E04Try_xx** file, and leave it open to use in the next Try It.

Applying a new font size

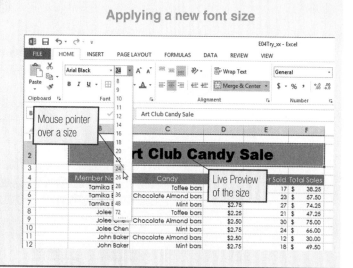

Merging and Centering Across Cells

- You can center a worksheet's title across the columns that contain the worksheet data.

- To center a label across several columns, use the **Merge & Center** button ▦ Merge & Center in the Alignment group of the HOME tab.

   ✓ *The Merge & Center command actually merges the selected cells into one large cell and then centers the data in the newly merged cell.*

   ✓ *You can align merge cells left or right instead of centering the data. Click the Merge & Center drop-down arrow and click Merge Across to merge the cells with the current alignment (left or right).*

- For Merge & Center to work properly, enter the data in the first cell in a range, and then select adjacent cells to the right.

- Merged cells act as a single cell. Applying formatting to a merged cell formats the entire merged area.

- You can unmerge, or separate, merged cells by selecting the cell and clicking the Merge & Center button ▦ Merge & Center again.

Try It!   Merging and Centering Across Cells

1 In the **E04Try_xx** file, drag over the range B2:F2 to select it.

2 On the HOME tab, in the Alignment group, click the Merge & Center button ⊞ Merge & Center ▾

3 Drag over the range B13:E13 to select it.

4 On the HOME tab, in the Alignment group, click the Merge & Center button ⊞ Merge & Center ▾

5 Leave the merged cell selected. On the HOME tab in the Styles group, click Total in the gallery of styles.

6 Save the **E04Try_xx** file, and leave it open to use in the next Try It.

Merge & Center aligns headings over all the data

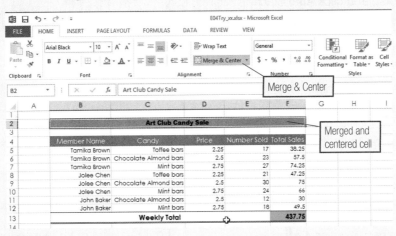

Applying Number Formats

- When formatting numerical data, you may want to change more than just the font and font size—you may want to also apply a **number format.**

- Number formats are grouped together in the Number group on the HOME tab.

- The number format determines the number of decimal places and the display of zeros (if any) before/after the decimal point.

- Number formats also include various symbols such as dollar signs, percentage signs, or negative signs.

- Changing the format of a cell does not affect the actual value stored there or used in calculations—it affects only the way in which that value is displayed.

- There are buttons for quickly applying three commonly used number formats:
  - **Accounting format** $ 21,008.00, which includes a decimal point with two decimal places, the thousands separator (comma), and a dollar sign aligned to the far left of the cell.
  - **Percent format** 32%, which includes a percentage sign and no decimal points.

✓ 32% is entered as **.32** in the cell. If you type 32 and apply the Percent format, you'll see 3200%.

  - **Comma format** 178,495.00, which includes two decimal places and the thousands separator (comma).

- Using the Number Format list, you can also apply a variety of other number formats such as Currency, Long Date, and Fraction.

- The **Currency format** is similar to Accounting format, except that the dollar sign is placed just to the left of the data, rather than left-aligned in the cell.

- If you don't see a number format you like, you can create your own by applying a format that's close. For example, you might apply the Accounting format and then change the number of decimal places using the Increase Decimal ⁺.₀₀ or Decrease Decimal ⁺.₀₀ buttons.

- You can also make selections in the Format Cells dialog box to design a custom number format. Click the Number group dialog box launcher ⌐ to open the dialog box.

Try It! Applying Number Formats

1 In the **E04Try_xx** file, click cell F5.

2 On the HOME tab, in the Number group, click the Accounting Number Format button **$ ▾**. Excel formats the cell with the Accounting format.

3 Click cell D5.

4 On the HOME tab, in the Number group, click the Number Format drop-down arrow > Currency. Excel formats the cell with the Currency format. Notice the difference between it and the Accounting format in cell F5.

5 Drag over the cell range D6:D12 to select it.

6 Click the Number Format arrow > Currency.

7 Drag over the range F6:F13 to select it.

8 Click the Accounting Number Format **$ ▾**.

9 Drag over the range E5:E12 to select it.

10 In the Number group, click the Increase Decimal button twice.

11 In the Number group, click the Decrease Decimal button twice.

12 Save and close the file, and exit Excel.

Applying Currency format

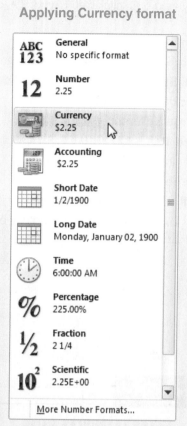

Lesson 4—Practice

In this project, you will apply font and number formats to cells, merge and center cells, apply cell styles, and apply a workbook theme using the skills you learned in this lesson.

DIRECTIONS

1. Start Excel, if necessary, and open the **E04Practice** file from the data files for this lesson.

2. Save the file as **E04Practice_xx** in the location where your teacher instructs you to store the files for this lesson.

3. Add a header that has your name at the left, the date code in the center, and the page number code at the right, and change back to **Normal** view.

4. Drag over the row headers for rows **1** through **4** to select them.

5. Click **HOME** > Clear ✎ > **Clear Formats**.

6. Click cell **A4**, type **11/30/14**, and press ⌷CTRL⌷ + ⌷ENTER⌷.

7. On the **HOME** tab, in the Number group, click the dialog box launcher to open the Format Cells dialog box. Date should already be selected in the Category list.

8. Click **14-Mar** in the Type list, and then click **OK**.

9. Click **PAGE LAYOUT** > Themes ⊞.

10. Move the mouse pointer over the **Facet** theme to view a Live Preview of its appearance.

11. Click the **Ion** theme to apply it.

12. Drag over the range **A1:I1** to select it.

13. Click **HOME** > **Merge & Center** Merge & Center ·

14. In the Styles group, click **Cell Styles** 📝, and click **Title**.

15. Drag over the range **A3:I3** to select it.

16. Click **Merge & Center** 🔲 Merge & Center ·

17. Click **Cell Styles** 📝 and then click **Heading 2**.

18. Drag over the range **A4:I4** to select it.

19. Click **Merge & Center** 🔲 Merge & Center ·

20. Click **Bold B**.

21. Drag over the range **D5:G5** to select it.

22. Click **Merge & Center** 🔲 Merge & Center ·

23. Click **Cell Styles** 📝 > **20% - Accent 3**.

24. Click cell **D7**, and type the following cell entries, pressing ENTER after each:

    a. 1

    b. 3

    c. 2

    d. 2

25. Click cell **E7**, and type the following cell entries, pressing ENTER after each:

    a. 2

    b. 4

    c. 2

    d. 1

26. Drag over the range **C7:C29** to select it.

27. Click **Accounting Number Format $ ·** .

28. Press CTRL + HOME . Your worksheet should look like the one shown in Figure 4-1.

29. **With your teacher's permission**, print the worksheet. Submit the printout or the file for grading as required.

30. Save and close the file, and exit Excel.

Figure 4-1

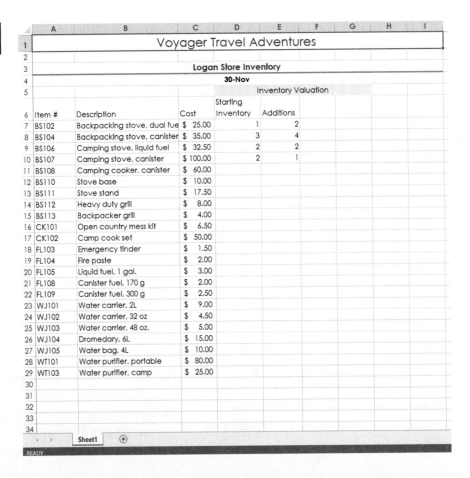

Lesson 4—Apply

As the Inventory Manager of the Voyager Travel Adventures retail store, you want to enhance the appearance of an inventory worksheet you have created. You have already compiled the inventory data, and you want to spruce up the worksheet prior to printing by adding some formatting.

DIRECTIONS

1. Start Excel, if necessary, and open the **E04Apply** file from the data files for this lesson.

2. Save the file as **E04Apply_xx** in the location where your teacher instructs you to store the files for this lesson.

3. Add a header that has your name at the left, the date code in the center, and the page number code at the right, and change back to **Normal** view.

4. Apply the **Organic** theme to the file. Notice how the fonts and colors in the worksheet change.

5. Select the range **I7:I29** and apply the **Percent** style. Then, format the data for two decimal places.

6. Select the range **G7:G29** and apply the **Accounting** number format.

7. Select the range **A6:I6** and apply the **Accent3** cell style and **Center** alignment.

8. Select the range **A7:A29** and apply the **60% - Accent3** cell style.

9. Click cell **A4** and apply the ***Wednesday, March 14, 2014** date format.

10. Go to cell **A1**. Your worksheet should look like the one shown in Figure 4-2.

11. **With your teacher's permission**, print the worksheet. Submit the printout or the file for grading as required.

12. Save and close the file, and exit Excel.

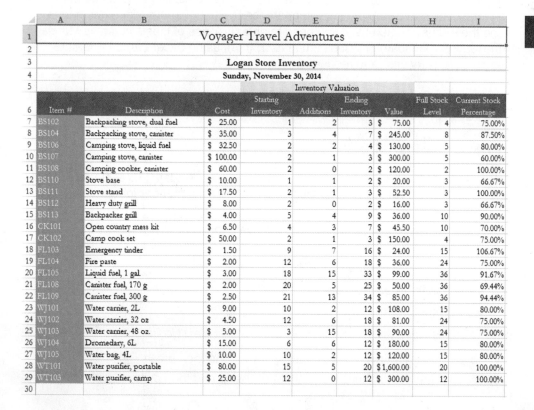

Figure 4-2

Item #	Description	Cost	Starting Inventory	Additions	Ending Inventory	Value	Full Stock Level	Current Stock Percentage
				Voyager Travel Adventures				
				Logan Store Inventory				
				Sunday, November 30, 2014				
				Inventory Valuation				
BS102	Backpacking stove, dual fuel	$ 25.00	1	2	3	$ 75.00	4	75.00%
BS104	Backpacking stove, canister	$ 35.00	3	4	7	$ 245.00	8	87.50%
BS106	Camping stove, liquid fuel	$ 32.50	2	2	4	$ 130.00	5	80.00%
BS107	Camping stove, canister	$ 100.00	2	1	3	$ 300.00	5	60.00%
BS108	Camping cooker, canister	$ 60.00	2	0	2	$ 120.00	2	100.00%
BS110	Stove base	$ 10.00	1	1	2	$ 20.00	3	66.67%
BS111	Stove stand	$ 17.50	2	1	3	$ 52.50	3	100.00%
BS112	Heavy duty grill	$ 8.00	2	0	2	$ 16.00	3	66.67%
BS113	Backpacker grill	$ 4.00	5	4	9	$ 36.00	10	90.00%
CK101	Open country mess kit	$ 6.50	4	3	7	$ 45.50	10	70.00%
CK102	Camp cook set	$ 50.00	2	1	3	$ 150.00	4	75.00%
FL103	Emergency tinder	$ 1.50	9	7	16	$ 24.00	15	106.67%
FL104	Fire paste	$ 2.00	12	6	18	$ 36.00	24	75.00%
FL105	Liquid fuel, 1 gal.	$ 3.00	18	15	33	$ 99.00	36	91.67%
FL108	Canister fuel, 170 g	$ 2.00	20	5	25	$ 50.00	36	69.44%
FL109	Canister fuel, 300 g	$ 2.50	21	13	34	$ 85.00	36	94.44%
WJ101	Water carrier, 2L	$ 9.00	10	2	12	$ 108.00	15	80.00%
WJ102	Water carrier, 32 oz	$ 4.50	12	6	18	$ 81.00	24	75.00%
WJ103	Water carrier, 48 oz.	$ 5.00	3	15	18	$ 90.00	24	75.00%
WJ104	Dromedary, 6L	$ 15.00	6	6	12	$ 180.00	15	80.00%
WJ105	Water bag, 4L	$ 10.00	10	2	12	$ 120.00	15	80.00%
WT101	Water purifier, portable	$ 80.00	15	5	20	$1,600.00	20	100.00%
WT103	Water purifier, camp	$ 25.00	12	0	12	$ 300.00	12	100.00%

Lesson 5

More on Cell Entries and Formatting

> ## ➤ What You Will Learn

Entering Dates
Filling a Series
Aligning Data in a Cell
Wrapping Text in Cells
Changing Column Width and Row Height
Using Keyboard Shortcuts

WORDS TO KNOW

Auto Fill
The feature that enables Excel to create a series automatically.

Date
A cell entry that indicates a date or time and is stored as a date code in Excel.

Default column width
The default number of characters that display in a column based on the default font.

Fill handle
A black box on the lower-right corner of the selected cell or range that you can use to fill (copy) a series or formula.

Key Tips
Keyboard shortcuts for choosing Ribbon commands that you display by pressing Alt.

Software Skills   Use dates to identify when you created a worksheet or to label a column or row of data by time period. After typing dates, labels, and numbers in a worksheet, you can improve its appearance by changing the alignment of data and the widths of columns. If you need to enter a series of labels (such as Monday, Tuesday, Wednesday) or values (such as 1, 2, 3), using Excel's Auto Fill feature saves data entry time and reduces errors.

What You Can Do

Entering Dates

■ Enter a **date** when you need to indicate the timing for data. Excel stores dates as special date codes, but automatically applies a Date number format depending on how you type in the date.

■ You can enter a date using one of these date formats:

  ● mm/dd/yy, as in 1/14/14 or 01/14/14

  ● mm/dd, as in 1/14

  ● dd-mmm-yy, as in 14-Jan-14

  ● dd-mmm, as in 14-Jan

    ✓ *The current year is assumed for any date entry that doesn't include a year.*

■ To enter today's date quickly, press CTRL + : and then press ENTER .

■ To enter the current time, press CTRL + SHIFT + : and then press ENTER .

- After entering a date, you can change its number format as needed. For example, you can change the date 1/14/14 to display as January 14, 2014.
- To enter a time, follow a number with a or p to indicate AM or PM, like this: 10:43 p.
- You can enter a date and time in the same cell, like this: 10/16/14 2:31 p.

Try It! **Entering Dates**

① Start Excel.

② Open the **E05Try** file from the data files for this lesson.

③ Save the file as **E05Try_xx** in the location where your teacher instructs you to store the files for this lesson.

④ Add a header that has your name at the left, the date code in the center, and the page number code at the right, and change back to Normal view.

⑤ Click cell C3 to select it.

⑥ Press CTRL + ;, and then press ENTER to insert the current date. It appears in the mm/dd/yyyy format.

⑦ Click cell C3 to select it again.

⑧ Click HOME > Number Format drop-down arrow > General. The date code for the date appears in the cell. The date code that you see will vary depending on the date you entered.

⑨ Click HOME > Number Format drop-down arrow > Short Date.

⑩ Save the **E05Try_xx** file, and leave it open to use in the next Try It.

A date code

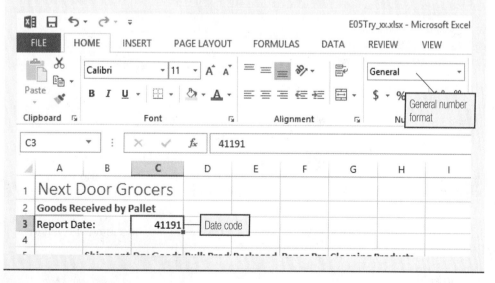

Filling a Series

- A **series** is a sequence of numbers (such as 1, 2, 3), dates (such as 10/21/14, 10/22/14, 10/23/14), times (such as 2:30, 2:45, 3:00), or text (such as January, February, March). The feature or process for creating a series in Excel is called **Auto Fill.**

- To enter a series based on the active cell, drag the **fill handle**, a small square in the lower-right corner of the active cell that turns into a plus sign (+), over the range of cells you want to fill with the series.

- Excel can create some series automatically. For example, type January in a cell, and then drag the fill handle down or to the right to create the series January, February, March, and so on.

- A yellow ScreenTip appears under the mouse pointer, displaying the cell values of the series as you drag. The series values appear in the cells after you release the mouse button.

- To create an incremental series (i.e., 1, 3, 5, 7), enter the data for the first and second cells of a series, select the two cells, and then drag the fill handle over the range of cells to fill.

- You can also use the fill handle to copy formatting only (such as bold, italics, and so on) from one cell to adjacent cells, and not its value, or the value only without formatting. To do so, click the Auto Fill Options button that appears when you perform the fill, and then click Fill Formatting Only or Fill Without Formatting.

Try It!   Filling in a Series

1 In the **E05Try_xx** file, click cell B6 to select it.

2 Type **4/2** and press ENTER . This enters the date with the format 2-Apr.

3 Type **4/9** and press ENTER . This is the second date in the sequence that you're entering.

4 Drag over the range B6:B7 to select it.

5 Drag the fill handle down until the ScreenTip reads *30-Apr*, and then release the mouse button.

> ✓ When you enter dates with the abbreviated format used in steps 2 and 3, Excel applies the year specified by your current system date, so your results may vary from those shown in this chapter.

6 Click cell C6 to select it.

7 Type **1** and press CTRL + ENTER .

8 Drag the fill handle right through cell G6, and then release the mouse button.

> ✓ Notice that a single number just repeats and doesn't automatically increment.

9 Click cell C7 to select it.

10 Type **2** and press ENTER .

11 Drag over the range C6:C7 to select it.

Filling a series

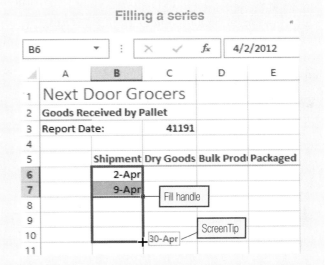

12 Drag the fill handle down until the ScreenTip reads *5*, and then release the mouse button.

13 With the range still selected, drag the fill handle right through column G. This fills the values across the columns, replacing the 1s already in row 6.

14 Save the **E05Try_xx** file, and leave it open to use in the next Try It.

Using Flash Fill

- When you have a series of labels in one column that you want to format, the Flash Fill feature in Excel can recognize the pattern in the text and change the format of the text for the series.

- Flash Fill can change the case of names that have been typed in lowercase to uppercase or change the format of phone numbers to include parentheses for the area code.

- Flash Fill only works when your text is in a single column.

- In the first cell next to the column you want to change, type the text the way you want it and press `ENTER`. Flash Fill begins to learn the pattern in the text.

- Next, type text into the second cell.

  ✓ If you select another cell or click on the Ribbon before typing in the second cell, the Flash Fill feature will not be available.

- When you type in the second cell, Flash Fill shows a preview of suggested changes for the rest of the series. Press `ENTER` to accept the suggestions.

  ✓ To continue typing without using Flash Fill suggestions, press the `ESC` key .

- You can use the Flash Fill Options button 🖹 to accept or undo the suggestions.

  ✓ If the Quick Analysis Lens displays, press the `ESC` key. You will learn about the Quick Analysis Lens in Chapter 2.

- Flash Fill also can separate labels (such as names or addresses) into different columns or combine labels from several columns into one.

- When you want to separate first and last names that are in one column, use Flash Fill to create two new columns with first names in one column and last names in another column.

- When you want to combine first names, middle initials, and last names that are in three columns, use Flash Fill to create a new column with the complete name.

- Flash Fill is case sensitive and works best with consistent labels. For example, all of the last names in a series need to be lowercase for Flash Fill to change the names to be uppercase.

  ✓ If the labels are not consistent, Flash Fill may not always separate the data elements correctly.

Try It! **Using Flash Fill**

1. In the **E05Try_xx** file, click cell I6 and type the following cell entries, pressing `ENTER` after each:

   a. **Michael W. Penn**
   b. **Rosie L. Patton**
   c. **Jameson P. Falcon**
   d. **Jon D. Stalwart**
   e. **Mia A. Dawson**

2. Click cell J6 to select it, type **Penn, Michael W.**, and press `ENTER`.

3. In cell J7, type **Pa**. The Flash Fill preview suggestions appear.

4. Press `ENTER` to fill cells J7:J10 with the series of last names, a comma, first names, and middle initials.

5. Click the Flash Fill Options button 🖹 > Undo Flash Fill.

6. Click the Undo button ↺ twice.

7. In cell J6, type **Michael**, and press `ENTER`.

8. In cell J7, type **Ro**, and press `ENTER`. Flash Fill fills the series of last names in cells J7:J10.

9. In cell K6, type **W.**, and press `ENTER`.

10. Click cell L6 to select it, type **Penn**, and press `ENTER`.

11. In cell L7, type **Pa**.

12. Click the Flash Fill Options button 🖹 > Accept Suggestions.

13. Drag over the range J6:L10 to select it.

14. On the HOME tab, in the Editing group, click Clear ✎ Clear ▾ > Clear All.

15. Save the **E05Try_xx** file, and leave it open to use in the next Try It!

Aligning Data in a Cell

- When you type a label, Excel automatically aligns it to the left of the cell. Excel aligns values and dates to the right by default.

- In addition, cell entries are aligned along the bottom edge of the cell.

- To improve the appearance of a worksheet, you can change the alignment (both vertically and horizontally) of column labels, row labels, and other data.

- To align data, select the cells to format and use the buttons in the Alignment group on the HOME tab.

- Align data between the top and bottom sides of a cell using the Top Align ≡, Middle Align ≡, or Bottom Align ≡ buttons.

- Align data between the left and right sides of a cell using the Align Left ≡, Center ≡, or Align Right buttons ≡.

  ✓ Use the Decrease Indent ≤ and Increase Indent ≥ buttons to add or remove space at the left end of the cell for left-aligned entries.

Try It!   Aligning Data in a Cell

1. In the **E05Try_xx** file, drag over the range B6:B10 to select it.

2. On the HOME tab, click the Align Text Left button ≡.

3. Drag over the range C6:G10 to select it.

4. On the HOME tab, click the Center button ≡.

5. Drag over the range A1:I1 to select it.

6. On the HOME tab, click Merge & Center
   ⊞ Merge & Center .

7. On the HOME tab, click Cell Styles 🖌 > Accent5.

   ✓ If you are working on a widescreen monitor, the Cell Styles button will change to the Styles gallery.

8. On the HOME tab, click Increase Font Size A˄ five times.

9. On the HOME tab, click Middle Align ≡.

   ✓ You will only see a subtle vertical alignment change in cell A1 at this point.

10. Save the **E05Try_xx** file, and leave it open to use in the next Try It.

Center aligned cells

Wrapping Text in Cells

- When a cell with a long label entry is too wide to display, you can use the **wrap text** feature to wrap the text to multiple lines.

- The Wrap Text button 📑 is in the Alignment group on the HOME tab of the Ribbon. Click it to apply and remove wrapping in the selected cell or range.

- Wrapping sometimes causes a line of text to break within a word, so you may need to adjust the column width for some columns after applying the wrapping.

Try It! **Wrapping Text in Cells**

① In the **E05Try_xx** file, click cell A2 to select it.

② On the HOME tab, click the Wrap Text button 📑.

 ✓ *You will correct the column widths soon.*

③ Drag over the range B5:I5 to select it.

④ On the HOME tab, click Wrap Text 📑.

⑤ Save the **E05Try_xx** file, and leave it open to use in the next Try It.

Changing Column Width and Row Height

- In a workbook file using the default Office theme, the default column width is 8.43 characters in the Calibri, 11 point font. The **default column width** varies in characters depending on the theme applied.

- You can quickly adjust a column to fit the longest entry in that column by double-clicking the right border of the column header, as you've seen in earlier lessons. Drag the right border to resize the width manually.

- The default row height in a workbook using the Office theme is 15 points.

- In some cases, such as when you apply a new number format, the column width increases automatically.

- In some cases, such as when you increase the font size of text or wrap text in a cell, the row height increases automatically.

- Double-click the bottom border of the row header to fit the row size automatically. Drag the border to resize it manually.

- Drag over multiple column or row headers or over cells in multiple columns or rows to resize all the selected rows or columns at once.

- Clicking the Format button 📅 in the Cells group on the HOME tab opens a menu with commands for automatically sizing (AutoFit Row Height and AutoFit Column Width) or manually sizing (Row Height and Column Width) rows and columns.

Try It! **Changing Column Width and Row Height**

① In the **E05Try_xx** file, move the mouse pointer over the right border of the column A column header until you see the resizing pointer, which is a vertical bar with left and right arrows.

② Drag right until the ScreenTip shows a width of 10.00, and then release the mouse button to finish resizing the column.

③ Drag over the range B5:G5 to select it.

④ On the HOME tab, click Format 📅 > Column Width.

Changing column width by dragging

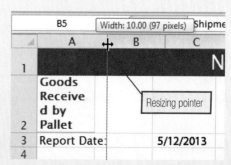

(continued)

Try It!   **Changing Column Width and Row Height** *(continued)*

5 Type **9.57** in the Column width text box of the Column Width dialog box, and then click OK.

6 Move the mouse pointer over the bottom border of the row 1 row header until you see the resizing pointer.

7 Drag down until the ScreenTip shows a height of 42.00, and then release the mouse button to finish resizing the row.

8 Save the **E05Try_xx** file, and leave it open to use in the next Try It.

Using Keyboard Shortcuts

■ You can use **keyboard shortcuts**—combinations of two or more keys pressed together or in sequence—to perform many commands in Excel.

✓ *Many keyboard shortcuts are the same as they've been in previous versions of Excel, such as* CTRL *+* O *to display the Open pane.*

■ Several of the formatting choices have keyboard shortcuts, such as CTRL + B for applying bold. Move the mouse pointer over a Ribbon button, and the ScreenTip lists a keyboard shortcut if one exists.

■ Pressing the ALT key displays **Key Tips**, which are keys you can press to select commands on the Ribbon.

■ After pressing ALT , press the Key Tip for the desired Ribbon tab, and then the Key Tip for the command.

✓ *The Help topic "Keyboard shortcuts in Excel 2013" explains Key Tips in detail and lists all the available keyboard shortcuts.*

■ You learned earlier about keyboard techniques for navigating and making selections, such as using the arrow keys to move from cell to cell.

Try It!   **Using Keyboard Shortcuts**

1 In the **E05Try_xx** file, click cell C3 to select it.

2 Press ALT . The tab Key Tips appear onscreen.

3 Press P . The Page Layout tab appears.

4 Press ALT twice to redisplay the tab Key Tips.

5 Press H . The HOME tab appears.

6 Press J . The Cell Styles gallery opens.

7 Press ↓ four times to select the 20%-Accent1 style, and then press ENTER .

8 Press ↓ three times and ← once to select cell B6.

9 Press and hold SHIFT and press ↓ four times to select the range B6:B10.

10 Press CTRL + B to apply bold to the selection.

11 Press CTRL + I to apply italics to the selection.

12 Press CTRL + S to save the file.

13 Press ALT + F to display the the Backstage view.

14 Press C to exit Excel.

Lesson 5—Practice

In this project, you will align data in cells, wrap text in cells, change column width and height, fill a series of cells with data, and use keyboard shortcuts.

DIRECTIONS

1. Start Excel, if necessary, and open the **E05Practice** file from the data files for this lesson.
2. Save the file as **E05Practice_xx** in the location where your teacher instructs you to store the files for this lesson.
3. Add a header that has your name at the left, the date code in the center, and the page number code at the right, and change back to **Normal** view.
4. Click cell **J3**, type **7/6/14**, and press `ENTER`.
5. Click cell **D6**, type **Jan**, and press `CTRL` + `ENTER`.
6. Drag the **fill handle** right through cell **I6** to automatically fill with the series of month labels.
7. Drag over the range **D7:I7** to select it.
8. Drag the **fill handle** down through cell **I14**. This fills all the selected cells with the values from the selection.
9. Click cell **D14**, type **25**, and press `TAB`.
10. Type **50**, and press `TAB`.
11. Drag over the range **D14:E14** to select it.
12. Drag the **fill handle** right through cell **I14**. Excel fills the cells with a series that increments based on the first two entries.
13. Drag over the range **C6:J6** to select it.
14. Press `ALT` + `H` to select the HOME tab and display its Key Tips.
15. Press `A` + `R` to align the labels to the right.
16. Click cell **C3** to select it.
17. In the HOME tab, click **Wrap Text**.
18. Click cell **C7** to select it.
19. Type **Clark, Joe** and press `ENTER`.
20. In cell C8, type **Hi** and press `ENTER`. Flash Fill fills the range C8:C14 with the series.

21. Drag over the range A7:B14 to select it.
22. On the HOME tab, click **Clear** > **Clear Contents**.
23. Drag over the column headers for columns A and B to select them.
24. Move the mouse over the **column B** header right border until you see the resizing pointer, and drag left until the ScreenTip displays a width of **1.00**. Release the mouse button to resize the columns.
25. Click the **column J** header.
26. Double-click the **column J** header right border. This automatically AutoFits the selected column.
27. Drag over the column headers for columns D through I to select them.
28. On the HOME tab, click **Format** > **Column Width**.
29. Type **8.43** in the Column width text box in the Column Width dialog box, and then click **OK**.
30. Double-click the **column C** header right border to AutoFit the column.
31. Double-click the **row 3** and **row 6** header bottom borders to AutoFit the rows.
32. Click cell **C1** to select it.
33. On the HOME tab, click **Format** > **Row Height**.
34. Type **52** in the Row height text box in the Row Height dialog box, and then click **OK**.
35. On the HOME tab, click **Middle Align**. Press `CTRL` + `S` to save the file. Your worksheet should look like the one shown in Figure 5-1 on the next page.
36. **With your teacher's permission**, print the worksheet. Submit the printout or the file for grading as required.
37. Press `ALT` + `F` and then `C` to close the file.

Figure 5-1

		Serenity Health Club							
	Client Account Tracking								7/6/2014
		Payments by Month							
	Client Name	Jan	Feb	Mar	Apr	May	Jun		Total
	Clark, Joe	$150	$150	$150	$150	$150	$150		$900
	Higgins, Mary	$150	$150	$150	$150	$150	$150		$900
	Stevens, Gary	$150	$150	$150	$150	$150	$150		$900
	Roberts, Paul	$150	$150	$150	$150	$150	$150		$900
	Moyer, Anne	$150	$150	$150	$150	$150	$150		$900
	Santos, Antonio	$150	$150	$150	$150	$150	$150		$900
	Jones, Brett	$150	$150	$150	$150	$150	$150		$900
	Stewart, Dorothy	$25	$50	$75	$100	$125	$150		$525
	Totals	$1,075	$1,100	$1,125	$1,150	$1,175	$1,200		$6,825

Lesson 5—Apply

You are the Accounts Receivable Supervisor at the Serenity Health Club. You need to compile data on client payments and extra services sold in a worksheet and improve its formatting.

DIRECTIONS

1. Start Excel, if necessary, and open the **05Apply** file from the data files for this lesson.
2. Save the file as **E05Apply_xx** in the location where your teacher instructs you to store the files for this lesson.
3. Add a header that has your name at the left, the date code in the center, and the page number code at the right, and change back to **Normal** view.
4. Click cell **A3**, type **7-6-14**, and press [ENTER].
5. Click cell **G3** to select it.
6. Wrap the text and align the text right.
7. Click cell **A1** and top align the data.
8. Adjust the height of row 1 using AutoFit.
9. Click cell **C6** and fill to cell **G6** to fill with a series of label entries.
10. Click cell **A8**. Drag the **fill handle** down to **A11** to fill four week labels.

11. Select the range **C8:C9**.
12. Drag the **fill handle** down to cell **C11** to fill with a series of increasing values.
13. Click cell **B8**, type **Week 1**, and press [ENTER].
14. In cell **B9**, type **Week 2**.
15. Drag the **fill handle** down to cell **B11** to fill the series of capitalized labels.
16. Select the range **A8:A11** and clear the contents of the cells.
17. Select the range **D8:D9**.
18. Drag the **fill handle** down to cell **D11** to fill a series of decreasing values.
19. Select the range **A5:G6**.
20. Wrap the text in the selection.
21. With the range still selected, apply bold to the entries.
22. With the range still selected, change the column width to **13.5**.

Lesson 6

Working with Ranges

➤ **What You Will Learn**

Selecting Ranges
Entering Data by Range
Making a Range Entry Using a Collapse Dialog Box Button

WORDS TO KNOW

Contiguous range
A block of adjacent cells in a worksheet.

Noncontiguous range
Cells in a worksheet that act as a block, but are not necessarily adjacent to each other.

Collapse Dialog box button
A button in a dialog box that you click to downsize a dialog box to make a selection on the sheet, and then click again to restore the dialog box to its regular size.

Range
A block of cells in an Excel worksheet.

Software Skills   Select a group of cells (a range) to copy, move, or erase the data in them in one step, or to quickly apply the same formatting throughout the range. You also can fill a range of cells with an entry, or perform calculations on cell ranges—creating sums and averages, for example. Some dialog boxes include a Collapse Dialog box button that enables you to specify a range entry in a text box.

What You Can Do

Selecting Ranges

- A **range** is an area made up of two or more cells.
- When you select cells A1, A2, and A3, for example, the range is indicated as A1:A3.
- The range A1:C5 is defined as a block of cells that includes all the cells in columns A through C in rows 1 through 5.
- A range of cells can be contiguous (all cells are adjacent to each other or in a solid block) or noncontiguous (not all cells are adjacent to each other).
- To select a **contiguous range**, drag over it. You also can click the first cell, press and hold SHIFT , and use the arrow keys to extend the selection or click the cell that's at the lower-right corner of the range to select.
- To select a **noncontiguous range**, select the first portion of the range. Then press and hold the CTRL key while dragging over additional areas or clicking additional cells. Release the CTRL key when finished selecting all the noncontiguous areas.
- When a range is selected, the active cell is displayed normally (with a white background), but the rest of the cells appear highlighted.

  ✓ *You also can assign a name to a range and use it to select or refer to the range. See "Using Named Ranges" in Lesson 13.*

- Clicking the column or row header selects the entire row or column. You also can press CTRL + SPACE to select the column holding the active cell or SHIFT + SPACE to select the row holding the active cell.

Try It!   Selecting Ranges

1 Start Excel.

2 Open the **E06Try** file from the data files for this lesson.

3 Save the file as **E06Try_xx** in the location where your teacher instructs you to store the files for this lesson.

4 Add a header that has your name at the left, the date code in the center, and the page number code at the right, and change back to Normal view.

5 With cell A1 selected, press and hold the SHIFT key while pressing ➡ four times.

6 On the HOME tab, click Merge & Center ▦ Merge & Center .

7 Drag over the range A5:A10 to select it.

A noncontiguous range selection

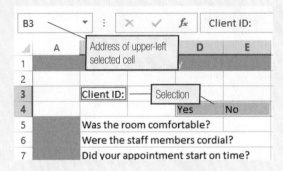

8 On the HOME tab, click Cell Styles ▦, and then click Accent6.

9 Drag over the range D4:E4 to select it. Press and hold the CTRL key, and click cell B3.

10 On the HOME tab, click Cell Styles ▦, and then click Accent6.

11 Click the column C column header to select the column.

12 On the HOME tab, click Cell Styles ▦, and then click Accent6.

13 Drag over the range B5:B10 to select it.

14 On the HOME tab, click Wrap Text ▦.

15 Move the mouse pointer over the right border of the column B column header and drag right until the ScreenTip shows a width of 20.00.

16 On the HOME tab, click Format ▦ > AutoFit Row Height.

17 Move the mouse pointer over the right border of the column C column header and drag left until the ScreenTip shows a width of 1.00.

18 Save the E06Try_xx file, and leave it open to use in the next Try It.

Entering Data by Range

- In the last lesson, you learned how to enter data by using the fill handle. There are a couple of other methods you can use to fill a range.

- To fill all the cells in a selected range with the same entry, first select the range. Then type the desired entry, and press CTRL + ENTER .

- The Fill button ▼ in the Editing group on the HOME tab offers choices that enable you to fill cells in the desired direction in a selected range and to create custom series. For example, you can click Down to fill down the column, or Right to fill across the row. Click Series to create a series to fill.

Try It!   Entering Data by Range

1 In the **E06Try_xx** file, drag over the range A5:A10 to select it.

2 Type **1** and press `ENTER` .

3 On the HOME tab, click Fill `▼` > Series.

4 In the Series dialog box, make sure the Columns and Linear options are selected and that 1 appears in the Step value text box, and then click OK.

5 Drag over the range D5:D6 to select it.

6 Press and hold `CTRL` , and click cells E7, D8, D9, and E10.

✓ *Be sure to release the* `CTRL` *key when you finish.*

7 Type **X**, and press `CTRL` + `ENTER` . Excel fills all the selected cells with the entry.

8 Save the changes to **E06Try_xx**, and leave it open to use in the next Try It.

Filling a range

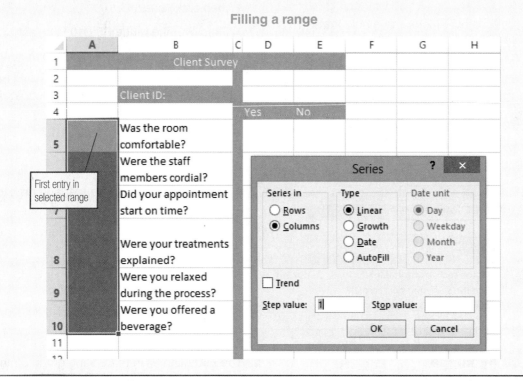

Making a Range Entry Using a Collapse Dialog Box Button

- You will most likely set options in Excel using the buttons on the Ribbon, however, occasionally, you may use a dialog box.

- Dialog boxes appear when you click the dialog box launcher `⌐` within a particular group on the Ribbon.

- To enter cell addresses or ranges in a dialog box, you can click the **Collapse Dialog box button** on the right end of the text box to shrink the dialog box so you can see the worksheet and select the range, rather than type it.

- After selecting the range, click the Collapse Dialog button to restore the dialog box to its normal size, and then finalize your selections.

| Try It! | **Making a Range Entry Using a Collapse Dialog Box Button** |

❶ In the **E06Try_xx** file, on the PAGE LAYOUT tab, in the Page Setup group, click the dialog box launcher ⌐.

❷ Click the Sheet tab.

❸ Click the Collapse Dialog box button 🔲 at the right end of the Print area text box.

❹ Drag over the range A1:E10 to select it and enter it in the text box.

❺ Click the Collapse Dialog box button 🔲 again.

❻ Click OK.

❼ Save and close the file, and exit Excel.

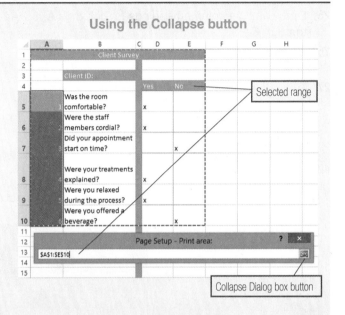

Using the Collapse button

Lesson 6—Practice

In this project, you will select a range of cells and fill a series using the skills you learned in this lesson.

DIRECTIONS

1. Start Excel, if necessary, and open the **E06Practice** file from the data files for this lesson.

2. Save the file as **E06Practice_xx** in the location where your teacher instructs you to store the files for this lesson.

3. Add a header that has your name at the left, the date code in the center, and the page number code at the right, and change back to **Normal** view.

4. Click cell **B25**, type **Frieda**, and press TAB.

5. Type **Randall**, and press ENTER.

6. Click cell B26, type **John**, and press TAB.

7. Type **Henson**, and press ENTER.

8. Drag over the range **A1:E1** to select it, and on the HOME tab, click **Merge & Center** 🔲 Merge & Center.

9. Drag over the range **A2:E2** to select it, and on the HOME tab, click **Merge & Center** 🔲 Merge & Center.

10. Drag over the range **A4:E5** to select it, and on the HOME tab, click **Cell Styles** 🔲 > **Accent2**.

11. Drag over the range **A9:E9** to select it, and click **HOME > Cell Styles** 🔲 > **Accent2**.

12. Drag over the range **A5:E5** to select it, and on the HOME tab, click **Wrap Text** 🔲 > **Center** ≡.

13. Click cell **A6** to select it.

14. Type **1**, and press ENTER.

15. Drag over the range **A6:E6** to select it.

16. On the HOME tab, click **Fill** 🔽 > **Series**.

17. Make sure that the Rows and Linear options are selected and that **1** is entered as the Step value, and click **OK**.

18. Drag over the range **D11:D12** to select it.

19. Press and hold CTRL, and click cells **D15**, **D18**, **D21**, **D22**, and **D26**. Be sure to release CTRL after clicking the last cell.

20. Type **3**, and press CTRL + ENTER.

21. Click cell **D19** to select it.

22. Type **4**, and press CTRL + ENTER.

23. Select the range **D19:D20** to select it.
24. On the HOME tab, click **Fill** ⬇ > **Down**.
25. Drag over the column headings for columns A through E.
26. Right-click the selected column headings, and click **Column Width**.
27. Type **13** in the Column width text box, and click **OK**.
28. Press ⌃ CTRL + HOME . Your worksheet should look like the one in Figure 6-1.
29. **With your teacher's permission**, print the worksheet. Submit the printout or the file for grading as required.
30. Save and close the file, and exit Excel.

Figure 6-1

	A	B	C	D	E
1	Overview Academy				
2	**Instructor Performance Ratings**				
3					
4	Scale: 1-5				
5	Unacceptable	Needs Improvement	Acceptable	Exceeds Expectations	Outstanding
6	1	2	3	4	5
7					
8					
9	Course	First Name	Last Name	2013 Rating	2014 Rating
10	Band	Angela	Green		
11	Business	Markus	Wright	3	
12	Calculus	Vincent	Gambel	3	
13	Chemistry	Linda	Brown		
14	Computer Basic	Robert	Cardo		
15	Computer Grap	Phyllis	Weaver	3	
16	Computer Prog	Ramon	Ramirez		
17	English	Terry	Kaminsky		
18	Fine Arts	Stella	Andrews	3	
19	French	Francoise	Martine	4	
20	Geometry	Allen	Chang	4	
21	Health/Phys Ed	Axel	Jones	3	
22	History	Fred	Wilson	3	
23	Life Manageme	Stewart	Bing		
24	Science	Carl	Tyrell		
25	Social Studies	Frieda	Randall		
26	Spanish	John	Henson	3	

Lesson 6—Apply

You are the Principal of Overview Academy, a small private school. You want to create a worksheet to track instructor performance ratings from two prior years. You need to finish entering some of the worksheet data, including the ratings, apply some formatting, and specify the range to print.

DIRECTIONS

1. Start Excel, if necessary, and open the **E06Apply** file from the data files for this lesson.

2. Save the file as **E06Apply_xx** in the location where your teacher instructs you to store the files for this lesson.

3. Add a header that has your name at the left, the date code in the center, and the page number code at the right, and change back to **Normal** view.

4. Adjust the width of **column A** using AutoFit.

5. Drag over the range **A8:E8** to select it.

6. Open the **Format Cells** dialog box, and click the **Alignment** tab, if necessary.

7. Open the **Horizontal** drop-down list and click **Fill**. Then click **OK**. This fills the selected range with the symbol character in cell A8, another way of creating a border.

8. Select the following non-contiguous cells: **D10, E10, E17, E18, E22, E23,** and **E25**.

9. Type **4**, and press `CTRL` + `ENTER` .

10. Click cell **E11** to select it.

11. Type **5**, and press `CTRL` + `ENTER` .

12. Fill the range **E12:E14** with the same value.

13. Enter the following data in the blank cells in column D:
    a. 5
    b. 5
    c. 2
    d. 2
    e. 5
    f. 5
    g. 2

14. Enter the following data in the blank cells in column E:
    a. 3
    b. 3
    c. 5
    d. 5
    e. 4
    f. 3
    g. 2

15. Open the **Page Setup** dialog box, and on the **Sheet** tab, set the Print area to **A1:E26**. Your worksheet should look like the one in Figure 6-2 on the next page.

16. **With your teacher's permission**, print the worksheet. Submit the printout or the file for grading as required.

17. Save and close the file, and exit Excel.

Figure 6-2

	A	B	C	D	E
1			Overview Academy		
2			**Instructor Performance Ratings**		
3					
4	Scale: 1-5				
5	Unacceptable	Needs Improvement	Acceptable	Exceeds Expectations	Outstanding
6	1	2	3	4	5
7					
8	●●●				
9	Course	First Name	Last Name	2013 Rating	2014 Rating
10	Band	Angela	Green	4	4
11	Business	Markus	Wright	3	5
12	Calculus	Vincent	Gambel	3	5
13	Chemistry	Linda	Brown	5	5
14	Computer Basics	Robert	Cardo	5	5
15	Computer Graphics	Phyllis	Weaver	3	3
16	Computer Programming	Ramon	Ramirez	2	3
17	English	Terry	Kaminsky	2	4
18	Fine Arts	Stella	Andrews	3	4
19	French	Francoise	Martine	4	5
20	Geometry	Allen	Chang	4	5
21	Health/Phys Ed.	Axel	Jones	3	4
22	History	Fred	Wilson	3	4
23	Life Management	Stewart	Bing	5	4
24	Science	Carl	Tyrell	5	3
25	Social Studies	Frieda	Randall	2	4
26	Spanish	John	Henson	3	2
27					

Lesson 7

Creating Formulas

➤ What You Will Learn

Entering a Formula
Using Arithmetic Operators
Editing a Formula
Copying a Formula Using the Fill Handle
Using the SUM Function

Software Skills   Creating formulas to perform calculations in Excel provides one of its powerful benefits: automatic recalculation. When you make a change to a cell that is referenced in a formula, Excel automatically recalculates the formula to reflect the change and displays the new formula result.

What You Can Do

Entering a Formula

- A **formula** is a worksheet instruction that performs a calculation.
- Enter a formula in the cell where the result should display.
- As you type a formula, it displays in the cell and in the formula bar.
- If you enter a long formula in a cell, that text may not fully display in the formula bar. You can expand the formula bar (make it taller) by clicking the Expand Formula Bar button ⌄ at the right end of the formula bar.
- When you select a cell that has a formula, the answer displays in the cell while the formula appears in the formula bar when the cell is selected.
- Use cell or range references, values, and mathematical operators in formulas.

    ✓ *A formula can also contain Excel's predefined functions, which are covered in Lesson 11, or use named ranges, which are covered in Lesson 13.*

- You must start each formula by typing the equal sign (=). For example, the formula =B2+B4+B6 adds together the values in those three cell locations.
- When you change the value in a cell that is referenced in a formula, the answer in the formula cell automatically changes.
- When typing a percentage as a value in a formula, you can enter it with the percent symbol or as a decimal.
- You can click a cell or drag a range to enter its address in the formula. This method can be more accurate than typing cell or range addresses.

WORDS TO KNOW

Arithmetic (mathematical) operators
Symbols used in mathematical operations: + for addition, - for subtraction, * for multiplication, / for division, and ^ for exponentiation.

Formula
An instruction Excel uses to calculate a result.

Order of precedence
The order in which Excel performs the mathematical operations specified in a formula, based on the types of mathematical operators used.

SUM function
A built-in calculation used to add a range of values together.

Try It!   Entering a Formula

1 Start Excel.

2 Open the **E07Try** file from the data files for this lesson.

3 Save the file as **E07Try_xx** in the location where your teacher instructs you to store the files for this lesson.

4 Add a header that has your name at the left, the date code in the center, and the page number code at the right, and change back to Normal view.

5 Click cell F4 to select it.

6 Type **=D4+E4**, and press [ENTER] .

7 Click cell D5 to select it.

8 Type **=**, click cell B5, type *****, and click cell C5.

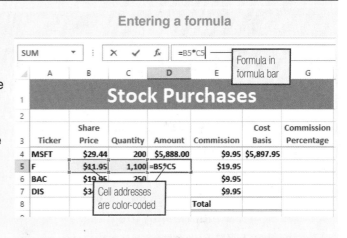

Entering a formula

	Ticker	Share Price	Quantity	Amount	Commission	Cost Basis	Commission Percentage
				Stock Purchases			
4	MSFT	$29.44	200	$5,888.00		$9.95	$5,897.95
5	F	$11.95	1,100	=B5*C5		$19.95	
6	BAC	$19.95	250			$9.95	
7	DIS	$3	Cell addresses are color-coded			$9.95	
8					Total		

Formula in formula bar: =B5*C5

9 Press [ENTER] to finish the formula.

10 Save the **E07Try_xx** file, and leave it open to use in the next Try It.

Using Arithmetic Operators

- Use the following standard **arithmetic (mathematical) operators** in formulas:
  - +   Addition
  - -   Subtraction
  - *   Multiplication
  - /   Division
  - ^   Exponentiation

- Excel performs mathematical operations in a particular order, called **order of precedence**. This is the order in which Excel calculates:
  1. Operations enclosed in parentheses.
  2. Exponentiation.
  3. Multiplication and division.
  4. Addition and subtraction.

- When a formula has multiple operators of the same precedence level, such as multiple multiplication operations, Excel performs the calculations from left to right.

- Keeping the order of mathematical operations in mind, the easiest way to control which part of a complex formula is calculated first is to use parentheses. Here are two examples:

=8+3*5   result: 23

Excel multiplies first, then adds.

=(8+3)*5   result: 55

Excel adds the values in parentheses, then multiplies.

Try It!   Using Arithmetic Operators

1 In the **E07Try_xx** file, click cell G4 to select it.

2 Type **=E4/F4** and press [ENTER].

3 Press [◁] to select cell F5.

4 Type **=B5*C5+E5** and press [TAB].

> ✓ *The formula you just entered is an alternate way of performing a calculation you created earlier. You could also enter this formula as =D5+E5 to calculate the correct result.*

5 In cell G5, type **=E5/(B5*C5+E5)** and press [ENTER].

> ✓ *The formula you just entered is an alternate way of performing a calculation you created in cell G4. You could also enter this formula as =E5/F5 to calculate the correct result.*

6 Save the **E07Try_xx** file, and leave it open to use in the next Try It.

Editing a Formula

- Excel automatically provides assistance in correcting common mistakes in a formula (for example, omitting a closing parenthesis).
- You can edit a formula as needed to update its calculation or if you see an error message such as #NUM! or #REF! in the cell.

- Editing a formula works just like editing any other data in a cell. Click the cell, and then press [F2] or double-click the cell to enter edit mode. Work in the cell or the formula bar to make the changes, and then press [ENTER] or click the Enter button ✔ on the formula bar to finish the entry.

> ✓ *Function lock must be enabled to use the function keys.*

Try It!   Editing a Formula

1 In the **E07Try_xx** file, click cell F5 to select it, and press [F2] to enter edit mode.

> ✓ *If needed, press the F Lock key to turn function lock on.*

2 In cell F5, drag over B5*C5, click cell D5 to replace the selection, and press [TAB] to finish the change.

3 With cell G5 selected, drag over (B5*C5+E5) in the formula bar to select it.

4 Type **F5** to replace the selected part of the formula, and press [ENTER].

5 Save the **E07Try_xx** file, and leave it open to use in the next Try It.

Editing in the formula bar

	SUM ▾	:	✕ ✓ *fx*	=E5/(B5*C5+E5)		
⊿	A	B	C	D	E	F	G

Stock Purchases

	A	B	C	D	E	F	G
3	Ticker	Share Price	Quantity	Amount	Commission	Cost Basis	Commission Percentage
4	MSFT	$29.44	200	$5,888.00	$9.95	$5,897.95	0.1687%
5	F	$11.95	1,100	$13,145.00	$19.95	$13,145.00	=E5/(B5*C5+E
6	BAC	$19.95	250		$9.95		
7	DIS	$34.09	350		$9.95		
8					Total		

Copying a Formula Using the Fill Handle

- You can use the fill feature to copy a formula that you've created to the cells below or to the right of it.
- Excel automatically adjusts cell addresses so the filled formulas apply to the correct data.

> ✓ *Lesson 8 explains more about how and why Excel adjusts cell and range addresses.*

- Drag the fill handle over the range of cells to fill with the formula.
- Also use the Fill button 🔽 in the Editing group on the HOME tab to fill formulas.

Try It!   **Copying a Formula Using the Fill Handle**

1 In the **E07Try_xx** file, click cell D5 to select it.

2 Drag the fill handle down through cell D7 to fill the formula.

3 Click cell F5 to select it.

4 Drag the fill handle down through cell F7 to fill the formula.

5 Click cell G5 to select it.

6 Drag the fill handle down through cell G7 to fill the formula.

7 Save the **E07Try_xx** file, and leave it open to use in the next Try It.

Using the SUM Function

■ The most basic and perhaps most often used function is the **SUM function**, which adds the values in the specified cells or range together.

■ You can enter the SUM function by typing it into the cell just like any other cell entry. For example, you could enter =SUM(A6,A9,B12) or =SUM(A6:B9).

  ✓ *Formulas and functions are not case sensitive, so an entry like =sum(a6:b9) would calculate correctly. This book shows cell addresses, formulas, and functions in uppercase to make them easier to read in the text.*

■ Enclose the cell addresses or range to sum in parentheses, and use commas to separate individual cell references.

■ Enter the SUM function more quickly using one of the following three methods:

  ● Press ALT + =.

  ● Click the Sum button Σ in the Editing group on the HOME tab. Note that this button is also called the AutoSum.

  ● Click the AutoSum button Σ AutoSum ▾ in the Function Library group on the FORMULAS tab.

Try It!   **Using the Sum Function**

1 In the **E07Try_xx** file, click cell F8 to select it.

2 On the HOME tab, click AutoSum Σ. Excel automatically starts the formula and selects the range above it.

  ✓ *If the selected range is incorrect, you can drag to change it.*

3 Press ENTER to finish the SUM formula.

4 Save and close the file, and exit Excel.

Summing a column of data

Lesson 7—Practice

In this project, you will add basic formulas to a spreadsheet using the skills you learned in this lesson.

DIRECTIONS

1. Start Excel, if necessary, and open the **E07Practice** file from the data files for this lesson.

2. Save the file as **E07Practice_xx** in the location where your teacher instructs you to store the files for this lesson.

3. Add a header that has your name at the left, the date code in the center, and the page number code at the right, and change back to **Normal** view.

4. Click cell **B12**, type **=B8+B9+B10+B11**, and press [ENTER] twice.

5. Type **=B12/G12**, and press [ENTER] . Excel should display a #DIV/0! error message because cell G12 is currently empty.

6. Click cell **C12** to select it.

7. Type **=sum(C8:C11)**, and press [ENTER] .

8. Click cell **G8** to select it.

9. Type **=B8+C8+D8+E8+F8**, and press [ENTER] . Your worksheet should look like the one shown in Figure 7-1.

10. **With your teacher's permission**, print the worksheet. Submit the printout or the file for grading as required.

11. Save and close the file, and exit Excel.

Figure 7-1

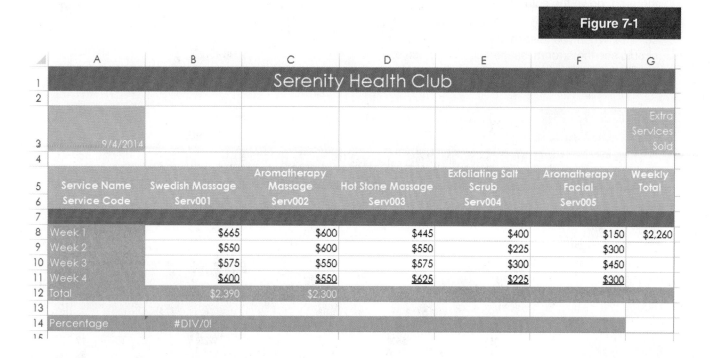

	A	B	C	D	E	F	G
1	Serenity Health Club						
2							
3	9/4/2014						Extra Services Sold
4							
5	Service Name	Swedish Massage	Aromatherapy Massage	Hot Stone Massage	Exfoliating Salt Scrub	Aromatherapy Facial	Weekly Total
6	Service Code	Serv001	Serv002	Serv003	Serv004	Serv005	
7							
8	Week 1	$665	$600	$445	$400	$150	$2,260
9	Week 2	$550	$600	$550	$225	$300	
10	Week 3	$575	$550	$575	$300	$450	
11	Week 4	$600	$550	$625	$225	$300	
12	Total	$2,390	$2,300				
13							
14	Percentage	#DIV/0!					
15							

Lesson 7—Apply

You are the Accounts Receivable Supervisor at the Serenity Health Club. You have some new data in a spreadsheet, and need to add basic formulas to calculate the data.

DIRECTIONS

1. Start Excel, if necessary, and open the **E07Apply** file from the data files for this lesson.

2. Save the file as **E07Apply_xx** in the location where your teacher instructs you to store the files for this lesson.

3. Add a header that has your name at the left, the date code in the center, and the page number code at the right, and change back to **Normal** view.

4. Click cell **D12** to select it and sum the values in the cells above.

5. Drag the fill handle right through cell **G12** to fill the formula.

6. Click cell **G8** and double-click the fill handle to fill the entry down the column.

7. Click cell **B14** and drag the fill handle right through cell **F14**. When you release the mouse button, you should see the error message #DIV/0! in each of the filled cells. This is because Excel changed the reference to cell G12 and you don't want it to do that.

8. Edit each of the formulas in the range **C14:F14** to change the divisor (the right cell address) to **G12**.

9. Select the range **B14:F14**. Look in the status bar next to the view buttons. The sum displayed there should be 100.00%, meaning that the corrected formulas each accurately calculate the percentage of the total. Your worksheet should look like the one shown in Figure 7-2.

   ✓ *When you want to see a quick sum of cells without building a formula, drag over the cells and check the status bar.*

10. **With your teacher's permission**, print the worksheet. Submit the printout or the file for grading as required.

11. Save and close the file, and exit Excel.

Figure 7-2

	A	B	C	D	E	F	G
1				Serenity Health Club			
2							
3	9/4/2014						Extra Services Sold
4							
5	Service Name	Swedish Massage	Aromatherapy Massage	Hot Stone Massage	Exfoliating Salt Scrub	Aromatherapy Facial	Weekly Total
6	Service Code	Serv001	Serv002	Serv003	Serv004	Serv005	
7							
8	Week 1	$665	$600	$445	$400	$150	$2,260
9	Week 2	$550	$600	$550	$225	$300	$2,225
10	Week 3	$575	$550	$575	$300	$450	$2,450
11	Week 4	$600	$550	$625	$225	$300	$2,300
12	Total	$2,390	$2,300	$2,195	$1,150	$1,200	$9,235
13							
14	Percentage	25.88%	24.91%	23.77%	12.45%	12.99%	
15							
16						Sum of selected cells	

Sheet1

READY   AVERAGE: 20.00%   COUNT: 5   SUM: 100.00%   100%

Lesson 8

Copying and Pasting

➤ **What You Will Learn**

Copying and Pasting Data
Copying Formats
Copying Formulas Containing a Relative Reference
Copying Formulas Containing an Absolute Reference

Software Skills Excel provides many time-saving shortcuts to help you enter data and build formulas in your worksheets. For example, you can use the copy and paste features to reuse data and formulas in the same worksheet, in another worksheet, or in another workbook. You also can copy formats. When copying formulas, you need to understand how to keep a cell reference from changing if needed.

What You Can Do

Copying, Cutting, and Pasting Data

- When you **copy** data, the copy is placed on the **Clipboard.**
- After you copy data, **paste** it to place the copy from the Clipboard to the new location.
- You can copy labels, values, and formulas to another cell, a range of cells, another worksheet, or another workbook. You also can copy Excel data to documents created in other programs, such as Word.
- To copy a selected cell or range of data to a new location, use the Copy ⧉ and Paste ▣ buttons in the Clipboard group on the HOME tab of the Ribbon.

  ✓ CTRL + C and CTRL + V are the shortcuts for copying and pasting, respectively.

- If the cells to which you want to copy data are adjacent to the original cell, you can use the fill handle to copy the data.
- Excel automatically copies the formats applied to data, which overrides any formatting in the destination cell.
- You can copy just the data and formulas without copying formatting.

  ✓ Clicking the bottom half of the Paste button, with the arrow on it, displays a menu with additional paste options. For example, you can paste formulas, formulas with number formatting, keep the column widths, and so on.

- Pasting overwrites data in the destination cell or range.

- You can link data as you paste it so the data changes automatically whenever the original data changes. Lesson 36 explains how to link data.

Try It! Copying, Cutting, and Pasting Data

1 Start Excel.

2 Open the **E08Try** file from the data files for this lesson.

3 Save the file as **E08Try_xx** in the location where your teacher instructs you to store the files for this lesson.

4 Add a header that has your name at the left, the date code in the center, and the page number code at the right, and change back to Normal view.

5 Click cell H5 to select it.

6 On the HOME tab, click Cut ✂.

7 Click cell E5 to select it.

8 On the HOME tab, click Paste 📋.

9 Drag over the range A3:E4 to select it.

10 On the HOME tab, click Copy 📑.

11 Click cell A13 to select it.

12 On the HOME tab, click Paste 📋.

13 Drag over the range A5:C11 to select it.

14 On the HOME tab, click Copy 📑.

15 Click cell A15 to select it.

16 On the HOME tab, click the Paste drop-down arrow > Values 📋. Excel pastes the range without pasting the formatting applied in the original range.

17 Press ESC to remove the selection marquee from the copied range.

   ✓ A selection marquee is a visible dashed line around a selected area.

18 Click cell B21 to select it. You still need a formula in this cell, so you need to update it.

19 Type **=MEDIAN(B15:B20** and press ENTER . Excel automatically fills in the closing parenthesis for you.

20 Save the **E08Try_xx** file, and leave it open to use in the next Try It.

Copied range

	A	B	C	D	E	F	G	H
1	Expense Analysis							
2								
3	Qtr 1							
4	Salesperson	Expenses		Accounts	Expense p	Amount Above or Below Median		
5	Jones	$ 3,500		6	583.3333	-1549.5		
6	Smith	$ 2,995		2				
7	Thomas	$ 6,599		4				
8	Weisbard	$ 8,055		5				
9	Vegas	$ 2,933		2				
10	Lewis	$ 7,800		4				
11	Median	$ 5,050						
12								
13	Qtr 1							
14	Salesperson	Expenses		Accounts	Expense p	Amount Above or Below Median		
15								
16								
17								

Copying Formats

- You can copy formatting from one cell to another, without copying the original cell's value.
- The Format Painter button 🖌 in the Clipboard group on the HOME tab enables you to copy formatting from one cell to another.
- **Format Painter** copies a cell's font, font size, font color, border, fill color, number formats, column widths (in some cases), cell alignment, and conditional formatting (formatting that depends on the current value in a cell).

- Select the cell with the formatting to copy, and then on the HOME tab, in the Clipboard group, click Format Painter 🖌. Click a destination cell or drag over a destination range to apply formatting in that location.
- To paste the formatting to multiple areas, double-click the Format Painter button 🖌. It will remain on until you click it again or press ESC to turn it off.

Try It! Copying Formats

1. In the **E08Try_xx** file, click cell E4 to select it.
2. On the HOME tab, click Wrap Text 🖹.
3. On the HOME tab, click Format Painter 🖌.
4. Drag over cells A4:D4 to copy the wrapping to them.
5. Click the column header for column C, and drag its right border to the right to resize the column to a width of 9.00.
6. Click cell E4 to select it.
7. On the HOME tab, click Format Painter 🖌.

8. Drag over cells D14:E14 to copy the wrapping to them.
9. Click cell B5 to select it.
10. Double-click the Format Painter button 🖌.
11. Drag over cells D5:E11 to copy the number formatting.
12. Scroll down and drag over cells B15:B21 to copy the number formatting.
13. Press ESC.
14. Save the **E08Try_xx** file, and leave it open to use in the next Try It.

Copying Formulas Containing a Relative Reference

- Formulas often have **relative references** to cells. This means that if you copy the formula to another location, the cell reference changes to reflect the position of its copied location relative to the original location.

- For example, the formula =B4+B5 entered in column B becomes =C4+C5 when copied to column C, =D4+D5 when copied to column D, and so on.
- Relative references make it easy to copy formulas across a row to total values above, for example.
- Relative references also work best when you want to fill formulas across a row or down a column.

Try It! Copying Formulas Containing a Relative Reference

1. In the **E08Try_xx** file, scroll down so row 4 is the first row visible.
2. Click cell D5 to select it.
3. On the HOME tab, click Copy 📋.
4. Drag over the range D6:D10 to select it.

5. Press ENTER. Excel pastes the formula to fill the destination range.

   ✓ In some cases, you can select a range or click in the upper-left cell of a range and press ENTER to complete a paste rather than using the Paste button.

6. Drag over the range D5:D10 to select it.

(continued)

Try It!   **Copying Formulas Containing a Relative Reference** *(continued)*

A pasted formula with relative references

D5			f_x	=B5/C5	
⊿	A	B	C	D	E
4	Salesperson	Expenses	Accounts	Expense per Account	Amount Above or Below Median
5	Jones	$ 3,500	6	$ 583	$ (1,550)
6	Smith	$ 2,995	2	$ 1,498	
7	Thomas	$ 6,599	4	$ 1,650	
8	Weisbard	$ 8,055	5	$ 1,611	
9	Vegas	$ 2,933	2	$ 1,467	
10	Lewis	$ 7,800	4	$ 1,950	
11	Median	$ 5,050			

⑦ Press CTRL + C .

⑧ Click cell D15 to select it.

⑨ Press CTRL + V .

⑩ Click cell B15 to select it.

⑪ Type **4240** and press ENTER . The value in cell D15 recalculates as you'd expect.

⑫ Click cell D15 to select it. The cell references in the formula have been updated to refer correctly to other cells on row 15.

⑬ Save the **E08Try_xx** file, and leave it open to use in the next Try It.

Copying Formulas Containing an Absolute Reference

- Sometimes, you do not want a cell reference to change when you copy the formula, so you need to create an **absolute reference**.

- To make a cell reference absolute, enter a dollar sign ($) before both the column letter and row number of that cell in the formula.

- For example, the formula =$B$4+$B$5 contained in a cell in column B remains =$B$4+$B$5 when copied to column C. The cell addresses do not adjust based on the new formula location.

- You can also create mixed cell references, where the column letter part of a cell address is absolute, and the row number is relative, or vice-versa.

- For example, the formula =B$4+B$5 contained in a cell in column B changes to =C$4+C$5 when copied to any cell in column C. The cell addresses partially adjust based on the new formula location.

- Press the F4 key as you type a cell reference in a formula to change to an absolute reference. Pressing F4 additional times cycles through the mixed references and then returns to a relative reference.

Try It!   **Copying a Formula Using an Absolute Reference**

① In the **E08Try_xx** file, click cell E5 to select it.

② Drag the fill handle down through cell E10 to fill the formula. Cell E8 displays an error message, so you know there must be a problem with the copied formula.

③ Click cell E5 to select it again. Notice that it subtracts the median value calculated in cell B11 from Jones' expenses. You need for each of the formulas in the column to subtract the value in B11 rather than changing, so you need to change to an absolute reference for cell B11.

Copying a formula with an absolute reference

⊿	A	B	C	D	E	F
1	Expense Analysis					
2				Absolute reference		
3	Qtr 1					
4	Salesperson	Expenses	Accounts	Expense per Account	Amount Above or Below Median	
5	Jones	$ 3,500	6	$ 583	$ (1,550)	
6	Smith	$ 2,995	2	$ 1,498	$ (2,055)	
7	Thomas	$ 6,599	4	$ 1,650	$ 1,550	
8	Weisbard	$ 8,055	5	$ 1,611	$ 3,006	
9	Vegas	$ 2,933	2	$ 1,467	$ (2,117)	
10	Lewis	$ 7,800	4	$ 1,950	$ 2,751	
11	Median	$ 5,050				
12						

(continued)

Try It!   **Copying a Formula Using an Absolute Reference** *(continued)*

4   Press F2 to enter edit mode.

5   Press F4 to add dollar signs for the row letter and column number for cell B11 in the formula, and then press ENTER to finish the change.

6   Click cell E5 to select it.

7   Drag the fill handle down through cell E10 to fill the formula. Now it fills correctly.

8   With the range E5:E10 still selected, on the HOME tab, click Copy.

9   Click cell E15 to select it.

10   On the HOME tab, click Paste. Look at the formula bar. The absolute reference in the formula still refers to cell B11, but for this set of data, you need for it to refer to cell B21.

11   Click cell E15 to select it.

12   Use the method of your choice to change the absolute reference in the formula from $B$11 to **$B$21**.

13   With cell E15 selected, drag the fill handle down through cell E20 to fill the formula.

14   Save and close the file, and exit Excel.

Lesson 8—Practice

In this project, you will copy and paste formatting and formulas using the skills you learned in this lesson.

DIRECTIONS

1. Start Excel, if necessary, and open the **E08Practice** file from the data files for this lesson.

2. Save the file as **E08Practice_xx** in the location where your teacher instructs you to store the files for this lesson.

3. Add a header that has your name at the left, the date code in the center, and the page number code at the right for each sheet, and change back to **Normal** view.

4. Click cell **D9** to select it.

5. Click **HOME > Copy**.

6. Drag over the range **D10:D19** to select it.

7. On the HOME tab, click **Paste**.

8. Drag over the range **J9:K19** to select it.

9. On the HOME tab, click **Copy**.

10. Click cell **B9** to select it.

11. On the HOME tab, click **Paste**.

12. Drag over the range J9:K19 to select it and clear the contents. Your worksheet should look like the one shown in Figure 8-1 on the next page.

13. **With your teacher's permission,** print both worksheets. Submit the printouts or the file for grading as required.

14. Save and close the file, and exit Excel.

Figure 8-1

▲	A	B	C	D	E	F	G
1	Voyager Travel Adventures						
2							
3	Eco Wilderness Adventure						
4	Tell City Thrill Seekers Club			Discount amount			35%
5	10/6/14-10/12/14			Commission			0
6							
7							
8	Item	Their Cost per Unit	Units	Their Total Cost	Our Cost per Unit	Our Total Cost	Our Profit
9	Bus to white water launch point (30 adventurers, max)	$1,125	1	$1,125	731.25		
10	White water raft, first day (4 adventurers max)	$450	3	$1,350			
11	White water raft, second day (4 adventurers max)	$450	3	$1,350			
12	River gear rental	$110	12	$1,320			
13	Transportation of gear to hike point	$1,500	1	$1,500			
14	Camping gear rental per person	$25	12	$300			
15	Hiking guides (1 per 4 adventurers), three days	$150	9	$1,350			
16	Rock climbing gear rental per person	$125	12	$1,500			
17	Food and water, per person	$275	12	$3,300			
18	Bus return trip (30 adventurers, max)	$1,675	1	$1,675			
19	Adventurer's insurance	$315	12	$3,780			
20				$18,550		0	0

Lesson 8—Apply

As an Adventure Coordinator for Voyager Travel Adventures, you make all the arrangements necessary to create a unique and thrilling adventure vacation for your clients. Today, the Tell City Thrill Seekers Club has asked for an estimate of expenses per person for a special trip that combines white water rafting, back country hiking, and rock climbing. You have started both a trip budget for the club and a profit worksheet. To complete the two worksheets, you need to copy formulas, data, and formatting.

DIRECTIONS

1. Start Excel, if necessary, and open the **E08Apply** file from the data files for this lesson.

2. Save the file as **E08Apply_xx** in the location where your teacher instructs you to store the files for this lesson.

3. Add a header that has your name at the left, the date code in the center, and the page number code at the right for each sheet, and change back to **Normal** view.

4. Click cell **I9** to select it, and copy the formula.

5. Click cell **E9** to select it, and paste the formula. An error message appears in cell E9, so you know there's a problem with the formula. Notice that to calculate the discounted price, the formula has to use the discount percentage in cell G4. That cell reference needs to be changed to an absolute reference for the formula to copy correctly.

6. In Edit mode, change the **C4** cell reference, to an absolute reference to cell **G4**.

7. Also in Edit mode, change the **#REF!** cell reference to **B9**.

8. Copy cell **E9** and paste it to the range **E10:E19**.

9. Delete the contents of cell **I9**.

10. Enter the formula **=C9*E9** in cell **F9**. Copy or fill the formula down through cell **F19**.

11. Enter the formula **=D9-F9** in cell **G9**. Copy or fill the formula down through cell **G19**.

12. Select cells **F20:G20**, and apply the **Total** cell style to them.

13. Click cell **G5**, and apply the **Currency** number format to it.

14. Click the cell range **F20:G20**, and apply the **Currency** number format. Apply the Total cell style to the same range. Your worksheet should look like the one shown in Figure 8-2.

15. **With your teacher's permission**, print the worksheet. Submit the printout or the file for grading as required.

16. Save and close the file, and exit Excel.

Figure 8-2

	A	B	C	D	E	F	G
1	Voyager Travel Adventures						
2							
3	Eco Wilderness Adventure						
4	Tell City Thrill Seekers Club			Discount amount			35%
5	10/6/14-10/12/14			Commission			$649.25
6							
7							
8	Item	Their Cost per Unit	Units	Their Total Cost	Our Cost per Unit	Our Total Cost	Our Profit
9	Bus to white water launch point (30 adventurers, max)	$1,125	1	$1,125	$731.25	$731.25	$393.75
10	White water raft, first day (4 adventurers max)	$450	3	$1,350	$292.50	$877.50	$472.50
11	White water raft, second day (4 adventurers max)	$450	3	$1,350	$292.50	$877.50	$472.50
12	River gear rental	$110	12	$1,320	$71.50	$858.00	$462.00
13	Transportation of gear to hike point	$1,500	1	$1,500	$975.00	$975.00	$525.00
14	Camping gear rental per person	$25	12	$300	$16.25	$195.00	$105.00
15	Hiking guides (1 per 4 adventurers), three days	$150	9	$1,350	$97.50	$877.50	$472.50
16	Rock climbing gear rental per person	$125	12	$1,500	$81.25	$975.00	$525.00
17	Food and water, per person	$275	12	$3,300	$178.75	$2,145.00	$1,155.00
18	Bus return trip (30 adventurers, max)	$1,675	1	$1,675	$1,088.75	$1,088.75	$586.25
19	Adventurer's insurance	$315	12	$3,780	$204.75	$2,457.00	$1,323.00
20				$18,550		$12,057.50	$6,492.50

Lesson 9

Techniques for Moving Data

➤ What You Will Learn

Inserting and Deleting Cells
Inserting, Deleting, Hiding, and Unhiding Columns and Rows
Cutting and Pasting Data
Using Drag-and-Drop Editing
Transposing Columns and Rows

WORDS TO KNOW

Cut
The command used to remove data from a cell or range of cells and place it on the Clipboard.

Drag-and-drop
A method used to move or copy the contents of a range of cells by dragging the border of a selection from one location in a worksheet and dropping it in another location.

Transpose
A method to rearrange data by switching the positions of columns and rows.

Software Skills   After you create a worksheet, you may want to rearrange data or add more information. For example, you may need to insert additional rows to a section of your worksheet because new employees have joined a department or been promoted. With Excel's editing features, you can easily add, delete, and rearrange cells and entire rows and columns. You can also move or drag and drop sections of the worksheet with ease.

What You Can Do

Inserting and Deleting Cells

- You can insert or delete cells when necessary to change the arrangement of the data on the worksheet.

- When you select a cell or range of cells, you can use the Insert and Delete buttons in the Cells group on the HOME tab to insert and delete cells. You also can click the drop-down arrows for these buttons for more commands, or right-click a selected cell and use the Insert and Delete commands on the shortcut menu.

- The Insert or Delete button will add or remove the number of cells specified by your selection.

- When you insert a cell in a worksheet, existing cells shift their position down. For example, if you select cell B2 and then insert a cell, the data that was in cell B3 is shifted down and becomes cell B4.

- When you select a range of cells and then click the Insert or Delete buttons, the Insert or Delete dialog box will open.

- You can choose the direction to shift the surrounding cells in the Insert or Delete dialog box, for example, right or down.

■ After inserting a cell or group of cells, you can use the Format Options button to choose whether or not formatting should be applied to the new cell(s).

■ When you delete a cell, existing cells shift left or up to close the gap. Any data in the rows or columns you select for deletion is erased.

Try It!   Inserting and Deleting Cells

1 Start Excel.

2 Open the **E09Try** file from the data files for this lesson.

3 Save the workbook as **E09Try_xx** in the location where your teacher instructs you to store the files for this lesson.

4 Add a header that has your name at the left, the date code in the center, and the page number code at the right, and change back to Normal.

5 Click cell C6 to select it.

6 On the HOME tab, in the Cells group, click the Insert button.

✓ Be sure to click the top part of the Insert button, not the drop-down arrow on the bottom part.

7 Click the Insert Options button ✦ ▾ next to the cell, and click Format Same As Below.

8 Type **3091**, and press CTRL + ENTER . Notice that the number is formatted for currency.

9 Right-click on cell C6, select delete, make sure Shift cells up is selected, and click OK.

10 Save the **E09Try_xx** file, and leave it open to use in the next Try It.

The Delete dialog box

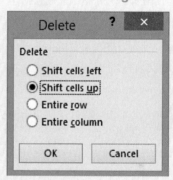

Inserting, Deleting, Hiding, and Unhiding Columns and Rows

■ You can insert or delete columns or rows when necessary to change the arrangement of the data on the worksheet.

■ When you select a row or column, or multiple rows or columns, you can use the Insert and Delete buttons in the Cells group on the HOME tab to insert and delete columns and rows. You also can right-click a selected column or row's heading and use the Insert and Delete commands on the shortcut menu.

✓ Drag over multiple row or column headings to select multiple rows or columns. Then, using the shortcut menu to insert or delete will add or remove the number of rows or columns specified by your selection.

■ When you insert column(s) in a worksheet, existing columns shift their position to the right. For example, if you select column C and then insert two columns, the data that was in column C is shifted to the right and becomes column E.

■ If you insert row(s) in a worksheet, existing rows are shifted down to accommodate the newly inserted row(s). For example, if you select row 8 and insert two rows, the data that was in row 8 is shifted down to row 10.

■ After inserting a column or row, you can use the Insert Options button ✦ ▾ to choose whether or not formatting from a nearby row or column should be applied to the new rows or columns.

■ When you delete a column or row, existing columns and rows shift left or up to close the gap. Any data in the rows or columns you select for deletion is erased.

■ You can also hide columns or rows temporarily and then redisplay them as needed. Right-click the column/row heading and click Hide. Drag over headings surrounding the hidden row/column, right-click, and click Unhide.

Try It!   **Inserting, Deleting, Hiding, and Unhiding Columns and Rows**

1 In the **E09Try_xx** file, right-click the column B column heading and click Hide on the shortcut menu.

2 Drag across column headings A though C and right-click the selected headings. Click Unhide on the shortcut menu.

3 Click the column B column heading to select the column.

4 On the HOME tab, click Delete ⯐. Excel removes the column.

  ✓ *Be sure to click the top part of the Delete button, not the drop-down arrow on the bottom part.*

5 Click the column C column heading to select it.

6 On the HOME tab, click Insert ⯐.

  ✓ *Be sure to click the top part of the Insert button, not the drop-down arrow on the bottom part.*

7 Make the following entries in the new column, starting in cell C3:

February

8282

9087

10443

9731

8367

8 Fill the formulas from cells B9 and B10 to the right to cells C9 and C10.

9 Right-click the row 8 row heading and click Hide on the shortcut menu.

10 Drag across row headings 7 though 9 and right-click the selected headings. Click Unhide on the shortcut menu.

11 Click the row 8 row heading to select it.

12 On the HOME tab, click Insert ⯐.

13 Make the following entries in the new row, starting in cell A8:

Vegas

8042

6639

8088

14 Save the **E09Try_xx** file, and leave it open to use in the next Try It.

Cutting and Pasting Data

■ To move data from one place in the worksheet to another, use the Cut ✂ and Paste 📋 options in the Clipboard group on the HOME tab. This removes the data from its original location.

■ When you **cut** data from a location, it is temporarily stored on the Clipboard. That data is then copied from the Clipboard to the new location when you paste.

■ If data already exists in the location you wish to paste to, Excel overwrites it.

■ Instead of overwriting data with the Paste command, you can insert the cut cells and have Excel shift cells with existing data down or to the right.

■ When you move data, its formatting moves with it. You can override this and move just the data using choices on the Paste button's drop-down list.

Try It!   **Cutting and Pasting Data**

1 In the **E09Try_xx** file, drag over the range **A8:E9** to select it.

2 On the HOME tab, in the Clipboard group, click Cut ✂.

3 Click cell G4 to select it.

4 On the HOME tab, in the Clipboard group, click Paste 📋.

✓ *Be sure to click the top part of the Paste button, not the drop-down arrow on the bottom part.*

5 Save the changes to **E09Try_xx** file, and leave it open to use in the next Try It.

Using Drag-and-Drop Editing

- The **drag-and-drop** feature enables you to use the mouse to copy or move a range of cells simply by dragging them.

- To use drag-and-drop, select a range to copy or move, and then you use the border surrounding the range to drag the data to a different location. When you release the mouse button, the data is "dropped" in that location.

- An outline of the selection appears as you drag it to its new location on the worksheet.

- You can use drag-and-drop to move data and to copy it. To copy data using drag-and-drop, simply hold down the CTRL key as you drag.

- Insert, delete, move, and copy operations may affect formulas, so you should check the formulas after you have used drag-and-drop to be sure that they are correct.

- When a drag-and-drop action does not move data correctly, use the Undo feature to undo it.

Try It!   **Using Drag-and-Drop Editing**

1 In the **E09Try_xx** file, drag over the range A7:E7 to select it.

2 Point to the border of the selection. When the mouse pointer changes to a four-headed arrow, drag down one row. When the ScreenTip reads A8:E8, release the mouse button.

3 Drag over the range G4:K4 to select it.

4 Use drag-and-drop to move the selection to row 7 of the sales data.

5 Click the row 9 row heading to select it.

6 On the HOME tab, click Delete 🗙.

7 Save the changes to **E09Try_xx** file, and leave it open to use in the next Try It.

Moving a range with drag-and-drop

	A	B	C	D	E
1	Sales Review				
2					
3	Salesperson	January	February	March	Total
4	Jones	$7,659	$8,282	$12,000	$27,941
5	Smith	$9,930	$9,087	$3,930	$22,947
6	Thomas	$5,909	$10,443	$6,965	$23,317
7	Weisbard	$5,056	$9,731	$7,933	$22,720
8					
9	Lewis A8:E8	$7,698	$8,367	$10,111	$26,176
10	Total	$36,252	$45,910	$40,939	$123,101
11	Average	$7,250	$9,182	$8,188	$24,620

Transposing Columns and Rows

- You can use the **transpose** feature to rearrange the columns and rows of data in a worksheet.

- To use the transpose feature, select the data you want to transpose, which can include row or column labels, and then copy it.

  ✓ *You must use Copy* 📋 *with the transpose feature; you cannot use Cut* ✂ *.*

- Transposed data must be placed in blank cells.

- To place the transposed data, right-click the first cell where you want the tranposed data to be pasted, and choose Transpose 📋 in the Paste Options menu.

- Transposing may affect formulas, so you should check the formulas after you have used the transpose feature to be sure that they are correct.

- When a transpose action does not move data correctly, use the Undo feature to undo it.

Try It!   **Transposing Columns and Rows**

---

1 In the **E09Try_xx** file, select the cell range A3:D8.

2 On the HOME tab, in the Clipboard group, click Copy 📋.

3 Right-click cell A13.

4 In the Paste Options menu, click Transpose 📋. The column headings have now been transposed to row headings, and vice versa. Notice that the data has been transposed also.

5 Save and close the file, and exit Excel.

The Transpose button in the
Paste Options drop-down menu

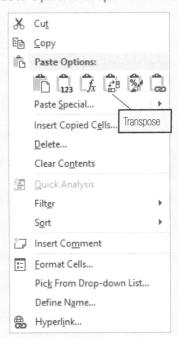

Lesson 9—Practice

In this project, you will insert, delete, hide, and unhide columns and rows using the skills you learned in this lesson.

DIRECTIONS

1. Start Excel, if necessary, and open the **E09Practice** file from the data files for this lesson.
2. Save the file as **E09Practice_xx** in the location where your teacher instructs you to store the files for this lesson.
3. Add a header that has your name at the left, the date code in the center, and the page number code at the right, and change back to **Normal** view.
4. Click the **row 14** row heading to select it.
5. On the HOME tab, click **Insert** 🖫.
6. Click the **row 4** row heading to select it.
7. Move the mouse pointer over the border of the selection, press and hold `CTRL`, and drag the selection down to **row 15**. When you release the mouse button, Excel copies the selection.

8. Click cell **A15** to select it, type **Hourly Employees**, and press `ENTER`.
9. Click the **column D** column heading to select it.
10. On the HOME tab, click **Delete** 🖫.
11. Right-click the **row 14** row heading and select **Hide**.
12. Click the row headings for **rows 13-15**, right-click, and select **Unhide**.
13. **With your teacher's permission**, print the worksheet. Submit the printout or the file for grading as required.
14. Save and close the file, and exit Excel.

Lesson 9—Apply

You are the Payroll Manager at Whole Grains Bread. The conversion to an in-house payroll system is next week, and you want to test out a payroll worksheet the staff will use to collect and enter payroll data in the computer system. You need to finish entering data and formulas in the worksheet. This will require adding, deleting, hiding, and unhiding rows and columns, and moving data by cutting and pasting and drag-and-drop techniques. You also will transpose the hourly employee data to show a different way of presenting this information.

DIRECTIONS

1. Start Excel, if necessary, and open the **E09Apply** file from the data files for this lesson.
2. Save the file as **E09Apply_xx** in the location where your teacher instructs you to store the files for this lesson.
3. Add a header that has your name at the left, the date code in the center, and the page number code at the right, and change back to **Normal** view.
4. Select the range **B5:J13** and move it left one column.

5. Select the range **B16:H24** and move it left one column.
6. Adjust column widths as needed.
7. Select the range **G5:I13**, press and hold the `CTRL` key, and use drag-and-drop to copy the data to the range **H16:J24**.

   ✓ When using drag-and-drop to copy data, remember to use the `CTRL` key.

8. Select **row 12**, and insert a new row.
9. Cut the range **A22:D22**, and paste it in the new **row 12**.

10. In row 12, change the Rate to **765**. For the rest of the columns, fill the formulas down from the row above to row 12.

11. Delete **row 22**.

12. Select **row 15** and hide the row.

13. Select **column B** and hide the column.

14. Select the cell range **A17:J24**.

15. On the HOME tab, in the Clipboard group, click **Copy** 📋.

16. Right-click cell **A27**.

17. In the Paste Options menu, click **Transpose** 📋. Adjust the column widths, if necessary. Your worksheet should look like the one shown in Figure 9-1.

18. **With your teacher's permission**, print the worksheet. Submit the printout or the file for grading as required.

19. Save and close the file, and exit Excel.

Figure 9-1

	A	C	D	E	F	G	H	I	J	K
1				**Whole Grains Bread**						
2	Home Office Payroll									
3										
4	Salaried Employees									
5	Employee Name	Rate		Regular Hours	Gross Pay	Fed Tax	SS Tax	State Tax	Net Pay	
6	Anthony Splendoria	$ 2,175.00		40.00	$2,175.00	$ 543.75	$ 169.65	$ 65.25	$1,396.35	
7	Eileen Costello	$ 1,895.00		40.00	$1,895.00	$ 473.75	$ 147.81	$ 56.85	$1,216.59	
8	Carol Chen	$ 895.00		40.00	$ 895.00	$ 223.75	$ 69.81	$ 26.85	$ 574.59	
9	Marty Gonzales	$ 684.00		40.00	$ 684.00	$ 171.00	$ 53.35	$ 20.52	$ 439.13	
10	Maria Nachez	$ 1,665.00		40.00	$1,665.00	$ 416.25	$ 129.87	$ 49.95	$1,068.93	
11	Mika Gritada	$ 1,023.00		40.00	$1,023.00	$ 255.75	$ 79.79	$ 30.69	$ 656.77	
12	Vickie Helms	$ 765.00		40.00	$ 765.00	$ 191.25	$ 59.67	$ 22.95	$ 491.13	
13	Randall Lohr	$ 1,545.00		40.00	$1,545.00	$ 386.25	$ 120.51	$ 46.35	$ 991.89	
14	Abe Rittenhouse	$ 1,231.00		40.00	$1,231.00	$ 307.75	$ 96.02	$ 36.93	$ 790.30	
16	Hourly Employees									
17	Employee Name	Rate		Regular Hours	Overtime Hours	Gross Pay	Fed Tax	SS Tax	State Tax	Net Pay
18	Thomas Cortese	$ 8.25		40.00	2.00	$ 354.75	$ 53.21	$ 27.67	$ 10.64	$ 263.22
19	Javier Cortez	$ 7.75		40.00	3.00	$ 344.88	$ 51.73	$ 26.90	$ 10.35	$ 255.90
20	Allen Gaines	$ 7.25		40.00	6.00	$ 355.25	$ 53.29	$ 27.71	$ 10.66	$ 263.60
21	Freda Gage	$ 8.00		40.00	3.00	$ 356.00	$ 53.40	$ 27.77	$ 10.68	$ 264.15
22	Isiah Herron	$ 10.95		40.00	5.50	$ 528.34	$ 79.25	$ 41.21	$ 15.85	$ 392.03
23	Thomas Kaminski	$ 9.75		40.00	4.00	$ 448.50	$ 67.28	$ 34.98	$ 13.46	$ 332.79
24	Chris Nakao	$ 11.25		40.00	3.00	$ 500.63	$ 75.09	$ 39.05	$ 15.02	$ 371.46
25										
26										
27	Employee Name	Javier Cortez	Allen Gaines	Freda Gage	Isiah Herron	Thomas Kaminski	Chris Nakao			
28	Employee ID	21154	23455	27855	33252	37881	29958			
29	Rate	$ 7.75	$ 7.25	$ 8.00	$ 10.95	$ 9.75	$ 11.25			
30	Regular Hours	40.00	40.00	40.00	40.00	40.00	40.00			
31	Overtime Hours	3.00	6.00	3.00	5.50	4.00	3.00			
32	Gross Pay	$ 344.88	$ 355.25	$ 356.00	$ 528.34	$ 448.50	$ 500.63			
33	Fed Tax	$ 51.73	$ 53.29	$ 53.40	$ 79.25	$ 67.28	$ 75.09			
34	SS Tax	$ 26.90	$ 27.71	$ 27.77	$ 41.21	$ 34.98	$ 39.05			
35	State Tax	$ 10.35	$ 10.66	$ 10.68	$ 15.85	$ 13.46	$ 15.02			
36	Net Pay	$ 255.90	$ 263.60	$ 264.15	$ 392.03	$ 332.79	$ 371.46			

Lesson 10

Sheet, Display, and Print Operations

➤ What You Will Learn

Displaying, Printing, and Hiding Formulas
Printing Titles
Changing Orientation
Scaling a Printout
Previewing and Printing a Worksheet

Software Skills   A few of the options available for adjusting a printout make a great difference in how easy it is to read the worksheet data. Repeating rows or columns with labels on multipage printouts ensures that the data will be identified on every page; choosing the right page orientation ensures enough columns will fit on screen; and scaling a printout to fit to a specified number of pages helps ensure that rows or columns aren't "orphaned" from the rest of the data. You might also want to display and print formulas to review them and preview the worksheet so you can see how it will look when printed.

What You Can Do

Displaying, Printing, and Hiding Formulas

- The **Show Formulas** command displays formulas in cells in which they are entered rather than formula results.

- Showing formulas enables you to review the worksheet to ensure that the formulas refer to the correct cells and ranges and accurately perform the desired calculations.

- Print the worksheet with the formulas displayed to create a printout of the formulas for later reference.

- Use the Show Formulas button 🔣 in the Formula Auditing group on the FORMULAS tab to turn formula display on and off. You also can press CTRL + `.

  ✓ *The accent grave character (`) is on the same key as the tilde, typically found to the left of the 1 on the row of numbers at the top of the keyboard or beside the Spacebar in rarer cases.*

WORDS TO KNOW

Orientation
The position for displaying and printing text either horizontally across the shorter side of a page, the default Portrait orientation, or along the wider side of the page, Landscape orientation.

Print titles
Row and column labels that reprint on each page of a printout.

Scale
Adjust the size proportionately.

Show Formulas
A command that enables you to display the formulas in a worksheet so that you can check them.

Try It! — Displaying, Printing, and Hiding Formulas

1. Start Excel, if necessary, and open the **E10Try** file from the data files for this lesson.

2. Save the file as **E10Try_xx** in the location where your teacher instructs you to store the files for this lesson.

3. Scroll down so that row 105 is visible.

4. Click FORMULAS > Show Formulas 🔢 .

5. Click FILE > Print.

6. Under Settings, click No Scaling > Custom Scaling > Fit Sheet on One Page.

✓ It's often necessary to scale the sheet when formulas are displayed because the formula display makes the columns wider.

7. **With your teacher's permission**, print the worksheet by clicking the Print button. Otherwise, click the Back button ⊖ .

8. Press ⌨CTRL + ⌨ to toggle off the formula display.

✓ The ⌨ is usually above the ⌨TAB key.

9. Save the **E10Try_xx** file, and leave it open to use in the next Try It.

Formulas displayed in worksheet

	A	B	C	D	E	F
94	KLAC	KLA-Tencor	32.25	1:29pm	5.482B	3.356
95	MGM	MGM Resorts International	12.42	1:29pm	5.481B	-37.953
96	CEA	China Eastern Air	48.25	1:12pm	5.441B	0
97	FLS	Flowserve Corp.	96.88	1:29pm	5.431B	25.771
98	LM	Legg Mason Inc.	33.09	1:29pm	5.411B	3.915
99	RDY	Dr. Reddy's Labor	31.6	1:28pm	5.335B	2.587
100	AIG	American International	39.49	1:29pm	5.334B	-9.384
101	ATI	Allegheny Technology	53.28	1:29pm	5.250B	2.216
102						
103						
104						
105	Averages		=AVERAGE(C4:C101)			=AVERAGE(F4:F101)
106						
107						

Printing Titles

■ Using the Sheet tab of the Page Setup dialog box, you can specify rows or columns with the **print titles** that need to appear on every page of a printout.

✓ Print titles do not affect or replace worksheet headers or footers.

■ You also can use the Print Titles button 🖨 in the Page Setup group of the PAGE LAYOUT tab on the Ribbon to add print titles.

✓ Click the dialog box launcher for the Page Setup group to open the Page Setup dialog box.

■ The row and column labels make it possible for you to identify the data on every page, which is useful when the sheet has many rows or many columns of information.

Try It!   **Printing Titles**

1. In the **E10Try_xx** file, add a header that has your name at the left, the date code in the center, and the page number code at the right, and change back to Normal view.

2. Click PAGE LAYOUT > Print Titles 🖾.

3. On the Sheet tab in the Page Setup dialog box, click in the Rows to repeat at top text box, click the Collapse Dialog box button, and then click the row 3 row header. The row address for row 3, which holds the labels for the columns of data, appears in the box.

4. Click OK.

5. Save the **E10Try_xx** file, and leave it open to use in the next Try It.

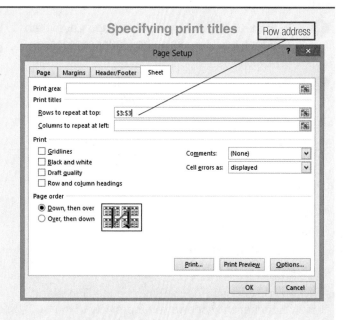

Specifying print titles

Changing Orientation

- You can change the **orientation** to help a worksheet fit better on paper.
- The default orientation is Portrait (tall or vertical).

- Changing to Landscape (wide or horizontal) orientation allows for more columns to fit on each page when a worksheet has many columns.
- Change orientation on the Page tab of the Page Setup dialog box, or use the Orientation button 🖾 choices in the Page Setup group of the PAGE LAYOUT tab.

Try It!   **Changing Orientation**

1. In the **E10Try_xx** file, click PAGE LAYOUT > Orientation 🖾 > Landscape.

2. Save the **E10Try_xx** file, and leave it open to use in the next Try It.

Scaling to Fit

- You can **scale** the data to print to a larger or smaller size to help it fill a page or print on fewer pages.
- Specify scaling in the Scaling section of the Page tab of the Page Setup dialog box.

- You can scale the printout to a percentage of normal size, or specify how many pages wide and tall it should be.

  ✓ *For many worksheets, changing to Landscape orientation and then scaling to 1 page wide prevents orphaned columns on a nearly blank page.*

- You also can use the choices in the Scale to Fit group on the Page Layout tab to specify the printout Width and Height in number of pages or a Scale percentage.

Try It!   *Scaling to Fit*

1 In the **E10Try_xx** file, click the Page Layout tab, and then click the dialog box launcher for the Scale to Fit group.

2 On the Page sheet, click the Fit to button, and then adjust the accompanying text box entries to set up the printout to be 1 page(s) wide by 2 tall.

3 Click the Print Preview button.

4 At the bottom of Backstage view, click the Next Page (right arrow) button to display the second page of the printout.

5 Save the **E10Try_xx** file, and leave it open to use in the next Try It.

Previewing and Printing a Worksheet

■ You may print the selected worksheet(s), an entire workbook, or a selected data range.

　✓ *You learn how to print an entire workbook and a selected range in Lesson 20.*

■ When you choose FILE > Print, the the Backstage view automatically shows you a preview of the printout. Review it carefully and adjust print settings there before printing.

■ Settings you can change appear in the middle column of the Backstage view. These include specifying how many copies to print, what printer to use, page orientation, page size, margins, and scaling.

Try It!   *Previewing and Printing a Worksheet*

1 In the **E10Try_xx** file, click FILE > Print.

2 In the Settings area, in the Orientation option, check that Portrait Orientation is selected.

3 Under Settings, click the Page Setup link.

4 In the Page Setup dialog box, click the Margins tab.

5 Click the Horizontally and Vertically check boxes under Center on page to select them, and then click OK.

6 Review the changes in the preview.

7 **With your teacher's permission,** print the worksheet by clicking the Print button. Otherwise, click the Back button ⊙ to return to your document.

8 Save and close the file, and exit Excel.

　✓ *Notice that when you save a file from the Backstage view, you exit the Backstage view.*

(continued)

Try It!   **Previewing and Printing a Worksheet** *(continued)*

Preparing and previewing before printing

Print

Copies: 1

Print

Printer

Snagit 11
Ready

Printer Properties

Choose print settings here

Settings

Print Active Sheets
Only print the active sheets

Pages: [ ] to [ ]

Collated
1,2,3 1,2,3 1,2,3

Portrait Orientation

Letter
8.5" x 11"

Normal Margins
Left: 0.7" Right: 0.7"

Fit Sheet on One Page
Shrink the printout so that it...

Page Setup

E10Try_xx - Excel

Lesson 10—Practice

In this project, you will review and print formulas, change the page orientation and scaling, and preview and print a worksheet using the skills you learned in this lesson.

DIRECTIONS

1. Start Excel, if necessary, and open the **E10Practice** file from the data files for this lesson.
2. Save the file as **E10Practice_xx** in the location where your teacher instructs you to store the files for this lesson.
3. Add a header that has your name at the left, the date code in the center, and the page number code at the right, and change back to **Normal** view.
4. Click **FORMULAS** > **Show Formulas** . The formulas instead of the formula results are now displayed on the worksheet.

5. Click **FILE** > **Print**.
6. Under Settings, click **Portrait Orientation** > **Landscape Orientation**.
7. Under Settings, click **No Scaling** > **Fit Sheet on One Page**.
8. **With your teacher's permission**, print the chart sheet. Submit the printout or the file for grading as required.
9. Save and close the file, and exit Excel.

Lesson 10—Apply

You are the Chief Financial Officer for Hyland Manufacturing. You are finalizing the company's balance sheet for fiscal year 2014. You want to review and print the formulas, and preview and print the finished worksheet.

DIRECTIONS

1. Start Excel, if necessary, and open the **E10Apply** file from the data files for this lesson.
2. Save the file as **E10Apply_xx** in the location where your teacher instructs you to store the files for this lesson.
3. Add a header that has your name at the left, the date code in the center, and the page number code at the right, and change back to **Normal** view.

4. Display formulas instead of formula results on the worksheet.
5. Change the print settings so that the sheet fits on one page.
6. **With your teacher's permission**, print the worksheet. Submit the printout or the file for grading as required.
7. Save and close the file, and exit Excel.

End-of-Chapter Activities

➤ Excel Chapter 1—Critical Thinking

Safety Consulting Services

You have recently started your own business providing safety consulting services to large businesses. You need to create a worksheet to help you track, report, and bill work for each client at two billing rates. You will create and format the sheet, and then enter example data to test how it works.

DIRECTIONS

1. Start Excel, if necessary, and create a new, blank file if necessary.
2. Save the file as ECT01_xx in the location where your teacher instructs you to store the files for this chapter.
3. Add a header that has your name at the left, the date code in the center, and the page number code at the right, and change back to **Normal** view.
4. Enter the following data:

A1	Timesheet
A3	Client Name
A5	Rate A
A6	Rate B
B5	50
B6	75
D5	Weekly Retainer
F5	1750
A8	Day
B8	Date
C8	Hours Rate A
D8	Hours Rate B
E8	Amount Rate A
F8	Amount Rate B
G8	Total
D17	Total
D18	Percentage of Retainer

5. Enter **Monday** in cell A9. Fill the days Monday through Sunday down through cell A15.
6. Enter **4/2/14** in cell B9. Fill the date entry down the column through **4/8/2014** in cell B15.
7. Insert a column to the left of **column C**.

8. Enter **Monday 4/2/2014** in cell **C9** of the new column C.
9. Enter **Tuesday 4/3/2014** in cell **C10**.
10. Use Flash Fill to fill the series in the range **C9:C15** with the day and date combined.
11. Delete **column C**.
12. Enter the formula **=C9*$B$5** in cell **E9**. Fill the formula down through cell **E15**.
13. Enter the formula **=D9*$B$6** in cell **F9**. Fill the formula down through cell **F15**.
14. In cell **G9**, enter a formula that adds the values in cells **E9** and **F9**. Fill the formula down through cell **G15**.
15. In cell **E17**, enter a formula with the SUM function that totals the values above. Fill the formula right through cell **G17**.
16. In cell **G18**, enter a formula that divides the overall total in cell **G17** by the weekly retainer amount in cell **F5**.
17. Apply the **Ion** theme to the file.
18. Apply the **Title** cell style to cell A1, and merge and center cells **A1:G1**.
19. Apply the **60%-Accent1** style to the label in cell **A3**, then copy the formatting to the other labels in the document (except for the dates).
20. Wrap and center align the range **A8:G8**. Adjust column widths as necessary to display all text.
21. Merge the range **D18:F18**.
22. In cells **B5**, **B6**, and **F5**, apply the **Currency** format with zero decimal places to the entries.
23. Apply the **Currency** format with two decimal places to all the other cells calculating dollar values.

24. Format cell **G18** as a **Percentage** with one
decimal place.

25. Enter the following sample data to test the sheet:

C9	2.25
D9	4.5
C10	2
D10	1.25

26. With your teacher's permission, print the
worksheet. Submit the printout or the file for
grading as required. Your worksheet should look
like the one in Illustration 1A.

27. Save and close the file, and exit Excel.

Illustration 1A

	A	B	C	D	E	F	G
1				Timesheet			
2							
3	Client Name						
4							
5	Rate A	$50		Weekly Retainer		$1,750	
6	Rate B	$75					
7							
8	Day	Date	Hours Rate A	Hours Rate B	Amount Rate A	Amount Rate B	Total
9	Monday	4/2/2014	2.25	4.50	$112.50	$337.50	$450.00
10	Tuesday	4/3/2014	2.00	1.25	$100.00	$93.75	$193.75
11	Wednesday	4/4/2014			$0.00	$0.00	$0.00
12	Thursday	4/5/2014			$0.00	$0.00	$0.00
13	Friday	4/6/2014			$0.00	$0.00	$0.00
14	Saturday	4/7/2014			$0.00	$0.00	$0.00
15	Sunday	4/8/2014			$0.00	$0.00	$0.00
16							
17				Total	$212.50	$431.25	$643.75
18				Percentage of Retainer			36.8%

➤ Excel Chapter 1—Portfolio Builder

Personal Budget

You want to save for a car and need to get a better handle on your income and expenses in order to do so. In this project, you finish a basic budget worksheet by adding formulas and by making sure items are arranged properly. You'll apply attractive formatting and adjust the print settings.

DIRECTIONS

1. Start Excel, if necessary, and open the **EPB01** file from the data files for this chapter.

2. Save the file as **EPB01_xx** in the location where your teacher instructs you to store the files for this chapter.

3. Add a header that has your name at the left, the date code in the center, and the page number code at the right, and change back to **Normal** view.

4. Insert a column to the left of **column C**.

5. Use Flash Fill to fill the range **C9:C12** with the combined text from columns A and B.

6. Copy the data from the range **C9:C12** and paste it to the range **A9:A12**.

7. Resize **column A**.

8. Delete **columns B** and **C**.

9. Enter the formula **=B5+B6** in cell **B7**. Fill the formula across through cell G7.

10. In cell **B13**, enter a formula that sums **B9:B12**. Fill the formula across through cell G13.

11. Insert a blank row above the *Expenses* row.

12. Review the items in the *Expenses* section. You realize that the Gifts row really belongs in the *Income* area.

13. Insert a new row 6, drag-and-drop row 13 to row 6, and then delete the blank row 13.

14. Click cell **B8**, and review its formula in comparison with the original formula you created in step 4. Because it totals specific cells, it does not include the Gifts data that you have moved to the *Income* section. Edit the formula to correct the calculation, and then copy or fill it across the row.

15. In cell **B15**, enter a formula that subtracts the expense subtotal from the income subtotal. Fill the formula across through cell G15.

16. Add a blank row above the *Surplus* row.

17. Apply a different theme to the workbook.

18. Format the labels as desired and apply the **Accounting** format with zero decimal places to the numeric data.

19. Hide row 2.

20. Display formulas.

21. Preview the sheet, scaling to fit the sheet on one page with the formulas displayed.

22. **With your teacher's permission**, print the worksheet. Submit the printouts or the file for grading as required.

23. Save and close the file, and exit Excel.

(Courtesy ChaKrit/Shutterstock)

Chapter 2

Working with Formulas and Functions

Lesson 11

Getting Started with Functions

➤ What You Will Learn

Using Functions (SUM, AVERAGE, MEDIAN, MIN, and MAX)
Inserting a Function
Using AutoCalculate
Inserting Subtotals

WORDS TO KNOW

Argument
The values and other inputs that a function uses to calculate the result. You specify the cell or range that holds the value(s) for each argument or input a particular value.

AutoCalculate
A feature that temporarily performs the following calculations on a range of cells without the user having to enter a formula: AVERAGE, COUNT, MIN, MAX, or SUM.

Formula AutoComplete
A feature that speeds up the manual entry of functions.

Function
A predefined formula that performs a specific calculation using the inputs you specify.

Function name
The name given to one of Excel's predefined formulas.

Nest
To use a function as an argument within another function.

Software Skills   Use an Excel function to help you write a formula to perform more advanced calculations in your worksheets. Excel's Insert Function feature provides a list of available functions and "fill-in-the-blanks" assistance to complete a formula. Excel's AutoCalculate feature allows you to quickly calculate the AVERAGE, COUNT, COUNTA, MAX, MIN, or SUM for a cell range without entering a formula. The Function Library group also enables you to select functions by category.

What You Can Do

Using Functions (SUM, AVERAGE, MEDIAN, MIN, and MAX)

■ Excel provides built-in formulas called **functions** to perform special calculations.

■ To create a formula with a function, enter these elements in the following order:
  - The equal sign (=).
  - The **function name**, in upper- or lowercase letters.
  - An open parenthesis to separate the arguments from the function name.
  - The **argument(s)** identifying the data required to perform the function.
  - A close parenthesis to end the argument.

■ For example, =SUM(A1:A40) adds the values in the cells specified by the argument, which in this case is a single range of cells A1 through A40.

■ Most functions allow multiple arguments, separated by commas. For example, =SUM(A1:A40,C1:C40) adds the values in the ranges A1:A40 and C1:C40.

■ A function may be inserted into a formula. For example, =B2/SUM(C3:C5) takes the value in cell B2 and divides it by the sum of the values in the range C3:C5.

■ When a function is used as an argument for other functions, it is **nested** within those functions.

- For example, =ROUND(SUM(B12:B23),2)) totals the values in the range, B12:B23, and then rounds that total to two decimal places.
- Following are commonly used functions:
  - =SUM( ) adds the values in a range of cells.
  - =AVERAGE( ) returns the arithmetic mean of the values in a range of cells.
  - =COUNT( ) counts the cells containing numbers in a range of cells (blank cells or text entries are ignored).
  - =COUNTA( ) counts the number of non-blank cells.
  - =MAX( ) finds the highest value in a range of cells.
  - =MIN( ) finds the lowest value in a range of cells.
  - =ROUND( ) adjusts a value to a specific number of digits.

  ✓ When a cell is formatted to a specified number of decimal places, only the display of that value is affected. The actual value in the cell is still used in all calculations. For example, if a cell contains the value 13.45687, and you decide to display only the last two decimal places, then the value 13.46 will display in the cell, but the value, 13.45687, will be used in all calculations.

- If you are familiar with a formula and its required arguments, you can type it into the cell where you want the result to display. The formula name must be typed correctly.
- After you type =, the function name, and the opening parenthesis, a ScreenTip shows you what argument(s) to enter for the function.
- When you type = and then type the beginning of a function name, the **Formula AutoComplete** feature displays a list of possible matching function names. Use the ⬇ key to select the desired function, and then press TAB to enter it in the formula.

  ✓ You also can use Formula AutoComplete to enter other listed items such as a range name.

- Use the drop-down arrow on the AutoSum button Σ in the Editing Group on the HOME tab to quickly insert a SUM, AVERAGE, COUNT, MAX, or MIN function. The AutoSum button Σ is also located in the Function Library group on the FORMULAS tab.

Try It!   **Using Functions (SUM, AVERAGE, MEDIAN, MIN, and MAX)**

1 Start Excel.

2 Open the **E11TryA** file from the data files for this lesson.

3 Add a header that has your name at the left, the date code in the center, and the page number code at the right, and change back to Normal view.

4 Click cell B10 to select it.

5 Type **=sum(**, and then drag over the range **B5:B9** to select it.

6 Press ENTER . Excel adds the closing parenthesis for you and displays the formula result in the cell.

7 Press ⬇ once to select cell B12.

8 Type **=av**. Press ⬇ once to select AVERAGE.

9 Press TAB, type **B5:B9** to specify that range as the argument, and press ENTER to finish the formula and select cell B13.

10 On the HOME tab, in the Editing group, click the AutoSum drop-down arrow Σ AutoSum ▾ , and then click Max. Type or select the range **B5:B9**, and press ENTER to complete the formula and select cell B14.

11 On the FORMULAS tab, in the Function Library group, click the AutoSum drop-down arrow Σ AutoSum ▾ , and then click Min. Type or select the range **B5:B9**, and press ENTER to complete the formula and select cell B15.

12 Save the **E11TryA_xx** file, and leave it open to use in the next Try It.

(continued)

Try It!   **Using Functions (SUM, AVERAGE, MEDIAN, MIN, and MAX)** *(continued)*

Typing a Function

| SUM | ▼ | : | ✕ | ✓ | *fx* | =sum(B5:B9 |

◢	A	B	C	D	E
1		eGame Mania			
2		First Quarter Store Sales Analysis			
3					
4	Store	Jan	Feb	Mar	Qtr 1
5	Cedar Creek #212	$ 23,548	$ 27,943	$ 25,418	$ 76,909
6	Glen Lake #278	$ 22,987	$ 25,673	$ 24,998	$ 73,658
7	Offingham #114	$ 23,872	$ 23,772	$ 24,118	$ 71,762
8	Maplehurst #234	$ 22,744	$ 24,565	$ 23,748	$ 71,057
9	Twin Oaks #137	$ 22,958	$ 25,848	$ 23,998	$ 72,804
10	Totals	=sum(B5:B9			

Drag to select range for argument

Type in function name

Selecting a function with Formula AutoComplete

12	Average	=av			
13	Maximum		*fx* AVEDEV		
14	Minimum		*fx* AVERAGE	Returns the average (arithmetic mean) of its arguments, which can be numbers or names, arrays, or references that contain numbers
15	Median		*fx* AVERAGEA		
16			*fx* AVERAGEIF		
17			*fx* AVERAGEIFS		

Inserting a Function

- If you know what category a function falls in, you can insert it by clicking the FORMULAS tab, clicking the category name in the Function Library group, and then clicking the function.

- Clicking More Functions displays a menu with additional categories. Click the desired category, and then the desired function.

- If you need to search for a function, click the Insert Function button *fx* on the formula bar. You also can click the Insert Function button *fx* in the Function Library group of the FORMULAS tab. Either method opens the Insert Function dialog box.

- In the Insert Function dialog box, you can type a brief description of the function you want to use to display a list of corresponding functions. For example, you could type the description "add numbers" to find a function you could use to add a column of numbers.

- You can also display functions by typing the name of the function (if you know it), or by choosing a category from the Or select a category list.

- When you enter a formula using Insert Function, Excel automatically enters the equal sign (=) in the formula.

- After you select a function and click OK in the Insert Function dialog box, the Function Arguments dialog box appears to prompt you to enter the arguments needed for the function.

- In the Function Arguments dialog box, you can select cells instead of typing them by using the Collapse Dialog button 🔲 located at the right of each text box.

  ✓ *You also can type another function as an argument for the current function.*

- Required argument names appear in bold.

- As you enter the arguments, the value of that argument is displayed to the right of the text box.

- Excel calculates the current result and displays it at the bottom of the dialog box.

  ✓ *If you need help understanding a particular function's arguments, click the Help on this function link, located in the lower left-hand corner of the dialog box.*

| **Try It!** | **Inserting a Function** |

① With cell B15 still selected in the **E11TryA_xx** file, on the FORMULAS tab, click More Functions ▦ > Statistical, and then scroll down and click MEDIAN.

② In the Number1 text box of the Function Arguments dialog box, type **B5:B9** to replace the suggested entry, and click OK.

③ Click cell C10 to select it.

④ Click the Insert Function button *fx* on the formula bar.

⑤ Click the Or select a category list drop-down arrow, and click Math & Trig.

⑥ Scroll down the Select a function list, click SUM, and then click OK.

⑦ In the Function Arguments dialog box, make sure that C5:C9 appears in the Number1 text box, and then click OK.

⑧ Use the fill handle to copy the formula from cell C10 to D10:E10.

⑨ Select the range B12:B15, and use the fill handle to copy the formulas from those cells to C12:E15 to the right.

⑩ Adjust the column widths if needed.

⑪ Save the **E11TryA_xx** file, and close it.

The Insert Function dialog box

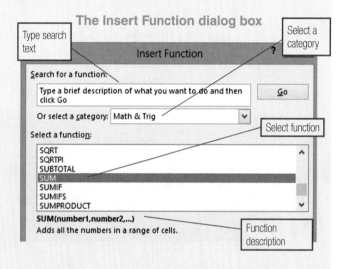

Using AutoCalculate

■ To quickly calculate the AVERAGE, COUNT, COUNTA, MAX, MIN, or SUM for a cell range without entering a formula, use **AutoCalculate**.

■ Select the range, and the Average, Count (COUNTA), and Sum results appear on the Status bar.

■ To control which function results appear on the Status bar, right-click the Status bar and click one of the six functions that appear.

| **Try It!** | **Using AutoCalculate** |

① In the **E11TryA_xx** file, drag over the range E5:E9 to select it.

② Observe the Status bar. The Average calculated by AutoComplete should match the result in cell E12. The Sum calculated by AutoComplete should match the result in cell E10.

③ With the range E5:E9 still selected, right-click the Status bar, click Maximum, and press [ESC].

④ Observe the Status bar. It now includes a Max value that should match the result shown in cell E13.

⑤ Right-click the Status bar, click Maximum, and press [ESC].

⑥ Click cell A1 to select it.

⑦ Save the **E11TryA_xx** file, and close it.

(continued)

Try It!   **Using AutoCalculate** *(continued)*

Working with AutoCalculate

Select calculations to show

Customize Status Bar	
✓ Cell Mode	Ready
✓ Flash Fill Blank Cells	
✓ Flash Fill Changed Cells	
✓ Signatures	Off
✓ Information Management Policy	Off
✓ Permissions	Off
Caps Lock	Off
Num Lock	On
✓ Scroll Lock	Off
✓ Fixed Decimal	Off
Overtype Mode	
✓ End Mode	
Macro Recording	Not Recording
✓ Selection Mode	
✓ Page Number	
✓ Average	$73,238
✓ Count	5
Numerical Count	
Minimum	
Maximum	$76,909
✓ Sum	$366,190
✓ Upload Status	
✓ View Shortcuts	
✓ Zoom Slider	
✓ Zoom	100%

AutoCalculate results on status bar

AVERAGE: $73,238   COUNT: 5   SUM: $366,190   100%

Inserting Subtotals

- With the Subtotal feature, you can quickly insert subtotals between similar rows in an Excel list without having to create custom functions.

  ✓ *You cannot use the Subtotal feature with an Excel table. You will learn more about Excel tables in the Lesson 12.*

- Instead of entering formulas or using functions to total a field for particular rows, you can use the Subtotal feature. For example, you can subtotal a sales list to compute the amount sold by each salesperson on a given day.

- The Subtotal feature does the following:
  - Calculates subtotals for all rows that contain the same entry in one column. For example, if you select the field Salesperson, Excel will create subtotals for each salesperson.
  - Inserts the totals in a row just below that group of data.
  - Calculates a grand total.
  - Inserts a label for each group totaled/subtotaled.
  - Displays the outline controls.

    ✓ *The outline controls allow you to control the level of detail displayed.*

- For the Subtotal feature to work, all records containing values that contribute to that subtotal (or other calculation) must be sorted together.

  ✓ *You will learn about sorting data in Lesson 31.*

- Excel inserts a subtotal line whenever it detects a change in the value of the chosen field—for instance, a change from each sales office name.

- Also, if the subtotal line is to show the average pledge amount for all callers to the Sacramento office, then each pledge must contain "Sacramento" in one column—preferably one with a meaningful field name, such as "Office."

- When you click the Subtotal button on the DATA tab, a dialog box displays from which you can make several choices:

  - *At each change in*—Select the field name by which you want to total.

  - *Use function*—Select a function.

  - *Add subtotal to*—Select one or more fields to use with the database function you selected.

  - *Replace current subtotals*—Select this option to create a new subtotal within a database, removing any current subtotals. Deselect this option to retain current subtotals.

- *Page break between groups*—Places each subtotaled group on its own page.

- *Summary below data*—Inserts the subtotals/ grand total below each group, rather than above it.

- *Remove All*—Removes all subtotals.

- Subtotals act just like any other formula or function; if you change the data, the total will recalculate automatically.

- The Subtotal feature displays the outline controls around the worksheet frame. With the outline controls, you can hide or display the records within any given group.

  ✓ *You will learn more about working with outlines in Lesson 34.*

Try It! **Creating Subtotals**

① Open the **E11TryB** file from the data files for this lesson.

② Save the workbook as **E11TryB_xx** in the location where your teacher instructs you to store the files for this lesson.

③ Add a header that has your name at the left, the date code in the center, and the page number code at the right, and change back to Normal.

④ Select the range A5:G29 and click DATA > Subtotal 🖽.

⑤ In the At each change in drop-down list, select Item Type, if necessary.

  ✓ *A new subtotal will be calculated at each change within the column you choose here.*

⑥ In the Use function box, select Sum.

⑦ In the Add Subtotal to box, select Items Sold and Value Sold. Unselect PriceperCase, if necessary.

⑧ Select Replace current subtotals, and Summary below data, if necessary.

⑨ Click OK. Notice that the item types are now subtotaled.

⑩ Save the **E11TryB_xx** file, and close it.

The Subtotal dialog box

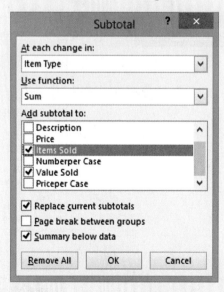

Lesson 11—Practice

In this project, you will insert functions into formulas and create subtotals using the skills you learned in this lesson.

DIRECTIONS

1. Start Excel, if necessary, and open the **E11Practice** file from the data files for this lesson.

2. Save the workbook as **E11Practice_xx** in the location where your teacher instructs you to store the files for this lesson.

3. Add a header that has your name at the left, the date code in the center, and the page number code at the right, and change back to **Normal** view.

4. In cell **E4**, enter the formula **=sum(B4,C4)**, and press TAB.

5. In cell **F4**, enter the formula **=sum(B4,D4)**, and press CTRL + ENTER.

6. Drag over the range **E4:F4** to select it, and then double-click the fill handle to copy the formulas down through row 14.

7. Click cell **B16** to select it.

8. Type **=B11**, and press CTRL + ENTER.

9. Drag the fill handle right through cell **F16** to fill the formula across.

10. Select the range **A3:G14** and click **DATA > Subtotal**.

11. In the **At each change in** drop-down list, select **Lot**.

12. In the **Use function** box, select **Count**.

13. Select **Replace current subtotals** and **Summary below**, if necessary.

14. Click **OK**.

15. Press CTRL + HOME. Your worksheet should look like the one shown in Figure 11-1.

16. **With your teacher's permission**, print the worksheet. Submit the printout or the file for grading as required.

17. Save and close the file, and exit Excel.

Figure 11-1

	A	B	C	D	E	F	G
1		Bid Results - Canal Street Home Restoration Project					
2							
3			Unit Bid	Option Pkg. #1	Option Pkg. #2	Base Bid + #1	Base Bid + #2	Lot
4	BJW, Ltd.	$ 97,854	$ 6,981	$ 9,726	$ 104,835	$ 107,580	Lot A
5	Craftsman, Inc.	$ 89,475	$ 7,051	$ 8,974	$ 96,526	$ 98,449	Lot A
6	Meguro Construction	$ 92,441	$ 6,200	$ 9,795	$ 98,641	$ 102,236	Lot A
7	Mendoza Inc.	$ 88,459	$ 7,500	$ 8,945	$ 95,959	$ 97,404	Lot A
8						Lot A Count	4
9	New Mark Designs	$ 99,487	$ 5,985	$ 9,760	$ 105,472	$ 109,247	Lot B
10	Ravuru Renovations	$ 92,335	$ 6,193	$ 8,554	$ 98,528	$ 100,889	Lot B
11	Renovation Ventures	$ 91,415	$ 6,300	$ 10,000	$ 97,715	$ 101,415	Lot B
12	Restoration Architecture	$ 89,445	$ 6,115	$ 9,784	$ 95,560	$ 99,229	Lot B
13						Lot B Count	4
14	TOH Construction	$ 91,225	$ 6,451	$ 10,800	$ 97,676	$ 102,025	Lot C
15	Williams Brothers Renovators, Ltd.	$ 96,485	$ 5,531	$ 9,875	$ 102,016	$ 106,360	Lot C
16	Woo Home Designs	$ 93,415	$ 6,751	$ 10,633	$ 100,166	$ 104,048	Lot C
17						Lot C Count	3
18						Grand Count	11
19	Analysis						
20	Restoration Architecture	$ 89,445	$ 6,115	$ 9,784	$ 95,560	$ 99,229	
21	Average of All Bids						
22	Difference (+/-)						
23	Lowest Bid						
24	Difference (+/-)						
25	Highest Bid						
26	Difference (+/-)						
27							
28	Median						

Lesson 11—Apply

You're the owner of Restoration Architecture, a large design and construction firm specializing in the remodeling, redesign, and restoration of existing properties. You submitted a bid to restore several homes purchased by a neighborhood revitalization organization. The group solicited bids from a number of firms. You want to analyze the bidding results to evaluate how competitive your bid was.

DIRECTIONS

1. Start Excel, if necessary, and open the **E11Apply** file from the data files for this lesson.

2. Save the workbook as **E11Apply_xx** in the location where your teacher instructs you to store the files for this lesson.

3. Add a header that has your name at the left, the date code in the center, and the page number code at the right, and change back to **Normal** view.

4. Click cell **B20**, type **=av**, click **AVERAGE** in the Formula AutoComplete list, and press TAB. Drag over the range **B6:B16** to enter it in the formula, and finish the formula.

5. Use the fill handle to fill the formula across the row.

6. In cell **B21**, enter a formula that subtracts the value in cell **B20** from the value in cell **B19**. Fill the formula across the row.

7. Use the **AutoSum** button **Σ** to enter a formula in cell **B22** that finds the lowest (MIN) value in the range **B6:B16**. Fill the formula across the row.

8. In cell **B23**, enter a formula that subtracts the value in cell **B22** from the value in cell **B19**. Fill the formula across the row.

9. Use the **More Functions** button **▦ Statistical** submenu to enter a formula in cell **B24** that finds the highest (MAX) value in the range **B6:B16**. Fill the formula across the row.

10. In cell **B25**, enter a formula that subtracts the value in cell **B24** from the value in cell **B19**. Fill the formula across the row.

11. Use the **Insert Function** button **ƒx** on the formula bar to enter a formula in cell **B27** that finds the median value in the range **B6:B16**. Fill the formula across the row.

12. Select the range **F6:F16**. Observe the AutoCalculate results in the status bar.

13. Select the range **A5:G16** and click **DATA > Subtotal** ▦.

14. In the **At each change in** drop-down list, select **Lot**.

15. In the **Use function** box, select **Count**.

16. Select **Replace current subtotals** and **Summary below**, if necessary.

17. Click **OK**. Adjust column widths as necessary to display all data. Your worksheet should look like the one shown in Figure 11-2 on the next page.

18. **With your teacher's permission**, print the worksheet. Submit the printout or the file for grading as required.

19. Save and close the file, and exit Excel.

Figure 11-2

	A	B	C	D	E	F	G	H
1	Bid Results - Canal Street Home Restoration Project							
2								
3	No. of homes to be restored:	11						
4								
5		Unit Bid	Option Pkg. #1	Option Pkg. #2	Base Bid + #1	Base Bid + #2	Lot	
6	BJW, Ltd.	$ 97,854	$ 6,981	$ 9,726	$ 104,835	$ 107,580	Lot A	
7	Craftsman, Inc.	$ 89,475	$ 7,051	$ 8,974	$ 96,526	$ 98,449	Lot A	
8	Meguro Construction	$ 92,441	$ 6,200	$ 9,795	$ 98,641	$ 102,236	Lot A	
9	Mendoza Inc.	$ 88,459	$ 7,500	$ 8,945	$ 95,959	$ 97,404	Lot A	
10						Lot A Count	4	
11	New Mark Designs	$ 99,487	$ 5,985	$ 9,760	$ 105,472	$ 109,247	Lot B	
12	Ravuru Renovations	$ 92,335	$ 6,193	$ 8,554	$ 98,528	$ 100,889	Lot B	
13	Renovation Ventures	$ 91,415	$ 6,300	$ 10,000	$ 97,715	$ 101,415	Lot B	
14	Restoration Architecture	$ 89,445	$ 6,115	$ 9,784	$ 95,560	$ 99,229	Lot B	
15						Lot B Count	4	
16	TOH Construction	$ 91,225	$ 6,451	$ 10,800	$ 97,676	$ 102,025	Lot C	
17	Williams Brothers Renovators, Ltd.	$ 96,485	$ 5,531	$ 9,875	$ 102,016	$ 106,360	Lot C	
18	Woo Home Designs	$ 93,415	$ 6,751	$ 10,633	$ 100,166	$ 104,048	Lot C	
19						Lot C Count	3	
20						Grand Count	11	
21								
22	Analysis							
23	Restoration Architecture	$ 89,445	$ 6,115	$ 9,784	$ 95,560	$ 99,229		
24	Average of All Bids	$ 92,912	$ 6,460	$ 9,713	$ 99,372	$ 102,626		
25	Difference (+/-)	$ (3,467)	$ (345)	$ 71	$ (3,812)	$ (3,397)		
26	Lowest Bid	$ 88,459	$ 5,531	$ 8,554	$ 95,560	$ 97,404		
27	Difference (+/-)	$ 986	$ 584	$ 1,230	$ -	$ 1,825		
28	Highest Bid	$ 99,487	$ 7,500	$ 10,800	$ 105,472	$ 109,247		
29	Difference (+/-)	$(10,042)	$ (1,385)	$ (1,016)	$ (9,912)	$ (10,018)		
30								
31	Median	$ 92,335	$ 6,300	$ 9,784	$ 98,528	$ 102,025		
32								

Lesson 12

Using Excel Tables

➤ What You Will Learn

Creating an Excel Table
Formatting an Excel Table
Sorting and Filtering an Excel Table
Converting a Table to a Range

Software Skills   Formatting a range as an Excel table enables you to apply formatting and create calculations more easily. You also can sort and filter the data in the table to organize it for analysis. You'll learn how to create and format a table, perform calculations, and sort and filter in this lesson, as well as how to convert a table back to a regular range of cells.

What You Can Do

Creating an Excel Table

- An **Excel table** is a range of data with special features that enable you to reference a column of data in a formula more naturally and build formulas more easily.
- You can perform other functions with the special column headers in an Excel table such as sorting and filtering data.
- Excel tables are best for data that's organized primarily by columns, because some automatic totals and other functions can be inserted by column, and not by row.
- You create a table by clicking in a range of data that includes headings for every column, and then using the Table button 🏛 in the Tables group of the INSERT tab.
- You select an overall table format and other formatting settings on the TABLE TOOLS DESIGN tab.
- Excel automatically names the table, although you can change the table name.
- You can reference the table name and table column headers in formulas. References to the table and columns are called **structured references**.
- Adding a formula in a cell in the column to the right of the table automatically creates a calculated column that becomes part of the table.
- Structured references make the formulas easy to understand and also adjust automatically when you add data to the table.

WORDS TO KNOW

Banded rows or columns
The shading of alternating rows or columns to make a table easier to read.

Column specifier
The structured reference to a table column, which consists of the table column header name in square brackets.

Criterion
A value, some text, or an expression that defines the type of content you want to see.

Excel table
Data arranged in columns and specially formatted with column headers that contain commands that allow you to sort, filter, and perform other functions on the table.

Filter
Hide nonmatching rows in a table or list of data according to the criterion or criteria you specify.

Sort
Arrange the rows in a table or list of data in a new order according to the entries in one or more columns.

Structured references
Using the table name or a table column header in a formula to refer to data in the entire table or specified column.

Table style
A combination of cell color, border, shading, and other formatting attributes applied to a table.

Total row
A row you can display below a table to calculate data in the columns above using a function you choose.

- For example, =SUM(SalesDept[Jan]) totals the range of cells in the Jan column in the SalesDept table.
- The structured reference to a table column header is called a **column specifier**.
- To enter formulas that reference table data, use Formula AutoComplete so it can supply you with valid table names, column specifiers, and other structured references.
- In a formula, you enclose column specifiers and structured references in square brackets, and precede them with the table name, as in =AVERAGE(Sales[June])
- Excel provides several structured references you can use to refer to specific areas in a table.
  - [#ALL]—refers to the entire table range, including column headers, table data, and the totals row (if any).
  - [#DATA]—refers to the table data range.
  - [#HEADERS]—refers to the cells in the header row.
  - [#TOTALS]—refers to the cells in the total row.
  - [#THISROW]—refers to table cells located in the same row as the formula. This might include non-data cells.
- For example, =SUM(SalesDept[[#TOTALS], [April]:[June]]) totals the values in the Totals cells in columns April through June.
- You can display the **total row** below the table data range and set it up to perform calculations using the functions you specify.

 Creating an Excel Table

❶ Start Excel.

❷ Open the **E12Try** file from the data files for this lesson.

❸ Save the workbook as **E12Try_xx** in the location where your teacher instructs you to store the files for this lesson.

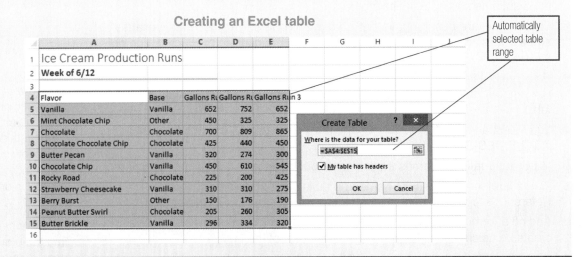

Creating an Excel table

(continued)

Try It! | **Creating an Excel Table** *(continued)*

4 Add a header that has your name at the left, the date code in the center, and the page number code at the right, and change back to Normal view.

5 Click cell B7 to select it.

6 Click the INSERT tab > Table ▦. The Create Table dialog box appears, suggesting the correct range as the data range for the table.

    ✓ *Because the selected cell is in a range of data that has column header labels, Excel can identify the proper range for the table. Otherwise, you can drag to select the desired range.*

7 Click OK. Excel automatically creates the table, applies a table style, and displays the TABLE TOOLS DESIGN tab.

8 On the TABLE TOOLS DESIGN tab, in the Table Styles group, click the More button ▾ and then click Table Style Medium 7 under Medium in the gallery.

9 Click cell F5 to select it.

10 Type =[Gallons Run 1]+[Gallons Run 2] +[Gallons Run 3] and press ᴇɴᴛᴇʀ . Excel automatically adds a new column to the table and copies the formula with structured references in the whole column.

    ✓ *This formula's structured references are the column headers, or column labels for the table. Notice that you didn't need to type in the table name in this instance.*

11 Press ᴄᴛʀʟ + ᴢ three times to undo the new column.

12 With cell F5 still selected, on the HOME tab, click AutoSum Σ, and press ᴇɴᴛᴇʀ . This method also creates a formula with structured references and adds a new column to the table.

13 Change the entry in cell F4 to Gallons Total.

14 Click TABLE TOOLS DESIGN > Total Row. The total row appears below the table data. Note that by default, Total is entered in cell A16, and a sum formula in cell F16.

    ✓ *Note that the function used to create the sum is actually a SUBTOTAL function.*

15 Change the entry in cell A16 to **Averages**.

Calculating with structured references

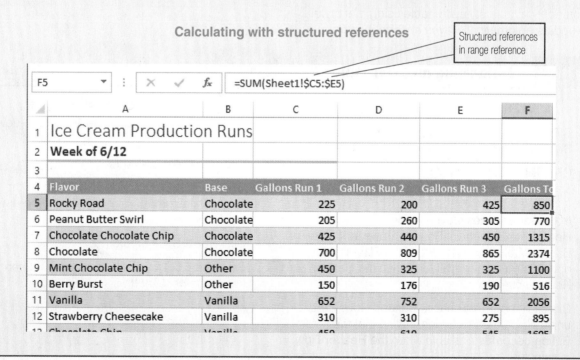

	A	B	C	D	E	F
1	Ice Cream Production Runs					
2	Week of 6/12					
3						
4	Flavor	Base	Gallons Run 1	Gallons Run 2	Gallons Run 3	Gallons To
5	Rocky Road	Chocolate	225	200	425	850
6	Peanut Butter Swirl	Chocolate	205	260	305	770
7	Chocolate Chocolate Chip	Chocolate	425	440	450	1315
8	Chocolate	Chocolate	700	809	865	2374
9	Mint Chocolate Chip	Other	450	325	325	1100
10	Berry Burst	Other	150	176	190	516
11	Vanilla	Vanilla	652	752	652	2056
12	Strawberry Cheesecake	Vanilla	310	310	275	895
13	Chocolate Chip	Vanilla	450	610	545	1605

F5 · ✕ ✓ *fx* =SUM(Sheet1!$C5:$E5)

Structured references in range reference

(continued)

Try It!   **Creating an Excel Table** *(continued)*

⑯ Click cell F16, click the down arrow button, and then click None to remove the sum.

⑰ Click cell C16, click the down arrow button, and click Average.

⑱ Add Average calculations for cells D16 and E16.

⑲ Drag over the range C16:E16 to select it.

⑳ On the HOME tab, click the dialog box launcher for the Number group.

㉑ In the Format Cells dialog box, on the Number tab, in the Category list, click Number. Reduce the Decimal places entry to 0, and then click OK.

㉒ Save the **E12Try_xx** file, and leave it open to use in the next Try It.

Formatting an Excel Table

■ **Table styles** include various formatting elements you can apply to column headings or totals and title and heading styles.

■ To select a table style, click the More drop-down button ⊽ in the Table Styles group on the TABLE TOOLS DESIGN tab.

■ You also can select a table style from the Format as Table ⊞ drop-down gallery in the Styles group on the HOME tab.

■ As you move the mouse over the table styles shown in the gallery, the worksheet automatically shows a Live Preview of the new style.

■ If you apply a table style, the table using that style will update automatically if you change themes.

■ You can control the appearance of rows and columns by using the Table Style Options on the TABLE TOOLS DESIGN tab.

■ Table Style Options include bolding the first and last column, including a header and total row, **banded rows and columns**, or including a filter button to sort and display data.

■ Checking a selection in the Table Style Options will include the table formatting element and unchecking a selection will remove it.

■ You can remove the entire table style by clicking the Clear button ⊞ from the More styles gallery in the Table Styles group on the TABLE TOOLS DESIGN tab.

Try It!   **Formatting an Excel Table**

❶ In the **E12Try_xx** file, click cell A5 to select it.

❷ Click the Format as Table button ⊞ in the Styles group on the HOME tab.

❸ Click Table Style Light 7.

❹ Click the TABLE TOOLS DESIGN tab.

❺ In the Table Styles Options group, uncheck Header Row, uncheck Banded Rows, and check Banded Columns. Notice that the Filter Button option is no longer available when the Header Row is unselected.

❻ Check Header Row, check Banded Rows, and uncheck Banded Columns. Notice that the Filter Button becomes available when the Header Row is selected.

❼ On the TABLE TOOLS DESIGN tab, in the Table Styles group, click the More drop-down button ⊽.

❽ Click the Clear button ⊞.

❾ On the TABLE TOOLS DESIGN tab, in the Table Styles group, click the More drop-down button ⊽.

❿ Click Table Style Medium 7.

⓫ Save the **E12Try_xx** file, and leave it open to use in the next Try It.

Sorting and Filtering an Excel Table

- Each column header in an Excel table has a down arrow button. Clicking the button displays a menu with choices for changing the display of the table rows.

- Using a column header menu, you can **sort** the table, or change the order of the rows according to the entries in the column header by which you're sorting.

- You can sort in ascending order: A to Z, lowest to highest, or least recent to most recent.

- You also can sort in descending order: Z to A, highest to lowest, or most recent to least recent.

- Clearing a sort does not undo the sort. So, either use Undo to remove a sort immediately or add a column that numbers the rows so that you can return the rows to their original order.

- To sort by multiple columns, use the Sort button in the Sort & Filter group on the DATA tab. In the Sort dialog box, specify the top level sort in the first Sort by row, then to sort within those results, use the Add Level button to sort by another field within those results.

- To limit the list to display only rows that have a particular entry (**criterion**) in one of the columns, **filter** the list.

- For example, you can filter a list of sales transactions to show transactions for only one client or salesperson.

- Choose (Select All) or Clear Filter from *"Column"* in the column header menu to remove the filter.

Try It!   Sorting and Filtering an Excel Table

1. In the **E12Try_xx** file, click the down arrow button for the Base column header.

2. In the menu, click Sort A to Z. Notice that the rows change order and are listed according to the entry in the Base column.

   ✓ *Look at the entries in the Flavor column. They are not sorted. For example, the rows with the Vanilla base appear in this order according to Flavor: Vanilla, Butter Pecan, Chocolate Chip, Strawberry Cheesecake, and Butter Brickle.*

3. Select the range B5:B15.

4. Click DATA > Sort.

5. In the Sort dialog box, click the Add Level button. In the Then by drop-down list that appears, choose Flavor. Open the Order drop-down list for that row, and click Z to A.

6. Click OK.

   ✓ *The rows reorder so that the Flavor column entries now appear in descending order within each Base grouping. The rows with the Vanilla base now appear in this order according to Flavor: Vanilla, Strawberry Cheesecake, Chocolate Chip, Butter Pecan, and Butter Brickle.*

7. Click the down arrow button for the Base column header.

8. In the menu, click the check box beside (Select All) to uncheck it. Then, click the check box beside Chocolate to check it and click OK.

   ✓ *The table changes to show results based on the filtered data only.*

9. Click the down arrow button for the Base column header.

10. In the menu, click Clear Filter From "Base".

11. On the DATA tab, click Sort.

12. Click the Delete Level button twice, and then click OK.

13. Save the **E12Try_xx** file, and leave it open to use in the next Try It.

(continued)

Try It!   **Sorting and Filtering an Excel Table** *(continued)*

Use a column header menu to sort or filter the table

◢	A	B	C	D	E	F
1	Ice Cream Production Runs					
2	Week of 6/12					
3						
4	Flavor ▼	Base ▼	Gallons Run 1 ▼	Gallons Run 2 ▼	Gallons Run 3 ▼	Gallons ▼
5	A↓ Sort A to Z		652	752	652	2056
6	Z↓ Sort Z to A		450	325	325	1100
7	Sort by Color ▶		700	809	865	2374
8			425	440	450	1315
9	▼ Clear Filter From "Base"		320	274	300	894
10	Filter by Color ▶		450	610	545	1605
11	Text Filters ▶		225	200	425	850
12			310	310	275	895
13	Search ⌕		150	176	190	516
14	☑ (Select All)		205	260	305	770
15	☑ Chocolate		296	334	320	950
16	☑ Other		380	408	423	
17	☑ Vanilla					

Sort choices

Filter choices

Converting a Table to a Range

- Converting a table to a range removes the special table functionality.

- The converted range retains any formatting you applied.

- Use the Convert to Range button 🖳 in the Tools group of the TABLE TOOLS DESIGN tab to convert the table, or right-click the table, point to Table, and click Convert to Range in the submenu.

Try It!   **Converting a Table to a Range**

1 In the **E12Try_xx** file, click any cell in the table.

2 Click TABLE TOOLS DESIGN > Convert to Range 🖳.

3 In the dialog box that appears to ask you to confirm the conversion, click Yes.

4 Click cell F6 to select it. Notice that the structured references have been converted to regular references.

5 Click cell C16 to select it. Notice that the formula is a subtotal formula.

6 Save the **E12Try_xx** file, and close it.

Lesson 12—Practice

In this project, you will create a table, perform calculations, sort and filter the table, and convert the table to a range using the skills you learned in this lesson.

DIRECTIONS

1. Start Excel, if necessary, and open the **E12Practice** file from the data files for this lesson.

2. Save the workbook as **E12Practice_xx** in the location where your teacher instructs you to store the files for this lesson.

3. Add a header that has your name at the left, the date code in the center, and the page number code at the right, and change back to **Normal** view.

4. In cell **G5**, enter the formula **=sum(D5:F5)**, and press CTRL + ENTER .

5. Double-click the fill handle to fill the formula down the column.

6. Click cell **C8** to select it.

7. Click the **INSERT** > **Table** 🏢 .

8. In the Create Table dialog box, click **OK**.

9. On the **TABLE TOOLS DESIGN** tab, in the Table Styles group, click the **More** button 🔽, and click **Table Style Medium 23** under Medium.

10. Click the down arrow button for the Type column header.

11. In the menu, click **Sort A to Z**.

12. Right-click anywhere in the table > **Table** > **Convert to Range** > **Yes** to confirm that you want to convert the table to a normal range.

13. Use **Undo** to undo the conversion of the table to a normal range.

14. Change the label in cell **A4** to **Project**. Your worksheet should look like the one in Figure 12-1.

15. **With your teacher's permission,** print page one of the worksheet. Submit the printout or the file for grading as required.

16. Save and close the file, and exit Excel.

Figure 12-1

	A	B	C	D	E	F	G	H
1	Restoration Architecture							
2	3rd Qtr Revenues by Project							
3								
4	Project ▾	Type ▾	Project Manager ▾	July ▾	August ▾	September ▾	Qtr 3 Totals ▾	
5	18 South Pendleton Ave.	Commercial	Jansen	$ 7,855	$ 27,958	$ 31,225	$ 67,038	
6	Old Barn Quilts	Commercial	Nolo	$ 4,522	$ 12,889	$ 18,645	$ 36,056	
7	Faster Library	Public	Nolo	$ 41,325	$ 78,945	$ 85,664	$ 205,934	
8	Cramer Theater	Public	Timson	$ 125,995	$ 285,941	$ 275,884	$ 687,820	
9	Freemont Park Amphitheater	Public	Jansen	$ 72,145	$ 63,145	$ 21,778	$ 157,068	
10	Rossen House	Residential	Jansen	$ 328,118	$ 456,221	$ 298,485	$ 1,082,824	
11	512 N. Oak Street	Residential	Nolo	$ 32,995	$ 28,445	$ 18,445	$ 79,885	
12								

Lesson 12—Apply

You are the Chief Financial Officer (CFO) of Restoration Architecture, and it's time for the quarterly revenue recap. You want to organize the information in a table so that you can add formulas and sort and filter to make the information easier to follow.

DIRECTIONS

1. Start Excel, if necessary, and open the **E12Apply** file from the data files for this lesson.

2. Save the workbook as **E12Apply_xx** in the location where your teacher instructs you to store the files for this lesson.

3. Add a header that has your name at the left, the date code in the center, and the page number code at the right, and change back to **Normal** view.

4. In cell **H5**, enter a function to calculate the average revenues for July, August, and September.

5. Change the column header for the new calculated column to **Qtr 3 Averages** and adjust the column width.

6. Add a total row to the table using the **TABLE TOOLS DESIGN** tab.

7. Change the entry in cell **A12** to **Averages**.

8. Remove the calculation from cell **H12**, and add average calculations to cells **D12:G12**.

9. Sort the table in ascending order by **Type**.

10. Filter the table to show only projects by **Jansen**.

11. Adjust column widths if needed. Your worksheet should look like the one in Figure 12-2.

12. **With your teacher's permission,** print page one of the worksheet. Submit the printout or the file for grading as required.

13. Save and close the file, and exit Excel.

Figure 12-2

	A	B	C	D	E	F	G	H
1	Restoration Architecture							
2	3rd Qtr Revenues by Project							
3								
4	Project	Type	Project Manager	July	August	September	Qtr 3 Totals	Qtr 3 Averages
5	18 South Pendleton Ave.	Commercial	Jansen	$ 7,855	$ 27,958	$ 31,225	$ 67,038	$ 22,346
9	Freemont Park Amphitheater	Public	Jansen	$ 72,145	$ 63,145	$ 21,778	$ 157,068	$ 52,356
10	Rossen House	Residential	Jansen	$ 328,118	$ 456,221	$ 298,485	$ 1,082,824	$ 360,941
12	Averages			$ 136,039	$ 182,441	$ 117,163	$ 435,643	
13								

Lesson 13

Working with the NOW Function and Named Ranges

➤ What You Will Learn

Using the NOW Function to Display a System Date
Using Named Ranges

Software Skills   If you don't add a header or footer including the date print code to a worksheet, you can instead insert the NOW function to add the system date and time to any cell on the sheet. Many users find it easier to reference a cell or range of cells using a descriptive name rather than cell addresses. Using range names makes worksheet formulas easier to understand, as well as helping with other operations such as formatting and printing.

What You Can Do

Using the NOW Function to Display a System Date

- When you need to include a date and time that automatically updates on the worksheet, insert the NOW function. Rather than performing a calculation, this function displays the current system date and time.
- The NOW function doesn't require any arguments, so you enter it as =NOW().
- The results of the now function are **volatile**, meaning that they change based on the current system date and time when you open the workbook file rather than reflecting values on a worksheet.
- When you enter the NOW function in a cell, Excel automatically applies a date format that includes the time to the cell. You can change to another format if desired.
- You can enter the NOW function by typing it in, using Formula AutoComplete, or inserting it as you've learned earlier in the chapter.

WORDS TO KNOW

Name Box
The box at the far-left end of the formula bar that you can use to create and navigate to named ranges.

Range name
An identifying label assigned to a group of cells. Also known as defined name.

Volatile
A function that updates and displays a new result each time you open the workbook.

Try It! Using the NOW Function to Display a System Date

1. Start Excel.
2. Open the **E13Try** file from the data files for this lesson.
3. Save the file as **E13Try_xx** in the location where your teacher instructs you to store the files for this lesson.
4. Add a header that has your name at the left, the date code in the center, and the page number code at the right, and change back to Normal view.
5. Click cell A2 to select it.
6. Type **=NOW()** and press CTRL + ENTER . The date and time appear in the cell.

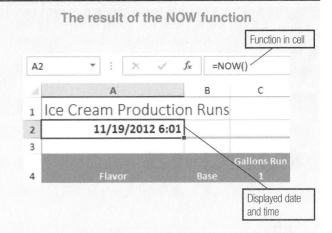

The result of the NOW function

Function in cell

Displayed date and time

7. Save the **E13Try_xx** file, and leave it open to use in the next Try It.

Using Named Ranges

- You create a descriptive **range name** for a range of cells (or a single cell) in order to reference it by name rather than by cell addresses.
- After naming a range, you can use the range name any place the range address might otherwise be entered—within a formula, defining the print range, selecting a range to format, and so on.
- As you learned in Lesson 13, you don't have to name ranges to use column labels in formulas. Instead, you can format your data as an Excel table.
- If you use the range name in a formula, you can use Formula AutoComplete to enter it quickly.
- You can also insert range names in a formula using the Use in Formula button ƒ list in the Defined Names group of the FORMULAS tab.
- If a range name is defined within a worksheet, it can only be used within that sheet, unless you precede it with the sheet name and an exclamation point, as in *Sheet1!RangeName*.
- If defined within a workbook, the range name can be used on any sheet in that workbook.
- A range name may use up to 255 characters, although short descriptive names are easier to read and remember.

- Range naming rules include:
  - No spaces allowed. Use the underscore character in place of a space.
  - Do not use range names that could be interpreted as a cell address or a number, such as Q2 or Y2012.
  - A range name may include letters, numbers, underscores (_), backslashes (\), periods (.), and question marks (?).
  - Do not begin a range name with a number.
  - Range names are not case sensitive, so you can use uppercase or lowercase letters.
  - Avoid using your column labels as range names, because they could create errors if you should format the range as a table and attempt to use range names as table names or vice versa.
- You can define a range name using the **Name Box** at the left end of the formula bar. Type a name and press ENTER .
- You also can use the Define Name button in the Defined Names group of the FORMULAS tab to define a range name. This method enables you to select the scope where the name applies (a particular worksheet or the entire workbook), and to enter a comment which might help in identifying the purpose of the range name.

- Right-click a selected range, and click Define Range to begin the naming process.
- If you have a lot of named ranges in a workbook, you can insert a list of named ranges with their corresponding cell references in the worksheet.

- If you are working with a list or table of data, you may need to sort the data prior to assigning range names.
- Use the Name Manager dialog box, opened from the Defined Names group on the FORMULAS tab, to edit or delete named ranges.

Try It!   Using Named Ranges

1 In the **E13Try_xx** file, select the range C5:C8.

2 Click in the Name Box, type **ChocRun1**, and press ENTER .

3 Use the technique in step 2 to assign the following names to the specified ranges:
D5:D8................**ChocRun2**
E5:E8 ....**ChocRun3**
F5:F8 .... **ChocTotal**

4 Select the range C9:C10, right-click it, and click Define Name. Type **OthRun1** in the Name text box of the New Name dialog box, and then click OK.

5 Use the technique in step 4 to assign the following names to the specified ranges:
D9:D10................ **OthRun2**
E9:E10 .... **OthRun3**
F9:F10.................. **OthTotal**

6 Select the range C11:C15. Click FORMULAS > Define Name ⊡. Type **VanRun1** in the Name text box of the New Name dialog box, and then click OK.

7 Use the technique in Step 6 to assign the following names to the specified ranges:
D11:D15 .... **VanRun2**
E11:E15............... **VanRun3**
F11:F15................**VanTotal**

8 Click in the Name Box, type **ChocRun1**, and press ENTER . Excel selects the range that you named ChocRun1 earlier.

9 Click cell C16. Type **=sum(ChocRun1,OthRun1,VanRun1)**, and press TAB.

10 Type **=sum(cho**, press ↓ to select ChocRun2, and press TAB. Type **,OthRun2,VanRun2** and press TAB.

✓ *Step 10 is an example of using Formula AutoComplete to enter a range name.*

11 Use the techniques of your choice to enter formulas that total the Gallons Run 3 and Gallons Total columns.

✓ *Named ranges are absolute references, so you can't fill them.*

12 Select cell C18, and enter the formula **=sum(ChocRun1)**. Continue by entering the following formulas:

C19 ....=sum(OthRun1)
C20 .... =sum(VanRun1)
D18 ....=sum(ChocRun2)
D19 ....=sum(OthRun2)
D20 .... =sum(VanRun2)
E18 ....=sum(ChocRun3)
E19 ....=sum(OthRun3)
E20 .... =sum(VanRun3)
F18........ =sum(ChocTotal)
F19...........=sum(OthTotal)
F20..........=sum(VanTotal)

13 Save the **E13Try_xx** file, and close it.

(continued)

Try It!   Using Named Ranges *(continued)*

Using range names in formulas

Formula with range names

F16 | : | × ✓ fx | =SUM(ChocTotal,OthTotal,VanTotal)

⊿	A	B	C	D	E	F
1	Ice Cream Production Runs					
2	11/19/2012 6:24					
3						
4	Flavor	Base	Gallons Run 1	Gallons Run 2	Gallons Run 3	Gallons Total
5	Rocky Road	Chocolate	225	200	425	850
6	Peanut Butter Swirl	Chocolate	205	260	305	770
7	Chocolate Chocolate Chip	Chocolate	425	440	450	1315
8	Chocolate	Chocolate	700	809	865	2374
9	Mint Chocolate Chip	Other	450	325	325	1100
10	Berry Burst	Other	150	176	190	516
11	Vanilla	Vanilla	652	752	652	2056
12	Strawberry Cheesecake	Vanilla	310	310	275	895
13	Chocolate Chip	Vanilla	450	610	545	1605
14	Butter Pecan	Vanilla	320	274	300	894
15	Butter Brickle	Vanilla	296	334	320	950
16	Totals		4,183	4,490	4,652	13,325
17						
18	Chocolate Subtotal		1,555	1,709	2,045	5,309
19	Other Subtotal		600	501	515	1,616

Formula result

Lesson 13—Practice

In this project, you will insert the NOW function to add the system date and time to a cell using the skills you learned in this lesson.

DIRECTIONS

1. Start Excel, if necessary, and open the **E13Practice** file from the data files for this lesson.

2. Save the workbook as **E13Practice_xx** in the location where your teacher instructs you to store the files for this lesson.

3. Add a header that has your name at the left, the date code in the center, and the page number code at the right, and change back to **Normal** view.

4. In cell **C2**, enter the formula =**NOW()**, and press CTRL + ENTER .

5. Drag over the range **A4:H11** to select it.

6. Click **DATA > Sort** ⬇.

7. In the Sort dialog box, click the **Sort by** down arrow, and click **Project Manager**.

8. Click **OK**.

9. Drag over the range **A5:H11** to select it.

10. Click the **HOME** tab, in the Styles group click **Cell Styles** 🗗, and then click **40% - Accent1**. Your worksheet should look like the one shown in Figure 13-1 on the next page.

11. **With your teacher's permission,** print the worksheet. Submit the printout or the file for grading as required.

12. Save and close the file, and exit Excel.

Figure 13-1

	A	B	C	D	E	F	G	H
1	Restoration Architecture							
2	3rd Qtr Revenues by Project		2/3/2014 7:56					
3								
4	Project	Type	Project Manager	July	August	September	Qtr 3 Totals	Qtr 3 Averages
5	18 South Pendleton Ave.	Commercial	Jansen	$ 7,855	$ 27,958	$ 31,225	$ 67,038	$ 22,346
6	Freemont Park Amphitheater	Public	Jansen	$ 72,145	$ 63,145	$ 21,778	$ 157,068	$ 52,356
7	Rossen House	Residential	Jansen	$ 328,118	$ 456,221	$ 298,485	$ 1,082,824	$ 360,941
8	Old Barn Quilts	Commercial	Nolo	$ 4,522	$ 12,889	$ 18,645	$ 36,056	$ 12,019
9	Faster Library	Public	Nolo	$ 41,325	$ 78,945	$ 85,664	$ 205,934	$ 68,645
10	512 N. Oak Street	Residential	Nolo	$ 32,995	$ 28,445	$ 18,445	$ 79,885	$ 26,628
11	Cramer Theater	Public	Timson	$ 125,995	$ 285,941	$ 275,884	$ 687,820	$ 229,273
12	Averages			$ 87,565	$ 136,221	$ 107,161	$ 330,946	$ 110,315
13								
14	Jansen Totals							
15	Nolo Totals							
16	Timson Totals							
17								
18	Overall Total							

Lesson 13—Apply

As the CFO of Restoration Architecture, you review a great deal of financial and other data. So you want to add features that make your worksheets faster to use, such as a date that updates automatically and named ranges to make it easier to build and review formulas. In this exercise, you'll modify a recent revenue analysis worksheet so it updates with the current date and time and includes range names for use in calculations.

DIRECTIONS

1. Start Excel, if necessary, and open the **E13Apply** file from the data files for this lesson.

2. Save the workbook as **E13Apply_xx** in the location where your teacher instructs you to store the files for this lesson.

3. Add a header that has your name at the left, the date code in the center, and the page number code at the right, and change back to **Normal** view.

4. Select the range **D5:D7**. Use the Name Box to assign the name **JansenJuly** to the range.

5. Also use the Name Box to assign the following range names:
   a. E5:E7   **JansenAugust**
   b. F5:F7   **JansenSeptember**
   c. G5:G7   **JansenTotal**

6. Select the range **D8:D10**. Right-click the range and click **Define Name**. Type **NoloJuly** in the **Name** text box of the New Name dialog box, change the **Scope** to **Sheet1**, and click **OK**.

7. Use the same technique used in step 6 to assign the following range names and limit their scope to Sheet1:
   a. E8:E10   **NoloAugust**
   b. F8:F10   **NoloSeptember**
   c. G8:G10   **NoloTotal**

8. Use the method of your choice to assign the following range names:
   a. D11   **TimsonJuly**
   b. E11   **TimsonAugust**
   c. F11   **TimsonSeptember**
   d. G11   **TimsonTotal**

9. Click **D14**, and enter a formula that sums the **JansenJuly** range.

10. Enter formulas that total the other three Jansen ranges in cells **E14:G14**.

11. Enter formulas that sum the ranges for the other two project managers in the applicable cells in the range **D15:G16**.

12. Click cell **D18** and enter a formula that sums the July ranges for all three project managers. (Hint: The first formula is =SUM(JansenJuly,NoloJuly, TimsonJuly).)

13. Enter formulas that sum the August, September, and Total data for the three project managers in cells **E18:G18**. Your worksheet should look like the one shown in Figure 13-2.

14. With your teacher's permission, print the worksheet. Submit the printout or the file for grading as required.

15. Save and close the file, and exit Excel.

Figure 13-2

	A	B	C	D	E	F	G	H
1	Restoration Architecture							
2	3rd Qtr Revenues by Project		2/3/2014 8:21					
3								
4	Project	Type	Project Manager	July	August	September	Qtr 3 Totals	Qtr 3 Averages
5	18 South Pendleton Ave.	Commercial	Jansen	$ 7,855	$ 27,958	$ 31,225	$ 67,038	$ 22,346
6	Freemont Park Amphitheater	Public	Jansen	$ 72,145	$ 63,145	$ 21,778	$ 157,068	$ 52,356
7	Rossen House	Residential	Jansen	$ 328,118	$ 456,221	$ 298,485	$ 1,082,824	$ 360,941
8	Old Barn Quilts	Commercial	Nolo	$ 4,522	$ 12,889	$ 18,645	$ 36,056	$ 12,019
9	Faster Library	Public	Nolo	$ 41,325	$ 78,945	$ 85,664	$ 205,934	$ 68,645
10	512 N. Oak Street	Residential	Nolo	$ 32,995	$ 28,445	$ 18,445	$ 79,885	$ 26,628
11	Cramer Theater	Public	Timson	$ 125,995	$ 285,941	$ 275,884	$ 687,820	$ 229,273
12	Averages			$ 87,565	$ 136,221	$ 107,161	$ 330,946	$ 110,315
13								
14	Jansen Totals			$ 408,118	$ 547,324	$ 351,488	$ 1,306,930	
15	Nolo Totals			$ 78,842	$ 120,279	$ 122,754	$ 321,875	
16	Timson Totals			$ 125,995	$ 285,941	$ 275,884	$ 687,820	
17								
18	Overall Total			$ 612,955	$ 953,544	$ 750,126	$ 2,316,625	
19								

Lesson 14

Working with IF Functions

➤ What You Will Learn

Understanding IF Functions
Nesting Functions
Using SUMIF and SUMIFS Functions
Using COUNTIF and COUNTIFS Functions
Using the AVERAGEIF Function

Software Skills   IF functions enable you to test for particular conditions and then perform specific actions based on whether those conditions exist or not. For example, with an IF function, you could calculate the bonuses for a group of salespeople on the premise that bonuses are only paid if a sale is over $1,000. With the SUMIF function, you could total up the sales in your Atlanta office, even if those sales figures are scattered through a long list of sales figures. With the COUNTIF function, you could count the number of sales that resulted in a bonus being paid. With the AVERAGEIF function, you could find the average bonus amount paid out.

What You Can Do

Understanding IF Functions

- IF() is a Logical function.
- With an IF function, you can tell Excel to perform one of two different calculations based on whether your data matches a logical test.
- For example, you can use an IF function to have Excel calculate a 10% bonus if total sales are over $500,000 and just a 3% bonus if they are not.
- The format for an IF function is: =IF(logical_test,value_if_true,value_if_false)
  - The *logical test* is a condition or **expression** whose result is either true or false.
  - If the condition is true, the formula displays the *value_if_true* argument in the cell.
  - If the condition is false, the formula displays the *value_if_false* argument in the cell.
- For example, to calculate the bonus described above, you would type **=IF(B2>500000,B2*.10,B2*.03)**
- The above function says, "If total sales (cell B2) are greater than $500,000, then take total sales times 10% to calculate the bonus. Otherwise, take total sales times 3%."

WORDS TO KNOW

Expression
A type of equation (such as B6>25) that returns a value, such as TRUE or FALSE. Excel uses expressions to identify cells to include in certain formulas such as IF and SUMIF.

Nesting
Using a function as an argument within another function.

- Notice that in the IF function, the value, $500,000, is entered without the dollar sign or the comma.

- You can have text appear in a cell instead of a calculated value. For example, you might type **=IF(B2>500000,"We made it!","Good try.")** to display the words *We made it!* if total sales are over $500,000, or the words *Good try.* if they are not.

- Surround the text you want to appear with quotation marks ("") in the formula.

  ✓ *The ampersand (&) may be used inside the function to join text.*

- IF functions may use the comparison operators below to state the condition:

=	Equals
<>	Not equal to
>	Greater than
>=	Greater than or equal to
<	Less than
<=	Less than or equal to

- Like any other function, you can enter an IF function manually, use Formula AutoComplete, or use the Insert Function dialog box or Function Library group drop-down lists to help.

Try It!   **Understanding IF Functions**

1 Start Excel.

2 Open the **E14Try** file from the data files for this lesson.

3 Save the workbook as **E14Try_xx** in the location where your teacher instructs you to store the files for this lesson.

4 Add a header that has your name at the left, the date code in the center, and the page number code at the right, and change back to Normal view.

5 Click cell F4 to select it.

6 Click FORMULAS > Logical 🔲 > IF. The Function Arguments dialog box appears.

7 Type **d4>=20** in the Logical_test text box, and press TAB.

8 Type **Yes** in the Value_if_true text box, and press TAB.

  ✓ *The Function Arguments dialog box adds the quotation marks around text entries for you.*

9 Type **No** in the Value_if_false text box, and press TAB.

10 Click OK. Because the entry in cell D4 is 17 (less than 20), a result of No displays in cell F4.

11 Drag the fill handle down to fill the formula through cell F21.

12 Click the Auto Fill Options button > Fill Without Formatting.

13 Save the **E14Try_xx** file, and leave it open to use in the next Try It.

Building an IF function

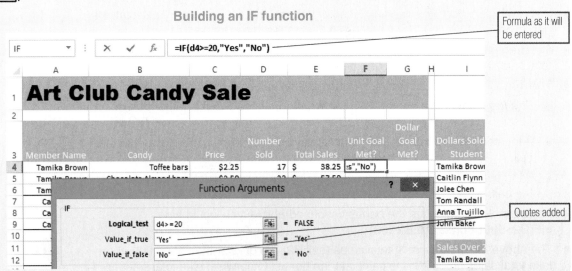

Nesting Functions

- You can **nest** any function as one of the arguments for another function in a formula.

- The arguments in IF functions often use nested functions, either in the logical test or of the possible outcome values, or both.

- For example, consider the formula:
  =IF(C3>92,"A",IF(C3>83,"B",IF(C3>73,"C", IF(C3>65,"D","F"))))

- The above formula says that if the average score in cell C3 is greater than 92, then the student gets an A; if the score is less than or equal to 92 but greater than 83, the student gets a B; if the score is less than or equal to 83 but greater than 73, the student gets a C; and so on.

Try It!   Nesting Functions

1 In the **E14Try_xx** file, click cell G4 to select it.

2 Click the Insert Function button *fx* on the formula bar.

3 Open the Or select a category list, and click Logical. In the Select a function list, click IF. Click OK. The Function Arguments dialog box appears.

4 Type **E4>=60** in the Logical_test text box, and press [TAB].

5 Type **Yes** in the Value_if_true text box, and press [TAB].

6 Type **No** in the Value_if_false text box, and press [TAB].

7 Click OK. Because the entry in cell E4 is less than $60, a result of No displays in cell G4.

8 Drag the fill handle down to fill the formula through cell G21.

9 Click the Auto Fill Options button > Fill Without Formatting.

10 Save the **E14Try_xx** file, and leave it open to use in the next Try It.

Using SUMIF and SUMIFS Functions

- SUMIF() is a Math & Trig function that uses a condition to add certain data.

- If the condition is true, then data in a corresponding cell is added to the total; if it is false, then the corresponding data is skipped.

- Here is how you enter a SUMIF function: =SUMIF(range,criteria,sum_range).

  - The *range* is the range of cells you want to review.

  - The *criteria* is an expression that is either true or false, and defines which cells should be added to the total.

  - If you specify an optional *sum_range*, values from the sum_range on the rows where the range data results in a true result for the *criteria* are added to the total.

  - If you do not specify a sum_range, the formula adds the values from the *range* rows that evaluate as true.

- Use the same comparison operators (such as >,<>, etc.) as for an IF function in the criteria. However, here, you must enclose the condition in quotation marks ("") if it is not a cell reference.

- For example, if you had a worksheet listing sales for several different products, you could total only sales for chocolate by using this formula: =SUMIF(D2:D55,"Chocolate",G2:G55).

  - Assume in this example that column D contains the name of the product being sold and column G contains the total amount for that sale. If column D contains the word *Chocolate*, then the amount for that sale (located in column G) is added to the running total.

- You can leave the last argument off if you want to sum the same range that you're testing; for example: =SUMIF(G2:G10,"<=500"). This formula calculates the total of all values in the range G2 to G10 that are less than or equal to 500.

- SUMIFS is a function similar to SUMIF except that it allows you to enter multiple qualifying conditions.

- The format for a SUMIFS statement is: =SUMIFS(sum_range,criteria_range1,criteria1,criteria_range2,criteria2,etc.).

  - The *criteria_range1* is the first range of cells you want to test.

  - The *criteria1* is an expression that is either true or false, and defines which cells should be added to the total.

  - If the criteria1 result is true, the corresponding cell in sum_range is added to the total.

  - If the criteria1 result is false, the corresponding cell in sum_range is not added to the total.

- You can add conditions and additional ranges to test as needed. You can specify the same range to test or use a different one.

- All ranges, the sum_range and the criteria ranges, must be the same size and shape.

- Using the earlier example, if you wanted to total all the sales of chocolate bars and toffee bars, you could use a formula such as: =SUMIFS(G2:G55, D2:D55,"Chocolate Bars",D2:D55,"Toffee Bars").

- Again, column D contains the name of the product being sold, and column G contains the total amount for that sale.

Try It! **Using SUMIF and SUMIFS Functions**

---

❶ In the **E14Try_xx** file, click cell K4 to select it.

❷ Click the Insert Function button *fx* on the formula bar.

❸ Open the Or select a category list, and click Math & Trig. In the Select a function list, click SUMIF. Click OK. The Function Arguments dialog box appears.

❹ Drag over the range A4:A21 to specify it in the Range text box, press [F4] to make the range address absolute, and press [TAB].

  ✓ *Because you will be copying the formula, you need to make the range references absolute.*

❺ Click cell I4 to specify it in the Criteria text box, and press [TAB].

  ✓ *Using a cell reference rather than typing in the student name in this case will enable you to fill the formula down and get an accurate result for each student.*

❻ Drag over the range E4:E21 to specify it in the Sum_range text box, press [F4] to make the range address absolute, and press [TAB].

❼ Click OK. Excel calculates a total of $170.00 in sales for the specified student.

❽ Drag the fill handle down to fill the formula through cell K9.

❾ Click cell K12 to select it.

❿ Click the Insert Function button *fx* on the formula bar.

⓫ Open the Or select a category list, and click Math & Trig. In the Select a function list, click SUMIFS. Click OK. The Function Arguments dialog box appears.

⓬ Drag over the range E4:E21 to specify it in the Sum_range text box, press [F4] to make the range address absolute, and press [TAB].

Using the SUMIF function

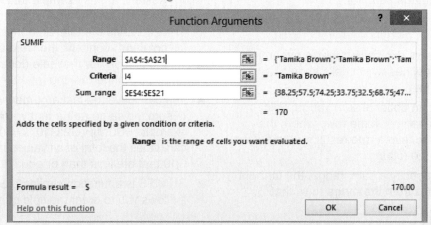

Try It!   **Using SUMIF and SUMIFS Functions** *(continued)*

⑬ Drag over the range A4:A21 to specify it in the Criteria_range1 text box, press F4 to make the range address absolute, and press TAB.

⑭ Click cell I12 to specify it in the Criteria1 text box, and press TAB.

⑮ Drag over the range D4:D21 to specify it in the Criteria_range2 text box, press F4 to make the range address absolute, and press TAB.

⑯ Type >20 in the Criteria2 text box.

⑰ Click OK. Excel calculates a total of $131.75 for sales where the specified student sold more than 20 units of a product.

⑱ Drag the fill handle down to fill the formula through cell K17.

⑲ Save the **E14Try_xx** file, and leave it open to use in the next Try It.

Specify as many criteria as needed with the SUMIFS function

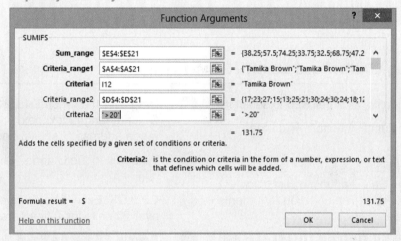

Using COUNTIF and COUNTIFS Functions

- COUNTIF is a Statistical function that uses a criteria to count the number of items in a range.

  ✓ *You learned about two similar functions, COUNT and COUNTA, in Lesson 11.*

- If the result of the criteria is true, then the item is added to a running count; if it is false, then the item is skipped.

- The format for a COUNTIF function is: =COUNTIF(range, criteria).

  - The *range* is the range of cells holding the values to test (and count).

  - The *criteria* is an expression that is either true or false, defining which cells should be counted.

- Use the same comparison operators as for the IF function when writing the criteria. As for SUMIF, you must enclose the condition in quotation marks ("") if it is not a cell reference.

- For example, if you want to count the number of individual Chocolate Bars sales in the earlier example, you could use this formula: =COUNTIF(D2:D55,"Chocolate Bars"). Assume here that column D contains the name of the product being sold; for each cell in column D that contains the words *Chocolate Bars*, 1 is added to the running total of the number of chocolate bar sales.

- Because Chocolate Bars is a text label, you must enclose it in quotation marks ("").

- To compute the number of chocolate bars sold or the value of those sales, use SUMIF.

- You can combine functions to create complex calculations: =SUMIF(D3:D13,"PASS",C3:C13)/ COUNTIF(D3:D13,"PASS"). This formula computes the average score of all the students who passed the course. Assume that column D contains the words *Pass* or *Fail* based on the student's final score. The final score is located in column C. The formula sums the scores of all the students who passed and divides that by the number of students who passed, calculating an average score for passing students.

- COUNTIFS is a function similar to COUNTIF except that it allows you to enter multiple qualifying conditions.
- The format for a COUNTIFS statement is: =COUNTIFS(criteria_range1,criteria1,criteria_range2,criteria2,etc.).
  - The *criteria_range1* is the range of cells you want to test.
  - The *criteria1* is an expression that is either true or false, and defines which cells should be counted.
  - You can add additional conditions and ranges to test as needed. You can specify the same range to test or use a different one.
  - All ranges must be the same shape and size.

- Using the earlier example, if you wanted to count all Chocolate Bars sales with a value over $100, you could use a formula such as: =COUNTIFS(D2:D55,"Chocolate Bars",G2:G55, ">100").
- Again, column D contains the name of the product being sold, and column G contains the total amount for that sale.
- Since there are 54 rows in the two ranges, the highest answer you might get is 54. A row is counted only if it contains both the words Chocolate Bars in column D, and a value greater than 100 in column G.

Try It! Using COUNTIF and COUNTIFS Functions

1. In the **E14Try_xx** file, click cell K20 to select it.

2. Click the Insert Function button *fx* on the formula bar.

3. Open the Or select a category list, and click Statistical. In the Select a function list, click COUNTIFS. Click OK. The Function Arguments dialog box appears.

4. Drag over the range B4:B21 to specify it in the Criteria_range1 text box, press [F4] to make the range address absolute, and press [TAB].

5. Type **I20** to specify it in the Criteria1 text box, and press [TAB].

6. Drag over the range D4:D21 to specify it in the Criteria_range2 text box, press [F4] to make the range address absolute, and press [TAB].

7. Type **>20** in the Criteria2 text box, and press [TAB].

8. Click OK. Excel calculates a total of 3 sales of over 20 units for Toffee bars.

9. Drag the fill handle down to fill the formula through cell K22.

10. Save the **E14Try_xx** file, and close it.

Using multiple criteria to count with the COUNTIFS function

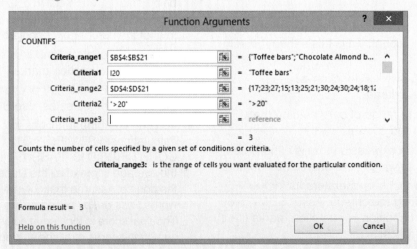

Using the AVERAGEIF Function

- AVERAGEIF is a Statistical function that uses a condition to return the average of all cells in a range that meet specific criteria.

- The IF portion of the function indicates what data meets the specific criteria and the AVERAGE portion calculates the mean or average.

- If the result of the criteria is true, then AVERAGEIF will calculate the average. If the result is false, then the item is skipped.

- The format for an AVERAGEIF statement is: =AVERAGEIF(range,criteria,average_range).

  - The *range* is the range of cells holding the values to test (and average).

  - The *criteria* is an expression that is either true or false, defining which cells should be averaged.

  - If you specify an optional *average_range*, values from the average_range on the rows where the range data results in a true result for the criteria are calculated.

- If you do not specify a average_range, the formula averages the values from the range rows that evaluate as true.

- Use the same comparison operators as for the IF function when writing the criteria. You must enclose the condition in quotation marks ("") if it is a text label and not a cell reference.

- For example, if you had a worksheet listing sales of different types of chocolate bars and you wanted to know the average sale for each chocolate bar, you could use this formula: =AVERAGEIF(D2:D55,"Chocolate Bar",G2:G55).

  - Assume in this example that column D contains the name of the product being sold and column G contains the total amount for that sale. If column D contains the words *Chocolate Bar*, then the amount for that sale (located in column G) is added to the averaged total.

Try It!   **Using the AVERAGEIF Function**

1 In the **E14Try_xx** file, click cell K25 to select it.

2 Click the Insert Function button *fx* on the formula bar.

3 Open the Or select a category list, and click Statistical. In the Select a function list, click AVERAGEIF. Click OK. The Function Arguments dialog box appears.

4 Drag over the range B4:B21 to specify it in the Range text box, press F4 to make the range address absolute, and press TAB.

  ✓ *Because you will be copying the formula, you need to make the range references absolute.*

5 Click cell I25 to specify it in the Criteria text box, and press TAB.

Using the AVERAGEIF function to find the average for a specific criterion

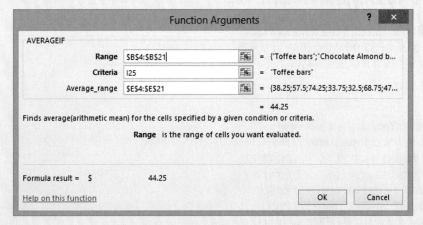

Formula result = $ 44.25

Help on this function

(continued)

Try It!   **Using the AVERAGEIF Function** *(continued)*

6 Drag over the range E4:E21 to specify it in the Average_range text box, press ⟦F4⟧ to make the range address absolute, and press OK. Excel calculates an average of $44.25 in sales for the specified candy bar.

7 Drag the fill handle down to fill the formula through cell K27.

8 Save the **E14Try_xx** file, and close it.

Lesson 14—Practice

In this project, you will use IF functions to perform calculations using the skills you learned in this lesson.

DIRECTIONS

1. Start Excel, if necessary, and open the **E14Practice** file from the data files for this lesson.

2. Save the workbook as **E14Practice_xx** in the location where your teacher instructs you to store the files for this lesson.

3. Add a header that has your name at the left, the date code in the center, and the page number code at the right, and change back to **Normal** view.

4. Enter the date **12/3/14** in cell **B4**, and increase the column width as needed to display the date.

5. Click cell **U8**. Notice that the Name Box displays the name already assigned to this cell. All the cells holding prices have names assigned.

6. Because your company gives a discount for white bread on Mondays, you need to enter a formula in cell U8 to calculate the discounted amount for that day of the week. Use the **IF** function with a nested **WEEKDAY** function in the formula. The formula should return a value of $2.00 if the date in cell B4 is a Monday, and $2.55 if it is not.

   ✓ *Hint: Use =IF(WEEKDAY(argument)=something,then do this, else do this).*

   ✓ *The WEEKDAY function requires one argument, in parentheses. The required argument is the address of the cell that contains the date to look at, which in this case is cell B4. WEEKDAY returns a value from 1 to 7, telling you what day of the week the date you provide as the first argument is. By default, Sunday is counted as day 1, so if the date in cell B4 is a Monday, WEEKDAY() will return a value of 2.*

7. Enter a similar formula in cell **U9**, charging $2.00 for wheat bread if it's Monday and $2.60 if it's not. Notice the values calculated in the Order Total column.

8. Change the date in cell **B4** to **12/8/14**. Notice how the Order Total values recalculate to reflect that the date is now a Monday.

9. Undo the change to return the date in cell B4 to 12/3/14.

10. Display the formulas, and increase the width of column U so that the two new formulas display completely. Your worksheet should look like the one in Figure 14-1 on the next page.

11. **With your teacher's permission,** print the Price List print area. Submit the printout or the file for grading as required.

12. Save and close the file, and exit Excel.

Figure 14-1

	T	U
	Price List	
	White Bread	=IF(WEEKDAY(B4)=2,2,2.55)
	Wheat Bread	=IF(WEEKDAY(B4)=2,2,2.6)
	Honey Wheat Bagel	1.1
	Blueberry Bagel	1.25
	Cinnamon Bagel	1.25
	Wheat Rolls	0.32
	White Rolls	0.3
	Garlic Bread	2.25
	Blueberry Muffin	1.95
	Bran Muffin	1.85
	Croissant	1.32
	Baguette	1.95

Lesson 14—Apply

You're the manager of a Whole Grains Bread store in Olympia, Washington, and you've been developing a new worksheet for tracking retail bread sales. You've just learned about various IF functions, and, along with some other new functions you've discovered, you know you can refine the worksheet so that it's simple for your employees to use. With the sales analysis the worksheet will provide, you can refine the retail end of your business to maximize your profits.

DIRECTIONS

1. Start Excel, if necessary, and open the **E14Apply** file from the data files for this lesson.

2. Save the workbook as **E14Apply_xx** in the location where your teacher instructs you to store the files for this lesson.

3. Add a header that has your name at the left, the date code in the center, and the page number code at the right, and change back to **Normal** view.

4. In cell **C36**, use the **COUNT** function to create a formula that counts the number of coupon sales. (Refer to Figure 14-2 throughout this exercise to double-check that you are getting the correct results.) Remember that the COUNT function counts how many cells in the range contain numbers (values or formula results).

Figure 14-2

34			
35	**Daily Summary**		
36	Coupon Sales	11	$146.46
37	Sales w/o Coupon	13	$289.84
38	Credit Sales	14	$271.98
39	Cash Sales	10	$164.32
40	Total Sales	24	$436.30
41	Credit Sales < $10	2	$ 15.48
42	Average Credit Sale		$ 19.43
43			

5. In cell **C37**, use the **COUNTBLANK** function to create a formula that counts the number of non-coupon sales.

6. In cell **C38**, use the **COUNTIF** function to create a formula that counts the number of credit card sales, using x as the criteria.

7. In cell **C39**, use the **COUNTIF** function to create a formula that counts the number of cash sales, using x as the criteria.

8. In cell **C40**, use the **COUNT** function to count the number of sales for the day, based on the Total Sale column.

9. In cell **C41**, use the **COUNTIFS** function to create a formula that counts the number of credit card sales for less than $10.

   ✓ *Calculations like this could help you determine whether your business should continue to accept credit card payments for small purchases.*

10. In cell **D36**, use the **SUMIF** function to create a formula that calculates the revenue from coupon sales.

11. In cell **D37**, use the **SUMIF** function to create a formula that calculates the revenue from non-coupon sales.

   ✓ *Hint: You want to find blank values ("") in the Coupon column and add the values from the corresponding rows in the Total Sale column.*

12. In cell **D38**, use the **SUMIF** function to create a formula that calculates the revenue from credit card sales.

13. In cell **D39**, use the **SUMIF** function to create a formula that calculates the revenue from cash sales.

14. In cell **D40**, use the method of your choice to make a cell reference to the cell with the sum of Total Sales.

15. In cell **D41**, use the **SUMIFS** function to total the value of credit card sales less than $10.

16. In cell **D42**, use the **AVERAGEIFS** function to find the average credit sale.

17. Apply the **Accounting** cell style to **D36:D42**, and adjust column widths as needed. Your worksheet should look like Figure 14-2 on the previous page.

18. **With your teacher's permission,** print the worksheet. Submit the printout or the file for grading as required.

19. Save and close the file, and exit Excel.

Lesson 15

Working with Text Functions

➤ What You Will Learn

Using the CONCATENATE Function
Using the UPPER and LOWER Functions
Using the LEFT, RIGHT, and MID Functions
Using the TRIM Function

Software Skills Excel's text functions help you manage the text data in your worksheets. For example, the CONCATENATE function would allow you to join together first and last names. Then you could use the UPPER and LOWER functions to correct any capitalization of the names. With the RIGHT, LEFT, and MID functions, you could separate the parts of a phone number into area code, prefix, and line number. Finally, you could use the TRIM function to remove unwanted spaces in the text.

What You Can Do

Using the CONCATENATE Function

■ You can use **concatenation** to join together cell data.

■ CONCATENATE is a Text function that joins together words, cell references, blank spaces, or numbers.

✓ *You learned in Lesson 5 that FlashFill also can be used to concatenate data.*

■ Access Text functions from the Text button ▣ in the Function Library on the FORMULAS tab.

■ You also can access Text functions from the Insert Function button *fx* on the formula bar. In the Function Arguments dialog box, click Text in the Or select a category list and then click a text function name in the Select a function list.

■ The CONCATENATE function requires a text argument.

■ You can add up to 255 text entries to the CONCATENATE function. Each entry must be separated by a comma.

WORDS TO KNOW

Case
The use of capital (uppercase) and small letters (lowercase) in text.

Concatenation
The linking of elements together in a series.

- The format for a CONCATENATE function is: =CONCATENATE(text1,text2).
  - In this example, *text1* is the first text item to be concatenated and *text2* is the second text item to be concatenated.
  - If *text1* is the word *voice* and *text2* is the word *mail*, then the returned result is *voicemail*.
- The CONCATENATE function does not automatically leave a blank space between words or other data.

- You must specify any spaces or punctuation that you want to appear in the results as an argument enclosed in quotation marks; for example, =CONCATENATE(A1," ",B1). The second argument in this example is a space character (" ").
  - In this example, the returned result is the contents of cell A1, a space, and the contents of cell B1.

Try It!   **Using the CONCATENATE Function**

1. Start Excel.

2. Open the **E15Try** file from the data files for this lesson.

3. Save the workbook as **E15Try_xx** in the location where your teacher instructs you to store the files for this lesson.

4. Add a header that has your name at the left, the date code in the center, and the page number code at the right, and change back to Normal.

5. Click cell D4 to select it.

6. Click the Insert Function button *fx* on the formula bar. The Insert Functions dialog box appears.

7. Open the Or select a category list, and click Text. In the Select a function list, click CONCATENATE. Click OK. The Function Arguments dialog box appears.

8. In the Text1 arguments box, type **A4**, and press [TAB].

9. In the Text2 arguments box, type " " (a quotation mark, space, and another quotation mark), and press [TAB].

10. In the Text3 arguments box, type **B4**, and click OK.

11. Drag the fill handle down to fill the formula through cell D9.

12. Save the **E15Try_xx** file, and leave it open to use in the next Try It.

Using the CONCATENATE function

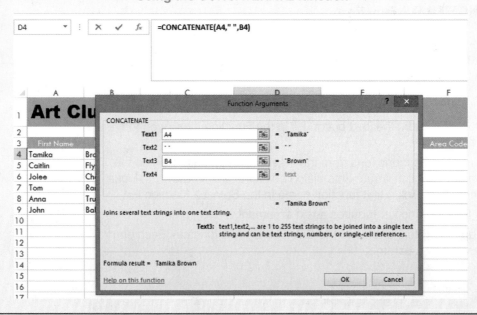

Using the UPPER and LOWER Functions

- When text data is imported or copied into an Excel spreadsheet, you may have to correct the capitalization.

- UPPER and LOWER Text functions can change the **case** of text. The UPPER function capitalizes text, and the LOWER function lowercases text.

- Both UPPER and LOWER functions require a text argument. The argument can be a cell reference or text.

  ✓ *When using text in an argument, you must enclose the text in quotation marks.*

- The format for an UPPER function is: =UPPER(text).

  - For example, the argument *text* can be a reference to a cell, and will return a result of all uppercase text in that cell.

- The format for a LOWER function is: =LOWER(text).

  - For example, the argument *text* can be typed text such as *INCOME STATEMENT,* which will return a result of all lowercase text (i.e., *income statement*).

- The LOWER function only affects letters; it does not change numbers or characters such as ampersands (&), percentage signs (%), or parentheses (()).

| **Try It!** | **Using the UPPER and LOWER Functions** |

1 In the **E15Try_xx** file, click cell D12 to select it.

2 Type **=UPPER(D4)** and press [ENTER] . The text is now all uppercase.

3 Drag the fill handle down to fill the formula through cell D17.

4 Clear the contents of the cell range D12:D17.

5 Click cell C12 to select it.

6 Click the Insert Function button *fx* on the formula bar.

Using the LOWER function to change the case of text

(continued)

Try It!   **Using the UPPER and LOWER Functions** *(continued)*

7 In the Function Arguments dialog box, click Text in the Or select a category list, click LOWER in the Select a function list, and click OK. The Function Arguments dialog box appears.

8 In the Text box, type **"PENCIL"** and click OK.

9 Drag and drop the cell C12 to replace cell C5.

10 Click OK to replace the current data.

11 Click cell C12 to select it.

12 Click FORMULAS > Text 🅰 > LOWER. The Function Arguments dialog box appears.

13 In the Text box, type **"WOOD"** and click OK.

14 Drag and drop the cell C12 to replace cell C9.

15 Click OK to replace the current data.

16 Save the **E15Try_xx** file, and leave it open to use in the next Try It.

Using the LEFT, RIGHT, and MID Functions

- You can use Excel's LEFT, RIGHT, and MID functions to remove unwanted characters from your data.

- You also can use these functions to extract specific characters from your data.

  ✓ *All of your data must be consistent in the cells where you choose to use the LEFT, RIGHT, and MID functions.*

- The LEFT function targets characters from the left side, and the RIGHT function targets characters from the right side of your data.

  - For example, you can use the LEFT function to extract a first name from a cell containing a first, middle, and last name.

  - In the above example, you can use the RIGHT function to extract a last name.

- The format for a LEFT function is: =LEFT(Text, Num_chars).

- The format for a RIGHT function is: =RIGHT(Text, Num_chars).

  - *Text* is the argument that contains the character you want to extract. This also can be a cell reference.

  - *Num_chars* is the number of characters you want the function to extract.

- The MID function targets characters in the middle of your data.

  - For example, you can use the MID function to extract a middle name from a cell containing a first, middle, and last name.

- The format for a MID function is: =MID(Text, Start_num, Num_chars).

  - *Text* is the argument that contains the character you want to extract.

  - *Start_num* is the position of the first characters you want the function to extract.

  - *Num_chars* is the number of characters you want the function to remove or extract.

  ✓ *When using text in an argument, you must enclose the text in quotation marks.*

Try It!   Using the LEFT, RIGHT, and MID Functions

1. In the **E15Try_xx** file, click cell F4 to select it.

2. Click the Insert Function button f_x on the formula bar.

3. In the Insert Function dialog box, click Text in the Or select a category list, click LEFT in the Select a function list, and click OK. The Function Arguments dialog box appears.

4. In the Text box, type **E4** and press TAB.

5. In the Num_chars box, type **5** and click OK. The area code is extracted from the phone number.

6. Drag the fill handle down to fill the formula through cell F9.

7. Click cell G4 to select it.

8. Click the Insert Function button f_x on the formula bar.

9. In the Insert Function dialog box, click Text in the Or select a category list, click MID in the Select a function list, and click OK. The Function Arguments dialog box appears.

10. In the Text box, type **E4** and press TAB.

11. In the Start_num box, type **7** and press TAB.

12. In the Num_chars box, type **3** and click OK. The prefix is extracted from the phone number.

13. Drag the fill handle down to fill the formula through cell G9.

14. Click cell H4 to select it.

15. Type **=RIGHT(E4,3)** and press ENTER. The extension is extracted from the phone number.

16. Drag the fill handle down to fill the formula through cell H9.

17. Save the **E15Try_xx** file, and leave it open to use in the next Try It.

Using the MID function

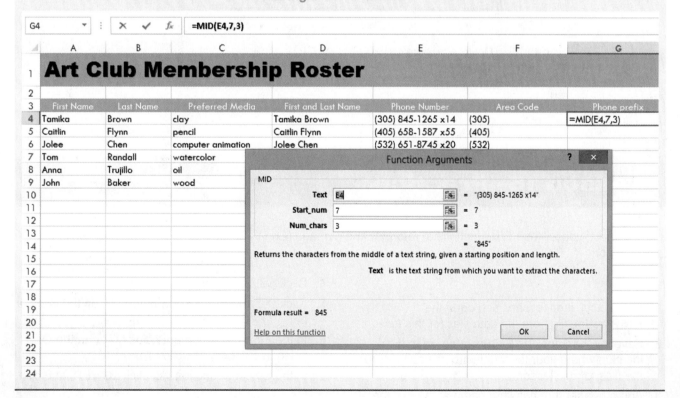

Using the TRIM Function

- You can use Excel's TRIM function to remove unwanted spaces from your data.

- The format for a TRIM function is: =TRIM(Text).
  - *Text* is the argument that contains the character you want to extract. This also can be a cell reference.

Try It!   **Using the TRIM Function**

1. In the **E15Try_xx** file, click cell C12 to select it.

2. Click FORMULAS > Text A > TRIM. The Function Arguments dialog box appears.

3. In the Text box, type **C6** and click OK. The ten spaces are trimmed from the text in cell C6. Notice that the space between words is not removed.

4. Clear the contents of cell C12.

5. Save the **E15Try_xx** file, and close it.

Using the TRIM function to remove unwanted spaces

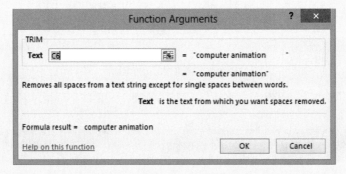

Lesson 15—Practice

In this project, you will use Text functions to reformat and manage text in a worksheet using the skills you learned in this lesson.

DIRECTIONS

1. Start Excel, if necessary, and open the **E15Practice** file from the data files for this lesson.

2. Save the workbook as **E15Practice_xx** in the location where your teacher instructs you to store the files for this lesson.

3. Add a header that has your name at the left, the date code in the center, and the page number code at the right, and change back to **Normal** view.

4. Click cell **D6** to select it.

5. Click the **Insert Function** button *fx* on the formula bar.

6. In the Function Arguments dialog box, in the Or select a category list, click **Text**.

7. In the Select a function list, click **LOWER**, and click **OK**.

8. In the Function Arguments dialog box, in the Text box, type **C6** and click **OK**.

9. Drag the fill handle down to fill the formula through cell **D13**.

10. Click cell **A18** to select it.

11. Click the **Insert Function** button _fx_ on the formula bar.

12. In the Insert Functions dialog box, open the Or select a category list, and click **Text**.

13. In the Select a function list, click **CONCATENATE**, and click **OK**.

14. In the Function Arguments dialog box, in the Text1 arguments box, type **A6**, and press TAB.

15. In the **Text2** arguments box, type "**: ", and press** TAB.

16. In the **Text3** arguments box, type **D6**, and click **OK**.

17. Drag the fill handle down to fill the formula through cell **A25**. Adjust the column width.

18. Select cell **C18** to select it.

19. Click the **Insert Function** button _fx_ on the formula bar.

20. In the Insert Function dialog box, open the Or select a category list, and click **Text**.

21. In the Select a function list, click **RIGHT**, and click **OK**.

22. In the **Function Arguments** dialog box, in the **Text** box, type **B6**, and press TAB.

23. In the **Num_chars** box, type **5**, and click **OK**.

24. Drag the fill handle down to fill the formula through cell **C25**.

25. Select cell **E18** to select it.

26. Type =**TRIM(E6)**, and click **OK**. Adjust the column width, if necessary.

27. Drag the fill handle to fill the series through cell **E25**. Your worksheet should look like Figure 15-1.

28. **With your teacher's permission**, print the worksheet. Submit the printout or the file for grading as required.

29. Save and close the file, and exit Excel.

Figure 15-1

	A	B	C	D	E
1	Whole Grains Bread				
2	Affiliate Retail Stores				
3					
4					
5	Store Name	Store Address	Store Code		Manager
6	ABC Bakery	234 SE 183RD Street, Portland, oR 97321	1B-2c	1b-2c	Jay Ray Burns
7	Baked Goods, Inc.	19 houston Ave., austin, tx 73301	10k-104D	10k-104d	Margie Ann Jackson
8	Better Breads, Corp.	923 1sT St., Seattle, WA 98101	3B-84d	3b-84d	Jose Angelo Marquez
9	Great Harvester	10 Market StrEET, San Diego, ca 92101	18e-99X	18e-99x	Mark Dean Smith
10	More Better Bread	2-b NorTH Wygandt Rd., DES moines, io 50301	4p-14w	4p-14w	Rob Beau Washington
11	My Best Bread, Inc.	209 9th AVE., BalTIMOre, Md 21201	8t-8O	8t-8o	Richard Benjamin Tiller
12	Very Best Bread	100 Charleston AveNUE, Boise, ID 83702	33d-1y	33d-1y	Diane Lea Ross
13	Your Whole Bread Store	88 wickersham lane, Lexington, KY 40505	8r-9P	8r-9p	Paris Renee Mills
14					
15					
16					
17	Store Name & Code		Store ZIP Code		Manager
18	ABC Bakery: 1b-2c		97321		Jay Ray Burns
19	Baked Goods, Inc.: 10k-104d		73301		Margie Ann Jackson
20	Better Breads, Corp.: 3b-84d		98101		Jose Angelo Marquez
21	Great Harvester: 18e-99x		92101		Mark Dean Smith
22	More Better Bread: 4p-14w		50301		Rob Beau Washington
23	My Best Bread, Inc.: 8t-8o		21201		Richard Benjamin Tiller
24	Very Best Bread: 33d-1y		83702		Diane Lea Ross
25	Your Whole Bread Store: 8r-9p		40505		Paris Renee Mills

Lesson 15—Apply

You're the manager of a Whole Grains Bread store in Olympia, Washington, and you've been sent a worksheet with information about other affiliate retail bread stores. The names in the worksheet have not been consistently typed and there are extra spaces within the cells. You've just learned about various Text functions, and you want to reformat the text in the worksheet so that it looks more professional.

DIRECTIONS

1. Start Excel, if necessary, and open the **E15Apply** file from the data files for this lesson.

2. Save the workbook as **E15Apply_xx** in the location where your teacher instructs you to store the files for this lesson.

3. Add a header that has your name at the left, the date code in the center, and the page number code at the right, and change back to **Normal** view.

4. In cell **A18**, use the **TRIM** function to create a formula that removes the extra spaces in the text.

5. Fill the formula down through cell **A25**.

6. In cell **B18**, use the **UPPER** function to create a formula that changes the text in cell **B6** to uppercase.

7. Fill the formula down through cell **B25**.

8. In cell **C18**, use the **LEFT** function to create a formula that extracts the area code. Remember to include the parentheses.

9. Fill the formula down through cell **C25**.

10. In cell **D18**, use the **MID** function to create a formula that extracts the phone prefix. Remember to count the space as a character for the start_num value.

11. Fill the formula down through cell **D25**.

12. In cell **E18**, use the **RIGHT** function to create a formula that extracts the phone line number (the last four digits of the phone number).

13. Fill the formula down through cell **E25**.

14. In cell **F18**, use the **CONCATENATE** function to create a formula that combines the first, middle, and last name of the manager. Remember to insert a space between each name.

15. Fill the formula down through cell **F25**. Adjust the column width, if necessary. Your worksheet should look like Figure 15-2.

16. **With your teacher's permission**, print the worksheet. Submit the printout or the file for grading as required.

17. Save and close the file, and exit Excel.

Figure 15-2

F18   fx   =CONCATENATE(D6," ",E6," ",F6)

	A	B	C	D	E	F
1	Whole Grains Bread					
2	**Affiliate Retail Stores**					
3						
4					Manager First	Manager
5	Store Name	Store Address	Phone Number	Name	Middle Name	Manager Last Name
6	ABC Bakery	234 SE 183RD Street, Portland, oR 97321	(205) 234-1323	Jay	Ray	Burns
7	Baked Goods, Inc.	19 houston Ave., austin, tx 73301	(562) 298-1593	Margie	Ann	Jackson
8	Better Breads, Corp.	923 1ST St., Seattle, WA 98101	(245) 684-3292	Jose	Angelo	Marquez
9	Great Harvester	10 Market StrEET, San Diego, ca 92101	(402) 982-2341	Mark	Dean	Smith
10	More Better Bread	2-b NorTH Wygandt Rd., DES moines, io 50301	(602) 723-2360	Rob	Beau	Washington
11	My Best Bread, Inc.	209 9th AVE., BalTIMOre, Md 21201	(263) 988-2086	Richard	Benjamin	Tiller
12	Very Best Bread	100 Charleston AveNUE, Boise, ID 83702	(835) 205-0944	Diane	Lea	Ross
13	Your Whole Bread Store	88 wickersham lane, Lexington, KY 40505	(839) 490-2005	Paris	Renee	Mills
14						
15						
16						
17	Store Name	Store Address	Area Code	Phone Prefix	Phone Line Number	Manager Name
18	ABC Bakery	234 SE 183RD STREET, PORTLAND, OR 97321	(205)	234	1323	Jay Ray Burns
19	Baked Goods, Inc.	19 HOUSTON AVE., AUSTIN, TX 73301	(562)	298	1593	Margie Ann Jackson
20	Better Breads, Corp.	923 1ST ST., SEATTLE, WA 98101	(245)	684	3292	Jose Angelo Marquez
21	Great Harvester	10 MARKET STREET, SAN DIEGO, CA 92101	(402)	982	2341	Mark Dean Smith
22	More Better Bread	2-B NORTH WYGANDT RD., DES MOINES, IO 50301	(602)	723	2360	Rob Beau Washington
23	My Best Bread, Inc.	209 9TH AVE., BALTIMORE, MD 21201	(263)	988	2086	Richard Benjamin Tiller
24	Very Best Bread	100 CHARLESTON AVENUE, BOISE, ID 83702	(835)	205	0944	Diane Lea Ross
25	Your Whole Bread Store	88 WICKERSHAM LANE, LEXINGTON, KY 40505	(839)	490	2005	Paris Renee Mills

Lesson 16

Using Frozen Labels and Panes

➤ What You Will Learn

Freezing Labels While Scrolling
Splitting a Worksheet into Panes

Software Skills   When working with a large worksheet, you can freeze row and/ or column labels to keep them in view, so that you can always identify your data no matter how far you've scrolled. You also can split the worksheet window into two or four panes, enabling you to view multiple parts of a worksheet at the same time—in order to compare or copy data, for example.

What You Can Do

Freezing Labels While Scrolling

■ When you need to keep labels or titles in view at the top or left edge of the worksheet as you scroll through it, you can **freeze** them in place.

   ✓ Note that freezing rows and columns onscreen does not freeze them in a printout.

■ Position the insertion point in the column to the right or the row below the data to be frozen, and then use the Freeze Panes button 🔳 in the Window group on the VIEW tab of the Ribbon.

■ You can freeze just the column labels, the row labels, or both.

■ Click a cell to specify which rows and columns to freeze. Rows above and columns to the left of the selected cell will be frozen. To freeze only rows, make sure you click a cell in column A. To freeze only columns, click a cell in row 1.

■ You also can instantly freeze either the top row or the first column of the worksheet.

■ Thin lines indicate the borders of the frozen area. You can scroll the area outside of these borders, and the frozen row/column labels will remain in view.

■ To remove the freeze, use the Unfreeze Panes command found on the Freeze Panes drop-down list.

WORDS TO KNOW

Freeze
A method to keep specified rows and columns—usually ones containing labels for data—in view when scrolling through a worksheet.

Panes
Sections or areas in a window that enable you to see different parts of the worksheet at the same time.

Try It! Freezing Labels While Scrolling

1 Start Excel.

2 Open the **E16Try** file from the data files for this lesson.

3 Save the workbook as **E16Try_xx** in the location where your teacher instructs you to store the files for this lesson.

4 Add a header that has your name at the left, the date code in the center, and the page number code at the right, and change back to Normal view.

5 Click cell C4 to select it.

6 Click View > Freeze Panes 🔲 > Freeze Panes.

✓ *Use the Freeze Top Row or Freeze First Column choices to freeze row 1 or column A.*

7 Scroll down and to the right until cell I70 is visible. Notice how rows 1 through 3 and columns A and B remain visible onscreen.

8 On the VIEW tab, click Freeze Panes 🔲 > Unfreeze Panes. The scrolling panes are removed and the worksheet scrolls back up.

9 Save the **E16Try_xx** file, and leave it open to use in the next Try It.

Frozen panes

Splitting a Worksheet into Panes

■ When you need to view different parts of a large worksheet at the same time, possibly at different zoom levels, split the worksheet horizontally or vertically into **panes**.

✓ *Panes also do not affect the appearance of a printout.*

■ To split a worksheet, use the Split button 🔲 in the Window group of the VIEW tab.

■ Click a cell to specify where the panes appear. The pane divider bars appear to the left of and above the selected cell.

■ You also can drag the horizontal or vertical split boxes on the scroll bars to split the window into panes. Use the split box at the top of the vertical ruler to split the window horizontally. Use the split box found at the right end of the horizontal ruler to split the window vertically.

■ When you position the insertion point in a cell in row 1 and use the Split command, the vertical panes scroll together when scrolling up and down, and independently when scrolling left to right.

■ When you position the insertion point in a cell in column A and use the Split command, the horizontal panes scroll together when scrolling left to right, and independently when scrolling up and down.

■ When you need to cancel the split, click the Split button again.

Try It! — Splitting a Worksheet into Panes

1 In the **E16Try_xx** file, click cell C15 to select it.

2 On the VIEW tab, click Split ▭.

3 Drag the vertical divider bar so that column C displays completely in the left pane.

4 In the right pane, scroll right so that columns A through D scroll out of view.

5 In the bottom pane, scroll down until row 60 is visible.

6 Drag the split box on the vertical scroll bar down to just below row 15 to insert a horizontal split at that location.

7 Scroll left so that column A is once again visible.

8 Scroll the bottom pane down until you see the Screener Criteria Conditions in the range A112:B115.

9 Save the **E16Try_xx** file, and close it.

Scrolling panes

	A	B	C	E	F	G	H	I	J
1	Stock Screener								
2									
3	Ticker	Company Name	Last Trade	Mkt Cap	Return On Equity	Return On Assets	Forward PE	Price % change(close)	
4	PTR	PetroChina Company	$ 117.39	211.902B	13.836	7.32	6.9	2.515	
5	BHP	BHP Billiton Limited	$ 70.16	195.185B	22.72	10.275	9.53	3.435	
6	GE	General Electric	$ 16.33	174.294B	9.9	0.949	11.99	2.351	
7	BBL	BHP Billiton plc	$ 59.57	165.724B	22.72	10.275	7.42	3.69	
8	VALE	VALE S.A. America	$ 27.94	145.644B	10.047	4.384	6.56	3.944	
9	LFC	China Life Insura	$ 69.19	130.872B	0	0	28.91	2.717	
10	CEO	CNOOC Limited Com	$ 178.90	79.913B	17.647	11.098	8.29	2.381	
11	SNP	China Petroleum &	$ 82.87	71.848B	18.118	6.928	6.24	2.407	
12	V	Visa Inc.	$ 80.95	67.979B	11.795	7.791	16.39	5.075	
13	ABV	Companhia de Bebi	$ 107.34	66.168B	27.201	13.979	16.9	2.453	
14	WBK	Westpac Banking	$ 105.25	62.034B	11.673	0.694	10.35	2.553	
15	BBD	Banco Bradesco S.A.	$ 17.90	61.225B	21.41	1.654	9.97	2.579	
108									
109									
110									
111									
112	Large Cap Momentum								
113	Screener Criteria Conditions:								
114	Market Cap >=5b								
115	Price % Gain vs. Previous Close >=2								
116									
117									

Lesson 16—Practice

In this project, you will freeze a row label using the skills you learned in this lesson.

DIRECTIONS

1. Start Excel, if necessary, and open the **E16Practice** file from the data files for this lesson.

2. Save the workbook as **E16Practice_xx** in the location where your teacher instructs you to store the files for this lesson.

3. Add a header that has your name at the left, the date code in the center, and the page number code at the right, and change back to **Normal** view.

4. Scroll down to row 33, and make the following cell entries:
   a. **A33**   ZG020
   b. **B33**   Sleeping bag, 20 degrees
   c. **C33**   75
   d. **D33**   3
   e. **E33**   1
   f. **H33**   3

5. Press ⌨CTRL + ⌨HOME .

6. Click cell **A7** to select it.

7. Click **VIEW** > **Freeze Panes** 🔲 > **Freeze Panes**.

8. Scroll down again so that row 34 is visible, and make the following cell entries.

   a. **A34**   ZG030
   b. **B34**   Sleeping bag, 30 degrees
   c. **C34**   70
   d. **D34**   5
   e. **E34**   2
   f. **H34**   8

9. **With your teacher's permission,** print the worksheet. Submit the printout or the file for grading as required.

10. Save and close the file, and exit Excel.

Lesson 16—Apply

You manage the Logan retail store for Voyager Travel Adventures. You've made some updates to your inventory worksheet, and need to use the features that enable you to divide the worksheet into panes so that you can complete your evaluation of current inventory levels for summer outdoor gear.

DIRECTIONS

1. Start Excel, if necessary, and open the **E16Apply** file from the data files for this lesson.

2. Save the workbook as **E16Apply_xx** in the location where your teacher instructs you to store the files for this lesson.

3. Add a header that has your name at the left, the date code in the center, and the page number code at the right. After completing the header, change back to Normal view.

4. Click cell **D20**, and split the window into panes.

5. Scroll down the bottom pane to display the range title *Inventory Evaluation*.

6. In cell **C49**, enter a formula that sums the values in the range **F7:F34**, entering that range in the formula by dragging over it in the upper-right pane.

7. In cell **C50**, enter a formula that sums the Value column entries in the upper-right pane. Adjust the position of the vertical split divider once you enter the formula and widen the column if necessary.

8. In cell **C51**, enter a formula that calculates a carrying cost of 2.5% of the Item Value you just calculated in cell C50.

   ✓ *Hint: Multiply the Item Value by 2.5%.*

9. In cell **C52**, enter a formula that calculates the average of the Current Stock Percentage entries. Your worksheet should resemble Figure 16-1 on the next page.

10. **With your teacher's permission,** print the worksheet. Submit the printout or the file for grading as required.

11. Save and close the file, and exit Excel.

Figure 16-1

	A	B	C	D	E	F	G	H	I	J
15	BS113	Backpacker grill	$ 4.00	5	4	9	$ 36.00	10	90.00%	
16	CK101	Open country mess kit	$ 6.50	4	3	7	$ 45.50	10	70.00%	
17	CK102	Camp cook set	$ 50.00	2	1	3	$ 150.00	4	75.00%	
18	FL103	Emergency tinder	$ 1.50	9	7	16	$ 24.00	15	106.67%	
19	FL104	Fire paste	$ 2.00	12	6	18	$ 36.00	24	75.00%	
20	FL105	Liquid fuel, 1 gal.	$ 3.00	18	15	33	$ 99.00	36	91.67%	
21	FL108	Canister fuel, 170 g	$ 2.00	20	5	25	$ 50.00	36	69.44%	
22	FL109	Canister fuel, 300 g	$ 2.50	21	13	34	$ 85.00	36	94.44%	
23	WJ101	Water carrier, 2L	$ 9.00	10	2	12	$ 108.00	15	80.00%	
24	WJ102	Water carrier, 32 oz	$ 4.50	12	6	18	$ 81.00	24	75.00%	
25	WJ103	Water carrier, 48 oz.	$ 5.00	3	15	18	$ 90.00	24	75.00%	
26	WJ104	Dromedary, 6L	$ 15.00	6	6	12	$ 180.00	15	80.00%	
27	WJ105	Water bag, 4L	$ 10.00	10	2	12	$ 120.00	15	80.00%	
28	WT101	Water purifier, portable	$ 80.00	15	5	20	$ 1,600.00	20	100.00%	
29	WT103	Water purifier, camp	$ 25.00	12	0	12	$ 300.00	12	100.00%	
30	ZG005	Day pack, light	$ 35.00	3	1	4	$ 140.00	5	80.00%	
31	ZG009	Rugged pack, frameless	$ 55.00	2	2	4	$ 220.00	3	133.33%	
32	ZG010	Rugged pack, light frame	$ 65.00	2	1	3	$ 195.00	3	100.00%	
33	ZG020	Sleeping bag, 20 degrees	$ 75.00	3	1	4	$ 300.00	3	133.33%	
34	ZG030	Sleeping bag, 30 degrees	$ 70.00	5	2	7	$ 490.00	8	87.50%	
35										
36										
41										
42										
43										
44										
45										
46										
47										
48	Inventory Evaluation									
49	Items in Stock		297							
50	Item Value		$5,308.00							
51	Carrying Cost		$ 132.70							
52	Average Inventory Level		86.87%							
53										
54										

Lesson 17

Using Conditional Formatting and Find and Replace

> ## What You Will Learn

Applying Conditional Formatting
Using Find and Replace

WORDS TO KNOW

Color scales
A type of conditional formatting that applies a background fill color that varies depending on the relative value stored in each of the formatted cells.

Conditional formatting
Variable formatting that changes the formatting applied based on the contents of the cells in the formatting range.

Data bars
A type of conditional formatting that creates filled background bars reflecting the relative value stored in each of the formatted cells.

Highlight cells rules
A method of applying conditional formatting based on how cell contents compare with a specified criterion, such as a Less Than comparison.

Software Skills   Conditional formatting is a volatile type of formatting that changes depending on what the values or calculated results in the cells are. This type of formatting enables you to identify key data, and it updates automatically if you update worksheet values and formulas. The Find and Replace function in Excel works just like it does in Word, enabling you to update text information by changing spellings and words globally. You learn to use both of these features in this lesson.

What You Can Do

Applying Conditional Formatting

- When you want cells to have different formatting depending on their contents, you can apply **conditional formatting**.

- Excel 2013 offers more forms of conditional formatting than its predecessors. You can now apply these types of conditional formatting to a cell or range:

  - Use **highlight cells rules** to apply specified formatting to cells only when the contents meet a certain rule or criterion, such as being greater than 100 or text that contains a particular phrase.

  - To format the cells holding the highest or lowest values in a range, use **top/ bottom rules** conditional formatting. You can find the top or bottom 10 items or top or bottom 10%, or format values that are above or below average.

  - The **data bars** conditional formatting method creates a colored horizontal bar in every cell. The length of the colored bars varies according to the values in the cells, basically creating a chart of the data right within the range holding the values.

- Use the **color scales** type of conditional formatting when you want to apply different cell fill colors depending on the values in the cells.

- If you prefer graphical indicators of the relative values in cells, use **icon sets** conditional formatting. You can choose variations from four different types of icons, including ones that indicate ratings.

■ To apply conditional formatting to a selected range, click the Conditional Formatting button in the Styles group of the HOME tab. Click an overall conditional formatting type from the menu that appears, and then choose the specific type of conditional formatting to apply.

■ You can create a custom conditional format using the New Rule command, clear conditional formatting using the Clear Rules command, or edit a conditional format with the Manage Rules choice.

■ You also can apply conditional formatting using the Quick Analysis Lens. When you select a range of cells, the **Quick Analysis Lens** button appears to the bottom right of your data.

■ The formatting options available in the Quick Analysis Lens will change based on the type of data you select.

■ You also can use the Quick Analysis Lens to clear the format of cells.

✓ *You will learn more about the Quick Analysis Lens in Chapter 4.*

Icon sets
A type of conditional formatting that includes one of a set of icons reflecting the relative value stored in each of the formatted cells.

Quick Analysis Lens
A tool that provides formatting for data analysis.

Top/Bottom rules
Conditional formatting rules that format the highest or lowest values in the formatted range, or those that are above or below average.

Try It!   Applying Conditional Formatting

1. Start Excel.
2. Open the **E17Try** file from the data files for this lesson.
3. Save the workbook as **E17Try_xx** in the location where your teacher instructs you to store the files for this lesson.
4. Add a header that has your name at the left, the date code in the center, and the page number code at the right, and change back to Normal view.
5. Select the range with Q1 sales data, excluding the column titles.

   ✓ *The worksheet has predefined names for each of the ranges with quarterly sales (SalesQ1 through SalesQ4) and the average data (Average).*

6. On the HOME tab, click Conditional Formatting > Highlight Cell Rules > Greater Than.

7. In the Greater Than dialog box, change the suggested value to 3000. Open the with drop-down list and click Green Fill with Dark Green Text. Click OK.
8. Select the range with Q2 sales data.
9. Click the Quick Analysis Lens button > Data Bars.
10. Click the Quick Analysis Lens button > Clear Format.
11. Click Conditional Formatting > Top/Bottom Rules > Bottom 10 Items.
12. In the Bottom 10 Items dialog box, change the suggested value to 5. Click OK.
13. Select the range with Q3 sales data.
14. Click Conditional Formatting > Data Bars > Gradient Fill > Orange Data Bar.

(continued)

Try It! **Applying Conditional Formatting** *(continued)*

15 Select the range with Q4 sales data.

16 Click Conditional Formatting > Color Scales > Green-Yellow-Red Color Scale. (It's the first choice in the first row.)

17 Select the range with Average sales data.

18 Click Conditional Formatting > Icon Sets > Ratings > 3 Stars.

19 Reselect the range with the Q2 sales data.

20 Click Conditional Formatting > Manage Rules.

21 In the Conditional Formatting Rules Manager dialog box, click the Edit Rule button.

22 Under Edit the Rule Description, change the entry in the center text box to **15** and click the % of the selected range check box to check it, then click OK.

23 Click OK in the Conditional Formatting Rules Manager dialog box.

24 Save the **E17Try_xx** file, and leave it open to use in the next Try It.

Applying conditional formatting

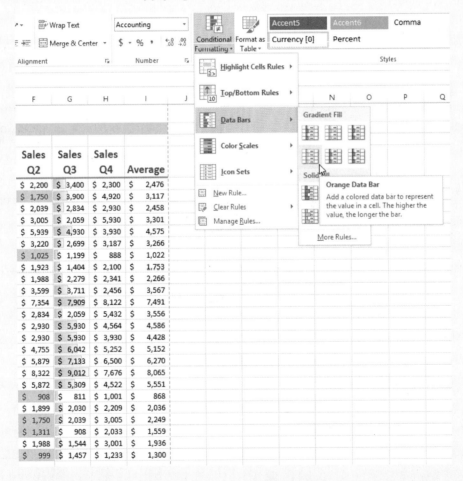

Using Find and Replace

- Similar to the Find and Replace feature used in Word 2013, Excel also offers Find and Replace, and you can use it to replace all or part of a cell entry.
- To open the Find and Replace dialog box, click HOME > Find & Select 🔍 > Replace.

- Enter the Find what and Replace with entries. Then, either use the Find Next and Replace buttons to replace selected entries, or Replace All to replace all entries.
- Click the Options button in the Find and Replace dialog box to display additional choices, such as the ability to find and replace formatting or search the entire workbook rather than just the current sheet.

Try It! **Using Find and Replace**

1 In the **E17Try_xx** file, select cell A1.

✓ As for a spell check, it's a good practice to start a find and replace from the top of the sheet.

2 On the HOME tab, click Find & Select 🔍 > Replace.

3 Type **Mens** in the Find what text box, press TAB, and type **M**.

4 Click the Options button to display all the options, and click the Match entire cell contents check box to check it.

5 Click the Replace All button, then click OK in the dialog box informing you that Excel made 12 replacements. Note that a number of entries in column B are replaced.

6 Change the Find what and Replace with entries to **Womens** and **W**, respectively, click the Replace All button, and click OK.

7 Change the Find What to **White** and Replace with to **Ivory**.

8 Click the Find Next button seven times to skip the first six instances of White in column D, rows 5 through 10.

9 Click the Replace button six times to replace the second six instances of White in rows 11 through 16.

10 Click the Match entire cell contents check box to clear it, and then click the Close button to close the Find and Replace dialog box.

11 Save the **E17Try_xx** file, and close it.

Lesson 17—Practice

In this project, you will find and replace terms in the worksheet using the skills you learned in this lesson.

DIRECTIONS

1. Start Excel, if necessary, and open the **E17Practice** file from the data files for this lesson.
2. Save the workbook as **E17Practice_xx** in the location where your teacher instructs you to store the files for this lesson.
3. Add a header that has your name at the left, the date code in the center, and the page number code at the right, and change back to **Normal** view.

4. On the HOME tab, click **Find & Select** 🔍 > **Replace**.
5. Type **Operations** in the **Find what** text box, and press TAB.
6. Type **Operating** in the **Replace with** box, and click the **Find Next** button.
7. Click **Replace** to replace the first match in cell A15.
8. Click in the worksheet, and press CTRL + HOME to return to cell A1.

9. Select the existing entry in the **Find what** text box in the Find and Replace dialog box, type **Expensives**, and press TAB.

10. Type **Expenses** in the **Replace with** box.

11. Click the **Replace All** button, and then click **OK** in the message box.

12. Click **OK** to confirm that Excel made two replacements.

13. Click the **Close** button to close the Find and Replace dialog box.

14. **With your teacher's permission,** print the worksheet. Submit the printout or the file for grading as required.

15. Save and close the file, and exit Excel.

Lesson 17—Apply

You are the CFO for Telson Tech, a small manufacturer of custom circuit boards. You are finalizing a Profit & Loss statement that compares this year's sales, expenses, and profit information with data from last year. You will use Find and Replace to fix some text errors, and then use conditional formatting to help evaluate the financial performance of your company.

DIRECTIONS

1. Start Excel, if necessary, and open the **E17Apply** file from the data files for this lesson.

2. Save the workbook as **E17Apply_xx** in the location where your teacher instructs you to store the files for this lesson.

3. Add a header that has your name at the left, the date code in the center, and the page number code at the right, and change back to **Normal** view.

4. Select the following noncontiguous cells and ranges (using the CTRL key):
   a. **D11**
   b. **D13:E13**
   c. **D21:E21**
   d. **D23:E23**
   e. **D27:E27**

5. Apply the **Green-White Color Scale** conditional format to the selection.

   ✓ *This formatting will apply deeper green shades to the revenue and profit items that have improved the most.*

6. Select the following noncontiguous cells and ranges:
   a. **D12 :E12**
   b. **D16:E19**
   c. **D25:E25**

7. Apply the **Red-White Color Scale** conditional format to the selection.

   ✓ *This formatting will apply deeper red shades to the expense items that have worsened (increased) the most.*

8. Select cell **B5**. Apply a highlight cell rules conditional format that changes the cell formatting to a Light Red Fill if the margin fell below 50%.

9. Select cell **B6**. Apply a highlight cell rules conditional format that changes the cell formatting to a Green Fill with Dark Green Text if the return exceeds 10%.

10. **With your teacher's permission,** print the worksheet. Submit the printout or the file for grading as required.

11. Save and close the file, and exit Excel.

Lesson 18

Rotating Entries and Resolving Errors

➤ What You Will Learn

Rotating Cell Entries
Resolving a #### Error Message

Software Skills   Rotating cell entries provides another choice you can use to better organize worksheet data and make it more attractive. One formatting problem—having columns that are two narrow—produces an #### error message. In this lesson, you learn how to apply rotation and how to fix column width errors.

WORDS TO KNOW

Rotate
To change the angle of the contents of a cell.

What You Can Do

Rotating Cell Entries

■ You can **rotate** the entry in a cell to change the angle of the entry.

■ The Orientation button ✸ in the Alignment group of the HOME tab offers five preset rotation choices.

  • Angle Counterclockwise: 45 degrees, right end angled up.

  • Angle Clockwise: -45 degrees, left end angled up.

  • Vertical Text: Does not rotate the letters, but stacks them top to bottom.

  • Rotate Text Up: 90 degrees, right end up.

  • Rotate Text Down: -90 degrees, left end up.

■ You also can specify a custom rotation in the Orientation area on the Alignment tab in the Format Cells dialog box. The Format Cell Alignment command at the bottom of the Orientation menu is another way to display that dialog box.

■ You can use rotation in conjunction with other formatting methods, such as cell merging.

Try It! Rotating Cell Entries

1 Start Excel.

2 Open the **E18Try** file from the data files for this lesson.

3 Save the workbook as **E18Try_xx** in the location where your teacher instructs you to store the files for this lesson.

4 Add a header that has your name at the left, the date code in the center, and the page number code at the right, and change back to Normal view.

5 Drag over the range A5:A10 to select it.

6 On the HOME tab, click the Merge & Center drop-down arrow ⊞ Merge & Center ▾ > Merge Cells.

7 On the HOME tab, click the Orientation ≫ > Angle Counterclockwise.

8 Repeat the techniques in steps 6 and 7 to merge and rotate the following ranges:
A11:A16
A17:A22
A23:A28

9 Double-click the right border of the column A column header to AutoFit the column width to the rotated values.

10 On the HOME tab, click the Border drop-down arrow ⊞ > Bottom Border to apply bottom borders to these ranges:
A10:I10
A16:I16
A22:I22
A28:I28

11 Save the **E18Try_xx** file, and leave it open to use in the next Try It.

Rotating a cell entry

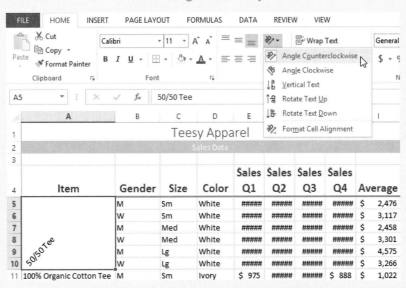

Resolving a #### Error Message

■ If a column is too narrow to display a value, formula result, or date entry in a cell, the cell will fill with pound signs (#).

■ You can correct this error by using any technique to increase the column width until all #### errors disappear from the column.

Try It!   **Resolving a #### Error Message**

1   In the **E18Try_xx** file, double-click the right border of the column E column header to resize the column. All #### errors should disappear from the column.

2   Drag over the column headers for columns F through H to select those columns.

3   On the HOME tab, click Format 🖼 > AutoFit Column Width. All #### errors should disappear from the selected columns.

4   Save the **E18Try_xx** file, and close it.

Lesson 18—Practice

In this project, you will fix column widths using the skills you learned in this lesson.

DIRECTIONS

1. Start Excel, if necessary, and open the **E18Practice** file from the data files for this lesson.

2. Save the workbook as **E18Practice_xx** in the location where your teacher instructs you to store the files for this lesson.

3. Add a header that has your name at the left, the date code in the center, and the page number code at the right, and change back to **Normal** view.

4. Click the column **E** column header.

5. On the **HOME** tab, click **Format** 🖼 > **AutoFit Column Width**.

6. Drag over the column headers for columns **I** and **J** to select them.

7. Double-click the right border of the column **I** column header. Your worksheet should look like Figure 18-1.

8. **With your teacher's permission,** print the worksheet. Submit the printout or the file for grading as required.

9. Save and close the file, and exit Excel.

Figure 18-1

Whole Grains Bread

	A	B	C	D	E	F	G	H	I	J	K
1	Whole Grains Bread										
2	Home Office Payroll										
3											
4	Salaried Employees										
5	Employee Name	Employee ID	Rate		Regular Hours	Gross Pay	Fed Tax	SS Tax	State Tax	Net Pay	
6	Anthony Splendoria	38748	$ 2,175.00		40.00	$2,175.00	$ 543.75	$ 169.65	$ 65.25	$1,396.35	
7	Eileen Costello	21544	$ 1,895.00		40.00	$1,895.00	$ 473.75	$ 147.81	$ 56.85	$1,216.59	
8	Carol Chen	38448	$ 895.00		40.00	$ 895.00	$ 223.75	$ 69.81	$ 26.85	$ 574.59	
9	Marty Gonzales	61522	$ 684.00		40.00	$ 684.00	$ 171.00	$ 53.35	$ 20.52	$ 439.13	
10	Maria Nachez	34789	$ 1,665.00		40.00	$1,665.00	$ 416.25	$ 129.87	$ 49.95	$1,068.93	
11	Mika Gritada	22785	$ 1,023.00		40.00	$1,023.00	$ 255.75	$ 79.79	$ 30.69	$ 656.77	
12	Vickie Helms	31851	$ 765.00		40.00	$ 765.00	$ 191.25	$ 59.67	$ 22.95	$ 491.13	
13	Randall Lohr	38514	$ 1,545.00		40.00	$1,545.00	$ 386.25	$ 120.51	$ 46.35	$ 991.89	
14	Abe Rittenhouse	22854	$ 1,231.00		40.00	$1,231.00	$ 307.75	$ 96.02	$ 36.93	$ 790.30	
15											
16	Hourly Employees										
17	Employee Name	Employee ID	Rate		Regular Hours	Overtime Hours	Gross Pay	Fed Tax	SS Tax	State Tax	Net Pay
18	Thomas Cortese	21875	$ 8.25		40.00	2.00	$ 354.75	$ 53.21	$ 27.67	$ 10.64	$263.22
19	Javier Cortez	21154	$ 7.75		40.00	3.00	$ 344.88	$ 51.73	$ 26.90	$ 10.35	$255.90
20	Allen Gaines	23455	$ 7.25		40.00	6.00	$ 355.25	$ 53.29	$ 27.71	$ 10.66	$263.60
21	Freda Gage	27855	$ 8.00		40.00	3.00	$ 356.00	$ 53.40	$ 27.77	$ 10.68	$264.15
22	Isiah Herron	33252	$ 10.95		40.00	5.50	$ 528.34	$ 79.25	$ 41.21	$ 15.85	$392.03
23	Thomas Kaminski	37881	$ 9.75		40.00	4.00	$ 448.50	$ 67.28	$ 34.98	$ 13.46	$332.79
24	Chris Nakao	29958	$ 11.25		40.00	3.00	$ 500.63	$ 75.09	$ 39.05	$ 15.02	$371.46
25											

Lesson 18—Apply

You are the Payroll Manager at Whole Grains Bread. Your assistant worked on a version of the payroll worksheet and introduced errors in the column formatting, so you need to make corrections. You also want to use rotated cell entries to improve worksheet formatting.

DIRECTIONS

1. Start Excel, if necessary, and open the **E18Apply** file from the data files for this lesson.

2. Save the workbook as **E18Apply_xx** in the location where your teacher instructs you to store the files for this lesson.

3. Add a header that has your name at the left, the date code in the center, and the page number code at the right, and change back to **Normal** view.

4. Select rows 4 and 16 (at the same time), and delete them from the sheet.

5. Insert a new column A, and move the entries in cells **B1:B2** left to **A1:A2**.

6. Select the range **A5:A13**, and merge it into one cell.

7. Enter **Salaried** in the merged cell A5, apply the **Accent1** cell style, and increase the text size to **24**.

8. Change the Orientation for the merged cell A5 to **Rotate Text Up**. Apply Middle and Center alignment.

9. Repeat the techniques used in steps 6 through 8 to merge **A16:A22** and create a rotated label that says **Hourly** to match the salaried label formatting.

10. Select column **F** and double-click its right column border to AutoFit the column width. Your worksheet should look like Figure 18-2.

11. **With your teacher's permission,** print the worksheet. Submit the printout or the file for grading as required.

12. Save and close the file, and exit Excel.

Figure 18-2

	A	B	C	D	E	F	G	H	I	J	K	L
1	Whole Grains Bread											
2	Home Office Payroll											
3												
4		Employee Name	Employee ID	Rate		Regular Hours	Gross Pay	Fed Tax	SS Tax	State Tax	Net Pay	
5	Salaried	Anthony Splendoria	38748	$ 2,175.00		40.00	$ 2,175.00	$ 543.75	$ 169.65	$ 65.25	$ 1,396.35	
6		Eileen Costello	21544	$ 1,895.00		40.00	$ 1,895.00	$ 473.75	$ 147.81	$ 56.85	$ 1,216.59	
7		Carol Chen	38448	$ 895.00		40.00	$ 895.00	$ 223.75	$ 69.81	$ 26.85	$ 574.59	
8		Marty Gonzales	61522	$ 684.00		40.00	$ 684.00	$ 171.00	$ 53.35	$ 20.52	$ 439.13	
9		Maria Nachez	34789	$ 1,665.00		40.00	$ 1,665.00	$ 416.25	$ 129.87	$ 49.95	$ 1,068.93	
10		Mika Gritada	22785	$ 1,023.00		40.00	$ 1,023.00	$ 255.75	$ 79.79	$ 30.69	$ 656.77	
11		Vickie Helms	31851	$ 765.00		40.00	$ 765.00	$ 191.25	$ 59.67	$ 22.95	$ 491.13	
12		Randall Lohr	38514	$ 1,545.00		40.00	$ 1,545.00	$ 386.25	$ 120.51	$ 46.35	$ 991.89	
13		Abe Rittenhouse	22854	$ 1,231.00		40.00	$ 1,231.00	$ 307.75	$ 96.02	$ 36.93	$ 790.30	
14												

	A	B	C	D	E	F	G	H	I	J	K	L
15		Employee Name	Employee ID	Rate		Regular Hours	Overtime Hours	Gross Pay	Fed Tax	SS Tax	State Tax	Net Pay
16	Hourly	Thomas Cortese	21875	$ 8.25		40.00	2.00	$ 354.75	$ 53.21	$ 27.67	$ 10.64	$ 263.22
17		Javier Cortez	21154	$ 7.75		40.00	3.00	$ 344.88	$ 51.73	$ 26.90	$ 10.35	$ 255.90
18		Allen Gaines	23455	$ 7.25		40.00	6.00	$ 355.25	$ 53.29	$ 27.71	$ 10.66	$ 263.60
19		Freda Gage	27855	$ 8.00		40.00	3.00	$ 356.00	$ 53.40	$ 27.77	$ 10.68	$ 264.15
20		Isiah Herron	33252	$ 10.95		40.00	5.50	$ 528.34	$ 79.25	$ 41.21	$ 15.85	$ 392.03
21		Thomas Kaminski	37881	$ 9.75		40.00	4.00	$ 448.50	$ 67.28	$ 34.98	$ 13.46	$ 332.79
22		Chris Nakao	29958	$ 11.25		40.00	3.00	$ 500.63	$ 75.09	$ 39.05	$ 15.02	$ 371.46
23												
24												

Lesson 19

Managing Worksheets and Performing Multi-Worksheet Operations

➤ What You Will Learn

Inserting, Deleting, Copying, Moving, and Renaming Worksheets
Changing the Color of a Worksheet Tab
Hiding Sheets
Grouping Worksheets for Editing and Formatting
Creating a Summary Worksheet
Updating a Summary Worksheet

Software Skills Use workbook sheets to divide and present data in logical chunks. For example, rather than placing an entire year's sales on one sheet, create a sales sheet for each month. You can add, delete, move, and rename sheets as needed. You can group sheets to work on them simultaneously, such as applying the same formatting to all the selected sheets. You also can combine data from different worksheets to perform summary calculations. When you do this, you can still change data on the individual worksheets. Excel recalculates the summary formula results to reflect the changes.

What You Can Do

Inserting, Deleting, Copying, Moving, and Renaming Worksheets

■ The sheet tab displays the name of the sheet. The **active sheet tab** name appears in bold.

■ You can add or delete worksheets as needed, using the Insert ⊞ and Delete ⊠ drop-down lists in the Cells group of the HOME tab. You also can use the Insert Worksheet tab ⊕ that appears to the right of the right-most sheet in the workbook.

■ You also can right-click a sheet tab to display a shortcut menu that allows you to insert, delete, rename, move, and copy worksheets.

WORDS TO KNOW

Active sheet tab
The selected worksheet; the tab name of an active sheet is bold.

Grouping
Worksheets that are selected as a unit; any action performed on this unit will affect all the worksheets in the group.

■ You do not need to delete unused sheets from a workbook, since they do not take up much room in the file; however, if you plan on sharing the file, you may want to remove unused sheets to create a more professional look.

■ When you copy a worksheet, you copy all of its data and formatting. However, changes you later make to the copied sheet do not affect the original sheet.

■ Moving sheets enables you to place them in a logical order within the workbook.

■ Renaming sheets make it easier to keep track of the data on individual sheets.

Try It!   Inserting, Deleting, Copying, Moving, and Renaming Worksheets

1 Start Excel.

2 Open the **E19TryA** file from the data files for this lesson.

3 Save the workbook as **E19TryA_xx** in the location where your teacher instructs you to store the files for this lesson.

4 Add a header that has your name at the left, the date code in the center, and the page number code at the right, and change back to Normal view.

5 Click the Insert Worksheet tab ⊕ to insert a new, blank sheet named Sheet2.

6 Click Sheet1, and then click Sheet2.

7 On the HOME tab, click Delete drop-down arrow ⬚ > Delete Sheet. Excel removes the new sheet from the workbook.

8 Right-click the Sheet1 tab and click Rename.

9 Type **2012**, and press [ENTER].

10 Right-click the 2012 sheet tab, and click Move or Copy.

11 In the Move or Copy dialog box, click (move to end) in the Before sheet list, click the Create a copy check box to check it, and click OK. The new sheet appears, with the name 2012 (2).

12 Double-click the name on the new sheet tab, type **2013**, and press [ENTER].

Shortcut menu with commands for working with sheets

13 Select the 2012 sheet. Drag it to the right of the 2013 sheet tab. As you drag, the mouse pointer includes a page and a black triangle shows you the move location. When you release the mouse button, the sheet moves into that new position.

14 Create a copy of the 2012 sheet, name the copy **2014**, and move it to the far left to make it the first sheet.

15 Save the **E19TryA_xx** file, and leave it open to use in the next Try It.

Changing the Color of a Worksheet Tab

- Change the color of a worksheet's tab to further distinguish sheets with different types of data.

- Choosing a tab color from the current theme colors enables you to maintain a color-coordinated look. If you change themes, the colors in the worksheet and the colors of your tabs will change to those in the new theme.

- If you change the color of a sheet tab, that color appears when the tab is not selected.

- When a colored sheet tab is clicked, its color changes to white, with a small line of its original color at the bottom of the tab. For example, an orange sheet tab changes to white with a thin orange line at the bottom.

Try It! Changing the Color of a Worksheet Tab

1 In the **E19TryA_xx** file, right-click the 2014 sheet tab, point to Tab Color, and click the Green, Accent 6 color in the top row.

2 Right-click the 2013 sheet tab, point to Tab Color, and click the Blue, Accent 1 color in the top row.

3 Right-click the 2012 sheet tab, point to Tab Color, and click the Orange, Accent 2 color in the top row.

4 Save the **E19TryA_xx** file, and leave it open to use in the next Try It.

Hiding Sheets

- Hide a worksheet temporarily when you need to put sensitive data out of sight.

- Hiding a sheet simply hides its sheet tab from view.

- Access the Hide & Unhide feature by clicking Format in the Cells group on the HOME tab. The Hide & Unhide submenu is in the Visibility group.

- The Hide & Unhide submenu includes the Hide Sheet and Unhide Sheet commands. You also can right-click the sheet tab and use the Hide and Unhide commands.

- Hiding provides a simple layer of protection, but does not provide any real security for confidential data because the Unhide commands become active whenever a sheet is hidden.

- If you rename your worksheets and hide the ones you don't want seen, it's difficult for a user to detect that a sheet is hidden because the sheet names are no longer sequential.

Try It! Hiding Sheets

1 In the **E19TryA_xx** file, click the 2013 sheet tab to select it.

2 On the HOME tab, in the Cells group, click Format ⊞ > Hide & Unhide > Hide Sheet.

3 Right-click the 2012 sheet tab, and click Hide.

4 On the HOME tab, click Format ⊞ > Hide & Unhide > Unhide Sheet.

5 Select 2013 in the Unhide sheet list of the Unhide dialog box, and click OK.

6 Save the **E19TryA_xx** file, and leave it open to use in the next Try It.

Grouping Worksheets for Editing and Formatting

■ If you want to work on several worksheets simultaneously, select multiple worksheets and create a **grouping**.

■ Grouped sheet tabs appear white when selected, the name of the active sheet tab appears in bold, and [Group] appears in the title bar.

■ To group adjacent sheets, click the first sheet tab and SHIFT + click on the last one. Or, CTRL + click to select nonadjacent sheets.

■ When you select a grouping, any editing, formatting, or new entries you make to the active sheet are simultaneously made to all the sheets in the group.

■ For example, you can select a group of sheets and format, move, copy, or delete them in one step. You can also add, delete, change, or format the same entries into the same cells on every selected worksheet.

■ Remember to deselect the grouping when you no longer want to make changes to all the sheets in the group. Right-click one of the selected sheet tabs, and click Ungroup Sheets.

Try It!   Grouping Worksheets for Editing and Formatting

1. In the **E19TryA_xx** file, click the 2014 sheet tab, and then SHIFT + click the 2013 sheet tab.

2. Select the range E5:H28.

3. On the HOME tab, click Clear ✐ Clear ▾ > Clear Contents.

4. Select cell A2.

5. On the HOME tab, in the Styles group, click Accent2.

6. Right-click the 2014 sheet tab, and click Ungroup Sheets.

7. Click the 2013 sheet tab. The changes you made appear on this tab as well as the 2014 tab.

8. Save the **E19TryA_xx** file, and close it.

Creating a Summary Worksheet

■ A formula on one worksheet can refer to cells in another worksheet in the same workbook file.

✓ Formulas also can refer to cells in other workbook files.

■ As when using a named range for another sheet, a reference to a cell on another sheet includes the sheet name and an exclamation point, as in Income!E9.

✓ Lesson 13 covered using named ranges.

■ You can type in references to cells on another sheet, or to save time, enter the reference by pointing (clicking the sheet tab and then clicking the cell to enter in the formula).

Try It!   Creating a Summary Worksheet Using Reference Formulas

1. Start Excel, if necessary.

2. Open the **E19TryB** file from the data files for this lesson.

3. Save the workbook as **E19TryB_xx** in the location where your teacher instructs you to store the files for this lesson.

4. Click the Qtr 1 sheet tab, and then SHIFT +click the Summary sheet tab to group the sheets. (You are grouping the sheets to apply the header to all three sheets.)

5. Add a header that has your name at the left, the date code in the center, and the sheet name code at the right, and change back to Normal view.

(continued)

Try It!   **Creating a Summary Worksheet Using Reference Formulas** *(continued)*

6 Right-click the Summary sheet tab, and click Ungroup Sheets.

7 Click cell B5 on the Summary sheet.

8 Type **=sum(**, click the Qtr 1 sheet tab, click cell B5 on that sheet, and type a , (comma).

9 Click the Qtr 2 sheet tab, click cell B5 on that sheet, press CTRL + ENTER .

10 Fill the formula down through cell B10.

11 Click cell C5 in the Summary sheet.

12 Type **=sum(**, click the Qtr 1 sheet tab, click cell D5 on that sheet, and type a , (comma).

✓ *If a Formula AutoComplete tip appears in the way, you can drag it to another location before clicking cell D5.*

13 Click the Qtr 2 sheet tab, click cell D5 on that sheet, and press CTRL + ENTER .

Formula referencing other sheets

Sheet names

B5	▼	:	×	✓	f_x	=SUM('Qtr 1'!B5,'Qtr 2'!B5)

◢	A	B	C	D	E	F
1		Expense Analysis				
2						
3	Summary					
4	Salesperson	Total Expenses	Expense per Account			
5	Jones	$ 7,000				

14 Fill the formula down through cell C10, and apply the Currency with zero decimal place cell style to the selected range.

15 Save the **E19TryB_xx** file, and leave it open to use in the next Try It.

Updating a Summary Worksheet

■ Formulas that summarize or perform calculations using data from other sheets work just like regular formulas.

■ Just change entries on the referenced sheets as desired, and formulas on the summary sheet will recalculate results accordingly.

Try It!   **Updating a Summary Worksheet**

1 In the **E19TryB_xx** file, review the data calculated on the Summary sheet. For example, the totals for Thomas are $13,198 and $3,300, respectively.

2 Click the Qtr 2 sheet tab.

3 Change the entries in the range B5:B10 to these values:
4250
3300
4599
6654
4952
7300

4 Click the Summary sheet tab, and review its data again. Now the totals for Thomas are $11,198 and $2,800.

5 Save the **E19TryB_xx** file, and close it.

Lesson 19—Practice

In this project, you will insert and copy worksheets, and color and rename tabs, using the skills you learned in this lesson.

DIRECTIONS

1. Start Excel, if necessary, and open the **E19Practice** file from the data files for this lesson.

2. Save the workbook as **E19Practice_xx** in the location where your teacher instructs you to store the files for this lesson.

3. Add a header that has your name at the left, the date code in the center, and the sheet name code at the right, and change back to **Normal** view.

4. Click the **Insert Worksheet** button to the right of the Monday sheet tab. A blank Sheet1 appears.

5. Right-click the tab for the new sheet, and click **Rename**. Type **Notes**, and press ENTER .

6. Right-click the **Monday** sheet tab, and click **Move or Copy**.

7. In the Move or Copy dialog box, click **(move to end)**, click the **Create a copy** check box to check it, and click **OK**.

8. Double-click the new sheet tab, type **Tuesday**, and press ENTER .

9. Right-click the new sheet tab, point to **Tab Color**, and click **Orange, Accent 2, Lighter 40%**.

10. Repeat steps 6 to 9 to create another copy of the Monday sheet, naming the copy **Wednesday** and assigning the **Green, Accent 6, Lighter 40%** color to the sheet tab.

11. Drag the **Notes** sheet tab to the far right of the other tabs, and reselect the **Monday** sheet. The tabs should now appear as shown in Figure 19-1.

12. **With your teacher's permission,** print the **Monday** worksheet. Submit the printout or the file for grading as required.

13. Save and close the file, and exit Excel.

Figure 19-1

Lesson 19—Apply

As the Manager of Spa Services at Serenity Health Club, you are reviewing the popularity of four services provided by a particular group of associates. You've developed a worksheet to total the invoiced amounts for these services on a daily basis. You've created the first day's sheet, and need to copy and update it for additional days of the week. You also want to create a summary worksheet.

DIRECTIONS

1. Start Excel, if necessary, and open the **E19Apply** file from the data files for this lesson.

2. Save the workbook as **E19Apply_xx** in the location where your teacher instructs you to store the files for this lesson.

3. On each sheet, add a header that has your name at the left, the date code in the center, and the sheet name code at the right, and change back to **Normal** view.

4. Group the **Monday, Tuesday, Wednesday,** and **Summary** sheets.

5. Increase the font size in cell **A3** to **14**.

6. Select **row 11**, wrap the text, apply bold, and align the text to the center.

7. Adjust column widths as needed.

8. Change the entry in cell **C7** to **65**.

9. Ungroup the sheets. Make sure that your changes have been applied to all four sheets.

10. In cell **C6** on the **Summary** sheet, enter a formula that averages cell C6 on the **Monday**, **Tuesday**, and **Wednesday** tabs, and press `CTRL` + `ENTER`. Your workbook should look like Figure 19-2.

11. **With your teacher's permission,** print one of the worksheets. Submit the printout or the file for grading as required.

12. Save and close the file, and exit Excel.

Figure 19-2

	A	B	C	D	E	F	G	H	I	J	K	L	M	N
1														
2	Serenity Health Club													
3	Services Tracking													
4	Date:													
5														
6		Massage	$75											
7		Herbal Wrap	$65											
8		Facial	$75											
9		Revitalizer	$175											
10														
11	Client Name	Member #	M	HW	F	R	Massage	Herbal Wrap	Facial	Revital-izer	Invoice Total			
12									0	0	0	0		
13								0	0	0	0	0		
14								0	0	0	0	0		
15								0	0	0	0	0		
16								0	0	0	0	0		
17								0	0	0	0	0		
18								0	0	0	0	0		
19								0	0	0	0	0		
20								0	0	0	0	0		
21								0	0	0	0	0		
22								0	0	0	0	0		
23								0	0	0	0	0		
24								0	0	0	0	0		
25								0	0	0	0	0		
26								0	0	0	0	0		
27								0	0	0	0	0		
28								0	0	0	0	0		
29								0	0	0	0	0		
30								0	0	0	0	0		
31								0	0	0	0	0		
32								0	0	0	0	0		
33								0	0	0	0	0		
34								0	0	0	0	0		
35								0	0	0	0	0		
36								0	0	0	0	0		
37	Totals							0	0	0	0	0		

Monday | Tuesday | Wednesday | **Summary** | ⊕

Lesson 20

Modifying Print Options

➤ What You Will Learn

Printing a Selection
Printing All the Worksheets in a Workbook
Inserting Page Breaks
Using the Page Break Preview
Setting the Print Area
Repeating Row and Column Labels
Selecting Other Sheet Tab Options

WORDS TO KNOW

Gridlines
Light gray lines that mark the cell borders.

Page break
A code inserted in a document that forces what follows to begin on a new page; a page break is represented on your screen as a dashed line in the worksheet.

Page Break Preview
A view that allows you to move and delete page breaks and redefine the print area.

Print area
The specified range of cells to be printed.

Print titles
Row and column labels that are reprinted on each page of a worksheet printout.

Software Skills   Excel gives you great flexibility in printing. If you need to print only part of a worksheet, you can select and print a specific area. Or, if you need to print all worksheets in a workbook to share comprehensive information, you can do so. If you are not satisfied with Excel's default page layout settings, you can change them manually. For example, if a worksheet doesn't fit on one page, Excel automatically sets page breaks for you. These page breaks indicate where a new page will start when printing. If you prefer, you can manually set your own page breaks before printing. If you need to print only part of a worksheet, you can temporarily change the print area. When your printout includes multiple pages, you can set the row and column labels to appear on each page, making it easier for you and others to locate data. You can also use other sheet tab options to speed up the printing process or display data in a manner that makes it easier to read.

What You Can Do

Printing a Selection

■ In some cases, you may prefer not to print all the data on a sheet. For example, you may want to print only the data that performs a certain set of calculations.

■ To print an area of the worksheet, select that range. Then, when you click FILE > Print, select Print Selection using the first drop-down list under Settings. (It normally says Print Active Sheets, until you change it.)

Try It!   Printing a Selection

1. Start Excel.

2. Open the **E20Try** file from the data files for this lesson.

3. Save the workbook as **ETry20_xx** in the location where your teacher instructs you to store the files for this lesson.

4. Add a header that has your name at the left, the date code in the center, and the sheet name code at the right, and change back to Normal view.

5. Select the range A8:C9.

6. Click FILE > Print.

7. Click the top option under Settings, which initially reads Print Active Sheets, and click Print Selection on the menu. The Preview immediately shows you that only the selection will print. You could then click the Print button to send it to the printer.

8. Click Save to save your changes to the file, and return to the HOME tab.

9. Leave the **ETry20_xx** file open to use in the next Try It.

Printing a worksheet selection.

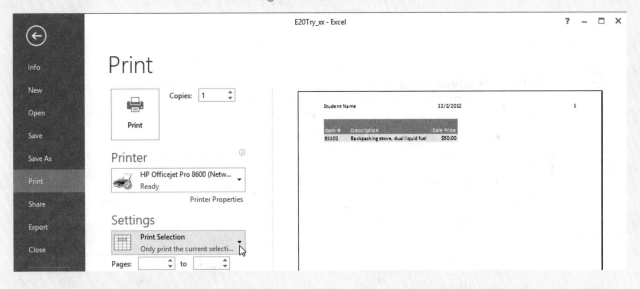

Printing All the Worksheets in a Workbook

- Workbooks with multiple sheets of data often contain information that needs to be shared with others for making business decisions.

- Excel enables you to print all the sheets in a workbook file in a single print operation, to save you the trouble of printing each sheet individually.

- Click FILE > Print, select Print Entire Workbook using the first drop-down list under Settings. (It normally says Print Active Sheets, until you change it.)

Try It!   Printing All the Worksheets in a Workbook

① In the ETry20_xx file, click FILE > Print.

② Click the top option under Settings, which by default reads Print Active Sheets but in this instance will read Print Selection due to the last Try It, and click Print Entire Workbook on the menu.

③ Use the Next button below the preview to view the print preview of all four sheets. Notice that the page breaks need to be adjusted.

④ Save the ETry20_xx file, and leave it open to use in the next Try It.

Inserting Page Breaks

- When worksheet data will not fit on one page, Excel inserts automatic **page breaks** based on the paper size, margins, and scaling options.

- Automatic page breaks appear as dashed lines on the worksheet.

  ✓ *Page breaks appear on the worksheet after you adjust Page Setup options, preview the worksheet, or print it.*

- If you prefer, you can override automatic page breaks and set manual page breaks before printing.

- While automatic page breaks (those created by Excel, based on your page setup options) appear as dashed lines, manual page breaks (those you create by either moving the automatic page breaks, or inserting new ones) display on the worksheet as solid lines.

Try It!   Setting Manual Page Breaks

① In the ETry20_xx file, click cell A30.

  ✓ *Unless you click in row 1, a horizontal page break will be inserted above the cell you click.*

  ✓ *Unless you click in column A, a vertical page break will be inserted to the left of the cell you click.*

② On the PAGE LAYOUT tab, click the Breaks button.

③ Click Insert Page Break.

  ✓ *Automatic page breaks that follow a manual page break will adjust automatically.*

④ Save the changes to the ETry20_xx file, and leave it open to use in the next Try It.

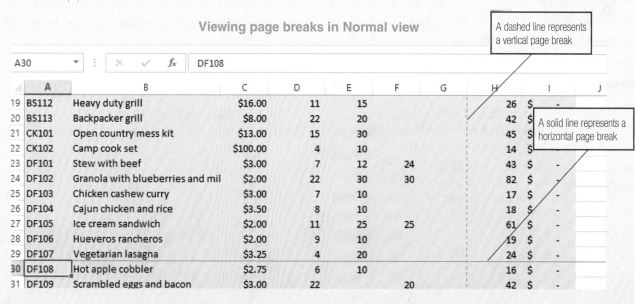

Viewing page breaks in Normal view

A dashed line represents a vertical page break

A solid line represents a horizontal page break

Using Page Break Preview

- **Page Break Preview** is a special view that displays both automatic and manual page breaks, and allows you to adjust them.

- You can change to Page Break Preview using the Page Break Preview button ▦ on the VIEW tab of the Ribbon or the Page Break Preview button 🔳 on the Status bar.

  ✓ *You can also see where page breaks occur in Normal and Page Layout views.*

- When you display a worksheet in Page Break Preview, lines appear, subdividing the worksheet into sections.
  - Each section represents a different print page.
  - Each section is marked in the center with a large page number displayed in light gray.
  - You can change the page breaks by dragging these lines.

- In Page Break Preview, when you drag a dashed line (automatic page break) to move it, it changes to a solid line (manual page break).

- In Page Break Preview, drag a dashed line off the worksheet to remove the page break and reset the page breaks.
  - Page breaks can be inserted and removed in any view, by clicking the cell located below or to the right of the page break and using the Breaks button ⊟ in the Page Setup group on the PAGE LAYOUT tab on the Ribbon

- You can also edit worksheet data and resize the print area from Page Break Preview.
  - The Print Area button in the Page Setup group on the PAGE LAYOUT tab also lets you adjust the print area.

- If you adjust a page break to include a few more columns or rows on a page, Excel automatically adjusts the scale (font size) to make that data fit on the page.

- You can also use Page Break Preview to adjust how embedded charts print.

  ✓ *Embedded charts and other objects cover page breaks, so sometimes it can be difficult to see that a chart spans two pages.*

Try It!   **Changing Page Breaks Using Page Break Preview**

1 In the **ETry20_xx** file, click the VIEW tab, then click the Page Break Preview button ▦.

OR

Click the Page Break Preview button 🔳 on the Status bar.

Page breaks viewed in Page Break Preview

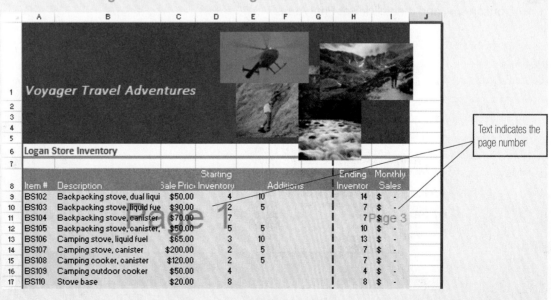

Text indicates the page number

(continued)

Try It! Changing Page Breaks Using Page Break Preview *(continued)*

② Drag the dashed line between column G and H to the right margin of column I.

✓ *The automatic page break dashed line changes to a solid line.*

✓ *When a manual page break is moved outside of the print area, the automatic page break is restored.*

③ Drag the solid blue line between column I and J to the right margin off the worksheet.

④ Save the changes to the **ETry20_xx** file, and leave it open to use in the next Try It.

Setting the Print Area

- To print only a selected area of data on a worksheet, adjust the **print area**.

- You can set the print area using Page Break Preview, the Print Area button on the PAGE LAYOUT tab of the Ribbon, or the Page Setup dialog box.

- In Normal view, the print area appears on the worksheet with a dashed border.

- In Page Break Preview, the print area appears in full color, while data outside the area to be printed appears on a gray background.

- You can define a unique print area for each worksheet in your workbook.

- You can set multiple print areas by first setting one print area, selecting the second print area, clicking the Print Area button on the PAGE LAYOUT tab, and select Add to Print Area.

- To print the entire worksheet again, you must either clear the print area setting or reset the print area to include all the data.

Try It! Setting the Print Area

① In the **ETry20_xx** file, switch to Page Break Preview, if necessary.

② Select A1:I20 as the range to print.

③ On the PAGE LAYOUT tab, click the Print Area button, and then click Set Print Area.

④ On the PAGE LAYOUT tab, click the Print Area button > Clear Print Area.

⑤ Save the changes to the **ETry20_xx** file, and leave it open to use in the next Try It.

Setting the print area

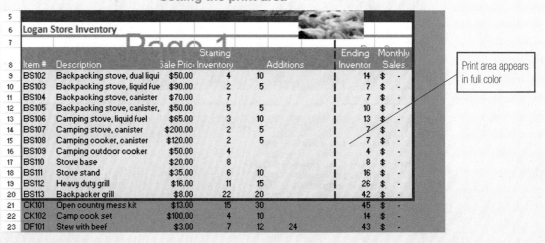

Repeating Row and Column Labels

- Using the Sheet tab of the Page Setup dialog box, you can select to reprint the **print titles** on each page of a worksheet printout.

- You can also use the Print Titles button in the Page Setup group on the PAGE LAYOUT tab to add print titles.

- Without the row and column labels printed on each page, it might be difficult to decipher your data.

Try It!   Repeating Row and Column Labels

1. In the **ETry20_xx** file, click the PAGE LAYOUT tab, then click the Print Titles button 🖨.

2. On the Sheet tab, click the Collapse Dialog box button on the Rows to repeat at top box.

3. Select rows 1 through 8.

4. Click the Expand Dialog box button.

5. In the Columns to repeat at left, type **$A:$C**.

6. Click OK.

7. Save the changes to the **ETry20_xx** file, and leave it open to use in the next Try It.

The Sheet tab in the Page Setup dialog box

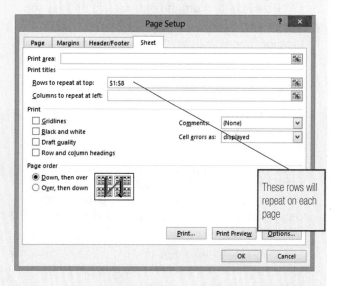

These rows will repeat on each page

Selecting Other Sheet Tab Options

- The Sheet tab of the Page Setup dialog box provides an option for printing **gridlines** with your data.
  - You can also choose to print gridlines using the Gridlines Print option on the PAGE LAYOUT tab of the Ribbon.

- You can print your worksheet in black and white (even if it includes color fills or graphics), in draft mode (faster printing, lower quality), with your comments, and with errors displayed.

- For large worksheets, you can specify the page order (the order in which data is selected to be printed on subsequent pages).

- You can add gridlines to your printouts to make your data more readable.

Try It!   Selecting Sheet Tab Options

1. In the **ETry20_xx** file, click the PAGE LAYOUT tab, if necessary.

2. Click the Page Setup dialog box launcher 🖳.

3. In the Page Setup dialog box, click the Sheet tab.

4. In the Print section, click Draft quality.

5. In the Print section, click Gridlines.

6. Click OK.

7. Save the changes to the **ETry20_xx** file, and close it.

Lesson 20—Practice

In this project, you will set page breaks before printing, change the print area, use other sheet tab options, and print a worksheet using the skills you learned in this lesson.

DIRECTIONS

1. Start Excel, if necessary, and open the **E20Practice** file from the data files for this lesson.

2. Save the workbook as **E20Practice_xx** in the location where your teacher instructs you to store the files for this lesson.

3. Add a header that has your name at the left, the date code in the center, and the sheet name code at the right, and change back to **Normal** view.

4. Click **FILE** > **Print**. A preview of the worksheet appears in the preview pane.

5. Click the **Next Page** button at the bottom of the preview pane to move through the entire printout. Notice that the worksheet is set to print on four pages, but the chart is split up and impossible to interpret.

6. Click the **Back** button ⊙.

7. Click the **PAGE LAYOUT** tab. Notice the page breaks indicated by the dashed lines.

8. On the PAGE LAYOUT tab, click the **Orientation** button 🗗 and select **Landscape**.

9. Click **FILE** > **Print**. Notice the changes to the preview.

10. Click the **Back** button ⊙.

11. On the **VIEW** tab, click the **Page Break Preview** button ▦. The worksheet appears in Page Break Preview.

12. Drag the automatic page break located between columns G and H to the right of column K of the worksheet data on page 1.

13. Drag the automatic page break located below row 54 up to the bottom of row 37. Your worksheet should look like Figure 20-1 on the next page.

14. On the PAGE LAYOUT tab, click the Page Setup dialog box launcher ⌐.

15. In the Page Setup dialog box, click the **Sheet** tab and select **Draft Quality** in the Print area. Click **Print** to view the preview.

16. **With your teacher's permission**, print the worksheet in draft quality. Submit the printout or the file for grading as required.

17. Save and close the file, and exit Excel.

Figure 20-1

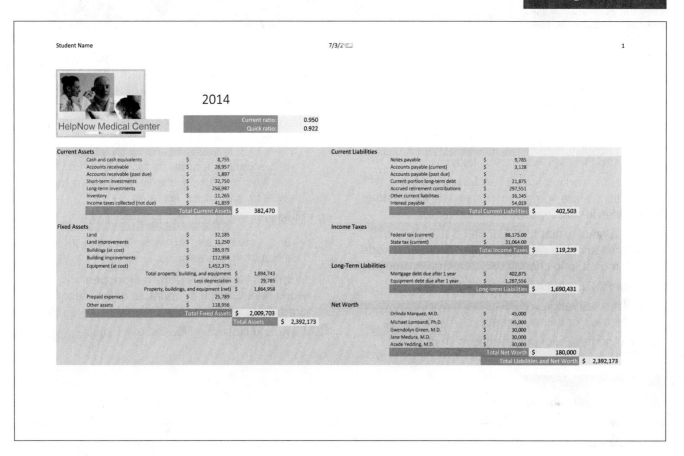

Student Name   7/3/2⊂   1

2014

HelpNow Medical Center

| | Current ratio: | 0.950 |
| | Quick ratio: | 0.922 |

Current Assets

Cash and cash equivalents	$	8,755
Accounts receivable	$	28,957
Accounts receivable (past due)	$	1,897
Short-term investments	$	32,750
Long-term investments	$	256,987
Inventory	$	11,265
Income taxes collected (not due)	$	41,859
Total Current Assets	$	382,470

Fixed Assets

Land	$	32,185
Land improvements	$	11,250
Buildings (at cost)	$	285,975
Building improvements	$	112,958
Equipment (at cost)	$	1,452,375
Total property, building, and equipment	$	1,894,743
Less depreciation	$	29,785
Property, buildings, and equipment (net)	$	1,864,958
Prepaid expenses	$	25,789
Other assets	$	118,956
Total Fixed Assets	$	2,009,703
Total Assets	$	2,392,173

Current Liabilities

Notes payable	$	9,785
Accounts payable (current)	$	3,128
Accounts payable (past due)	$	
Current portion long-term debt	$	21,875
Accrued retirement contributions	$	297,551
Other current liabilities	$	16,145
Interest payable	$	54,019
Total Current Liabilities	$	402,503

Income Taxes

Federal tax (current)	$	88,175.00
State tax (current)	$	31,064.00
Total Income Taxes	$	119,239

Long-Term Liabilities

Mortgage debt due after 1 year	$	402,875
Equipment debt due after 1 year	$	1,287,556
Long-term Liabilities	$	1,690,431

Net Worth

Orlinda Marquez, M.D.	$	45,000
Michael Lombardi, Ph.D.	$	45,000
Gwendolyn Green, M.D.	$	30,000
Jane Medura, M.D.	$	30,000
Azade Yedding, M.D.	$	30,000
Total Net Worth	$	180,000
Total Liabilities and Net Worth	$	2,392,173

Lesson 20—Apply

As the new franchise director at HelpNow Medical Center, you've spent a lot of time creating reports that describe your company's fiscal strength. The balance sheet is ready for printing, but you want to add a repeating row and column label and modify the print settings so it will print exactly as you want.

DIRECTIONS

1. Start Excel, if necessary, and open the **E20Apply** file from the data files for this lesson.

2. Save the workbook as **E20Apply_xx** in the location where your teacher instructs you to store the files for this lesson.

3. Add a header that has your name at the left, the date code in the center, and the sheet name code at the right, and change back to **Normal** view.

4. Click **PAGE LAYOUT** > **Print Titles** 🗒.

5. Set the cell range **A1:B9** as the repeating row (print title) for this worksheet.

6. Change the sheet print setting to **Draft quality**.

7. Create two print areas (**A1:K37** and **A39:K71**). Refer to Figures 20-2 and 20-3.

   ✓ *Hint: Set one print area and then select the second print area. When you click the Print Area button on the Page Layout tab, select Add to Print Area.*

8. Display the worksheet in Print Preview.

   ✓ *Because you selected two different ranges for the print area, they print on separate pages.*

9. **With your teacher's permission**, print the worksheet. Submit the printout or the file for grading as required.

10. Save and close the file, and exit Excel.

Figure 20-2

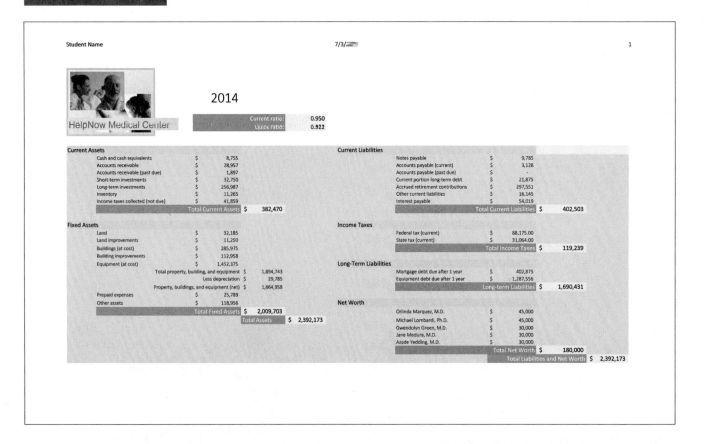

Figure 20-3

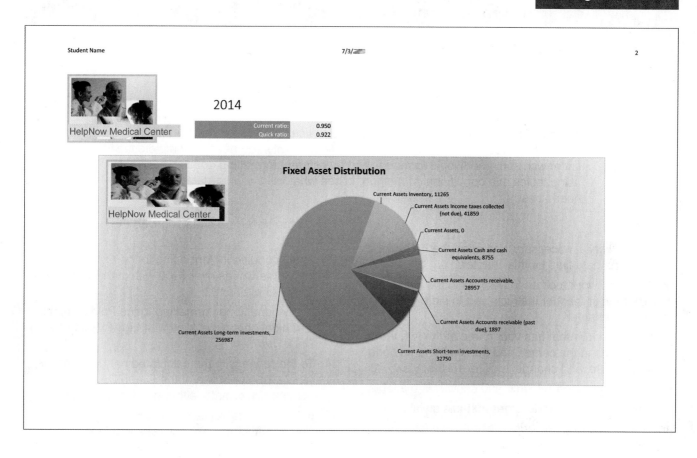

Student Name   7/3/   2

2014

HelpNow Medical Center

| Current ratio: | 0.950 |
| Quick ratio: | 0.922 |

Fixed Asset Distribution

HelpNow Medical Center

Current Assets Inventory, 11265

Current Assets Income taxes collected (not due), 41859

Current Assets, 0

Current Assets Cash and cash equivalents, 8755

Current Assets Accounts receivable, 28957

Current Assets Accounts receivable (past due), 1897

Current Assets Long-term investments, 256987

Current Assets Short-term investments, 32750

End-of-Chapter Activities

➤ Excel Chapter 2—Critical Thinking

Client Activity Worksheet

You have a business called Fry Landscape Services. You have created a worksheet to record and evaluate monthly client activity. You need to complete the sheet with some additional formulas, and try different formatting options, such as using tables and conditional formatting, to see what will suit your data analysis needs best.

DIRECTIONS

1. Start Excel, if necessary, and open the **ECT02** file from the data files for this chapter.

2. Save the workbook as **ECT02_xx** in the location where your teacher instructs you to store the files for this chapter.

3. Add a header that has your name at the left, the date code in the center, and the sheet name code at the right, and change back to **Normal** view.

4. Select the range **A4:D32**, and convert it to a table.

5. Apply the **Table Style Light 20** table style.

6. Add a total row, and adjust it so a *Sum total* displays for the **Fee** column only.

7. In cell **G5**, enter a formula that sums only the fees that have been paid.

8. In the range **G7:G10**, enter formulas that sum only the fees paid for each type of service.

9. Rename **Sheet1** to **Version1**.

10. Copy the **Version1** sheet, naming the copy **Version2** and placing it after the copied sheet.

11. On the **Version2** sheet, convert the table back to a range.

12. Apply conditional formatting to the **Fee** column that highlights values over $100 with a **Yellow Fill with Dark Yellow Text**.

13. Apply conditional formatting to the Paid column that highlights *No* entries with **Light Red Fill with Dark Red Text**.

14. To the range with the calculated paid values **(G7:G10)**, apply one of the Green Data Bar conditional formats (either gradient or solid).

15. In both sheets, replace the Customer name *Tayson* with **Tyler**. Your sheet should resemble Illustration 2A on the next page.

16. Set **row 4** as the print titles on both sheets.

17. **With your teacher's permission,** print the workbook. Submit the printouts or the file for grading as required.

18. Save and close the file, and exit Excel.

Fry Landscape Services

Client Activity

Customer	Service	Fee		Paid
Hoover	Mowing	$	75	Yes
Jackson	Trimming	$	60	Yes
Tyler	Mowing	$	75	Yes
Renfro	Mowing	$	100	No
Allen	Aeration	$	100	Yes
Friend	Other	$	65	Yes
Keeger	Mowing	$	50	Yes
Tyler	Other	$	85	Yes
Hoover	Other	$	150	No
Poland	Mowing	$	75	Yes
Manders	Other	$	125	Yes
Nodine	Mowing	$	100	No
Welty	Aeration	$	100	Yes
Tyler	Mowing	$	50	Yes
Guertler	Aeration	$	100	Yes
Fanson	Mowing	$	100	No
Molton	Mowing	$	200	Yes
Davis	Other	$	100	Yes
Fiver	Trimming	$	50	No
Olson	Mowing	$	75	Yes
Erland	Mowing	$	100	No
Walton	Aeration	$	100	Yes
Stilson	Trimming	$	60	Yes
Reece	Mowing	$	125	Yes
Anders	Other	$	200	Yes
Tyler	Aeration	$	100	Yes
Branson	Mowing	$	75	Yes
Carson	Other	$	275	No
Total		**$ 2,870**		

Amount Collected	$ 1,995
Aeration Paid	$ 500
Mowing Paid	$ 800
Other Paid	$ 575
Trimming Paid	$ 120

➤ Excel Chapter 2—Portfolio Builder

Fundraising Worksheet

You are the Executive Director of Crossmont Services, a nonprofit organization that provides food assistance to needy families in Crossmont County. Your organization is holding a ball as a fundraiser. You created a budget for the ball and just entered actual information after the event. Now you need to evaluate the actual information to see if the event was a financial success. You will work with a summary worksheet and use formatting to help identify trouble spots so you can plan the event more effectively next year.

DIRECTIONS

1. Start Excel, if necessary, and open the **EPB02** file from the data files for this chapter.

2. Save the workbook as **EPB02_xx** in the location where your teacher instructs you to store the files for this chapter.

3. Group **Sheet1** through **Sheet3**.

4. Add a header that has your name at the left, the sheet name code in the center, and the page number code at the right, and change back to **Normal** view.

5. Format cell **A1** with the **Title** cell style.

6. Format range **A2:E2** with the **Heading 3** cell style.

7. Format the range **A4:E4** with the **Heading 3** cell style, and rotate it using the **Angle Counterclockwise** setting.

8. In cell **D2**, enter the date and time using the **NOW** function.

9. Adjust column widths as needed, and then ungroup the worksheets.

10. Rename the sheets as follows:
    Sheet1   **Expenses**
    Sheet2   **Income**
    Sheet3   **Summary**

11. On the **Expenses** sheet, select the range **C5:C13**. Review the AutoCalculate results on the status bar.

12. In cells **B14** and **C14** of the **Expenses** sheet, enter formulas using the SUM function to calculate the values above. Adjust column widths, as necessary.

13. In cells **B9** and **C9** of the **Income** sheet, enter formulas using the SUM function to calculate the values above. Adjust column widths, as necessary.

14. In cells **B5:C5** of the **Summary** sheet, enter formulas that summarize the applicable data from the other two sheets.

    ✓ *Hint: Subtract the Expenses from the Income.*

15. On the **Income** sheet, change the actual ticket sales value to **53500**.

16. Return to the **Summary** sheet to review the recalculated results. Review the revised results, which appear in Illustration 2B.

17. **With your teacher's permission,** print all worksheets in the workbook in one print operation. Submit the printouts or the file for grading as required.

18. Save and close the file, and exit Excel.

Illustration 2B

⁄	A	B	C	D	E
1	Crossmont Services				
2	**Fundraising Ball Budget**			7/3/2014 3:26	
3					
4		Estimated	Actual	Difference $	Difference %
5	Event Profit	$ 52,200	$ 53,275	$ 1,075	2.06%
6					

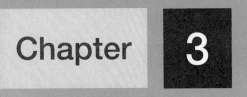
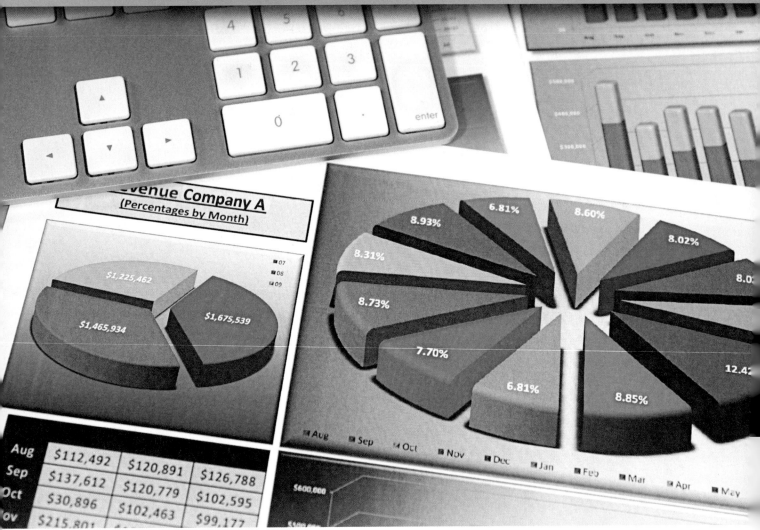

Chapter 3

(Courtesy Chad McDermott/Shutterstock)

Charting Data

Lesson 21

Building Basic Charts

> ## ➤ What You Will Learn

Understanding Chart Basics
Selecting Chart Data
Reviewing Chart Elements
Creating a Chart
Using Recommended Charts
Changing Chart Types
Selecting a Chart
Resizing, Copying, Moving, or Deleting a Chart

WORDS TO KNOW

Categories
In most cases, each column of charted worksheet data contains a category. Selecting multiple rows of chart data creates multiple categories. The chart displays categories along the horizontal axis.

Chart
A graphic that compares and contrasts worksheet data in a visual format. A chart is also known as a graph.

Chart sheet
A chart that occupies its own worksheet.

Column chart
The default chart type that displays each data point as a vertical column.

Data marker
The shape—bar, column, line, pie slice, and so on—representing each data point of a chart.

Software Skills A chart presents Excel data in a graphical format—making the relationship between data items easier to understand. To present your data in the best format, you must select the proper chart type. For example, if you wanted to highlight your department's recent reduction in overtime, you might use a column or bar chart. Or, to compare your division's sales to those of other divisions, you might use a pie chart.

What You Can Do

Understanding Chart Basics

■ **Charts** provide a way of presenting and comparing data in a graphical format.
■ You can create **embedded charts** or **chart sheets**.
■ When you create an embedded chart, the chart exists as an object in the worksheet alongside the data.
■ When you create a chart sheet, the chart exists on a separate sheet in the workbook.
■ All charts are linked to the charted data, which appears in the **plot area**. (The plot area is contained within the overall chart area.) When you change worksheet data linked to the charted **data points**, the **data markers** in the chart plot area change automatically.

Selecting Chart Data

- To create a chart, you first select the data to plot.
- The selection should not contain blank columns or rows.
- If the data is not in a single range, press CTRL and select each range separately, making sure not to select blank rows or columns that may separate the ranges.
- You can select multiple ranges to plot on a single chart.
- You can hide columns or rows you do not wish to chart.

  ✓ *The selection should include the labels for the data when possible.*

- A blank cell in the upper-left corner of a selection tells Excel that the data below and to the right of the blank cell contains labels for the values to plot.
- Excel assumes each row includes a series. However, you may change the orientation as desired.

Reviewing Chart Elements

- As you move the mouse pointer over a chart, the name of the chart element appears in a ScreenTip.
- A chart may include some or all of the parts shown in Figure 21-1.
- In this example, each community is a **data series** listed on its own row in the worksheet. On the chart, each data series is represented on the chart by a different data marker—columns in the example.
- The **legend** at the right is a key that identifies the series by name.
- Each kind of data for each item is a data point. For each series in the example there are three data points—Planned, Started, and Completed—as noted on the **horizontal axis** (X axis). These are the **categories** of data.

Data points
The specific values plotted on a chart.

Data series
A set of related data points to be charted. In most cases, each row of charted worksheet data holds a data series. Selecting multiple columns of data for a chart creates multiple data series. The chart presents each data series in its own color bar, line, or column.

Embedded chart
A chart placed as an object within a worksheet.

Horizontal axis
The horizontal scale of a chart on which categories are plotted, sometimes called the X axis.

Legend
A key that identifies each of the data series in a chart.

Plot area
The area that holds the data points on a chart.

Vertical axis
The vertical scale of a chart on which the values from each category is plotted, sometimes called the Y axis.

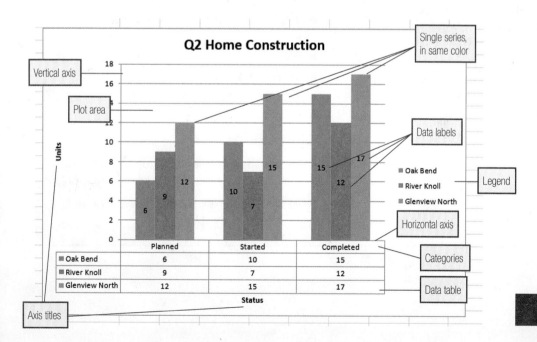

Figure 21-1

- If desired, you can identify each specific data point by displaying data labels. These labels appear on or near the data markers.

- For charts that use axes (generally all charts except pie charts and some 3-D charts), the **vertical axis** or Y axis provides the scale for the values being charted.

  ✓ *For bar charts the axes are reversed. The vertical axis charts categories and the horizontal axis charts values.*

  ✓ *3-D charts typically have a third axis representing the amount of 3-D rotation.*

- The horizontal axis title describes the categories data. (Status in the example.)

- The vertical axis title describes the types of values being plotted. (Units in the example.)

- The chart title identifies the chart overall and axis titles describe the axes. You have to add these titles when you want them to appear.

- So a user can easily view the data that's plotted on the chart, you can add a data table below the chart.

- The data table looks like a small worksheet, and it lists the data used to create the chart.

- You can view chart options using the three buttons that appear in the upper right corner next to the selected chart: Chart Elements, Chart Styles, and Chart Filters.

  ✓ *The Chart Elements, Chart Styles, and Chart Filters buttons provide a limited selection of the most commonly used formatting choices.*

- You can use the Chart Elements button to select the chart elements you want to display. The chart elements available will vary depending on the type of chart you select.

  ✓ *You will learn about Chart Styles and Chart Filters in Lesson 25.*

Try It!   **Reviewing Chart Elements**

1. Start Excel.

2. Open the **E21Try** file from the data files for this lesson.

3. Save the file as **E21Try_xx** in the location where your teacher instructs you to store the files for this lesson.

4. Add a header that has your name at the left, the date code in the center, and the page number code at the right, and change back to Normal view.

5. On the Example sheet, scroll down until you can see the entire chart.

6. Move the mouse pointer over the title at the top of the chart. A ScreenTip that reads *Chart Title* appears.

7. Using Figure 21-1 as a guide, move the mouse pointer over these areas of the chart to view the ScreenTips, verifying that you've identified the correct parts of the chart:

   - Legend
   - Any data marker for the Oak Bend series
   - Any data marker for the River Knoll series
   - Any data marker for the Glenview North series
   - Plot area
   - Vertical axis
   - Title for each axis
   - Data table

8. Click the chart to select it.

9. Click the Chart Elements button ⊞ to the right of the chart and review the available elements.

10. Save the **E21Try_xx** file, and leave it open to use in the next Try It.

Creating a Chart

- The first step to creating a chart is selecting the data to chart on the worksheet, as discussed earlier in the lesson.
- Create charts using the buttons in the Charts group on the INSERT tab.
- The buttons in the group enable you to create each type of chart: Column; Bar; Stock, Surface or Radar; Line; Area; Combo; Pie or Doughnut; and Scatter or Bubble charts.
- Each chart type contains chart subtypes, which are variations on the selected chart type.

- After selecting data to chart—including labels for the data—press ALT + F1 to insert an embedded default column chart on the worksheet.

  ✓ After selecting the data to chart, pressing the F11 key will create a column chart on its own *chart sheet*.

  ✓ Lesson 25 explains how to use the Chart Tools contextual tabs to work with elements, such as adding chart text.

- You can also insert an embedded default **column chart** by selecting the data and using the CHARTS feature in the Quick Analysis tool that appears in the lower right of your selection.
- The theme applied to the workbook file determines the chart's color scheme.

Try It!   **Creating a Chart**

1 In the **E21Try_xx** file, select the Practice sheet.

2 Add a header that has your name at the left, the date code in the center, and the page number code at the right, and then change back to Normal view.

3 Drag over the range A5:D8 to select it.

4 On the INSERT tab, click the Insert Bar Chart button 📊▾ , and click 3-D Clustered Bar in the 3-D Bar group.

5 Drag the new chart so that its upper-left corner is over cell F2. Notice how the charted data is selected in the worksheet.

6 Leave the data selected, and press ALT + F1. A default column chart appears.

OR

With the data selected, click the Quick Analysis tool that appears in the lower right of your selection, click CHARTS, and click the first Clustered Column.

7 Drag the new chart so that its upper-left corner is over cell F18. Compare how the different chart types present the same data.

8 Save the **E21Try_xx** file, and leave it open to use in the next Try It.

A new bar chart

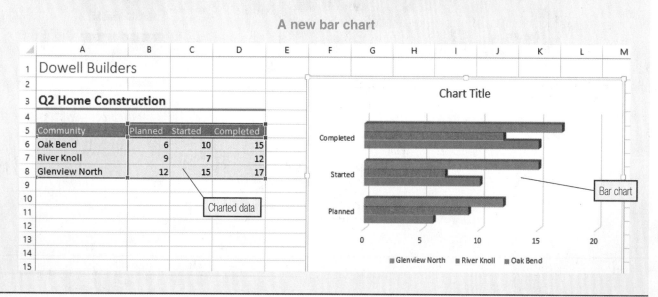

Using Recommended Charts

- Excel's Recommended Charts feature examines your data and provides recommended chart types based on the type of your data.
- When you select your data, the Quick Analysis tool ⧉ appears in the lower-right corner next to the chart.
- You can click the Quick Analysis tool, and then select CHARTS to view and preview the recommended charts.

- You can also access Recommended Charts by clicking on the INSERT tab, and clicking the Recommended Charts button.
- Use the More Charts button if you want to view additional recommended charts. The Insert Charts dialog box will open.

  ✓ *You can also access More Charts in the Charts group on the INSERT tab.*

Try It! **Using Recommended Charts**

① In the **E21Try_xx** file, drag over the range A5:D8 to select it again.

② At the bottom right of the data, click the Quick Analysis tool ⧉.

③ Click CHARTS, and click the first Stacked Column chart. Notice that the Community names are the horizontal axis labels.

④ Drag the new chart so that its upper-left corner is over cell P2.

⑤ Save the **E21Try_xx** file, and leave it open to use in the next Try It.

Viewing Recommended Charts in the Quick Analysis tool

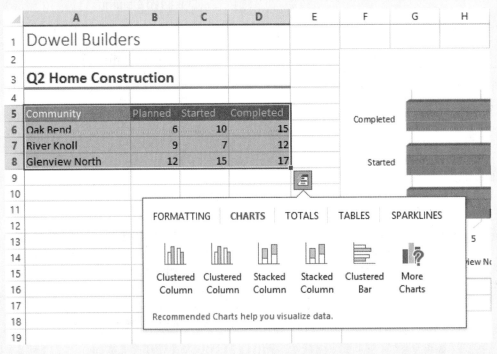

Changing Chart Types

- After creating a chart, you can easily change its chart type.

- Select the chart and click Change Chart Type ▮▮ in the Type group of the CHART TOOLS DESIGN tab to open the Change Chart Type dialog box.

- Column charts, the default chart type, compare individual or sets of values. The height of each bar corresponds to its value in the worksheet, relative to other values in the chart.

  ✓ *Most chart types also have 3-D subtypes.*

- Line charts connect points of data, making them effective for showing changes over time, such as trends.

- Circular pie charts show the relationship of each value in a single series to the total for the series. The size of a pie wedge represents the percentage that value contributes to the total, and adding data labels clarifies the proportions even more.

  ✓ *Charting one more series of data in a pie chart results in an inaccurate chart because Excel will combine all selected series into a single chart.*

- A bar chart is basically a column chart turned on its side. Like column charts, bar charts compare the values of various items.

- Area charts are like "filled in" line charts; you can use area charts to track changes over time.

- Scatter charts, also called XY charts, represent data points as dots. The dots for each series appear in a different color. Any overall direction to the position of the dots reveals a trend.

- Excel also offers many specialty chart types such as Stock, Surface, Doughnut, Bubble, and Radar.

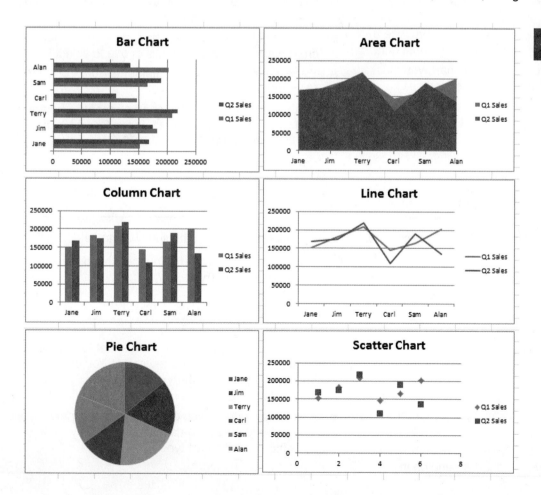

Figure 21-2

Try It!   Changing Chart Types

1 In the **E21Try_xx** file, click the bar chart that you created first (positioned starting in cell F2) to select it.

2 On the CHART TOOLS DESIGN tab, click Change Chart Type ▮▮ . The Change Chart Type dialog box appears.

3 In the list at the left, click the Area chart type. Notice that the chart choices have different horizontal axis labels.

4 Click the 3-D Area choice above Area.

5 Click OK. Observe the changes. You determine that the 3-D Area chart is too imprecise for the data, so you will change the chart again.

6 On the CHART TOOLS DESIGN tab, click Change Chart Type ▮▮ . The Change Chart Type dialog box appears.

7 In the list at the left, click the Line chart type.

8 Click the Line with Markers choice above Line.

9 Click OK.

10 Save the **E21Try_xx** file, and leave it open to use in the next Try It.

Selecting a Chart

- You can copy a chart and then edit it to produce a different chart that uses the same worksheet data.
- To resize, copy, move, or format a chart, you must first select it by clicking anywhere on the chart.
- A selected chart is surrounded by a border with evenly spaced square handles at the corners and middle of each side.
- Use the square handles on the border of a selected chart to resize the chart.
- Once the chart itself is selected, click an individual chart element such as an axis or title to select it.
- You can select some chart elements from the Chart Elements button ➕ .
- To select from all available chart elements, use the Add Chart Element button ▮▮ in the Chart Layouts group on the CHART TOOLS DESIGN tab.

Try It!   Selecting a Chart

1 In the **E21Try_xx** file, click the column chart with the upper-left corner in cell F18. The border with the square handles appears.

2 Click the line chart above it to select it, instead.

3 Click the legend on the line chart to select it.

4 Save the **E21Try_xx** file, and leave it open to use in the next Try It.

Resizing, Copying, Moving, or Deleting a Chart

- You can resize, copy, or move an embedded chart as needed using the same methods as for moving and resizing other objects.
- You can't resize a chart on a chart sheet; however, you can copy or move the chart around on the sheet.
- You can move a chart on a chart sheet to another sheet, creating an embedded object. You can reverse the process when needed to change an embedded chart into a chart sheet.
- If you copy a chart, you can change the copied chart type to present data in a different way, such as using another chart type.

| Try It! | **Resizing, Copying, Moving, or Deleting a Chart** |

1 In the **E21Try_xx** file, click the border of the line chart itself to reselect the whole chart.

2 Press `DEL`.

3 Click the stacked bar chart with the upper-left corner starting at cell P2, and drag it so that its upper-left corner starts at cell F2.

4 With the chart still selected, click HOME > Copy.

5 Click the New sheet button ⊕.

6 On the HOME tab, click Paste.

7 With the chart still selected, drag it down so its upper-left corner is on cell B3.

8 Drag the lower-right handle down to cell K21 to increase the chart size.

9 Reset the page break to fit the chart on one page.

10 Save the **E21Try_xx** file, and close it.

Lesson 21—Practice

In this project, you will create a chart, change its chart type, and resize the chart using the skills you learned in this lesson.

DIRECTIONS

1. Start Excel, if necessary, and open the **E21Practice** file from the data files for this lesson.

2. Save the file as **E21Practice_xx** in the location where your teacher instructs you to store the files for this lesson.

3. Group the sheets. Add a header that has your name at the left, the date code in the center, and the page number code at the right, and change back to **Normal** view. Ungroup the sheets.

4. Select the product names in the range **A6:L6**.

5. Scroll down, press and hold `CTRL`, and drag over the daily sales figures in the range **A31:L31**.

6. Click **INSERT > Insert Line Chart** 📈 ▾ > **Line with Markers** in the 2-D Line group.

7. With the new chart still selected, click **HOME > Cut** ✂.

8. Click the **Charts** sheet tab.

9. On the **HOME** tab, click **Paste** 📋.

10. Drag the chart so its upper-left corner is in cell **B2**.

11. Drag the lower-right corner of the chart up and to the left, through cell **G12**. Your chart should resemble Figure 21-3 on the next page.

12. **With your teacher's permission**, print the **Charts** worksheet. Submit the printout or the file for grading as required.

13. Save and close the file, and exit Excel.

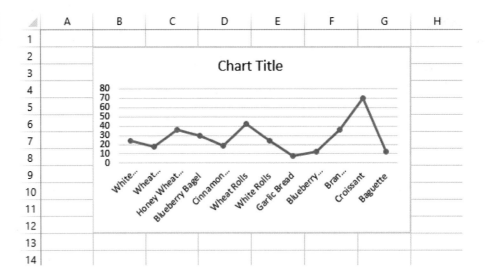

Lesson 21—Apply

The modifications you made to your daily bread sales worksheet is working out very well. Now, as manager of a Whole Grains Bread store, you're ready to analyze the data further with charts. Being able to visually compare the sales of the various items in your retail store will help you to produce the right products you need to maximize profits. In this project, you will add two charts.

DIRECTIONS

1. Start Excel, if necessary, and open the **E21Apply** file from the data files for this lesson.

2. Save the file as **E21Apply_xx** in the location where your teacher instructs you to store the files for this lesson.

3. Group the sheets. Add a header that has your name at the left, the date code in the center, and the page number code at the right, and change back to **Normal** view. Ungroup the sheets.

4. Go to the **Daily Sales** sheet and scroll down to the Daily Summary area.

5. Select the nonadjacent ranges **A38:A39** and **D38:D39**.

6. Insert a pie chart using the **3-D Pie** subtype.

7. Cut the new pie chart from the **Daily Sales** sheet, and paste it on the **Charts** sheet.

8. Drag the chart down so its upper-left corner is over cell **B16**.

9. Resize the chart so that its lower-right cell is over cell **G27**.

10. Change the chart type to a column chart, **3-D Clustered Column** subtype.

11. Deselect the chart.

12. **With your teacher's permission**, print the **Charts** worksheet. Submit the printout or the file for grading as required.

13. Save and close the file, and exit Excel.

Lesson 22

Showing Percentages with a Pie Chart

➤ What You Will Learn

Calculating Percentages
Creating a Pie Chart on a Chart Sheet

Software Skills   Finding relative percentages of values provides a way to measure performance or compare parts to a whole. You can build formulas from scratch to calculate percentages, or you can create a pie chart, which automatically calculates percentages. You can also place a pie chart on a separate chart sheet so you can print it separately and manage it more easily.

What You Can Do

Calculating Percentages

- A percentage is a calculation of proportion. It tells you how much one value represents when compared with a total.

- Calculate a percentage of a total by dividing the individual value by the total value.

    ✓ *For example, if you want to find the chocolate ice cream sales percentage of total ice cream sales, substitute the division operator for "percentage of" to see how to structure your formula: =chocolate sales/total sales.*

- If you know the percentage you need to calculate of a value, use multiplication and specify the percentage as a decimal.

- For example, if you want to calculate 25% of total sales, change the percentage to a decimal and substitute the multiplication operator for "of" to see how to structure your formula: =.25*total sales.

Try It!   **Calculating Percentages**

1 Start Excel.

2 Open the **E22Try** file from the data files for this lesson.

3 Save the file as **E22Try_xx** in the location where your teacher instructs you to store the files for this lesson.

4 Add a header that has your name at the left, the date code in the center, and the page number code at the right, and change back to Normal view.

5 Click cell J4 to select it.

6 Use the method of your choice to enter the formula that calculates the first student's sales as a percentage of the Weekly Total sales: =I4/E22.

7 Press F4 to make the reference to cell E22 an absolute reference, which changes the formula to =I4/$E$22, and press CTRL + ENTER .

✓ *You can also manually type the dollar signs.*

8 Use the fill handle to fill the formula down through cell J9.

9 Use the same process to create formulas in cells J12:J14 to calculate each type of candy's percentage of Weekly Total sales.

10 In cell G17, enter a formula that calculates 33% of the Weekly Total sales in cell E22, or =.33*E22.

11 Save the **E22Try_xx** file, and leave it open to use in the next Try It.

Finding a percentage

	Number Sold	Total Sales	Dollars Sales by Student			Percentage of Total
	17	$ 38.25	Tamika Brown		$ 170.00	=I4/$E$22
	23	$ 57.50	Caitlin Flynn		$ 135.00	
	27	$ 74.25	Jolee Chen		$ 188.25	
	15	$ 33.75	Tom Randall		$ 177.00	
	13	$ 32.50	Anna Trujillo		$ 155.00	
	25	$ 68.75	John Baker		$ 131.25	
	21	$ 47.25				
	30	$ 75.00	Sales by Item			
	24	$ 66.00	Toffee bars		$ 265.50	
	30	$ 67.50	Chocolate Almond bars		$ 322.50	
	24	$ 60.00	Mint bars		$ 368.50	
	18	$ 49.50				
	12	$ 27.00	33% of Total Sales?			
	27	$ 67.50				
	22	$ 60.50				
	23	$ 51.75				
	12	$ 30.00				
	18	$ 49.50				
		$ 956.50				

Student's sales

Total sales

Creating a Pie Chart on a Chart Sheet

- A pie chart automatically calculates the total of the values in the selected range, and represents each individual value as a percentage of that total.

  ✓ *Lesson 25 will explain how to make changes such as adding percentage data labels to pie slices, and Lesson 23 will explain other changes specific to working with slices.*

- After you create a pie chart, you can move it to its own chart sheet using the Move Chart button 📊 in the Location group on the CHART TOOLS DESIGN tab.

- This opens the Move Chart dialog box, where you can click New sheet, enter a chart sheet name, and then click the OK button.

- Or, you can select data to chart and press ⌘ to create a column chart on a new chart sheet, and then change the chart to a pie chart.

- When you insert a header or footer on a chart sheet, the Page Setup dialog box appears, with the Header/Footer tab selected. Click the Custom Header or Custom Footer button, and then use the dialog box that appears to specify what information appears in each section of the header or footer.

Try It!   **Creating a Pie Chart on a Chart Sheet**

① In the **E22Try_xx** file, use `CTRL` to select the nonadjacent ranges G4:G9 and I4:I9.

② Click INSERT > Insert Pie or Doughnut Chart > Pie in the 2-D Pie group

③ On the CHART TOOLS DESIGN tab, in the Location group, click Move Chart 📊 .

④ Click the New sheet option button, and type **Student Pie Chart** as the name for the new sheet.

⑤ Click OK. Review the chart.

⑥ Click INSERT > Header & Footer 📄 .

⑦ On the Header/Footer tab, click Custom Header.

⑧ In the Left section edit box, type your name, and press `TAB`.

⑨ In the Center section edit box, click the Insert Date button 📅 , and press `TAB`.

⑩ In the Right section edit box, click the Insert Page Number button 📄 , and press OK twice.

⑪ Click FILE > Print, and preview the chart sheet with the custom header.

⑫ Save the **E22Try_xx** file, and close it.

Lesson 22—Practice

In this project, you will add percentage calculations using the skills you learned in this lesson.

DIRECTIONS

1. Start Excel, if necessary, and open the **E22Practice** file from the data files for this lesson.

2. Save the file as **E22Practice_xx** in the location where your teacher instructs you to store the files for this lesson.

3. Add a header that has your name at the left, the date code in the center, and the page number code at the right, and change back to **Normal** view.

4. In cell **F5**, enter the formula =E5/$E$9, and press CTRL + ENTER .

5. Drag the fill handle to fill the formula down through cell **F8**.

6. In cell **G5**, enter the formula =.05*E5, and press CTRL + ENTER .

7. Drag the fill handle to fill the formula down through cell **G8**, as shown in Figure 22-1.

8. **With your teacher's permission**, print the worksheet. Submit the printout or the file for grading as required.

9. Save and close the file, and exit Excel.

Figure 22-1

	A	B	C	D	E	F	G	H
1	Telson Tech							
2	Q3 Sales							
3								
4	Rep	July	August	September	Total	Percentage	5% Bonus	
5	Parker	$ 65,000	$ 45,982	$ 68,256	$ 179,238	27.96%	$ 8,962	
6	Jones	$ 35,990	$ 62,834	$ 51,045	$ 149,869	23.38%	$ 7,493	
7	Anderson	$ 51,030	$ 22,930	$ 73,454	$ 147,414	22.99%	$ 7,371	
8	Chen	$ 46,113	$ 29,288	$ 89,224	$ 164,625	25.68%	$ 8,231	
9	Total	$ 198,133	$ 161,034	$ 281,979	$ 641,146			
10								

Lesson 22—Apply

You are the vice president of sales for Telson Tech. You are performing a review of quarterly sales, and you want to review how the sales made by individual sales reps contribute to overall revenue. You also want to calculate 5% bonus values. You will develop formulas to find percentages, and create reviewing percentages via a pie chart.

DIRECTIONS

1. Start Excel, if necessary, and open the **E22Apply** file from the data files for this lesson.

2. Save the file as **E22Apply_xx** in the location where your teacher instructs you to store the files for this lesson.

3. Select the nonadjacent ranges **A5:A8** and **E5:E8**.

4. Insert a pie chart using the **3-D Pie** subtype.

5. Move the chart to its own sheet named **Sales Percentage Pie**. The finished chart should resemble Figure 22-2.

6. Add a header to the chart sheet that has your name at the left, the date code in the center, and the page number code at the right, and change back to **Normal** view.

7. **With your teacher's permission**, print the chart sheet. Submit the printout or the file for grading as required.

8. Save and close the file, and exit Excel.

Figure 22-2

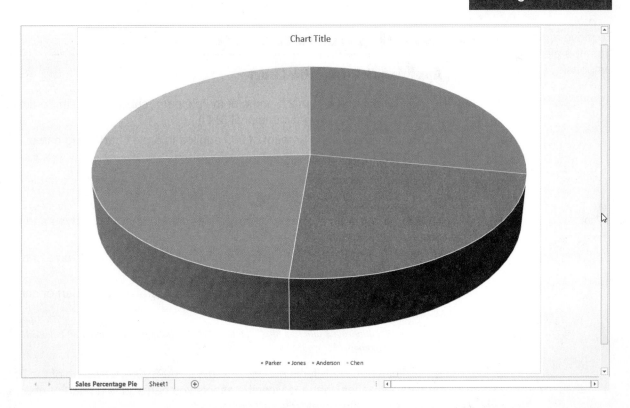

Lesson 23

Enhancing a Pie Chart

➤ What You Will Learn

Applying 3-D to a Pie Chart
Rotating Slices in a Pie Chart
Exploding and Coloring a Pie Chart
Formatting the Chart Area of a Pie Chart

WORDS TO KNOW

Chart area
The overall background for the chart and all its elements, such as titles.

Explode
To move a pie slice away from the pie chart, for emphasis.

Software Skills   With the themes available in Excel, even a basic pie chart looks attractive. However, you can present the data even more effectively by working with several pie chart formatting settings. You can work with the amount of 3-D applied to the pie chart, rotate the slices to a new position, explode a slice or change slice color, and add formatting to the area behind the chart.

What You Can Do

Applying 3-D to a Pie Chart

■ As you saw in Lesson 22, some of the pie chart subtypes are three-dimensional (3-D) rather than two dimensional (2-D).

■ You can change the amount of 3-D applied to a pie chart using one of the 3-D subtypes.

✓ *Some users believe that excessive 3-D distorts the appearance of the chart, making interpreting the data more difficult.*

■ If the chart does not use a 3-D subtype, change to a 3-D subtype and then adjust the rotation.

■ You can adjust rotation for either an embedded chart or chart on a chart sheet. Be sure to select the embedded chart to change it.

■ You can apply formatting and effects, such as rotation, to a chart or chart element using the Format task pane.

✓ *When you select a different chart element, the task pane displays available options for the new chart element.*

■ You can use the Effects button ◻ in the CHART OPTIONS tab of the Format Chart Area task pane to view the effects you can add to a chart or chart element. Click a heading to view specific effect options.

- You can also right-click to view the shortcut menu, and select Format Chart Area.
- When you right-click a chart and click 3-D Rotation, the 3-D Rotation options will display.

- With 3-D ROTATION selected the Format Chart Area dialog box, change the entries in the X Rotation and Y Rotation boxes to adjust the amount of horizontal and vertical rotation, respectively.

Try It!   **Applying 3-D to a Pie Chart**

1. Start Excel.

2. Open the **E23Try** file from the data files for this lesson.

3. Save the file as **E23Try_xx** in the location where your teacher instructs you to store the files for this lesson.

4. Display the Student Pie Chart sheet, if necessary, and add a header that has your name at the left, the date code in the center, and the page number code at the right.

5. Select the chart, and click CHART TOOLS DESIGN > Change Chart type ▮▮ > 3-D Pie > OK.

6. Right-click the chart > 3-D Rotation.

7. Change the Y Rotation value to 50°.

8. Close the Format Chart Area pane.

9. Save the **E23Try_xx** file, and leave it open to use in the next Try It.

Rotating the pie chart

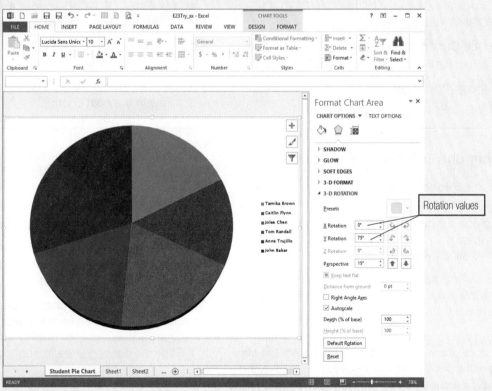

Rotating Slices in a Pie Chart

- You can rotate a pie chart's slices to help enhance a chart's appearance. For example, a pie chart might look best visually with the thinnest slices at the bottom.
- You can select the pie chart itself or a slice to apply the rotation.
- The Chart Elements drop-down list in the Current Selection group will display your selection.

    ✓ *If you select the pie chart itself, the Chart Elements drop-down box displays Series "xx," where "xx" is the name of the data series.*

    ✓ *If you select a slice, the Chart Elements drop-down box displays Series "xx" Point, where "xx" is the name of the data point.*

- After selecting the pie chart or slice you want to rotate, click the Format Selection button ✍ in the Current Selection group on the CHART TOOLS FORMAT tab to display the SERIES OPTIONS.
- Use the slider below Angle of first slice to rotate the pie chart.

Try It!   Rotating Slices in a Pie Chart

1. In the **E23Try_xx** file, with the chart sheet and chart still selected, click the CHART TOOLS FORMAT tab.

2. In the Current Selection group, click the Chart Elements drop-down arrow > Series 1.

3. Click Format Selection ✍.

4. In the Format Data Series task pane, in the SERIES OPTIONS, under Angle of first slice, drag the slider right to a setting of 280.

5. Click the Close button ✕ on the Format Data Series task pane.

6. Save the **E23Try_xx** file, and leave it open to use in the next Try It.

Exploding and Coloring a Pie Chart

- You can **explode** a pie slice to separate it from the others and emphasize it.
- To explode a single slice, first click the pie, then click the slice to select it individually. Drag the selected slice away from the rest of the slices.

    ✓ *To explode all slices, select the entire pie chart, click the Format Selection button, and drag the slider under Pie Explosion.*

- You can also change the coloring for the entire chart or a single slice or data point. Select the slice, and on the CHART TOOLS FORMAT tab click the Format Selection button ✍. The Format Data Point task pane appears. Click the Fill&Line button ◇, and click FILL.

- You can select Solid fill, and then use the Color button to select a color. Note that you can also fill a slice with a gradient, picture, or pattern.
- You can also change the coloring by right-clicking on the entire chart or element, and using the Fill button ◇▾.

    ✓ *Use the techniques described here to change the coloring for elements in any chart type.*

- To recolor the entire chart, click CHART TOOLS DESIGN, and then click the More button in the Chart Styles group to display a gallery of styles. Click the desired style to apply it.

    ✓ *Chart styles typically do not change any separate formatting you've applied previously, such as changing rotation.*

Try It!   Exploding and Coloring a Pie Chart

1 In the **E23Try_xx** file, with the chart sheet and chart still selected, click CHART TOOLS DESIGN, and click the More button ⊽ in the Chart Styles group, if necessary.

2 Click Style 3 from the gallery, which is third from the left in the first row.

3 Click the chart, and then click the slice for Jolee Chen, who was the top seller. It is the orange slice beside the legend. Right-click the selected slice, and then click Format Data Point on the shortcut menu.

4 In the Format Data Point task pane, click the Fill & Line button ◇ > FILL.

5 Under FILL, click the Solid fill option button.

6 Click the Color button, and then click Green under Standard Colors.

7 Click the Close button ✕ on the task pane.

8 With the green slice still selected, drag it away from the pie to explode it.

9 Save the **E23Try_xx** file, and leave it open to use in the next Try It.

Formatting the Chart Area of a Pie Chart

■ The **chart area** is the background that holds all of the elements of the chart, including the plot area.

■ You can fill the chart area with a solid color, gradient, picture or texture, or pattern, just as for individual data points and series.

   ✓ Use the techniques described here to change the formatting of the chart area for any type of chart.

■ Select the chart area, and then use the Format Selection button ⬙ in the Chart Layouts group to open the Format Chart Area task pane, where you can apply the formatting.

■ Be careful when applying a picture or texture fill. If the fill is too busy looking, it can make other elements of the chart, such as axis labels, difficult to read.

Try It!   Formatting the Chart Area of a Pie Chart

1 In the **E23Try_xx** file, with the chart sheet and chart still selected, click CHART TOOLS FORMAT > Chart Elements drop-down arrow > Chart Area.

2 Click Format Selection ⬙.

3 Make sure FILL is selected, and click the Gradient fill option button.

4 Click the Preset gradients button, and then click Light Gradient - Accent 5, which is the fifth from the left on the top row.

5 Click the Close button ✕ on the task pane.

6 Save the **E23Try_xx** file, and close it.

Lesson 23—Practice

In this project, you will change worksheet data and update an existing pie chart using the skills you learned in this lesson.

DIRECTIONS

1. Start Excel, if necessary, and open the **E23Practice** file from the data files for this lesson.
2. Save the file as **E23Practice_xx** in the location where your teacher instructs you to store the files for this lesson.
3. On the **Sales Percentage Pie** chart sheet, add a header that has your name at the left, the date code in the center, and the page number code at the right, and change back to **Normal** view.
4. Click the **Sheet1** sheet tab.
5. Right-click the row **7** row header, and click **Insert**.
6. Enter the following data across the new row to cell E7:

   Bronsky
   8504
   9250
   11904
   15172

7. Select cells **F6:G6**, and use the fill handle to fill the formulas down to row 7.
8. Change the entry in cell **B8** to **31030**.
9. Click the **Sales Percentage Pie** sheet tab to return to that sheet. As shown in Figure 23-1, the chart has automatically updated to reflect the data changes.
10. **With your teacher's permission**, print the chart sheet. Submit the printout or the file for grading as required.
11. Save and close the file, and exit Excel.

Figure 23-1

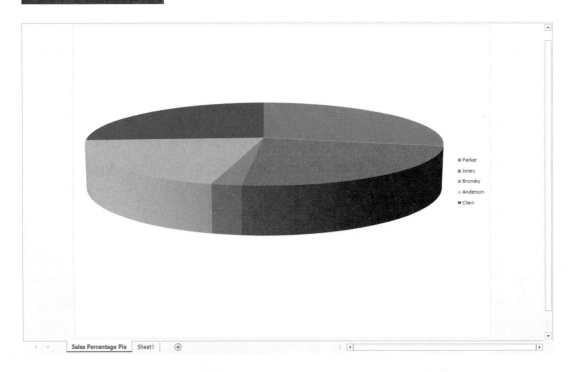

Lesson 23—Apply

As vice president of sales for Telson Tech, you are continuing the review of quarterly sales. You've received updates to the sales data, so you want to make those changes. You also want to enhance the pie chart by working with 3-D settings, exploding the slice for the leading salesperson, and applying coloring.

DIRECTIONS

1. Start Excel, if necessary, and open the **E23Apply** file from the data files for this lesson.

2. Save the file as **E23Apply_xx** in the location where your teacher instructs you to store the files for this lesson.

3. On the **Sales Percentage Pie** chart sheet, add a header that has your name at the left, the date code in the center, and the page number code at the right, and change back to **Normal** view.

4. Right-click the **chart area** > **3-D Rotation**.

5. In the Format Chart Area task pane, change the **Y Rotation** to **20°**.

6. Select the pie chart series. The Format Data Series task pane will appear.

    ✓ *Make sure the Chart Elements drop-down displays Series 1.*

7. Click the **Series Options** button ◨, drag the slider under **Angle of first slice** right to a setting of **150**, and then click the Close button on the task pane.

8. Explode the blue slice for **Parker** at the bottom of the chart.

9. Format the exploded slide to fill it with the **Granite** texture.

10. Apply a **Gold, Accent 4, Lighter 60%** solid fill to the chart area.

11. **With your teacher's permission**, print the chart sheet. Submit the printout or the file for grading as required.

12. Save and close the file, and exit Excel.

Lesson 24

Adding Special Elements to a Chart or Sheet and Updating a Chart

➤ **What You Will Learn**

Inserting a Text Box in a Chart
Using WordArt in a Worksheet
Updating a Chart

Software Skills   Even though a chart is graphical in itself, you can still enhance
it with other elements. For example, you can add a text box with information to
elaborate on a particular data point, or use WordArt to create a jazzy title. You can
also change the actual data charted.

What You Can Do

Inserting a Text Box in a Chart

■ When you need to be able to position text freely on a chart, chart sheet, or
worksheet, you can insert a **text box**.

■ A text box can hold any text you specify, and it can be sized, positioned, and
formatted.

■ To insert a text box on a chart, make sure the chart is selected first.

■ Use the Text Box [A] in the Text group of the INSERT tab, and click on the
location where you want to insert the text box.

■ You can also click and hold, and then drag the mouse pointer to insert a text box
with the dimensions you outline.

■ You can reposition a text box by selecting it and dragging it to the desired
position.

■ Use the HOME tab and DRAWING TOOLS FORMAT tab choices to apply
desired formatting.

Try It!   **Inserting a Text Box in a Chart**

1   Start Excel.

2   Open the **E24Try** file from the data files for this lesson.

3   Save the file as **E24Try_xx** in the location where your teacher instructs you to store the files for this lesson.

4   On the Student Pie Chart Sheet, add a header that has your name at the left, the date code in the center, and the page number code at the right, and change back to Normal view.

5   Click INSERT > Text Box 🅰.

6   Click on the exploded pie slice to create a text box.

7   Type **Great job!** in the text box.

8   Drag over the text in the text box.

9   Using the tools in the Font group of the HOME tab, increase the font size to 20 and change the font color to White, Background 1.

10   Resize the text box so the text is on one line, and reposition the text to fit on the pie slice, if needed.

11   Save the **E24Try_xx** file, and leave it open to use in the next Try It.

Using WordArt in a Worksheet

- You can create a **WordArt** object to add decorative text on a worksheet or chart sheet.

- You can also apply WordArt styles to existing text, such as a chart title.

  ✓ *You will learn more about adding and working with chart text formatting in Lesson 25.*

- Use the WordArt button 🄰 in the Text group on the INSERT tab to create a WordArt object.

- When you create WordArt, you choose from a gallery of styles that are compatible with the theme applied to the workbook file.

- You can format the WordArt object using the choices on the DRAWING TOOLS FORMAT tab.

- Use the HOME tab and DRAWING TOOLS FORMAT tab choices to change the font size and apply desired formatting.

Try It!   **Using WordArt in a Worksheet**

1   In the **E24Try_xx** file, with the chart sheet and chart selected, click INSERT > WordArt 🄰.

2   In the gallery, click the Fill - Red, Accent 2, Outline 2 - Accent 2 style, which is on the top row, third from left. The WordArt object appears with placeholder text.

3   Type **Top**, press ENTER , and type **Sellers**.

4   Drag the WordArt object to the upper-right corner of the chart area. The WordArt object can overlap the pie slice.

5   Click below the legend to deselect the WordArt.

6   Select the *Great job!* text box, and click DRAWING TOOLS FORMAT.

7   In the WordArt Styles group, click the More button ⊽.

8   Click the Fill - Blue, Accent 4, Soft Bevel style, which is on the top row, fifth from the left.

9   Save the **E24Try_xx** file, and leave it open to use in the next Try It.

Updating a Chart

- In Lesson 23, you saw how adding data within the range of charted data was automatically added to the pie chart and changes made to the chart data also resulted in automatic chart updates. In other cases, you may need to make your own changes to the charted data to update the chart.

- For example, you may want to sort the charted range to present the data in a different order, or remove part of the charted range from the chart.

  ✓ *Sorting data does change the order of the pie slices, so be sure to fix that.*

- Make any changes you want to the chart data first.

- Then, with the chart selected, click CHART TOOLS DESIGN > Select Data 🔲. Change the entry in the Chart data range text box as needed, either by typing a new range or using the Collapse Dialog button 🔲.

  ✓ *If the chart is on the chart sheet, Excel automatically displays the sheet holding the charted data.*

- When you change the data of a chart, Excel's chart engine animates the change within the chart. The chart animation feature can show you how the changed data will affect the chart overall.

Try It!   Updating a Chart

1 In the **E24Try_xx** file, click the Sheet1 sheet to select it.

2 Select the range G3:J9.

3 Click DATA > Sort 🔣.

4 In the Sort dialog box, click the My data has headers box.

5 In the Sort by drop-down list, select Percentage of Total.

6 Review the Sort On drop-down list, and make sure it reads Values.

7 In the Order drop-down list, select Largest to Smallest, and click OK.

8 Click the Student Pie Chart sheet tab.

9 Select the chart, and click CHART TOOLS DESIGN > Select Data 🔲.

10 In the Select Data Source dialog box, change the range to:

=Sheet1!$G$4:$G$6,Sheet1!$I$4:$I$6

This will eliminate the bottom three contributors from the chart.

11 Click OK.

12 Drag the green slice back to the rest of the pie, right-click it, and click Reset to Match Style.

13 Select the *Great job!* text box and drag it over the top slice for Jolee Chen, the top seller.

14 Click below the legend to deselect the text box.

15 Save the **E24Try_xx** file, and close it.

Lesson 24—Practice

In this project, you will insert a WordArt object and reposition it using the skills you learned in this lesson.

DIRECTIONS

1. Start Excel, if necessary, and open the **E24Practice** file from the data files for this lesson.

2. Save the file as **E24Practice_xx** in the location where your teacher instructs you to store the files for this lesson.

3. On the **Sales Percentage Pie** chart sheet, add a header that has your name at the left, the date code in the center, and the page number code at the right, and change back to **Normal** view.

4. With the chart sheet displayed, click **INSERT > WordArt** $\mathcal{A}$.

5. In the gallery, click the **Fill - Orange, Accent 2, Outline - Accent 2** style, which is on the top row, third from the left.

6. Type **Q3 Sales by Rep**.

7. Drag the WordArt object above the chart, and click outside it to deselect it.

8. **With your teacher's permission**, print the chart sheet. Submit the printout or the file for grading as required.

9. Save and close the file, and exit Excel.

Lesson 24—Apply

As vice president of sales for Telson Tech, you continue to work with the quarterly sales worksheet and chart. You also will add a text box to explain the exploded pie slice, and update chart information.

DIRECTIONS

1. Start Excel, if necessary, and open the **E24Apply** file from the data files for this lesson.

2. Save the file as **E24Apply_xx** in the location where your teacher instructs you to store the files for this lesson.

3. On the **Sales Percentage Pie** sheet, add a header that has your name at the left, the date code in the center, and the page number code at the right, and change back to **Normal** view.

4. On **Sheet1**, select the range **A4:G9**, and sort the data by the **Total** column, from smallest to largest, making sure that the **My data has headers** check box is checked.

5. Click the Sales Percentage Pie sheet, and click **CHART TOOLS DESIGN > Select Data** .

6. Use the method of your choice to change the selected ranges to **A6:A9** and **E6:E9**, to eliminate the Bronsky data.

7. Drag the exploded slice back to the pie, right-click it, and click **Reset to Match Style**.

8. Rotate the pie so that the gold slice for Parker is at the lower right, and then explode that slice.

   ✓ *You can use an X Rotation of more than 200°.*

9. Add a text box at the center-bottom with the following text:
   Bronsky data eliminated because she was in training.
   Parker was top seller.

10. Format the text box text with the **Gradient Fill - Blue, Accent 1, Reflection** WordArt style.

11. Deselect the text box.

12. **With your teacher's permission**, print the chart sheet. Submit the printout or the file for grading as required.

13. Save and close the file, and exit Excel.

Lesson 25

Completing Chart Formatting

➤ What You Will Learn

Changing Data Series Orientation
Formatting a Chart
Formatting a Chart Element
Changing Chart Text
Enhancing the Chart Plot Area
Formatting Category and Value Axes

WORDS TO KNOW

Chart layout
A formatting arrangement that specifies the location and sizes of chart elements, such as the chart title and legend.

Object
Any element on a worksheet or chart that can be manipulated independently. Some chart elements are also objects.

Tick marks
Lines of measurement along the category and value axis.

Walls
The areas of a 3-D chart that frame the data series. These can include side walls and a back wall.

Software Skills　There are many ways in which you can enhance your chart: you can add and format chart text, add color or a pattern to the chart plot area, format the value and category axes so that the numbers are easier to read, and add a legend.

What You Can Do

Changing Data Series Orientation

■ When you create a chart, Excel assumes the data series are arranged in rows.

■ For example, if you had a worksheet with several stores listed in different rows, and sales for each month listed in columns, then each store would be a different data series and be represented with a unique color.

■ If you switched the orientation of the data series from columns to rows, then the sales in the columns would become the series rather than the categories.

■ Use the Switch Row/Column button 🔲 in the Data group on the CHART TOOLS DESIGN tab to change the data orientation for the selected chart.

Try It!   Changing Data Series Orientation

1   Start Excel.

2   Open the **E25Try** file from the data files for this lesson.

3   Save the file as **E25Try_xx** in the location where your teacher instructs you to store the files for this lesson.

4   Group the sheets. Add a header that has your name at the left, the date code in the center, and the page number code at the right, and change back to Normal view. Ungroup the sheets.

✓ *You may need to adjust the page breaks after adding the headers.*

5   Click the Practice sheet tab, and click the chart.

6   Click CHART TOOLS DESIGN > Switch Row/Column ⊞ . The statuses become the series and the communities become the categories.

7   Save the **E25Try_xx** file, and leave it open to use in the next Try It.

Formatting a Chart

■ When a chart is created, it contains a legend and labels along each axis.

■ Apply a different **chart layout** to add common features such as a chart title, axis titles, and data table.

■ You can also select individual chart elements such as a legend or a chart title, and add or remove them from your chart layout to personalize it.

■ You can use the shortcut buttons that appear at the upper right corner outside of the chart to format chart elements and chart styles. Use the Filter shortcut button to display selected data elements of a chart.

■ In addition to its default chart layout, every new chart is formatted with a default style.

■ The Chart Layouts and Chart Styles galleries are found on the CHART TOOLS DESIGN tab.

■ As you learned in Lesson 23, you can quickly recolor and format the selected chart by simply changing chart styles. The technique presented in that lesson works for any chart type.

■ Regardless of the style you select, you can still apply manual formatting to any selected chart element using special Format dialog boxes.

■ You can use the Quick Layout button in the Chart Layouts group to change the layout of the chart to one of Excel's preset layouts.

■ You can also quickly change the coloring of a chart using the Change Colors button in the Chart Styles group.

Try It!   Formatting a Chart

1   In the **E25Try_xx** file, click the Large Chart sheet tab to select it.

2   Click the chart to select it.

3   Click CHART TOOLS DESIGN > Quick Layout button ▦ > Layout 9, which is third from the left in the third row of the gallery. The layout adds a placeholder chart title and axis titles.

4   Click CHART TOOLS DESIGN > Chart Styles More button ⏷ > Style 8. This applies a dark background and lighter formatting to the chart.

5   Click the Chart Title placeholder to select it.

6   Click HOME > Font Color drop-down arrow **A** ⏷ , and apply the Orange, Accent 2, Lighter 40% color.

7   Save the **E25Try_xx** file and leave it open to use in the next Try It.

(continued)

Chart formatting tools

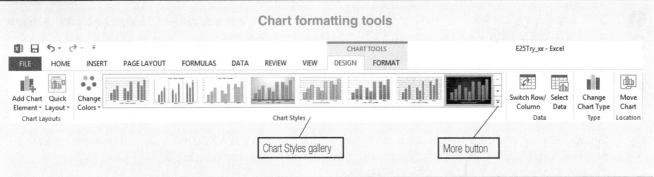

Chart Styles gallery

More button

Formatting a Chart Element

■ Before you can resize, move, or delete a chart element, also called an **object**, you must first select it.

■ By adding, resizing, moving, or deleting the parts of your chart, you may make it more attractive and easier to read.

■ If you resize an object that contains text, the font size of the text changes correspondingly.

■ When you delete an object from a chart, the remaining parts of the chart are enlarged to fill the gap.

■ You can also use the CHART ELEMENTS shortcut button ⊞ to select the chart elements you want to display.

■ You can change the value represented by a column or bar by resizing it.

■ You can format chart elements, such as the legend, the axis labels, and data labels.

■ You can format some of the chart elements as a group, for example, in a 3-D chart you can format the side and back **walls** at the same time by selecting Walls in the Chart Elements drop-down list of the CHART TOOLS FORMAT tab.

1 In the **E25Try_xx** file, on the Large Chart sheet with the chart selected, click the legend to select it.

2 Drag the legend to the lower-right corner of the chart area.

3 Click the horizontal Axis Title placeholder to select it.

4 Press DEL to delete the placeholder.

5 Click the CHART ELEMENTS shortcut button ⊞, and click the Legend checkbox to deselect it.

6 Move the mouse pointer to the right of the Legend element, and click the More arrow ▶ that appears.

✓ *If using a touch device, touch to the right of the Legend element to display the More arrow.*

7 Click Right. Notice that the Legend chart element checkbox is selected, and the legend is now placed to the right of the chart.

8 Save the **E25Try_xx** file, and leave it open to use in the next Try It.

Changing Chart Text

- You can edit chart text or change its formatting. For example, you can change the size, font, and attributes of a chart's title.

- Usually, you can select a new text object or placeholder, type the new text, and press ENTER to update the text. The text you type appears in the formula bar.

  ✓ *Double-clicking the text with the text object will insert the cursor within the placeholder text, which you can delete and replace with your own text.*

- You can also click within a text box and edit the text, and then click outside the text box to finish the change.

- The Data Labels options in the Chart Elements shortcut menu provides options for displaying individual chart labels and varying their position.

- Click the More Options button at the bottom of the menu to display the Format Data Labels task pane.

- For charts with multiple series, you have to format the data labels for each series independently.

  ✓ *Click the drop-down arrow next to LABEL OPTIONS in the Format Data Labels task pane to change labels or chart elements.*

Try It!   **Changing Chart Text**

① In the **E25Try_xx** file, on the Large Chart sheet click the chart to select it, and click the Chart Title placeholder to select it.

② Type **Buildout Status**, and press ENTER .

③ Click the vertical Axis Title placeholder to select it.

④ Type **Units**, and press ENTER .

⑤ Click HOME > Increase Font Size $A^{\uparrow}$ four times to make the axis title larger.

⑥ Click the Chart Elements shortcut menu ➕ , click the More arrow next to the Data Labels option, and click Inside End. Data labels are added to the column chart bars.

⑦ Click one of the data labels for the River Knoll series. Notice that the entire River Knoll series data labels are now selected.

⑧ On the CHART TOOLS FORMAT tab, click the Text Fill drop-down arrow, and then click Automatic. The text becomes black.

⑨ Click above the legend to deselect all objects.

⑩ Save the **E25Try_xx** file, and leave it open to use in the next Try It.

Enhancing the Chart Plot Area

- In Lesson 23, you learned how to apply a background to the chart area. You can use that same method to apply a fill to the chart area for any chart type.

- You can also apply a separate fill to the smaller plot area.

- You can:
  - Add a border around the background area.
  - Apply a color to the background.
  - Apply a fill effect, such as a gradient (a blend of two colors), texture (such as marble), pattern (such as diagonal stripes), or picture (a graphic file).
  - Add a shadow effect behind the border.
  - Shape the corners to create a 3-D look.

- To select the plot area, click it or choose Chart Area in the Chart Elements drop-down list in the Current Selection group on the CHART TOOLS DESIGN tab. Click the Format Selection button 🌫 to display the Format Chart Area task pane and its formatting options.

- You can also use the choices in the CHART TOOLS FORMAT Shape Styles group to change the plot area formatting.

- You can remove a plot area fill by right-clicking on the plot area, and clicking Fill > No fill.

Try It! | **Enhancing the Chart Plot Area**

1 In the **E25Try_xx** file, in the Large Chart sheet, click CHART TOOLS FORMAT > Chart Elements drop-down list arrow > Plot Area.

2 Click Format Selection 💅.

3 In the Format Plot Area task pane, click FILL > No fill.

4 On the CHART TOOLS FORMAT tab, click Shape Fill drop-down arrow 🎨 Shape Fill ▾ > Gray-50%, Accent 3, Lighter 80% (seventh choice in the second row of Theme Colors).

5 Click above the legend to deselect the plot area.

6 Save the **E25Try_xx** file, and leave it open to use in the next Try It.

Formatting the plot area

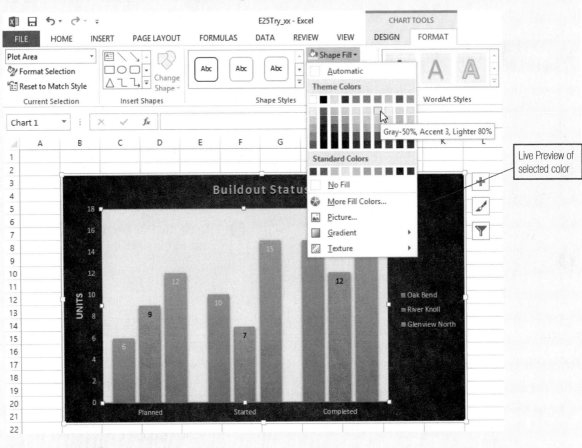

Formatting Category and Value Axes

- Categories and data series are plotted along the category or horizontal axis.

- The vertical or value axis provides a scale for the values of the data for most chart types. (For example, for bar charts, the axes are reversed.)

- You can change the font, size, color, attributes, alignment, and placement of text or numbers along both the category and value axes.

- You can add a color fill, border, line, shadow, or 3-D effect to the labels along either axis.

- You can also change the appearance of the **tick marks**, or add or remove gridlines.

- In addition, you can adjust the scale used along the value axis.

- You can use the Axes option in the Chart Elements shortcut menu to control whether either axis displays overall.

- You can also select an axis in the Chart Elements drop-down list on the CHART TOOLS FORMAT tab, and make changes in the Format Axis task pane.
- You can control whether the axis includes major gridlines, minor gridlines, or both, by clicking More Options in the Gridlines option of the Chart Elements shortcut menu. Use the task pane to make changes to the gridlines.

- After selecting an axis, use CHART TOOLS DESIGN > Format Selection to see more detailed settings.

Try It! **Formatting Category and Value Axes**

1 In the **E25Try_xx** file, with the Large Chart sheet and chart selected, click the Chart Elements shortcut button ➕ > Axes arrow > More Options. The Format Axis task pane opens.

2 Below Format Axis, click the AXIS OPTIONS drop-down arrow > Vertical (Value) Axis.

3 Click the Axis Options button ▮▮▮, and expand the AXIS OPTIONS submenu.

4 Under Units, in the Minor box, change the entry to 1.

5 Scroll down if necessary, expand the TICK MARKS submenu, and select Inside in the Major type drop-down list.

6 Click the Close button ✕ on the task pane.

7 Save the **E25Try_xx** file, and close it.

Lesson 25—Practice

In this project, you will change the data orientation and layout of a chart using the skills you learned in this lesson.

DIRECTIONS

1. Start Excel, if necessary, and open the **E25Practice** file from the data files for this lesson.
2. Save the file as **E25Practice_xx** in the location where your teacher instructs you to store the files for this lesson.
3. Group the sheets. Add a header that has your name at the left, the date code in the center, and the page number code at the right, and change back to **Normal** view. Ungroup the sheets.
4. Click the **Charts** sheet tab to select it.
5. Click the bottom pie chart and press the ⌈DEL⌋ key to remove it.

6. Click the top chart to select it, and click **HOME** > **Copy** ▣.
7. Click cell **B25** > **HOME** > **Paste** ▣.
8. Click **CHART TOOLS DESIGN** > **Switch Row/ Column** ▦.
9. Scroll up and compare the appearance of the top chart with that of the bottom chart. As shown in Figure 25-1 on the next page, changing the data orientation reduced the categories but increased the number of series.
10. **With your teacher's permission**, print the **Charts** sheet. Submit the printout or the file for grading as required.
11. Save and close the file, and exit Excel.

Figure 25-1

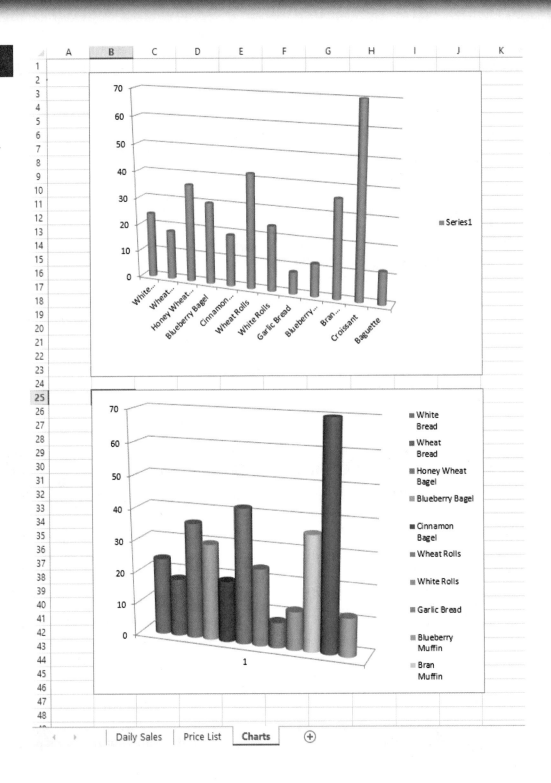

Lesson 25—Apply

The charts you created to analyze daily bread sales at your Whole Grains Bread retail store are almost completed. Before printing, you want to format them to make them more professional looking and easier to understand.

DIRECTIONS

1. Start Excel, if necessary, and open the **E25Apply** file from the data files for this lesson.

2. Save the file as **E25Apply_xx** in the location where your teacher instructs you to store the files for this lesson.

3. Group the sheets. Add a header that has your name at the left, the date code in the center, and the page number code at the right, and change back to **Normal** view. Ungroup the sheets.

4. Click the **Charts** sheet tab.

5. Select the horizontal axis for the top chart, and format it so it displays without axis labels.

6. On the same chart display data labels that are the category names.

7. Use the Format Data Labels task pane to show the category name only.

8. Use the TEXT OPTIONS in the Format Data Labels task pane to change the text direction to Rotate all text 270°.

9. Select the **Croissant** data label, and move it just to the left of the top of its data point cylinder, within the plot area.

10. Delete the legend.

11. Add a chart title above the chart that reads **Daily Sales**.

12. Add an **Orange, Accent 2, Lighter 40%** fill to the walls.

13. Select the data marker (cylinder) for the Croissant data point, and change its fill color to **Green, Accent 6, Darker 50%**.

14. Scroll down, if necessary, and select the bottom chart.

15. Apply the **Style 10** chart style.

16. Change the position of the legend to **Right**.

17. Add a rotated vertical axis title that reads **Unit Sales**, and increase its font size to **16** pts.

18. Select the Chart Area, and use the Format Chart Area task pane to add a **Pink tissue paper** texture fill set to **25%** transparency to the chart area.

19. Scroll to compare the charts. They should resemble Figure 25-2 on the next page.

20. **With your teacher's permission**, print the **Charts** sheet. Submit the printout or the file for grading as required.

21. Save and close the file, and exit Excel.

Figure 25-2

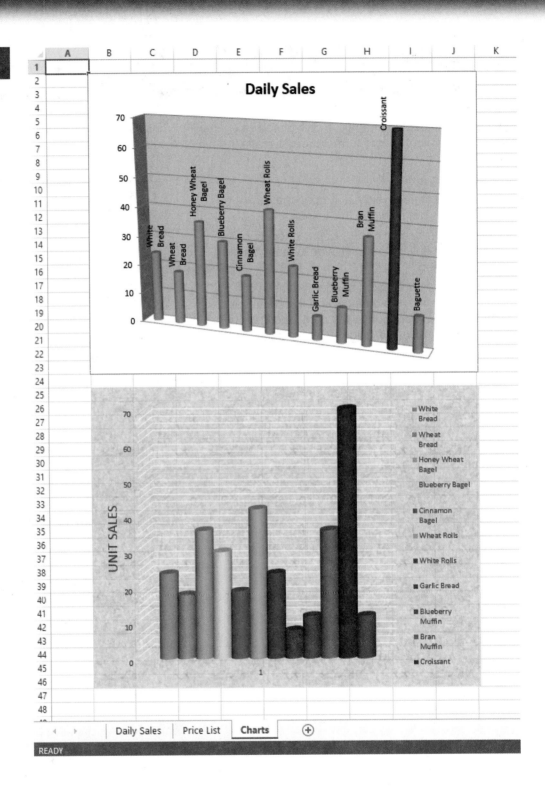

Lesson 26

Comparing and Analyzing Data

➤ What You Will Learn

Using Parentheses in a Formula
Calculating a Value After an Increase
Performing What-If Analysis
Creating a Line Chart to Compare Data

Software Skills Forecasting is an important business function. You can't plan for the future unless you can anticipate how various scenarios will develop and play out numerically. Excel offers a number of techniques that you can use to evaluate data based on your answer to the question, "What if?" In this lesson, you will explore the use of parentheses in formulas, calculating a value based on a percentage increase, creating a formula that performs a basic what-if analysis, and using a line chart to visualize the what-if scenario.

What You Can Do

Using Parentheses in a Formula

■ Parentheses, along with operator precedence, control the order of calculations in formulas.

✓ *Lesson 7 first introduced the concept of how to use parentheses in formulas. This lesson provides more examples.*

■ When there are multiple nested pairs of parentheses, Excel calculates from the innermost pair, working outward.

■ Improperly placed parentheses can cause logic flaws in a formula Excel might not necessarily flag with an error message or indicator. Look at the use of parentheses if your formula results are not what you expected.

Try It!   **Using Parentheses in a Formula**

1   Start Excel.

2   Open the **E26Try** file from the data files for this lesson.

3   Save the file as **E26Try_xx** in the location where your teacher instructs you to store the files for this lesson.

4   Add a header that has your name at the left, the date code in the center, and the page number code at the right, and change back to Normal view.

5   Select cell F6 and enter =((B6/C6)+(D6/E6))/2.

   ✓ *The parentheses cause the formula to calculate the individual quarterly averages, and then average the two values.*

6   Use the fill handle to copy the formula from cell F6 through F11.

7   Save the **E26Try_xx** file, and leave it open to use in the next Try It.

Calculating a Value After an Increase

■   In Lesson 22, you learned how to calculate the percentage of a total value represented by a single value. In that case, you create a formula that divides the individual value by the total value to yield the percentage.

■   You also learned in that lesson that to find a particular percentage of a value, you convert the percentage to a decimal, and then multiply.

■   Calculating the result of an increase works the same as calculating a percentage of a value, in most cases. That's because increases are often stated in terms of percentage increases.

■   So while you still convert to a decimal and multiply, you first add 1 (to represent 100% of the original value) to the decimal, so the result reflects the original value with the percentage increase added.

   ●   For example, suppose you pay a $215 membership fee this year and that value is in cell B2. The fee will go up 15% next year, and that value (.15) is in cell B3. To find the new fee, use the formula =(1+B3)*B2, or simply =1.15*B2.

Try It!   **Calculating a Value After an Increase**

1   In the **E26Try_xx** file, select cell G6.

2   Assume that Q3 travel expenses will be 2% more than the average for the first two quarters. Enter the formula =F6*1.02 in the cell.

3   Use the fill handle to copy the formula from cell G6 through G11.

4   Save the **E26Try_xx** file, and leave it open to use in the next Try It.

A formula that calculates an increase

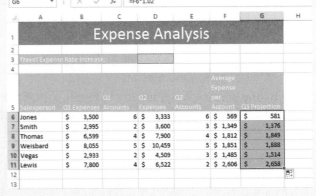

Performing What-If Analysis

- A **what-if analysis** entails looking at how future results might change based on varying inputs or data.

- For example, businesses often want to plan for sales increases or decreases, tax increases or decreases, or other expense increases or decreases.

- You can perform some what-if analyses in Excel simply by creating formulas that refer to an input cell whose entry you can change to see differing results.

  ✓ *Lesson 34 covers built-in tools that help automate what-if analysis. These tools include what-if data tables, Goal Seek, and Solver.*

Try It!   Performing What-If Analysis

1. In the **E26Try_xx** file, select cell G6.

2. Change the formula to calculate the increased projected quarterly expense amount using an absolute reference to D3. The formula should read =F6*(1+$D$3).

3. Use the fill handle to copy the formula from cell G6 through G11.

4. Enter **2.5** in cell D3. Note how the column G values update.

5. Enter **3.5** in cell D3. Review the new values in column G again.

6. Save the **E26Try_xx** file, and leave it open to use in the next Try It.

Creating a Line Chart to Compare Data

- Line charts provide a great data analysis tool.

- Not only do line charts identify data points, but they also show how data changed between data points. You can draw the lines further to anticipate how data might change beyond the charted timeframes.

- When performing what-if analysis, charting the most recent actual data and the projected data as separate series provides an idea of how the projected data varies based on changes in projected inputs.

Try It!   Creating a Line Chart to Compare Data

1. In the **E26Try_xx** file, select the nonadjacent ranges A5:A11 and F5:G11.

2. Click INSERT > Insert Line Chart 〽️ ⁻ > Line with Markers.

3. Drag the chart down below the sheet data.

4. Change the entry in cell D3 to **7.5**. View the results in the chart.

5. Save the **E26Try_xx** file, and close it.

(continued)

Try It! **Creating a Line Chart to Compare Data** (continued)

A line chart that shows a what-if analysis result

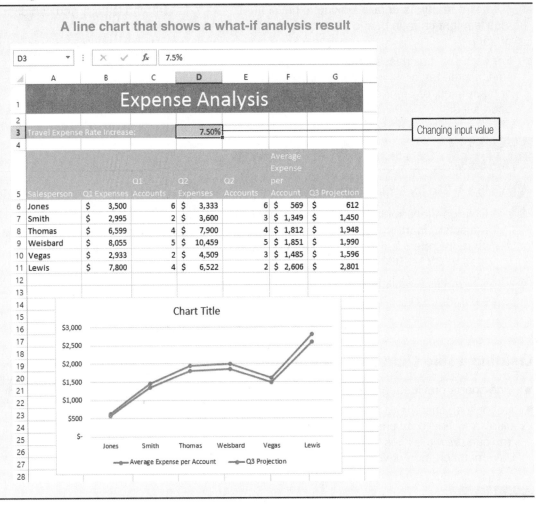

Changing input value

Lesson 26—Practice

In this project, you will use parentheses in formulas to calculate a value based on a percentage increase using the skills you learned in this lesson.

DIRECTIONS

1. Start Excel, if necessary, and open the **E26Practice** file from the data files for this lesson.
2. Save the file as **E26Practice_xx** in the location where your teacher instructs you to store the files for this lesson.
3. Add a header that has your name at the left, the date code in the center, and the page number code at the right, and change back to **Normal** view.
4. Click cell **B14**.
5. Enter a formula that adds the 2013 tax rates and multiplies by the Q1 2013 wages. It should be =($B$7+$B$8+$B$9)*B13.

6. Use the fill handle to copy the formula from cell B14 through F14. Increase column widths, as necessary.
7. Copy the formula from cell **B14** to cell **B16**.
8. Edit the absolute references in the copied formula in cell B16 to refer to column C. Edit the relative cell reference to refer to cell B15.
9. Use the fill handle to copy the formula from cell B16 to F16. Your worksheet should look like the one shown in Figure 26-1.
10. **With your teacher's permission**, print the worksheet. Submit the printout or the file for grading as required.
11. Save and close the file, and exit Excel.

Figure 26-1

	A	B	C	D	E	F
1	Cantrell Resources					
2	2014 Projections					
3						
4	Proposed State Tax Increase					
5						
6		2013	2014			
7	Av. Federal Tax Rate	25.00%	25.00%			
8	State Tax Rate	6.00%	6.00%			
9	Other Payroll Taxes	15.30%	15.30%			
10						
11						
12		Q1	Q2	Q3	Q4	Total
13	2013 Wages	$626,254.00	$832,999.00	$709,241.00	$906,888.00	$3,075,382.00
14	2013 Withholding	$289,955.60	$385,678.54	$328,378.58	$419,889.14	$1,423,901.87
15	2014 Wages (+1.9%)					
16	2014 Withholding	$ -	$ -	$ -	$ -	$ -

Lesson 26—Apply

You are the CEO for Cantrell Resources, a firm that provides temporary labor, placement, and payroll services. The state legislature in your state is debating a possible increase in the state income tax for next year. You are already anticipating that gross wages will increase by 1.9% for the coming year, so you want to examine how different increased state tax levels will affect quarterly withholding taxes for your firm by adding the formulas and charts needed to make these projections.

DIRECTIONS

1. Start Excel, if necessary, and open the **E26Apply** file from the data files for this lesson.

2. Save the file as **E26Apply_xx** in the location where your teacher instructs you to store the files for this lesson.

3. Add a header that has your name at the left, the date code in the center, and the page number code at the right, and change back to **Normal** view.

4. Select cell **C8**, and enter a formula that multiples 1 plus the input rate in cell **C4** times the previous tax rate in cell **B8**.

5. In cell **B15**, create a formula that increases the wages in cell **B13** by **1.9%**. Fill the formula through cell **F15**, and adjust column widths, as necessary.

6. Enter **1** as the base rate in cell **C4**.

7. Select the noncontiguous ranges **A12:E12**, **A14:E14**, and **A16:E16**.

8. Insert a line chart using the **Line with Markers** subtype.

9. Adjust the minimum bound of the vertical axis to a minimum value of **250000**, and a maximum value of **450000**.

   ✓ *Use the Minimum and Maximum text boxes in the Bounds group in the AXIS OPTIONS of the Format Axis task pane.*

10. If necessary, adjust the Major units to a value of **20000**, and adjust the Minor units to a value of **4000**.

11. Remove the decimal places from the axis display.

   ✓ *See the NUMBER choices in the Format Axis task pane.*

12. Increase the size of the chart as desired and position it below the data.

13. Change the entry in cell **C4** to **4**. Observe the calculations in the data and the chart. Your chart should resemble Figure 26-2 on the next page.

14. **With your teacher's permission**, print the worksheet. Submit the printout or the file for grading as required.

15. Save and close the file, and exit Excel.

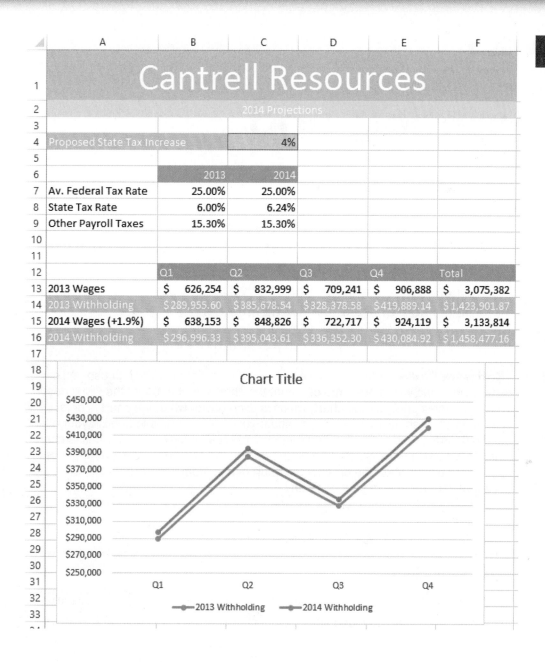

Lesson 27

Chart Printing and Publishing

➤ What You Will Learn

Printing a Chart
Preparing and Printing a Chart Sheet
Publishing a Chart to the Internet/Intranet

WORDS TO KNOW

Intranet
A private network of computers within a business or organization.

Publish
The process of saving data to an intranet or Internet.

Software Skills   After creating a chart, you may want to print it out so you can share your data with others. You can print the chart with the rest of the worksheet data, or simply print just the chart, which is even easier when the chart is on a separate chart sheet. Another way to share your information is to publish your chart to the Internet, or to your company's intranet. You can even make your online chart *interactive*, so that users can change the data in the chart as well as view it. This is especially useful when the data for the chart comes from several sources, such as different departments in your company.

What You Can Do

Printing a Chart

■ Embedded charts typically print with the worksheet on which they are located.

■ If you select an embedded chart before choosing the Print command, you will only be able to print the chart.

■ Typical print settings, such as changing the orientation and scaling, are available when printing a chart.

| Try It! | **Printing a Chart** |

1 Start Excel.

2 Open the **E27Try** file from the data files for this lesson.

3 Save the file as **E27Try_xx** in the location where your teacher instructs you to store the files for this lesson.

4 On the Example sheet, add a header that has your name at the left, the date code in the center, and the page number code at the right, and change back to Normal view.

5 Make sure the Example sheet is selected.

6 Click FILE > Print. Examine the preview of the printout. Under Settings, notice that the Print Active Sheets option is set to only print the active sheets.

7 **With your teacher's permission**, click the Print button to print the sheet and chart.

8 Save the **E27Try_xx** file, and leave it open to use in the next Try It.

Preparing and Printing a Chart Sheet

- When printing a chart sheet, the Print Active Sheet option is selected by default so that only the chart sheet prints. You would have to change that setting to print the whole workbook.

- When you insert a header or footer on a chart sheet using INSERT > Header & Footer 📄, the Page Setup dialog box appears with the Header/Footer tab selected. Use the Custom Header or Custom Footer button to build a header or footer.

  ✓ You also have to use this method to add a header or footer to an embedded chart if you want to print it by itself.

- The FILE > Print command also enables you to print the chart sheet.

| Try It! | **Preparing and Printing a Chart Sheet** |

1 In the **E27Try_xx** file, click the Large Chart sheet.

2 Click the Buildout Status chart to select it, and then click INSERT > Header & Footer 📄.

3 Click the Custom Header button. The Header dialog box appears.

4 Using the sections in the dialog box, add a header that has your name at the left, the date code in the center, and the page number code at the right, and then click OK twice.

5 Click FILE > Print. Examine the preview of the printout. Notice that the Large Chart sheet is using a different orientation than the Example sheet.

6 **With your teacher's permission**, click the Print button to print the chart.

7 Save the **E27Try_xx** file, and leave it open to use in the next Try It.

Publishing a Chart to the Internet/Intranet

- The process of saving worksheet data to the Internet or your company's **intranet** is called **publishing**.

- To publish a chart on the Internet or an intranet, Excel converts the chart to HTML format.

- There are actually two different HTML formats: Web Page (HTM) and Single File Web Page (MHT).

- HTM or HTML format is the standard Web page format in which the text and page format is stored in one file, and the graphics and other elements are stored in separate files linked to the main file.

- MHT or MHTML format is a single file Web page format in which the text, page format, and supporting graphics for a Web page are stored in one file.

- Both formats work perfectly well in most Web browsers; the MHT format does make it easier to relocate a Web page file if needed.

- If the chart is an embedded chart, the chart and its supporting data is published.

- You can publish a chart sheet or the entire workbook.

- Choose the Web format to save to from the Save as type drop-down list in the Save As dialog box. After choosing one of the Web formats, click the Publish button to open the Publish as Web Page dialog box, where you can navigate to a Web destination.

- In the Publish as Web Page dialog box, you must also open the Choose drop-down list under Item to publish, and then click Entire workbook. Otherwise, only the current sheet will be published, even if you chose Entire workbook in the Save As dialog box.

- Once your data is published, you can republish it when needed to update the data.

- You can have Excel automatically republish the data whenever you change the workbook, using the AutoRepublish option in the Publish as Web Page dialog box.

- You can also save Web page data on your hard disk, and transfer it to a Web location using another method.

  ✓ *When transferring Web page data to a Web location, be sure to transfer all the subfolders and contents created when the Web page was published; otherwise, the Web page will not display correctly.*

- Using an HTML editor, you can make changes to the Web page after it's saved to improve its appearance.

Try It!   **Publishing a Chart to the Internet/Intranet**

1 In the **E27Try_xx** file, make sure the Large Chart sheet is selected.

2 Click FILE > Save As.

3 Browse to the location where your teacher instructs you to store the files for this lesson.

4 In the File name box enter **E27Try_HTM_xx**. Open the Save as type drop-down list, and click Single File Web Page.

5 Click the Change Title button [Change Title...], type **Progress in Construction** as the title, and click OK.

6 Click the Selection: Chart button.

7 Click the Publish button [Publish...].

8 If necessary, use the Browse button to specify the location where your teacher instructs you to store the files for this lesson.

9 Click the Open published web page in browser check box, and then click the Publish button [Publish].

10 View the published chart in the system's Web browser, and then close the browser.

11 Save and close the **E27Try_xx** file, and exit Excel.

Publishing settings

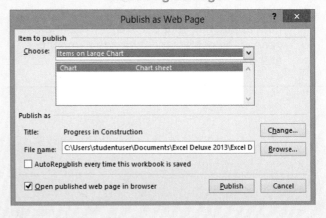

Lesson 27—Practice

In this project, you will print a worksheet and a chart using the skills you learned in this lesson.

DIRECTIONS

1. Start Excel, if necessary, and open the **E27Practice** file from the data files for this lesson.
2. Save the file as **E27Practice_xx** in the location where your teacher instructs you to store the files for this lesson.
3. For the **Data** sheet, add a header that has your name at the left, the date code in the center, and the page number code at the right, and change back to **Normal** view.
4. Click **FILE** > **Print**. Notice that the right side of the data and chart are cut off, and that 1 of 2 appears at the bottom of the preview to indicate the number of pages in the file.
5. Under Settings, change the orientation to **Landscape**.

6. **With your teacher's permission**, print the worksheet.
7. On the **Data** sheet, click the chart to select it.
8. Click **INSERT** > **Header & Footer** > **Custom Header**.
9. In the text edit boxes, type your name at the left, the date code in the center, and the page number code at the right.
10. Click **OK** twice.
11. **With your teacher's permission**, print the chart. Submit the printout or the file for grading as required.
12. Save and close the file, and exit Excel.

Lesson 27—Apply

You are the CFO of Restoration Architecture and you've been preparing an important report for the CEO on fourth quarter revenues. The most important part is the chart you've prepared. You're going to print it out for inclusion in the final report, and publish the chart to the Web.

DIRECTIONS

1. Start Excel, if necessary, and open the **E27Apply** file from the data files for this lesson.
2. Save the file as **E27Apply_xx** in the location where your teacher instructs you to store the files for this lesson.
3. For both the **Revenue Chart** and **Data** sheets, add a header that has your name at the left, the date code in the center, and the page number code at the right, and change back to **Normal** view.
4. Preview the Revenue Chart sheet.
5. **With your teacher's permission**, print the sheet.
6. Save the chart sheet as a Single File Web Page in the location where your teacher instructs you to store the files for this lesson.

7. Click **Selection: Chart**.
8. Add a title of **Q4 Revenue Chart**.
9. Click **Save**.
10. In the Publish as Web Page dialog box, click the **Open published web page in browser** check box to select it if it isn't already selected.
11. Click **Publish**, and view the published chart in the Web browser program.
12. Close the browser.
13. **With your teacher's permission**, print the chart sheet. Submit the printout or the file for grading as required.
14. Save and close the file, and exit Excel.

Lesson 28

Using Charts in Other Files

➤ What You Will Learn

Pasting a Picture of a Chart
Embedding a Chart in a Word Document
Linking a Chart
Editing a Linked or Embedded Chart

WORDS TO KNOW

Embed
To insert an object in a destination document so that it can still be edited by the source application. When you double-click an embedded object, the source application (or its tools) appear, so you can edit the object. The original object remains unchanged because no link exists.

Link
A reference in a destination document to an object (such as a chart) in a source document. Changes to the linked object in the source document are automatically made to the object in the destination document.

Software Skills   You can link or embed an Excel chart into another document, such as a Word document. If the source data is likely to change, you should link the data to its source, so that your chart will automatically update. This is especially useful when the source data is updated by several different people in your organization. You can also embed the chart in your Word document to ensure that your changes will not affect the original data.

What You Can Do

Pasting a Picture of a Chart

- The simplest way to include an Excel chart within another document, such as a Word document, is to paste its picture.

- The advantage of using a picture of a chart is that it will not significantly affect the size of your Word file.

- The disadvantage of using a chart picture is that the data is static—meaning if the data changes in the original Excel workbook, the picture of the chart is not updated.

- To update the picture, you would need to change the data in Excel and paste a new picture.

- After pasting the chart, click the Paste Options button that appears to the lower-right of the chart and then click Picture to paste the chart as a picture.

| **Try It!** | **Pasting a Picture of a Chart** |

1 Start Excel.

2 Open the **E28TryA** file from the data files for this lesson.

3 Save the file as **E28TryA_xx** in the location where your teacher instructs you to store the files for this lesson.

4 Add a header that has your name at the left, the date code in the center, and the page number code at the right, and change back to Normal view.

5 Start Word.

6 Open the **E28TryB** file from the data files for this lesson.

7 Save the document as **E28TryB_xx** in the location where your teacher instructs you to store the files for this lesson.

8 Press CTRL + END and type your name.

9 Press ↑ three times to position the insertion point where you'd like the chart to appear.

10 In the **E28TryA_xx** workbook, on the Expenses tab, click the chart.

11 On the HOME tab, click Copy 📋.

12 In the **E28TryB_xx** Word document, on the HOME tab, click Paste 📋.

13 Click the Paste Options button, and click the Picture button 🖼.

14 Drag the sizing handle in the upper-left corner of the chart to make the chart smaller, so it will fit within the margins of the page.

15 Save the **E28TryB_xx** file, and leave it open to use in the next Try It.

Embedding a Chart in a Word Document

■ When you **embed** a chart in a Word document, the chart data is also copied to the Word file and stored there.

■ Making data or formatting changes to an embedded chart does not affect the original data or chart, since there is no link to the original chart.

✓ *Although this lesson discusses pasting charts into another document, you can use these same procedures to embed worksheet data rather than chart data. You can also use these procedures to share data in PowerPoint. See Excel Lesson 45 to learn more about using Paste Special.*

■ An embedded chart in the destination file may also be displayed as an icon.

■ After pasting the chart, you can use the Paste Options button that appears to the lower right of the chart to select either Use Destination Theme & Embed Workbook or Keep Source Formatting & Embed Workbook to insert the chart.

✓ *Rather than pasting and then choosing a paste method, you can use the HOME > Paste > Paste Options to choose the paste method when performing the initial paste. This is true of all the procedures covered in this lesson.*

| **Try It!** | **Embedding a Chart in a Word Document** |

1 In the **E28TryB_xx** Word file, double-click the pasted chart picture. Notice that Excel does not open.

✓ *If the Format Chart Area task pane opens, click Close to close it.*

2 With the picture selected, press DEL to remove the picture from the file.

3 On the HOME tab, click the Paste button drop-down arrow ▾.

✓ *Because the chart is already on the Clipboard, there is no need to copy it again. However, if you copy any other data or information in a situation like this, you would need to return to Excel and select and copy the chart again.*

(continued)

Try It!   **Embedding a Chart in a Word Document** *(continued)*

4 In the Paste Options drop-down options, click the Keep Source Formatting & Embed Workbook button .

5 Double-click the chart. Notice that the Chart Tools contextual tabs appear on Word's Ribbon.

6 Save the **E28TryB_xx** file, and leave it open to use in the next Try It.

Linking a Chart

- If you want to be able to edit your chart after pasting it into another document, you can **link** the chart.

- When you paste a chart into a destination file (Word document) as a linked chart, it remains connected to its source data (in Excel).

- When you change the data or chart formatting in a linked chart and open the destination file again, the link causes the destination chart to update as well.

- The link also enables you to start Excel from within the destination file (from within Word, for example), display the chart, and make your changes.

- To maintain the link, the files must remain in their original locations.

- Linked data in the destination file may also be displayed as an icon.

- After pasting the chart, click the Paste Options button that appears to the lower right of the chart and then click either Use Destination Theme & Link Data or Keep Source Formatting & Link Data to establish the link.

Try It!   **Linking a Chart**

1 In the **E28TryB_xx** Word file, double-click the pasted chart picture. Notice that the Format Chart Area task pane opens, but that Excel does not open.

2 With the embedded chart selected, press DEL to remove the chart from the file.

3 On the HOME tab, click the Paste button drop-down arrow .

4 In the Paste Options drop-down options, click the Use Destination Theme & Link Data button .

5 Double-click the chart. Notice that the Chart Tools contextual tabs appear on Word's Ribbon.

6 Save the **E28TryB_xx** file and leave it open to use in the next Try It.

Editing a Linked or Embedded Chart

- Because linked data is stored in the source document, you can open that document in Excel to edit a linked chart. Save the source document to preserve the changes.

- When you change the worksheet data in Excel, the corresponding chart is updated.

- Open the destination document and the chart is either updated automatically or when you manually update the link.

- You can open Excel from within the destination document if you like, rather than starting Excel separately.

- Click a linked or embedded chart to display Excel's CHART TOOLS tabs in the destination application.

  ✓ *When you make formatting changes to a chart either in the source or destination workbook for a linked chart, those changes do not flow between the two chart locations.*

- Right-click a linked or embedded chart and click Edit Data to open the Excel window for editing data.

■ If the data is linked, the source document opens in Excel. If the data is embedded, the Excel window shows the Chart name in the title bar, indicating the data is stored in the destination file, with the embedded chart.

■ Make the changes you need. For a linked chart, save the source worksheet and close the Excel window. For an embedded chart, simply close the Excel window.

■ If you've updated a source linked chart and the updates don't appear in the destination document, click the chart in the destination document and use the Refresh Data button on the CHART TOOLS DESIGN tab.

Try It!   **Editing a Linked or Embedded Chart**

1. In Word, save the **E28TryB_xx** file and close it.

2. In the **E28TryA_xx** Excel file, select the chart title.

3. Edit the title to read **Projected 2014 Expenses**.

4. Click cell A6 and change its entry to **Computers & Software**.

5. Change the entries for book expenses in cells B4 and C4 to **375** and **450**, respectively.

6. Save the **E28TryA_xx** file, and exit Excel.

7. In Word, open the **E28TryB_xx** file.

8. Click the chart to select it > CHART TOOLS DESIGN tab > Refresh Data. Notice that the changes to the book expenses and the new series name appear in the chart. The title does not change, because that is a formatting change.

9. Save the **E28TryB_xx** file, and exit Word.

Lesson 28—Practice

In this project, you will paste a chart in a Word document as a picture using the skills you learned in this lesson.

DIRECTIONS

1. Start Excel, if necessary, and open **E28PracticeA** from the data files for this lesson.

2. Save the file as **E28PracticeA_xx** in the location where your teacher instructs you to store the files for this lesson.

3. Group the sheets. Add a header that has your name at the left, the date code in the center, and the page number code at the right, and change back to **Normal** view. Ungroup the sheets.

4. Open **E28PracticeB** from the data files for this lesson.

5. Save the document as **E28PracticeB_xx** in the location where your teacher instructs you to store the files for this lesson.

6. Type the date and your name in the *Date Prepared* and *Prepared By* headings, respectively.

7. In Word, add a footer that has your name at the left, the date code in the center, and the page number code at the right.

   ✓ The Blank (Three-Columns) Footer will provide a footer similar to the heading you have been using in the Excel exercises.

   ✓ To insert a page number in a Word footer, click the Type Here placeholder > Page Number > Current Position > Plain Number.

   ✓ Click Close Header and Footer on the HEADER & FOOTER TOOLS DESIGN tab to close the header or footer and return to your document.

8. In the **E28PracticeA_xx** Excel file, click the **2014 Charts** tab.

9. Click the top chart to select it.

10. On the HOME tab, click **Copy** 📋.

11. In the **E28PracticeB_xx** Word file, click below the Asset Summary heading, and click **HOME** > **Paste** drop-down arrow ᵖᵃˢᵗᵉ > **Picture** 📷. The picture appears in the document.

12. **With your teacher's permission**, print the Word document. Submit the printout or the file for grading as required.

13. Save and close both files, and exit Word and Excel.

Lesson 28—Apply

As CFO of Hyland Manufacturing, you need to prepare an executive summary of balance sheet data for the board of directors. You've prepared the charts, and you need to incorporate the charts in the executive summary Word document.

DIRECTIONS

1. Start Excel, if necessary, and open **E28ApplyA** from the data files for this lesson.

2. Save the file as **E28ApplyA_xx** in the location where your teacher instructs you to store the files for this lesson.

3. Group the sheets. Add a header that has your name at the left, the date code in the center, and the page number code at the right, and change back to **Normal** view. Ungroup the sheets.

4. Open **E28ApplyB** from the data files for this lesson.

5. Save the document as **E28ApplyB_xx** in the location where your teacher instructs you to store the files for this lesson.

6. In the **E28ApplyB_xx** document, type the date and your name in the *Date Prepared* and *Prepared By* headings, respectively.

7. Add a footer that has your name at the left, the date code in the center, and the page number code at the right.

8. In the Excel file, click the **2014 Charts** tab.

9. Select and copy the top chart.

10. In the Word document, paste the chart using the destination theme and link the data under the Asset Summary heading.

11. Repeat steps 8 through 10 to paste and link the bottom chart under the Liability Summary heading. Review the appearance of both charts.

12. In the Excel file, click the **2014 Balance Sheet** sheet tab.

13. Change the entry in cell **B15** to **4095**.

14. Change the entry in cell **E19** to **1813**.

15. Save the **E28ApplyA_xx** Excel file, and exit Excel.

16. In the Word document, review the changes to the charts, particularly the Liabilities chart.

17. **With your teacher's permission**, print the Word document. Submit the printout or the file for grading as required.

18. Save the **E28ApplyB_xx** Word file, and exit Word.

Lesson 29

Making Special Purpose Charts

➤ What You Will Learn

Creating Organization Charts
Creating Other SmartArt Diagrams

Software Skills   With an organization chart, you can easily show the relationship between objects or people. For example, you could show how your department is organized. With other conceptual charts, you could show the progress of a project—from conception to completion, areas of overlapping responsibility within a department or on a group project, or the cycle of events with a school or calendar year.

What You Can Do

Creating Organization Charts

- To show relationships within a group such as an office, the government, or a school, create an **organization chart**.

- An organization chart is just one of many **SmartArt graphics** you can insert on a worksheet.

- On the INSERT tab, use the SmartArt button 🖼 to open the Choose a SmartArt Graphic dialog box. The Hierarchy group in the Choose a SmartArt Graphic dialog box provides a selection of organization and layout charts.

- When you start an organization chart, Excel provides a sample chart showing several basic relationships.

- Enter data for the organization chart using the Text Pane, which displays a bulleted list that shows the relationship between people.

    ✓ *Use the Text Pane button* 🗔 *on the SMARTART TOOLS DESIGN tab to open and close the Text Pane.*

- You can paste this list from another source or enter it manually.

- Use the Add Shape button on the SmartArt Tools Design tab to add the desired relationships.

WORDS TO KNOW

Organization chart
Displays the relationships within an organization, such as the managers in an office, the people they manage, and who they report to.

SmartArt graphic
A pre-drawn graphic used to illustrate a specific data relationship, such as a list, process, cycle, hierarchy, matrix, pyramid, or other relationship.

- You can add shapes before, after, above, or below the currently selected shape. You can also add an assistant shape.

- If you add a shape before or after, that shape is placed on the same level in the hierarchy as the current shape.

- If you add a shape above or below, the shape is placed above or below the current shape in the organizational hierarchy.

  ✓ *After typing text in the Text Pane, press* ENTER *to create another shape at the same level. Use* SHIFT + TAB *to decrease the level, or* TAB *to increase the level.*

- An assistant shape is placed out to one side, indicating a different relationship than an employee-manager or employee-employee relationship.

- Remove shapes (relationships) you don't need for your chart by selecting the shape, and pressing DEL .

- For other graphics such as charts, you can select from predefined layouts and styles, and apply them with a single click. The SMARTART TOOLS DESIGN tab offers Layouts and SmartArt Styles galleries.

- You can also apply your own formatting (outlines, fills, shadows, glows, and other effects) to individual shapes and the background. These choices are on the SMARTART TOOLS FORMAT tab.

- You can format the text of individual shapes or the whole chart.

- Using the Layout button in the Create Graphic group on the SMARTART TOOLS DESIGN tab, you can change the way in which relationships are displayed within the chart.

  ✓ *If you've already created an organization chart or other SmartArt graphic in Word or PowerPoint, you can save time by simply copying and pasting it into Excel.*

Try It!   Creating Organization Charts

1 Start Excel, and create a new blank workbook file.

2 Save the file as **E29Try_xx** in the location where your teacher instructs you to store the files for this lesson.

3 Add a header that has your name at the left, the date code in the center, and the page number code at the right, and change back to Normal view.

4 Click PAGE LAYOUT > Orientation 🖼 > Landscape.

5 Click INSERT > SmartArt 🖼 .

6 In the list at the left, click Hierarchy.

7 In the list in the middle, click the third layout in the top row, Name and Title Organization Chart, and click OK.

8 In the Text Pane that appears to the left of the chart, type the following names in order, clicking the next placeholder after finishing each one:
Aliyah Brown
Linda Williams
Bill Whittaker
Marlow Aronstein
Katie Martin

9 Click the smaller text box at the lower right of each shape, and type the following titles:
President
Assistant
HR Director
Product Director
Sales Director

10 Click the Katie Martin shape > SMARTART TOOLS DESIGN > Add Shape drop-down arrow > Add Shape Below.

11 In the new shape, add **Ron Crane** and **Deputy Sales Director** as the name and title.

12 On the SMARTART TOOLS DESIGN tab, click the SmartArt Styles More button ⬇, and click Polished, the first style under 3-D.

13 Click the Linda Williams shape to select it.

14 Click SMARTART TOOLS FORMAT > Shape Fill 🪣 Shape Fill ▾ > Green, Accent 6, Darker 25%.

15 With the Linda Williams shape still selected, click SMARTART TOOLS FORMAT > Shape Outline 📝 > Green, Accent, Lighter 80%.

(continued)

Try It!   **Creating Organization Charts** *(continued)*

16   Click the Close button on the Text Pane.

17   Drag the chart up so its upper-left corner is over cell B2.

18   Save the **E29Try_xx** file and leave it open to use in the next Try It.

Organization chart with names and titles added

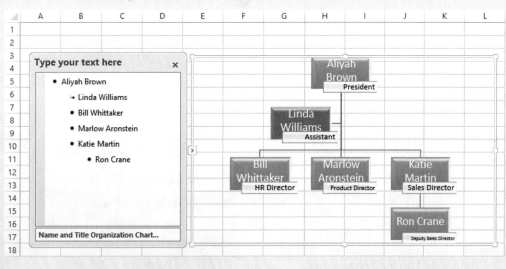

Creating Other SmartArt Diagrams

■ In addition to organization charts, Excel enables you to create several other types of conceptual charts using the Choose a SmartArt Graphic dialog box.

■ You can choose these overall diagram types from the list at the left side of the dialog box.

✓ *You can use the Office.com choice to see the latest added diagrams available for download.*

■ There are numerous layouts available for each of the SmartArt diagram types.

■ After you create the diagram, you can easily change from one layout to another until you find the one that properly conveys the relationship between your data items. You can use the More button ⊡ in the Layouts group on the SMARTART TOOLS DESIGN tab to view the layouts. You can use the More Layouts button at the bottom of the menu to change to another type of diagram. The More Layouts choice at the bottom of the menu even enables you to change to another type of diagram.

Try It!   **Creating Other SmartArt Diagrams**

1   In the **E29Try_xx** file, click INSERT > SmartArt ⌨. The SmartArt Graphic Dialog box opens.

2   In the list at the left, click Cycle.

3   In the list in the middle, click the first layout in the second row, Continuous Cycle, and click OK.

4   Drag the new chart down below the organization chart. Scroll down, if necessary.

5   On the SMARTART TOOLS DESIGN tab, in the Create Graphic group, click Text Pane ⌨.

(continued)

Try It!   Creating Other SmartArt Diagrams *(continued)*

6 In the Text Pane, type the following text for the boxes, clicking the next placeholder after finishing each one:

Startup

Initial Diagnostics

Operational Cycle

Cleaning Cycle

Auto Power Cycle

7 Click Text Pane ⊞ to close the Text Pane.

8 With the mouse pointer still in the Auto Power Cycle box, click Add Bullet ⊞ .

9 Type **Manual power cycle every 14 days**.

10 On the SMART TOOLS DESIGN tab, in the SmartArt Styles group, click Change Colors ∴ > Colorful > Colorful Range - Accent Colors 2 to 3 (the second choice in the Colorful group).

11 Click SMARTART TOOLS FORMAT > Shape Fill ⬗ Shape Fill ▾ > Gradient > Dark Variations > From Center (second on the second row).

12 Click SMARTART TOOLS DESIGN > Layouts More button ▼ > More Layouts.

13 In the list at the left, click List.

14 In the list in the middle, click the second layout in the second row, Vertical Box List, and click OK.

15 Click the Close button on the Text Pane to close the Text Pane.

16 Save and close the file, and exit Excel.

Cycle diagram with fill gradient

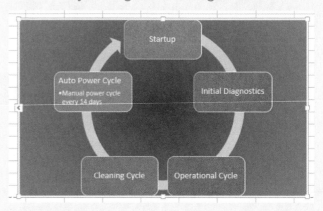

Lesson 29—Practice

In this project, you will use SmartArt to create a process diagram using the skills you learned in this lesson.

DIRECTIONS

1. Start Excel, if necessary, and open **E29Practice** from the data files for this lesson.

2. Save the file as **E29Practice_xx** in the location where your teacher instructs you to store the files for this lesson.

3. Add a header that has your name at the left, the date code in the center, and the page number code at the right, and change back to **Normal** view.

4. Click **INSERT** > SmartArt 🖼 .

5. In the list at the left, click **Process**.

6. In the middle list, click **Vertical Chevron List**, and click **OK**.

7. In the Text Pane, add the following text:

Rapid Prototyping

   Reduced Time

   Reduced Waste

Production Pilot

   Build Process

   Document Process

Testing

   Safety Testing

   Performance Testing

8. After the last entry, press ENTER and then SHIFT + TAB. This creates another shape at the top level.

9. Type **Production Release**, press ENTER and then TAB. This indents to the bullet-level shape.

10. Type **Continuous Quality Improvement**, press ENTER, and then type **RFID Tracking**.

11. On the SMARTART TOOLS DESIGN tab, click **Text Pane** to hide the Text Pane.

12. Drag the diagram up so its upper-left corner is on cell **B4**. Your chart should resemble Figure 29-1.

13. **With your teacher's permission**, print the worksheet. Submit the printout or the file for grading as required.

14. Save and close the file, and exit Excel.

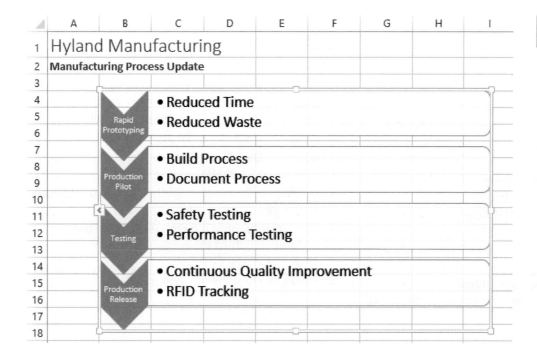

Figure 29-1

Lesson 29—Apply

You are the Chief Operating Officer (COO) of Hyland Manufacturing. The company has developed a new manufacturing process, and you need to provide information about it to key customers to reassure them that their future orders will be handled seamlessly under the new process. You will send two SmartArt diagrams—one that illustrates the process itself, and another that is an organization chart of the team managing the process.

DIRECTIONS

1. Start Excel, if necessary, and open **E29Apply** from the data files for this lesson.
2. Save the file as **E29Apply_xx** in the location where your teacher instructs you to store the files for this lesson.
3. Add a header that has your name at the left, the date code in the center, and the page number code at the right, and change back to **Normal** view.
4. Create an organization chart using the **Horizontal Organization Chart** layout.
5. Delete the Assistant shape (the text box above the relationship line).
6. Enter **Production Director** in the top level box on the left.
7. Enter **Engineering Manager**, **Quality Manager**, and **Production Manager** in the three stacked text boxes.

8. Right-click the Engineering Manager box, click **Change Shape**, and click the **Pentagon** block arrow.
9. Apply the **Pentagon** block arrow shape to the other two lower-level boxes.
10. Drag the organization chart below the process chart, so its upper-left corner is over cell **B20**.
11. Apply the **Inset** SmartArt style to both charts.
12. Apply the **Dark 2 Fill** colors under Primary Theme Colors to both charts.
13. Deselect both charts. Your charts should resemble Figure 29-2.
14. **With your teacher's permission**, print the worksheet. Submit the printout or the file for grading as required.
15. Save and close the file, and exit Excel.

Figure 29-2

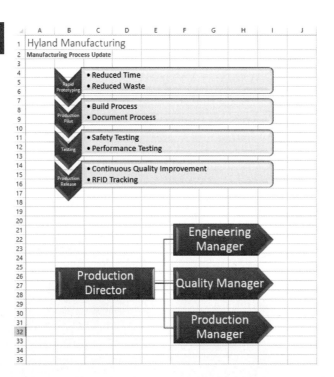

End-of-Chapter Activities

➤ Excel Chapter 3—Critical Thinking

Investment Portfolio

You are a certified financial planner with Solid Investments, LLC. You are putting some sample data together to help illustrate stock performance and investment potential and risk for new clients who are also new to investing overall. You will chart historical stock price data, create formulas that show how a sample portfolio of investments will change if the market goes up or down, and chart that sample portfolio data.

DIRECTIONS

1. Start Excel, if necessary, and open **ECT03** from the data files for this chapter.

2. Save the file as **ECT03_xx** in the location where your teacher instructs you to store the files for this chapter.

3. Group the named sheets. Add a header that has your name at the left, the date code in the center, and the page number code at the right, and change back to **Normal** view. Ungroup the sheets.

4. On the **Ford Historical Prices** sheet, select the range **A5:E27**, and insert a **Stock** chart using the **Open-High-Low-Close** subtype.

5. Apply the **Layout 1** layout to the chart, and the **Style 3** chart style.

6. Change the scale of the primary vertical axis so that its minimum value is **9**. This scales the data bars so that they are easier to interpret.

7. Change the chart title to **Ford June 2010**.

8. Drag the chart so its upper-left corner is over cell **I3**.

9. Go to the **Portfolio Analysis** tab.

10. In cell **E8**, enter a formula that will recalculate the value from the Total column based on an increase percentage entered in cell **D4**. Use an absolute reference to cell **D4**.

11. Copy the formula in cell **E8** down through cell **E12**.

12. In cell **F8**, enter a formula that will recalculate the value from the Total column based on a decrease percentage entered in cell **D5**. Use an absolute reference to cell D5.

    ✓ *You can use a similar formula to the one you created in step 10, but subtract, instead.*

13. Copy the formula in cell **F8** down through cell **F12**. Adjust column widths, if necessary.

14. To test your formulas, enter **7** in cell **D4** and **5** in cell **D5**. Verify that the values in column E increased by 7% and that the values in column F decreased by 5%. If not, correct your formulas.

15. Select the ranges **D7:F7** and **D13:F13** and insert a **Clustered Column** chart.

16. Add a title above the chart that reads **Sample Portfolio Results**.

17. Move the chart so its upper-left corner is over cell **I4**.

18. Adjust the page breaks in Page Break Preview for both worksheets to print on a single page.

    ✓ *Adjust the Print Settings to Print Entire Workbook and Fit Sheet on One Page, as needed.*

19. **With your teacher's permission**, print the workbook. Submit the printouts or the file for grading as required.

20. Save and close the file, and exit Excel.

➤ Excel Chapter 3—Portfolio Builder

Sales Data Chart and Web Page

You are the CFO for Teesy Apparel, a T-shirt manufacturer. You have developed a worksheet with quarterly sales data that also tracks sales by product line and size. You need to chart all this information for future production planning, and create a SmartArt diagram that ranks potential new product ideas. After you chart the data, you will publish the data as a Single File Web Page to the company intranet to give the planning team easier access.

DIRECTIONS

1. Start Excel, if necessary, and open **EPB03** from the data files for this chapter.

2. Save the file as **EPB03_xx** in the location where your teacher instructs you to store the files for this chapter.

3. Create a **Clustered Column** chart of the quarterly sales totals on its own chart sheet. Name the sheet **Q Sales**.

4. Use the Select Data Source dialog box to assign the range ='Sales Data'!$E$4:$H$4 as the horizontal axis label range. (Hint: Select an existing axis label entry, and click **Edit**.)

5. Add a title above the chart that reads **Strong Quarterly Product Sales**.

6. Apply chart **Style 16** to the chart.

7. On the **Sales Data** sheet, create **3-D Pie** charts for the Sales by Product Line and Sales by Size data, placing each chart on its own sheet and giving the sheets appropriate names.

8. Apply the **Layout 1** layout to each pie chart, and make the chart title the same as the sheet name.

9. Apply a solid fill of **Gold, Accent 4, Lighter 80%** to each of the pie chart areas.

10. Explode the smallest slice for each pie chart.

11. Add a sheet titled **Potential Products**.

12. Insert a **Matrix** SmartArt diagram that uses the **Grid Matrix** layout.

13. Open the Text Pane, and use it to add these entries to the diagram:

    Organic Cotton Socks

    Organic Cotton Sweatshirts

    Natural Dyes Line

    Children's Tees

14. Hide the Text Pane, apply **Colorful - Accent Colors** to the diagram, and drag it to the upper-left corner of the worksheet.

15. On the **Sales Data** sheet, select cell **A1**. Publish the entire workbook as a **Single File Web Page**, adding **Teesy Apparel** as a title. (Hint: In the Publish as Web Page dialog box, remember to also open the Choose drop-down list under Item to publish, and then click Entire workbook.) Save the Web page as **EPB03_HTM_xx**.

16. The workbook opens in your Web browser. If necessary, allow blocked content to be viewed in the browser. The file has a tab for every tab in the worksheet, as shown in Illustration 3A on the next page. Click the various tabs to review the charts that you have created. Close the Web browser when you finish.

17. For all chart sheets and worksheets, add a header that has your name at the left, the date code in the center, and the page number code at the right, and change back to **Normal** view.

18. **With your teacher's permission**, print all worksheets in the workbook, scaling each to fit a single page. Submit the printouts or the file for grading as required.

19. Save and close the file, and exit Excel.

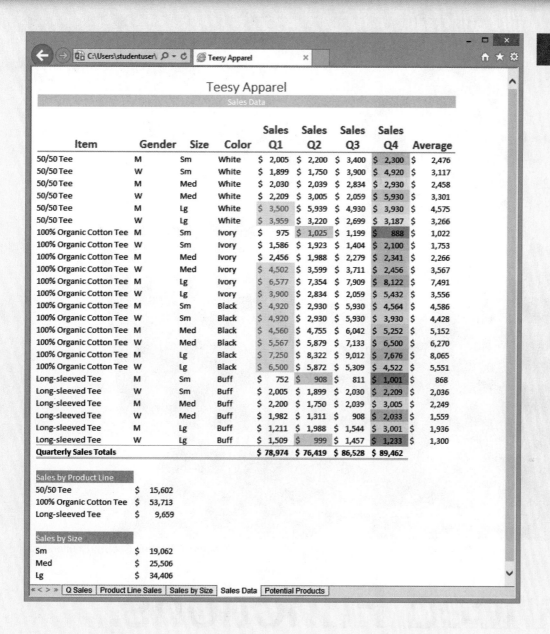

Teesy Apparel
Sales Data

Item	Gender	Size	Color	Sales Q1	Sales Q2	Sales Q3	Sales Q4	Average
50/50 Tee	M	Sm	White	$ 2,005	$ 2,200	$ 3,400	$ 2,300	$ 2,476
50/50 Tee	W	Sm	White	$ 1,899	$ 1,750	$ 3,900	$ 4,920	$ 3,117
50/50 Tee	M	Med	White	$ 2,030	$ 2,039	$ 2,834	$ 2,930	$ 2,458
50/50 Tee	W	Med	White	$ 2,209	$ 3,005	$ 2,059	$ 5,930	$ 3,301
50/50 Tee	M	Lg	White	$ 3,500	$ 5,939	$ 4,930	$ 3,930	$ 4,575
50/50 Tee	W	Lg	White	$ 3,959	$ 3,220	$ 2,699	$ 3,187	$ 3,266
100% Organic Cotton Tee	M	Sm	Ivory	$ 975	$ 1,025	$ 1,199	$ 888	$ 1,022
100% Organic Cotton Tee	W	Sm	Ivory	$ 1,586	$ 1,923	$ 1,404	$ 2,100	$ 1,753
100% Organic Cotton Tee	M	Med	Ivory	$ 2,456	$ 1,988	$ 2,279	$ 2,341	$ 2,266
100% Organic Cotton Tee	W	Med	Ivory	$ 4,502	$ 3,599	$ 3,711	$ 2,456	$ 3,567
100% Organic Cotton Tee	M	Lg	Ivory	$ 6,577	$ 7,354	$ 7,909	$ 8,122	$ 7,491
100% Organic Cotton Tee	W	Lg	Ivory	$ 3,900	$ 2,834	$ 2,059	$ 5,432	$ 3,556
100% Organic Cotton Tee	M	Sm	Black	$ 4,920	$ 2,930	$ 5,930	$ 4,564	$ 4,586
100% Organic Cotton Tee	M	Sm	Black	$ 4,920	$ 2,930	$ 5,930	$ 3,930	$ 4,428
100% Organic Cotton Tee	M	Med	Black	$ 4,560	$ 4,755	$ 6,042	$ 5,252	$ 5,152
100% Organic Cotton Tee	W	Med	Black	$ 5,567	$ 5,879	$ 7,133	$ 6,500	$ 6,270
100% Organic Cotton Tee	M	Lg	Black	$ 7,250	$ 8,322	$ 9,012	$ 7,676	$ 8,065
100% Organic Cotton Tee	W	Lg	Black	$ 6,500	$ 5,872	$ 5,309	$ 4,522	$ 5,551
Long-sleeved Tee	M	Sm	Buff	$ 752	$ 908	$ 811	$ 1,001	$ 868
Long-sleeved Tee	W	Sm	Buff	$ 2,005	$ 1,899	$ 2,030	$ 2,209	$ 2,036
Long-sleeved Tee	M	Med	Buff	$ 2,200	$ 1,750	$ 2,039	$ 3,005	$ 2,249
Long-sleeved Tee	W	Med	Buff	$ 1,982	$ 1,311	$ 908	$ 2,033	$ 1,559
Long-sleeved Tee	M	Lg	Buff	$ 1,211	$ 1,988	$ 1,544	$ 3,001	$ 1,936
Long-sleeved Tee	W	Lg	Buff	$ 1,509	$ 999	$ 1,457	$ 1,233	$ 1,300
Quarterly Sales Totals				$ 78,974	$ 76,419	$ 86,528	$ 89,462	

Sales by Product Line

50/50 Tee	$ 15,602
100% Organic Cotton Tee	$ 53,713
Long-sleeved Tee	$ 9,659

Sales by Size

Sm	$ 19,062
Med	$ 25,506
Lg	$ 34,406

« < > » | Q Sales | Product Line Sales | Sales by Size | Sales Data | Potential Products

(Courtesy Stephen Coburn/Shutterstock)

Chapter 4

Advanced Functions, PivotCharts, and PivotTables

303

Lesson 30

Working with Hyperlinks

➤ What You Will Learn

Using a Hyperlink in Excel
Creating a Hyperlink in a Cell
Modifying Hyperlinks
Modifying Hyperlinked Cell Attributes
Removing a Hyperlink

WORDS TO KNOW

Hyperlink
Text or graphics linked to related information in the same workbook, another workbook, or another file.

URL
Short for Uniform Resource Locator. The address or location of a page or file on the Internet.

Web pages
Documents (frequently including multimedia elements) that can be accessed with a Web browser.

Software Skills   A hyperlink can connect a worksheet to specific locations within any worksheet in any workbook, or to information on the Internet or a company intranet. Using a hyperlink is a convenient way to provide quick access to related information. For example, in a sales worksheet, you could provide a hyperlink to an area in the workbook (or in another workbook) that provides product costs or other revenues.

What You Can Do

Using a Hyperlink in Excel

- A **hyperlink** is text or a graphic that, when clicked, displays related information elsewhere in the worksheet or in another file.
  - You can link to information in the same worksheet, another worksheet in the same workbook, another workbook, or anywhere on the Internet.
  - You can also link to any other file, such as a Word document, sound file, graphic image or movie, as shown in Figure 30-1 on the next page.
  - These files may be located on your hard disk, the company network, the Internet or an intranet.
    - ✓ *If you link to other files, make sure that the location of the file you are linking to will not change.*
  - You can link to your e-mail address, to help the user send you an e-mail message.
  - You can also create a new workbook to link to.
- When you move the mouse pointer over a hyperlink, it changes to a pointing hand 🖑.
  - This change helps you distinguish hyperlinks from regular text, and hyperlink graphics from regular pictures.
  - Because the mouse pointer changes to a hand when over a hyperlink, you must use special techniques to select the link for editing.

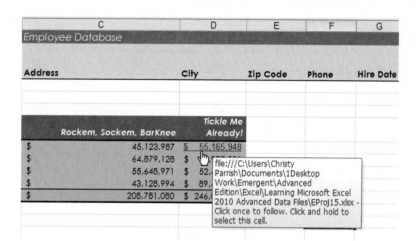

Figure 30-1

- When a mouse pointer moves over a hyperlink, a ScreenTip appears, displaying the **URL** of the linked file or e-mail address.
  - You can override this default ScreenTip with a short description of the linked file or e-mail address.
- Text hyperlinks are typically formatted in a different color and underlined.
  - When you click a text hyperlink and then later return to it, you'll probably notice that it has changed to purple underlined text.
  - This change helps you quickly identify the links you've used (and those you haven't).
- Clicking a hyperlink moves you to the associated location.
  - If the hyperlink involves another file, that file is opened automatically.
  - If you want the user to move to a particular place within a worksheet, you might want to create a range name so that you can use that name in the link.
    - ✓ If you don't want to create a range name, you can still link to a specific place within a worksheet by typing its cell address.
- You can create hyperlinks that connect a user to data in the current workbook or workbooks located on a company intranet.

- You can also connect to data on the Internet.
  - You can connect to Excel files or to HTML/MHTML files, since Excel can display either.
  - This capability allows you to include links to related **Web pages** (since they're coded in HTML or MHTML) within your worksheets.
- You can include hyperlinks in ordinary Excel worksheets or in workbooks that you have converted to HTML format.

Creating a Hyperlink in a Cell

- If you want to create a hyperlink, enter the text or graphic image before you follow the steps to create the hyperlink.
- Normally, you insert a hyperlink using the Insert Hyperlink dialog box.
- If you want to create a hyperlink to a Web page or an intranet document, you can bypass the Insert Hyperlink dialog box and type the Web page address (URL) or intranet location into a cell.
  - Excel will instantly recognize the address as a URL, and create a hyperlink from it automatically.
  - A Web address might look like this: http://www.fakeco.com/augsales.html
- You can also type an e-mail address directly in a cell, and Excel will convert it to a hyperlink. When a user clicks this type of hyperlink, an e-mail message is automatically created, with the recipient's address included.

Try It!   Creating a Hyperlink to Another File

1. Start Excel, and open **E30TryA** from the data files for this lesson.

2. Save the file as **E30TryA_xx** in the location where your teacher instructs you to store the files for this lesson.

3. For all worksheets, add a header that has your name at the left, the date code in the center, and the page number code at the right, and change back to Normal view.

4. On the Sept Sales worksheet, click cell B8 > INSERT > Hyperlink 🔗.

5. Navigate to the data files for this lesson and click **E30TryB**.

6. In the Link to menu on the left, check that Existing File or Web Page is selected, and click OK.

7. Save the **E30TryA_xx** file, and leave it open to use in the next Try It.

The Insert Hyperlink dialog box

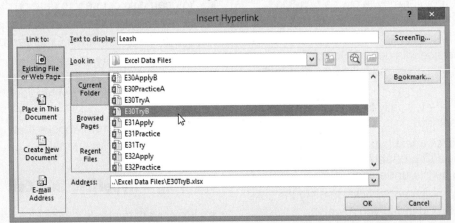

Try It!   Creating a Hyperlink to a Web Page

1. In the **E30TryA_xx** file, click cell B6.

2. Click INSERT > Hyperlink 🔗.

3. Check that Existing File or Web Page is selected, and type **http://www.akc.org/** in the Address box.

4. Click OK.

5. Save the **E30TryA_xx** file, and leave it open to use in the next Try It.

Try It!   Inserting a Hyperlink to a Location in the Current Workbook

1. In the **E30TryA_xx** file, click cell D7.

2. Click INSERT > Hyperlink 🔗.

3. Click Place in This Document.

4. In the Or select a place in this document section, select Customers.

5. Click OK.

6. Save the **E30TryA_xx** file, and leave it open to use in the next Try It.

(continued)

Try It!   **Inserting a Hyperlink to a Location in the Current Workbook** *(continued)*

Creating a hyperlink to a location in the current workbook

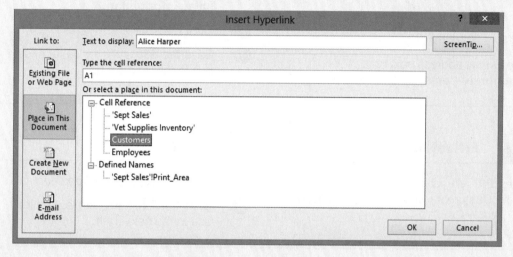

Try It!   **Inserting a Hyperlink to a New Workbook**

1 In the **E30TryA_xx** file, click cell B10.

2 Click INSERT > Hyperlink 🔗.

3 Click Create New Document.

4 In the Name of the new document box, type **E30TryC_xx.xlsx**.

5 Click Change, if necessary, and select the location your teacher instructs you to store files for this lesson.

✓ *When linking files, the file locations must stay the same for the links to remain intact.*

6 Under When to edit, click Edit the new document later option button, and click OK.

7 Save the **E30TryA_xx** file, and leave it open to use in the next Try It.

Creating a hyperlink to a new workbook

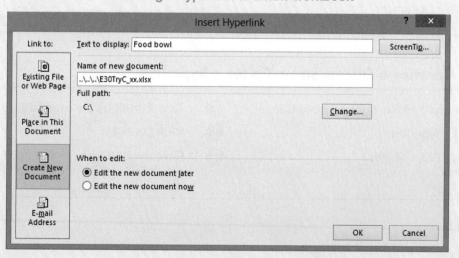

Try It!   **Inserting a Hyperlink to an E-mail Address**

1 In the **E30TryA_xx** file, click cell C3.

2 Click INSERT > Hyperlink 🖳 .

3 Click E-mail Address.

4 In the E-mail address box, type **accounting@petes_pets.com**.

5 In the Subject box, type **Request for additional sales information**.

6 Click OK.

7 Save the **E30TryA_xx** file, and leave it open to use in the next Try It.

Try It!   **Activating a Hyperlink**

1 In the **E30TryA_xx** file, click the hyperlink in cell D7. The Customers worksheet is displayed.

2 Click the Sept Sales worksheet tab.

3 Save the **E30TryA_xx** file, and leave it open to use in the next Try It.

Modifying Hyperlinks

- You can modify a hyperlink by providing a custom ScreenTip, by changing the destination for the link, or by editing the screen text.

Try It!   **Modifying a Hyperlink**

1 In the **E30TryA_xx** file, select cell C8, and press the left arrow key ⬅ one time.

2 Type **Collar**.

3 Right-click cell D7 > Edit Hyperlink.

4 Change the destination of the link by clicking Place in This Document.

5 Click Employees in the destination list, type **A6** in the Type the cell reference box, and click OK.

6 Save the **E30TryA_xx** file, and leave it open to use in the next Try It.

Try It!   **Creating a Custom ScreenTip for a Hyperlink**

1 In the **E30TryA_xx** file, right-click cell C3.

2 Select Edit Hyperlink.

3 Click ScreenTip ScreenTip... .

4 Type **E-mail us for more information**.

5 Click OK twice.

6 Save the **E30TryA_xx** file, and leave it open to use in the next Try It.

(continued)

Try It!   **Creating a Custom ScreenTip for a Hyperlink** *(continued)*

Creating a custom ScreenTip for a hyperlink

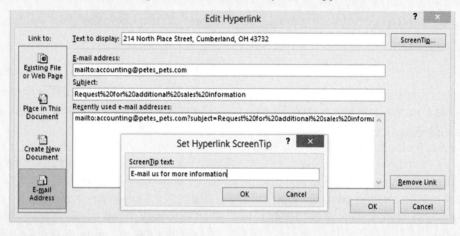

Modifying Hyperlinked Cell Attributes

■ When you add a hyperlink to a cell, you might find that the resulting link colors do not look good with the existing formatting of the worksheet.

■ You can modify the appearance of hyperlinked cells using the Cell Styles button on the HOME tab. You can also manually change your worksheet's formatting, including theme and font colors and other text attributes.

Try It!   **Modifying Hyperlinked-Cell Attributes**

1. In the **E30TryA_xx** file, select cells A3:F3.
2. Click HOME > Cell Styles 🖳.

3. In the Cell Styles gallery, select Accent1 in the Themed Cell Styles.

4. Save the **E30TryA_xx** file, and leave it open to use in the next Try It.

Removing a Hyperlink

■ There are many ways to remove a hyperlink from a worksheet depending on whether you want to eliminate the hyperlink itself or remove the cell contents as well.

Try It!   **Removing a Hyperlink**

1. In the **E30TryA_xx** file, right-click cell B6.
2. Select Remove Hyperlink.

3. Save the **E30TryA_xx** file, and close it.

Lesson 30—Practice

In this project, you will insert a hyperlink and create custom screen tip text using the skills you learned in this lesson.

DIRECTIONS

1. Start Excel, if necessary, and open the **E30PracticeA** file from the data files for this lesson.
2. Save the file as **E30PracticeA_xx** in the location where your teacher instructs you to store the files for this lesson.
3. Add a header that has your name at the left, the date code in the center, and the page number code at the right, and change back to **Normal** view.
4. Open the **E30PracticeB** file from the data files for this lesson.
5. Save the file as **E30PracticeB_xx** in the location where your teacher instructs you to store the files for this lesson.
6. Add a header that has your name at the left, the date code in the center, and the page number code at the right, and change back to **Normal** view.
7. Save and close the **E30PracticeB_xx** file.

8. Create a link to Akemi's medical history:
   a. Click cell **A6** > **INSERT** > **Hyperlink** 🔗 .
   b. Click the **Existing File or Web Page** button on the Link to bar.
   c. In the Look in list, browse to the folder where the files for this lesson are stored, and click the **E30PracticeB_xx** file from the list.
   d. Click **ScreenTip**, type **Akemi's medical history** in the ScreenTip text box, and click **OK**.
   e. Click **OK** to create the hyperlink.
9. Click cell **A6** to test the hyperlink. Accept the conditions of the security warning, if needed. The **E30PracticeB_xx** file should appear onscreen.

   ✓ *Remember that when you click a link, only the linked workbook appears on the screen, unless you arrange the view so you can see both.*

10. Close the **E30PracticeB_xx** file.
11. Save and close the **E30PracticeA_xx** file, and exit Excel.

Lesson 30—Apply

You've been put in charge of tracking patient services at Wood Hills Animal Clinic. You've put together a patient worksheet listing the various pets that have recently visited the clinic and a separate worksheet listing owner information. Before you get too far on your project, you want to test out its usability by adding hyperlinks that connect each pet with its owner's personal data.

DIRECTIONS

1. Start Excel, if necessary, and open **E30ApplyA** from the data files for this lesson.
2. Save the file as **E30ApplyA_xx** in the location where your teacher instructs you to store the files for this lesson.
3. Add a header that has your name at the left, the date code in the center, and the page number code at the right, and change back to **Normal** view.

4. Open the **E30ApplyB** file from the data files for this lesson.
5. Save the file as **E30ApplyB_xx** in the location where your teacher instructs you to store the filesfor this lesson.
6. Add a header that has your name at the left, the date code in the center, and the page number code at the right, and change back to **Normal** view.
7. Save and close the **E30ApplyB_xx** file.

8. Create a hyperlink to information about Akemi's owner:

   a. Click cell **E6** > **INSERT** > **Hyperlink** 🔗.

   b. Click the **Existing File or Web Page** button on the Link to bar, if necessary.

   c. In the Look in list, browse to the folder where the files for this lesson are stored, and select the **E30ApplyB_xx** file from the list.

   d. Create a ScreenTip that says **View owner information**.

   e. Click the **Bookmark** button.

   f. Select the range name **woo_daniel**, and click **OK**.

   g. Click **OK** to create the hyperlink.

9. Test the hyperlink on the worksheet. See Figure 30-2.

   ✓ *The linked workbooks have been arranged onscreen so you can see how they are linked. To do the same click VIEW > Arrange All > Cascade, and resize the windows.*

10. Close the **E30ApplyB_xx** file.

11. Save and close the file, and exit Excel.

Figure 30-2

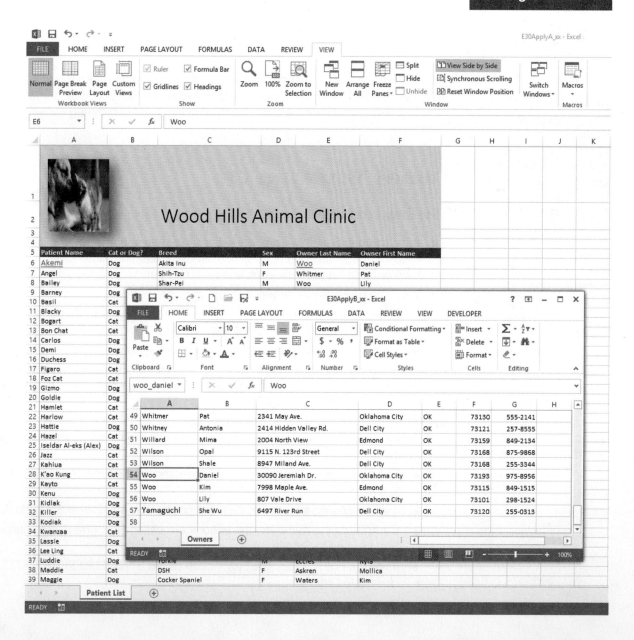

Lesson 31

Using Advanced Sort

➤ What You Will Learn

Sorting Excel Items
Understanding the Rules for Advanced Sorting
Sorting on Multiple Columns
Removing a Sort

WORDS TO KNOW

Ascending order
An arrangement of items in alphabetical order (A to Z) or numerical order (1, 2, 3, and so on). Dates are arranged from oldest to most recent.

Descending order
An arrangement of items in reverse alphabetical order (Z to A) or reverse numerical order (10, 9, 8, and so on). Dates are arranged from newest to oldest.

Key
One level within a sort. For example, you might sort a list by last name (one key) and then sort duplicate last names by first name (another key).

Software Skills   Entering data in random order might make the job a bit easier, but trying to find information in a disorganized spreadsheet is time consuming. So the first order of business after entering data into a list is ordering (or sorting) the data.

What You Can Do

Sorting Excel Items

■ After entering data into an Excel list or table, you can arrange the items in any order: alphabetically (for example, a list of names), or numerically (a price list), or date order (a list of employees and their hire dates).

■ Lists can be sorted in **ascending order** or **descending order.**
   ● Ascending order will arrange labels alphabetically (A to Z), numbers from smallest to largest, and dates from oldest to most recent.
   ● Descending order is the reverse of ascending order.

■ You can sort any contiguous data in the worksheet; it doesn't have to be a list or table. For example, you might want to sort an expense report to list all the expenses in order by account number.

■ You can sort data by using the sort buttons on the DATA tab, the HOME tab or with the down-arrow button that appears beside the field names in the top row of an Excel table.
   ● The sort buttons change names depending on the type of data you're trying to sort.
   ● If you're sorting text, the buttons are called Sort A to Z and Sort Z to A.
   ● If you're sorting numbers, the buttons are called Sort Smallest to Largest and Sort Largest to Smallest.
   ● If you're sorting dates, the buttons are called Sort Oldest to Newest and Sort Newest to Oldest.

Understanding the Rules for Advanced Sorting

- Excel sorts data based on the actual cell content, not the displayed results.
- If you choose to sort in ascending order, items are arranged as follows:
  - Numeric sort—Numbers are sorted from the largest negative number to the largest positive number. For example, -3, -2, -1, 0, 1, 2, and so on.
  - Alphanumeric sort—Labels (text or text/number combinations) are sorted first by symbols, then by letters.
  - Hyphens (-) and apostrophes (') are ignored in alphanumeric sorts if the cell's contents are identical apart from a hyphen or apostrophe, in which case the cell containing the symbol is placed last.
  - If names in the list contain spaces (for example, de Lancie), the sort results may differ from what you expect. Because spaces sort to the top of the list, de Lancie lands above Dean and Debrazzi.
  - When number/text combinations are sorted alphanumerically, combinations like 1Q through 11Q, for example, sort like this 10Q, 11Q, 1Q, 2Q, 3Q, and so on.

- Dates are sorted chronologically. For example, 1/10/14 would come before 2/12/14.
- If a cell in the sort column is blank, that record is placed at the end of the list.
- As an example of sorted records, consider this list:
  - Jay's Grill   1256 Adams Ave.
  - CompuTrain   12 Brown Street
  - Central Perk
  - Carriage Club   Carriage Center
  - Giving Tree   Mark Building
- If the list is sorted by address (ascending order), you'll end up with:
  - Compu Train   12 Brown Street
  - Jay's Grill   1256 Adams Ave.
  - Giving Tree   Mark Building
  - Carriage Club   Carriage Center
  - Central Perk
- Notice that the record that doesn't contain an address is placed last when you sort by address.
- Using the Sort Options dialog box, you can sort left to right (across a row) rather than top to bottom (down a column). This option is useful if your list is organized with a horizontal rather than a vertical orientation.
- You also can sort with case sensitivity. In a case-sensitive sort, capital letters are sorted after lowercase letters, so kit appears above Kit.

Try It! Sorting a List in Ascending or Descending Order

1. Start Excel, and open **E31Try** from the data files for this lesson.
2. Save the file as **E31Try_xx** in the location where your teacher instructs you to store the files for this lesson.
3. For all worksheets, add a header that has your name at the left, the date code in the center, and the page number code at the right, and change back to Normal view.
4. Click cell B8 on the Employees worksheet.
5. Click DATA > Sort A to Z.
6. On the DATA tab, click Sort Z to A. Notice that the names are sorted from highest to lowest.
7. Save the E31Try_xx file, and leave it open to use in the next Try It.

The Sort & Filter Group

Try It!   Sorting in a Table in Ascending or Descending Order

① In the **E31Try_xx** file, click the arrow next to the First Name column heading.

② Click Sort A to Z $\overset{A}{Z}\downarrow$.

③ Click the arrow next to the Hire Date column heading.

④ Click Sort Newest to Oldest $\overset{Z}{A}\downarrow$.

⑤ Save the **E31Try_xx** file, and leave it open to use in the next Try It.

Try It!   Sorting in a Table by Formatting

① In the **E31Try_xx** file, click the arrow next to the Last Name column heading.

② Select Sort by Color.

③ Select the Green fill color.

④ Save the **E31Try_xx** file, and leave it open to use in the next Try It.

Table sort options

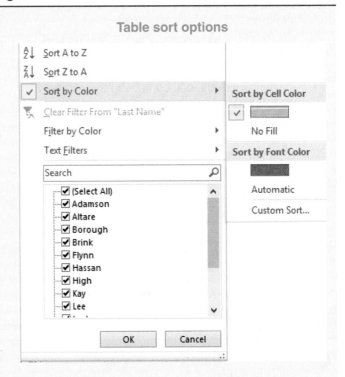

Sorting on Multiple Columns

■ Data can be sorted using one or more **keys**.

■ For example, an employee listing could be sorted by ZIP code. Employees with duplicate ZIP codes are then sorted by surname (last name), and those with duplicate surnames are sorted by given name (first name) for a total of three keys.

■ You can use the Sort dialog box to create a custom sort that contains multiple sort levels.

Try It!   Creating a Custom Sort

1 In the **E31Try_xx** file, click cell B8, if needed.

2 Click DATA > Sort 🔽.

   ✓ *Notice that the last sort appears as the first sort level.*

3 Click the Add Level button 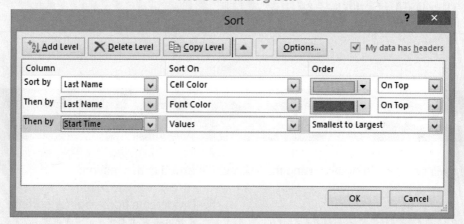, click the Column Then by down arrow, and select Last Name.

4 In the level you added, click the Sort On down arrow, and select Font Color.

5 Click the Automatic down arrow and select the Red font color.

6 Click the Add Level button ⬆, click the new Column Then by down arrow, and select Start Time.

7 Click OK.

8 Save the **E31Try_xx** file, and leave it open to use in the next Try It.

The Sort dialog box

Column	Sort On	Order
Sort by Last Name	Cell Color		On Top
Then by Last Name	Font Color		On Top
Then by Start Time	Values	Smallest to Largest

Removing a Sort

- You can undo a sort if you click the Undo button immediately after completing the sort.

- If you don't undo a sort immediately, the original sort order is lost.

- To protect your data, always save the workbook prior to sorting.

   ✓ *If something goes wrong, close the workbook without saving changes, and open the previously saved version.*

- If you want to keep your original sort order as well as the new, sorted list, copy the original list to another sheet in the workbook and then sort.

- Another way to restore the original record order of data that has been sorted is to include a unique field in every record.

  - For example, you could include a field called Record Number, and fill in unique numbers for each record. (Make sure all numbers are the same length.)

  - To restore the original order, sort by the Record Number column.

Try It! **Removing a Sort**

① In the **E31Try_xx** file, right-click the column F heading and select Insert. A table column is inserted to the left and becomes the new column F.

② In cell F5, type **Record Number**.

③ In cell F6, type **1**, and in cell F7 type **2**.

④ Select cells F6 and F7, and drag the fill handle down to cell F20 so that AutoFill completes the record number list.

⑤ Click cell A11 > DATA > Sort A to Z ↕.

⑥ Click the arrow next to the Hire Date column heading.

⑦ Click Sort Oldest to Newest.

⑧ Click Undo ↺.

⑨ Click the arrow next to the Record Number heading.

⑩ Click Smallest to Largest.

⑪ Save the **E31Try_xx** file, and close it.

Lesson 31—Practice

In this project, you will sort a table of data using the skills you learned in this lesson.

DIRECTIONS

1. Start Excel, if necessary, and open **E31Practice** from the data files for this lesson.

2. Save the file as **E31Practice_xx** in the location where your teacher instructs you to store the files for this lesson.

3. Add a header that has your name at the left, the date code in the center, and the page number code at the right, and change back to **Normal** view.

4. Click the arrow next to the Breed field name and click **Sort A to Z**.

5. Divide cats from dogs by sorting:
   a. Click cell **B8**.
   b. Click **DATA > Sort A to Z**.
   ✓ *Notice that the cat breeds and the dog breeds are still sorted alphabetically as well because of the sort you performed earlier.*

6. **With your teacher's permission**, print the worksheet. It should look similar to Figure 31-1 on the next page.

7. Save and close the file, and exit Excel.

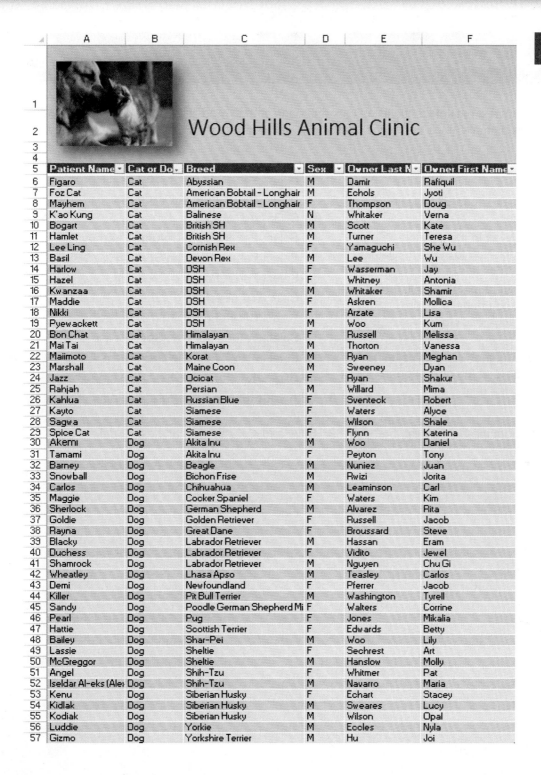

Figure 31-1

	A	B	C	D	E	F
5	Patient Name	Cat or Do	Breed	Sex	Owner Last N	Owner First Name
6	Figaro	Cat	Abyssian	M	Damir	Rafiquil
7	Foz Cat	Cat	American Bobtail – Longhair	M	Echols	Jyoti
8	Mayhem	Cat	American Bobtail – Longhair	F	Thompson	Doug
9	K'ao Kung	Cat	Balinese	N	Whitaker	Verna
10	Bogart	Cat	British SH	M	Scott	Kate
11	Hamlet	Cat	British SH	M	Turner	Teresa
12	Lee Ling	Cat	Cornish Rex	F	Yamaguchi	She Wu
13	Basil	Cat	Devon Rex	M	Lee	Wu
14	Harlow	Cat	DSH	F	Wasserman	Jay
15	Hazel	Cat	DSH	F	Whitney	Antonia
16	Kwanzaa	Cat	DSH	M	Whitaker	Shamir
17	Maddie	Cat	DSH	F	Askren	Mollica
18	Nikki	Cat	DSH	F	Arzate	Lisa
19	Pyewackett	Cat	DSH	M	Woo	Kum
20	Bon Chat	Cat	Himalayan	F	Russell	Melissa
21	Mai Tai	Cat	Himalayan	M	Thorton	Vanessa
22	Maiimoto	Cat	Korat	M	Ryan	Meghan
23	Marshall	Cat	Maine Coon	M	Sweeney	Dyan
24	Jazz	Cat	Ocicat	F	Ryan	Shakur
25	Rahjah	Cat	Persian	M	Willard	Mima
26	Kahlua	Cat	Russian Blue	F	Sventeck	Robert
27	Kayto	Cat	Siamese	F	Waters	Alyce
28	Sagwa	Cat	Siamese	F	Wilson	Shale
29	Spice Cat	Cat	Siamese	F	Flynn	Katerina
30	Akemi	Dog	Akita Inu	M	Woo	Daniel
31	Tamami	Dog	Akita Inu	F	Peyton	Tony
32	Barney	Dog	Beagle	M	Nuniez	Juan
33	Snowball	Dog	Bichon Frise	M	Rwizi	Jorita
34	Carlos	Dog	Chihuahua	M	Leaminson	Carl
35	Maggie	Dog	Cocker Spaniel	F	Waters	Kim
36	Sherlock	Dog	German Shepherd	M	Alvarez	Rita
37	Goldie	Dog	Golden Retriever	F	Russell	Jacob
38	Rayna	Dog	Great Dane	F	Broussard	Steve
39	Blacky	Dog	Labrador Retriever	M	Hassan	Eram
40	Duchess	Dog	Labrador Retriever	F	Vidito	Jewel
41	Shamrock	Dog	Labrador Retriever	M	Nguyen	Chu Gi
42	Wheatley	Dog	Lhasa Apso	M	Teasley	Carlos
43	Demi	Dog	Newfoundland	F	Pferrer	Jacob
44	Killer	Dog	Pit Bull Terrier	M	Washington	Tyrell
45	Sandy	Dog	Poodle German Shepherd Mi	F	Walters	Corrine
46	Pearl	Dog	Pug	F	Jones	Mikalia
47	Hattie	Dog	Scottish Terrier	F	Edwards	Betty
48	Bailey	Dog	Shar-Pei	M	Woo	Lily
49	Lassie	Dog	Sheltie	F	Sechrest	Art
50	McGreggor	Dog	Sheltie	M	Hanslow	Molly
51	Angel	Dog	Shih-Tzu	F	Whitmer	Pat
52	Iseldar Al-eks (Ale	Dog	Shih-Tzu	M	Navarro	Maria
53	Kenu	Dog	Siberian Husky	F	Echart	Stacey
54	Kidlak	Dog	Siberian Husky	M	Sweares	Lucy
55	Kodiak	Dog	Siberian Husky	M	Wilson	Opal
56	Luddie	Dog	Yorkie	M	Eccles	Nyla
57	Gizmo	Dog	Yorkshire Terrier	M	Hu	Joi

Lesson 31—Apply

You are responsible for adding new patients to the list of cats and dogs at the Wood Hills Animal Clinic. However, the records system adds new patients at the end of the patients list. You need to use Excel to sort the entries alphabetically.

DIRECTIONS

1. Start Excel, if necessary, and open **E31Apply** from the data files for this lesson.

2. Save the file as **E31Apply_xx** in the location where your teacher instructs you to store the files for this lesson.

3. Add a header that has your name at the left, the date code in the center, and the page number code at the right, and change back to **Normal** view.

4. Sort the table by cat or dog, then sex (males first), then breed (see Figure 31-2 on the next page):

   a. Click anywhere inside the table.

   b. Click **DATA** > **Sort**.

   c. Select **Cat or Dog?** from the **Sort by** list.

   d. Select **Values** from the **Sort On** list.

   e. Select **A to Z** from the **Order** list.

   f. Click **Add Level**.

   g. Select **Sex** from the **Column Then by** list.

   h. Select **Values** from the **Sort On** list.

   i. Select **Z to A** from the **Order** list.

   j. Click **Add Level**.

   k. Select **Breed** from the **Then by** list.

   l. Select **Values** from the **Sort On** list

   m. Select **A to Z** from the **Order** list.

   n. Click **OK**.

5. **With your teacher's permission**, print the worksheet.

6. Save and close the file, and exit Excel.

Figure 31-2

	A	B	C	D	E	F
1						
2			**Wood Hills Animal Clinic**			
3						
4						
5	Patient Name	Cat or Do	Breed	Sex	Owner Last Na	Owner First Na
6	Figaro	Cat	Abyssian	M	Damir	Rafiquil
7	Foz Cat	Cat	American Bobtail – Longhair	M	Echols	Jyoti
8	K'ao Kung	Cat	Balinese	M	Whitaker	Verna
9	Hamlet	Cat	British SH	M	Turner	Teresa
10	Bogart	Cat	British SH	M	Scott	Kate
11	Basil	Cat	Devon Rex	M	Lee	Wu
12	Kwanzaa	Cat	DSH	M	Whitaker	Shamir
13	Pyewackett	Cat	DSH	M	Woo	Kum
14	Mai Tai	Cat	Himalayan	M	Thorton	Vanessa
15	Maiimoto	Cat	Korat	M	Ryan	Meghan
16	Marshall	Cat	Maine Coon	M	Sweeney	Dyan
17	Rahjah	Cat	Persian	M	Willard	Mima
18	Mayhem	Cat	American Bobtail – Longhair	F	Thompson	Doug
19	Lee Ling	Cat	Cornish Rex	F	Yamaguchi	She Wu
20	Maddie	Cat	DSH	F	Askren	Mollica
21	Nikki	Cat	DSH	F	Arzate	Lisa
22	Harlow	Cat	DSH	F	Wasserman	Jay
23	Hazel	Cat	DSH	F	Whitney	Antonia
24	Bon Chat	Cat	Himalayan	F	Russell	Melissa
25	Jazz	Cat	Ocicat	F	Ryan	Shakur
26	Kahlua	Cat	Russian Blue	F	Sventeck	Robert
27	Sagwa	Cat	Siamese	F	Wilson	Shale
28	Spice Cat	Cat	Siamese	F	Flynn	Katerina
29	Kayto	Cat	Siamese	F	Waters	Alyce
30	Akemi	Dog	Akita Inu	M	Woo	Daniel
31	Barney	Dog	Beagle	M	Nuniez	Juan
32	Snowball	Dog	Bichon Frise	M	Rwizi	Jorita
33	Carlos	Dog	Chihuahua	M	Leaminson	Carl
34	Sherlock	Dog	German Shepherd	M	Alvarez	Rita
35	Blacky	Dog	Labrador Retriever	M	Hassan	Eram
36	Shamrock	Dog	Labrador Retriever	M	Nguyen	Chu Gi
37	Wheatley	Dog	Lhasa Apso	M	Teasley	Carlos
38	Killer	Dog	Pit Bull Terrier	M	Washington	Tyrell
39	Bailey	Dog	Shar-Pei	M	Woo	Lily
40	McGreggor	Dog	Sheltie	M	Hanslow	Molly
41	Iseldar Al-eks (Alex	Dog	Shih-Tzu	M	Navarro	Maria
42	Kodiak	Dog	Siberian Husky	M	Wilson	Opal
43	Kidlak	Dog	Siberian Husky	M	Sweares	Lucy
44	Luddie	Dog	Yorkie	M	Eccles	Nyla
45	Gizmo	Dog	Yorkshire Terrier	M	Hu	Joi
46	Tamami	Dog	Akita Inu	F	Peyton	Tony
47	Maggie	Dog	Cocker Spaniel	F	Waters	Kim
48	Goldie	Dog	Golden Retriever	F	Russell	Jacob
49	Rayna	Dog	Great Dane	F	Broussard	Steve
50	Duchess	Dog	Labrador Retriever	F	Vidito	Jewel
51	Demi	Dog	Newfoundland	F	Pferrer	Jacob
52	Sandy	Dog	Poodle German Shepherd Mix	F	Walters	Corrine
53	Pearl	Dog	Pug	F	Jones	Mikalia
54	Hattie	Dog	Scottish Terrier	F	Edwards	Betty
55	Lassie	Dog	Sheltie	F	Sechrest	Art
56	Angel	Dog	Shih-Tzu	F	Whitmer	Pat
57	Kenu	Dog	Siberian Husky	F	Echart	Stacey

Lesson 32

Using Advanced Filtering

➤ What You Will Learn

Using AutoFilter to Filter Tables
Using AutoFilter to Filter by Custom Criteria
Filtering Items without Creating a Table
Filtering by Using Advanced Criteria
Removing an In-Place Advanced Filter
Extracting Filtered Rows
Using Sum, Average, and Count in a Filtered Table
Using Slicers

WORDS TO KNOW

Calculated column
A special column that can be added to a table, in which a single formula is automatically applied to each row.

Criteria range
Area of the worksheet in which you specify the criteria for selecting records from the list or table.

Excel table
Data arranged in columns and specially formatted with column headers that contain commands that allow you to sort, filter, and perform other functions on the table.

Extract
Copy records that match specified criteria to another place in the worksheet where they can be changed, sorted, formatted, printed, and so on.

Software Skills   When you're looking for particular records in a long list, you can use a filter to reduce the number of records to the ones you want to view right now. You can use an advanced filter to extract the matching records and then format, sort, and make other changes to them without affecting the records in the list. This is handy when you want to print or format a subset of the list. In addition, advanced filters let you create complex criteria using formulas, multiple conditions applied to a single field, and so on, to filter the list.

What You Can Do

Using AutoFilter to Filter Tables

- You can use the AutoFilter feature to find pertinent information in a worksheet quickly.
- Use AutoFilter to filter the data in multiple columns.
- When you use AutoFilters, the AutoFilter drop-downs take the place of the column headers when scrolling through long **lists** so that you can easily see your categories.
- You can access the AutoFilter search settings by clicking the AutoFilter drop-downs.

| Try It! | **Using AutoFilter to Filter Tables** |

1. Start Excel, and open **E32Try** from the data files for this lesson.

2. Save the file as **E32Try_xx** in the location where your teacher instructs you to store the files for this lesson.

3. For both worksheets, add a header that has your name at the left, the date code in the center, and the page number code at the right, and change back to Normal view.

4. On the Sept Sales worksheet, click the arrow ⌄ next to the Salesperson heading.

5. Deselect the (Select All) option, select Alice Harper, and click OK.

6. Hover on the Filter indicator for the Salesperson column to see the ScreenTip.

7. Save the **E32Try_xx** file, and leave it open to use in the next Try It.

Use the Filter Indicator to see your filter criteria

Salesperson	Cost	Sales Incentive
Alice Harper	Salesperson: Equals "Alice Harper"	$ 3.56
Alice Harper	$ 9.25	$ -
Alice Harper	$ 11.50	$ -

Using AutoFilter to Filter by Custom Criteria

■ In Excel 2013, you can search for specific criteria within an AutoFilter. This allows you to quickly jump to the information you want without having to scroll through a long list of values.

■ You can set up an AutoFilter based on specific numeric or text values, formatting, or based on specific custom criteria.

| Try It! | **Using AutoFilter to Filter by Custom Criteria** |

1. In the **E32Try_xx** file, on the Sept Sales worksheet, click the arrow next to the Cost heading.

2. Point to Number Filters, and select Greater Than from the list.

3. In the box to the right of the is greater than box, type **15**, and click OK.

4. Click the arrow next to the Description heading.

5. Point to Text Filters, and select Custom Filter from the list.

6. In the first box, scroll down and click does not contain, and in the second box, type **puppy**.

Filter
Hide nonmatching rows in a table or list of data according to the criterion or criteria you specify.

List
A range of Excel data organized primarily in columns.

Slicer
An easy-to-use filtering component that contains a set of buttons to enable you to quickly filter data.

Total row
A row you can display below a table to calculate data in the columns above using a function you choose.

(continued)

Using AutoFilter to Filter by Custom Criteria *(continued)*

7 Check that the And option button is selected, and in the first box of the second row, select *does not end with*.

8 In the second box, type **n**. Click OK.

9 Click the arrow next to the *Product Type* heading.

10 Point to Filter by Color, and select the blue fill color.

11 Save the **E32Try_xx** file, and leave it open to use in the next Try It.

The Custom AutoFilter dialog box

Custom AutoFilter

Show rows where:
Description

does not contain | puppy

● And   ○ Or

does not end with | n

Use ? to represent any single character
Use * to represent any series of characters

OK   Cancel

Filtering Items Without Creating a Table

- As mentioned earlier, you do not need to convert a list into an **Excel table** in order to **filter** its data.
- A table, however, does give you several advantages. With a table, you can:
  - Create formulas that reference the columns in the table by their name.
  - Format the table with a single click.

- Add a **total row** that allows you to select from a range of functions that sum, average, count, or perform other operations on the data in a column.
- Add a **calculated column** that allows you to enter a formula and have that formula copied instantly throughout the column. For example, you could link to Microsoft Excel data during a presentation.

Filtering Items Without Creating a Table

1 In the **E32Try_xx** file, click the Pet Supplies Inventory worksheet tab.

2 Click anywhere in the range A5:H32 > DATA > Filter.

  ✓ *Arrow buttons appear next to each column name.*

3 Click the arrow next to the Current Inventory heading.

4 Point to Number Filters, and select Less Than Or Equal To from the list.

5 In the second box of the first row, type **10**, and click OK.

6 Click the arrow next to the *Description* heading.

7 Deselect the (Select All) option.

8 Type **Collar** in the Search box. Click OK.

9 Save the **E32Try_xx** file, and leave it open to use in the next Try It.

(continued)

Filtering Items without Creating a Table *(continued)*

A list offers most of the same filter features as a table

	A	B	C	D	E	F	G	H
1								
2			Pete's Pets					
3			214 North Place Street, Cumberland, OH 43732					
4			*Pet Supplies Inventory*					
5	Product # ▼	Description ▼	Pr ▼	Current Invento ▼	Reorder Wh ▼	Number per Ca ▼	My Co ▼	Price per Ca ▼

Filter dropdown menu:
- A↓ Sort A to Z
- Z↓ Sort Z to A
- Sort by Color ▶
- ▽ Clear Filter From "Description"
- Filter by Color ▶
- Text Filters ▶
- collar ✕
  - ☑ (Select All Search Results)
  - ☐ Add current selection to filter
  - ☑ Lg. Collar - Black
  - ☑ Lg. Collar - Blue
  - ☑ Lg. Collar - Green
  - ☑ Lg. Collar - Red
  - ☑ Sm.Collar - Blue
  - ☑ Sm.Collar - Green
  - ☑ Sm.Collar - Red
  - [OK] [Cancel]

Row	Price	Current Inventory	Reorder When	Number per Case	My Cost	Price per Case
6	12.95	6	3	10	3.47	$ 34.70
8	12.95	8	3	10	3.47	$ 34.70
9	12.95	5	3	10	3.47	$ 34.70
10	17.5	4	4	12	5.25	$ 63.00
11	17.5	4	4	12	5.25	$ 63.00
12	17.5	4	4	12	5.25	$ 63.00
13	17.5	4	4	12	5.25	$ 63.00
16	3.5	6	25	100	0.64	$ 64.00
18	13.75	9	10	25	7.6	$ 190.00
19	15.25	6	10	25	9.8	$ 245.00
20	22.5	3	5	5	11.75	$ 58.75
21	29.75	6	5	5	14.3	$ 71.50
24	21.75	6	5	5	12.75	$ 63.75
25	23.5	4	5	5	14.8	$ 74.00
26	24.25	8	5	5	15.3	$ 76.50
40 Product #	Description	Price	Current Inventory	Reorder When	Number per Case	My Cost	Price per Case
41 24514	Sm.Collar - Red	12.95	6	3	10	3.47	$ 34.70

Removing a Filter from a List

1 In the **E32Try_xx** file, in the Pet Supplies Inventory worksheet, click any cell in the list.

2 Click DATA > Filter ▼.

✓ *This process will redisplay all records and remove the filter arrows from a list, but not a table.*

3 Save the **E32Try_xx** file, and leave it open to use in the next Try It.

Filtering by Using Advanced Criteria

- With an advanced filter, you can filter records to hide records that do not match the criteria you specify—in much the same way as with a regular filter.
- Prior to using an advanced filter, you must first set up your **criteria range**.
- An advanced filter allows you to enter more complex criteria than a regular filter:
  - Instead of selecting criteria from a drop-down list, you enter it in a special area in the workbook—perhaps a worksheet unto itself—set aside for that purpose.
  - In the marked cells of this criteria range, you enter the items you want to match from the list, or expressions that describe the type of comparison you wish to make.
  - You then open a dialog box in which you specify the range where the list or table is contained, the range containing the criteria, and the range to which you want records copied/extracted (if applicable).
- To set up the criteria range, copy the field names from the top of the list to another area of the worksheet, or to a separate worksheet in the same workbook.

  ✓ *The labels in the criteria range must exactly match the labels used in the list, which is why you should copy them rather than typing them.*

Guidelines for Entering Criteria

- After the criteria range is established, you enter criteria in the criteria range, below the field names you copied.
  - For example, to display only records belonging to Smith, you might type Smith under the Last Name field name in the criteria range you've established.
- If you want to establish an AND condition, where two or more criteria must be true for a record to match, then type the criteria under their proper field names in the same row.
  - For example, to display records where the quantity on hand is over 25 AND the cost is less than $10, type both criteria in the same row, each in their respective column.

- If you want to establish an OR condition, where any of two or more criteria will qualify a record as a match, then type the criteria under their proper field names, but in separate rows.
- When you enter text, Excel looks for any match beginning with that text. For example, typing Sam under the First Name label would match records such as Sam, Samuel, and Samantha.
- You can use wildcards when entering text criteria.
  - A question mark (?) can be used to replace a single character in a specific position within the text. For example, type Sm?th under the Last Name label to get Smith and Smyth.
  - An asterisk (*) can be used to replace one or several characters within the text. For example, type Sm*th under the Last Name label to get Smith, Smyth, Smouth, and Smaningfith.
  - Because ? and * are assumed to be wildcards, if you want to find records that actually contain those characters, you must precede them with a tilde (~). For example, type RJ4~?S2 to get RJ4?S2.
- You can use operators to compare text, numbers, or dates.
  - Operators include < (less than), > (greater than), <= (less than or equal to), >= (greater than or equal to), <> (not equal to), and = (equal to). For example, type >256000 under the Annual Salary label to get all records that contain an annual salary over $256,000.
  - You can use operators with dates as well. For example, type >=01/01/08 under the Hire Date label to get all records with a hire date on or after January 1, 2008.
  - You can also use operators with text, as in <M, which will display all records beginning with the letters A through L.
- You can use formulas to specify criteria.
  - For example, to display only records where the total sale (stored in column G) is greater than the average of column G, you could enter something like this for cell G5: =G5>AVERAGE($G$5:$G$21).

    ✓ *G5 in this example is the first cell in the list or table in column G.*

- You could also use the label cell (G4) or the label itself, as in this formula: ="Total Sales">AVERAGE($G$5:$G$21).

- The comparison cell address uses relative cell addressing, while the rest of the formula must use absolute cell addresses (preceded by $).

■ To use a formula to specify criteria, type it in a cell that doesn't have a label above it.

 ✓ For this reason, it's usually best to type a formula in the first column to the right of the criteria range you originally established.

- Be sure to redefine the criteria range to include the cell that contains the formula and the blank cell above it.

- You can use more than one formula by typing the second formula in the next column, and adjusting the criteria range again.

 ✓ If you need to use two formulas, and either one may be true in order to get a match, then type them in the same column in different rows.

 ✓ See examples in the next section for placement of formulas in the criteria range.

Examples of Advanced Criteria

■ To display records for Smith and Jones from the sample shown here, type these criteria, in two rows, under the Name field:

Name	Computer	Sale Amt.
Smith		>1300
Jones		

 ✓ As on the preceding pages, the following examples show typical list or table field names. Be sure to copy the actual field names from your own list/table to the criteria range.

■ To display records for Jones where the total sale amount is over $1,300, type these criteria in one row under the appropriate field names:

Name	Computer	Sale Amt.
Jones		>1300

 ✓ You could also display these records with the proper selections from two columns in filtered list or table.

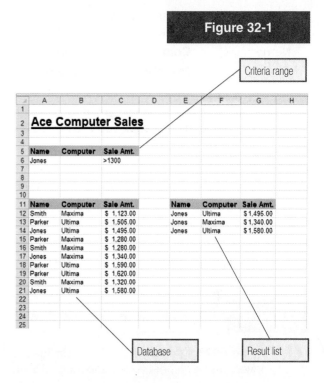

Figure 32-1

Criteria range

Database

Result list

■ To display Smith's sales records of Maxima computers with a total sales amount more than $1,250, type this in one row:

Name	Computer	Sale Amt.
Smith	Maxima	>1250

 ✓ Again, you could display these records using a regular filter.

■ To display records for both Smith and Jones that have a sale amount over $1,250, type this in two rows:

Name	Computer	Sale Amt.
Smith		>1250
Jones		>1250

■ To display records that have a sale amount over $1,250 or that involve Maxima computers (no matter what amount), type this in two rows:

Name	Computer	Sale Amt.
	Maxima	
		>1250

■ To display records of sales of Maxima computers over $1,250, type this in one row:

Name	Computer	Sale Amt.
	Maxima	>1250

- To display records of sales of Maxima or Ultima computers over $1,250, type this in two rows:

Name	Computer	Sale Amt.
	Maxima	>1250
	Ultima	>1250

- To display records whose sale amount is greater than or equal to the average, type this in a cell without a label:

Sale Amt.

=C2>AVERAGE($C$2:$C$17)

✓ Be sure to include the cell in which you type the formula and the blank cell above it, within the criteria range.

✓ The formula includes an expression of comparison, featuring the > operator, and which evaluates to TRUE or FALSE.

- To display records whose sale amounts are between $1,250 and $2,000, type this in two cells without a label in the same row, but in different columns:

Computer	Sale Amt.
=C2>1250	=C2<2000

✓ Place formulas in cells without a label above them.

- To display records whose total sale is greater than the average OR over $2,000, type this in two rows, but in the same column:

Sale Amt.

=C2>AVERAGE($C$2:$C$17)

=C2>2000

Try It!   **Setting Up a Criteria Range and an Advanced Filter**

1 In the **E32Try_xx** file, in the Pet Supplies Inventory worksheet, select the range A5:H5.

2 Click HOME > Copy.

✓ Typically, you create a criteria range above or to the right of the list or table, separated from it by a few rows or columns, although you can create a separate Criteria worksheet if you like.

3 Click cell J5 and press CTRL + V. Adjust the column widths as necessary.

✓ Remember that formulas, if you use them, must be entered in cells that don't have a label above them.

4 Type the following criteria.

Cell	Type
K7	Cat*
M6	<10
N6	<10
P7	>1.00

5 Click any cell within the range A6:H32 > DATA > Advanced.

6 If necessary, select Filter the list, in-place.

7 In the List range text box, type **$A$6:$H$32** or select the range containing the list or table.

8 In the Criteria range text box, select the range J5:Q7.

✓ Include the criteria label(s) with the criteria.

✓ If the criteria includes a formula, include the blank cell(s) above the cell(s) containing the formula.

9 Click OK.

10 Save the **E32Try_xx** file, and leave it open to use in the next Try It.

(continued)

Setting up an advanced filter

G	H	I	J	K	L	M	N	O	P	Q
My Cost	Price per Case		Product #	Description	Price	Current Inventory	Reorder When	Number per Case	My Cost	Price per Case
3.47 $	34.70					<10	<10			
3.47 $	34.70			Cat*					>1.00	
3.47 $	34.70									
3.47 $	34.70									
5.25 $	63.00									
5.25 $	63.00									
5.25 $	63.00									
5.25 $	63.00									
0.5 $	50.00									
0.53 $	53.00									
0.64 $	64.00									
4.1 $	82.00									
7.6 $	190.00									
9.8 $	245.00									
11.75 $	58.75									
14.3 $	71.50									
0.75 $	18.75									
0.75 $	18.75									
12.75 $	63.75									
14.8 $	74.00									
15.3 $	76.50									
1.75 $	24.50									
1.8 $	25.20									
1.9 $	26.60									
2.2 $	79.20									
2.3 $	82.80									
2.4 $	86.40									

Advanced Filter ? ✕

Action
◉ Filter the list, in-place
◯ Copy to another location

List range: $A$5:$H$32
Criteria range: $J$5:$Q$7
Copy to:

☐ Unique records only

OK   Cancel

Removing an In-Place Advanced Filter

- Unlike a regular filter, an advanced filter applied in-place to a list or table (rather than copied to another area of the worksheet) isn't easily detectable.

- If the row numbers in the list or table are blue and the filter down-arrow buttons aren't visible, an advanced filter is in place.

- To remove an in-place advanced filter, click in the list/table and click the Clear button on the DATA tab.

Try It! **Removing an In-Place Advanced Filter**

1. In the **E32Try_xx** file, in the Pet Supplies Inventory worksheet, click any cell in the table or list within the cell range A4:H6.
2. Click DATA > Clear.
3. Click the Sept Sales worksheet tab, and click any cell in the table or list with the cell range A5:F45.
4. Click DATA > Clear.
5. Save the **E32Try_xx** file, and leave it open to use in the next Try It.

Extracting Filtered Rows

- With an advanced filter, you can **extract** (copy) records to another place in the worksheet.

- The extracted records are copied to another area of the worksheet (called the results list). You can edit them as needed.

- The results list must appear in the same worksheet as the source list from which its records were copied.

  ✓ *The destination range must be located in the same worksheet as the list or table.*

✓ *If you indicate a single cell as the Copy to range, Excel copies the filtered results to cells below and to the right of the cell, overwriting existing data without warning.*

- You can change, format, print, sort, delete, and otherwise manipulate the extracted records.

- Even if you alter the extracted records, it won't affect the original records in the list or table.

- This allows you to create a customized, professional-looking report with the extracted records.

- You can even delete some of the extracted records if you don't want to work with them; again, this does not affect the original data.

Try It!   **Extracting Filtered Rows**

1 In the **E32Try_xx** file, click the Pet Supplies Inventory worksheet tab.

  ✓ *For this exercise, you'll use the same criteria and range as before.*

2 Click any cell within the table or list within the cell range A5:H32 > DATA > Advanced ▼ .

3 Select Copy to another location.

4 In the Copy to text box, type **$A$40**.

5 Click OK.

6 Save the **E32Try_xx** file, and leave it open to use in the next Try It.

Using Sum, Average, and Count in a Filtered Table

- Using tables provides a lot of flexibility when it comes to managing columnar data.

  - For example, it's easy to add totals and perform other calculations on the columns in a table by simply adding a total row.

  - Once a total row is added, click in the total row at the bottom of a column you want to calculate, and choose an available function such as SUM, AVERAGE, or MIN.

  - You can select a different function for each column, or none at all.

  - You can also enter text in the total row if needed.

- You can temporarily hide the total row when needed.

- Another easy way to add calculations to a table is to use calculated columns.

  - A calculated column can be located in a blank column inserted between existing table columns, or in the first blank column to the right of a table.

  - To create a calculated column, type a formula in the blank column you've inserted in the table, or in a blank column to the right of the table.

  - The formula is instantly copied down the column.

  - If new rows are added to the table, the formula is copied to that new row automatically.

Try It!	**Using Sum, Average, and Count in a Filtered Table**

① In the **E32Try_xx** file, click the Sept Sales worksheet tab.

② Click in the list with the cell range A5:F45 > TABLE TOOLS DESIGN > Total Row.

③ Click cell F46, and click the down arrow that appears to the right of the cell. Select Sum, if necessary.

④ Click cell E46, and click the down arrow. Select Average.

⑤ Click cell D46, and click the down arrow. Select Count.

⑥ Save the **E32Try_xx** file, and leave it open to use in the next Try It.

Working with a Total Row in a filtered table

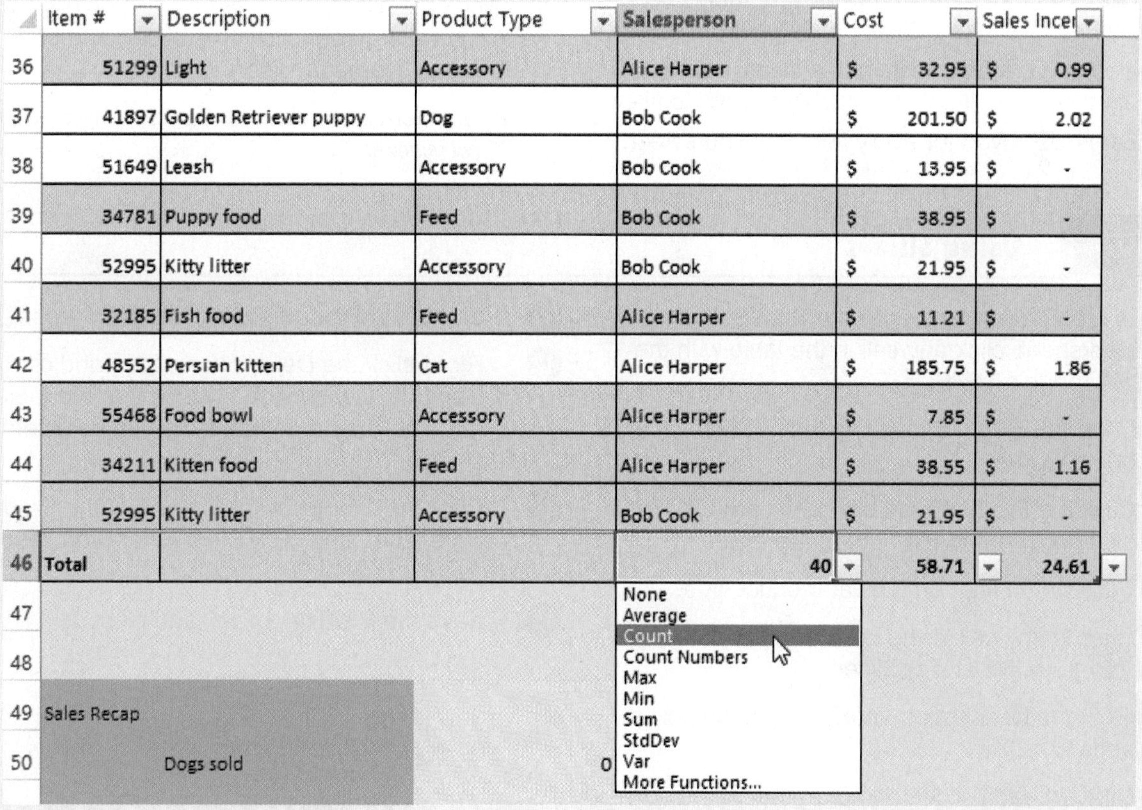

	Item #	Description	Product Type	Salesperson	Cost	Sales Incer
36	51299	Light	Accessory	Alice Harper	$ 32.95	$ 0.99
37	41897	Golden Retriever puppy	Dog	Bob Cook	$ 201.50	$ 2.02
38	51649	Leash	Accessory	Bob Cook	$ 13.95	$ -
39	34781	Puppy food	Feed	Bob Cook	$ 38.95	$ -
40	52995	Kitty litter	Accessory	Bob Cook	$ 21.95	$ -
41	32185	Fish food	Feed	Alice Harper	$ 11.21	$ -
42	48552	Persian kitten	Cat	Alice Harper	$ 185.75	$ 1.86
43	55468	Food bowl	Accessory	Alice Harper	$ 7.85	$ -
44	34211	Kitten food	Feed	Alice Harper	$ 38.55	$ 1.16
45	52995	Kitty litter	Accessory	Bob Cook	$ 21.95	$ -
46	Total			40 ▼	58.71 ▼	24.61 ▼
47				None		
48				Average		
49	Sales Recap			Count		
50		Dogs sold		0 Count Numbers		

Menu options shown: None / Average / Count / Count Numbers / Max / Min / Sum / StdDev / Var / More Functions...

Using Slicers

- When you filter on multiple criteria, it is not always easy to see which filters are being used.

- **Slicers** provide buttons that you can click to filter data in a table.

- You can use slicers to quickly see the current filtering state when you filter on multiple items.

- If you have multiple tables, you can create a slicer for each table.

- You can insert a slicer using the Slicer button 📊 in the Filter group on the INSERT tab.

- You can select the data you want your table to display from the Insert Slicers dialog box.

- To select more than one item in a slicer, hold down CTRL , and click the items on which you want to filter.

- A slicer is displayed for every field that you select.

- After you create a slicer, it appears on the worksheet alongside the table. If needed, you can move a slicer to another location on the worksheet.

- If you have more than one slicer, the slicers are displayed in layers.

- Select the item or items on which you want to filter from the Insert Slicers dialog box.

- To remove a filter, click the Clear Filter button 🔻 on the slicer.

- You can change the slicer settings or apply slicer styles from the SLICER TOOLS OPTIONS tab.

- You can resize a slicer.

- Click on a slicer, and press DEL to delete a slicer. You also can right-click on a slicer, and click Remove "Name of slicer."

  ✓ *When you delete a slicer, the filter(s) applied to your data are not removed.*

Try It!   Using Slicers

1 In the **E32Try_xx** file, on the Sept Sales worksheet, click any cell in the table with the cell range A5:F46.

2 Click INSERT > Slicer. The Insert Slicers dialog box appears.

3 Click the Product Type box, and click OK. The slicer appears to the right of the table.

4 Click Cat to filter on the cat product type.

5 Click in any cell in the table with the cell range A5:F46 > INSERT > Slicer.

6 Click the Description and Salesperson boxes, and click OK.

7 Click on each slicer, and drag the slicers so you can see all three of them.

8 On the Product Type slicer, click Dog.

9 On the Description slicer, scroll down, and click Scottie puppy. Notice that the Salesperson slicer automatically filters on Bob Cook because he is the only salesperson to sell a Dog that was a Scottie puppy.

10 On the Description slicer, click the Clear Filter button 🔻. Notice that all dogs are now showing.

11 Select the Product Type slicer, and press DEL

12 Right-click the Description slicer, and click Remove "Description." Notice that the table remains filtered on the items you selected in the slicers.

13 Click the filter arrow at the end of the Product Type label, and click Clear Filter From "Product Type."

14 Save the **E32Try_xx** file, and close it.

An example of a slicer

Product Type 🔻
Accessory
Cat
Dog
Feed
Fish

Lesson 32—Practice

In this project, you will filter a large data table using the skills you learned in this lesson.

DIRECTIONS

1. Start Excel, if necessary, and open **E32Practice** from the data files for this lesson.
2. Save the file as **E32Practice_xx** in the location where your teacher instructs you to store the files for this lesson.
3. Add a header that has your name at the left, the date code in the center, and the page number code at the right, and change back to **Normal** view.
4. Display only the heart medications:
   a. Click on any cell in the table > **INSERT** > **Slicer**.
   b. In the **Insert Slicers** dialog box, click the **For use on** box > **OK**.
   c. Move the slicer so the entire table is visible, if necessary.
   d. In the **For use on slicer**, click **Heart**.
   e. Sort the records by price by clicking the arrow next to **Item Cost**, and choosing **Sort Smallest to Largest**.
5. **With your teacher's permission**, adjust the print settings, and print the worksheet.
6. Right-click the For use on slicer, and click "Remove For use on."

   ✓ *Remember that removing a slicer does not clear its filter.*

7. Display only items with 100 or more units remaining in inventory:
   a. Clear the filter by clicking **DATA** > **Clear**.
   b. Click the arrow next to **Total Items2**, and point to **Number Filters**.

   c. Select **Greater Than Or Equal To** from the list.
   d. In the box to the right of is greater than or equal to, enter **100**, and click **OK**.
8. Add a total row:
   a. Click anywhere in the table, then click **TABLE TOOLS DESIGN** > **Total Row**.
   b. Click the cell at the bottom of the **Total Items2** column, click the arrow, and click **Average**.
   c. Click the cell at the bottom of the **Total Items** column, click the arrow, and click **Sum**.
9. Display the top **15** selling items:
   a. Clear the filter by clicking **DATA** > **Clear**.
   b. Click the arrow next to **Total Sales** heading, point to **Number Filters**, and click **Top 10**.
   c. In the center box of the Top 10 AutoFilter dialog box, choose **15**, then click **OK**.
10. Select **A1:K95** and click **Page Layout** > **Print Area** > **Set Print Area**.
11. **With your teacher's permission**, print the worksheet. It should look similar to Figure 32-2 on the next page.

    ✓ *To print the selected print area, you may need to change the print settings to Print Selection, Landscape Orientation, and No Scaling.*

12. Save and close the file, and exit Excel.

Figure 32-2

Wood Hills Animal Clinic
August Drug Sales

Drug	For use on	To treat	No. of Cases	Items per Case	Loose Items	Total Items	Total Items2	No. Sold	Item Cost	Total Sales
						Starting Inventory	Ending Inventory			
Droncit Tapewormer	De-wormer	Dog or Cat	6	100	88	688	432	256	$ 28.95	$ 7,411.20
Enacard	Heart	Dog or Cat	12	22	20	284	61	223	$ 25.00	$ 5,575.00
Enacard	Heart	Dog or Cat	14	30	3	423	222	201	$ 31.95	$ 6,421.95
Anipryl	Endocrine	Dog	12	20	19	259	152	107	$ 53.00	$ 5,671.00
Enacard	Heart	Dog or Cat	10	30	14	314	158	156	$ 32.95	$ 5,140.20
Bomazeal Senior	Arthritis	Dog	14	50	42	742	382	360	$ 24.95	$ 8,982.00
Proin	Incontinence	Dog	15	35	33	558	390	168	$ 30.00	$ 5,040.00
Tapazole	Hyperthyroidism	Cat	15	30	29	479	358	121	$ 49.00	$ 5,929.00
Heartgard Plus Blue	Heartworm	Dog	18	75	42	1,392	968	424	$ 14.95	$ 6,338.80
Soloxine	Hyperthyroidism	Dog or Cat	18	20	17	377	51	326	$ 36.95	$ 12,045.70
Revolution	Heartworm	Dog	21	32	6	678	325	353	$ 26.95	$ 9,513.35
Soloxine	Hyperthyroidism	Dog or Cat	21	20	4	424	186	238	$ 40.00	$ 9,520.00
Advantage Green	Flea	Dog	22	25	14	564	268	296	$ 19.95	$ 5,905.20
Heartgard Plus Green	Heartworm	Dog	22	75	36	1,686	1,296	390	$ 19.95	$ 7,780.50
Heartgard Plus Brown	Heartworm	Dog	30	75	19	2,269	918	1,351	$ 24.95	$ 33,707.45
Total						11,137	411			$ 134,981.35

Lesson 32—Apply

You're continuing to put together the inventory tracking sheet for Wood Hills Animal Clinic, and it's looking pretty good. It's your job now to make some sense of all this data. You plan to use filtering to organize the information, and make printouts based on particular data the boss has requested.

DIRECTIONS

1. Start Excel, if necessary, and open **E32Apply** from the data files for this lesson.

2. Save the file as **E32Apply_xx** in the location where your teacher instructs you to store the files for this lesson.

3. On all three sheets, add a header that has your name at the left, the date code in the center, and the page number code at the right, and change back to **Normal** view.

4. Set up a criteria range for an advanced filter:

   a. Click the **New sheet** button, and create a new worksheet.

   b. Name the new worksheet **Criteria**, and move it after the **Drug Sales for Cats** worksheet.

   c. In the **Drug Sales for Dogs** worksheet, copy cells **A7:K7**, and paste them in the Criteria worksheet in the same position.

   d. Adjust columns widths as necessary to be readable.

5. Use the Criteria worksheet to select the records from the Drug Sales for Dogs worksheet, featuring only those medications for dogs with sales over $2000 and where less than 150 items are left in inventory:

   a. In the **Criteria** worksheet, in the cell under **To treat**, type **Dog**.

   b. In the cell under **Total Items2**, type **<150**.

   c. In the cell under **Total Sales**, type **>2000**.

   d. Switch to the **Drug Sales for Dogs** worksheet, and click any cell in the list range.

   e. Click **DATA > Advanced**.

   ✓ Under List range, the range $A$7:$K$94 should already appear.

   f. Next to Criteria range, click the **Collapse Dialog Box** button.

   g. Switch to the Criteria worksheet, select the range **A7:K8**.

   ✓ The criteria range should always include the entire field names row, plus as many rows beneath it that include criteria values or expressions, in their entirety.

h. Click the **Restore Dialog Box** button, then choose **Copy to another location**.

i. Next to **Copy to**, click the **Collapse Dialog Box** button.

j. Select cell **O7** in the **Drug Sales for Dogs** worksheet.

k. Click the **Restore Dialog Box** button to return to the dialog box, click **OK**.

　✓ *Excel will copy all records that match the given criteria, including field names, and will format these records exactly as they appear in their original cells, except for their column width.*

l. Adjust column widths as necessary.

6. Select the range **O1:Y17** > **Page Layout** > **Print Area** > **Set Print Area**.

7. **With your teacher's permission**, print the worksheet. It should look similar to Figure 32-3.

　✓ *To print the selected print area, you may need to change the print settings to Print Selection, Landscape Orientation, and No Scaling.*

8. Save and close the file, and exit Excel.

Figure 32-3

Student Name   12/19/2012   1

Wood Hills Animal Clinic

August Drug Sales for Dogs

Results

Drug	For use on	To treat	No. of Cases	Items per Case	Loose Items	Total Items	Total Items2	No. Sold	Item Cost	Total Sales
Enacard	Heart	Dog or Cat	6	30	8	188	126	62	$ 41.00	$ 2,542.00
Soloxine	Hyperthyroidism	Dog or Cat	6	20	6	126	74	52	$ 38.50	$ 2,002.00
Revolution	Heartworm	Dog	7	32	21	245	146	99	$ 25.95	$ 2,569.05
Anipryl	Endocrine	Dog	8	20	11	171	110	61	$ 49.00	$ 2,989.00
Anipryl	Endocrine	Dog	9	20	4	184	135	49	$ 60.00	$ 2,940.00
Revolution	Heartworm	Dog	9	32	27	315	145	170	$ 27.95	$ 4,751.50
Deramaxx	Anti-inflamatory	Dog	10	12	8	128	67	61	$ 62.50	$ 3,812.50
Lotagen	Skin Wounds	Dog or Cat	10	15	9	159	104	55	$ 72.15	$ 3,968.25
Enacard	Heart	Dog or Cat	12	22	20	284	61	223	$ 25.00	$ 5,575.00
Soloxine	Hyperthyroidism	Dog or Cat	18	20	17	377	51	326	$ 36.95	$ 12,045.70

Lesson 33

Using Advanced Functions to Predict Trends

➤ **What You Will Learn**

Creating Predictions and Estimations
Using FORECAST
Using TREND
Using GROWTH

WORDS TO KNOW

Sparklines
A tiny chart that can
be used to show trend
patterns.

Step
Used to calculate a future
value. The step is the
difference between two
existing values.

Trend
A mathematical prediction
of future values based on
the relationship between
existing values.

Software Skills   When it comes to business accounting, a crystal ball that
predicts the future would come in handy pretty often. Imagine being able to predict
sales so accurately you never order too many parts, carry too much inventory, or
schedule too many staff members. Excel doesn't come with a crystal ball, but it does
provide some nifty equivalents, such as sparklines, and the FORECAST, TREND,
and GROWTH functions.

What You Can Do

Creating Predictions and Estimations

■ In Excel, you can use the AutoFill feature to create a series of data, such as April,
May, June.

■ You also can use AutoFill to predict many kinds of future values.

■ AutoFill calculates future values by examining the **trend** of existing values.

■ With AutoFill, you can choose from two different trend formulas: linear or growth.

   ● Linear trend—the **step** is calculated by determining the average difference
     between the existing values. The step is then added to the second value.

     ✓ *For example, in the series 21, 37, the next value would be 53 (37-21=16; 16+37=53).*

   ● Growth trend—the step is calculated by dividing the second selected value by
     the first selected value. The step is then multiplied by the second value.

     ✓ *For example, in the series 21, 37, the next value would be 65.19048 (37/21=1.761905;
       37*1.761905=65.19048).*

■ To determine which tool to use, follow this pattern:

   ● If existing values seem to follow a straight curve, use the linear trend method.

   ● If existing values seem to go up and down a lot, use the growth trend method.

- You can also create a linear trend or growth trend estimate using the Fill button in the Editing group on the HOME tab.

  ✓ *If you want to create an estimate based on more than one set of numbers instead, select Trend from the Insert Series dialog box. You also can enter a specific Step or Stop value.*

- You can use **Sparklines**, as shown in Figure 33-1, to quickly show a trend graphically inside a single cell.

- You also can insert a Column or Win/Loss sparkline to show a trend in these formats.

		Actual			Predicted			Trends
		July	August	September	October	November	December	
12	Flours	$ 2,250.35	$ 2,901.77	$ 1,770.00	$ 2,000.00	$ 3,000.00	$ 1,600.00	
13	Milk & Buttermilk	$ 277.95	$ 358.41	$ 95.09	$ 174.23	$ 400.61	$ 83.68	
14	Eggs	$ 165.05	$ 212.82	$ 156.00	$ 162.12	$ 213.66	$ 141.50	
15	Sugars	$ 859.45	$ 908.00	$ 294.02	$ 528.69	$ 1,044.25	$ 322.47	
16	Butter	$ 2,141.71	$ 2,761.67	$ 1,733.00	$ 1,932.00	$ 2,843.37	$ 1,567.45	
17	Oil	$ 333.29	$ 429.76	$ 214.00	$ 267.84	$ 456.03	$ 192.56	
18	Oats	$ 1,565.06	$ 2,018.10	$ 535.42	$ 981.05	$ 2,255.74	$ 471.18	
19	Cornmeal	$ 1,543.74	$ 991.00	$ 1,528.00	$ 1,506.71	$ 1,010.70	$ 1,705.11	
20	Yeast	$ 2,844.30	$ 3,667.65	$ 973.05	$ 1,782.94	$ 4,099.53	$ 856.31	
21	Fruit	$ 1,566.74	$ 1,020.00	$ 1,536.00	$ 1,521.17	$ 1,043.18	$ 1,712.36	
22	Herbs & Spices	$ 1,222.02	$ 576.00	$ 1,418.00	$ 1,305.07	$ 546.84	$ 1,608.36	

Figure 33-1

Sparklines

Try It!   Using AutoFill to Complete a Series and Create Trends

1. Start Excel, and open **E33Try** from the data files for this lesson.

2. Save the file as **E33Try_xx** in the location where your teacher instructs you to store the files for this lesson.

3. Add a header that has your name at the left, the date code in the center, and the page number code at the right, and change back to Normal view.

4. Select cells B2:G2.

5. Click the AutoFill handle + and drag to the right to cell J2.

6. Select cells B3:G3.

7. Right-click the AutoFill handle +, and drag to the right to cell J3.

8. Release the mouse button at cell J3.

9. In the shortcut menu, select Linear Trend.

10. Select cells B4:G4.

11. Right-click the AutoFill handle +, and drag to the right to cell J4.

12. Release the mouse button at cell J4.

13. In the shortcut menu select Growth Trend.

14. Save the changes to the **E33Try_xx** file, and leave it open to use in the next Try It.

AutoFill shortcut menu

- Copy Cells
- Fill Series
- Fill Formatting Only
- Fill Without Formatting
- Fill Days
- Fill Weekdays
- Fill Months
- Fill Years
- Linear Trend
- Growth Trend
- Flash Fill
- Series...

Try It!   Using the Fill Button to Create a Linear Trend

1. In the **E33Try_xx** file, select cells B5:J5.

2. On the HOME tab, click the Fill button ⬇ > Series.

3. In the Series in group, click Rows, if necessary.

4. Select Linear as the Type.

5. Click OK.

6. Save the changes to the **E33Try_xx** file, and leave it open to use in the next Try It.

The Series dialog box

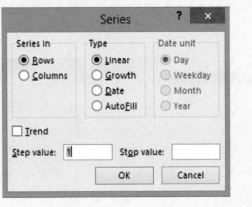

Try It!   Using Sparklines to Instantly Chart Trends

1. In the **E33Try_xx** file, select cells B5:J5, if needed.

2. On the INSERT tab, click the Line button 〰 to show the trend in a line chart.

3. In the Create Sparklines dialog box, enter **$L$5** in the Location Range box.

4. Click OK.

5. Save the changes to the **E33Try_xx** file, and leave it open to use in the next Try It.

The Create Sparklines dialog box

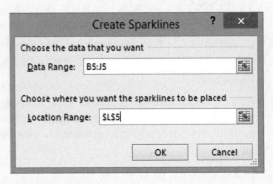

Using FORECAST

- The FORECAST function uses a "linear trend" formula to calculate future values.

- FORECAST examines the x-values and their relationship to the y-values, and then, given a new x-value, it calculates the matching y-value.

- Use FORECAST when existing values follow more or less a straight line, with little or no variance (ups or downs).

- FORECAST plots new values along a straight line formed by existing values.

- The FORECAST function requires two sets of related variables—x values and y values.

Try It!   **Using the FORECAST Function**

1. In the **E33Try_xx** file, click D14.
2. Type =.
3. Type **FORECAST**.

   ✓ *Notice that when you begin typing the name of the function, Excel provides a list of functions. You can double-click the function of your choice instead of typing the entire name.*

4. Type (.

5. Select D13.
6. Type ,.
7. Select B3:J3.
8. Type ,.
9. Select B2:J2.
10. Type), and press [ENTER].
11. Save the changes to the **E33Try_xx** file, and leave it open to use in the next Try It.

Using TREND

- TREND, like FORECAST, plots new values along the straight line formed by the plotted positions of existing values.
- Use the TREND function when existing values follow more or less a straight line when plotted on a chart.
- The TREND function uses a "linear trend" method of calculating future values.

- You only need known y-values to make a prediction using TREND.
- You can input known x-values in the TREND equation to improve the accuracy of the prediction.
- If you also input a new x-value as an argument, it will produce the same result as FORECAST.
- TREND uses the formula, $y=mx+b$ to plot new values along a straight line.
- If you tell TREND to set the value of b to zero, the x value will be adjusted to begin plotting its trend line at zero.

Try It!   **Using the TREND Function**

1. In the **E33Try_xx** file, click D15.
2. Type =.
3. Type **TREND**.
4. Type (.
5. Select cells B4:J4 and skip to Step 6.

   OR

   If desired, add known x-value(s):
   - Type ,.
   - Select B2:J2.

If desired, add new x-value(s):
- Type ,.
- Select D13.

If desired, set the intercept to zero:
- Type ,.
- Type **FALSE**.

6. Type).
7. Press [ENTER].
8. Save the changes to the **E33Try_xx** file, and leave it open to use in the next Try It.

Using GROWTH

- The GROWTH function predicts future values using an exponential growth formula, $y=b*m^x$.

- The trend line created by the GROWTH function is curved, not straight.

- Like TREND, the GROWTH function requires only known y-values.

- You can improve the accuracy by supplying known x-values and new x-values if they're available.

Try It!   **Using the GROWTH Function**

1. In the **E33Try_xx** file, click D16.
2. Type = .
3. Type **GROWTH**.
4. Type (.
5. Select B5:J5.
6. Type ,.
7. Select B2:J2.
8. Type ,.

9. Select D13 and skip to Step 10.

   OR

   If desired, set the intercept to zero:
   - Type ,.
   - Type **FALSE**.
10. Type).
11. Press ENTER.
12. Save the **E33Try_xx** file, and close it.

Lesson 33—Practice

In this project, you will create a FORECAST function using the skills you learned in this lesson.

DIRECTIONS

1. Start Excel, if necessary, and open the **E33Practice** file from the data files for this lesson.
2. Save the workbook as **E33Practice_xx** in the location where your teacher instructs you to store the files for this lesson.
3. For all the worksheets, add a header that has your name at the left, the date code in the center, and the page number code at the right, and change back to **Normal** view.
4. Switch to the **FORECAST** sheet, if necessary, and click cell **E13**.
5. Type **=FORECAST(**.
6. Click cell **E12** and press F4 twice. This will make the row part of the address absolute.

   ✓ You want to use the value entered in row 12 of each column as the new x-value for the y-value you wish to calculate.

7. Type , (comma), and select the range **B13:D13**.
8. Press F4 three times to make the column part of the range address absolute.

   ✓ As you copy the formula, you want it to always refer to the known y-values in columns B, C, and D.

9. Type , (comma), and select the range **B12:D12**.
10. Press F4 to make the range address absolute.

   ✓ As you copy the formula, you want it to always refer to the known x-values in cells B12:D12, which correspond to the new x value entered in row 12 of columns E through G.

11. Type), and press ENTER to complete the formula.
12. Select cell **E13**, and on the HOME tab, click **Copy** to place the formula on the Office Clipboard.
13. Press SHIFT + click cell **G22** to select the cells where you want to enter the projected fourth quarter data.

14. On the HOME tab, click the **Paste** down arrow and select **Formulas** to fill the range **E13:G22** while maintaining the worksheet formatting. Your worksheet should look like Figure 33-2.

15. **With your teacher's permission,** print the **FORECAST** worksheet. Submit the printout or the file for grading as required.

16. Save and close the file, and exit Excel.

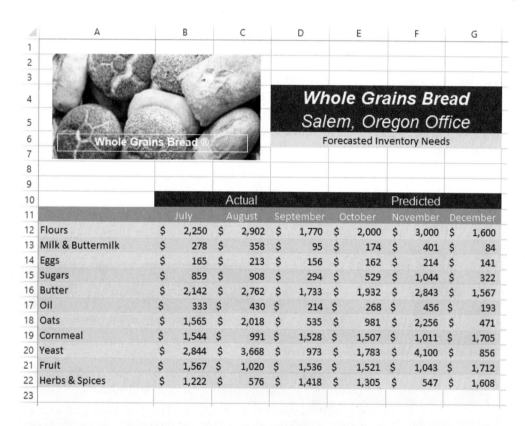

Figure 33-2

	A	B	C	D	E	F	G
				Actual		Predicted	
		July	August	September	October	November	December
12	Flours	$ 2,250	$ 2,902	$ 1,770	$ 2,000	$ 3,000	$ 1,600
13	Milk & Buttermilk	$ 278	$ 358	$ 95	$ 174	$ 401	$ 84
14	Eggs	$ 165	$ 213	$ 156	$ 162	$ 214	$ 141
15	Sugars	$ 859	$ 908	$ 294	$ 529	$ 1,044	$ 322
16	Butter	$ 2,142	$ 2,762	$ 1,733	$ 1,932	$ 2,843	$ 1,567
17	Oil	$ 333	$ 430	$ 214	$ 268	$ 456	$ 193
18	Oats	$ 1,565	$ 2,018	$ 535	$ 981	$ 2,256	$ 471
19	Cornmeal	$ 1,544	$ 991	$ 1,528	$ 1,507	$ 1,011	$ 1,705
20	Yeast	$ 2,844	$ 3,668	$ 973	$ 1,783	$ 4,100	$ 856
21	Fruit	$ 1,567	$ 1,020	$ 1,536	$ 1,521	$ 1,043	$ 1,712
22	Herbs & Spices	$ 1,222	$ 576	$ 1,418	$ 1,305	$ 547	$ 1,608

Lesson 33—Apply

You are the owner of a Whole Grains Bread store in Salem, Washington, and you've been looking for a way to manage inventory more effectively. After learning about Excel's forecasting functions, you've decided to give them a try and see how good they are at predicting your future inventory needs.

DIRECTIONS

1. Start Excel, if necessary, and open the **E33Apply** file from the data files for this lesson.

2. Save the workbook as **E33Apply_xx** in the location where your teacher instructs you to store the files for this lesson.

3. For all worksheets, add a header that has your name at the left, the date code in the center, and the page number code at the right, and change back to **Normal** view.

4. On the **TREND** worksheet, use a simple **TREND** formula to calculate the Flours projection for October.

5. Copy the formula for the rest of the year.

6. In cell **E13**, create a **TREND** formula that projects inventory expenses for Milk & Buttermilk based on its relationship to the flours usage.

   ✓ *Hint: Use the Flours expense for July-Sept as the known x-values and the Flours expense for October as the new x-value.*

7. Use this TREND formula to project the rest of the expenses for the fourth quarter of October, November, and December. (Keep the existing formatting.)

8. On the **GROWTH** worksheet, use a simple **GROWTH** formula to calculate the Flours projection for October.

9. Copy the formula for the rest of the year.

10. In cell **E13**, create a **GROWTH** formula that projects inventory expenses for Milk & Buttermilk based on its relationship to the flours usage.

   ✓ Hint: Use the Flours expense for July-Sept as the known x-values and the Flours expense for October as the new x-value.

11. Use this **GROWTH** formula to project the rest of the expenses for the fourth quarter. (Keep the existing formatting.)

12. Apply the Accounting formatting to all expenses in the workbook, and widen the columns, as necessary. Your **GROWTH** worksheet should look like Figure 33-3.

13. Check the spelling in the workbook.

14. **With your teacher's permission,** print the TREND and GROWTH worksheets. Submit the printouts or the file for grading as required.

15. Save and close the file, and exit Excel.

Figure 33-3

Whole Grains Bread
Salem, Oregon Office
Forecasted Inventory Needs

| | Actual | | | Predicted | | |
	July	August	September	October	November	December
Flours	$ 2,250.35	$ 2,901.77	$ 1,770.00	$ 2,549.38	$ 2,514.61	$ 1,885.29
Milk & Buttermilk	$ 277.95	$ 358.41	$ 95.09	$ 277.96	$ 267.27	$ 131.47
Eggs	$ 165.05	$ 212.82	$ 156.00	$ 188.71	$ 186.88	$ 156.57
Sugars	$ 859.45	$ 908.00	$ 294.02	$ 769.29	$ 744.46	$ 411.04
Butter	$ 2,141.71	$ 2,761.67	$ 1,733.00	$ 2,399.13	$ 2,365.14	$ 1,826.68
Oil	$ 333.29	$ 429.76	$ 214.00	$ 362.14	$ 354.62	$ 242.63
Oats	$ 1,565.06	$ 2,018.10	$ 535.42	$ 1,565.10	$ 1,504.95	$ 740.28
Cornmeal	$ 1,543.74	$ 991.00	$ 1,528.00	$ 1,204.79	$ 1,221.65	$ 1,571.08
Yeast	$ 2,844.30	$ 3,667.65	$ 973.05	$ 2,844.37	$ 2,735.05	$ 1,345.37
Fruit	$ 1,566.74	$ 1,020.00	$ 1,536.00	$ 1,230.78	$ 1,247.10	$ 1,582.84
Herbs & Spices	$ 1,222.02	$ 576.00	$ 1,418.00	$ 820.15	$ 843.77	$ 1,410.67

Lesson 34

Using Advanced Functions for Data Analysis

➤ **What You Will Learn**

Using the PMT Function
Creating What-If Data Tables
Solving a Problem with Goal Seek
Using Solver to Resolve Problems
Working with Outlines

Software Skills   What-if analysis allows you to determine the optimal values for a given situation. For example, if you know that you can only spend a maximum of $32,000 this year on new computers, you could adjust the monthly budget amount so you could spend the total amount by the end of the year and yet still remain within your department's monthly budgetary constraints. You can use Excel's data features—Goal Seek, Solver, and Auto Outline—to improve and manage list or table data.

What You Can Do

Using the PMT Function

- You can use the PMT (payment) function to calculate a loan payment amount given the principal, interest rate, and number of payment periods.

  ✓ *The PMT result is equal to your principal and interest for the loan, but does not include any other payment parts such as taxes, escrow, points, closing fees, and so on.*

- The arguments for the PMT function are: =PMT(rate,nper,pv).
  - rate: Interest rate per period (for example, annual interest rate/12).
  - nper: Number of payment periods (for example, years*12).
  - pv (present value): The total amount that a series of future payments is worth now (for example, the principal).

    ✓ *The principal is the amount of the loan after any down payment that might have been paid.*

WORDS TO KNOW

Data table
A method of performing what-if analysis, involving a column (and possibly a row) of variables and a formula that Excel solves over and over, using each of the variables. The result is a table of answers.

Goal Seek
A method of performing what-if analysis in which the result (the goal) is known, but the value of a single dependent variable is unknown.

Input cell
A cell in a data table to which your formula refers. Excel copies a variable into this cell, solves the formula, and then goes on to the next variable to create a series of answers.

Outline
A feature that allows groups of data to be displayed or hidden.

Solver
A method of performing what-if analysis in which the result is known, but more than a single variable is unknown. Also, there may be additional constraints upon the final result.

Substitution values
A special name given to the variables used in a data table.

Variable
An input value that changes depending on the desired outcome.

What-if analysis
Excel's term for a series of tools that perform calculations involving one or more variables.

- For example, if you wish to calculate a monthly payment for a $175,000 loan at a 9% annual rate of interest for 25 years, you must enter **.09/12** as the monthly rate and enter **25*12** to get the total number of payments (nper): **=PMT(.09/12,25*12,175000)**

- Both the rate and the number of payment periods (nper) must be in the same timeframe or format, such as monthly or annually.

- You must enter the present value as a negative to get a positive number for the result, as in: **=PMT(.09/12,25*12,-175000)**

| Try It! | **Using the PMT Function** |

1. Start Excel, and open the **E34Try** file from the data files for this lesson.

2. Save the file as **E34Try_xx** in the location where your teacher instructs you to store the files for this lesson.

3. For all worksheets, add a header that has your name at the left, the date code in the center, and the page number code at the right, and change back to Normal view.

4. Click the PMT worksheet tab to make that sheet active, and click D7.

5. Type =.

6. Type **PMT**.

7. Type (.

8. Click cell D6, and type /12.

    ✓ *This breaks the interest rate into a monthly amount. The rate is a percentage, or .09.*

9. Type ,.

10. Click cell D5, and type *12.

    ✓ *For example, 3*12. The term is the number of years.*

11. Type ,.

12. Type – (minus), and click cell D4.

    ✓ *When you type a minus sign before the principal, the payment amount will appear as a positive amount.*

13. Type).

14. Press ENTER .

15. Save the **E34Try_xx** file, and leave it open to use in the next Try It.

Loan payment calculation using PMT

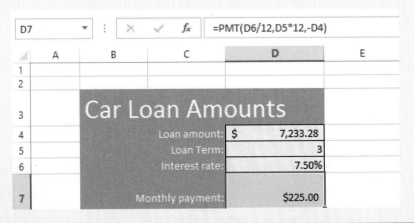

Creating What-If Data Tables

■ Use **what-if analysis** to evaluate different situations and find the best solution.

■ For example, a what-if table can help you figure out the maximum mortgage you can afford if you want to keep your payments at $1,000 per month given various interest rates.

■ The **variables** used in a data table are called **substitution values**, because Excel substitutes each value in the given formula when evaluating the what-if situation.

■ Excel uses the **input cell** as a working area during the analysis—it can be blank, or it can contain one of the variables (typically, the first one in the variables list).

✓ *The what-if formula must refer to this input cell.*

■ Excel places each variable into the input cell as it solves each equation.

■ **Data tables** can be either one-input or two-input.

■ In a one-input data table, you enter one series of variables, which are then substituted in a formula to come up with a series of answers.

● You can enter the variables, such as the varying interest rates in this example, in a single column or a single row.

● You then enter a formula in a cell either one row up and one column to the right, or one row down and one column to the left (for variables entered in a row).

● The formula points to the input cell, which typically contains a value equal to the first variable in your list.

■ In a two-input data table, you enter two series of variables, thus increasing the number of possible solutions.

✓ *For example, you can enter both the loan rates and several different loan terms (15-, 20-, 25-, or 30-year) to determine what amounts you can afford under varying plans.*

■ In a two-input data table, you enter one set of variables in a row, and the other set in a column to the left of the first row variable.

● You enter the formula in the cell intersected by the variable row and variable column.

● The formula refers to two input cells, which again can be blank, or may be filled with the first variable.

■ After entering the variables, formula, and input cell precisely, you use a command on the DATA tab to generate the values in the input table.

Try It!   Creating a One-Input Data Table

1 In the **E34Try_xx** file, select the One Input Table worksheet.

2 In cell C12, type **=D8**, and press ENTER.

   ✓ To enter additional formulas, type them in the cells to the right of the formula cell (if you entered variables in a column), or in the cells below the formula cell (if you entered variables in a row).

3 Select the range B12:C19.

   ✓ Select cells containing the formula and substitution values.

   ✓ Do not select the input cell.

4 Click DATA > What-If Analysis 📊 > Data Table.

5 In the Column input cell box, type **D8**.

6 Click OK.

7 Save the **E34Try_xx** file, and leave it open to use in the next Try It.

A one-variable what-if analysis

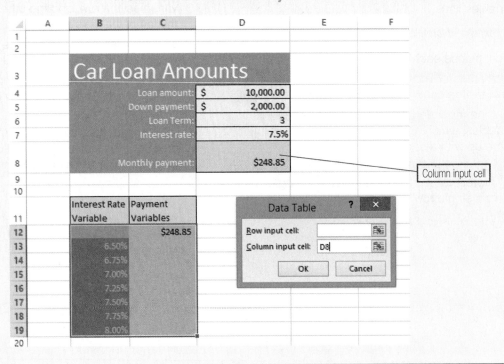

Try It!   Creating a Two-Input Data Table

1 In the **E34Try_xx** file, select the Two Input Table worksheet.

2 In cell B6, type **=C21**, and press `ENTER`.

3 Select B6:I13, or all the cells in the data table range.

   ✓ *Select cells containing the formula and the substitution values.*

4 On the DATA tab, click What-If Analysis ▣ > Data Table.

5 In the Row input cell, type **C20**.

6 In the Column input cell box, type **C18**.

   ✓ *Excel will automatically create absolute references by adding dollar signs to cell addresses entered in the Data Table dialog box.*

7 Click OK.

8 Save the **E34Try_xx** file, and leave it open to use in the next Try It.

A two-variable what-if analysis

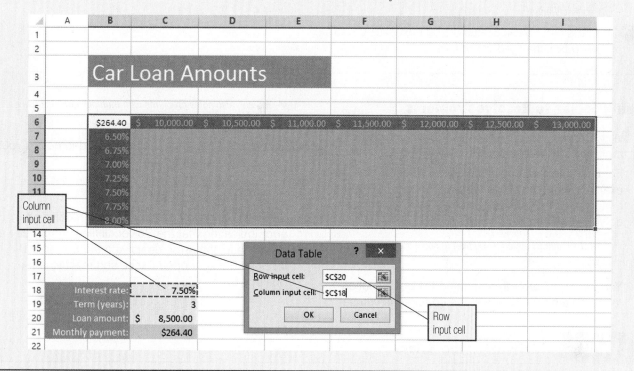

Solving a Problem with Goal Seek

- Use **Goal Seek** when you know the result (the goal), but you do not know the value of one of the input variables.

- Goal Seek tests possible variables until it finds the input value that produces the desired result.

- For example, you could use Goal Seek to determine the exact amount you could borrow at 9.25% and keep the payment at $1,000 a month.

- When you input your known variables into Goal Seek, the Goal Seek Status dialog box will show whether it found a solution and, if so, the solution. The values on the worksheet are also changed.

Try It!   Using Goal Seek

1 In the **E34Try_xx** file, select the Goal Seek worksheet.

2 On the DATA tab, click What-If Analysis ▦? > Goal Seek.

3 In the Set cell box, type **D9**.

4 In the To value box, type **350**.

5 In the By changing cell box, type **D6**.

6 Click OK.

✓ *Goal Seek finds a solution and displays it in the Goal Seek Status dialog box. The values on the worksheet are also changed.*

7 In the Goal Seek Status dialog box, click OK to keep the changed cell values.

8 Save the **E34Try_xx** file, and leave it open to use in the next Try It.

The Goal Seek Status dialog box

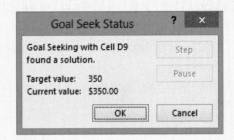

Using Solver to Resolve Problems

■ With **Solver**, you can resolve problems involving more than one variable with a known result.

■ For example, you could use Solver to determine the exact amount you could borrow, spending $1,000 a month, using various interest rates and various down payments.

✓ *Use the Value Of option if you plan to solve for a specific result.*

■ You can use Solver to determine the best solution to a problem that fits within the constraints you set.

✓ *You can also solve problems with multiple variables using a PivotTable, which is covered in Lesson 36.*

■ You must first activate the Solver Add-in before you can use the Solver feature.

■ You can enable the Solver Add-in from the Excel Options on the FILE tab.

■ When working with Solver, you may receive an error indicating that the Solver.dll file cannot be found. To fix the error, deactivate the Solver add-in, close Excel, reopen Excel, and reactivate the Solver add-in.

Try It!   Activating the Solver

1 In the **E34Try_xx** file, click FILE > Options.

2 In the Excel Options dialog box, click Add-Ins.

3 In the Manage drop-down box, select Excel Add-ins > Go.

4 In the Add-Ins dialog box, click Solver Add-in > OK.

5 Save the **E34Try_xx** file, and leave it open to use in the next Try It.

Try It!   Using Solver

1. In the **E34Try_xx** file, select the Solver worksheet.

2. On the DATA tab, in the Analysis group, click Solver 📈.

3. In the Solver Parameters dialog box, click Max.

4. In the Set Objective box, type **I4**.

5. In the By Changing Variable Cells box, type **F5**.

6. Click the Add button to add a constraint.

7. In the Cell Reference box, type **F5**.

8. Select <= from the descriptor drop-down list.

9. In the Constraint box, type **I7**.

10. Click OK.

    ✓ Note that the cell reference in the Solver Parameters dialog box makes your cell references absolute.

11. Click Solve.

    ✓ Solver finds a solution and displays it in a dialog box. The values on the worksheet are also changed.

12. Click OK to keep the changed cell values. Adjust the column widths, as needed.

    ✓ You can save the scenario, restore your previous values, or print reports from the dialog box that appears.

13. Save the **E34Try_xx** file, and leave it open to use in the next Try It.

The Solver Parameters dialog box

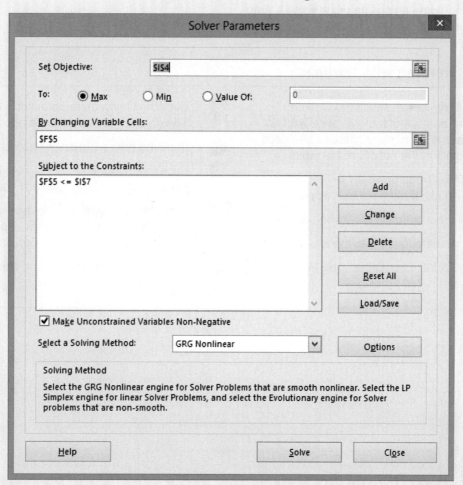

Working with Outlines

- If you have a list of data that you want to group and summarize, you can create an **outline** of up to eight levels, one for each group.
- You can use an outline to quickly display summary rows or columns, or to reveal the detail data for each group.
- You can create an outline of rows, an outline of columns, or an outline of both rows and columns.
- Each column of the data that you want to outline needs to have a label in the first row, similar facts in each column, and no blank rows or columns within the range.
- Outline features are located in the Outline group on the DATA tab.
- To create an outline, select a cell in the range of cells you want to outline, and click the Group button.
- You can quickly create an outline using Excel's Auto Outline feature.

✓ For the Auto Outline feature to function, the rows of your data need be located below or above a summary row, or a subtotal.

✓ You learned about the SUBTOTAL function and creating a subtotal in Lesson 11.

- You can access Auto Outline from the Group button's drop-down arrow.
- Once you create an outline, the outline controls appear. Row outline controls appear to the left of the list or table. Column outline controls appear above the list or table.
- You can expand or collapse the data in your outline by clicking the plus ⊞ and minus ⊟ outline control buttons.
- You can remove an outline by using the Clear Outline button from the Ungroup button's drop-down arrow.

Try It!　　Working with Outlines

1. In the **E34Try_xx** file, select the Outline worksheet, and select the cell range A6:G37. Notice that the list already contains two cells with subtotals at the bottom of the table.

2. Click DATA > Group down arrow ᴳʳᵒᵘᵖ > Auto Outline. The row outline controls appear.

3. Click the minus button ⊟ to the left of row 20.

4. Click the minus button ⊟ to the left of row 29.

5. On the DATA tab, click Group. The Group dialog box appears.

6. Click the Columns radio button, and click OK. The column outline controls appear.

7. Click the minus button ⊟ above column F.

8. Click the minus button ⊟ to the left of row 37. Notice that all of the rows are now collapsed.

9. Click the plus button ⊞ to the left of row 37. Notice that the rows are now expanded, except for the rows you previously collapsed.

10. Save the **E34Try_xx** file, and close it.

Lesson 34—Practice

In this project, you will use Solver to create a bid projection using the skills you learned in this lesson.

DIRECTIONS

1. Start Excel, if necessary, and open the **E34Practice** file from the data files for this lesson.

2. Save the workbook as **E34Practice_xx** in the location where your teacher instructs you to store the files for this lesson.

3. For all worksheets, add a header that has your name at the left, the date code in the center, and the page number code at the right, and change back to **Normal** view.

4. Select the **Bid Sheet** worksheet, if necessary.

5. On the **DATA** tab, click the **Solver** button. The Solver Parameters dialog box opens.

6. In the **Set Objective** box, click the **Collapse Dialog box** button.

7. Click cell **E14**, and click the **Expand Dialog box** button.

8. Click **Value Of**, and type **300000** in the text box.

9. In the **By Changing Variable Cells** box, click the **Collapse Dialog box** button.

10. Hold down CTRL , and click cells **B20** and **D7**.

11. Click the **Expand Dialog** box button.

12. Click **Add** to open the Add Constraint dialog box.

13. In the **Cell Reference** box, type **B20**.

14. Click **less than or equal** from the descriptor list.

15. Type **22** in the **Constraint** box.

16. Click **Add** to add a second constraint.

17. In the **Cell Reference** box, type **D7**.

18. Click **less than or equal** from the descriptor list.

19. Type **10** in the **Constraint** box, and click **OK** to return to the Solver Parameters dialog box.

20. Click **Solve**.

21. In the **Solver Results** dialog box, select **Keep Solver Solution** and click **OK**. Your document should look like the one shown in Figure 34-1.

22. **With your teacher's permission,** print the **Bid Sheet** worksheet. Submit the printout or the file for grading as required.

   ✓ *If printing, adjust the page breaks, and change the print settings, as necessary.*

23. Save and close the file, and exit Excel.

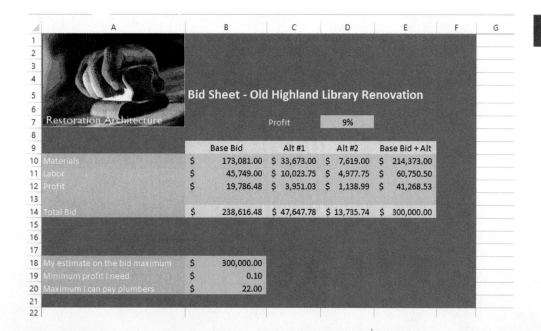

Figure 34-1

Lesson 34—Apply

As the owner of Restoration Architecture, you're always watching the bottom line. You're preparing a bid for the renovation of your town's library, and you want to run the numbers through Excel before submitting it. You'll create data tables to compute the cost of the small construction loan you'll need if you get the job, and the estimated amount of any increased costs you might encounter if the job runs over deadline.

DIRECTIONS

1. Start Excel, if necessary.
2. Open the **E34Apply** file from the data files for this lesson.
3. Save the workbook as **E34Apply_xx** in the location where your teacher instructs you to store the files for this lesson.
4. For all worksheets, add a header that has your name at the left, the date code in the center, and the page number code at the right, and change back to **Normal** view.
5. Create a two-input what-if analysis on the **Labor** worksheet. Set up the table as shown in Figure 34-2 on the next page:
   a. Type the following formula in cell C19: **=H19*H20**.
      ✓ *This calculates the changes in cost when construction finishes early or late.*

   b. Select the data range **C19:F25**.
   c. Use **H20** for the **Row input cell**.
   d. Use **H19** for the **Column input cell**.
6. Create another two-input table on the **Loan** worksheet. Set up the table as shown in Figure 34-3 on the next page:
   a. In cell **A9**, create a PMT formula using the values in cells **C6**, **C7**, and **F6**.
      ✓ *Be sure to enter the principle value as a negative.*

   b. Select the data range **A9:F15**.
   c. Use **C7** for the **Row input cell**.
   d. Use **C6** for the **Column input cell**.
7. **With your teacher's permission,** print the **Labor** and **Loan** worksheets. Submit the printout or the file for grading as required.
8. Save and close the file, and exit Excel.

Figure 34-2

	A	B	C	D	E	F	G	H	I
1									
2									
3									
4									
5		Estimated Labor Costs - Old Highland Library Renovation							
6									
7	Restoration Architecture								
8			Hours Estimated to Complete Work				Labor Cost		
9		Base Bid	Alt #1	Alt #2	Totals Hours	Hourly Rate Current Quotes	Base Bid	Alt #1	Alt #2
10	Masonary	215.00			215.00	$ 29.75	$ 6,396.25	$ -	$ -
11	Carpentry	1,245.00	325.00	114.00	1,684.00	$ 18.75	$ 23,343.75	$ 6,093.75	$ 2,137.50
12	Electrical	322.00	95.00	85.75	502.75	$ 27.00	$ 8,694.00	$ 2,565.00	$ 2,315.25
13	Roofers	96.00	21.00		117.00	$ 15.00	$ 1,440.00	$ 315.00	$ -
14	Plumbing	235.00	42.00	21.00	298.00	$ 22.00	$ 5,170.00	$ 924.00	$ 462.00
15									
16	Total Bid	2,113.00	483.00	220.75	2,816.75		$ 45,044.00	$ 9,897.75	$ 4,914.75
17									
18				Alt #2	Alt #1	Base			
19			$ 4,423.28	$ 4,914.75	$ 9,897.75	$ 45,044.00		$ 4,914.75	
20		1-Week Early	90%	4,423.28	8,907.98	40,539.60		90%	
21	Estimated Cost	On Time	100%	4,914.75	9,897.75	45,044.00			
22	Reductions/Increases	1 Week Late	112%	5,504.52	11,085.48	50,449.28			
23	for Schedule Changes	2 Weeks Late	126%	6,192.59	12,471.17	56,755.44			
24		3 Weeks Late	132%	6,487.47	13,065.03	59,458.08			
25		4 Weeks Late	141%	6,929.80	13,955.83	63,512.04			
26									

Figure 34-3

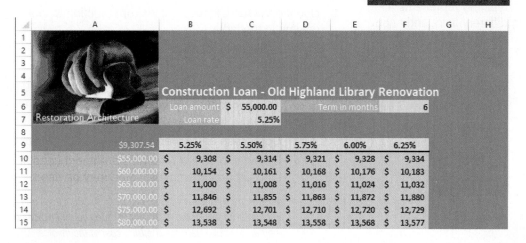

	A	B	C	D	E	F	G	H
1								
2								
3								
4								
5		Construction Loan - Old Highland Library Renovation						
6		Loan amount	$ 55,000.00		Term in months		6	
7	Restoration Architecture	Loan rate	5.25%					
8								
9		$9,307.54	5.25%	5.50%	5.75%	6.00%	6.25%	
10		$55,000.00	$ 9,308	$ 9,314	$ 9,321	$ 9,328	$ 9,334	
11		$60,000.00	$ 10,154	$ 10,161	$ 10,168	$ 10,176	$ 10,183	
12		$65,000.00	$ 11,000	$ 11,008	$ 11,016	$ 11,024	$ 11,032	
13		$70,000.00	$ 11,846	$ 11,855	$ 11,863	$ 11,872	$ 11,880	
14		$75,000.00	$ 12,692	$ 12,701	$ 12,710	$ 12,720	$ 12,729	
15		$80,000.00	$ 13,538	$ 13,548	$ 13,558	$ 13,568	$ 13,577	

Lesson 35

Using LOOKUP Functions

➤ **What You Will Learn**

Creating Lookup Functions

WORDS TO KNOW

Range name
The name given to a set
of adjacent cells. You
might name a range in
order to make it more
convenient to reference
that range in a formula
or a function, such as
VLOOKUP.

Table
A series of columns and
rows used to organize
data. Each column
typically represents a
different field, and each
row represents an entire
record.

Software Skills   With the lookup functions, you can look up information in
a table based on a known value. For example, you can look up the salesperson
assigned to a particular client. At the same time, you can look up that client's
address and phone number. You can also look up the sales discount for a particular
customer or calculate the bonuses for a group of salespeople based on a bonus
structure. If needed, you can nest a function, such as SUM, within a lookup function
in order to look up a sum total within a table. For example, you might want to look up
the total cost of the items in an invoice to calculate the cost of delivering them.

What You Can Do

Creating Lookup Functions

- The lookup functions, VLOOKUP and HLOOKUP, locate a value in a **table**.
- Use the VLOOKUP (vertical lookup) function to look up data in a particular
  column in the table.
- The VLOOKUP function uses this format: =VLOOKUP(item,table-range,column-
  position)
  - *Item* is the text or value for which you are looking.
    - The item to look up must be located in the first column of the VLOOKUP
      table.
    - Uppercase and lowercase are treated the same.
    - Depending on the true/false argument used, if an exact match is not
      found, the next smallest value may be used.
  - ✓ *You can use a function here to calculate the item's value. For example, you can use the SUM*
    function to calculate the total cost of items on an invoice and look up the delivery costs in
    another table to determine the total cost of the invoice.

- *Table-range* is the range reference or **range name** of the lookup table.
  - Do not include the row containing the column labels.
  - If you are going to copy the lookup function, you should express the range as an absolute reference or as a range name.
- *Column-position* is the column number in the table from which the matching value should be returned.
  - ✓ *The far-left column of the table is one; the second column is two, etc.*
- Use the HLOOKUP (horizontal lookup) function to look up data in a particular row in the table.

- You may use a similar formula in a horizontal lookup table:
  =HLOOKUP(item,table-range,row-position).
  - *Item* is the text or value for which you are looking.
  - *Table-range* is the range reference or range name of the lookup table.
    - ✓ *Do not include the column that contains the row labels in this range.*
  - *Row-position* is the row number in the table from which the matching value should be returned.

Try It!   Inserting the VLOOKUP Function

1   Start Excel, and open **E35Try** file from the data files for this lesson.

2   Save the file as **E35Try_xx** in the location where your teacher instructs you to store the files for this lesson.

3   Add a header that has your name at the left, the date code in the center, and the page number code at the right, and change back to Normal view.

4   Click cell I18.

5   Type =.

6   Type **VLOOKUP(**.

    ✓ *This function's syntax appears in a ScreenTip underneath the selected cell formula. You can click the function's name in the ScreenTip in order to display the related Help screen.*

7   Type **.0725** in the lookup_value position.

    ✓ *This can be an actual value or item or a reference to the cell containing the value or item.*

    ✓ *You can click a cell in the worksheet to insert a cell reference.*

8   Type **,**.

9   Type **B6:I13** for the table_array.

    ✓ *You can also select cells in the worksheet for the cell range.*

10   Type **,**.

11   Type **4** for the col_index_num (column number).

12   Type **)**, and press ENTER .

13   Save the **E35Try_xx** file, and leave it open to use in the next Try It.

Try It!   Inserting an HLOOKUP Function Using the Function Wizard

1 In the **E35Try_xx** file, select cell I19.

2 Type =.

3 Type **HLOOKUP(**.

4 Click the Insert Function button *f*× on the formula bar.

✓ *This opens the Function Wizard that can help you format the function's arguments.*

5 In the Lookup_value box, type **10500**.

6 Click in the Table_array box, and select cells B6:I13.

✓ *You can use the Collapse Dialog box and Expand Dialog box buttons to hide or expand the dialog box for the selection, if necessary.*

7 In the Row_index_num box, type **MATCH(0.0675,B7:B13)+1**.

✓ *By using the MATCH function, you can have the HLOOKUP function locate the appropriate row index item for you.*

8 Click OK.

9 Save the **E35Try_xx** file, and close it.

The Function Arguments dialog box

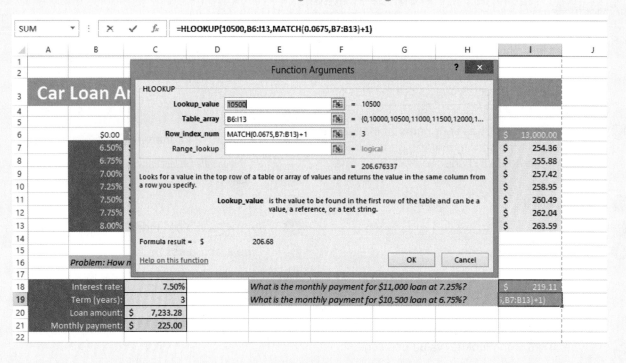

Lesson 35—Practice

In this project, you will create VLOOKUP functions to perform income tax calculations using the skills you learned in this lesson.

DIRECTIONS

1. Start Excel, if necessary, and open the **E35Practice** file from the data files for this lesson.

2. Save the workbook as **E35Practice_xx** in the location where your teacher instructs you to store the files for this lesson.

3. For all worksheets, add a header that has your name at the left, the date code in the center, and the page number code at the right, and change back to **Normal** view.

4. Select the **1040** worksheet, if necessary.

5. Click cell **F50**. You'll use this cell to enter a formula to look up your tax based on the provided taxable amount.

6. Type **=VLOOKUP(**, and click the Insert Function button *fx* on the formula bar to open the Function Arguments dialog box.

7. Click in the **Lookup_value** box, and click cell **F49**.

   ✓ *You also can use the Collapse and Expand Dialog box buttons.*

8. Click in the **Table_array** box, click the **Tax Table** worksheet, and select the cell range **A4:C304**.

9. In the **Column_index_num** box, type **2** (the married filing joint column).

10. Click **OK**. Your worksheet should look like Figure 35-1 on the next page.

11. **With your teacher's permission,** print the **1040** worksheet. Submit the printout or the file for grading as required.

    ✓ *If printing, adjust the page breaks, and change the print settings, as necessary.*

12. Save and close the file, and exit Excel.

Figure 35-1

	A	B	C	D	E	F
45	37b	Married filing separately and spouse itemizes				
46	38	Deduction (married jointly)				$ 7,850.00
47	39	Subtract line 38 from line 36				$ 78,530.23
48	40	Multiply $3,000 by tot. exemptions...				$ 12,000.00
49	41	Taxable income				$ 66,530.23
50	42	Tax				$ 11,758.00
51	43	Alternative minimum tax				
52	44	Add lines 42 and 43				$ 11,758.00
53	45	Foreign tax credit				
54	46	Credit for child and dependent care expenses			$ 682.00	
55	47	Credit for elderly or disabled				
56	48	Education credits				
57	49	Retirement savings credit				
58	50	Child tax credit			$ 1,200.00	
59	51	Adoption credit				
60	52	Credits from form 8396 or 8859				
61	53	Other credits from form 3800 or 8801				
62	54	Total credits				$ 1,882.00
63	55	Subtract line 54 from line 44				$ 9,876.00
64	56	Self-employment tax				
65	57	Social security tax and Medicare tax on tip income				
66	58	Tax on IRAs				
67	59	Advanced EIC payments				
68	60	Household employment taxes				
69	61	Total tax				$ 9,876.00
70	62	Federal income tax withheld			$ 9,761.40	
71	63	2010 estimated tax payments				
72	64	Earned income credit				
73	65	Excess social security tax and tier 1 RRTA tax withheld				
74	66	Additional child tax credit				
75	67	Amount paid with extension to file				
76	68	Other payments				
77	69	Total payments				$ 9,761.40
78	70	This is the amount you OVERPAID				$ -
79	71a	Amount to be refunded to you				$ -
80	72	Amount to be applied to 2011 tax				
81	73	The amount you OWE				$ 114.60
82	74	Estimated tax penalty				

Amount you owe

Lesson 35—Apply

After learning about the power of Excel's lookup functions, you've decided to use them to make tax time a bit easier. You want to add several lookup functions to your income tax worksheets.

DIRECTIONS

1. Start Excel, if necessary, and open **E35Apply** from the data files for this lesson.
2. Save the workbook as **E35Apply_xx** in the location where your teacher instructs you to store the files for this lesson.
3. Select the **Student Loan** worksheet, if necessary.
4. Add a header that has your name at the left, the date code in the center, and the page number code at the right, and change back to **Normal** view.
5. In cell **F7**, enter a formula to look up the deduction limit, which is based on your filing status. Make sure the formula takes the following into consideration:

   a. Use the **IF** function to determine your filing status.
   b. If the text entered in cell **B7** is equal to "married, filing jointly," then use an **HLOOKUP** function that looks up the value **2** in the table, and displays the dollar amount shown below it.

   c. If the text in cell **B7** is anything else, use **HLOOKUP** to look up the value **1** and display the dollar amount below it.
   d. The **Row Index** for both **HLOOKUP** functions is 2, because the dollar amounts are located in row 2 of the table.
6. Your worksheet should look like Figure 35-2. **With your teacher's permission,** print the **Student Loan** worksheet. Submit the printout or the file for grading as required.

   ✓ If printing, adjust the page breaks, and change the print settings, as necessary.

7. Save and close the file, and exit Excel.

	A	B	C	D	E	F
1	Student Loan Interest Deduction Worksheet - 1040 Line 25					
2	Line	Description				Amount
3	1	Interest paid				$ 778.56
4	2	1040, line 22				$ 92,808.79
5	3	1040, lines 23,24,27-33a				$ 1,200.00
6	4	Subtract line 3 from line 2				$ 91,608.79
7	5	Married, filing jointly				$ 100,000.00
8	6	Is line 4 > 5?				No
9	7	Divide line 6 by $30,000				$ -
10	8	Multiply line 1 by 7				$ -
11	9	Student loan interest deduction				$ 778.56
12						
13						
14			1	2		
15		Limit	$50,000.00	$100,000.00		
16						

Figure 35-2

Lesson 36

Working with PivotTables and PivotCharts

> ➤ **What You Will Learn**
>
> Creating PivotTables
> Using the PivotTable Fields Task Pane
> Applying PivotTable Styles
> Creating PivotCharts

Software Skills   PivotTables make it easier to analyze complex data. For example, if you had a database containing lots of information, such as sales data by product, store, region, and salesperson, you can summarize it in a PivotTable. With the table, you can display totals by region for each product, or you can rearrange the table to display sales totals by office and individual salesperson. You also can combine the tables to display totals by region, office, salesperson, and product. PivotTable can become very hard to navigate depending on their complexity. You can use a PivotChart to visually present your data, and quickly analyze a subset of your data using the filtering controls.

WORDS TO KNOW

Database
An organized collection of records. For example, in an employee database, one record might include:

Employee name
Date of hire
Address
Phone number
Salary rate

Field
A single element of a record, such as "Phone number." Multiple related fields, such as one employee's name, address, phone number, etc., make up one record.

PivotChart
A chart based on PivotTable data.

What You Can Do

Creating PivotTables

- A **PivotTable** allows you to summarize complex data, such as a company's sales or accounting records. (See Figure 36-1 on the next page.)

- The advantage of the PivotTable over a regular table of information is that it lets you quickly change how data is summarized.

- For example, you can change from a report that summarizes sales data by region and office to one that summarizes the same data by salesperson and product.

- The source data for your PivotTable can be an external **database**, text file, or query file, or a range or table within an Excel workbook.

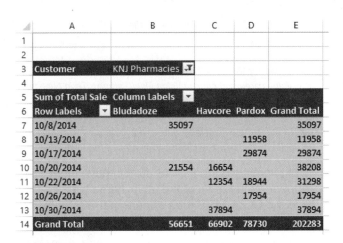

Figure 36-1

PivotTable
A rearrangeable table that allows you to analyze complex data in a variety of ways.

Report filter
A field from the database that you can use to filter or limit the data displayed within the PivotTable.

	A	B	C	D	E
1					
2					
3	Customer	KNJ Pharmacies			
4					
5	Sum of Total Sale	Column Labels			
6	Row Labels	Bludadoze	Havcore	Pardox	Grand Total
7	10/8/2014	35097			35097
8	10/13/2014			11958	11958
9	10/17/2014			29874	29874
10	10/20/2014	21554	16654		38208
11	10/22/2014		12354	18944	31298
12	10/26/2014			17954	17954
13	10/30/2014		37894		37894
14	Grand Total	56651	66902	78730	202283

Try It!   Creating PivotTables with Excel Data

1 Start Excel, and open **E36Try** from the data files for this lesson.

2 Save the file as **E36Try_xx** in the location where your teacher instructs you to store the files for this lesson.

3 For all worksheets, add a header that has your name at the left, the date code in the center, and the page number code at the right, and change back to Normal view.

4 On the DATA worksheet, click cell A5.

5 Click INSERT > PivotTable.

> ✓ The range or table containing the cell you selected earlier should appear in the Select a table or range box. If the selection is wrong, you can select the correct range yourself.

6 Select Existing Worksheet.

7 In the Location box, type **PivotTable!$A$5**.

8 Click OK.

9 Save the **E36Try_xx** file, and leave it open to use in the next Try It.

Create PivotTable dialog box

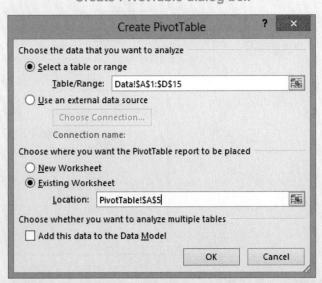

Using the PivotTable Fields Task Pane

- The PivotTable Field List allows you to control each of the **fields** (columns) in your original data.

- When you insert a PivotTable in a worksheet, Excel creates the framework for your PivotTable. You then use the items on the PivotTable Fields task pane to arrange (and rearrange) the data to create the table you want.

- To change the way your data is summarized, drag the field name into the report area boxes at the bottom of the PivotTable Fields task pane.

- The PivotTable has four areas into which you can drag your fields: FILTERS, COLUMNS, ROWS, and VALUES.

- Drag numerical items into the VALUES area to summarize them.

- ✓ The default format for values on the PivotTable is a sum of the items.

- ✓ To modify the format of the data, click the field item in the Values area and choose Value Field Settings. Then choose the type of value you want, such as Sum, and click OK.

- ✓ In the sample PivotTable shown in Figure 36-1, the Total Sale item was placed in the body area of the PivotTable.

- Drag items into the ROWS area to have them appear as the rows of the table. Items that you drag into the COLUMNS area appear in the columns of the table.

- ✓ In the sample PivotTable shown in Figure 36-1, the Sales Date item was added to the row area, and the Drug Purchased item was added to the column area of the table (see Figure 36-2 to see where to add the items).

Figure 36-2

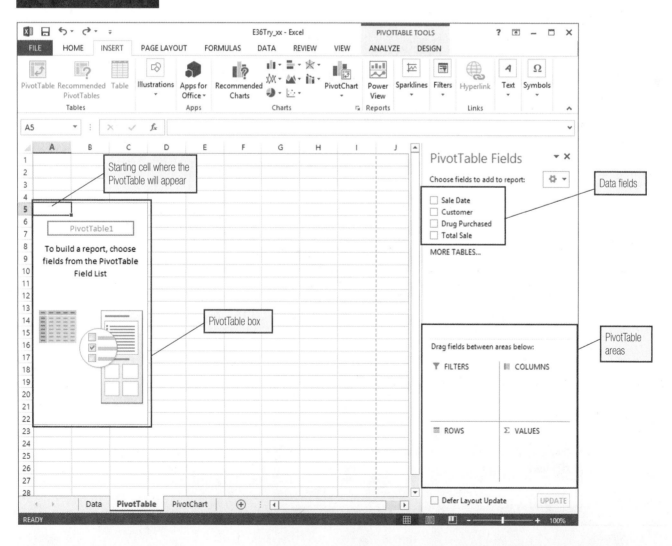

- You can also filter the entire table by dragging a field to the FILTERS area.
- When you use **Report filters**, only the items relating to a particular category are displayed.

  ✓ *In the sample PivotTable shown in Figure 36-1, the Customer item was added to the FILTERS area.*

- When you add an item to a PivotTable, that item becomes a button with a down arrow.
- You can limit what's displayed in the PivotTable by clicking the down arrow on the appropriate item and selecting the item(s) you want to display.

  ✓ *For example, you could click the down arrow on a Sale Date field, and choose a specific date. The PivotTable data would then be limited to activity on that date.*

✓ *In the sample PivotTable shown in Figure 36-1 the down arrow on the Customer button was clicked, and "KNJ Pharmacies" was selected. A user could further limit the report to display only the drug sales for Bludadoze and Pardox, or only the sales for 10/22.*

- To rearrange a table, drag fields from area to area at the bottom of the PivotTable Fields List.
- If you don't want to see the changes to the PivotTable as you go, click the Defer Layout Update option. Then, when you're ready, click the Update button.
- To remove an item from a PivotTable, deselect it in the PivotTable Fields List.

Try It! Using the PivotTable Fields Task Pane

1. In the **E36Try_xx** file, click in the PivotTable box on the worksheet.
2. In the PivotTable Fields task pane, drag the Drug Purchased field into the COLUMNS area.
3. Drag the Sale Date field from the PivotTable Fields task pane into the ROWS area.
4. Drag the Total Sale field to the VALUES area.

✓ *This item is typically a numerical item, such as total sales.*

5. Drag the Customer field to the FILTERS area.

✓ *To rearrange a table, drag fields from area to area at the bottom of the PivotTable Fields List.*

6. Save the **E36Try_xx** file, and leave it open to use in the next Try It.

The PivotTable Fields task pane and Field List

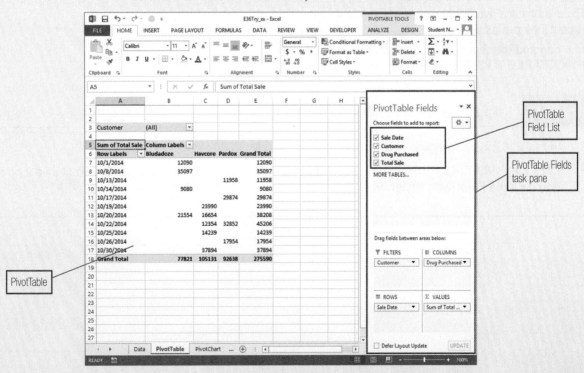

Try It!   **Filtering Report Data**

1 In the **E36Try_xx** file, click anywhere within the PivotTable on the PivotTable worksheet.

2 Click the Customer (All) down arrow.

3 Select KNJ Pharmacies.

4 Click OK.

5 Save the **E36Try_xx** file, and leave it open to use in the next Try It.

The Filtered PivotTable

▲	A	B	C	D	E
1					
2					
3	Customer	KNJ Pharmacies ▾T			
4					
5	Sum of Total Sale	Column Labels ▾			
6	Row Labels ▾	Bludadoze	Havcore	Pardox	Grand Total
7	10/8/2014	35097			35097
8	10/13/2014			11958	11958
9	10/17/2014			29874	29874
10	10/20/2014	21554	16654		38208
11	10/22/2014		12354	18944	31298
12	10/26/2014			17954	17954
13	10/30/2014		37894		37894
14	Grand Total	56651	66902	78730	202283

PivotTable drop-down arrows allow you to filter data

Applying PivotTable Styles

■ After creating a PivotTable report, you can use Excel's built in PivotTable designs to make your report look professional.

■ You can find the PivotTable Styles on the PIVOTTABLE TOOLS DESIGN tab.

Try It!   **Applying a PivotTable Style**

1 In the **E36Try_xx** file, click inside the PivotTable.

2 Click the PIVOTTABLE TOOLS DESIGN tab, and click the PivotTable Styles More button ▾.

3 Click Pivot Style Dark 2.

4 Save the **E36Try_xx** file, and leave it open to use in the next Try It.

Creating Pivot Charts

- After creating a PivotTable report, you can create a **PivotChart** that illustrates the data summarized in the report.

- You can publish your PivotTable/PivotChart to the Internet or your company's intranet.

- You also can create a PivotChart without first creating a PivotTable. This is called a decoupled PivotChart.

- You can create a standalone PivotChart using an external data connection to an external data source.

- You can filter the data on a PivotChart as you might filter the data on a PivotTable; select the items you want to show from the appropriate drop-down buttons on the chart.

- You can format and move a PivotChart as you would a regular chart.

Try It!   **Creating a PivotChart from a PivotTable**

1 In the **E36Try_xx** file, click inside the PivotTable.

2 Click INSERT > PivotChart.

3 Click the Area type, and click 3-D Area as the chart subtype.

4 Click OK.

5 Save the **E36Try_xx** file, and leave it open to use in the next Try It.

A PivotChart

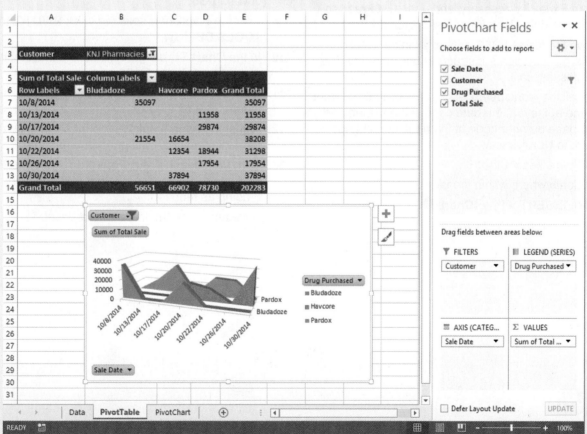

Try It!	**Moving a PivotChart**

1 In the **E36Try_xx** file, click the PivotChart to select it.

2 Click PIVOTCHART TOOLS ANALYZE > Move Chart 🖳.

3 Select Object in, and click the down arrow.

4 Select PivotChart, and click OK.

5 In the PivotChart worksheet, click on the PivotChart to select it, and drag it so that its upper right corner is over B3.

6 Save the **E36Try_xx** file, and close it.

Lesson 36—Practice

In this project, you will create and format a PivotChart using the skills you learned in this lesson.

DIRECTIONS

1. Start Excel, if necessary, and open **E36Practice** from the data files for this lesson.

2. Save the file as **E36Practice_xx** in the location where your teacher instructs you to store the files for this lesson.

3. For all the worksheets, add a header that has your name at the left, the date code in the center, and the page number code at the right, and change back to **Normal** view.

4. Click the **Report** tab.

5. Click anywhere within the table.

6. Click **INSERT** > **PivotChart** ▮▪.

7. Click **Column** > **3-D Clustered Column**.

8. Drag the PivotChart so the upper-left corner is covering G5.

9. With the PivotChart selected, click **PIVOTCHART TOOLS DESIGN**.

10. In the **Chart Styles** group, click the **More** button ⤓ of the Chart Styles Gallery.

11. Click **Style 3**. Your worksheet should resemble Figure 36-3 on the next page.

12. Adjust the page breaks and print settings so that the table and chart will print on one page.

13. **With your teacher's permission**, print the Report worksheet. Submit the printout or the file for grading as required.

14. Save and close the file, and exit Excel.

Figure 36-3

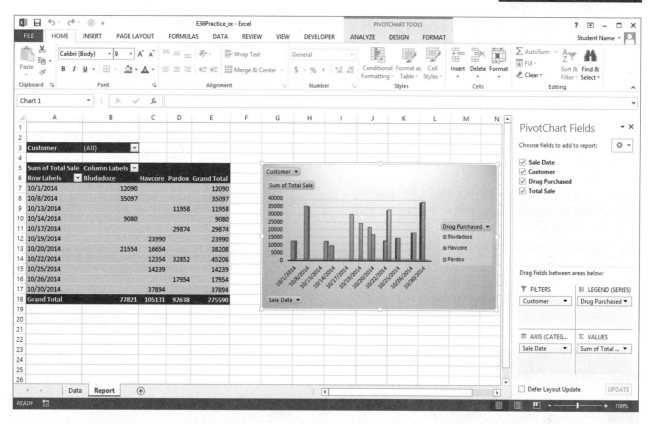

Lesson 36—Apply

As the Inventory Manager at Voyager Travel Adventures, you are well aware of the inventory problems at the Logan store. Sometimes the store carries too much of an item, and other times it carries so little there is nothing on the floor to sell. Carrying too many items that don't sell wastes space that costs a lot to rent and makes it difficult to restock the items you do carry. Carrying low inventory on popular items causes customers to get frustrated when they are told they have to come back. You want to use the inventory figures from the previous month to create a PivotTable and PivotChart that will help you quickly see where the problems are.

DIRECTIONS

1. Start Excel, if necessary, and open the **E36Apply** file from the data files for this lesson.

2. Save the workbook as **E36Apply_xx** in the location where your teacher instructs you to store the files for this lesson.

3. For all worksheets, add a header that has your name at the left, the date code in the center, and the page number code at the right, and change back to **Normal** view.

4. On the **Total Inventory** worksheet, click cell **A9** to indicate the data range for the PivotTable.

5. On the INSERT tab, click **PivotTable** 🗐. The Create PivotTable dialog box opens.

6. In the Table/Range box, make sure the data range is **'Total Inventory'!$A$8:$L$134**, indicating that the range consists of cells A8:L134 on the Total Inventory worksheet.

7. Click **Existing Worksheet**.

8. Click in the **Location** box, click the **Collapse Dialog box** button, click the **PivotTable** worksheet tab, and click cell **A11**.

9. Click **OK**. A blank PivotTable appears with the PivotTable Fields task pane on the right.

10. Check that cell **A11** on the **PivotTable** worksheet is selected, and set up the PivotTable as follows, as shown in Figure 36-4:

    a. Drag the **Category** field to the **ROWS** area.
    b. Drag the **Subcategory** field to the **COLUMNS** area.
    c. Drag the **Monthly Revenue** field to the **VALUES** area.
    d. Drag the **Type** field to the **FILTERS** area.
    e. Click the **Type** drop-down arrow, select **Men**, and click **OK**.

11. Apply the **Pivot Style Dark 5** style to the PivotTable.

12. Apply the **Accounting** number format to the cell range **B13:D17**. Adjust column widths, if necessary.

13. Create a PivotChart from your table as shown in Figure 36-5 on the next page:

    a. Click **Bar** > **Clustered Bar Chart**.
    b. Use **Cut** and **Paste** to place the PivotChart on the PivotChart worksheet.
    c. Right-click the **X-axis label**, and click **Format Axis**.
    d. Click the **NUMBER** arrow, and format so that there are no decimal places.
    e. Close the Format Axis task pane.
    f. Reposition the PivotChart so that the upper-left corner is at edge of cell B3.
    g. Resize the PivotChart so that the lower-right corner is at the edge of cell K22.

14. **With your teacher's permission,** print the workbook. Submit the printout or the file for grading as required.

15. Save and close the file, and exit Excel.

Figure 36-4

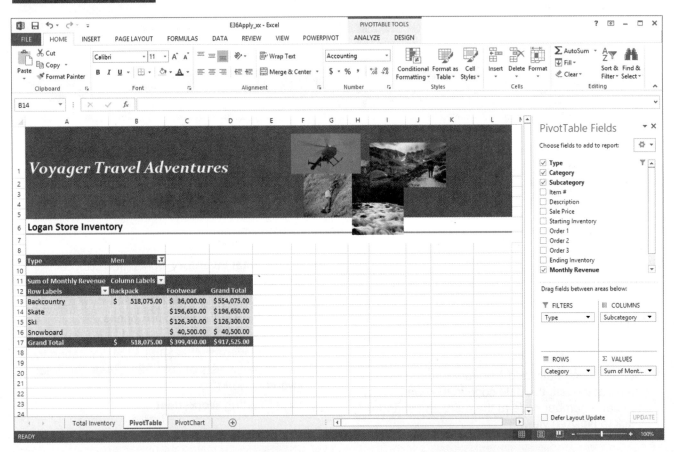

Figure 36-5

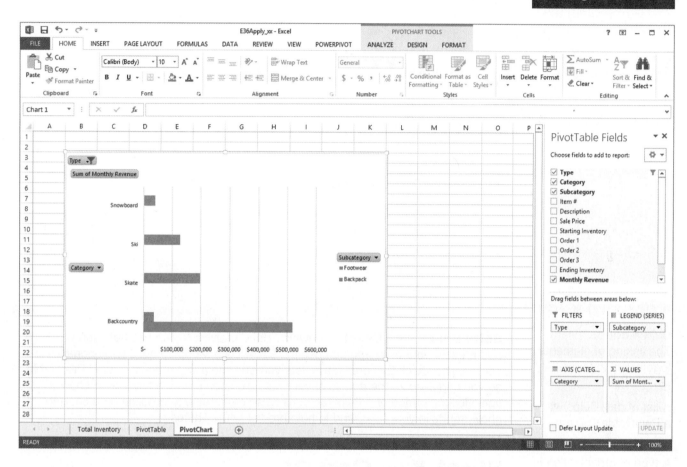

Lesson 37

Working with the Excel Data Model

> ## ➤ What You Will Learn
>
> Understanding the Excel Data Model
> Drilling into PivotTable Data
> Using a PivotTable Timeline
> Using a Trendline

WORDS TO KNOW

Data Model
The linking of elements together in a series.

Field List
A list of data fields within a PivotTable.

Hierarchy
A type of organization in which items (e.g., data) are ranked one above the other.

Linear
A pattern of data points that looks like a line.

Quick Explore
A feature in Excel that allows you to navigate data tables and drill into specific data.

Timeline
A feature in Excel that filters dates and time, and can zoom in on a specific time period.

Trendline
A feature in Excel that shows trends in the data series of a chart.

Software Skills   Excel has powerful data analysis features to help you visualize and present your data. You can use the Excel Data Model to build a relational data source. The Quick Explore feature lets you drill into a Data Model–based PivotTable so you can analyze the details of your data. You can create a timeline to show a specific time period of a PivotTable. You also can create a trendline on a chart to show trends in your data, and to help predict future values.

What You Can Do

Understanding the Excel Data Model

- A **Data Model** is a feature in Excel 2013 that allows you to integrate data from multiple tables.
- The Excel Data Model is displayed as a collection of tables in a **Field List** as shown in the Fields task pane.
- You can use the Excel Data Model to build a relational data source inside a workbook.
- An Excel Data Model is automatically created when you use data in PivotTables, PivotCharts, and Power View reports.

  ✓ *You will learn about Power View in Lesson 38.*

- The Excel Data Model can contain a single table or multiple tables.
- You can add data from other tables to modify and enhance the same Excel Data Model used in PowerPivot.

  ✓ *You can only add a table once to a Data Model.*

Drilling into PivotTable Data

- Drilling into large amounts of data in a PivotTable **hierarchy** can be a time-consuming task with lots of expanding, collapsing, and filtering.
- The **Quick Explore** feature in Excel 2013 lets you drill into a Data Model-based PivotTable hierarchy so you can analyze the details of your data.
- The Quick Explore feature acts like a filter to help you navigate to the data you want to see.

  ✓ *You must have at least two PivotTables in your data model to use the Quick Explore feature.*

- The Quick Explore button 🔎 appears whenever you select an item in a PivotTable field.

  ✓ *You can only drill down one item at a time.*

- You also can right-click an item, and select Quick Explore from the menu.
- When working with multiple tables, it is recommended to name the tables so you can keep track of them.
- You can name a PivotTable from the PivotTable Name box in the PivotTable group on the PIVOTTABLE TOOLS ANALYZE tab.

  ✓ *Remember that you cannot use spaces or special characters in a table name.*

Try It! **Drilling into PivotTable Data**

① Start Excel, if necessary, and open the **E37TryA** file from the data files for this lesson.

② Save the file as **E37TryA_xx** in the location where your teacher instructs you to store the files for this lesson.

③ For all worksheets, add a header that has your name at the left, the date code in the center, and the page number code at the right, and change back to Normal view.

④ Click the Inventory Description tab, and click any cell in the table.

⑤ Click INSERT > PivotTable 📊.

⑥ In the Create PivotTable dialog box, check that the table in the Table/Range box is Inv Description.

⑦ Under Choose where you want the PivotTable report to be placed, click Existing Worksheet.

⑧ Click the Collapse dialog box, select the cell E3 on the PivotTables worksheet, and click the Expand dialog box to return to the Create PivotTable dialog box.

⑨ Under Choose whether you want to analyze multiple tables, click the Add this data to the Data Model option.

⑩ Click OK. Notice that the OrderInfo PivotTable has already been created for you.

⑪ On the PIVOTTABLE TOOLS ANALYZE tab, in the PivotTable group, in the PivotTable Name box, type **InventoryTable**, and press ⏎.

⑫ Set up the InventoryTable with the following fields:

   a. Drag the Type field into the FILTERS area.

   b. Drag the Category field into the ROWS area.

   c. Scroll down, and click the Starting Inventory and the Ending Inventory check boxes. Notice that Excel automatically adds these sum fields to the VALUES area, and places the Values in the COLUMNS area.

⑬ Click cell E4. Notice that the Quick Explore feature appears outside the lower-right corner of the cell.

⑭ Click Quick Explore 🔎.

⑮ Click Description. Notice that the Drill To box includes Description.

⑯ Click Drill To Description.

⑰ Save the **E37TryA_xx** file, and close it.

Using a PivotTable Timeline

- You can use a PivotTable **timeline** to show dates, filter by time, and zoom in on a specific time period.
- You can insert a timeline from the Filter group on the PIVOTTABLE TOOLS ANALYZE tab.
- Once you insert a timeline, you can make changes to the time period on the fly.
- To move a timeline, select the timeline, and drag it to the desired location on the worksheet.

- To resize a timeline, select the timeline, and use the sizing handles to change its size.
- You can apply a Timeline Style to customize the look of a timeline.
- You can clear a timeline by using the Clear Filter button in the Filter group on the PIVOTTABLE TOOLS ANALYZE tab.

  ✓ *To remove a timeline, you also can right-click the timeline, and click Remove Timeline.*

Try It!   **Using a PivotTable Timeline**

1. Open the **E37TryB** file from the data files for this lesson.

2. Save the file as **E37TryB_xx** in the location where your teacher instructs you to store the files for this lesson.

3. For all worksheets, add a header that has your name at the left, the date code in the center, and the page number code at the right, and change back to Normal view.

4. Click the PivotTable tab.

5. Click in any cell in the PivotTable.

6. In the PIVOTTABLE TOOLS ANALYZE tab, in the Filter group, click the Insert Timeline 🔣 button. The Insert Timelines dialog box appears.

7. Click the Sale Date box, and click OK.

8. Drag the timeline so that the upper-left corner is at the edge of cell B18.

9. Click the MONTHS down arrow, and click DAYS.

10. Scroll to the right, and under OCT 2014, click 1.

11. Save the **E37TryB_xx** file, and leave it open to use in the next Try It.

A PivotTable timeline

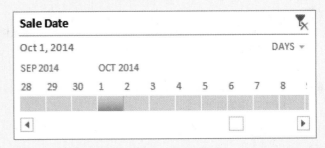

Using a Trendline

- You can show trends in your data using a **trendline** in a chart you have created.
- For example, you can extend a trendline beyond your data to help predict future values.
- A **linear** trendline creates a best-fit straight line for simple data.
- Use a linear trendline to show data that is increasing or decreasing at a steady rate.
- You also can show moving averages with a trendline in a chart you have created.

- You can add a trendline to a 2-D chart that is not stacked (such as an area, bar, column line, stock, scatter, or bubble chart).

  ✓ *You cannot use trendlines with stacked, 3-D, radar, pie, surface, or doughnut charts.*

- Access the trendline feature using the Chart Elements button ⊞ next to the upper-right corner of your chart.
- The trendline will begin on the first data point of your data series.
- To choose a different type of trendline, hover the mouse pointer over Trendline, and click the arrow.

- You also can choose More Options, and the Format Trendline task pane will display.
- You can create multiple trendlines on the same chart.

- To delete a trendline, click on the trendline to select it, and press the [DEL] key.
- To remove all trendlines, uncheck the Trendline box in the CHART ELEMENTS menu.

| **Try It!** | **Using a Trendline** |

1 In the **E37TryB_xx** file, click the PivotChart tab.

2 Click the chart to select it, and click the Chart Elements button [+].

3 Click the Trendline box. The Add Trendline dialog box appears.

4 Click Pardox, and click OK.

5 Click the Trendline box to deselect it. The trendline is deleted.

6 In the CHART ELEMENTS menu, hover the mouse pointer over Trendline, and click the arrow.

7 Click Linear Forecast.

8 In the Add Trendline dialog box, click Havcore, and click OK.

9 Save and close the file.

A linear forecast trendline

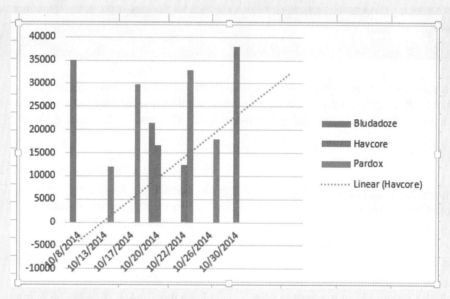

Lesson 37—Practice

In this project, you will drill into a PivotTable to view detailed data using the skills you learned in this lesson.

DIRECTIONS

1. Start Excel, if necessary, and open the **E37Practice** file from the data files for this lesson.

2. Save the file as **E37Practice_xx** in the location where your teacher instructs you to store the files for this lesson.

3. For all worksheets, add a header that has your name at the left, the date code in the center, and the page number code at the right, and change back to **Normal** view.

4. Click the **PivotTable** tab, and click cell **C24**.

5. Click the **Quick Explore** button 🔎 that appears outside the lower-right corner of the cell.

6. Click **Item #**, and click **Drill To Item #**.

7. **With your teacher's permission**, print the worksheet. Submit the printout or the file for grading as required.

8. Save and close the file, and exit Excel.

Lesson 37—Apply

You're the chief financial officer of A-1 Pharmacy based in Portland, Oregon, and you've been sent a worksheet with information about the company's annual drug sales. You want to review data from previous years to see whether the company's profits have increased or decreased. You also want to forecast a trend for next year's profits.

DIRECTIONS

1. Start Excel, if necessary, and open the **E37Apply** file from the data files for this lesson.

2. Save the workbook as **E37Apply_xx** in the location where your teacher instructs you to store the files for this lesson.

3. For all worksheets, add a header that has your name at the left, the date code in the center, and the page number code at the right, and change back to **Normal** view.

4. Click the Report tab.

5. Click any cell in the PivotTable.

6. Click **PIVOTTABLE TOOLS ANALYZE** > **Insert Timeline** 📊.

7. In the Insert Timelines dialog box, click the **Year** box, and click **OK**.

8. Drag the timeline so that the upper-left corner is at the edge of cell A18.

9. Drag the resizing handle in the lower-right corner to the edge of cell E26.

10. Click the **MONTHS** down arrow, and click **YEARS**.

11. Click **2012**. Notice that the PivotTable data is now filtered to the chosen year, and the PivotChart only shows that year's data.

12. Click **Clear Filter** 🔻.

13. Click the chart to select it, and click **Chart Elements** ➕.

14. In the CHART ELEMENTS menu, hover the mouse pointer over Trendline, and click the arrow.

15. Click **Linear Forecast**.

16. In the Add Trendline dialog box, click **Bludadoze** > **OK**.

17. Repeat steps 13–15 to add trendlines for Havcore and Pardox. Your worksheet should look like Figure 37-1 on the next page.

18. **With your teacher's permission**, print the worksheet. Submit the printout or the file for grading as required.

19. Save and close the file, and exit Excel.

Figure 37-1

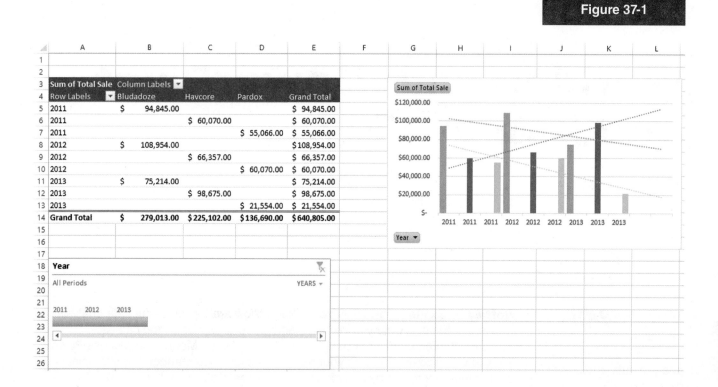

Lesson 38

Working with PowerPivot and Power View

> ## ➤ What You Will Learn

Using PowerPivot
Understanding Power View

Software Skills   PowerPivot and Power View are two powerful data analysis features of Excel to help you visualize and present your data. You can use PowerPivot to enhance your data within the Excel Data Model. You can use Power View to visualize and present your data in an interactive manner. For example, you could prepare a report by first modifying the Excel Data Model with PowerPivot, and then present the report with Power View.

Using PowerPivot

- PowerPivot is an Excel add-in that provides a richer modeling environment that allows you to enhance your data within the Excel Data Model.
- The data model you see in a workbook in Excel is the same data model you see in the PowerPivot window.
- You must first activate the PowerPivot Add-in before you can use PowerPivot.
- You can enable the PowerPivot Add-in from the Excel Options on the FILE tab.

  ✓ *The Microsoft Office PowerPivot for Excel 2013 add-in is a COM Add-in.*

- You can use **PowerPivot** to work with the Excel Data Model directly. Use the Manage button ⧉ in the Data Model group on the POWERPIVOT tab.
- You can view data in PowerPivot in the Data view or the Diagram view.

  ✓ *The Ribbon will provide available features depending on which view and which data item you select.*

- To resize the view of the tables in the Diagram view, click on the display, and drag the edge or corner.

■ You can use PowerPivot to add data from other tables to modify and enhance the Excel Data Model.

✓ *You can only add a table once to the Excel Data Model.*

■ You also can delete data or tables from the Excel Data Model using PowerPivot.

■ With PowerPivot, you also can perform advanced data modeling such as importing data into PowerPivot, managing that data when you import into PowerPivot, and creating relationships among your data from different data sources and between multiple tables.

Try It! Activating PowerPivot

① Open Excel, if necessary, and click FILE > Options.

② In the Excel Options dialog box, click Add-Ins.

③ In the Manage drop-down box, select COM Add-ins > Go.

④ In the COM Add-Ins dialog box, click the Microsoft Office PowerPivot for Excel 2013 box.

⑤ Click OK. The POWERPIVOT tab appears on the Ribbon.

Try It! Using PowerPivot

① Open the **E38Try** file from the data files for this lesson.

② Save the file as **E38Try_xx** in the location where your teacher instructs you to store the files for this lesson.

③ For all worksheets, add a header that has your name at the left, the date code in the center, and the page number code at the right, and change back to Normal view.

④ Click the PivotTable tab.

⑤ Click POWERPIVOT > Manage 📖 . The PowerPivot for Excel window opens.

⑥ In the PowerPivot for Excel window, on the Home tab, in the View group, click Diagram View 🖻 .

⑦ Resize the display of each of the two tables, if necessary.

⑧ Click Data View 📰 .

⑨ Right-click the WomenInventoryTable tab, and click Delete.

⑩ Click Yes to confirm that you want to permanently delete the table.

⑪ Click the Close button ⊠ to close the PowerPivot window.

⑫ In the Excel worksheet, click the Women's Inventory tab. Notice that the table you deleted from the Excel Data Model did not delete the table from your worksheet.

⑬ Click in any cell in the table.

⑭ On the POWERPIVOT tab, click Add to Data Model 📇 .

⑮ Click the Close button ⊠ to close the PowerPivot window.

⑯ Save the **E38Try_xx** file, and close it.

(continued)

Try It!   **Using PowerPivot** *(continued)*

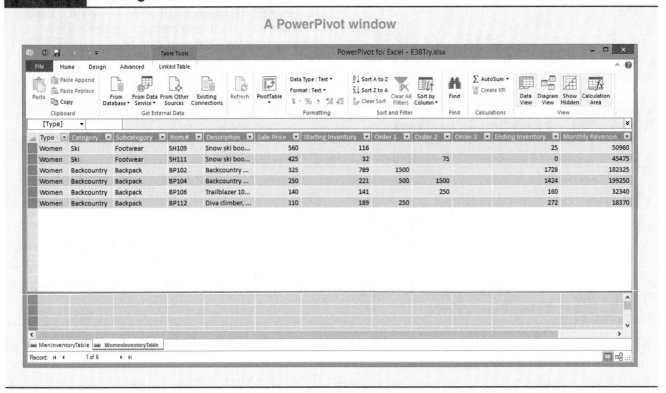

A PowerPivot window

Understanding Power View

- **Power View** is an interactive feature in Excel to visualize and present your data. See Figure 38-1 on the next page for reference.

- You can interact with data in the same Excel workbook as a Power View sheet.

- You can view data from multiple tables in a Power View sheet.

  ✓ *In Power View, you can only drill down one item at a time.*

- Power View requires Silverlight, a free plug-in from Microsoft. The first time you insert a Power View sheet, Excel asks you to enable the Power View add-in.

- If you don't have Silverlight, click Install Silverlight. After you have followed the steps for installing Silverlight, in Excel click Reload.

  ✓ *If the Power View Field List has the message Power View needs data to work with, go back to the sheet that has data in your workbook, select the range of cells containing your data, and click Power View on the INSERT tab.*

- You can create another sheet for the Power View or add the data to a sheet you have already created.

- Power View adds the range to the Field List and adds the data directly to the Power View sheet.

Figure 38-1

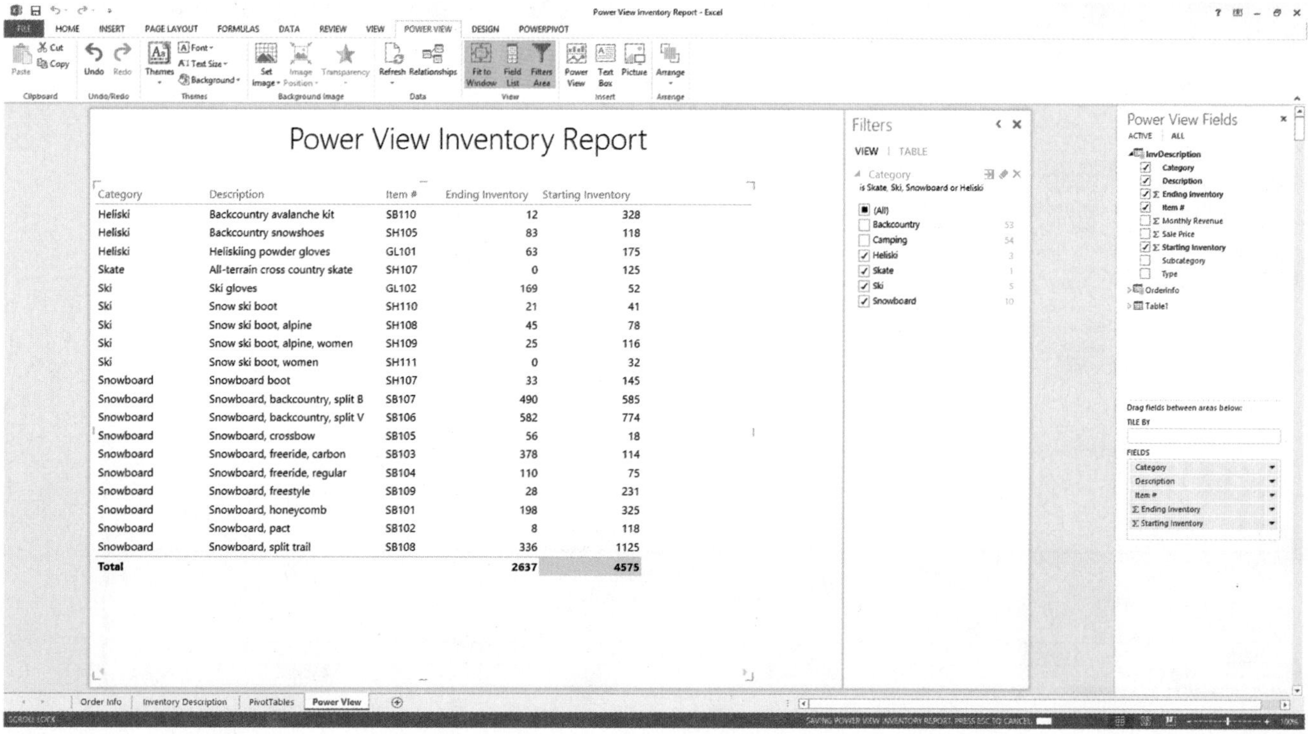

Lesson 38—Practice

In this project, you will add table data to the Excel Data Model using the skills you learned in this lesson.

DIRECTIONS

1. Start Excel, if necessary, and open the **E38Practice** file from the data files for this lesson.

2. Save the file as **E38Practice_xx** in the location where your teacher instructs you to store the files for this lesson.

3. For all worksheets, add a header that has your name at the left, the date code in the center, and the page number code at the right, and change back to **Normal** view.

4. On the **Data** tab, click any cell in the table.

5. Click **POWERPIVOT** > **Add to Data Model** 📷.

6. Your PowerPivot for Excel window should look like Figure 38-2 on the next page.

7. Click the **Close** button ⌧ to close the PowerPivot window.

8. Save and close the file, and exit Excel.

Figure 38-2

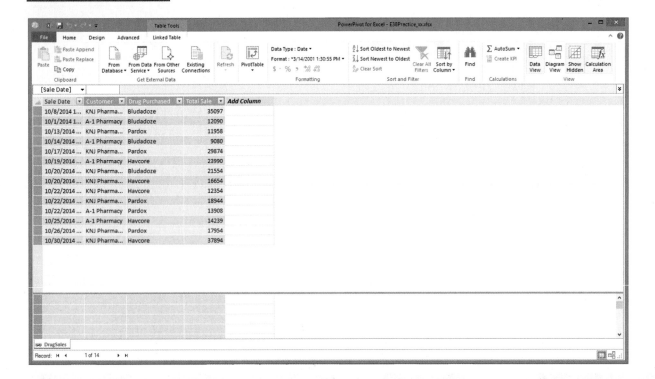

Lesson 38—Apply

You're the sales manager for A-1 Pharmacy and KNJ Pharmacies, and you've been sent a worksheet with information about the month's drug sales. You want to prepare a report for a board meeting. Before you can create a report, you need to make sure that the current data is available in the Excel Data Model. You may have used another version of the worksheet, so you want to delete any existing table data from the Excel Data Model. You then want to add the current table data to the Excel Data Model.

DIRECTIONS

1. Start Excel, if necessary, and open the **E38Apply** file from the data files for this lesson.

2. Save the workbook as **E38Apply_xx** in the location where your teacher instructs you to store the files for this lesson.

3. For all worksheets, add a header that has your name at the left, the date code in the center, and the page number code at the right, and change back to **Normal** view.

4. Click the **PivotTable** tab.

5. Click **POWERPIVOT** > **Manage** 📖 . The PowerPivot for Excel window opens.

6. In the PowerPivot for Excel window, right-click the **DrugSales** tab > **Delete**.

7. Click **Yes** to confirm that you want to permanently delete the table.

8. Click the **Close** button ⊠ to close the PowerPivot window.

9. In the Excel worksheet, on the **Data** tab, select the cell range **A1:D15**.

10. Click **Add to Data Model** 📷 .

11. Your PowerPivot for Excel window should look like Figure 38-2, shown previously.

12. Click the **Close** button ⊠ to close the PowerPivot window.

13. Save and close the file, and exit Excel.

End-of-Chapter Activities

➤ Excel Chapter 4—Critical Thinking

Revenue PivotTable

You're the owner of Whole Grains Bread company, and you want to analyze the past year's sales for each of your stores. You've compiled a database of revenues, and with it you'll create a PivotTable you can rearrange as you like, creating as many different revenue reports as you wish. After creating a PivotTable that lists quarterly revenues by city, you'll use its data to predict possible earnings amounts for next year. Finally, you'll use Solver to help you decide on the best price for a new product you'll introduce in your Oregon stores—tomato basil focaccia.

DIRECTIONS

1. Start Excel, if necessary.

2. Open the **ECT04** file from the data files for this chapter.

3. Save the workbook as **ECT04_xx** in the location where your teacher instructs you to store the files for this lesson.

4. For all worksheets, add a header that has your name at the left, the date code in the center, and the page number code at the right, and change back to **Normal** view.

5. Create a PivotTable using the information on the **Revenue** worksheet:

   a. Place the table on the **Analysis** worksheet, beginning in cell **A10**.
   b. Show each city on its own row.
   c. Show the quarterly totals in separate columns.
   d. Display the values or grand totals of the gross sales.
   e. Add a report filter that allows you to display each state separately.
   f. Apply a currency format with no decimal places to all numerical data.
   g. Display only the Oregon stores.
   h. Apply **Pivot Style Medium 5** style.
   i. Spell check the worksheet.
   j. **With your teacher's permission,** print the PivotTable **Analysis** worksheet (see Illustration 4A).

6. Copy the table data:

   a. Make sure that all cities and states are displayed by removing the **State** field from the **FILTERS** area.
   b. Select the range **B12:E27**, and copy it.
   c. Use Paste Special to paste only the values starting in cell **B9** of the **Forecast** worksheet.

7. Use the GROWTH function to predict future sales (see Illustration 4B):

   a. In cell **F9** of the **Forecast** worksheet, enter a formula that calculates the predicted sales for Bend, OR.
   b. Use the actual sales in cells **B9:E9** as the basis for the prediction.
   c. Copy the formula to the range **B10:B24** to fill Quarter 1.
   d. Copy the formula to the range **G9:I24** to fill Quarters 2–4.

8. Adjust column widths as needed.

9. Spell check the **Forecast** worksheet, and adjust the page breaks, if necessary.

10. **With your teacher's permission,** print the **Forecast** worksheet.

11. Use Solver to change the proposed price of tomato basil focaccia (cell **C15** of the **New Product** sheet) so that the projected weekly profit (cell **C19**) equals **$1,200** (see Illustration 4C):

    a. Allow the coupon discount in cell **D18** to also be changed as needed.
    b. Set constraints that limit the price point to a value between **$3.75** and **$4.25**.
    c. Set constraints that limit the coupon discount (cell **D18**) to a value between **0.50** and **0.75**.

12. Spell check the entire workbook, and adjust the page breaks, if necessary.

13. **With your teacher's permission,** print the **New Product** worksheet. Submit the printout or the file for grading as required.

14. Save and close the file, and exit Excel.

Illustration 4A

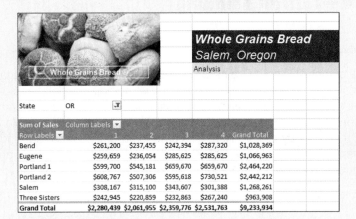

State	OR				

Sum of Sales	Column Labels				
Row Labels	1	2	3	4	Grand Total
Bend	$261,200	$237,455	$242,394	$287,320	$1,028,369
Eugene	$259,659	$236,054	$285,625	$285,625	$1,066,963
Portland 1	$599,700	$545,181	$659,670	$659,670	$2,464,220
Portland 2	$608,767	$507,306	$595,618	$730,521	$2,442,212
Salem	$308,167	$315,100	$343,607	$301,388	$1,268,261
Three Sisters	$242,945	$220,859	$232,863	$267,240	$963,908
Grand Total	$2,280,439	$2,061,955	$2,359,776	$2,531,763	$9,233,934

Illustration 4B

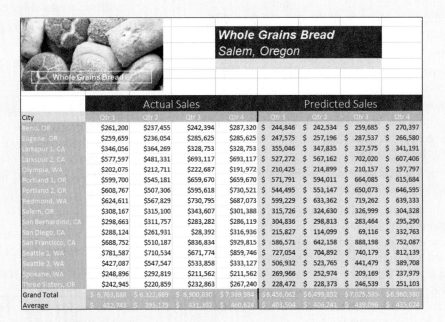

City	Actual Sales				Predicted Sales			
	Qtr 1	Qtr 2	Qtr 3	Qtr 4	Qtr 1	Qtr 2	Qtr 3	Qtr 4
Bend, OR	$261,200	$237,455	$242,394	$287,320	$ 244,846	$ 242,534	$ 259,685	$ 270,397
Eugene, OR	$259,659	$236,054	$285,625	$285,625	$ 247,575	$ 257,196	$ 287,537	$ 266,580
Larkspur 1, CA	$346,056	$364,269	$328,753	$328,753	$ 355,046	$ 347,835	$ 327,575	$ 341,191
Larkspur 2, CA	$577,597	$481,331	$693,117	$693,117	$ 527,272	$ 567,162	$ 702,020	$ 607,406
Olympia, WA	$202,075	$212,711	$222,687	$191,972	$ 210,425	$ 214,899	$ 210,157	$ 197,797
Portland 1, OR	$599,700	$545,181	$659,670	$659,670	$ 571,791	$ 594,011	$ 664,085	$ 615,684
Portland 2, OR	$608,767	$507,306	$595,618	$730,521	$ 544,495	$ 553,147	$ 650,073	$ 646,595
Redmond, WA	$624,611	$567,829	$730,795	$687,073	$ 599,229	$ 633,362	$ 719,262	$ 639,333
Salem, OR	$308,167	$315,100	$343,607	$301,388	$ 315,726	$ 324,630	$ 326,999	$ 304,328
San Bernardino, CA	$298,663	$311,757	$283,282	$286,119	$ 304,836	$ 298,813	$ 283,464	$ 295,290
San Diego, CA	$288,124	$261,931	$28,392	$316,936	$ 215,827	$ 114,099	$ 69,116	$ 332,763
San Francisco, CA	$688,752	$510,187	$836,834	$929,815	$ 586,571	$ 642,158	$ 888,198	$ 752,087
Seattle 1, WA	$781,587	$710,534	$671,774	$859,746	$ 727,054	$ 704,892	$ 740,179	$ 812,139
Seattle 2, WA	$427,087	$547,547	$533,858	$333,127	$ 506,932	$ 523,765	$ 441,479	$ 389,708
Spokane, WA	$248,896	$292,819	$211,562	$211,562	$ 269,966	$ 252,974	$ 209,169	$ 237,979
Three Sisters, OR	$242,945	$220,859	$232,863	$267,240	$ 228,472	$ 228,373	$ 246,539	$ 251,103
Grand Total	$ 6,763,888	$ 6,322,869	$ 6,900,830	$ 7,389,984	$6,456,062	$6,499,852	$7,025,535	$6,960,380
Average	$ 422,743	$ 395,179	$ 431,302	$ 460,624	$ 403,504	$ 406,241	$ 439,096	$ 435,024

Illustration 4C

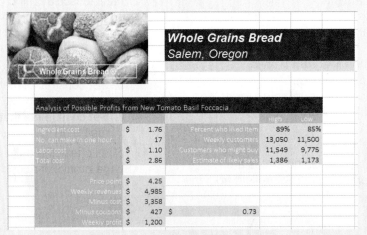

Analysis of Possible Profits from New Tomato Basil Foccacia

				High	Low
Ingredient cost	$	1.76	Percent who liked item	89%	85%
No. can make in one hour		17	Weekly customers	13,050	11,500
Labor cost	$	1.10	Customers who might buy	11,549	9,775
Total cost	$	2.86	Estimate of likely sales	1,386	1,173
Price point	$	4.25			
Weekly revenues	$	4,985			
Minus cost	$	3,358			
Minus coupons	$	427	$	0.73	
Weekly profit	$	1,200			

➤ Excel Chapter 4—Portfolio Builder

Lemonade Stand Projections

It's difficult to run any business, no matter how simple. Customer purchases are based on many things, some of them outside of your control, such as the weather and social trends. You might think that running a lemonade stand is easy, but it's not, as you'll find in this project. First, you'll gather data for 30 days of lemonade sales. You'll get the opportunity to make business decisions based on the weather and the cost of making your lemonade. In the end, you'll analyze your data using a PivotTable, and make predictions on future sales.

DIRECTIONS

1. Start Excel, if necessary.

2. Open the **EPB04** file from the data files for this chapter.

3. Save the file as **EPB04_xx** in the location where your teacher instructs you to store the files for this lesson.

4. For all worksheets, add a header that has your name at the left, the date code in the center, and the page number code at the right, and change back to **Normal** view.

5. On the Sales Data tab, in the **Day** column, enter the values **1** to **30**.

6. In the **Day of Week** column, enter the days of the week, beginning with Monday.

7. In the **Gross Profit** column, enter a formula that calculates revenue (the number of glasses sold multiplied by the amount you're charging per glass).

8. In the **Advertising** column, enter a formula that calculates the cost of advertising your stand (0.25 per sign).

9. In the **Cost to Make Lemonade** column, enter a formula that calculates your cost—the cost per glass times the number of glasses you made that day.

10. Finally, enter a formula to calculate your profit in the **Net Profit** column.

11. In the first cell under **Money at Start of Day**, enter $3.

12. In the **Money at End of Day** column, enter a formula that adds the net profit to the Money at Start of Day.

13. In the second cell under **Money at Start of Day**, enter a formula that displays the value in the first cell under **Money at End of Day**. Copy the formula down to cell N33.

14. Copy cells **N5** and **O5**. Highlight cells **N6:O33** and click **HOME > Paste** to record 30 days' worth of lemonade sales. Format the worksheet to create a professional appearance.

15. Use the data to create a PivotTable so you can analyze your results. Place the PivotTable on the **PivotTable** worksheet.

16. Modify the PivotTable to show the effects of weather and price on the number of glasses sold. You might also want to see if the day of the week had any effect on sales—your choice.

17. Format the PivotTable and worksheet, similar to that shown in Illustration 4D.

18. Use **Paste** to copy the values and formats in the **Gross Profit, Advertising, Cost to Make Lemonade**, and **Net Profit** data to the **Forecast** worksheet. Copy the data in the **Day** and **Day of Week** columns as well.

19. Use this data and the **TREND** function to predict another 15 days' worth of gross sales.

20. Use the **FORECAST** function to predict the advertising costs, and the cost to make lemonade. You want to have different formulas adjacent to each other, so choose to ignore the error indicated by the Error Checker.

21. Use a regular formula to calculate the predicted net profits.

22. After entering data, adjust column widths, spell check the worksheets, and adjust the page breaks. The worksheet should look similar to that shown in Illustration 4E.

23. **With your teacher's permission,** print the **Forecast** and **PivotTable** worksheets. Submit the printout or the file for grading as required.

24. Save and close the file, and exit Excel.

Illustration 4D

Lemonade Sales Analysis							

Day of Week	(All) ▼						

Count of GlassesSold	Column Labels ▼						
Row Labels ▼	$ -	$0.10	$0.12	$0.20	$0.25	$0.30	Grand Total
⊟ Cloudy				2	5	2	9
Cool				1	2	1	4
Storms					2	1	3
Sunny				1	1		2
⊟ Hot						5	5
Hot						4	4
Sunny						1	1
⊟ Rainy		1	1	1	3		6
Cool							
Storms		1	1	1	3		6
⊟ Sunny					2	7	9
Cool						1	1
Hot						3	3
Sunny					2	3	5
Grand Total		1	1	1	5	7	14	29

Illustration 4E

		Forecasted Sales			

Day	Day of Week	Gross Profit	Advertising	Cost to Make Lemonade	Net Profit
1	Monday	$ 7.50	$ 0.50	$ 2.10	$ 4.90
2	Tuesday	$ 3.60	$ 0.50	$ 2.40	$ 0.70
3	Wednesday	$ 0.12	$ 0.25	$ 0.72	$ (0.85)
4	Thursday	$ -	$ -	$ 0.12	$ (0.12)
5	Friday	$ 0.60	$ 0.75	$ 4.80	$ (4.95)
6	Saturday	$ 6.00	$ 0.50	$ 1.40	$ 4.10
7	Sunday	$ 1.00	$ 0.50	$ 1.50	$ (1.00)
8	Monday	$ 9.00	$ 0.75	$ 3.00	$ 5.25
9	Tuesday	$ 7.50	$ 0.50	$ 2.00	$ 5.00
10	Wednesday	$ 5.00	$ 0.50	$ 2.00	$ 2.50
11	Thursday	$ 15.00	$ 0.75	$ 3.50	$ 10.75
12	Friday	$ -	$ 0.50	$ 3.50	$ (4.00)
13	Saturday	$ 0.30	$ 0.50	$ 1.20	$ (1.40)
14	Sunday	$ -	$ -	$ 0.50	$ (0.50)
15	Monday	$ 0.30	$ 0.75	$ 1.60	$ (2.05)
16	Tuesday	$ 13.80	$ 0.75	$ 5.40	$ 7.65
17	Wednesday	$ 7.50	$ 0.50	$ 4.25	$ 2.75
18	Thursday	$ 9.00	$ 0.75	$ 2.40	$ 5.85
19	Friday	$ 12.00	$ 0.75	$ 3.60	$ 7.65
20	Saturday	$ 2.00	$ 0.50	$ 1.80	$ (0.30)
21	Sunday	$ 12.00	$ 0.75	$ 2.40	$ 8.85
22	Monday	$ 2.60	$ 0.50	$ 1.40	$ 0.70
23	Tuesday	$ 12.00	$ 0.75	$ 4.40	$ 6.85
24	Wednesday	$ -	$ -	$ -	$ -
25	Thursday	$ -	$ 0.50	$ 1.50	$ (2.00)
26	Friday	$ -	$ -	$ 0.15	$ (0.15)
27	Saturday	$ 8.70	$ 0.75	$ 3.20	$ 4.75
28	Sunday	$ 7.50	$ 0.50	$ 4.00	$ 3.00
29	Monday	$ -	$ -	$ 0.48	$ (0.48)
30	Tuesday	$ -	$ -	$ -	$ -
31	Wednesday	$ 4.67	0.47	$ 2.16	$ 2.04
32	Thursday	$ 4.68	0.47	$ 2.18	$ 2.02
33	Friday	$ 4.69	0.47	$ 2.17	$ 2.05
34	Saturday	$ 4.70	0.47	$ 2.19	$ 2.04
35	Sunday	$ 4.70	0.49	$ 2.23	$ 1.99
36	Monday	$ 4.71	0.47	$ 2.10	$ 2.14
37	Tuesday	$ 4.71	0.47	$ 2.14	$ 2.11
38	Wednesday	$ 4.72	0.47	$ 2.13	$ 2.12
39	Thursday	$ 4.72	0.46	$ 2.13	$ 2.13
40	Friday	$ 4.73	0.46	$ 2.16	$ 2.10
41	Saturday	$ 4.73	0.46	$ 2.17	$ 2.10
42	Sunday	$ 4.73	0.47	$ 2.20	$ 2.06
43	Monday	$ 4.73	0.46	$ 2.12	$ 2.15
44	Tuesday	$ 4.73	0.45	$ 2.11	$ 2.17
45	Wednesday	$ 4.73	0.46	$ 2.12	$ 2.15

(Courtesy auremar/Shutterstock)

Chapter 5

Advanced Formatting and Workbook Features

Lesson 39

Working with File Formats

> ## ➤ What You Will Learn

Ensuring Backward-Compatibility in a Workbook
Importing a File
Saving Excel Data in CSV File Format
Saving a Workbook As a PDF or an XPS File
Sending a Workbook
Sharing a Workbook

WORDS TO KNOW

CSV format
CSV stands for comma-separated value. A CSV file is a file format in which text is separated by commas. It is also known as a comma delimited file.

PDF format
PDF stands for Portable Document Format. It is a file format that preserves the original layout and formatting of most documents, so they can be viewed and shared.

XPS file
XPS stands for XML Paper Specification. This format retains the look and feel of an electronic document, much like electronic paper.

Software Skills   If you share Excel data, you can save that data in a format that's compatible with the program someone else is using, such as an older version of Excel. You can save your Excel data in many different formats, and use the Compatibility Checker to ensure that everything will work in the older program.

What You Can Do

Ensuring Backward-Compatibility in a Workbook

- Sometimes saving your workbook in a different format will result in a loss of some data—typically formatting changes.
- You can see which features might be lost before resaving a workbook in an older version of Excel by running Check Compatibility first.
- Check Compatibility scans the workbook, and lists any incompatibilities and the number of occurrences of an incompatibility.
  - Incompatibilities are grouped by severity.
  - You can copy this list of incompatibilities to a sheet in the workbook for further review.
- You can click the Find link in the Compatibility Checker to have Excel show you where the problem is.
- The Compatibility Checker will warn you if there are features or formatting that are not supported by the selected file format.
- For example, if you check the compatibility of an Excel 2003 worksheet and receive the formatting warning, in most cases, the worksheet will function properly in Excel 2003; it just might look a bit different.

  ✓ It's always best to test a converted workbook to make sure that it looks and works as you want it to before you send it to anyone.

Try It!   Using the Compatibility Checker

1 Start Excel, if necessary, and open the **E39TryA** file from the data files for this lesson.

2 Save the file as **E39TryA_xx** in the location where your teacher instructs you to store the files for this lesson.

3 Add a header that has your name at the left, the date code in the center, and the page number code at the right, and change back to Normal view.

4 Click FILE > Info > Check for Issues.

5 Select Check Compatibility.

6 Excel will display a list of potential problems. Scroll through the issues.

7 Click OK.

8 Save the **E39TryA_xx** file, and leave it open to use in the next Try It.

The Compatibility Checker report

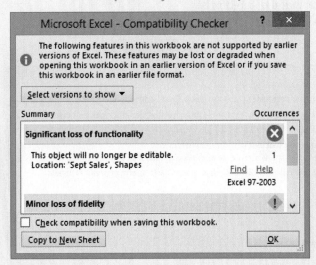

Importing a File

- You can import files with a different file format into Excel.

- For example, you may want to import data in a text file into your worksheet.

- You can import a file from Microsoft Access, a webpage, a text file, or a database-related file using the buttons in the Get External Data group on the DATA tab.

  ✓ If the Excel window is not full size, you can access the Get External Data group using the Get External Data button.

- When you import a text file, the Text Import Wizard can help you select the appropriate formatting for importing the text.

- Be careful when importing a file. You cannot use Undo to remove the imported data.

- If you do not want to keep the data you have imported, close the Excel file without saving the changes.

Try It!   **Importing a File**

1. In the **E39TryA_xx** file, click DATA.

2. In the Get External Data group, click From Text.

3. Browse to the **E39TryB.txt** file from the data files for this lesson.

4. Select the **E39TryB.txt** file > Import. The Text Import Wizard dialog box appears.

5. Click the Delimited option, and check that the Start import at row is 1, and click Next.

6. Under Delimiters, check that the Tab box is checked, and click Next.

7. Under Column data format, check that the General option is checked.

8. Click Finish. The Import Data dialog box appears.

9. Click in the Existing worksheet box, make sure the value is =$F$2.

10. Click OK.

11. Save the **E39TryA_xx** file, and leave it open to use in the next Try It.

The Text Import Wizard dialog box

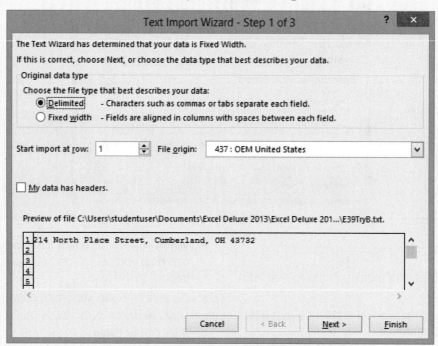

Saving Excel Data in CSV File Format

- Although many programs can open Excel files, you may occasionally need to save your workbook in a different format.

- For example, you might need to save a workbook in Excel 2003 format so that a colleague using an older version of Excel can open it.

- Besides converting a workbook to an earlier version of Excel, you can also convert your data to **CSV format**, which is compatible with almost every kind of spreadsheet or database software.

- The CSV file format maintains the functionality of your data, but the formatting is lost.

- You can also choose a CSV format for Macintosh or MS-DOS.

| **Try It!** | **Saving Excel Data in CSV File Format** |

(1) In the **E39TryA_xx** file, click FILE > Save As.

(2) In the Backstage view, browse to the location where your teacher instructs you to store files for this lesson.

(3) In the File name box, rename the file as **E39TryC_xx**.

(4) From the Save as type drop-down list, select CSV (Comma delimited).

✓ *Notice that there are two other CSV formats: one for Macintosh and one for MS-DOS. Choose the correct one for your computer.*

(5) Click Save.

(6) When Excel warns that features might not be compatible with CSV, click Yes to save the file as is.

(7) Save the **E39TryC_xx** file, and close it.

Saving a Workbook As a PDF or XPS File

- Besides converting a workbook to another spreadsheet format, you can also convert the file to **PDF format** and **XPS format**.

- You can use FILE > Save As to save a file in a different format.

- In order to view a workbook saved in PDF format, you need Adobe Reader, which is free, or Adobe Acrobat software.

- To make changes to a workbook saved as PDF, you can use Adobe Acrobat, or open the original Excel file in Excel, make your changes, and then resave the file in PDF format

- To view a worksheet saved in XPS format, you need an XPS viewer, available free from Microsoft.

  - To make changes to a workbook saved in XPS, open the original Excel file in Excel, make your changes, and resave the file.

| **Try It!** | **Saving a Workbook As a PDF or an XPS File** |

(1) Open the **E39TryA_xx** file from your solution files.

(2) In the SECURITY WARNING bar, click Enable Content.

✓ *Excel warns you when you open a file with an external data connection.*

(3) Click FILE > Export.

(4) Click Create PDF/XPS Document.

(5) Click Create PDF/XPS.

(6) Change the file name to **E39TryD_xx** and navigate to the location where your teacher instructs you to store files for this lesson.

(7) Click the Save as type drop-down arrow and choose either PDF or XPS Document.

(8) Click Publish.

✓ *If a file viewer such as Adobe Reader opens to display the file, right-click to access the file controls, click More, and click Close file. Then go to the Windows Start menu, and click Excel to return to Excel.*

(9) Save the **E39TryA_xx** file, and leave it open to use in the next Try It.

Sending a Workbook

- Excel files, like any other files, can be attached to e-mail messages for distribution.
- In the Backstage view, Excel's Share command will send a workbook as an e-mail attachment.
- When you use the Email Share feature, your default e-mail program opens a new blank message with the active Excel workbook attached to it.

✓ *If there is no e-mail application installed and configured on your PC, you cannot use this command. Ask your teacher for information on using a Web-based e-mail service such as Hotmail or Gmail.*

- You can also send a file as a PDF, an XPS file, or an Internet Fax.
- You can send a workbook as a link, so that everyone can work on the same copy.

✓ *To use the link command, you must first save the workbook in a shared location.*

Try It!   Sending a Workbook As an E-mail Attachment

1   In the **E39TryA_xx** file, click FILE.

2   Click Share > Email > Send as Attachment.

3   Verify that Send Using E-mail is selected, then, under Send Using E-mail, click Send as Attachment.

    ✓ *Your default e-mail application opens to a new message, with the workbook as an attachment.*

    ✓ *If a message to configure Outlook appears, close the message, and skip to step 5.*

4   Fill in a recipient's e-mail address in the To: box and, **with your teacher's permission**, click Send. Otherwise, close the e-mail application without sending.

5   Save the **E39TryA_xx** file, and exit Excel.

Sharing a Workbook

- Besides sharing a file as an email attachment, you can save your document to a SkyDrive location and share your document there.

- You can access the Share command from the FILE tab.
- You must have a Microsoft account to use SkyDrive.

Lesson 39—Practice

In this project, you will check a workbook for compatibility and save an Excel 2013 workbook in Excel 97-2003 format using the skills you learned in this lesson.

DIRECTIONS

1. Start Excel, if necessary, and open the **E39PracticeA** file from the data files for this lesson.

2. Save the file as **E39PracticeA_xx** in the location where your teacher instructs you to store the files for this lesson.

3. Add a header that has your name at the left, the date code in the center, and the page number code at the right, and change back to **Normal** view.

4. Use Check Compatibility to see if any features are incompatible with Excel 2003 format. Click **FILE > Info**.

5. Click **Check for Issues**.

6. Select **Check Compatibility**.

7. Review the Compatibility Checker report.

   a. Click Select Versions to Show, and click Excel 2007 to turn off that version of Excel.

   b. Click Select Versions to Show, and click Excel 2010 to turn off that version of Excel.

c. Note that some of the formatting (themes) are not compatible with the older version of Excel.

d. Click **OK**.

8. Resave the workbook as **E39PracticeB_xx** in the Excel 97-2003 workbook format in the location where your teacher instructs you to store the files for this lesson.

9. The Compatibility Checker opens again. Click **Continue**.

10. Save and close the file, and exit Excel.

Lesson 39—Apply

You've been working on a worksheet for Holy Habañero. Now you need to save the worksheet as a PDF to send to management. You'll also need to convert the worksheet to Excel 2003 format, which is being used by the manager of a different restaurant location.

DIRECTIONS

1. Start Excel, if necessary, and open the **E39ApplyA** file from the data files for this lesson.

2. Save the file as **E39ApplyA_xx** in the location where your teacher instructs you to store the files for this lesson.

3. Add a header that has your name at the left, the date code in the center, and the page number code at the right, and change back to **Normal** view.

4. Click **FILE** > **Export**.

5. Under Create a PDF/XPS Document, click **Create PDF/XPS Document**.

6. Rename the file as **E39ApplyB_xx**, and choose the location where your teacher instructs you to store the files for this lesson.

7. Click **Open file after publishing**, if necessary, and click **Publish**.

8. Look at the PDF file that opens, and then close the PDF.

9. Return to Excel, and in the **E39ApplyA_xx** file, click **FILE** > **Save As**.

10. Rename the file as **E39ApplyC_xx**.

11. In the Save as type drop-down list, select **CSV (MS-DOS)**.

12. Click **Save** to save the file in the location where your teacher instructs you to store the files for this lesson.

13. Click **Yes** at the prompt to continue saving in the CSV (MS-DOS) format.

14. Save and close all Excel files. Click **Yes** at any prompts to keep using the CSV (MS-DOS) format.

15. Open the **E39ApplyB_xx** to see what the CSV file looks like.

   ✓ *Remember the CSV format maintains the data but eliminates all formatting.*

16. Save and close the document, and exit Excel.

Lesson 40

Working with Graphics and Saving a Worksheet As a Web Page

Clip
A small file—clip art, photo, audio, or video—that can be inserted in a worksheet from the **Clip Art task pane**.

Clip art
Images that you can insert in any Office program, including Excel.

Clip Art task pane
A task pane that displays clip art matching the keywords you enter.

Cropping handle
A corner or side bracket along the border of a picture, enabling you to crop edges off of the corresponding side or corner.

Embed
A special process of copying data from one document to another, so that the tools from the original application are made available in the destination application for editing. Because no link to the original data is created, editing does not affect the original data.

➤ **What You Will Learn**

Inserting Graphics
Formatting Graphics
Saving a Worksheet As a Web Page
Embedding a Worksheet on a Web Page

Software Skills   Adding images can make it easier for a reader to digest a page full of figures and statistics. In this lesson, you will learn how to import pictures from image files and from clip art. You will also learn to save a worksheet in HTML format to publish it on the Internet or company intranet, and to add the data to an existing Web page.

What You Can Do

Inserting Graphics

■ You can insert **clip art** and other graphic images in a worksheet to enhance its appearance.

■ You can insert a **picture** from your computer using the Pictures button on the INSERT tab.

■ The Insert Picture dialog box initially opens to your Pictures Library.

■ In addition to the **clips** stored on your computer, you can insert other graphics or clip art from online sources.

■ You can search for clip art online using the Online Pictures button.

   ● The Insert Pictures window allows you to search for pictures by entering a keyword or phrase, such as "savings" or "goal."

   ● After displaying a list of matching pictures, you can preview and then insert any **picture** you wish.

   ● You can also view the properties of a clip, search for clip art in a similar style, and delete and copy the images.

- After inserting a picture, you can move and resize it as needed.

  ✓ *Audio and video files appear as icons when inserted in a worksheet, which can be moved and resized (to make smaller, for example) as desired.*

- Once you insert a picture, you can change it for another picture.
- To change a picture, click the Change Picture button on the PICTURE TOOLS FORMAT tab.
- You can also right-click on the picture, and click Change Picture.
- Then from the Insert Pictures dialog box, you can choose to insert a picture from a file or from an online source.

Try It!   Inserting a Picture

1. Start Excel, if necessary, and open the **E40Try** file from the data files for this lesson.
2. Save the file as **E40Try_xx** in the location where your teacher instructs you to store the files for this lesson.
3. Add a header that has your name at the left, the date code in the center, and the page number code at the right, and change back to Normal view.
4. Click cell C22.

5. Click INSERT > Pictures 🖼.
6. In the Insert Picture dialog box, navigate to the location where the data files for this lesson are stored, and select **E40Try_toy**.
7. Click Insert.

   ✓ *The picture will align with cell C22 but will overlap the words on the worksheet.*

8. Save the changes to the **E40Try_xx** file, and leave it open to use in the next Try It.

Try It!   Inserting an Online Picture

1. In the **E40Try_xx** file, select cell A1.
2. On the INSERT tab, click the Online Pictures button 🖼.
3. In the Office.com Clip Art search box, type **antique**, and click Search 🔍. A list of images matching the keyword is displayed.

4. Scroll through the list of available clip art until you find an appropriate image.
5. Click the image to select it, and click Insert.

   ✓ *The Insert Pictures window will close, and the picture will appear aligned against the upper-left corner of the active cell.*

6. Save the changes to the **E40Try_xx** file, and leave it open to use in the next Try It.

Excel Web App
A Microsoft feature that allows you to view and work with Excel workbooks directly on the Web site where the workbook is stored.

HTML
Hypertext Markup Language, used to publish information on the Internet

Intranet
A private network of computers within a business or organization.

Picture
A clip art image or photo that you can add to a worksheet.

Publishing
The process of saving data to an intranet or the Internet.

Shape
A predesigned object (such as a banner, rectangle, or star) that can be drawn with a single dragging motion.

Web browser
Software that enables you to view Web sites on the Internet.

Web page
Information published on the Internet, which can include text, graphics, and links to other pages.

World Wide Web
A network of computers located in businesses, research foundations, schools, and homes that allows users to share and search for information. Also called the Internet.

Try It!   **Changing One Picture for Another**

1 In the **E40Try_xx** file, click the picture in cell A1.

2 On the PICTURE TOOLS FORMAT tab, click the Change Picture button 🖼.

3 In the Insert Pictures dialog box, click From a file, and navigate to the location where the data files for this lesson are stored.

4 Select **E40Try_photo.jpg**, and click Insert.

5 Save the changes to the **E40Try_xx** file, and leave it open to use in the next Try It.

Formatting Graphics

- Once you've inserted clip art or a picture, you can adjust its appearance and other characteristics using options on the FORMAT tab.
  - You can make a color picture grayscale, sepia, washed out, or black and white.
  - You can make overall adjustments to a picture's contrast and brightness.
  - You can crop a picture to a smaller size.
  - You can crop a picture to fit within the borders of a **shape** you select.
  - You can right-click the picture, and access more formatting options with the Format Picture task pane.
- You can modify a clip the same way that you modify a shape, such as resizing, moving, rotating, adding a border or effect, or applying a style.
- When you resize some objects, such as photographs, Excel may automatically adjust the dimensions to keep the object in proportion.

- The changes you make to clip art or a picture in your worksheet (such as cropping) will not affect the original image.
- To crop a picture, click the picture to select it, click the Crop button, hover the mouse pointer over one of the **cropping handles** until it changes to the shape of the cropping handle, and drag the handle to crop to the desired dimension.
  - You can use a corner handle to crop from two sides.
  - You can use a side or top handle to crop from the corresponding side.
- Use the Reset Picture button in the Adjust group on the PICTURE TOOLS FORMAT tab to undo any formatting changes you have made and to reset the graphic to its original state.
- You can also use the Reset Picture button to reset the picture's size.

Try It!   **Cropping a Graphic**

1 In the **E40Try_xx** file, click the graphic in cell C22.

2 On the PICTURE TOOLS FORMAT tab, click the Crop button 🖼.

3 Rest the mouse pointer over the cropping handle in the top right corner until the pointer resembles a right angle ⌐.

4 Drag the top-right cropping handle toward the center of the image to remove excess white space.

5 Hover the mouse pointer over the bottom-left cropping handle, and drag to remove excess white space.

6 When you're done cropping, click the Crop button 🖼 again.

7 Save the **E40Try_xx** file, and leave it open to use in the next Try It.

(continued)

| Try It! | **Cropping a Graphic** *(continued)* |

Cropping a graphic

Cropping handles

...ies Fair is the middle of September.
...and staffing.

Shaded area
indicates area to be
cropped

| Try It! | **Resizing a Graphic Object** |

1 In the **E40Try_xx** file, click the clip art image in cell A1.

2 Rest the mouse pointer over the sizing handle in the bottom-right corner until the pointer resembles a diagonal double-headed arrow ⤡.

3 Drag the handle up and to the left to decrease the height and width of the shape to resemble the figure.

✓ *When you press the left mouse button, the pointer changes to a crosshair +.*

4 Click the toy image.

5 On the PICTURE TOOLS FORMAT tab, in the Size group, use the Width increment arrows to set the width of the shape to 1.3". Excel will automatically adjust the height proportionally.

6 Drag the toy graphic so that it is positioned next to the text in cell D22.

7 Save the **E40Try_xx** file, and leave it open to use in the next Try It.

Resizing a graphic using sizing handles

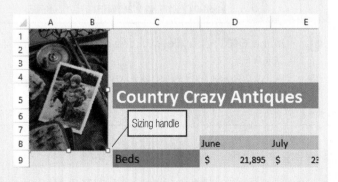

Sizing handle

Country Crazy Antiques

	June	July
Beds	$ 21,895	$ 2...

Try It!   Formatting a Graphic

1. In the **E40Try_xx** file, click the clip art image in cell A1.

2. On the PICTURE TOOLS FORMAT tab, in the Adjust group, click the Color button.

3. Under Color Saturation, click Saturation 66%.

4. Click Color, and under Color Tone, click Temperature 5300 K.

5. Click the toy clip art image in cell C22.

6. On the PICTURE TOOLS FORMAT tab, click Color > Set Transparent Color.

   ✓ *The cursor will change to a pointing wand. Aim the tip of the wand at the color in the object you want to make transparent.*

7. Click the white background on the graphic.

8. Click the toy clip art image.

9. On the PICTURE TOOLS FORMAT tab, click the Corrections button.

10. Under Brightness and Contrast, select Brightness: 0% (Normal) Contrast: -20%.

11. Click the clip art image in cell A1.

12. On the PICTURE TOOLS FORMAT tab, click the Picture Styles More button.

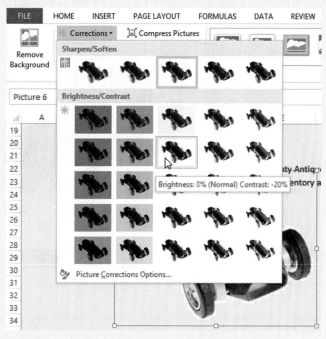

Changing color brightness and contrast

13. Select Beveled Oval, Black.

   ✓ *Live Preview enables you to see the effect of a style by hovering over the option.*

14. Save the **E40Try_xx** file, and leave it open to use in the next Try It.

Try It!   Resetting a Picture

1. In the **E40Try_xx** file, click the clip art image in cell A1.

2. On the PICTURE TOOLS FORMAT tab, click the Reset Picture button.

3. Save the changes to the **E40Try_xx** file, and leave it open to use in the next Try It.

Saving a Worksheet As a Web Page

- You can save an Excel worksheet in HTML format to make it easy to publish on the **World Wide Web**.

- Excel can save its worksheets in **HTML** format, or MHT format, a version of HTML in which all graphics are stored in a single file rather than in a series of separate ones.

- You can use a process called **publishing** to post files in in HTML/MHT format to the Internet or a company **intranet**.

- Once your data is published, you can republish it when needed to update the data.

- You can also have Excel automatically republish the data whenever you change the workbook, using the AutoRepublish option in the Publish as Web Page dialog box.

■ After saving a worksheet as a **Web page**, you must use a **Web browser**, such as Internet Explorer, to view that page.

✓ *You can also view the Web page by typing its address (file path) in the Address box of your Web browser.*

■ In the Publish as Web Page dialog box, you're given the option to immediately view the published page in your browser.

Try It!   **Saving a Worksheet or Workbook As a Web Page**

1 In the **E40Try_xx** file, press CTRL + HOME .

2 Hold the SHIFT key, and click cell I25 to select the cell range A1:I25.

3 Click FILE > Save As.

4 Click Computer, click Browse, and go to the location where your teacher instructs you to store the files for this lesson.

5 From the Save as type list, select Single File Web Page.

OR

From the Save as type list, select Web Page to save the worksheet's contents in separate files.

6 Type **E40Try_Web_xx** in the File name text box.

7 Next to Save, click Selection: $A$1:$I$25.

8 Change the title for the Web page.

✓ *The title appears in the title bar of the Web browser when viewed online.*

a. Click the Change Title button Change Title... .

b. In the Title box, type **Country Crazy Antiques**.

c. Click OK.

9 Click the Publish button Publish... . The Publish as Web Page dialog box appears.

10 Make sure that the Choose drop-down box reflects the range of cells selected.

✓ *You can choose the entire workbook, a range of cells (to publish the currently selected cells only), or a worksheet.*

11 If desired, select AutoRepublish every time this workbook is saved to automatically update the Web page each time you save the workbook.

✓ *If you don't select this option and you later make changes to the published data, you'll need to follow the steps under "Republishing a Worksheet or Workbook" to republish the data manually.*

12 Make sure that Open published web page in browser is selected, and click Publish Publish .

13 View the Web page in the Web browser, and close the Web browser.

14 In Excel, click Save.

15 In the dialog box warning that this workbook contains items that are automatically republished to Web pages each time the workbook is saved, check that Disable the AutoRepublish feature while this workbook is open is selected, and click OK.

16 Close the file.

Publish as a Web Page dialog box

| **Try It!** | **Republishing a Worksheet or Workbook** |

1 Open the **E40Try_xx** file, and select the cell range C5:F5.

2 On the HOME tab, click the down arrow next to the Fill Color button and select Gold, Accent 4, Darker 50%.

3 Select cells A1:I25, click FILE > Save As.

4 Click Computer, click Browse, and go to the location where your teacher instructs you to store the files for this lesson.

5 In the Save as type list, select Single File Web Page.

6 In the Save area, click Republish: $A$1:$I$25.

7 Click Publish [Publish...].

8 In the Choose list, make sure that Previously published items is selected. Notice that the range of cells (A1:I25) is reflected in the box below the Choose list.

9 Click Publish [Publish].

10 Save the **E40Try_xx** file, and close Excel.

| **Try It!** | **Opening a Web Page File in a Web Browser** |

✓ Use this procedure to open a published Web page that was not opened automatically by the Publish as Web Page dialog box.

1 Click File Explorer on the Desktop taskbar.

2 Navigate to the location where your teacher instructs you to store the files for this lesson, and double-click **E40Try_Web_xx** to open the file.

3 Click OK. Notice that Internet Explorer opens, and you can view your Web page.

4 Close Internet Explorer, and close File Explorer.

Embedding a Worksheet on a Web Page

- You can use the **Excel Web App** to **embed** Excel worksheet data on a Web page.
- Workbooks don't have to be created in Excel 2013 to be opened in the Excel Web App.

  ✓ For best compatibility, use spreadsheets created in Excel 2003 or later.

- You can use embedded spreadsheets to interactively collaborate with other people when you save your document to a SkyDrive location and share it.
- Use the Excel Web App to save your workbook to the SkyDrive. On the FILE tab, click Save & Send, and then click Save to Web.

  ✓ Remember, you must have a Microsoft account to use SkyDrive.

- To invite other people to work on the workbook, in SkyDrive, click the FILE tab in the Excel Web App, and then click Share. Add the people who you want to share the workbook with, click Save, and then compose a message.
- When you open a shared workbook from the SkyDrive, the Excel Web App opens the workbook in your browser.
- You can view and edit the embedded spreadsheet data as you would a regular Excel spreadsheet. You can also add tables, chart, hyperlinks, and functions.
- The Excel Web App saves changes to your workbook automatically.
- If you make your workbook available for collaboration, multiple people can work on the workbook at the same time.

- When you edit the workbook in the Excel Web App, you are able to see who else is working on the document in the status bar.

- If you want the full set of Excel capabilities, click the FILE tab, and click Open in Excel.

Lesson 40—Practice

In this project, you will insert and format a picture using the skills you learned in this lesson.

DIRECTIONS

1. Start Excel, if necessary, and open the **E40Practice** file from the data files for this lesson. If a security warning appears, click **Enable Content**.

2. Save the workbook as **E40Practice_xx** in the location where your teacher instructs you to store the files for this lesson.

3. For all worksheets, add a header that has your name at the left, the date code in the center, and the page number code at the right, and change back to **Normal** view.

4. On the **Usage** worksheet, click cell **A1**.

5. Click **INSERT > Pictures**.

6. Navigate to the location where the data files for this lesson are stored, click **E40_Intellidata_logo**, and click Insert.

7. On the PICTURE TOOLS FORMAT tab, click **Crop**.

8. Slide the bottom-middle cropping handle up to eliminate extra space at the bottom of the logo. The area to be eliminated will be outlined outside of the crop markers.

9. Click **Crop** again to save your changes to the logo.

10. Drag the lower-right sizing handle of the logo until the bottom edge of the image sits at row 3.

11. Click **HOME > Copy**.

12. Click cell **A17**, and on the HOME tab, click **Paste**. The logo will appear in the second panel of the worksheet.

13. Click cell **F1 > INSERT > Online Pictures**.

14. In the search text box, type **computer**, and click Search.

15. Scroll down until you locate the image shown at the top of Figure 40-1, or select a similar image.

16. Double-click the image to insert it in the worksheet.

17. Resize the graphic to the dimensions shown in Figure 40-1 on the next page.

18. **With your teacher's permission**, adjust the page break, and print the **Usage** worksheet with a landscape orientation. Submit the printout or the file for grading as required.

19. Save and close the file, and exit Excel.

Figure 40-1

Monthly Usage Breakdown

Diaz Used Auto Sales

	James Murphy	Kenesha Stevens	Tai Ling Wong	Julie Jung	Yolanda Dickerson	Totals
Message Management	1,385.00	563.00	925.00	777.00	1,298.00	4,948.00
E-Mail Auto-Respond	483.00	177.00	341.00	488.00	399.00	1,888.00
Online Sales Reports	18.00	8.00	4.00	13.00	8.00	51.00
Wireless Lead Alerts	529.00	507.00	516.00	808.00	424.00	2,784.00

Monthly Usage Breakdown

Diaz Used Auto Sales

	Message Management	E-Mail Auto-Respond	Online Sales Reports	Wireless Lead Alerts		
James Murphy	1,385.00	483.00	18.00	529.00		
Kenesha Stevens	563.00	177.00	8.00	507.00		
Tai Ling Wong	925.00	341.00	4.00	516.00		
Julie Jung	777.00	488.00	13.00	808.00	Message Management	3,562.56
Yolanda Dickerson	1,298.00	399.00	8.00	424.00	E-Mail Auto-Respond	1,793.60
Totals	4,948.00	1,888.00	51.00	2,784.00	Online Sales Reports	63.75
Charge per item	0.72	0.95	1.25	1.10	Wireless Lead Alerts	3,062.40
Total charge	3,562.56	1,793.60	63.75	3,062.40	Total invoice	8,482.31

Lesson 40—Apply

To complete the usage breakdown statement you designed for Intellidata Services, you need to add the corporate logo and some clip art from Microsoft's collection. When the design is complete, you want to share it with workers throughout the enterprise by publishing it to your company's Web site. That way, managers of individual stores can see how they are doing compared to other stores in their area. You also want to publish the results of a recent market analysis of a potential new product.

DIRECTIONS

1. Start Excel, if necessary, and open the **E40Apply** file from the data files for this lesson. If a security warning appears, click **Enable Content**.

2. Save the workbook as **E40Apply_xx** in the location where your teacher instructs you to store the files for this lesson.

3. For all worksheets, add a header that has your name at the left, the date code in the center, and the page number code at the right, and change back to **Normal** view.

4. Modify the clip art in cell **F1** as indicated in Figure 40-2 on the next page.

   a. Apply the picture style shown.

   b. Recolor the clip art as shown.

5. Publish the **Usage** worksheet as a single file Web page with the file name **E40Apply_Usage_xx**. Use the Web page title **2014 Usage Breakdown**. Use the AutoRepublish option. Display the page in your browser. (See Figure 40-2.)

   ✓ Notice that you cannot change any of the data. You can print it, however, using the File, Print command in the browser.

6. Publish the **New Product** worksheet as a single file Web page with the file name **E40Apply_ NewProduct_xx**. Use the Web page title **Profit Analysis**. Use the AutoRepublish option. Display the page in your browser.

7. Modify the **New Product** worksheet as shown in Figure 40-3 on the next page.

   a. Copy the Intellidata logo from the **Usage** worksheet to the **New Product** worksheet.

   b. Change the percentage of people who liked the item.

   c. Change the price point as shown.

   d. Save your changes.

8. Refresh your view in the Web browser. Or, close the existing Profit Analysis tab, and republish the **New Product** worksheet.

9. **With your teacher's permission**, print the Profit Analysis page from your Web browser. Submit the printout or the file for grading as required.

10. Save and close the files, and exit the programs.

Figure 40-2

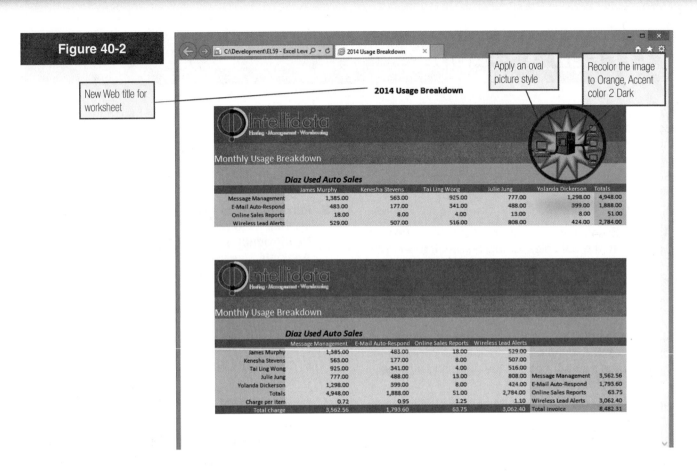

New Web title for worksheet

Apply an oval picture style

Recolor the image to Orange, Accent color 2 Dark

Figure 40-3

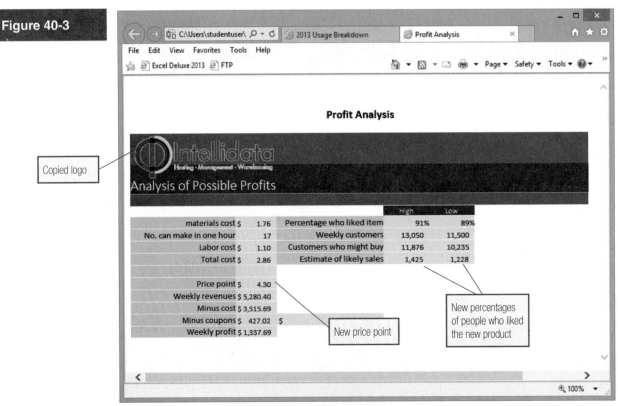

Copied logo

New price point

New percentages of people who liked the new product

Lesson 41

Working with Web Data

➤ What You Will Learn

Copying Data from a Web Page
Creating a Web Query

Software Skills   The Internet contains a vast amount of data, some of it useful, some of it not. When you find useful data, such as a table that lists the pricing structure for a supplier's services, you can copy this data to an Excel worksheet, where you can calculate, sort, format, and analyze it. You can also create a refreshable Web query to copy current data from the Web at the click of a button.

What You Can Do

Copying Data from a Web Page

- You can import data from the Internet or your company's intranet to use in Excel.
- You can use cut and paste to import data to a worksheet.
- After pasting data in a worksheet, you can use Paste Options to format it to suit your worksheet.
- You can also use the Paste Options button to convert the pasted data into a Web query.

WORDS TO KNOW

Web query
The process of pulling data from a Web page into an Excel worksheet.

Refresh
The process of updating the data copied to a worksheet through a query.

Try It!   **Copying Data from a Web Page**

1 Start Excel, if necessary, and open the **E41Try** file from the data files for this lesson.

2 Save the file as **E41Try_xx** in the location where your teacher instructs you to store the files for this lesson.

3 For all worksheets, add a header that has your name at the left, the date code in the center, and the page number code at the right, and change back to Normal view.

4 Open File Explorer, and browse to the location of the data files for this lesson.

5 Copy the **E41Try_Table** file, and paste the file in the location where your teacher instructs you to store the files for this lesson.

     ✓ *Linked files must be stored in the same folder.*

6 Open **E41Try_Table** from the data files for this lesson.

     ✓ *To open a file in Internet Explorer, click File on the Menu bar and then browse to where the file is located. Internet Explorer will open.*

7 In your Web browser, select all elements of currency table.

8 Press CTRL + C.

9 Return to Excel, and click cell A5 on the Web Data worksheet.

10 On the HOME tab, click the Paste button 📋.

11 Save the **E41Try_xx** file, and leave both files open to use in the next Try It.

Try It!   **Changing the Format of Pasted Data**

1 In the **E41Try_xx** file, click the Paste Options worksheet.

2 With your Web browser open to the **E41Try_Table** Web page, select the rows that contain the conversion data for the Euro and the British Pound.

3 Press CTRL + C.

4 Return to Excel, and click cell A4 of the Paste Options worksheet.

5 On the HOME tab, click Paste 📋.

6 Click the Paste Options button 📋 (Ctrl) ▾ > Match Destination Formatting 📋.

     ✓ *You can change the pasted data to a Web query by clicking Refreshable Web Query from the Paste Options menu; then follow the steps in the next procedure to create the query.*

7 Save the **E41Try_xx** file, and leave it open to use in the next Try It.

Using the Paste Options menu

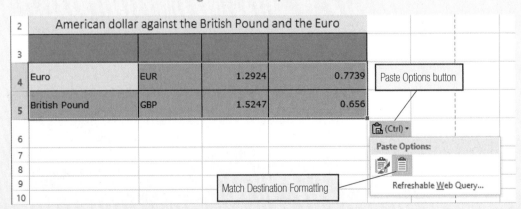

Creating a Web Query

- You can create a **Web query** by copying and pasting the data from a Web page directly into an Excel workbook, or by initiating a query in Excel with the Get External Data command.

- After a query is created, data from the associated Web page is copied to the worksheet.

- If the data on the Web page changes, you can refresh the query with the **Refresh** command on the Refresh All button drop-down menu in the Connections group on the DATA tab.

- To refresh all the queries in a workbook, you can use the Refresh All button.

  ✓ *You can set the query to update periodically by clicking the Properties button* ▦ *in the Connections group and setting the Refresh every XX minutes option.*

- You can also use the options in the Refresh All button to learn the status of a refresh operation or to stop a refresh operation.

- When a query is refreshed, current data from the associated Web page is copied to the worksheet, replacing the existing data.

- With the Connections button on the DATA tab, you can change the Web page and specific Web data associated with the query.

- With the Properties button on the DATA tab, you can update the query automatically, after a period of time you specify.

| **Try It!** | **Creating a Web Query** |

1 With your Web browser open to **E41Try_Table**, select the URL in the address bar.

2 Press `CTRL` + `C`.

3 In the **E41Try_xx** file, select the Query worksheet, and click cell A5.

4 Click the DATA tab, From Web button 🔲. (Click Yes if a Script Error message appears.)

5 In the New Web Query dialog box, select the URL in the Address box and press `CTRL` + `V`.

6 Click Go.

7 Click the yellow arrow next to the table, as shown in the figure.

✓ *Selected arrows will change to green check marks.*

✓ *If you click Import without selecting any tables, the entire page will be imported.*

8 Click Import.

9 In the Import Data dialog box, check that the Existing Worksheet box has =$A$5.

10 Click OK.

11 Close Internet Explorer.

12 Save the **E41Try_xx** file, and leave it open to use in the next Try It.

New Web Query dialog box

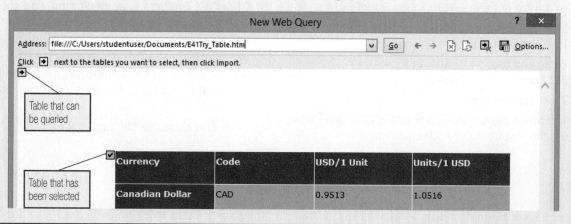

Try It!   **Refreshing a Web Query**

❶ In the **E41Try_xx** file, in the Query worksheet, click a cell within the query area (A5:D10).

❷ On the DATA tab, in the Connections group, choose a refresh option.

    a. To refresh all external data, click Refresh All 🗗.

    b. To refresh the currently selected query only, click the Refresh All drop-down arrow > Refresh.

✓ *To learn the status of a refreshing operation, choose Refresh Status.*

✓ *To stop a refresh operation, choose Cancel Refresh.*

❸ Save the **E41Try_xx** file, and close it.

Lesson 41—Practice

In this project, you will be using the skills you learned in this lesson.

DIRECTIONS

1. Start Excel, if necessary, and open the **E41Practice** file from the data files for this lesson.

2. Save the workbook as **E41Practice_xx** in the location where your teacher instructs you to store the files for this lesson.

3. Add a header that has your name at the left, the date code in the center, and the page number code at the right, and change back to **Normal** view.

4. Click cell A11 on the **Infusion Rates** worksheet.

5. Click **DATA > From Web** 🌐. The New Web Query dialog box opens.

6. Copy the file path for **E41Practice_Medication**.

    a. Open File Explorer, and navigate to the data files for this lesson.

    b. Press and hold [SHIFT], and right-click **E41Practice_Medication**.

    c. Click Copy as path.

7. Return to the New Web Query dialog box, and delete the text from the Address box.

8. Press [CTRL] + [V] to paste the file path text in the Address box.

9. In the Address box, delete the quotation marks (") from the beginning and end of the file path.

10. Click Go. (Click Yes if a Script Error message appears.) The preview window in the dialog box fills with the requested Web page.

    ✓ *Yellow tabs indicate all of the refreshable information that can be queried.*

11. Click the yellow arrows next to the table containing medication information. The arrow will turn into a green check mark.

12. Click **Import**. The Import Data dialog box opens.

13. Click **OK**. The data is pasted to the worksheet in a refreshable format. Refer to Figure 41-1 on the next page.

14. **With your teacher's permission,** adjust the page breaks, and print the **Infusion Rates** worksheet. Submit the printout or the file for grading as required.

15. Save and close the file, and exit Excel.

Figure 41-1

Updated Infusions Rates

HelpNow Medical Center

Medication	Conc	Units	Solution	Diluent	Note	Min Dose	Max Dose	Units
Alprostadil	0.01	mg/ml	500mcg/50ml	D5W		0.01	0.4	mcg/kg/min
	0.02	mg/ml	1mg/50ml	D5W		0.01	0.4	mcg/kg/min
Aminocaproic Acid	20	mg/ml	5000mg/250ml	D5W			33	mg/kg/hr
Aminophylline	1	mg/ml	500mg/500ml	D5W		0.5	2	mg/kg/hr
	8	mg/ml	2000mg/250ml	D5W		0.5	2	mg/kg/hr
Amiodarone	0.5	mg/ml	25mg/50ml	D5W		2	20	mg/kg/day
	5	mg/ml	250mg/50ml	D5W		2	20	mg/kg/day
Bumetanide	0.25	mg/ml	25mg/100ml	D5W		0.0025	0.014	mg/kg/hr
Cisatricurium	1	mg/ml	50mg/50ml	D5W		1	2	mcg/kg/min
	2	mg/ml	200mg/100ml	D5W		1	2	mcg/kg/min
Dexmedetomidine	0.004	mg/ml	200mcg/50ml	NS		0.2	0.7	mcg/kg/hr
Diltiazem	0.5	mg/ml	25mg/50ml	D5W		0.05	0.15	mg/kg/hr
	1	mg/ml	50mg/50ml	D5W		0.05	0.15	mg/kg/hr
Dobutamine	1000	mcg/ml	250mg/250ml	D5W	Premix	2	20	mcg/kg/min
	4000	mcg/ml	1000mg/250ml	D5W	Premix	2	20	mcg/kg/min
Dopamine	800	mcg/ml	200mg/250ml	D5W	Premix	2	20	mcg/kg/min
	3200	mcg/ml	800mg/250ml	D5W	Premix	2	20	mcg/kg/min
Epinephrine	0.01	mg/ml	0.5mg/50ml	D5W		0.05	2	mcg/kg/min
	0.02	mg/ml	1mg/50ml	D5W		0.05	2	mcg/kg/min
	0.12	mg/ml	6mg/50ml	D5W		0.05	2	mcg/kg/min
Esmolol	10	mg/ml	2500mg/250ml	0.59%Saline	Premix	25	1000	mcg/kg/min
Fenoldapam	0.04	mg/ml	10mg/250ml	D5W		0.1	0.5	mcg/kg/min
	0.08	mg/ml	20mg/250ml	D5W		0.1	0.5	mcg/kg/min
Fentanyl	10	mcg/ml	550mcg/55ml	NS	Premade	1	20	mcg/kg/hr
			1mg/100ml					
	50	mcg/ml	2.5mg/50ml			1	20	mcg/kg/hr
			12.5mg/250ml					
Furosemide	1	mg/ml	50mg/50ml	D5W		0.25	0.75	mg/kg/hr
	5	mg/ml	250mg/50ml	D5W		0.25	0.75	mg/kg/hr
	10	mg/ml	300mg/30ml	D5W		0.25	0.75	mg/kg/hr
			500mg/50ml					
Heparin	100	unit/ml	25000unit/250ml	D5W or 1/2NS	Premix	10	40	unit/kg/hr
Hydromorphone	0.2	mg/ml	10mg/50ml	D5W		7	20	mcg/kg/hr
			20mg/100ml					

Infusion Rates

Lesson 41—Apply

The workbooks with rate information for your company, HelpNow Medical Center, need to be updated. You can use Excel's Web query feature to update the clinic fees quickly and easily, and then you can copy the rate information from a Web page to a worksheet.

DIRECTIONS

1. Start Excel, if necessary, and open the **E41Apply** file from the data files for this lesson.

2. Save the workbook as **E41Apply_xx** in the location where your teacher instructs you to store the files for this lesson.

3. For all worksheets, add a header that has your name at the left, the date code in the center, and the page number code at the right, and change back to **Normal** view.

4. Click the **Clinic Fees** worksheet.

5. Use the Web page data to complete the worksheet, as follows:
   a. Open the **E41Apply_Fees** file in Internet Explorer.
   b. Copy the first seven rows under the heading *Services and Fees* in the Services and Fees table.
   c. On the **Clinic Fees** worksheet, click cell B11 > Paste.
   d. Select the cell range F12:H17, and drag the range to the cell range B12:D17.

   > ✓ *When copying content from a Web page, you may have to reformat the content after you paste it.*

   e. Copy the last five rows in the Services and Fees table.
   f. On the **Clinic Fees** worksheet, click cell B20 > Paste.
   g. Select the cell range F21:H24, and drag the range to the cell range B21:D24.
   h. Copy the entire Vaccinations table from the **E41Apply_Fees** file.
   i. On the **Clinic Fees** worksheet, click cell G10 > Paste.
   j. Delete rows H–L.

6. Format the worksheet like Figure 41-2 on the next page:
   a. Format cells A10:D10 with Orange, Accent 2 and Calibri, 14-point, bold white font.
   b. Use the Format Painter to copy the format to cells A19:D19 and G10:H10.
   c. Apply the Orange, Accent 2, Lighter 60% fill color to the range B11:D17.
   d. Apply the Orange, Accent 2, Lighter 60% fill color to the range B20:D24.
   e. Apply the Orange, Accent 2, Lighter 60% fill color to the range G11:H24.
   f. Remove the left cell border from the cell range B11:B17.
   g. Remove the right cell border from the cell range D11:D17.
   h. Remove the left cell border from the cell range B20:B24.
   i. Remove the right cell border from the cell range D20:D24.

7. Adjust the column widths, row heights, and page breaks as needed.

8. **With your teacher's permission,** print the **Clinic Fees** worksheet. Submit the printout or the file for grading as required.

9. Save and close the file, and exit Excel.

Figure 41-2

	A	B	C	D	E	F	G	H	I
1									
2									
3									
4				Project Clinic Fees					
5									
6		HelpNow Medical Center							
7				(fees for our south side Critical Care Clinic)					
8									
9									
10	Services and Fees						Vaccinations		
11		Minor illness examination		$69			Flu (Seasonal)	$25	
12		School Physical		$45			GARDASIL®(HPV)	1st dose - $214.99	
13		Skin conditions exam		$55				2nd dose - $184.99	
14		Minor injuries		$69				3rd dose - $184.99	
15		Wellness exams		$75			H1N1 Vaccine	$20	
16		Well Baby check ups		$100			Hepatitis B	3 doses at $79.99	
17		Health condition monitoring		$75-$125			Menactra (Meningitis)	$120.99	
18							MMR (Measles, Mumps, Rubella)	$95.99	
19	Testing Services						PPV (Pneumonia)	$63.99	
20		Strep testing		$69			Shingles	$219.99	
21		PPD/Tuberculosis testing		$50			Tdap (Tetanus, Diphtheria, Pertussis	$65	
22		Influenza A & B testing		$35			Varicella (Chicken Pox)	Two doses at $136.99	
23		H1N1 testing		$40					
24		Pregnancy testing		$55					
25									
26									

Lesson 42

Linking and Embedding Data

> ## ➤ What You Will Learn

Linking and Embedding Excel Data
Embedding Data
Linking Data
Editing Embedded Data
Editing Linked Data

WORDS TO KNOW

Embed
A special process of copying data from one document to another, so that the tools from the original application are made available in the destination application for editing. Because no link to the original data is created, editing does not affect the original data.

Link
A reference to data stored in another file. When that data is changed, the data is updated in the destination file automatically.

Software Skills   When you need to use Excel data within a file created in another program, such as a Word document or PowerPoint presentation, you can link the file to the Excel data and update it automatically when the Excel data is changed. If you'd like to make changes in the other file without affecting the original Excel data (or vice versa), you can embed the data instead of linking it.

What You Can Do

Linking and Embedding Excel Data

- If you copy data from Excel and paste it in another file, that data does not maintain any connection to its source. For many purposes, this is all you need.

- If you want to maintain a connection to the original Excel data, you can opt to **link** or **embed** it.

- Linked data is automatically changed when the original data is changed; embedded data is not.

- Typically, all Microsoft programs support linking and embedding, so you can apply the same processes to link or embed Excel data wherever you want, not just within Office documents.

Embedding Data

- With embedding, there is no direct link to the source data. Thus, you can make changes to the source data that do not affect the destination file and vice versa.

  ✓ *For example, if you change embedded Excel data within a Word document, the changes won't affect the original data in its Excel workbook.*

- When you embed Excel data in another document, that data is copied to the destination file, making the file larger than if you used linking.

- To embed files, use the Paste button's drop-down menu on the HOME tab.

- You can also click Picture 🖻 in the Other Paste Options group on the Paste Options menu to paste the data as a graphic.

- Although embedded data isn't tied to the source document, it does retain a connection to the source program. Consequently, you are able to use all of the tools from the source program when you need to make changes.

Try It! Embedding Excel Data in a PowerPoint Presentation

1 Start Excel, if necessary, and open the **E42Try** file from the data files for this lesson. If a security warning appears, click Enable Content.

2 Save the file as **E42Try_xx** in the location where your teacher instructs you to store the files for this lesson.

3 For all worksheets, add a header that has your name at the left, the date code in the center, and the page number code at the right, and change back to Normal view.

4 Start PowerPoint, and open the **E42Try_Grades** presentation from the data files for this lesson.

5 Save the presentation as **E42Try_Grades_xx** in the location where your teacher instructs you to store the files for this lesson.

6 In the Excel file, click the Sem 2 worksheet, and select the cell range A1:M30.

7 On the HOME tab, click Copy 🖹.

8 In the PowerPoint file, select slide 2. On the HOME tab, click the Paste drop-down arrow ^{Paste} > Paste Special.

9 In the Paste Special dialog box, select Microsoft Excel Worksheet Object.

10 Click OK.

OR

Click the Paste down arrow ^{Paste} > Embed 🖻.

11 Save both files and leave them open to use in the next Try It.

The Paste Special dialog box

Linking Data

- Use linking to create a special link between a source file and a destination file.
- When you create a link between files, the data in the destination file changes if you update the source file.
  - Thus, if you link Excel data to a Word document and then change that data, the changes are automatically updated within the Word document.

- Although linked data is updated automatically, you can change the link so that you update it manually.
- You can perform other maintenance tasks with the links in your destination file, such as breaking a link and retaining any local formatting changes whenever a link is updated.
- Linked data is not stored in the destination file, so the resulting file is smaller than if you embed data.
- You can display linked data as an icon within the source document; this does not affect the link's ability to keep that data current.

Try It!   **Linking Excel Data in a PowerPoint Presentation**

1 In the **E42Try_xx** Excel file, click the Grades worksheet, and select the cell range A4:E30.

2 On the HOME tab, click Copy 🗐.

3 In the **E42Try_Grades_xx** PowerPoint file, select slide 3.

4 On the HOME tab, click the Paste down arrow ᵖᵃˢᵗᵉ > Paste Special.

5 In the Paste Special dialog box, click Paste link.

6 In the As list, select Microsoft Excel Worksheet Object.

7 Click OK.

8 Save the changes to the **E42Try_Grades_xx** file, and leave it open to use in the next Try It.

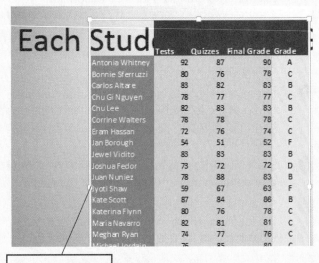

A linked object's container

Linked and embedded objects are contained in object containers that can be resized as needed

---

Editing Embedded Data

- When you double-click data embedded from an Excel workbook, the Ribbon within the destination application will change to display Excel's tools.
- The changes you make to embedded data will not alter the original data in the Excel workbook—the two sets of data are separate.

Try It!   Editing Embedded Data

1 In the **E42Try_Grades_xx** file, select slide 2.

2 Click the embedded data on slide 2.

   ✓ *The data is surrounded by a thick gray border, and Excel's Ribbon commands appear.*

3 Use the top-left and lower-right corner sizing handles to enlarge the object.

4 Double-click the embedded data, and note the changes to the Ribbon.

5 Select cells A1:M2.

6 On the HOME tab, click the Fill Color down arrow, and select Green, Accent 6.

7 Click outside the worksheet border.

8 Save the changes to the **E42Try_Grades_xx** file, and leave it open to use in the next Try It.

9 Save the **E42Try_xx** Excel file, and close it.

The source program's editing tools

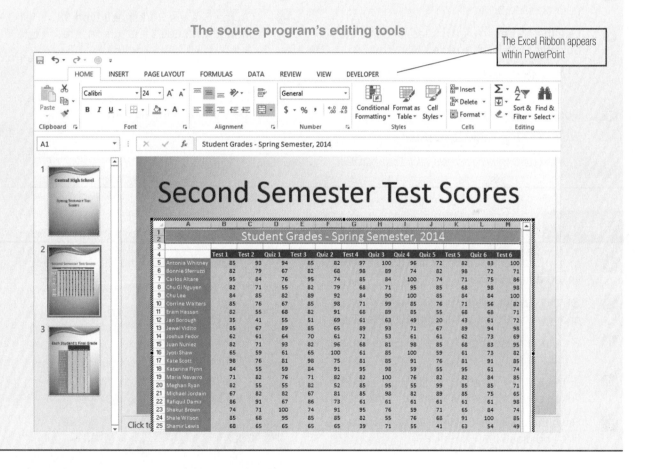

The Excel Ribbon appears within PowerPoint

Editing Linked Data

■ When you double-click data linked to an Excel workbook, Excel automatically starts and opens the workbook so you can make changes.

　✓ *For example, if you link Excel data in a Word document, you can open that Word document and double-click the data to start Excel so that you can make changes.*

■ After you make your changes and save them, the changes are automatically updated through the link to the destination file.

　✓ *If the destination file is not currently open, then the changes will be updated when it is opened later.*

Try It!　　**Editing Linked Data**

❶ In the **E42Try_Grades_xx** file, click the linked data on slide 3.

❷ Use the corner sizing handles to resize the object to better fit the slide.

　✓ *If the linked data blocks part of the title text, drag the linked data down.*

❸ Double-click the linked data.

　✓ *The **E42Try_xx** workbook should open.*

　✓ *If a security warning appears, click Enable Content.*

❹ Arrange the two programs side by side.

❺ On the Grades worksheet, type **93** in cell D9 to change Chu Lee's final grade. Press ENTER .

❻ Notice the change reflected in the PowerPoint presentation.

❼ Save the **E42Try_Grades_xx** file, and leave it open to use in the next Try It.

Try It!　　**Updating Links Manually**

❶ In the **E42Try_Grades_xx** file, double-click the linked data on slide 3.

❷ On the Grades worksheet, type **80** in cell D12 to change Jan Borough's final grade. Press ENTER .

❸ Save and close the **E42Try_xx** Excel file, and exit Excel.

❹ In the **E42Try_Grades_xx** file, right-click the linked object on slide 3 > Update Link.

❺ Save the changes to the **E42Try_Grades_xx** file, and close it.

Manually updating a linked object

	Tests	Quizzes	Final Grade	Grade
Antonia Whitney	92	87	90	A
Bonnie Sferruzzi	80	76	78	C
Carlos Altare	83	82	83	B
Chu Gi Nguyen	78	77	77	C
Chu Lee	82	83	93	A
Corrine Walters	78	78	78	C
Eram Hassan	72	76	74	C
Jan Borough	54	51	80	C
Jewel Vidito	83	83		
Joshua Fedor	73	72		
Juan Nuniez	78	88		
Jyoti Shaw	59	67		
Kate Scott	87	84		
Katerina Flynn	80	76		
Maria Navarro	82	81		
Meghan Ryan				
Michael Jordain				

Cut / Copy / Paste Options / Linked Worksheet Object / Update Link / Group

Manually update a linked object

Lesson 42—Practice

In this project, you will insert Excel data into a Word document using the skills you learned in this lesson.

DIRECTIONS

1. Start Excel, if necessary, and open the **E42Practice** file from the data files for this lesson.

2. Save the workbook as **E42Practice_xx** in the location where your teacher instructs you to store the files for this lesson.

3. For all worksheets, add a header that has your name at the left, the date code in the center, and the page number code at the right, and change back to **Normal** view.

4. Start Word, and open the **E42Practice_Projections** document from the data files for this lesson.

5. Save the document as **E42Practice_Projections_xx** in the location where your teacher instructs you to store the files for this lesson.

6. In the **E42Practice_xx** workbook, select the range **A10:G22** on the **FORECAST** worksheet.

7. On the HOME tab, click **Copy** .

8. In the **E42Practice_Projections_xx** document, click the second blank line under the last paragraph on the first page.

9. On the HOME tab, click the **Paste** down arrow ^{Paste}, and under Paste Options, click **Picture**. Your document should look similar to Figure 42-1.

10. **With your teacher's permission**, print the first page of the **E42Practice_Projections_xx** document.

11. Save and close both files, and exit Excel.

Figure 42-1

Whole Grains Bread
Salem Office #2994
3131 Court Street N. W.
Salem, OR 97302

September 30, 2014

Mrs. Eileen Costello
Whole Grains Bread
320 Magnolia Ave.
Larkspur, CA 94939

Dear Mrs. Costello,

Per your request of September 25, 2014, I have conducted a thorough inventory analysis, and have created predictions for fourth quarter inventory needs, using several popular methods.

Here is a listing of our actual inventory usage for the third quarter and our predicted fourth quarter needs, using the Forecast method:

	Actual			Predicted		
	July	August	September	October	November	December
Flours	$ 2,250.35	$ 2,901.77	$ 1,770.00	$ 2,000.00	$ 3,000.00	$ 1,600.00
Milk & Buttermilk	$ 277.95	$ 358.41	$ 95.09	$ 174.23	$ 400.61	$ 83.68
Eggs	$ 165.05	$ 212.82	$ 156.00	$ 162.12	$ 213.66	$ 141.50
Sugars	$ 859.45	$ 908.00	$ 294.02	$ 528.69	$ 1,044.25	$ 322.47
Butter	$ 2,141.71	$ 2,761.67	$ 1,733.00	$ 1,932.00	$ 2,843.37	$ 1,567.45
Oil	$ 333.29	$ 429.76	$ 214.00	$ 267.84	$ 456.03	$ 192.56
Oats	$ 1,565.06	$ 2,018.10	$ 535.42	$ 981.05	$ 2,255.74	$ 471.18
Cornmeal	$ 1,543.74	$ 991.00	$ 1,528.00	$ 1,506.71	$ 1,010.70	$ 1,705.11
Yeast	$ 2,844.30	$ 3,667.65	$ 973.05	$ 1,782.94	$ 4,099.53	$ 856.31
Fruit	$ 1,566.74	$ 1,020.00	$ 1,536.00	$ 1,521.17	$ 1,043.18	$ 1,712.36
Herbs & Spices	$ 1,222.02	$ 576.00	$ 1,418.00	$ 1,305.07	$ 546.84	$ 1,608.36

Lesson 42—Apply

As the owner of a Whole Grains Bread store in Salem, Oregon, you've been concerned about your inventory control. Using Excel, you created several worksheets using various forecasting functions to help you more accurately predict your needs. The corporate office has asked to review your figures, so you need to prepare a letter in Word, and then link and embed Excel data within it.

DIRECTIONS

1. Start Excel, if necessary, and open the **E42Apply** file from the data files for this lesson.

2. Save the workbook as **E42Apply_xx** in the location where your teacher instructs you to store the files for this lesson.

3. For all worksheets, add a header that has your name at the left, the date code in the center, and the page number code at the right, and change back to **Normal** view.

4. Start Word, and open the **E42Apply_Projections** file from the data files for this lesson.

5. Save the document as **E42Apply_Projections_xx** in the location where your teacher instructs you to store the files for this lesson.

6. Embed the data from range A10:G22 on the **TREND** worksheet to the second line under the Trend paragraph on page 2 in the **E42Apply_Projections_xx** document.

   ✓ Hint: Use the Paste Special dialog box.

7. Link the data from the **GROWTH** worksheet to the second line under the Growth paragraph on page 2 in the **E42Apply_Projections_xx** document.

8. Save the **E42Apply_Projections_xx** Word file, close the **E42Apply_xx** Excel file, and exit Excel.

9. Make changes to the embedded data in Word:
   a. Double-click the TREND data.
   b. Change the Milk & Buttermilk value for December to **185**, as shown in Figure 42-2 on the next page.
   c. Start Excel, open the **E42Apply_xx** Excel file, and view the **TREND** worksheet to verify that no changes are reflected there.
   d. Adjust the width of the embedded object to be about **6"** wide.

10. Make changes to the linked data in Word:
    a. Double-click the GROWTH data.
    b. Change the Milk & Buttermilk value for December to **185**, as shown in Figure 42-2 on the next page.
    c. Change the Oats value for December to **750**.
    d. Save the **E42Apply_xx** Excel file, and exit Excel.
    e. Adjust the width of the linked object to be about **6"** wide.

11. In the Word document, check that the data has been updated.

    ✓ If necessary, update the link manually to reflect the changes.

12. Spell check the document.

13. **With your teacher's permission**, print the **E42Apply_Projections_xx** document.

14. Save and close the file, and exit Excel.

Figure 42-2

Here is a listing of our actual inventory usage and our predicted fourth quarter needs, using the Trend method:

	Actual			Predicted		
	July	August	September	October	November	December
Flours	$ 2,250.35	$ 2,901.77	$ 1,770.00	$ 2,547.55	$ 2,583.55	$ 1,893.59
Milk & Buttermilk	$ 277.95	$ 358.41	$ 95.09	$ 298.19	$ 306.34	$ 185.00
Eggs	$ 165.05	$ 212.82	$ 156.00	$ 190.34	$ 192.19	$ 156.63
Sugars	$ 859.45	$ 908.00	$ 294.02	$ 810.98	$ 829.54	$ 473.83
Butter	$ 2,141.71	$ 2,761.67	$ 1,733.00	$ 2,431.02	$ 2,463.83	$ 1,835.02
Oil	$ 333.29	$ 429.76	$ 214.00	$ 370.88	$ 377.66	$ 247.81
Oats	$ 1,565.06	$ 2,018.10	$ 535.42	$ 1,679.01	$ 1,724.90	$ 845.42
Cornmeal	$ 1,543.74	$ 991.00	$ 1,528.00	$ 1,235.12	$ 1,217.26	$ 1,559.49
Yeast	$ 2,844.30	$ 3,667.65	$ 973.05	$ 3,051.39	$ 3,134.78	$ 1,536.44
Fruit	$ 1,566.74	$ 1,020.00	$ 1,536.00	$ 1,259.44	$ 1,242.24	$ 1,572.03
Herbs & Spices	$ 1,222.02	$ 576.00	$ 1,418.00	$ 889.90	$ 862.60	$ 1,385.75

Here is a listing of our actual inventory usage and our predicted fourth quarter needs, using the Growth method:

	Actual			Predicted		
	July	August	September	October	November	December
Flours	$ 2,250.35	$ 2,901.77	$ 1,770.00	$ 2,549.38	$ 2,514.61	$ 1,885.29
Milk & Buttermilk	$ 277.95	$ 358.41	$ 95.09	$ 277.96	$ 267.27	$ 185.00
Eggs	$ 165.05	$ 212.82	$ 156.00	$ 188.71	$ 186.88	$ 156.57
Sugars	$ 859.45	$ 908.00	$ 294.02	$ 769.29	$ 744.46	$ 411.04
Butter	$ 2,141.71	$ 2,761.67	$ 1,733.00	$ 2,399.13	$ 2,365.14	$ 1,826.68
Oil	$ 333.29	$ 429.76	$ 214.00	$ 362.14	$ 354.62	$ 242.63
Oats	$ 1,565.06	$ 2,018.10	$ 535.42	$ 1,565.10	$ 1,504.95	$ 750.00
Cornmeal	$ 1,543.74	$ 991.00	$ 1,528.00	$ 1,204.79	$ 1,221.65	$ 1,571.08
Yeast	$ 2,844.30	$ 3,667.65	$ 973.05	$ 2,844.37	$ 2,735.05	$ 1,345.37
Fruit	$ 1,566.74	$ 1,020.00	$ 1,536.00	$ 1,230.78	$ 1,247.10	$ 1,582.84
Herbs & Spices	$ 1,222.02	$ 576.00	$ 1,418.00	$ 820.15	$ 843.77	$ 1,410.67

Lesson 43

Working with Workbooks

➤ What You Will Learn

Creating a Workbook from a Template
Adding Values to Workbook Properties
Opening Multiple Workbooks
Changing from Workbook to Workbook
Comparing Workbooks

WORDS TO KNOW

Document Panel
A feature in Excel that contains the document properties.

Document properties
Document properties include details about your workbook such as the author, title, and subject. You can edit this information.

Template
A workbook with preset labels, formulas, and formatting that you can use to create commonly used worksheets, such as monthly invoices or balance sheets.

Software Skills   Excel provides a number of templates you can use to format a workbook and to guide you in the development of specific types of content. There will be many times when you want to work with several workbooks at the same time. Excel makes it easy to arrange several workbooks onscreen so you can view their contents at the same time.

What You Can Do

Creating a Workbook from a Template

■ To save time when creating a new workbook from scratch, select an Excel **template**.

■ Excel templates already have the formatting, formulas, and layout design created for you.

■ In the New view, you can search for templates on Office.com, or use templates already stored on your system.

    ✓ *You will need a live Internet connection to download a template from Office.com.*

■ When you perform a template search, Excel will display templates that are installed on your computer and templates available for downloading.

    ● You can also select a category from the Category pane to further refine your search.

■ You can also create additional templates for your own use, and store them on your computer.

■ You can access your stored templates from the PERSONAL tab on the New tab.

- In addition to using templates to create new workbooks, you can base a new workbook on a copy of an existing workbook.
- After a new workbook is created from the template, enter your data.

✓ *For example, if you start a new workbook using the Personal Monthly Budget template, enter your income where indicated, and then type the individual expense items you want to include in the budget.*

Try It! Creating a New Workbook from a Template

1 Start Excel, if necessary, and click Blank workbook, or click FILE > New and click Blank workbook if Excel is already open.

2 In the Suggested searches list, click Invoice > Basic Invoice > Create.

OR

If you cannot download the template from the Internet, you can use the Basic invoice.xltx template file from the data files for this lesson.

a. In Excel, click FILE > Open.

b. Browse to the data files for this lesson, and double-click the **E43Try_Basic invoice.xslx** file.

✓ *Double-clicking a template file in the Open dialog box will create a new workbook based on the template.*

3 Save the file as **E43Try_Invoice_xx** in the location where your teacher instructs you to store the files for this lesson.

4 Add a header that has your name at the left, the date code in the center, and the page number code at the right, and change back to Normal view.

5 Personalize the information as needed.

6 Save the **E43Try_Invoice_xx** file, and close it.

The New tab in the Backstage view

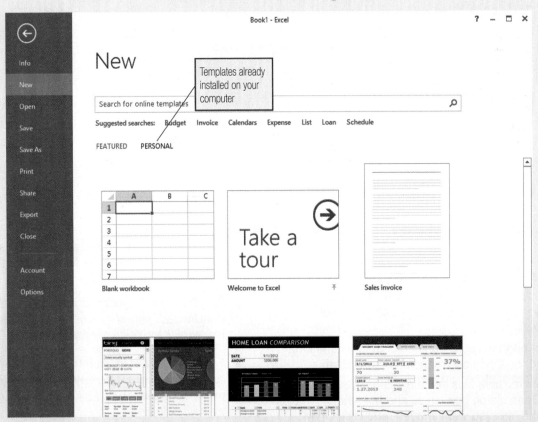

Adding Values to Workbook Properties

- You can add information, such as a title and subject, to the **document properties** of your workbook to.
- Document properties can also include information that is automatically maintained by Office programs, such as the name of the person who authored a workbook, the date when a document was created, and the document location.

- You can access the document properties from the Properties drop-down menu on the Info tab of the FILE tab.
- You can use the **Document Panel** to add or edit document properties. From the Properties drop-down menu, click Show Document Panel.
- When active, the Document Panel will appear below the Ribbon.
- You can also use the Advanced Properties button to add and edit additional properties.

Try It! Adding Values to Workbook Properties

1. Start Excel, if necessary, and open the **E43Try** file from the data files for this lesson.

2. Save the file as **E43Try_xx** in the location where your teacher instructs you to store the files for this lesson.

3. Add a header that has your name at the left, the date code in the center, and the page number code at the right, and change back to Normal view.

4. Click FILE > Info.

5. On the right side of the Info tab, click Properties > Show Document Panel. The Document Panel appears. Notice that Excel automatically entered the file location in the Location box.

6. In the Author box, type your name.

7. Click the Close button ✖ of the Document Panel.

8. Save and close the file.

The Document Properties panel

Document Properties ▼		Location:	C:\Users\studentuser\Documents\E43Try_xx.xlsx	✱ Required field ✖

Author: | Title: | Subject: | Keywords: | Category:

Status:

Comments:

Opening Multiple Workbooks

- In Microsoft Excel 2013, workbooks are displayed as separate Excel windows.
- In previous versions of Excel, multiple workbook windows were displayed inside a single Excel window.
- You can open multiple workbooks at the same time by using the Open command on the FILE tab.
- To select multiple files that are listed consecutively in the Open dialog box, press and hold the SHIFT key, select the files you want to open, and click Open.

- To select multiple files that are *not* listed consecutively in the Open dialog box, press and hold the CTRL key, select the files you want to open, and click Open.

  ✓ If you click a file that you do not want to select while holding down the CTRL key and you haven't released the CTRL key, you can click the file again to deselect.

  ✓ If you click a file that you do not want to select while holding down the CTRL key and you have released the CTRL key, you can press and hold the CTRL key again, and click the file you want to deselect.

Try It!   **Opening Multiple Workbooks**

1 In Excel, click FILE > Open.

2 Browse to the location of the data files for this lesson.

3 In the Open dialog box, press and hold the [CTRL] key.

4 While holding down the [CTRL] key, click the **E43Apply** file, and click the **E43Try** file. Click Open, if necessary.

5 Close both files without saving.

   ✓ *Closing all open files will close Excel.*

6 Start Excel, and click FILE > Open.

7 In the Open dialog box, press and hold the [SHIFT] key.

8 While holding down the [SHIFT] key, click the **E43Apply** file, and click the **E43Try** file. Notice that an additional Apply file and two Practice files are also selected.

9 Click Open.

10 Close all open files without saving, and exit Excel.

Changing from Workbook to Workbook

- When more than one workbook is open, use the Switch Windows button ⊞ on the VIEW tab to change to a different workbook; select the workbook from the displayed list of names.

- You can also change between workbooks by hovering the mouse point over the Excel button on the Windows taskbar, and choosing from the list of open workbooks that appears.

Try It!   **Changing to a Different Open Workbook**

1 Start Excel, and open the **43Try_Invoice_xx** file from the location where your teacher instructs you to store the files for this lesson.

2 Open the **E43Try_xx** file from the location where your teacher instructs you to store the files for this lesson.

3 Click VIEW > Switch Windows ⊞.

4 Click the **E43Try_Invoice_xx** file.

OR

Click any other open workbook window.

OR

Hover the mouse pointer over the Excel button on the Windows taskbar, and click one of the other open workbooks.

5 Leave the files open to use in the next Try It.

Comparing Workbooks

- If you want to view the contents of more than one workbook at the same time, you can arrange all open workbooks in one of four ways:
  - Tiled: arranges windows in small, even rectangles to fill the screen.
  - Horizontal: arranges windows one above the other.
  - Vertical: arranges windows side by side.
  - Cascade: creates a stack of windows with only the title bar in view.

- You can also choose View Side by Side or Arrange All on the VIEW tab to view multiple workbooks at the same time.
  - With the Synchronous Scrolling button ⊟ on the VIEW tab, you can view the exact same cells in each workbook by scrolling within one workbook.
  - To resize workbook windows so that they once again split the screen horizontally, use the Reset Window Position ⊞ button.

- The title bar of an active workbook's window is light gray, while the inactive workbook's title bar is white.

Try It!   Arranging Open Workbooks

❶ In the **E43Try_xx** file, click VIEW > Arrange All ⊟.

❷ In the Arrange Windows dialog box, select from four options:

- Tiled
- Horizontal
- Vertical
- Cascade

❸ Click OK.

✓ You may need to click Restore Down in the upper-right corner of the window to allow the window to arrange properly.

❹ Leave the files open to use in the next Try It.

The Arrange Windows dialog box

Try It!   Viewing Workbooks Side by Side

❶ In the **E43Try_Invoice_xx** file, click VIEW > View Side by Side 🗗.

✓ If the open workbooks are arranged one on top of the other, you can change them to side by side by clicking the Arrange All button ⊟ and then selecting Vertical.

❷ On the VIEW tab, click the Synchronous Scrolling 🗐, and scroll to C43 in one of the workbooks.

✓ Side-by-side workbooks are scrolled synchronously. To stop synchronous scrolling, click the Synchronous Scrolling button 🗐 to turn it off.

❸ Click the View Side by Side button 🗗 to end the side-by-side comparison.

❹ Close all open workbooks without saving.

Lesson 43—Practice

In this project, you will open multiple workbooks and arrange workbook windows using the skills you learned in this lesson.

DIRECTIONS

1. Start Excel, if necessary, click Open Other Workbooks, and browse to the location of the data files for this lesson.
2. In the Open dialog box, press and hold the ⎈CTRL key.
3. While holding down the ⎈CTRL key, click the **E43Practice** file, and click the **E43Practice_Schedule 7-20** file.
4. Click Open.
5. On the Windows taskbar, click the **Excel** button, and click the **E43Practice** file.
6. Save the **E43Practice** workbook as **E43Practice_xx** in the location where your teacher instructs you to store the files for this lesson.
7. Add a header that has your name at the left, the date code in the center, and the page number code at the right, and change back to **Normal** view.
8. Click VIEW > Arrange All ⊟.

9. In the Arrange Windows dialog box, select **Cascade** > **OK**. The two workbooks appear in an overlapped arrangement.

10. Click in the window of the **E43Practice_xx** workbook to activate it, and scroll within the workbook.

    ✓ *Notice that when you scroll, the two windows are not kept in synch.*

11. Maximize the **E43Practice_xx** workbook. The other workbook is no longer visible.

12. Click the **Excel** button on the Windows Taskbar, and select **E43Practice_Schedule 7-20**.

13. Click **VIEW** > **Side by Side** 🔲.

14. Scroll within the workbook. Notice that when you scroll, the two workbooks display the same cells—they are kept in synch with each other.

15. In the **E43Practice_xx** file, type the data as shown in Figure 43-1. Adjust the column widths and page breaks, as necessary.

16. **With your teacher's permission,** print the **E43Practice_xx** worksheet.

17. Save the **E43Practice_xx** file and close it.

18. Close the **E43Practice_Schedule 7-20** file without saving the changes, and exit Excel.

Figure 43-1

Student Name   7/8/2013   1

Whole Grains Bread
Salem, Oregon Office
Forecasted Inventory Needs

Whole Grains Bread
Bakery Schedule
Date: 7/21/2014

Customer	Item	Qty Needed	Qty Shipped	Still Needed
Café Latte	Bagels, various	25		25
Café Latte	Muffins, various	50		50
Village Green	Wheat Rolls	50		50
Java Café	Pastries, various	25		25
Village Green	Wheat Bread	20		20
Village Green	White Bread	12		12
Mike's Steak House	Wheat Rolls	1875		1875
Gribaldi's Restaurant	Garlic Bread	100		100
Gribaldi's Restaurant	Pastries, various	85		85
Java Café	Croissants	75		75
Java Café	Muffins, various	75		75
Green Street Market	Wheat Bread	325		325
Green Street Market	White Bread	325		325
Green Street Market	Baguettes	200		200
Green Street Market	Croissants	150		150
Green Street Market	Rolls	150		150

Lesson 43—Apply

You are the head chef at Whole Grains Bread. You need to create an invoice for a recent catering job.

DIRECTIONS

1. Start Excel, if necessary, and open the **E43Apply** file from the data files for this lesson.

2. Create a new workbook using the **Sales invoice** template.

   ✓ *You'll need to download the template from Office.com. You'll find the template listed in the Invoice category.*

   ✓ *If you cannot download the template, you can open the* **E43Apply_Sales invoice** *template file from the data files for this lesson, click FILE > Save As. Change the Save as type to Excel Template, and click OK. Excel will save the template to your Templates folder. After copying the template, use the My Templates category to open the template.*

3. Save the new workbook as **E43Apply_xx** in the location where your teacher instructs you to store the files for this lesson.

   ✓ *Be sure to save the workbook using the Excel workbook format (.xlsx).*

4. In the **E43Apply_xx** file, add a header that has your name at the left, the date code in the center, and the page number code at the right, and change back to **Normal** view.

5. Position the two workbooks side by side.

6. Use data in the **E43Apply** workbook to complete the invoice in the **E43Apply_xx** file for the Green Street Market:

   a. Use the data from the cell ranges **E26:E30** and **G26:G30** to fill in the sales data in the cell ranges **B17:B21** and **D17:D21**, respectively, on the **E43Apply_xx** file.

   b. On the invoice, delete the Your company logo and tagline placeholder shapes.

   c. In the **E43Apply** file, copy the logo and the product name, and paste them in cell B2 on the invoice.

   d. Replace both instances of Company Name with **Whole Grains Bread**. Remove the brackets from the text, as necessary.

   e. Replace the company address and contact information where appropriate on the invoice.

7. Replace the invoice date with today's date.

8. Close the **E43Apply** file.

9. In the **E43Apply_xx** file, complete the rest of the invoice as shown in Figure 43-2 on the next page.

   a. Replace the Contact at company and <Name> with your name.

   b. In cell **F4**, replace the purchase order number with **14102**.

   c. In cell **E28**, change the Credit to **500.00**.

   d. In cell **E30**, change the additional discount to **20%**.

   e. Change the name of the worksheet tab to **Invoice 2014**.

10. Adjust column widths, and page breaks, as necessary.

11. Spell check the worksheet.

12. **With your teacher's permission**, print the invoice.

13. Save and close the file, and exit Excel.

Student Name   7/9/2013   1

Whole Grains Bread ®

INVOICE

2354 Smith Street
Salem, OR 97301
Phone: (206) 555-1163
Fax:(206) 555-1164
bakers@wholegrains.com

Date	Today's Date
Invoice #	1111
For:	PO # 14102

Bill To:

Student Name
Whole Grains Bread
2354 Smith Street
Salem, OR 97301
(206) 555-1163

Quantity	Description	Unit price		Amount		10% Discount applied
325	Wheat Bread	$	2.00	$	585.00	✓
325	Wheat Bread	$	2.00	$	585.00	✓
200	Baguettes	$	1.95	$	351.00	✓
150	Croissants	$	1.32	$	178.20	✓
150	Rolls	$	0.32	$	48.00	
				$	0.00	
				$	0.00	
				$	0.00	
				$	0.00	
Subtotal				$	**1,747.20**	

Make all checks payable to Whole Grains Bread. If you
have any questions concerning this invoice, contact
Student Name (206) 555-1163, bakers@wholegrains.com.
Thank you for your business!

Credit	$	500.00
Additional discount		20%
Balance due	$	**897.76**

Figure 43-2

Lesson 44

Working with Comments and Modifying Page Setup

➤ What You Will Learn

Inserting Comments
Printing Multiple Copies of a Workbook or Worksheet
Modifying Page Setup
Using Page Layout View
Inserting Headers and Footers

Software Skills　You can add comments to your worksheet as helpful hints or reminders for yourself or for others who view the data. In addition, you can change the page setup of your worksheet, and use the available print options to control the printed output of a report. For example, if you need to fit the worksheet on one page, you can change the margins, print orientation, paper size, and scaling. You can add headers and footers to worksheets to repeat the same information at the top or bottom of each printed page.

What You Can Do

Inserting Comments

■ You can attach a text note to a cell by using the New Comment button on the REVIEW tab.

■ A red triangle appears in the upper-right corner of any cell with an attached **comment**.

■ To display a comment, hover the mouse pointer on the cell containing the comment indicator (the red triangle).

- Comments are marked with the user's name, so if more than one person works on a worksheet, each person's comments are easy to identify.

  ✓ *The name used to mark comments is stored on the General tab of the Excel Options dialog box, accessible through the FILE tab.*

- Comments help explain data, formulas, and labels used in a complex worksheet. You can insert comments as reminders to yourself, but they are especially useful for explaining a worksheet shared with others.

- If you want, you can display all the comments on a worksheet with a single command.

- You can resize or move comments, as you would any other object.

- You can also format the comment text using the commands on the HOME tab.

Try It!   **Creating Comments**

1. Start Excel, if necessary, and open the **E44Try_xx** file from the data files for this lesson.

2. Save the file as **E44Try_xx** in the location where your teacher instructs you to store the files for this lesson.

3. Click cell C8 to select it.

4. Click REVIEW > New Comment 🗒.

5. Type **Includes new tires**.

6. Click outside the comment box.

   ✓ *A red triangle now displays in the upper-right corner of the comment cell.*

7. Save the **E44Try_xx** file, and leave it open to use in the next Try It.

Try It!   **Displaying and Editing Comments**

1. In the **E44Try_xx** file, on the REVIEW tab, click the Show All Comments button 🗒.

   ✓ *All the comments on the worksheet are displayed.*

2. Click the Show All Comments 🗒 button again to hide the comments.

3. Hover the mouse pointer over cell B6.

   ✓ *A comment appears in a small box beside the cell.*

4. Click cell B6.

5. On the REVIEW tab, click the Edit Comment button 🗒.

6. Delete the words **scanner and** from the comment.

   ✓ *Drag a handle to increase or decrease the size of the comment box.*

7. Click outside the comment box.

8. Click cell E6.

9. On the REVIEW tab, click the Delete button 🗒.

10. Save the **E44Try_xx** file, and leave it open to use in the next Try It.

Printing Multiple Copies of a Workbook or Worksheet

- You can print multiple copies of your data by increasing the value in the Copies box on the Print tab in the Backstage view.

- If you print multiple copies of a multipage document, select Collated so that each copy is printed in order: page 1, 2, 3, and so on.

Try It!   Printing Multiple Copies

1   In the **E44Try_xx** file, click FILE > Print.

2   Type **3** in the Copies box.

   ✓ *You can also click the scroll buttons to set the number of copies.*

3   In the Settings area, click Collated, if necessary.

4   Click Save to save the **E44Try_xx** file, and leave it open to use in the next Try It.

Printing multiple copies

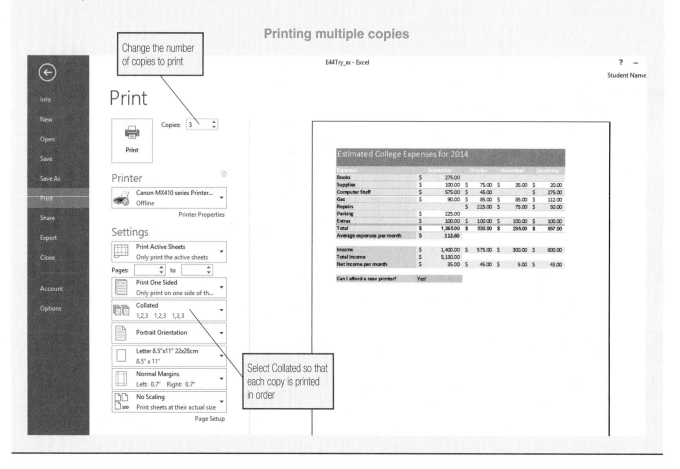

Modifying Page Setup

- Before you print, you can preview the printout so that you can make any changes to the **print options** as necessary to improve its appearance.

- From the Print tab, you can access the **Page Setup** dialog box where you can change the setup of the printout and instantly preview their effect.

- You can also make page setup changes by using commands from the PAGE LAYOUT tab on the Ribbon.
  - On the Ribbon, the page setup commands are divided into groups: Page Setup, Scale to Fit, and Sheet Options.

- With the Page Setup Dialog Box Launcher button ⌐ on the Ribbon, you can access the Page Setup dialog box to select other, less often used commands that are not shown on the Ribbon.

- In the Page Setup dialog box, the page setup commands are grouped on four tabs: Page, Margins, Header/Footer, and Sheet.

Changing Orientation

- You can print the worksheet in Portrait (vertical) or Landscape (horizontal) orientation.

- You can also use the Orientation button in the Page Setup group on the PAGE LAYOUT tab to change orientation.

Adjusting Page Scaling

- Reduce or enlarge information through the **scaling** options. Use the Fit to pages option to compress worksheet data to fill a specific number of pages in width and height.
- You can also use the Scale button and Width and Height boxes in the Scale to Fit group on the PAGE LAYOUT tab to set Scaling options.

Changing Paper Size

- You can change the paper size to print on a paper size other than 8½" × 11".
- You can also use the Size button in the Page Setup group on the PAGE LAYOUT tab to change paper size.

Changing Print Quality

- You can use the Page Setup dialog box to reduce the print quality to print draft output. Increase print quality by raising the dpi (dots per inch).

Changing Page Margins

- Increase or decrease the Top, Bottom, Left, or Right margins to control the distance between your data and the edge of the paper.
- Increase or decrease the Header or Footer margins to specify the distance between the top or bottom of the page and the header/footer.
- You can select from a few standard margin combinations using the Margins button on the Ribbon, or choose Custom Margins to set your own combination.
- You can center the worksheet horizontally and/ or vertically on the page.

Try It!   **Setting Page Setup Options**

1. In the **E44Try_xx** file, click the FILE tab.
2. Click Print, and review the page setup in the preview pane.
3. In the Settings area, click Portrait Orientation > Landscape Orientation.
4. Click No Scaling > Fit Sheet on One Page.
5. Click Normal Margins > Custom Margins. The Page Setup dialog box appears.
6. In the Top box, type **2**.
7. Click OK.
8. Click Save to save the **E44Try_xx** file, and leave it open to use in the next Try It.

Using Page Layout View

- You can use Page Layout view to view data as it will look when printed, and make adjustments.
  - You can change to Page Layout view using the Page Layout button on the VIEW tab, or the Page Layout button 🔲 on the Status bar.
- You can work in Page Layout view, or change to it as you're making your final adjustments for printing.
- In Page Layout view, you can see and make changes to your headers and footers and your margins.

- Rulers appear in Page Layout view by default, making it easy to adjust margins.
  - ✓ *For example, to change the left margin, move the mouse pointer to the margin edge on the ruler and, when it changes, drag to the left to narrow the margin, or to the right to widen it.*
- The rulers can also be used to adjust the size of graphics and charts to fit exact requirements.
- To use the ruler to adjust margins, drag the margin border. As you drag, a ScreenTip appears, showing you the changing margin's measurements.

Try It!   Using Page Layout View

1 In the **E44Try_xx** file, click the VIEW tab, then click the Page Layout button 📄.

2 On the ruler that runs along the left of the worksheet, drag the top margin border up to adjust the margin to 1.50 inches.

✓ *If the ruler is not visible, check the Ruler option in the Show group.*

3 Save the **E44Try_xx** file, and leave it open to use in the next Try It.

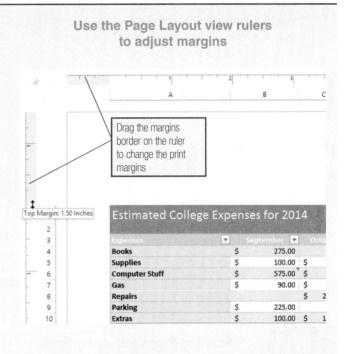

Use the Page Layout view rulers to adjust margins

Drag the margins border on the ruler to change the print margins

Inserting Headers and Footers

- When you want to repeat the same information at the top of each printed page, create a **header**.

- When you want to repeat the same information at the bottom of each printed page, create a **footer**.

- Header and footer information displays in Page Layout view and in the preview on the Print tab. They do not display in Normal View or Page Break Preview.

- To add a header or footer, you can use the Page Setup dialog box or the Page Layout view.

  - When you use the Page Setup dialog box, you make selections from the Header/Footer tab. You can also enter custom header or footer data in the Header or Footer dialog box, shown later in this section.

  - When you use Page Layout view, click the Header & Footer button 📄 on the INSERT tab to enter the header or footer directly in the worksheet.

  ✓ *If you prefer the structure of a dialog box, you might want to use Page Setup.*

- You can select a pre-designed header or footer or create customized ones.

  - You can create the header or footer using tools on the HEADER & FOOTER TOOLS DESIGN tab.

  - When creating a custom header/footer, type the text you want to use in the appropriate section of the dialog box: left, center, or right.

- Headers and footers are separated into three sections: left (text is left-aligned), center (text is center-aligned), and right (text is right-aligned).

- In Page Layout view, placeholder text such as *Click to add header* appears so you can add a header.

- Similar placeholder text appears for empty footers.

- Text may be entered on multiple lines as needed.

- You can also click buttons in the Header & Footer Elements group on the HEADER & FOOTER TOOLS DESIGN tab to insert print codes for the page number, number of pages, current date, current time (both reset at time of printing), page number, total pages, file path, file name, sheet name, or picture.

- You can insert a picture graphic (such as a company logo) in a custom header/footer.
  - If you add graphics or additional lines of text, you'll need to adjust the header/footer and top/bottom margins on the Margins tab to allow enough space for these elements to print.
  - Keep in mind that any graphic you use must be small in order to look proportional to the header/footer text.
  - Header/footer graphics do not appear in the regular worksheet window; in Page Layout view, you'll see the code &[Picture] instead.
  - To see a header/footer graphic you'll need to view the preview on the Print tab or print it.
- Excel does not have a built-in **watermark** feature, but you can simulate the look of a watermark by inserting a picture in the header.

- The font, font style, and font size of the custom header/footer may be changed using the tools on the HOME tab.
- You can set additional header or footer options from the Options group on the HEADER & FOOTER TOOLS DESIGN tab:
  - Different First Page allows you to create a unique first page header or footer.
  - Different Odd & Even Pages allows you to create unique headers or footers for even and odd pages.
  - Scale with Document allows header or footer text to shrink proportionately if you scale the worksheet for printing.
  - Align with Page Margins aligns the sides of the header or footer to the margins of the worksheet.

Try It! **Adding Built-In Headers and Footers in Page Layout View**

1. In the **E44Try_xx** file, click VIEW > Page Layout, if necessary.

2. Click the Click to add header placeholder text at the top of the page.

3. Click the HEADER & FOOTER TOOLS DESIGN tab, click the Header button, and select Page 1of ?.

   ✓ The question mark in the built-in header Page 1 of ? indicates the number of pages in your document.

4. On the HEADER & FOOTER TOOLS DESIGN tab, click the Footer button, and click Sheet1, Page 1.

   ✓ The comma in a header or footer indicates that data will be placed in separate cells.

5. Save the **E44Try_xx** file, and leave it open to use in the next Try It.

Try It! **Deleting Headers and Footers in Page Layout View**

1. In the **E44Try_xx** file, click the Page Layout view button in the Status bar, if necessary.

2. Click HEADER & FOOTER TOOLS DESIGN > Header > (none).

   ✓ Notice that you have deleted the header you created in the previous exercise.

3. Click HEADER & FOOTER TOOLS DESIGN > Footer > (none).

4. Save the **E44Try_xx** file, and leave it open to use in the next Try It.

Try It! Creating a Custom Header and Footer in Page Layout View

1 In the **E44Try_xx** file, click the Page Layout view button in the Status bar, if necessary.

2 Scroll to view the footer area, if necessary, and click the Click to add footer placeholder text at the bottom of the page.

3 Type **College Expenses** in the center footer section, and press ENTER to insert text on another line.

4 Scroll to view the header area, if necessary, and click the Click to add header placeholder text at the top of the page.

OR

On the HEADER & FOOTER TOOLS DESIGN tab, click the Go to Header button.

5 Type the appropriate text in the center header section.

OR

Click one of the buttons in the Header & Footer Elements group on the HEADER & FOOTER TOOLS DESIGN tab.

6 Save the **E44Try_xx** file, and leave it open to use in the next Try It.

Create custom headers and footers in Page Layout view

Expenses	September	October	November	December	January	February	March
Books	$ 275.00				$ 275.00		
Supplies	$ 100.00	$ 75.00	$ 35.00	$ 20.00	$ 125.00	$ 75.00	$ 45.00
Computer Stuff	$ 575.00	$ 45.00		$ 275.00	$ 50.00		

Estimated College Expenses for 2014

Try It!   **Creating Built-In Headers and Footers with the Page Setup Dialog Box**

1   In the **E44Try_xx** file, click the PAGE LAYOUT tab.

2   Click the Page Setup dialog box launcher ⌐ .

3   Click the Header/Footer tab.

4   Click the Header drop-down arrow, and click a header from the list.

5   Click the Footer drop-down arrow, and click a footer from list.

6   Click OK.

7   Save the **E44Try_xx** file, and leave it open to use in the next Try It.

Page Setup dialog box

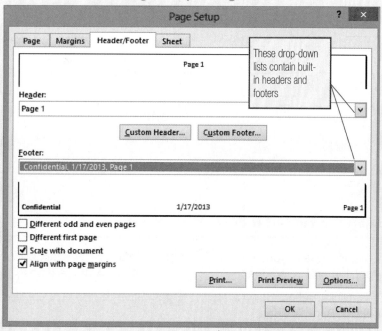

Try It!   **Creating Custom Headers and Footers with the Page Setup Dialog Box**

1   In the **E44Try_xx** file, click the PAGE LAYOUT tab, and click the Page Setup dialog box launcher ⌐ .

2   Click the Header/Footer tab.

3   Click the Header list arrow > (none).

4   Click Custom Header.

5   Type your name in the Left section, add the date code in the Center section, and add the page number code in the Right section.

6   Click OK.

7   Click the Footer list arrow > (none).

8   Click Custom Footer.

9   In the Right section, click the Insert File Name button ⌐ .

10   Click OK twice.

11   Save the **E44Try_xx** file, and leave it open to use in the next Try It.

(continued)

Try It!　　**Creating Custom Headers and Footers with the Page Setup Dialog Box** *(continued)*

Header dialog box

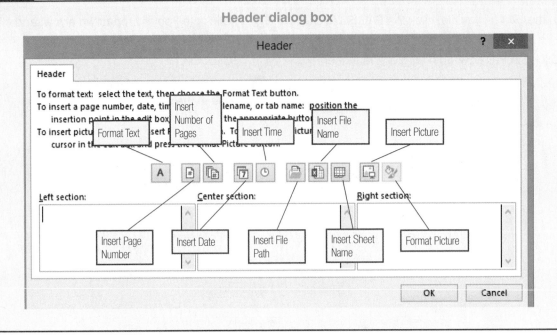

Try It!　　**Changing the Font of a Header or Footer**

1 In the **E44Try_xx** file, in Page Layout view, click in the left header section and select the text.

2 Click the HOME tab, click the Font down arrow `Calibri ▼`, and click Book Antiqua.

3 On the HOME tab, click the Increase Font Size button **A˄** three times.

4 Save the **E44Try_xx** file, and close it.

Lesson 44—Practice

In this project, you will create a custom footer and modify the page setup using the skills you learned in this lesson.

DIRECTIONS

1. Start Excel, if necessary, and open the **E44Practice** file from the data files for this lesson.

2. Save the workbook as **E44Practice_xx** in the location where your teacher instructs you to store the files for this lesson.

3. On the **Trip Budget** worksheet, click INSERT > **Header & Footer** 📄. The worksheet changes to Page Layout view, and the HEADER & FOOTER TOOLS DESIGN tab opens.

4. On the HEADER & FOOTER TOOLS DESIGN tab, click Go to Footer.

5. In the center footer section, type your name.

6. Click **FILE** > **Print**. The Print tab opens containing the printer settings and a preview of the printout.

7. Click **Portrait Orientation** > **Landscape Orientation**.

8. Click **No Scaling** > **Fit Sheet on One Page**. The entire worksheet now fits on a single page, as shown in Figure 44-1.

9. **With your teacher's permission**, print the **Trip Budget** worksheet.

10. Save and close the file, and exit Excel.

Figure 44-1

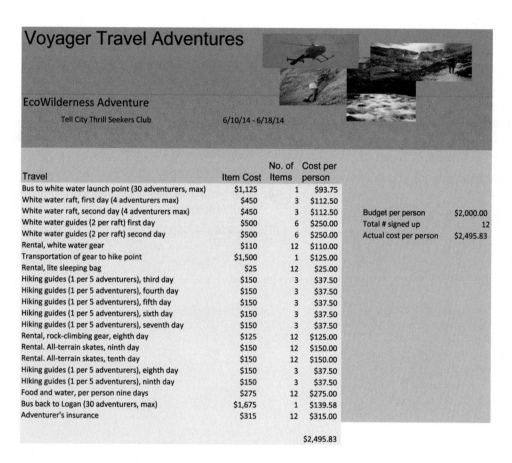

Voyager Travel Adventures

EcoWilderness Adventure

Tell City Thrill Seekers Club   6/10/14 - 6/18/14

Travel	Item Cost	No. of Items	Cost per person			
Bus to white water launch point (30 adventurers, max)	$1,125	1	$93.75			
White water raft, first day (4 adventurers max)	$450	3	$112.50			
White water raft, second day (4 adventurers max)	$450	3	$112.50	Budget per person	$2,000.00	
White water guides (2 per raft) first day	$500	6	$250.00	Total # signed up	12	
White water guides (2 per raft) second day	$500	6	$250.00	Actual cost per person	$2,495.83	
Rental, white water gear	$110	12	$110.00			
Transportation of gear to hike point	$1,500	1	$125.00			
Rental, lite sleeping bag	$25	12	$25.00			
Hiking guides (1 per 5 adventurers), third day	$150	3	$37.50			
Hiking guides (1 per 5 adventurers), fourth day	$150	3	$37.50			
Hiking guides (1 per 5 adventurers), fifth day	$150	3	$37.50			
Hiking guides (1 per 5 adventurers), sixth day	$150	3	$37.50			
Hiking guides (1 per 5 adventurers), seventh day	$150	3	$37.50			
Rental, rock-climbing gear, eighth day	$125	12	$125.00			
Rental. All-terrain skates, ninth day	$150	12	$150.00			
Rental. All-terrain skates, tenth day	$150	12	$150.00			
Hiking guides (1 per 5 adventurers), eighth day	$150	3	$37.50			
Hiking guides (1 per 5 adventurers), ninth day	$150	3	$37.50			
Food and water, per person nine days	$275	12	$275.00			
Bus back to Logan (30 adventurers, max)	$1,675	1	$139.58			
Adventurer's insurance	$315	12	$315.00			
			$2,495.83			

Student Name

Lesson 44—Apply

You are an adventure coordinator for Voyager Travel Adventures, and you have prepared a cost estimate for the Tell City Thrill Seekers Club's upcoming trip. The trip combines whitewater rafting, backcountry hiking, rock climbing, and all-terrain skating. You need to print the estimate, but you want to change the setup so it will print the way you want.

DIRECTIONS

1. Start Excel, if necessary, and open the **E44Apply** file from the data files for this lesson.

2. Save the workbook as **E44Apply_xx** in the location where your teacher instructs you to store the files for this lesson.

3. On the **Cost Analysis** worksheet, add comments as follow:

   a. Add a comment to cell **C11** indicating that this cost is based on using the Bluebird Cruiser.

   b. Add a comment to **C30** indicating that the bus will be provided by Adventure West.

4. Use the Show All Comments feature to view both comments together.

5. Delete the comment in cell **C11**.

6. On the **Cost Analysis** worksheet, create headers and footers as shown in Figure 44-2 on the next page.

   a. Use a built-in header in the center section.

   b. Press [ENTER] between the date and sheet name in the left footer section to create a second line.

   c. Use the **E44Apply_Voyager_Travel_Logo** file in the right footer section.

7. Change the bottom margin to 1.25".

8. Using the buttons on the PAGE LAYOUT tab, change the orientation of the **Cost Analysis** worksheet to landscape.

9. Spell check the workbook.

10. **With your teacher's permission**, print the **Cost Analysis** worksheet.

11. Save and close the file, and exit Excel.

Figure 44-2

Voyager Travel Adventures

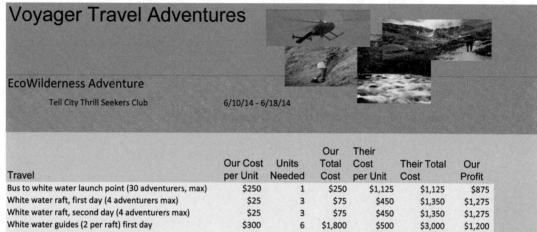

EcoWilderness Adventure

Tell City Thrill Seekers Club　　　　　　6/10/14 - 6/18/14

Travel	Our Cost per Unit	Units Needed	Our Total Cost	Their Cost per Unit	Their Total Cost	Our Profit
Bus to white water launch point (30 adventurers, max)	$250	1	$250	$1,125	$1,125	$875
White water raft, first day (4 adventurers max)	$25	3	$75	$450	$1,350	$1,275
White water raft, second day (4 adventurers max)	$25	3	$75	$450	$1,350	$1,275
White water guides (2 per raft) first day	$300	6	$1,800	$500	$3,000	$1,200
White water guides (2 per raft) second day	$300	6	$1,800	$500	$3,000	$1,200
Rental, white water gear	$12	12	$144	$110	$1,320	$1,176
Transportation of gear to hike point	$325	1	$325	$1,500	$1,500	$1,175
Rental, lite sleeping bag	$8	12	$90	$25	$300	$210
Hiking guides (1 per 5 adventurers), third day	$125	3	$375	$150	$450	$75
Hiking guides (1 per 5 adventurers), fourth day	$125	3	$375	$150	$450	$75
Hiking guides (1 per 5 adventurers), fifth day	$125	3	$375	$150	$450	$75
Hiking guides (1 per 5 adventurers), sixth day	$125	3	$375	$150	$450	$75
Hiking guides (1 per 5 adventurers), seventh day	$125	3	$375	$150	$450	$75
Rental, rock-climbing gear, eighth day	$20	12	$240	$125	$1,500	$1,260
Rental. All-terrain skates, ninth day	$35	12	$420	$150	$1,800	$1,380
Rental. All-terrain skates, tenth day	$35	12	$420	$150	$1,800	$1,380
Hiking guides (1 per 5 adventurers), eighth day	$125	3	$375	$150	$450	$75

7/10/2013
Cost Analysis　　　　　　　　　　　　　　　Student Name

Use Current Date and Insert Sheet Name buttons to create this footer section

Lesson 45

Using Copy and Paste Special

➤ What You Will Learn

Using Copy and Paste Options
Transposing Data
Combining Data with Copy and Paste Special

WORDS TO KNOW

Copied cells
Data copied to the
Clipboard.

Destination cells
The new location to
receive the pasted data.

Paste Special
An editing feature used
to control how data
is inserted from the
Clipboard to the current
file.

Transpose
An option that pastes
a column of data to a
row or a row of data to a
column in the current file.

Software Skills You can control how to paste data after you copy it to the Clipboard. For example, you may copy cells that contain formulas to the Clipboard but only want to paste the results. You can also use the time-saving Copy and Paste Special commands when you need to copy and combine data.

What You Can Do

Using Copy and Paste Special

- The **Paste Special** feature gives you control over how copied data is pasted.
- Some of the Paste Special options are available through the Paste button in the Clipboard group on the HOME tab of the Ribbon.

  ✓ *The Paste options available on the Paste button vary depending on the type of data copied.*

  - Paste 🗋: pastes the contents and the formatting of the copied cells.
  - Formulas ⌨: pastes only the formulas as shown in the Formula bar.
  - Formulas & Number Formatting 🗒: pastes formulas (not results) and the number formats, but no additional formatting, such as color fills.
  - Keep Source Formatting 📋: copies the formula contained in the copied cells along with the cell formatting.
  - No Borders 🗋: pastes the contents and formatting of the copied cells, except for borders.
  - Keep Source Column Widths 🗋: pastes the column widths of the selected cells.
  - Transpose 🗋: pastes a column of data in the copy area to a row or a row of data in the copy area to a column.
  - Values 🗋: pastes only the values as shown in the cells.

- Values & Number Formatting 🗒: pastes the results of formulas (and not the formulas themselves), along with number formats. Additional formatting, such as text colors, is not copied.
- Values & Source Formatting 🗒: pastes the values as shown in the cells along with the cell formatting.
- Formatting 🖌: pastes just the formatting of the copied cells.
- Paste Link 🗒: pastes a link to the data.
- Linked Picture 🗒: creates a link to the source image.
- Picture 🗒: pastes a picture of the data.

- Some paste options are only available through the Paste Special dialog box.
    - Comments: pastes only the comments attached to the copied cells.
    - Validation: pastes data validation rules for the copied cells.
    - Operation options, such as Add, Subtract, Multiply, and Divide, specify the mathematical operation to use when data from the copy area is combined with data in the paste area.
    - Skip blanks in the copy area so they do not overwrite data in the paste area.
- You can change the formatting that's copied after a paste operation using the Paste Options button 🗒 (Ctrl)▾ that appears on the worksheet next to the copied data.

Try It!   **Using Paste Special Commands on the Paste Options Menu**

1 Start Excel, if necessary, and open the **E45Try** file from the data files for this lesson.

2 Save the file as **E45Try_xx** in the location where your teacher instructs you to store the files for this lesson.

3 Add a header that has your name at the left, the date code in the center, and the page number code at the right, and change back to Normal view.

4 On Sheet1, click B11 > HOME > Copy 🗒.

5 Click cell C23 > Paste 🗒.

   ✓ Notice that the entire formula and the cell formatting is copied, which changes the value in the cell.

6 On the HOME tab, click the Paste down arrow ᴾᵃˢᵗᵉ▾ > Values 🗒.

7 Click cell C11 > HOME > Copy 🗒.

8 Click cell C24 > Paste down arrow ᴾᵃˢᵗᵉ▾ > Values & Number Formatting 🗒.

9 Click cell D11 > Copy 🗒.

10 Click cell C25 > Paste down arrow ᴾᵃˢᵗᵉ▾.

11 Hover the mouse over the various options to see how each affects the outcome in cell C25.

12 Click the Values & Source Formatting button 🗒.

13 Save the **E45Try_xx** file, and leave it open to use in the next Try It.

The Paste Options drop-down menu

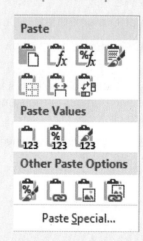

Try It!   Using the Paste Special Dialog Box

1 In the **E45Try_xx** file, click cell E11, and on the HOME tab, click Copy 📋.

2 Click cell C26 > Paste down arrow ᴾᵃˢᵗᵉ > Paste Special.

3 In the Paste Special dialog box, click Values and number formats > OK.

4 Click cell C28 > Copy 📋.

5 Select the range C23:C26, click the Paste down arrow ᴾᵃˢᵗᵉ > Paste Special.

6 In the Paste Special dialog box, click All using Source theme > OK. The cell data is deleted, and the cells return to the original format.

7 Save the **E45Try_xx** file, and leave it open to use in the next Try It.

Transposing Data

■ You can copy data in a column and then paste it into a row, or copy data in a row and then paste it into a column.

■ If you're **transposing** a group of cells containing formulas, Excel will adjust the cell references in the formulas so that they point to the correct transposed cells.

■ You can also transpose data with formulas and paste the formula values by selecting cells individually and selecting Paste Special options.

Try It!   Transposing Data

1 In the **E45Try_xx** file, on Sheet1, select the cell range B3:J3.

2 On the HOME tab, click Copy 📋.

3 Click cell B23 > Paste down arrow ᴾᵃˢᵗᵉ > Transpose 📋.

4 Select the cell range B11:J11 > Copy 📋.

5 Click cell C23 > Paste down arrow ᴾᵃˢᵗᵉ > Paste Special.

6 In the Paste Special dialog box, select both the Values and number formats and Transpose options, and click OK.

7 Save the **E45Try_xx** file, and leave it open to use in the next Try It.

Transposing data using the
Paste Special dialog box

Combining Data with Copy and Paste Special

- Using the Paste Special Operation commands, you can combine data as you paste it on top of existing data.

- When combining, Excel either adds, subtracts, multiplies, or divides the data in the **copied cells** with the data in the **destination cells**.

- Operation options include:
  - None: replaces destination cells with copied cells. This is the default setting.
  - Add: adds numeric data in copied cells to values in destination cells.
  - Subtract: subtracts numeric data in copied cells from values in destination cells.
  - Multiply: multiplies numeric data in copied cells by values in destination cells.
  - Divide: divides numeric data in copied cells by values in destination cells.

Try It!   **Combining Data with Copy and Paste Special**

1 In the **E45Try_xx** file, on Sheet1, select the cell range J4:J10.

2 On the HOME tab, click Copy 📋.

3 Click Sheet2 and click C4.

4 Click the Paste down arrow ^{Paste} > Paste Special.

5 In the Paste Special dialog box, under Operation, click Add.

6 Under Paste, select any additional Paste Special options as desired.

7 Click OK.

8 Save the **E45Try_xx** file, and close it.

Lesson 45—Practice

In this project, you will copy and paste data in various formats using the skills you learned in this lesson.

DIRECTIONS

1. Start Excel, if necessary, and open the **E45Practice** file from the data files for this lesson.

2. Create a new blank workbook, and save the workbook as **E45Practice_xx** in the location where your teacher instructs you to store the files for this lesson.

3. On the **Revenues** worksheet in the **E45Practice** file, select the cell range A1:E8 and, on the HOME tab, click **Copy** 📋.

   ✓ Because of the location of the graphic, you might find it easier to select this range by clicking cell G8 and dragging up to cell A1.

4. In the **E45Practice_xx** file, click cell A1 > Paste 📋. The data is copied, but the column widths are not right.

5. Click the **Paste Options** button 📋 (Ctrl)▾ > **Keep Source Column Widths**. Now the top rows of the sheet header match the rows copied from the **E45Practice** workbook.

6. Click cell B4, and edit the entry to read **3rd Qtr Revenue Analysis**.

7. On the **Revenues** sheet in the **E45Practice** workbook, select the cell range **A9:A16**, and click **Copy** 📋.

8. In the **E45Practice_xx** file, on Sheet1, click cell **A9** > **Paste** down arrow ^{Paste} > **Paste Special**.

9. In the Paste Special dialog box, click **Values and number formats** and **Transpose**, and click **OK**.

10. On the **Revenues** sheet in the **E45Practice** workbook, select the cell range **E9:E16**, and click **Copy** 📋.

11. In the **E45Practice_xx** file, on Sheet1, click cell **A11** > **Paste** down arrow ⬇️ > **Paste Special**.

12. Select **Values and number formats** and **Transpose**, and click **OK**. Refer to Figure 45-1.

13. Adjust the column widths and page breaks.

14. **With your teacher's permission**, print **Sheet1** in landscape orientation.

15. Save and close the **E45Practice_xx** file.

16. Close the **E45Practice** file.

Figure 45-1

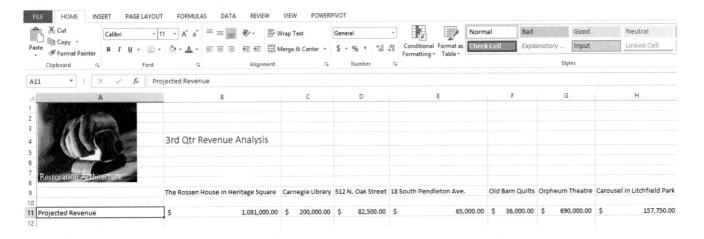

Lesson 45—Apply

You need to perform further third-quarter revenue analysis for Restoration Architecture. You'll use the Paste Special functions to transpose and reuse data, as well as add additional formulas and finalize print settings.

DIRECTIONS

1. Start Excel, if necessary, and open the **E45Apply_Revenues** file from the data files for this lesson.

2. Then, open **E45Apply** from the data files, and save the workbook as **E45Apply_xx**.

3. In the **E45Apply_xx** file, add a header that has your name at the left, the date code in the center, and the page number code at the right, and change back to **Normal** view.

4. Use the Paste Special dialog box to copy the formats from the **E45Apply_Revenues** file to the **E45Apply_xx** file as follows.

   a. Copy the formats from **A9:A16** and **E9:E16** to their corresponding rows in **E45Apply_xx**.

   b. Adjust the column widths.

   ✓ *Remember that the data is transposed.*

5. Select the cell range **B10:B16** in **E45Apply_Revenues** and transpose the values and number formats to **B10:H10** in the **E45Apply_xx** worksheet.

6. Add the data in ranges **C10:C16** and **D10:D16** on the **E45Apply_Revenue** worksheet to **B10:H10** in the **E45Apply_xx** worksheet. For each range, use the **Add** operation, **Values and number formatting**, and **Transpose** in the Paste Special dialog box.

7. On the **E45Apply_xx** worksheet, calculate the difference between the actual revenues and projected revenues for each project.

   a. Create a formula in **B12** that subtracts **B11** from **B10**.

   b. Copy that formula to the rest of the projects.

c. Format the cell range **B12:H12**. Use a different format for projects that earned less than the projected revenue, as shown in Figure 45-2.

d. Format the cell range **B10:H10** with an alternating fill of your choice, as shown in Figure 45-2.

8. **With your teacher's permission,** print the **E45Apply_xx** worksheet after making the following changes on the FILE > Print tab.

   a. Print Sheet1 in **Landscape Orientation**.

   b. Click **No Scaling**, and select **Fit Sheet on One Page**.

9. Save and close the file, and exit Excel.

Figure 45-2

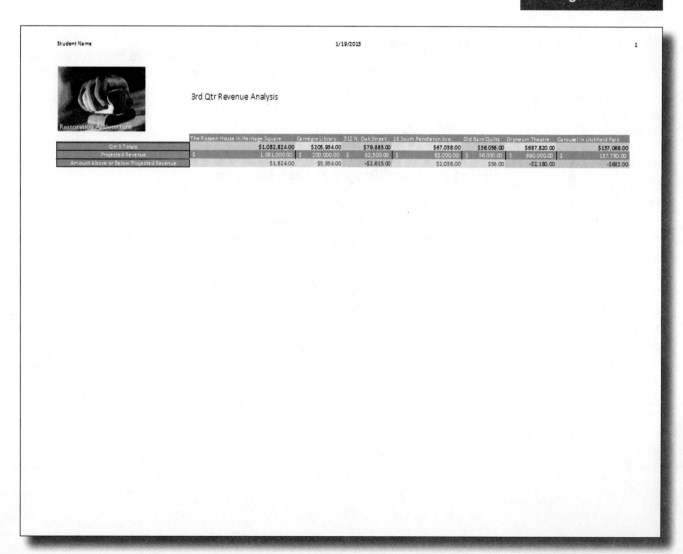

Lesson 46

Moving and Linking Data Between Workbooks

➤ **What You Will Learn**

Using Drag-and-Drop Between Windows
Linking Workbooks

WORDS TO KNOW

Drag-and-drop
To use the mouse to copy or move information from one location to another on a worksheet, between worksheets, or between workbooks.

Dependent
The workbook that references the data in the source.

External references
References to cells in other workbooks.

Link
A reference in a cell in a dependent workbook to data contained in a cell in a source workbook.

Source
The workbook that contains the data being referenced.

Software Skills   You can copy or move information between worksheets using the drag-and-drop procedure. By linking workbooks, you ensure that the destination file always contains the most recent information. Changes that you make in source workbooks will automatically appear in the destination workbooks.

What You Can Do

Using Drag-and-Drop Between Windows

- If you arrange open workbooks on the screen, you can use the **drag-and-drop** procedure to copy or move data between workbooks.
- To copy data, press the ⌈CTRL⌉ key while dragging the border of the selected range from the source to the destination workbook.
- To move data, drag the border of the selected range from the source to the destination workbook.

Try It! — Using Drag-and-Drop to Copy Data Between Windows

1. Start Excel, if necessary, and open the **E46Try** file from the data files for this lesson.

2. Click FILE > New > Blank workbook.

3. Save the new workbook as **E46Try_xx** in the location where your teacher instructs you to store the files for this lesson.

4. In the **E46Try_xx** file, add a header that has your name at the left, the date code in the center, and the page number code at the right, and change back to Normal view.

5. Click VIEW > Arrange All. The Arrange Windows dialog box appears.

6. Select Vertical > OK.

7. In the **E46Try_xx** file, on the VIEW tab, click View Side by Side 🔲.

   ✓ If you see only one workbook, click Reset Window Position on the VIEW tab to view the two open workbooks one above the other.

8. In the **E46Try** file, select the cell range A1:A33.

9. Press and hold CTRL, and drag the border of the selected range to cell A1 in the new workbook.

10. Release CTRL.

11. Save the **E46Try_xx** file, and leave it open to use in the next Try It.

Try It! — Using Drag-and-Drop to Move Data

1. In the **E46Try** file, select the range B3:B18.

2. Drag the border of the selected range to the **E46Try_xx** file. Position it so that the top cell is B3.

3. Save the **E46Try_xx** file, and leave it open to use in the next Try It.

Dragging data from one workbook to another

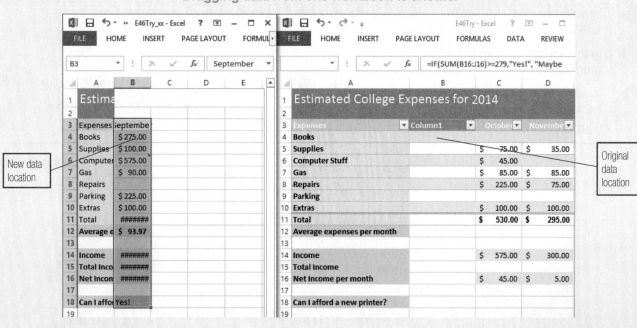

Linking Workbooks

- When you need to consolidate information from one or more workbooks into a summary workbook, create a **link**.
- The **source** workbook provides the original data.
- The **dependent** workbook contains the link to the **external references** in the source workbook.
- By default, workbook links update automatically. This means that as data in the source workbook is changed, the linked data in the dependent workbook is updated as well.
- If the dependent workbook is not open when data in the source workbook is changed, then the data in the dependent workbook will be changed later.

  ✓ *When you open a dependent workbook, you will be asked if you want to update it. You can choose to update at that time, or not to update at all.*

- You can link a file in one of three ways:
  - Copy data from the source workbook and paste it in the dependent workbook using the Paste Link option in the Paste Special dialog box. This creates an external reference that links the workbooks.
  - Type the external reference as a formula using the following format:

    =drive:\path\[file.xls]sheetname!reference

    For example:

    =Libraries\Documents\[report.xls]sheet1!H5

    ✓ *You may omit the path if the source and dependent files are saved in the same folder.*

  - While editing or creating a formula in the dependent workbook, you can include an external reference by selecting a cell or cells in the source workbook.
- When a cell in an external reference includes a formula, only the formula result displays in the dependent workbook.

  ✓ *To link to a cell while creating a formula, click the cell. For example, you could type =SUM(in a cell, then drag over cells located in another workbook, type) to complete the formula, and press* ENTER *. Links to the cells you selected are created automatically.*

- If possible, save linked workbooks in the same directory (folder). You should save the source workbook first, then save the dependent workbook.

Try It!   Linking Workbooks Using Paste Link

① Ensure that both the **E46Try** workbook and the **E46Try_xx** are arranged side by side.

② In the source workbook (**E46Try**), select the cell range C3:C16, and click Copy 🗐 .

③ In the **E46Try_xx** workbook, click cell C3 > HOME > Paste down arrow ⬇ᴾᵃˢᵗᵉ .

④ Click the Paste Link button 🗐 .

   OR

   Click Paste Special > Paste Link.

⑤ Save the **E46Try_xx** file and close the file.

⑥ Close the **E46Try** file without saving the changes.

(continued)

Try It!   Linking Workbooks Using Paste Link *(continued)*

Using Paste Link to connect data from one workbook to another

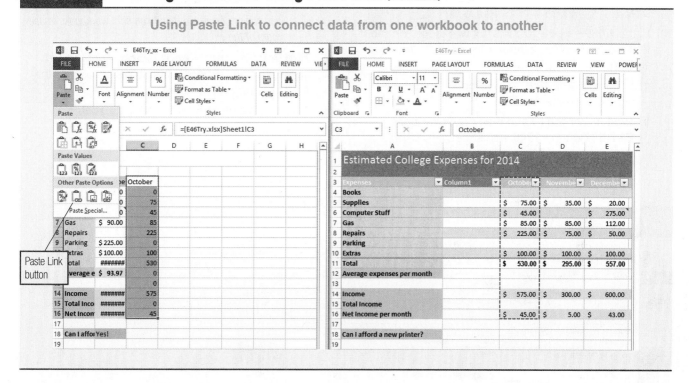

Lesson 46—Practice

In this project, you will copy and link data be workbooks using the skills you learned in this lesson.

DIRECTIONS

1. Start Excel, if necessary, and open the **E46Practice** file from the data files for this lesson.

2. Save the workbook as **E46Practice_xx** in the location where your teacher instructs you to store the files for this lesson.

3. In the **E46Practice_xx** file, for all worksheets, add a header that has your name at the left, the date code in the center, and the page number code at the right, and change back to **Normal** view.

4. Open the **E46Practice_TaxWS** file from the data files for this lesson. Save it as **E46Practice_TaxWS_xx** in the location your teacher instructs you to store the files for this lesson.

5. In the **E46Practice_TaxWS_xx** file, for all worksheets, add a header that has your name at the left, the date code in the center, and the page number code at the right, and change back to **Normal** view.

6. In the **E46Practice_TaxWS** file, click **VIEW** > **Arrange All** ⊟. The Arrange Windows dialog box opens.

7. Select **Horizontal** > **OK**. The two open workbook windows appear with one workbook above the other.

8. On the **1040** sheet of the **E46Practice_xx** workbook, scroll down to cell **F26**, click cell **F26** and click **Copy** 🖹.

   ✓ *Be careful to select the cell in row 26 and not the tax line item 26 (as indicated in column A).*

9. In the **E46Practice_TaxWS_xx** workbook, on the **IRA Deduction** worksheet, click cell **C6** > **HOME** > **Paste** down arrow ^{Paste} > **Paste Link**.

10. In the **E46Practice_TaxWS_xx** workbook, on the **IRA Deduction** worksheet, click cell **C7**, and type **=SUM(**.

   a. In the **E46Practice_xx** workbook, on the **1040** worksheet, click cell **E27**.

   b. Type a **comma (,)** and then drag over cells **E31:E37** on the **1040** worksheet.

    ✓ You may need to scroll down to select the cell range.

c. Type **)** to complete the formula, and press ENTER. Refer to Figure 46-1.

   ✓ You can minimize the Ribbon on both workbooks to see more of the worksheets.

11. **With your teacher's permission**, print the **IRA Deduction** worksheet. Submit the printout or the file for grading as required.

12. Save and close both files, and exit Excel.

Figure 46-1

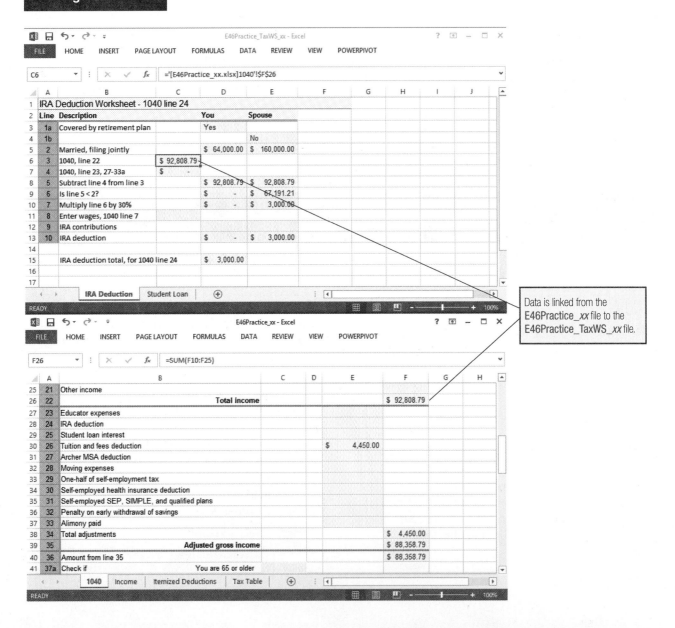

Lesson 46—Apply

You are an employee at Whole Grains Bread, and it's time to prepare your tax returns. Luckily, the company accountant has been showing you how she uses Excel to make tax preparation easier. You've entered most of the data, and now you want to determine if you can reduce your taxes further. You will use linking to pull data from the IncomeTax workbook into the special TaxWS workbook you've created.

DIRECTIONS

1. Start Excel, if necessary, and open the **E46Apply** file from the data files for this lesson. Save it as **E46Apply_xx** in the location where your teacher instructs you to store the files for this lesson.

2. In the **E46Apply_xx** file, for all worksheets, add a header that has your name at the left, the date code in the center, and the page number code at the right, and change back to **Normal** view.

3. Open the **E46Apply_TaxWS** file from the data files. Click **Enable Content**, and save it as **E46Apply_TaxWS_xx** in the location where you are storing files for this lesson.

4. In the **E46Apply_TaxWS_xx** file, for all worksheets, add a header that has your name at the left, the date code in the center, and the page number code at the right, and change back to Normal view.

5. Arrange the workbooks side by side in a vertical layout.

6. Copy and link data from the **E46Apply_xx** workbook to the **E46Apply_TaxWS_xx** workbook as follows:

Copy data from:		Link data to:	
Worksheet	**Cell**	**Worksheet**	**Cell**
1040	F10	IRA Deduction	C11
Income	B8	IRA Deduction	D12
Income	B17	IRA Deduction	E12
1040	F26	Student Loan	F4

7. Create a sum from data in the other workbook:

   a. On the **E46Apply_TaxWS_xx** workbook, on the **Student Loan** worksheet, click cell **F5**.

   b. Type **=SUM(** and drag over cells **E27:E28** on the **1040** worksheet in the **E46Apply_xx** workbook.

   c. Type a comma, and drag over cells **E31:E37** on the **1040** worksheet of the **E46Apply_xx** workbook.

   d. Type **)** and press ENTER .

8. Link data from the WSTax workbook back to the 1040 form:

Copy data from:		Link data to:	
Worksheet	**Cell**	**Worksheet**	**Cell**
IRA Deduction	D15	1040	E28

9. After looking it up in the tax tables, you discover that your federal income tax is $11,758. Enter this amount in cell F50 of the 1040 sheet in the **E46Apply_xx** workbook.

10. Widen column widths, as necessary. Refer to Figure 46-2 on the next page.

11. **With your teacher's permission**, print both the IRA Deduction and 1040 worksheets.

12. Save and close both workbooks, and exit Excel.

Figure 46-2

For Tax Filing 4/15/14

Form 1040

Line	Description	Amount			
6a	Yourself	1			
6b	Spouse	1			
6c	Dependents				
	Therese (222-22-2222)	1			
	Jorge (333-33-3333)	1			
6d	**Total exemptions**				4
7	Wages, salaries, tips, etc.				$ 88,740.00
8a	Taxable interest				$ 115.23
8b	Tax exempt interest				
9	Dividends				$ 78.56
10	Taxable refunds from state or local taxes				
11	Alimony				
12	Business income or (loss)				
13	Capital gain or (loss)				$ 3,875.00
14	Other gains or losses				
15a	Total IRA distributions	$31,598.00	15b	Taxable amount	$ -
16a	Total pensions and annuities		16b	Taxable amount	
17	Rental real estate				
18	Farm income or loss				
19	Unemployment compensation				
20a	Social Security benefits		20b	Taxable amount	
21	Other income				
22	**Total income**				$ 92,808.79
23	Educator expenses				
24	IRA deduction		$	1,200.00	
25	Student loan interest				
26	Tuition and fees deduction		$	4,450.00	
27	Archer MSA deduction				
28	Moving expenses				
29	One-half of self-employment tax				
30	Self-employed health insurance deduction				
31	Self-employed SEP, SIMPLE, and qualified plans				
32	Penalty on early withdrawal of savings				
33	Alimony paid				
34	Total adjustments				$ 5,650.00
35	**Adjusted gross income**				$ 87,158.79
36	Amount from line 35				$ 87,158.79
37a	Check if You are 65 or older				
	You are blind				
	Spouse is 65 or older				
	Spouse is blind				-
37b	Married filing separately and spouse itemizes				
38	Deduction (married jointly)				$ 7,850.00
39	Subtract line 38 from line 36				$ 79,308.79
40	Multiply $3,000 by tot. exemptions...				$ 12,000.00
41	Taxable income				$ 67,308.79
42	**Tax**				$ 11,758.00
43	Alternative minimum tax				
44	**Add lines 42 and 43**				$ 11,758.00
45	Foreign tax credit				
46	Credit for child and dependent care expenses		$	682.00	
47	Credit for elderly or disabled				
48	Education credits				
49	Retirement savings credit				
50	Child tax credit		$	1,200.00	
51	Adoption credit				
52	Credits from form 8396 or 8859				
53	Other credits from form 3800 or 8801				
54	Total credits				$ 1,882.00
55	Subtract line 54 from line 44				$ 9,876.00
56	Self-employment tax				
57	Social security tax and Medicare tax on tip income				
58	Tax on IRAs				
59	Advanced EIC payments				
60	Household employment taxes				
61	**Total tax**				$ 9,876.00
62	Federal income tax withheld		$	9,761.40	
63	2010 estimated tax payments				
64	Earned income credit				
65	Excess social security tax and tier 1 RRTA tax withheld				
66	Additional child tax credit				
67	Amount paid with extension to file				
68	Other payments				
69	**Total payments**				$ 9,761.40
70	This is the amount you OVERPAID				$ -
71a	Amount to be refunded to you				$ -
72	Amount to be applied to 2011 tax				
73	The amount you OWE				$ 114.60
74	Estimated tax penalty				

Lesson 47

Working with 3-D Formulas

➤ What You Will Learn

Creating 3-D Formulas
Duplicating a Workbook Window

Software Skills   You can create a 3-D formula to reference values in the same cells, across multiple worksheets. For example, you may want to total data from several worksheets into a summary worksheet. When you need to look at more than one of the worksheets in a workbook, create a duplicate workbook window.

What You Can Do

Creating 3-D Formulas

- Create a **3-D formula** when you want to summarize data from several worksheets into a single worksheet.

- A 3-D formula contains references to the same cell or range of cells on several worksheets in the same workbook. These cell references are called **3-D references**.

- You can refer to the same cell/range on consecutive worksheets (e.g., Sheet1, Sheet2, Sheet3) or non-consecutive worksheets (e.g., Sheet1 and Sheet4).
  Example: =Sheet1!G24+Sheet4!G24

  ✓ *This formula adds the values in the same cell (cell G24) of the non-consecutive worksheets Sheet1 and Sheet4.*

  Example: =SUM(Sheet1:Sheet3!G24)

  ✓ *This formula adds the values in the same cell (G24) in consecutive worksheets Sheet1, Sheet2, and Sheet3.*

- As you create or edit a formula, you can select the cells of a 3-D reference in the worksheets or type them in the formula.

- When typing a 3-D formula, use an exclamation point to separate the sheet name(s) from the cell reference(s); for example, April!G41+September!G41.

- Use a colon (:) between sheet names to indicate a range of worksheets; for example, April:June!B23:D45 or Sheet2:Sheet3!C21.

- Single quotation marks surround a sheet name that contains a space; for example,'NW Region'D14+'SW Region'D14 or 'Tax 2001':'Tax 2003'G23.

- Combine a 3-D reference with a function to create a formula that references data on different worksheets; for example, =SUM(Exp2000:Exp2002!C14:C22).

WORDS TO KNOW

3-D formula
An equation that references values across worksheets.

3-D reference
A reference to a value from any sheet or range of sheets used in a 3-D formula.

Duplicate workbook window
An option that allows you to view an exact copy of the active workbook.

Try It!   **Creating a 3-D Reference in a Formula**

1. Start Excel, if necessary, and open the **E47Try** file from the data files for this lesson.

2. Save the file as **E47Try_xx** in the location where your teacher instructs you to store the files for this lesson.

3. For all worksheets, add a header that has your name at the left, the date code in the center, and the page number code at the right, and change back to Normal view.

4. On the Grades worksheet, click cell B5.

5. Type **=AVERAGE('Sem 1:Sem 2'!H5**.

   ✓ *Remember to type single or double quotation marks surrounding sheet names that contain spaces.*

   ✓ *H5 is the cell that contains the first test score on each of the first two worksheets.*

6. Type **)** and press ENTER .

7. Save the **E47Try_xx** file, and leave it open to use in the next Try It.

Creating a 3-D reference to a cell
in a different worksheet

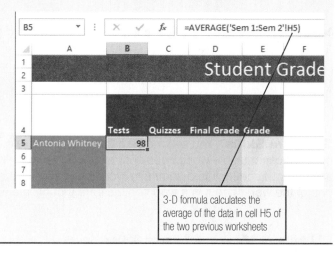

3-D formula calculates the average of the data in cell H5 of the two previous worksheets

---

Try It!   **Creating a 3-D Reference for a Range of Worksheets in a Formula**

1. In the **E47Try_xx** file, click cell C5 in the Grades worksheet.

2. Type **=AVERAGE('Sem 1:Sem 2'!B5:G5**.

   ✓ *Remember to type single or double quotation marks surrounding sheet names that contain spaces.*

   ✓ *B5:G5 is the range of cells that contain the first row of quiz scores on each of the first two worksheets.*

3. Type **)** and press ENTER .

4. Save the **E47Try_xx** file, and leave it open to use in the next Try It.

Creating a 3-D reference to a range of
cells in a different worksheet

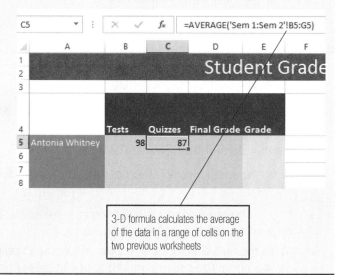

3-D formula calculates the average of the data in a range of cells on the two previous worksheets

Duplicating a Workbook Window

■ To view more than one worksheet of the active workbook at the same time on the screen, use the New Window button on the VIEW tab to make a **duplicate workbook window**.

　✓ *When the new workbook window appears, it is maximized; to see both windows you must arrange them on-screen.*

　● Use the Arrange All button on the VIEW tab to view the duplicate windows on the screen at the same time.

● In each window, click the sheet tab of the sheet you want to view.

● The number of duplicate windows that can be opened is determined by the amount of your system memory and the size of your monitor.

● You can add or edit data in the original or the duplicate window. All edits will be reflected in the other workbook automatically.

■ If you close a duplicate window, the workbook remains open.

Try It!　　**Duplicating a Workbook Window**

① In the **E47Try_xx** file, click the VIEW tab.

② Click the New Window button ⊞ New Window .

　✓ *The new window appears over the top of the old workbook.*

③ Click the Arrange All button ⊟.

④ Select the arrangement you prefer:
　■ Tiled　　■ Vertical
　■ Horizontal　■ Cascade

⑤ Click OK.

⑥ Close the duplicate window (**E47Try_xx:2**).

⑦ Save the changes to the **E47Try_xx** file, and close it.

Lesson 47—Practice

In this project, you will add 3-D formulas to a worksheet to summarize the data from several worksheets using the skills you learned in this lesson.

DIRECTIONS

1. Start Excel, if necessary, and open the **E47Practice** file from the data files for this lesson.

2. Save the workbook as **E47Practice_xx** in the location where your teacher instructs you to store the files for this lesson.

3. For all worksheets, add a header that has your name at the left, the date code in the center, and the page number code at the right, and change back to **Normal** view.

4. On the **Qtr 3** worksheet, in cell **C10**, type the formula =SUM(July:September!C10).

5. Enter the following 3-D formula in cell **C11**:
　a. Type =SUM(.

　b. Click cell **C11** of the **July** worksheet.

　c. Press [SHIFT], and click the tab of the **September** worksheet.

　d. Press [ENTER] to complete the formula.

6. Copy the formula from cell **C11** to the cell range **C12:C25**.

7. Copy the formulas in the cell range **C10:C25** to the cell range **D10:F25**. Refer to Figure 47-1 on the next page.

8. Adjust column widths to fit the data, if necessary.

9. **With your teacher's permission**, print the **Qtr 3** worksheet.

10. Save and close the file, and exit Excel.

Figure 47-1

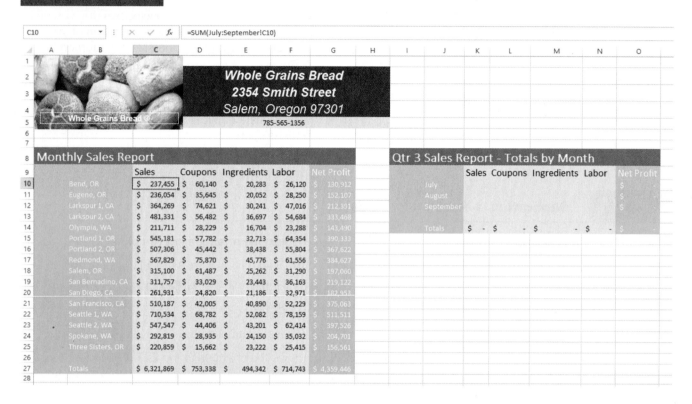

| C10 | ▾ | : | × | ✓ | *fx* | =SUM(July:September!C10) |

	Sales	Coupons	Ingredients	Labor	Net Profit
Bend, OR	$ 237,455	$ 60,140	$ 20,283	$ 26,120	$ 130,912
Eugene, OR	$ 236,054	$ 35,645	$ 20,052	$ 28,250	$ 152,107
Larkspur 1, CA	$ 364,269	$ 74,621	$ 30,241	$ 47,016	$ 212,391
Larkspur 2, CA	$ 481,331	$ 56,482	$ 36,697	$ 54,684	$ 333,468
Olympia, WA	$ 211,711	$ 28,229	$ 16,704	$ 23,288	$ 143,490
Portland 1, OR	$ 545,181	$ 57,782	$ 32,713	$ 64,354	$ 390,333
Portland 2, OR	$ 507,306	$ 45,442	$ 38,438	$ 55,804	$ 367,622
Redmond, WA	$ 567,829	$ 75,870	$ 45,776	$ 61,556	$ 384,627
Salem, OR	$ 315,100	$ 61,487	$ 25,262	$ 31,290	$ 197,060
San Bernadino, CA	$ 311,757	$ 33,029	$ 23,443	$ 36,163	$ 219,122
San Diego, CA	$ 261,931	$ 24,820	$ 21,186	$ 32,971	$ 182,953
San Francisco, CA	$ 510,187	$ 42,005	$ 40,890	$ 52,229	$ 375,063
Seattle 1, WA	$ 710,534	$ 68,782	$ 52,082	$ 78,159	$ 511,511
Seattle 2, WA	$ 547,547	$ 44,406	$ 43,201	$ 62,414	$ 397,526
Spokane, WA	$ 292,819	$ 28,935	$ 24,150	$ 35,032	$ 204,701
Three Sisters, OR	$ 220,859	$ 15,662	$ 23,222	$ 25,415	$ 156,561
Totals	$ 6,321,869	$ 753,338	$ 494,342	$ 714,743	$ 4,359,446

Monthly Sales Report

Qtr 3 Sales Report - Totals by Month

	Sales	Coupons	Ingredients	Labor	Net Profit
July					$ -
August					$ -
September					$ -
Totals	$ -	$ -	$ -	$ -	$ -

Lesson 47—Apply

As sales director at Whole Grains Bread, you designed a workbook to track three months' worth of sales at each of your various locations. It is almost complete, but you need to add 3-D formulas to summarize the monthly totals into a final set of totals for the quarter.

DIRECTIONS

1. Start Excel, if necessary, and open the **E47Apply** file from the data files for this lesson.

2. Save the workbook as **E47Apply_xx** in the location where your teacher instructs you to store the files for this lesson.

3. For all worksheets, add a header that has your name at the left, the date code in the center, and the page number code at the right, and change back to **Normal** view.

4. Duplicate the workbook window, and arrange the windows vertically.

5. Display the **July** worksheet in the left window, and the **Qtr 3** worksheet in the right window.

6. Use Paste Options to link the values in the range **C27:G27** on the **July** worksheet to the range **K10:O10** on the **Qtr 3** sheet.

7. In the left window, change to the **August** worksheet, and link the values in the range **C27:G27** to the range **K11:O11** in the **Qtr 3** sheet.

8. In the left window, change to the **September** worksheet, and link the values in the range **C27:G27** to the range **K12:O12** in the **Qtr 3** sheet.

9. In cells **K14:O14**, enter formulas to calculate totals for the quarterly sales, coupons, ingredients, labor costs, and net profit. Refer to Figure 47-2.

10. Close the duplicate window (the right window).

11. Adjust the column widths, as necessary.

12. Spell check the entire workbook.

13. **With your teacher's permission,** print the **Qtr 3** worksheet in Landscape Orientation on one page.

14. Save and close the workbook, and exit Excel.

Figure 47-2

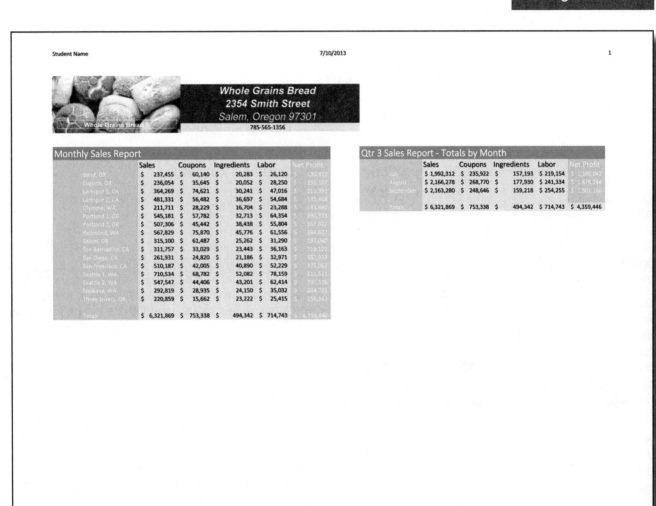

Lesson 48

Working with Data Validation and Macros

➤ **What You Will Learn**

Setting Data Validation
Adding the DEVELOPER Tab to the Ribbon
Managing Macro Security
Saving a Workbook That Contains Macros
Recording a Macro
Running a Macro

WORDS TO KNOW

Data validation
A feature in Excel that
you can use to define
restrictions on what data
can or should be entered
in a cell.

DEVELOPER tab
An optional Ribbon tab
that contains commands
for advanced users,
such as commands for
creating and managing
macros.

Error alert
A feature in Excel that
you can use to warn
users when they enter
invalid data.

Input message
A feature in Excel that
you can use to guide
users to enter valid data.

Macro
A series of recorded
actions that can be
replayed when needed.
The recorded actions are
carried out automatically
for the user.

Software Skills   Excel can help you improve the quality and efficiency of data
entered in your workbook. You can use data validation to assist users to enter
accurate and consistent data. You can create a macro to automate the performance
of a sequence of tasks.

What You Can Do

Setting Data Validation

■ You can use **data validation** to control the type of data or the values that users
enter into a single cell or a range of cells.

   ● For example, you may want to restrict the data entered in a cell to a certain
range of dates or make sure that only positive whole numbers are entered.

■ You can configure data validation to prevent users from entering data that is not
valid. You can also choose to allow users to enter invalid data, and then provide
feedback about the entered data.

■ The data validation commands are located on the DATA tab, in the Data Tools
group.

■ What users see when they enter invalid data into a cell depends on how you
configure the data validation in the Data Validation dialog box.

■ You can use data validation to restrict numbers, dates, and times inside or
outside of a specified range.

   ● For example, you can specify a time frame between today's date and seven
days from today's date.

- You can also use data validation to validate data based on formulas or values in other cells.
  - For example, you can use data validation to set a maximum limit for salary bonuses of $3,600, based on the overall projected payroll value. If users enter more than $3,600 in the cell, they will see a validation message.
- Use an **input message** to offer users guidance about the type of data that you want entered in the cell.
  - For example, in an accounting workbook, you can set a cell to only allow account numbers that are exactly nine characters long. When users select the cell, you can show them a message such as "Enter a nine-digit account number."
- You can choose to show an input message when the user selects the cell, and the input message will appear near the cell.
- Use an **error alert** to notify users when they enter invalid data in a cell.
  - For example, if users type a five-digit number in the cell that requires a nine-digit number, you can use data validation to display an error alert.
- Input messages and error alerts appear only when data is typed directly into the cell or cells with data validation.

  ✓ *Input messages and error alerts do not appear when a user enters data in the cell using copy or fill.*

- You can choose to visually alert users to cells with invalid data by using the Circle Invalid Data button.
- To remove data validation, select the cell or cell range with data validation, click Data Validation, and click the Clear All button in the Data Validation dialog box.

Macro security
A macro setting that enables or disables macros when the workbook is opened by a person other than the person who created the file. The default security setting is to disable macros.

VBA
Visual Basic for Applications, the programming language used to create macros.

.xlsm
The file extension that is used for an Excel 2007–2013 file that contains a macro.

Try It!   **Setting Data Validation**

1. Start Excel, if necessary, and open the **E48Try** file from the data files for this lesson.

2. Save the file as **E48Try_xx** in the location where your teacher instructs you to store the files for this lesson.

3. Add a header that has your name at the left, the date code in the center, and the page number code at the right, and change back to Normal view.

4. Adjust the column widths, as necessary.

5. On Sheet1, click the cell range B4:B10.

6. Click the DATA tab, and click Data Validation 🗏. The Data Validation dialog box appears.

7. In the Settings tab, in the Allow list, click the drop-down arrow, and click Decimal. The Ignore blank checkbox is checked by default.

8. In the Data list, check that between is selected.

9. In the Minimum text box, type **1**.

10. In the Maximum text box, type **500**.

11. Click the Input Message tab. The Show input message when cell is selected is checked by default.

12. In the Title text box, type **Overbudget**.

13. In the Input message text box, type **You might go over budget**.

14. Click OK. Notice that the amount in B6 is outside of the restricted range set in the data validation, and the input message appears.

15. Click cell B8, and type **600**. Press [ENTER]. Notice the error message that appears because you restricted the maximum value to 500.

(continued)

Try It!   **Setting Data Validation** *(continued)*

16   Click Cancel.

17   Save the **E48Try_xx** file, and leave it open to use in the next Try It.

The Data Validation dialog box

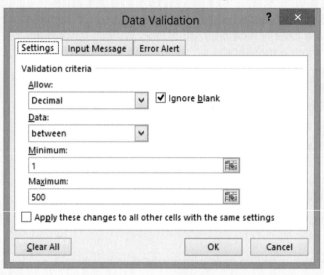

Adding the DEVELOPER Tab to the Ribbon

■ The **DEVELOPER tab** on the Ribbon contains useful commands for creating and running a **macro**.

■ The default setting is for Excel to not display the DEVELOPER tab.

■ You do not have to enable the DEVELOPER tab in order to record a macro; however, having the DEVELOPER tab available makes the process of recording and running macros easier.

■ After you add the DEVELOPER tab to the Ribbon, you can see the status of a macro in progress on the Status bar. When you record a macro, the command to stop a macro is available on the Status bar.

Try It!   **Adding the DEVELOPER Tab to the Ribbon**

1   In the **E48Try_xx** file, click FILE > Options.

2   Click Customize Ribbon.

3   Under Customize the Ribbon, in the Main Tabs list, click the Developer checkbox.

4   Click OK. The DEVELOPER tab appears.

5   Leave the **E48Try_xx** file open to use in the next Try It.

Managing Macro Security

- To minimize the risk of a macro virus or other malware threat contained in a macro, Excel has a **macro security** feature.
- Excel's default setting is to disable all macros, and to display a notification option when working with a file that contains macros.
- When you open a macro-enabled workbook, you can click Enable Content in the security warning notification to enable the macros.

Saving a Workbook That Contains Macros

- The default file extension for Excel 2013 is **.xlsx**. This file format cannot contain macros, by design, to avoid potential malware threats associated with macros.
- A workbook must be saved in .xlsm format in order to enable it to store macros.

  ✓ *When you save a file in .xlsm format, it does not overwrite the original in .xlsx format.*

Try It! **Saving a Workbook That Contains Macros**

1 In the **E48Try_xx** file, click FILE > Save As.

2 Navigate to the location where your teacher instructs you to store the files for this lesson.

3 Open the Save as type drop-down list, and click Excel Macro-Enabled Workbook.

4 Click Save, and leave the **E48Try_xx** file open to use in the next Try It.

Recording a Macro

- The macro recorder records every action you take and stores them in a macro that you can later play back to reproduce the steps.
- You can record a macro that includes steps such as typing text, selecting cells or cell ranges, clicking commands on the Ribbon, and formatting cells, rows, or columns.
- The macro recorder uses the Visual Basic for Applications (**VBA**) programming language to create macros.
- The commands for recording, creating, and deleting macros are available on the DEVELOPER tab on the Ribbon.
- When you record a macro, Excel records the actual addresses of the cells by default.
  - For example, if the active cell happens to be cell D2 when you begin recording a macro that makes the active cell bold, the macro will always make cell D2 bold, regardless of the position of the active cell when you run that macro.
- You can also record a macro that will perform the recorded action on the cell or cell range selected before running the macro.
- Recording a macro requires planning and some practice.
- It is not uncommon to have to record a macro several times because of errors made during the recording process.

- If you make a mistake while recording a macro, you can delete it by clicking the Macros button in the Code group on the DEVELOPER tab. In the Macro dialog box, click Delete.
- You can name a macro to make it easier to reference.
  - The first character of the macro name must be a letter.
  - You can use letters, numbers, or underscore characters in the name of a macro; however, you cannot use spaces in a macro name.
- You can assign a macro in three ways:
  - Define a shortcut key combination when you create the macro.

    ✓ *If you choose a shortcut key that Excel has already assigned to another action, the macro will override the other action in this workbook.*

  - Add the macro to the Quick Access Toolbar.

    ✓ *You can customize the Quick Access Toolbar by clicking the Customize Quick Access Toolbar button, selecting Macros in the Choose commands from list, and selecting the desired macro.*

  - Add the macro to the Ribbon.

    ✓ *You can customize the Ribbon from the Customize Ribbon tab in the Options tab of the FILE tab.*

Try It!   **Recording a Macro**

1 In the **E48Try_xx** file, on Sheet1, click the DEVELOPER tab.

2 In the Code group, click Record Macro 🖿. The Record Macro dialog box opens.

3 In the Macro Name text box, type **ColumnWidth**.

4 In the Shortcut key text box, type **w**.

✓ *The shortcut key must be different from any shortcut key Excel has already assigned to another action. CTRL + C is already assigned to the copy action.*

5 Check that the Store macro in list has This Workbook selected.

6 Click OK. The recording begins.

7 Press CTRL + HOME .

✓ *This will select cell A1 when the macro is run.*

8 Press CTRL + A .

✓ *This will select all cells in the worksheet.*

9 Click HOME > Format > AutoFit Column Width.

✓ *This will autofit the column width when the macro is run.*

10 Press CTRL + HOME .

11 Click the Stop Recording button ☐ on the Status bar. The recording stops.

12 Save and close the file.

The Record Macro dialog box

Running a Macro

■ You can run a macro in four ways:

● Use the Macros button on the DEVELOPER tab to open the Macro dialog box from which you can select the macro you want.

● Use a shortcut key combination that you define when you create the macro.

● Assign a macro to the Quick Access Toolbar, and run it from its button.

● Assign a macro to the Ribbon, and run it from its button.

Try It!   **Running a Macro**

1 Open the **E48Try_xx** file, from the data files for this lesson, and click Enable Content.

2 Click Sheet2.

3 Press CTRL + W . The macro runs on Sheet2.

4 Save and close the file.

Lesson 48—Practice

In this project, you will set data validation and an error alert using the skills you learned in this lesson.

DIRECTIONS

1. Start Excel, if necessary, and open the **E48Practice** file from the data files for this lesson.

2. Save the file as **E48Practice_xx** in the location where your teacher instructs you to store the files for this lesson.

3. For all worksheets, add a header that has your name at the left, the date code in the center, and the page number code at the right, and change back to **Normal** view.

4. Click the **Qtr3** worksheet.

5. Select the cell range **D10:F12**.

6. Click **DATA** > **Data Validation** ☒.

7. In the Settings tab, in the Allow list, click the drop-down arrow, and click Whole numbers. The Ignore blank checkbox is checked by default.

8. In the Data list, select **greater than or equal to**.

9. In the Minimum text box, type **225000**.

10. Click the **Input Message** tab, and uncheck **Show input message when cell is selected**.

11. Click the **Error Alert** tab. The Show error alert after invalid data is entered is checked by default.

12. In the **Style** list, select **Warning**.

13. In the **Title** text box, type **Low Profit**.

14. In the **Error message** text box, type **This will affect the Net Profit. Contact the store manager immediately.**

15. Click **OK**.

16. Complete the **Coupons**, **Ingredients**, and **Labor** columns with the data shown in Figure 48-1. Click **Yes** for each error alert.

17. **With your teacher's permission,** print the **Qtr3** worksheet. Submit the printout or the file for grading as required.

18. Save and close the file, and exit Excel.

Figure 48-1

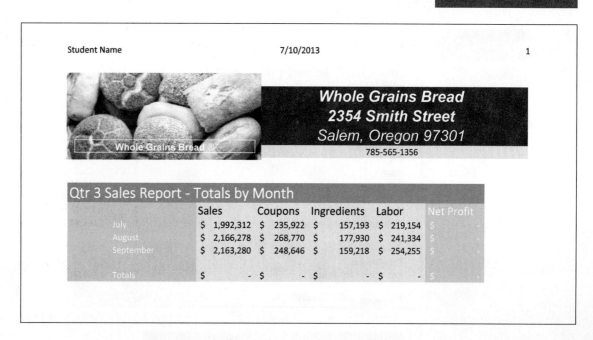

| | Student Name | | 7/10/2013 | | | 1 |

Whole Grains Bread
2354 Smith Street
Salem, Oregon 97301
785-565-1356

Whole Grains Bread ®

Qtr 3 Sales Report - Totals by Month

	Sales	Coupons	Ingredients	Labor	Net Profit
July	$ 1,992,312	$ 235,922	$ 157,193	$ 219,154	$ -
August	$ 2,166,278	$ 268,770	$ 177,930	$ 241,334	$ -
September	$ 2,163,280	$ 248,646	$ 159,218	$ 254,255	$ -
Totals	$ -	$ -	$ -	$ -	$ -

Lesson 48—Apply

You are a college student, and you have created a worksheet to estimate your monthly expenses. You want to create a header that contains your name, the current date, and the page number. You will create a macro to automate the process of inserting a header.

DIRECTIONS

1. Start Excel, if necessary, and open the **E48Apply** file from the data files for this lesson.

2. Click **FILE** > **Save As**. Navigate to the location where your teacher instructs you to store the files for this lesson.

3. Open the **Save as** type drop-down list, and click **Excel Macro-Enabled Workbook (*.xlsm)**.

4. Change the file name to **E48Apply_xx**. Click **Save**.

5. Click **DEVELOPER** > **Record Macro** 📇.

6. In the Macro Name text box, type **Header**. Check that the **Store macro in** list has **This Workbook** selected.

7. In the **Description** text box, type **Adds a header with my name at the left, the date code in the center, and the page number code at the right, and changes back to Normal view.**

8. Click **OK**.

9. Click **VIEW** > **Page Layout** 📄.

10. Click the left header cell, and type your name.

11. Click in the center header cell, click **HEADER & FOOTER TOOLS DESIGN**, and click **Current Date** 🗓.

12. Click in the right header cell, on the **HEADER & FOOTER TOOLS DESIGN** tab, click **Page Number** #.

13. Click cell **A1**.

14. Click **VIEW** > **Normal** ▦.

15. Click the **Stop Recording** button ⬜ on the Status bar.

16. Add a new worksheet.

17. Click **DEVELOPER** > **Macros** 🗒 > **Run**.

18. Click **VIEW** > **Page Layout** 📄. Refer to Figure 48-2.

19. **With your teacher's permission,** print the entire workbook. Submit the printout or the file for grading as required.

20. Save and close the file, and exit Excel.

Figure 48-2

Student Name		1/23/2013		1

Estimated College Expenses for 2014

Expenses		September
Books	$	275.00
Supplies	$	100.00
Computer Stuff	$	300.00
Gas	$	90.00
Repairs	$	75.00
Parking	$	225.00
Extras	$	100.00
Total	$	1,165.00
Average expenses per month	$	**1,158.00**
Income	$	1,400.00
Total Income	$	1,400.00
Net Income per month	$	1,400.00
Can I afford a new printer?	Yes!	

Expense Analysis

End-of-Chapter Activities

➤ Excel Chapter 5—Critical Thinking

Finalize and Package Bakery P&L Statements

You are the Accounting Manager at Whole Grains Bread, and you've been working on this quarter's profit and loss statement (income statement). You need to create 3-D formulas, link to data stored in two other workbooks, and then print the result.

DIRECTIONS

1. Start Excel, if necessary, and open the **ECT05_P&L** file from the data files for this chapter. Save the workbook as **ECT05_P&L_xx** in the location where your teacher instructs you to store the files for this chapter.

2. Open the **ECT05_Sales** file from the data files for this chapter.

3. Arrange the two workbooks on-screen in a tiled fashion.

4. Copy cell **K17** on the **Qtr 3** sheet of the **ECT05_Sales** workbook, and paste link it to cell **F11** of the **ECT05_P&L_xx** workbook.

5. Copy cell **L17** on the **Qtr 3** sheet of the **ECT05_Sales** workbook, and paste it as a link to cell **E26** of the **ECT05_P&L_xx** workbook.

6. Close the **ECT05_Sales** workbook without saving changes.

7. Open the **ECT05** file from the data files for this chapter.

8. Save the workbook as **ECT05_xx**. Maximize the workbook window.

9. Copy the cell range **N13:N28** on the **Opening** sheet of the **ECT05** workbook, and link it to the cell range **C13:C28** of the **Qtr 3** sheet in that same workbook.

10. Copy the cell range **N13:N28** on the **Ending** sheet and link it to the cell range **F13:F28** of the **Qtr 3** sheet in the **ECT05_xx** workbook.

11. In cell **D13** of the **Qtr 3** sheet, create a 3-D formula that sums the values in **N13** of the **July Purchases**, **August Purchases**, and **September Purchases** sheets in the **ECT05_xx** workbook.

12. Copy this 3-D formula down the cell range **D14:D28** on the **Qtr 3** sheet in the **ECT05_xx** workbook.

13. Select the cell range **C30:D30** on the **Qtr 3** sheet in the **ECT05_xx** workbook, and click **Copy**.

    a. Click cell **E14** in the **ECT05_P&L_xx** workbook.

    b. Use Paste Special to transpose the data and paste the values only.

    c. Copy cell **F30** on the **Qtr 3** sheet on the **ECT05_xx** workbook, and paste its value in cell **E17** of the **ECT05_P&L_xx** workbook.

14. Adjust the column widths as needed. Refer to Illustration 5A on the next page.

15. Spell check the workbooks.

16. Print the **ECT05_P&L_xx** workbook:

    a. Reduce the scaling to fit the sheet on one page.

    b. Add a custom header that includes the date on the left, and the text **Prepared by** followed by your name on the right.

    c. Preview and, **with your teacher's permission**, print the worksheet.

17. Print the **Qtr 3** worksheet in the **ECT05_xx** workbook:

    a. Use Portrait orientation.

    b. Add a custom footer with your name in the center and the page number on the right.

    c. Preview and, **with your teacher's permission**, print the entire workbook.

18. Save and close all files, and exit Excel.

Illustration 5A

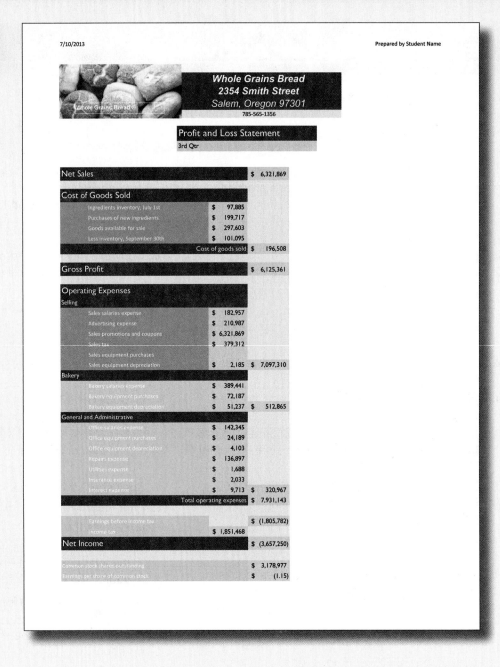

Whole Grains Bread
2354 Smith Street
Salem, Oregon 97301
785-565-1356

Profit and Loss Statement
3rd Qtr

Net Sales		$ 6,321,869
Cost of Goods Sold		
Ingredients inventory, July 1st	$ 97,885	
Purchases of new ingredients	$ 199,717	
Goods available for sale	$ 297,603	
Less inventory, September 30th	$ 101,095	
Cost of goods sold	$	196,508
Gross Profit		$ 6,125,361
Operating Expenses		
Selling		
Sales salaries expense	$ 182,957	
Advertising expense	$ 210,987	
Sales promotions and coupons	$ 6,321,869	
Sales tax	$ 379,312	
Sales equipment purchases		
Sales equipment depreciation	$ 2,185	$ 7,097,310
Bakery		
Bakery salaries expense	$ 389,441	
Bakery equipment purchases	$ 72,187	
Bakery equipment depreciation	$ 51,237	$ 512,865
General and Administrative		
Office salaries expense	$ 142,345	
Office equipment purchases	$ 24,189	
Office equipment depreciation	$ 4,103	
Repairs expense	$ 136,897	
Utilities expense	$ 1,688	
Insurance expense	$ 2,033	
Interest expense	$ 9,713	$ 320,967
Total operating expenses		$ 7,931,143
Earnings before income tax		$ (1,805,782)
Income tax	$ 1,851,468	
Net Income		$ (3,657,250)
Common stock shares outstanding		$ 3,178,977
Earnings per share of common stock		$ (1.15)

➤ Excel Chapter 5—Portfolio Builder

Publishing Bid Results

You work at the Michigan Avenue Athletic Club, and you've been put in charge of coordinating bids to have television monitors installed on all equipment throughout the facility. The plan is to phase in the installation over several months. You've received three bids for the work, and now you need to publish the findings on the company's Web site and prepare a coordinating memo to your boss. In addition, you were asked to do some research on the average price of a 50" flat screen television, since the upgrade plan includes installing two of them in the cycling studio.

DIRECTIONS

1. Start Excel, if necessary, and open the **EPB05** file from the data files for this chapter.

2. Save the workbook as **EPB05_xx** in the location where your teacher instructs you to store the files for this lesson.

3. Create a Web query:

   a. In the New Web Query dialog box, display the page **EPB05_Samsung50InchTV** from the data files for this chapter.

      ✓ *Click Allow blocked content, if necessary.*

   b. Click the yellow arrows next to the six items in the big table listing various televisions and their prices, and click **Import**.

   c. Import the data to cell **A7** of the **Samsung TV** worksheet.

4. Create another Web query:

   a. In the New Web Query dialog box, display the page **EPB05_Pioneer50InchTV** from the data files for this chapter.

   b. Click the yellow arrows next to each item in the big table listing various televisions and their prices, and click Import.

      ✓ *If asked to run scripts, click No.*

   c. Import the data to cell **A7** of the **Pioneer TV** worksheet.

5. Create a final Web query:

   a. In the New Web Query dialog box, display the page **EPB05_Philips50InchTV** from the data files for this chapter.

   b. Click the yellow arrows next to the six items in the big table listing various televisions and their prices, and click Import.

      ✓ *Click Allow blocked content, if necessary.*

   c. Import the data to cell **A7** of the **Philips TV** worksheet.

6. Publish the workbook as a single file web page:

   a. Use the file name **EPB05_xx.mht**.

   b. Publish the entire workbook

   c. Use the title **Upgrade Costs**.

   d. Turn on AutoRepublish

   e. Display the page in your Web browser. See Illustration 5B on the next page.

   f. Close the Web browser.

      ✓ *Click Allow blocked content, if necessary.*

7. Create a memo to your boss.

   a. Start Word, and open the **EPB05_Memo** document from the data files for this chapter.

   b. Save the document as **EPB05_Memo_xx** in the location where your teacher instructs you to store the files for this chapter.

   c. Replace *Student Name* with your own name.

   d. Change to the **EPB05_xx** workbook

   e. Select the range **A1:D20** on the **TV Screens for Equipment** worksheet, and click **Copy**.

   f. Link the data into the memo at the location shown in Illustration 5C on page 85. Keep the source formatting of the linked data.

   g. Adjust column widths of the linked data so the memo is only one page.

h. In the **EPB05_xx** workbook, type a formula in cell **E8** that computes the total cost for **Bid One**.

i. Copy that formula to cells **E14** and **E20**.

j. Apply cell formats to column E.

k. Change the value of the labor cost for **Bid Three** for the Workout Terrace cell (**D19**) to **$90**.

l. Save the **EPB05_xx** file, and return to Word. If needed, right-click the data and select **Update Link** to view your changes in the memo.

8. Spell check the memo.

9. **With your teacher's permission**, print the memo.

10. Save the memo and exit Word.

11. Save and close the workbook, and exit Excel.

Illustration 5B

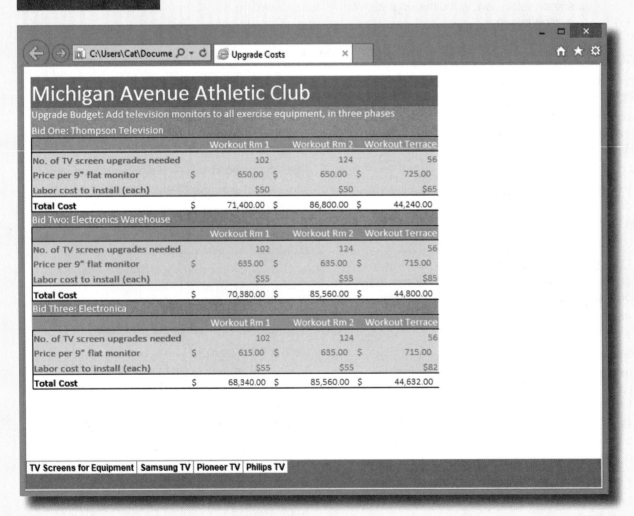

C:\Users\Cat\Docume   Upgrade Costs

Michigan Avenue Athletic Club

Upgrade Budget: Add television monitors to all exercise equipment, in three phases

Bid One: Thompson Television

		Workout Rm 1		Workout Rm 2		Workout Terrace
No. of TV screen upgrades needed		102		124		56
Price per 9" flat monitor	$	650.00	$	650.00	$	725.00
Labor cost to install (each)		$50		$50		$65
Total Cost	$	71,400.00	$	86,800.00	$	44,240.00

Bid Two: Electronics Warehouse

		Workout Rm 1		Workout Rm 2		Workout Terrace
No. of TV screen upgrades needed		102		124		56
Price per 9" flat monitor	$	635.00	$	635.00	$	715.00
Labor cost to install (each)		$55		$55		$85
Total Cost	$	70,380.00	$	85,560.00	$	44,800.00

Bid Three: Electronica

		Workout Rm 1		Workout Rm 2		Workout Terrace
No. of TV screen upgrades needed		102		124		56
Price per 9" flat monitor	$	615.00	$	635.00	$	715.00
Labor cost to install (each)		$55		$55		$82
Total Cost	$	68,340.00	$	85,560.00	$	44,632.00

TV Screens for Equipment | Samsung TV | Pioneer TV | Philips TV

**Michigan Avenue
Athletic Club**

Memo

To: Mr. Ray Peterson

From: Student Name

CC:

Date: June 23, 2014

Re: Status of Upgrade Bids

I've received the final bid for the addition of television monitors to all equipment throughout the facility. Here are the final numbers for your review:

Michigan Avenue Athletic Club

Upgrade Budget: Add television monitors to all exercise equipment, in three phases

Bid One: Thompson Television

	Workout Rm 1	Workout Rm 2	Workout Terrace	
No. of TV screen upgrades needed	102	124	56	
Price per 9" flat monitor	$ 650.00	$ 650.00	$ 725.00	
Labor cost to install (each)	$50	$50	$65	
Total Cost	$ 71,400.00	$ 86,800.00	$ 44,240.00	$ 202,440.00

Bid Two: Electronics Warehouse

	Workout Rm 1	Workout Rm 2	Workout Terrace	
No. of TV screen upgrades needed	102	124	56	
Price per 9" flat monitor	$ 635.00	$ 635.00	$ 715.00	
Labor cost to install (each)	$55	$55	$85	
Total Cost	$ 70,380.00	$ 85,560.00	$ 44,800.00	$ 200,740.00

Bid Three: Electronica

	Workout Rm 1	Workout Rm 2	Workout Terrace	
No. of TV screen upgrades needed	102	124	56	
Price per 9" flat monitor	$ 615.00	$ 635.00	$ 715.00	
Labor cost to install (each)	$55	$55	$90	
Total Cost	$ 68,340.00	$ 85,560.00	$ 45,080.00	$ 198,980.00

1

Chapter 6

(Courtesy Brocreative/Shutterstock)

Managing Large Workbooks

Lesson 49

Customizing the Excel Interface and Converting Text

> ## ➤ What You Will Learn
>
> Customizing the Quick Access Toolbar
> Customizing the Ribbon
> Customizing Excel Options
> Converting Text to Columns

Software Skills   Like other Office programs, Excel is designed to be customized to your needs. You can customize Excel Options, the Ribbon, and the Quick Access Toolbar to have easy access to the tools and features you use most often.

What You Can Do

Customizing the Quick Access Toolbar

- The Quick Access Toolbar (QAT) appears at the top-left corner of the Excel window. It provides a set of quick shortcuts to the most common functions and features.

- You can choose to show the Quick Access Toolbar below the Ribbon.

- By default the Quick Access Toolbar contains three buttons: Save, Undo, and Redo. You can also customize it by adding shortcuts to most other Excel features.

- To add any button to the Quick Access Toolbar, right-click it and select Add to Quick Access Toolbar.

- To remove a button from the Quick Access Toolbar, right-click it and choose Remove from Quick Access Toolbar.

- You can use the Quick Access Toolbar section of the Excel Options dialog box to add Excel features that don't appear on the tabs of the Ribbon.

- You can also use the Quick Access Toolbar section of the Excel Options dialog box to remove features or to reset any customizations.

Try It! — Customizing the Quick Access Toolbar

1 Start Excel, and create a new, blank workbook.

2 Click the REVIEW tab, right-click Spelling ✓, and click Add to Quick Access Toolbar.

3 Click Customize Quick Access Toolbar ⇟ > Sort Ascending.

4 Click FILE > Options > Quick Access Toolbar.

5 Click the Choose commands from drop-down arrow, and click Formulas Tab.

6 In the list of commands, click Average, and click the Add button [Add >>].

7 In the list below the Customize Quick Access Toolbar box, select Average, and click the Remove button [<< Remove].

8 Click the Reset button [Reset ▼] > Reset only Quick Access Toolbar.

9 Click Yes in the confirmation dialog box, and click OK. The Quick Access Toolbar is reset.

10 Leave the blank workbook and Excel open for the next Try It.

Customizing the Quick Access Toolbar

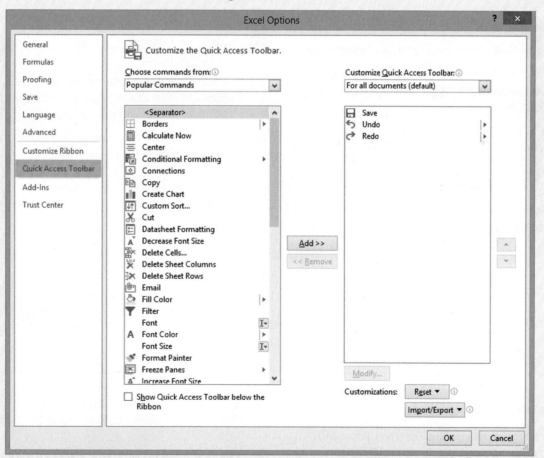

Customizing the Ribbon

- In Excel 2013 you can customize the Ribbon by adding commands that you use frequently or removing those commands that you don't use.

- You can create new groups on a Ribbon tab, and you can create a new tab with new groups.

- Commands for customizing the Ribbon are on the Customize Ribbon tab of the Excel Options dialog box.

- You can also use the Customize Ribbon section of the Excel Options dialog box to remove features or to reset any customizations.

Try It!   **Customizing the Ribbon**

1 In Excel, click FILE > Options to open the Excel Options dialog box.

2 Click Customize Ribbon.

3 On the right side of the dialog box, under Main Tabs, click to clear the check mark to the left of Page Layout.

4 Click the New Tab button New Tab .

5 In the Main Tabs box, click New Tab (Custom).

6 Click the Rename button Rename... , in the Display name box type **Learning Excel**, and click OK.

7 Click the Choose commands from drop-down arrow, and click Commands Not in the Ribbon.

8 In the commands list, scroll down, click Zoom In, and click the Add button Add >> .

9 In the commands list, click Zoom Out, and click the Add button Add >> .

10 Click OK to apply the change and close the Excel Options dialog box. Notice that the PAGE LAYOUT tab no longer appears on the Ribbon and that the new tab named New Tab displays.

11 Click New Tab to view the Learning Excel group of commands.

12 Click FILE > Options > Customize Ribbon.

13 Click the Reset button Reset ▾ > Reset all customizations.

14 Click Yes in the confirmation dialog box, and click OK. The Quick Access Toolbar and Ribbon are reset to the default settings.

15 Leave the blank workbook and Excel open to use in the next Try It.

Modified Ribbon

| FILE | HOME | INSERT | New Tab | FORMULAS | DATA | REVIEW | VIEW |

⊕ ⊖
Zoom Zoom
In   Out
Learning Excel

Customizing Excel Options

- There are more than 100 different options and settings that you can use to control the way Excel operates.

- Excel options are organized in categories, such as Formulas, Proofing, Save, and Add-Ins.

- You can view and set program options in the Excel Options dialog box accessed from the Backstage view.

- When you set up Microsoft Excel 2013 on your computer, you enter a user name and initials.

- Excel uses this information to identify you as the author of new workbooks that you create and save, and as the editor of existing workbooks that you open, modify, and save.

- In addition, your user name is associated with revisions that you make when you use the Track Changes features, and the initials are associated with comments that you insert.

- You can change the user name and initials using options in the General group in the Excel Options dialog box.

Try It!   Customizing Excel Options

1 In Excel, in the blank workbook, click FILE > Options.

2 On the General tab, under Personalize your copy of Microsoft Office, in the User name box, type your full name.

3 In the list on the left side of the dialog box, click Save to display the Save options.

4 Click Proofing to display the Proofing options.

5 Click Advanced, and scroll through the options.

6 Under Display options for this workbook, clear Show sheet tabs.

7 Under Display options for this worksheet, click the Gridline color button.

8 Select Blue (last color on the last row).

9 Click Cancel to close the Excel Options window without saving the changes.

10 Close the blank workbook without saving the changes, and leave Excel open to use in the next Try It.

Excel's advanced display options

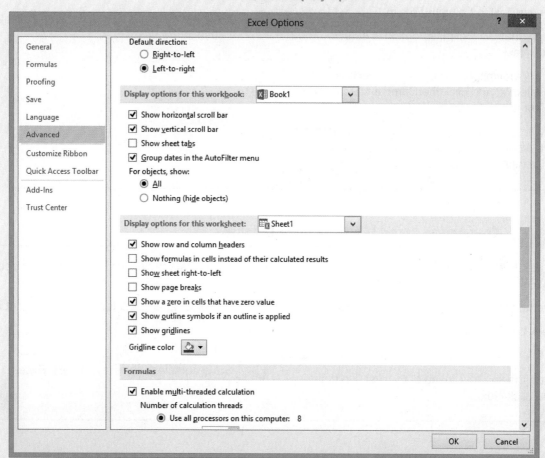

Converting Text to Columns

- When working with large amounts of text data in Excel, pre-planning is often critical.

  - For example, when creating a long list of customers, it's useful to place first names in one column and last names in another so that you can sort on the column with last names and arrange the customer list alphabetically.

- It is useful to separate out the parts of a customer's address into different columns—one each for street address, city, state, and ZIP Code—so the customer list can be sorted by state or ZIP Code.

- You can split the contents of one cell across several cells.

- You can split the contents of a single cell, a range, or an entire column in one step.

Try It!   Converting Delimited Text to Columns

1. In Excel, open the open the **E49Try** file from the data files for this lesson.

2. Save the file as **E49ATry_xx** in the location where your teacher instructs you to store the files for this lesson.

3. Select the cell range I6:I57.

4. Click DATA > Text to Columns 🖹 to display the Convert Text to Columns Wizard.

5. Verify that the Delimited option is selected, and click Next.

6. Under Delimiters, click the Tab check box to deselect it, and click the Comma check box to select it.

   ✓ After selecting the correct delimiter, the fields in the selected cell, range, or column will appear in the Data preview pane, separated by vertical lines.

7. To skip empty columns, click the Treat consecutive delimiters as one check box, and click Next.

8. In the Data preview window, click the last column to select it.

9. Under Column data format, click the Text option.

10. Click Finish.

11. Save the changes to the file, and leave it open to use in the next Try It.

Try It!   Converting Fixed Width Text to Columns

1. In the **E49Try_xx** file, select the cell range F6:F57.

2. On the DATA tab, click Text to Columns 🖹.

3. Click the Fixed width option, and click Next.

4. In the Data preview window, click 10 on the ruler.

5. Drag the line to the end of the first five digits, and click Next.

6. In the Data preview window, click the second column.

7. Under Column data format, click Do not import column (skip).

8. Click Finish.

9. Save and close the file, and exit Excel.

Lesson 49—Practice

Your manager at The Little Toy Shoppe wants you to create a newsletter to inform clients of new products and to entice them to return to the store on special sales days. Rob the intern has been keeping track of customer names and addresses in a new worksheet, but the worksheet is not formatted correctly. Unfortunately, Rob doesn't know the first thing about creating a workable database. In this project, you will take Rob's list and convert the data into usable columns.

DIRECTIONS

1. Start Excel, if necessary, and open **E49Practice** from the data files for this lesson.
2. Save the file as **E49Practice_xx** in the location where your teacher instructs you to store the files for this lesson.
3. Add a header to the worksheet that has your name at the left, the date code in the center, and the page number code at the right, and change back to **Normal** view.
4. Select the column headers for columns C and D, right-click the headers, and select **Insert** from the shortcut menu.
5. Select cells **E2** and **E3**, and drag them to cells **C2** and **C3**.
6. In cell **B5**, replace the text by typing **First Name**; type **Last Name** in cell **C5**.
7. Select the cell range **B6:B57**.
8. Click DATA > Text to Columns .
9. Verify that the **Delimited** option is selected, and click **Next**.
10. Under Delimiters, click the Comma check box to deselect it, click the **Space** check box to select it, and click **Next**.
11. Click the first column in the Data preview window, and under Column data format, click the **Text** option.
12. Click the second column in the Data preview window, and under Column data format, click the **Text** option.
13. Click **Finish**.
14. Click **OK** in the confirmation dialog box.
15. Click the **Customize Quick Access Toolbar** button , and click **Spelling**.
16. Click the **Customize Quick Access Toolbar** button , and click **Spelling** to remove it.
17. **With your teacher's permission**, print the worksheet. It should look similar to Figure 49-1 on the next page.
18. Save and close the file, and exit Excel.

Figure 49-1

	A	B	C	D	E	F	G
1							
2			The Little Toy Shoppe				
3			Customer Database				
4							
5	Title	First Name	Last Name		Address	City-State-Zip	Phone
6	Mrs.	Barbara	Adamson		7770 Dean Road	Cincinnati, OH 33240	844-1589
7	Mr.	Carlos	Altare		4125 Fairlinks Ave.	Carmel, IN 46231	298-1212
8	Mrs.	Diana	Bond		10208 E. Ridgefield Drive	Indian Blade, IN 46236	899-1712
9	Mrs.	Jan	Borough		7556 Hilltop Way	Cincinnati, OH 33254	291-3678
10	Mr.	Adam	Bounds		4943 Windridge Drive	Indianapolis, IN 42626	542-8151
11	Mrs.	Mary	Jane	Brink	704 Fairway Drive	Cincinnati, OH 33250	255-1655
12	Mr.	Shakur	Brown		5648 Hydcort	Indianapolis, IN 46250	842-8819
13	Mrs.	Rafiquil	Damir		14559 Senator Way	Indianapolis, IN 46226	844-9977
14	Mrs.	Diana	Dogwood		6311 Douglas Road	Wayne's Town, OH 33502	251-9052
15	Mrs.	Lucy	Fan		5784 N. Central	Indianapolis, IN 46268	255-6479
16	Mr.	Joshua	Fedor		1889 E. 72nd Street	Indian Blade, IN 46003	251-4796

Lesson 49—Apply

You are creating a newsletter to inform clients of new products and to entice them to return to the store on special sales days. You are working with a worksheet of customer names and addresses created by Rob the intern. However, the worksheet data is not in the most usable format. In this project, you will prepare the data and convert it into usable columns.

DIRECTIONS

1. Start Excel, if necessary, and open **E49Apply** from the data files for this lesson.
2. Save the file as **E49Apply_xx** in the location where your teacher instructs you to store the files for this lesson.
3. Add a header to the worksheet that has your name at the left, the date code in the center, and the page number code at the right, and change back to **Normal** view.
4. Notice that two of the names use all three columns; these names have two-part first names. Fix the names to appear in the correct columns.
   a. Type **Mary Jane** in cell **B11**, and type **Brink** in cell **C11**.
   b. Type **Chu Gi** in cell **B34**, and type **Nguyen** in cell **C34**.
   c. Delete column **D**.
5. Insert two columns between columns E and F.
6. Type **City** in cell **E5**, type **State** in cell **F5**, and type **ZIP Code** in cell **G5**.

7. Split the addresses in column E into two columns:

   a. Select the cell range **E6:E57**.

   b. Click Text to Columns 📇.

   c. Select the **Delimited** option and **Comma** as the delimiter used.

   d. Select **Text** as the format for first column.

8. Split the state and ZIP Codes in column F into two columns:

   a. Select the cell range **F6:F57**.

   b. Click Text to Columns 📇.

   c. Select the **Fixed Width** option.

   d. Add a delimiting line at the beginning of the Zip codes in the Data preview window.

   e. Select **Text** as the format for first column, and **General** for the second column.

9. Adjust the column widths as needed.

10. Customize the Quick Access Toolbar with the features of your choices.

11. Customize the Ribbon with the tabs and commands of your choice.

12. **With your teacher's permission**, print page 1 of the worksheet in landscape orientation. It should look similar to Figure 49-2.

13. Reset the Quick Access Toolbar and the Ribbon to their default settings.

14. Save and close the file, and exit Excel.

Figure 49-2

	Title	First Name	Last Name	Address	City	State	ZIP Code	Phone
6	Mrs.	Barbara	Adamson	7770 Dean Road	Cincinnati	OH	33240	844-1589
7	Mr.	Carlos	Altare	4125 Fairlinks Ave.	Carmel	IN	46231	298-1212
8	Mrs.	Diana	Bond	10208 E. Ridgefield Drive	Indian Blade	IN	46236	899-1712
9	Mrs.	Jan	Borough	7556 Hilltop Way	Cincinnati	OH	33254	291-3678
10	Mr.	Adam	Bounds	4943 Windridge Drive	Indianapolis	IN	42626	542-8151
11	Mrs.	Mary Jane	Brink	704 Fairway Drive	Cincinnati	OH	33250	255-1655
12	Mr.	Shakur	Brown	5648 Hydcort	Indianapolis	IN	46250	842-8819
13	Mrs.	Rafiquil	Damir	14559 Senator Way	Indianapolis	IN	46226	844-9977
14	Mrs.	Diana	Dogwood	6311 Douglas Road	Wayne's Town	OH	33502	251-9052
15	Mrs.	Lucy	Fan	5784 N. Central	Indianapolis	IN	46268	255-6479
16	Mr.	Joshua	Fedor	1889 E. 72nd Street	Indian Blade	IN	46003	251-4796
17	Mrs.	Michele	Floyd	3203 Wander Wood Ct	Indianapolis	IN	46220	291-2510
18	Mrs.	Jennifer	Flynn	9876 Wilshire Ave.	Cincinnati	OH	33240	975-0909
19	Ms.	Katerina	Flynn	4984 Wander Wood Lane	Indianapolis	IN	42626	542-0021
20	Mr.	Eram	Hassan	8123 Maple Ave.	Cincinnati	OH	33250	722-1487
21	Mrs.	Betty	High	7543 Newport Bay Drive	Cincinnati	OH	33250	722-1043
22	Mrs.	Addie	Howard	7960 Susan Drive, S.	Westland	IN	46215	849-3557
23	Mr.	Tyrell	Johnson	11794 Southland Ave.	Wayne's Town	OH	33505	846-9812
24	Mr.	Michael	Jordain	4897 Kessler Ave.	Indianapolis	IN	46220	255-1133
25	Mrs.	Ashley	Kay	8738 Log Run Drive, S.	Carmel	IN	46234	299-6136
26	Mrs.	Rhoda	Kuntz	567 W. 72nd Street	Indian Blade	IN	46003	251-6539
27	Ms.	Verna	Latinz	14903 Senator Way	Indianapolis	IN	46226	844-4333
28	Mr.	Wu	Lee	6467 Riverside Drive	Carmel	IN	46220	257-1253
29	Mr.	Chu	Lee	5821 Wilshire Ave.	Cincinnati	OH	33240	975-0484
30	Mr.	Shamir	Lewis	11684 Bay Colony Drive	Plainsville	IN	46234	297-1894
31	Mrs.	Martha	Luck	4131 Brown Road	Cincinnati	OH	33454	547-7430
32	Mrs.	Maria	Navarro	3847 Shipshore Drive	Indianapolis	IN	46032	873-9664
33	Mr.	Tony	Navarro	7998 Maple Ave.	Westland	IN	46215	849-1515
34	Mr.	Chu Gi	Nguyen	8794 Dean Road	Cincinnati	OH	33240	853-1277

Lesson 50

Formatting Cells

➤ What You Will Learn

Using Advanced Formatting of Dates and Times
Creating Custom Number Formats
Clearing Formatting from a Cell

Software Skills   Sometimes, in order to accommodate the various kinds of data in a worksheet, you have to apply various formatting techniques that you might not ordinarily use, such as adjusting the row heights, merging cells, and slanting column labels. Other refinements you may need to make include applying the proper format to data—even if that means removing existing formats and creating your own.

What You Can Do

Using Advanced Formatting of Dates and Times

- You can change the way a date or time is displayed by formatting a cell or cells before or after entering the date/time.
- You can apply several standard date and time formats. The most common ones are located on the Number Format list on the HOME tab of the Ribbon.
- Use the Format Cells dialog box to apply other standard date and time formats.
- You can customize the way you want dates displayed by creating a custom number format.
- After entering a date, you can change its number format as needed. For example, you can change the date 1/14/15 to display as January 14, 2015.

Try It! **Formatting a Date or Time with a Standard Format**

1 Start Excel, and open **E50Try** from the data files for this lesson.

2 Save the file as **E50Try_xx** in the location where your teacher instructs you to store the files for this lesson.

3 Select the cell range G6:G20.

4 On the HOME tab, in the Number group, click the Number Format drop-down arrow `Date ▾`, and click Short Date.

5 Select the cell range L6:M20, click the Number Format drop-down arrow `Date ▾`, and click Time.

6 Save the changes to the file, and leave it open to use in the next Try It.

Try It! **Formatting a Date or Time with a Custom Format**

1 In the **E50Try_xx** file, on the HOME tab, in the Number group, select the cell range G6:G20, click the Number Format drop-down arrow `Date ▾`, and click More Number Formats.

OR

Right-click the cell range G6:G20, and click Format Cells.

2 On the Number tab, in the Category box, click Custom.

3 In the Type box, click the d-mmm-yy option.

4 Click OK.

5 Double-click the column border between column G and column H to resize the column.

6 Save the changes to the file, and leave it open to use in the next Try It.

Applying a custom date format

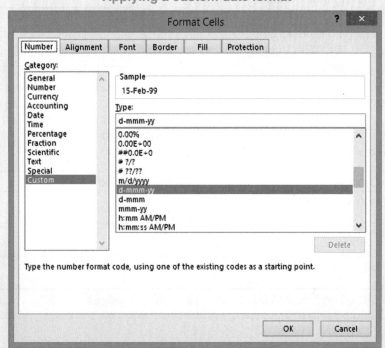

Creating Custom Number Formats

- When a number format doesn't fit your needs, you can create a custom number format:
  - Typically, you use a custom number format to preformat a column or row, prior to data entry. The custom format speeds the data entry process.
  - For example, if you need to type account numbers in the format AB-2342-CO, you can create a format that will insert the dashes for you. And if the account numbers all end in -CO, you can build that into the custom format as well.
- You create a custom number format by typing a series of special codes.
  - ✓ To speed the process, select an existing format and customize it.
- You can specify format codes for positive numbers, negative numbers, zeros, and text:
  - If you wish to specify all four formats, you must type the codes in the order listed above.
  - If you specify only two formats, you must type a code for positive numbers and zeros first, and type a code for negative numbers second.
  - If you specify only one format, all numbers in the row or column will use that format.
  - To separate the formats, use a semicolon, as in the following custom number format: $#,##0.00;[red]($#,##0.00);"ZERO";[blue].
  - This format displays positive numbers as $0,000.00, negative numbers in red and parentheses, a zero as the word ZERO, and text in blue.

- To specify a standard color, type any of the following in brackets: red, black, blue, white, green, yellow, cyan, and magenta.
- The following table shows examples of codes you can use in creating a format:

#	Digit placeholder for one number
0	Zero placeholder
?	Digit placeholder for multiple digits (e.g., ?? allows two digits or one digit)
@	Text placeholder
.	Decimal point (period)
%	Percentage
,	Thousands separator (comma)
$	Dollar sign
-	Negative sign
+	Plus sign
( )	Parentheses
:	Colon
_	Underscore (skips one character width)
[color]	Type the name of a standard color (red, black, blue, white, green, yellow, cyan, or magenta)

- Custom number formats are saved with the worksheet, so if you want to use a custom format on another worksheet, use the Format Painter to copy the format.

Examples of formats you can create:

Type	To Display	Using This Code
5.56	5.5600	#.0000
5641	$5,641	$#,##0
5641 and -5641	$5,641 and ($5,641) in red	$#,##0;[red]($#,##0)
5641 and -5641	$5,641.00 and ($5,641.00) in red	$#,##0.00;[red]($#,##0.00)

Try It!   Creating Custom Number Formats

1 In the **E50Try_xx** file, select the cell range N6:N20.

2 On the HOME tab, click the Number group dialog box launcher ⬚ to display the Format Cells dialog box.

3 In the Category box, click Custom.

4 Scroll through the Type list, and select 000-00-0000.

5 In the Type text box, place the insertion point before the first zero, and type **"AB-"**.

6 Place the insertion point after the last zero, and press BACKSPACE five times.

7 Click OK.

8 Click cell N6, type **35135**, and press ENTER . Notice the new format.

9 Save the changes to the file, and leave it open to use in the next Try It.

Creating a custom number format

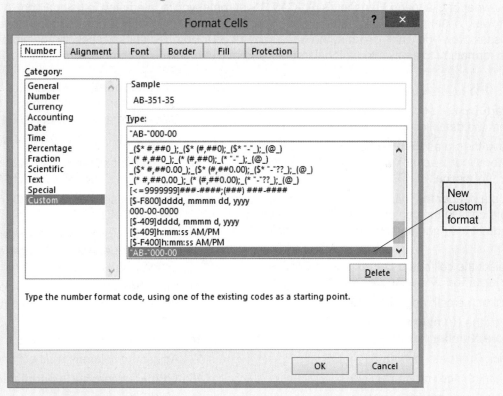

New custom format

Clearing Formatting from a Cell

■ Sometimes, you may want to keep the data in a cell, but remove the formatting you've applied.

■ Use the Clear button in the Editing group on the HOME tab to clear just the format of a cell, without clearing its contents.

Try It!   **Clearing Formatting from a Cell**

1 In the **E50Try_xx** file, select the cell range E6:E20.

2 On the HOME tab, in the Editing group, click Clear ✐ Clear ▾.

3 Click Clear Formats.

4 Save and close the file, and exit Excel.

Lesson 50—Practice

As the owner of Giancarlo Franchetti's Go-Cart Speedrome, you're interested in using Excel to help you manage your growing business. You've created a worksheet for tracking daily admissions and receipts for your American businesses. Now you want to format the worksheet for your European businesses. In this project, you will use custom formatting to apply international formats and make the worksheet more attractive.

DIRECTIONS

1. Start Excel, if necessary, and open **E50Practice** from the data files for this lesson.

2. Save the file as **E50Practice_xx** in the location where your teacher instructs you to store the files for this lesson.

3. Add a header that has your name at the left, the date code in the center, and the page number code at the right, and change back to **Normal** view.

4. Select the cell range **C8:H8**. Click **HOME > Orientation** ✎ ▾ > **Angle Counterclockwise**.

5. Select the cell range **B9:B20**.

6. Click the **Number Format** drop-down arrow > **More Number Formats**.

7. Click **Custom > d-mmm-yy > OK**.

8. Select the cell range **C9:D20**.

9. Click the **Number Format** drop-down arrow > **More Number Formats**.

   13. Click **Time > 13:30:55 > OK**.

10. Select the cell range **F21:H23**, right-click, and click **Format Cells**.

11. Click **Accounting**, click in the **Decimal places** box, and replace the zero with **2**. Click the **Symbol** drop-down arrow > **€ Euro (€ 123) > OK**.

   ✓ Scroll down to about one-third in the Symbol list.

12. Select the cell range **B21:H23**, click the **Borders** drop-down arrow ⊞ ▾ > **Thick Box Border**.

13. Select the cell range **C9:H20**, right-click, and click **Format Cells**.

14. Click **Fill** > click the **Pattern Color** drop-down arrow > **Blue, Accent 5, Lighter 80%** (the ninth option in the second row).

15. Click the **Pattern Style** drop-down arrow > **Vertical stripe** (the second option in the second row).

16. Click **OK**.

17. Adjust the columns widths if needed.

18. **With your teacher's permission**, print the document.

19. Save and close the file, and exit Excel.

Figure 50-1

Giancarlo Franchetti's Go-Cart Speedrome

Daily Admission Tracker
Week

(Track is closed Monday & Tuesday through the racing season)

Session Date	Start of Session	End of Session	Session Number	Adult	Child	Team Racers
5-Oct-13	12:30:00	14:30:00		127	198	17
5-Oct-13	15:15:00	17:15:00		175	189	32
8-Oct-13	15:30:00	17:30:00		78	81	2
9-Oct-13	15:30:00	17:30:00		137	102	3
10-Oct-13	15:30:00	17:30:00		94	122	17
10-Oct-13	18:00:00	20:00:00		145	201	38
10-Oct-13	20:30:00	22:30:00		212	56	27
11-Oct-13	11:30:00	13:30:00		148	198	56
11-Oct-13	13:45:00	15:45:00		126	155	28
11-Oct-13	16:00:00	18:00:00		141	168	17
12-Oct-13	18:15:00	20:15:00		165	255	41
12-Oct-13	20:30:00	22:30:00		256	32	19
Total Admissions				€ 1,804.00	€ 1,757.00	€ 297.00
Admission Price				€ 10.25	€ 7.50	€ 5.00
Total Receipts				€ 18,491.00	€ 13,177.50	€ 1,485.00

Lesson 50—Apply

You are the owner of Giancarlo Franchetti's Go-Cart Speedrome, and you've created a worksheet for tracking daily admissions and receipts for your European businesses. In this project, you will use custom and conditional formatting to make the data easier to read.

DIRECTIONS

1. Start Excel, if necessary, and open **E50Apply** from the data files for this lesson.
2. Save the file as **E50Apply_xx** in the location where your teacher instructs you to store the files for this lesson.
3. Add a footer that has your name at the left, the worksheet file name in the center, and the page number code at the right, and change back to **Normal** view.
4. Apply a custom number format to the Session Number column.
   a. Select the cell range **E9:E20**.
   b. Display the **Format Cells** dialog box, and on the **Number** tab, click **Custom**.
   c. Replace the contents of the **Type** box with the following text: **00-00-"Session "0**.
   d. Click **OK**.
5. In the following cells, enter the session numbers, without dashes:

F9	10051
F10	10052
F11	10081
F12	10091
F13	10101
F14	10102
F15	10103
F16	10111
F17	10112
F18	10113
F19	10121
F20	10122

6. Clear the formatting in the title area, and reformat as shown in Figure 50-2 on the next page:
   a. Select the cell range **A1:I7**.
   b. Clear the formats in the selected range.
   c. Apply **Blue-Gray, Text 2, Lighter 40%** fill color to the selection.
   d. Apply bold formatting to the selection.
   e. Change the point size of cell **C3** to **24 pt**.
   f. Adjust the height of row 3 to **65**.
7. Apply conditional formatting to the dates.
   ✓ *You learned about conditional formatting in Excel, Lesson 17.*
   a. Select the cell range **B9:B20**.
   b. On the HOME tab, click **Conditional Formatting** 🔲, point to **Highlight Cells Rules**, and click **Greater Than**.
   c. In the Greater Than dialog box, in the Format cells that are GREATER THAN box, replace the text with **=$B$13**.
   d. In the with box, click **Light Red Fill** > **OK**. The dates greater than 10 Oct are formatted with light red fill.
8. Edit and manage conditional formatting you applied to the dates.
   a. On the HOME tab, click **Conditional Formatting** 🔲 > **Manage Rules**.
   b. Click the **Edit Rule** button.
   c. In the Edit Formatting Rule dialog box, in the greater than box, click **equal to** > **OK**.
   d. Click **OK** to apply the changes and close the Conditional Formatting Rules Manager dialog box. The dates of 10 Oct are formatted with light red fill.
9. Adjust column widths if needed.
10. **With your teacher's permission**, adjust the page breaks and print the worksheet.
11. Save and close the file, and exit Excel.

Figure 50-2

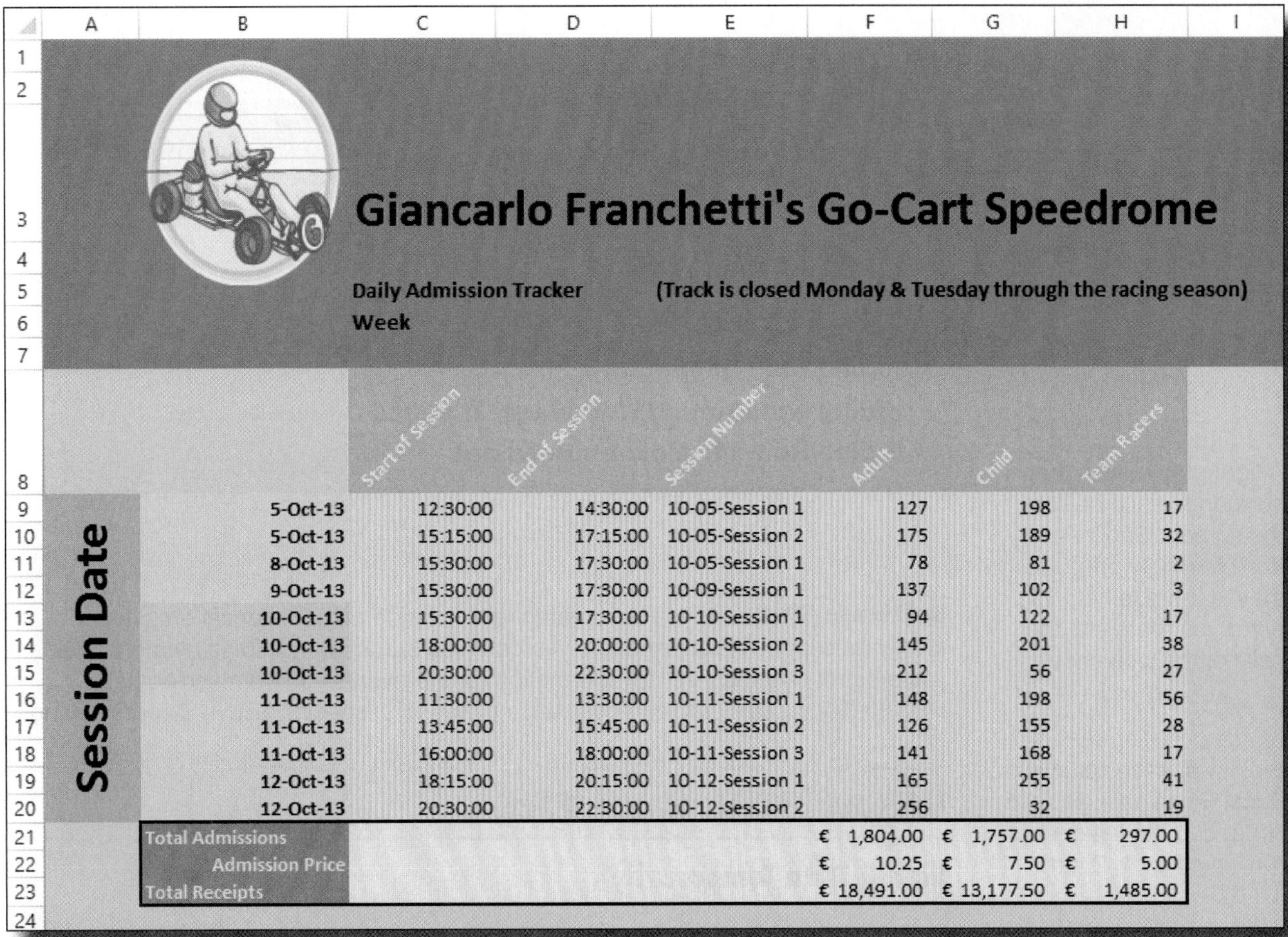

Giancarlo Franchetti's Go-Cart Speedrome

Daily Admission Tracker   (Track is closed Monday & Tuesday through the racing season)
Week

Session Date	Start of Session	End of Session	Session Number	Adult	Child	Team Racers
5-Oct-13	12:30:00	14:30:00	10-05-Session 1	127	198	17
5-Oct-13	15:15:00	17:15:00	10-05-Session 2	175	189	32
8-Oct-13	15:30:00	17:30:00	10-05-Session 1	78	81	2
9-Oct-13	15:30:00	17:30:00	10-09-Session 1	137	102	3
10-Oct-13	15:30:00	17:30:00	10-10-Session 1	94	122	17
10-Oct-13	18:00:00	20:00:00	10-10-Session 2	145	201	38
10-Oct-13	20:30:00	22:30:00	10-10-Session 3	212	56	27
11-Oct-13	11:30:00	13:30:00	10-11-Session 1	148	198	56
11-Oct-13	13:45:00	15:45:00	10-11-Session 2	126	155	28
11-Oct-13	16:00:00	18:00:00	10-11-Session 3	141	168	17
12-Oct-13	18:15:00	20:15:00	10-12-Session 1	165	255	41
12-Oct-13	20:30:00	22:30:00	10-12-Session 2	256	32	19
Total Admissions				€ 1,804.00	€ 1,757.00	€ 297.00
Admission Price				€ 10.25	€ 7.50	€ 5.00
Total Receipts				€ 18,491.00	€ 13,177.50	€ 1,485.00

Lesson 51

Hiding and Formatting Workbook Elements

WORDS TO KNOW

Gridlines
A light gray outline that surrounds each cell on the screen. Gridlines don't normally print; they're there to help you enter your data into the cells of the worksheet.

Headings
Markers that appear at the top of each column in Excel (such as A, B, and IX) and to the left of each row (such as 1, 2, and 1145).

Hide
To prevent Excel from displaying or printing certain data.

Unhide
To redisplay hidden data, worksheets, or workbooks.

View
A saved arrangement of the Excel display and print settings that you can restore at any time.

➤ **What You Will Learn**

Hiding Data Temporarily
Hiding and Printing Worksheet Gridlines
Hiding Row and Column Headings
Using Custom Views

Software Skills   If you have data that's considered confidential or is needed strictly as supporting information, you can hide it from view. Hiding elements helps you present only the relevant information, and prevents you from accidentally printing private data. You can customize a view with specific display or print settings.

What You Can Do

Hiding Data Temporarily

- To prevent data from displaying or printing in a workbook, you can **hide** the data.
- You can hide the contents of individual cells, whole rows or columns, and even whole worksheets.

  ✓ *Hiding data is useful for keeping important supporting or confidential information out of sight, but it won't prevent those who know Excel from exposing that data if they can get access to the workbook. If you need more security, review the protection options in Lesson 77.*

- When a row or column is hidden, the row number or column letter is missing from the worksheet frame. Hiding row 12, for example, leaves the row **headings** showing 11, 13, 14, and so on.
- Hiding a worksheet makes its tab disappear. If worksheets use a sequential numbering or naming scheme (such as Sheet1, Sheet2, Sheet3), the fact that a worksheet is hidden may be obvious.
- If you hide the contents of a cell, the cell appears to contain nothing, but the cell itself doesn't disappear from the worksheet.
- Even if a cell's contents are hidden, you can still display the contents in the Formula bar by selecting the cell.

- You can hide all the zeros in a worksheet to display blank cells. by typing three semicolons (;;;) in the Type list box of the Format Cells dialog box. The value of zero (0) will remain in the cell.
- If you hide a workbook, its contents aren't displayed even when the workbook is open. This feature is useful for storing macros that you want to have available but not necessarily in view.
- If you copy or move hidden data, it remains hidden.

- Because the data in hidden columns or rows doesn't print, you can use this feature to print noncontiguous columns or rows as if they were contiguous.
- To edit, format, or redisplay the contents of hidden rows, columns, or worksheets, **unhide** the rows, columns, or worksheet.

Try It!   Hiding and Redisplaying Cell Contents

1. Start Excel, and open **E51Try** from the data files for this lesson.
2. Save the file as **E51Try_xx** in the location where your teacher instructs you to store the files for this lesson.
3. On the Employees worksheet, click cell C4, and click the Number group dialog box launcher 🔽.
4. On the Number tab, in the Category list box, click Custom.
5. In the Type list box, remove the text, and type ;;;.
6. Click OK.
7. Click the Number Format drop-down arrow [Date ▾] > Text.
8. Save the changes to the file, and leave it open to use in the next Try It.

Try It!   Hiding All Zeros for Current Worksheet

1. In the **E51Try_xx** file, click FILE > Options > Advanced.
2. Under Display options for this worksheet, click the Show a zero in cells that have zero value check box to deselect it, and click OK.
3. Save changes to the file, and leave the file open to use in the next Try It.

Try It!   Hiding Rows or Columns

1. In the **E51Try_xx** file, click the column I heading.
2. On the HOME tab, click Format 📇.
3. Click Hide & Unhide > Hide Columns.
4. Right-click the row 6 heading.
5. Click Hide.

   OR

   Click and hold the border between rows 6 and 7, and drag up until row 6 disappears.
6. Save the changes to the file, and leave it open to use in the next Try It.

Try It!   Unhiding Rows or Columns

❶ In the **E51Try_xx** file, select the H and J column headings.

❷ Right-click the selection and select Unhide.

OR

Point just to the right of the column H heading until the pointer changes to ↔, and double-click.

❸ Point just below the row 5 heading border until the cursor changes to ⊹. Click, hold, and drag down until you reach the bottom of the name Carlos that was in cell A7, and release the mouse button.

OR

Select the 5 and 7 row headings, click Format ▦ > Hide & Unhide > Unhide Rows.

❹ Save the changes to the file, and leave it open to use in the next Try It.

Dragging to unhide a row

Unhide indicator

Try It!   Hiding and Unhiding Workbooks

❶ In the **E51Try_xx** file, click VIEW > Hide ▭. Notice the change to the Excel window.

❷ Click VIEW > Unhide ▭.

❸ In the Unhide dialog box, verify that **E51Try_xx** is selected, and click OK.

❹ Save the changes to the file, and leave it open to use in the next Try It.

Try It!   Hiding and Unhiding Worksheets

1 In the **E51Try_xx** file, click the Customers worksheet > HOME > Format 🖿 > Hide & Unhide > Hide Sheet.

OR

Right-click the Customers sheet tab > Hide.

2 Click HOME > Format 🖿 > Hide & Unhide > Unhide Sheet. In the Unhide dialog box, verify that the Customers worksheet is selected, and click OK.

OR

Right-click the Employees sheet tab > Unhide.

3 Save the changes to the file, and leave it open to use in the next Try It.

Hiding and Printing Worksheet Gridlines

- When presenting Excel data onscreen to a client, you might prefer to present it cleanly, without various on-screen elements such as **gridlines**.

- To turn off gridlines onscreen, select that option from the VIEW tab or select the View check box under Gridlines in the Sheet Options group of the PAGE LAYOUT tab on the Ribbon.

- Regardless of whether you display gridlines on the screen, they don't print unless you select the Print check box under Gridlines in the Sheet Options group of the PAGE LAYOUT tab on the Ribbon.

Try It!   Hiding Worksheet Gridlines

1 In **E51Try_xx**, on the Customers worksheet, click VIEW, and click the Gridlines check box to deselect it.

2 Save the changes to the file, and leave it open to use in the next Try It.

Hiding Row and Column Headings

- Column headings display the letter assigned to each column (such as A, B, and IX) .

- Row headings display the number assigned to each row (1, 2, 3, etc.).

- You can choose to not display the column and row headings; however, it is helpful to display them until you are finished entering data.

- Access the Headings option from the Show group of the VIEW tab.

- You can toggle the Headings option on and off.

Try It!   Hiding Row and Column Headings

1 In the **E51Try_xx** file, on the Customers worksheet, click VIEW.

2 In the Show group, click the Headings check box to deselect it.

3 On the VIEW tab, click Page Break Preview 🖿. Notice the headings are absent.

4 On the VIEW tab, click Page Layout 🖿.

5 On the VIEW tab, in the Show group, click the Headings check box to reselect it.

6 On the VIEW tab, click Normal 🖿.

7 Save the changes to the file, and leave it open to use in the next Try It.

Using Custom Views

- You can set up the display of a workbook and save that setup in a custom **view**.
  - For example, you could save one view of the worksheet with all cells displayed, another view with certain rows or columns hidden, and so on.
- Settings in a view include selected cells, current column widths, how the screen is split or frozen, window arrangements and sizes, filter settings, print setup, and defined print area (if any).
- When creating a view, you can specify whether to save the settings for hidden columns and rows, and print settings.

  ✓ *Hidden worksheets are always hidden in the view.*

- Because a custom view can control print settings, you can create the same arrangement of printed data each time you print from that view (for example, printing just the tax deductible expenses from a monthly expense workbook).

- The current view is saved with the workbook.
- You cannot create a custom view when a worksheet contains an Excel list or table. If one or more worksheets contain an Excel list or table, the Custom Views command is disabled for the entire workbook.
- In Excel 2010, you could save views of workbooks as workspaces. For example, you could open several workbooks, arrange them using the Arrange All command, and then save that view of the workbooks as a workspace so they would redisplay in the same way when you opened the workspace.
- The Save Workspace command is not available in Excel 2013, but you can open in 2013 workspaces you saved in the previous version of Excel. Open the .xlw workspace file the same way you open any Excel file.

Try It!   Creating a Custom View

1. In the **E51Try_xx** file, on the Customers worksheet, on the VIEW tab, notice that the Custom Views command is disabled.
2. Convert the data table to a range.
   a. Select the cell range A5:I57.
   b. Click TABLE TOOLS DESIGN > Convert to Range.
   c. Click Yes in the confirmation dialog box.
   d. Press CTRL + HOME.
3. Click VIEW > Custom Views > Add to display the Add View dialog box.
4. In the Name box type **Normal**, and click OK.
5. Click the Employees worksheet tab, click the H column heading, press and hold CTRL, and click the column headings I, O, and P.
6. Click HOME > Format > Hide & Unhide > Hide Columns.
7. Right-click the Customers worksheet tab, and click Hide.
8. On the Employees worksheet, click INSERT > Header & Footer > File Name.

9. Click FILE > Print > No Scaling > Fit Sheet on One Page.
10. Click Back to exit the Backstage view.
11. Click VIEW > Normal.
12. Click Custom Views > Add to display the Add View dialog box.
13. In the Name box, type **Schedule**, verify that both Print settings and Hidden rows, columns and filter settings options are selected, and click OK.
14. Save the changes to the file, and leave it open to use in the next Try It.

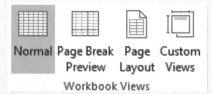

The Workbook Views group

Try It! Displaying a Custom View

1. In the **E51Try_xx** file, on the VIEW tab, click Custom Views ▣.

2. In the Custom Views dialog box, click Normal > Show. Notice that the Customers tab displays.

3. In the Custom Views dialog box, click Schedule > Show.

4. Save the changes to the file, and leave it open to use in the next Try It.

The Custom Views dialog box

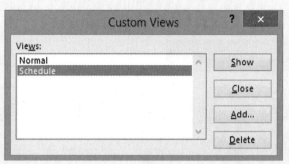

Try It! Deleting a Custom View

1. In the **E51Try_xx** file, on the VIEW tab, click Custom Views ▣.

2. In the Custom Views dialog box, click Schedule > Delete.

3. Click Yes in the confirmation dialog box.

4. In the Custom Views dialog box, click Close.

5. Save and close the file, and exit Excel.

Lesson 51—Practice

You are the bookkeeper for Intellidata Database Services, and you are working with a statistics report. You want to be able to view just the data for one of the three offices. You also want to set print options for that specific data.

DIRECTIONS

1. Start Excel, if necessary, and open **E51Practice** from the data files for this lesson.

2. Save the file as **E51Practice_xx** in the location where your teacher instructs you to store the files for this lesson.

3. For all worksheets, add a header that has your name at the left, the date code in the center, and the page number code at the right, and change back to **Normal** view.

4. On the **Usage statistics 0704** sheet, click VIEW > **Gridlines** to deselect the Gridlines check box for this sheet.

5. Click the row heading for row 8, press and hold CTRL, and click the row headings for 9, 12, 13, 16, 17, 20, 21, 24, and 25.

6. Click HOME > Format ▦ > Hide & Unhide > Hide Rows.

7. Click VIEW > Headings to deselect the Headings check box.

8. Click PAGE LAYOUT > Orientation ▣ > Landscape.

9. Click VIEW > Custom Views ▣ > Add

10. In the Name box, type **North**.

11. Verify that both **Print settings** and **Hidden rows, columns and filter settings** options are selected, and click **OK**.

12. **With your teacher's permission**, print page 1 of the worksheet. It should look similar to Figure 51-1.

13. Save and close the file, and exit Excel.

Figure 51-1

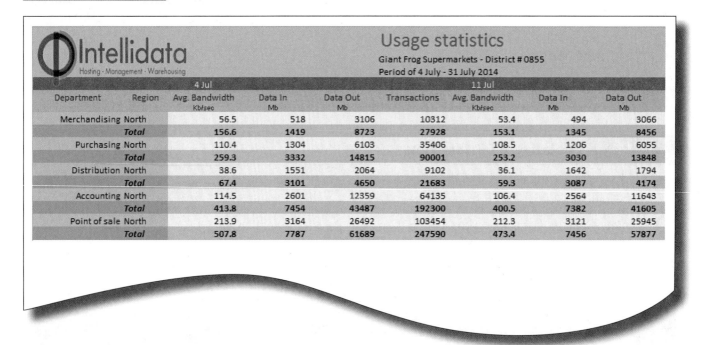

| Department | Region | 4 Jul | | | | 11 Jul | | |
		Avg. Bandwidth Kb/sec	Data In Mb	Data Out Mb	Transactions	Avg. Bandwidth Kb/sec	Data In Mb	Data Out Mb
Merchandising	North	56.5	518	3106	10312	53.4	494	3066
	Total	156.6	1419	8723	27928	153.1	1345	8456
Purchasing	North	110.4	1304	6103	35406	108.5	1206	6055
	Total	259.3	3332	14815	90001	253.2	3030	13848
Distribution	North	38.6	1551	2064	9102	36.1	1642	1794
	Total	67.4	3101	4650	21683	59.3	3087	4174
Accounting	North	114.5	2601	12359	64135	106.4	2564	11643
	Total	413.8	7454	43487	192300	400.5	7382	41605
Point of sale	North	213.9	3164	26492	103454	212.3	3121	25945
	Total	507.8	7787	61689	247590	473.4	7456	57877

Intellidata
Hosting · Management · Warehousing

Usage statistics
Giant Frog Supermarkets - District # 0855
Period of 4 July - 31 July 2014

Lesson 51—Apply

As the bookkeeper for Intellidata Database Services, your job is to produce three versions of one Web traffic statistics report, each of which is distributed to a different office. In this project, you will create multiple custom views of your worksheet.

DIRECTIONS

1. Start Excel, if necessary, and open **E51Apply** from the data files for this lesson.

2. Save the file as **E51Apply_xx** in the location where your teacher instructs you to store the files for this lesson.

3. For all worksheets, add a header that has your name at the left, the date code in the center, and the page number code at the right, and change back to **Normal** view.

4. Display the row and column headings.

5. Unhide rows 6 through 26.

6. Create a custom view on the **Usage statistics 0704** worksheet for the South offices.

   a. Click cell **B7**, press and hold [CTRL] , and click all the cells where the words *North* or *Central* appear in column B.

   b. Hide the rows for *North* and *Central*.

   c. Turn off the headings.

   d. **Add a Custom View named South** with the **Print settings** and **Hidden rows, columns and filter settings** options selected.

   ✓ *Since the department labels appear next to "North" for each group, they will disappear in the views for the South and Central offices.*

7. Display the row and column headings.

8. Unhide rows 7 through 25.

9. Create a custom view on the **Usage statistics 0704** worksheet for the Central offices.

   a. Press and hold [CTRL] , and click all the cells where the words *North* or *South* appear in column B.

   b. Hide the rows for *North* and *South*.

   c. View the worksheet in Custom View.

   d. Add a Custom View named **Central** with the **Print settings** and **Hidden rows, columns and filter settings** options selected.

10. Display the South view, and display the Central view. Your worksheet should look similar to Figure 51-2.

11. Unhide all of the rows, and display the row and column headings.

12. **With your teacher's permission**, print each of the three custom views.

13. Save and close the file, and exit Excel.

Figure 51-2

Intellidata
Hosting · Management · Warehousing

Usage statistics
Giant Frog Supermarkets - District # 0855
Period of 4 July - 31 July 2014

Department	Region	Avg. Bandwidth Kb/sec	Data In Mb	Data Out Mb	Transactions	Avg. Bandwidth Kb/sec	Data In Mb	Data Out Mb
		4 Jul				11 Jul		
	Central	51.6	495	2943	9103	49.6	487	2876
	Total	156.6	1419	8723	27928	153.1	1345	8456
	Central	89.1	1064	3946	29431	84.5	984	3761
	Total	259.3	3332	14815	90001	253.2	3030	13848
	Central	12.4	674	943	4121	9.8	584	874
	Total	67.4	3101	4650	21683	59.3	3087	4174
	Central	214.7	3169	21661	81355	205.6	3024	20461
	Total	413.8	7454	43487	192300	400.5	7382	41605
	Central	109.9	1974	15464	65467	97	1821	13467
	Total	507.8	7787	61689	247590	473.4	7456	57877

Lesson 52

Customizing Styles and Themes

➤ **What You Will Learn**

Customizing a Workbook Theme
Customizing a Cell Style
Merging Cell Styles
Customizing a Table Style

WORDS TO KNOW

Style
A collection of formatting settings that can be applied to characters or paragraphs.

Table
Data arranged in columns and specially formatted with column headers that contain commands that allow you to sort, filter, and perform other functions on the table.

Template
A document that contains formatting, styles, and sample text that you can use to create new documents.

Theme
A set of coordinated colors, fonts, and effects that can be applied to Office 2013 documents.

Software Skills   To make a worksheet look more professional, you might want to customize the standard themes Excel provides by choosing company-style fonts and colors. You can create custom cell and table styles to provide consistent formatting in a workbook. You can merge styles from other Excel workbooks so that you can use custom styles you created in other workbooks.

What You Can Do

Customizing a Workbook Theme

- A **theme** is a collection of fonts, colors, and effects that can be applied in a single click. For example, the default theme for the Normal **template** is Office.
- You can select a different set of existing fonts, colors, and effects and save them in a new theme.
- You can create your own custom set of colors or fonts for use with a theme.
- Themes you create are automatically added to a Custom group in the Themes gallery on the PAGE LAYOUT tab.
- When you save a custom theme, you change the template file of the current document.
- You can reset, or restore, the default template theme, even if you apply a different theme, or a custom theme.
- You can delete a custom theme that you no longer need. Deleting a custom theme does not affect existing documents formatted with that theme.

Try It!   **Customizing Theme Colors**

1 Start Excel, and open **E52TryA** file from the data files for this lesson.

2 Save the file as **E52TryA_xx** in the location where your teacher instructs you to store the files for this lesson.

3 Click PAGE LAYOUT > Colors ▦ > Customize Colors. The Create New Theme Colors dialog box displays.

4 Click the Accent 6 button, and click Blue, Accent 1, Lighter 40%.

5 Click the Accent 2 button, and click Blue, Accent 1, Darker 50%.

6 Click the Hyperlink button, and click Dark Blue, Hyperlink, Lighter 40%.

7 In the Name box, type your name, and click Save.

8 On the PAGE LAYOUT tab, click Colors ▦, right-click your custom theme, and click Delete.

9 Click Yes in the confirmation dialog box.

10 Save the changes to the file, and leave it open to use in the next Try It.

Creating a new theme color

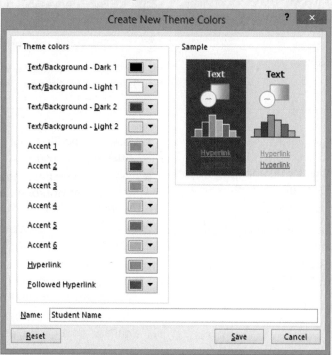

Try It!　**Customizing Theme Fonts**

1 In the **E52TryA_xx** file, on the PAGE LAYOUT tab, click Fonts A > Customize Fonts. The Create New Theme Fonts dialog box displays.

2 Click the Heading font drop-down arrow, and click Verdana.

3 Click the Body font drop-down arrow and select Tahoma.

4 In the Name box, type your name, and click Save.

5 On the PAGE LAYOUT tab, click Fonts A, right-click your custom font set, and click Delete.

6 Click Yes in the confirmation dialog box.

7 Save the changes to the file, and leave it open to use in the next Try It.

Try It!　**Saving and Deleting a New Theme**

1 In the **E52TryA_xx** file, on the PAGE LAYOUT tab, click Themes > Save Current Theme.

2 In the Name box, type your name, and click Save.

3 Click Themes > Facet.

4 Click Themes, and click your custom theme.

5 Click Themes, right-click your custom theme, and click Delete.

6 Click Yes in the confirmation dialog box.

7 Save the changes to the file, and leave it open to use in the next Try It.

Customizing a Cell Style

- A cell **style** includes settings for number, alignment, font border, fill, and protection properties.
- Excel comes with built-in cell styles.
- If you do not want to use a built-in cell style, you can create and save your own.
- You can access the Cell Styles gallery from the Styles group of the HOME tab of the Ribbon.

  ✓ *Depending on the width of your screen, you may need to click the Styles dialog box launcher to display the cell styles.*

- You can modify a cell style, and save it as a new, custom cell style.
- When you create a new cell style, it is saved in the current workbook. You can use it only in the workbook where you created it.
- Cell styles you create are automatically added to a Custom group in the Cell Styles gallery.
- You can delete a cell style that you no longer need. Deleting a custom cell style does not affect existing documents formatted with that cell style.
- To delete a cell style, access it from the Cell Style gallery, right-click it, and click Delete.

Try It!   Customizing a Cell Style

1   In the **E52TryA_xx** file, click cell A3, and format it with custom formatting.

     a. On the HOME tab, in the Font group, click Fill Color ☌ > Gold, Accent 4.

     b. Click the Font drop-down arrow > Arial.

     c. On the HOME tab, in the Alignment group, click Center ≡.

2   On the HOME tab, in the Styles group, click Cell Styles 💭.

     ✓ *Depending on the width of your screen, you may need to click the Styles dialog box launcher ⌐ to display the cell styles.*

3   Click New Cell Style. The Style dialog box displays.

4   In the Style name box, type your name. Verify that the cell style settings are the ones you applied.

5   Click OK.

6   Select the cell range A4:A7.

7   On the HOME tab, in the Styles group, click Cell Styles 💭, and click your custom cell style.

8   Save the changes to the file, and leave it open to use in the next Try It.

Creating a new cell style

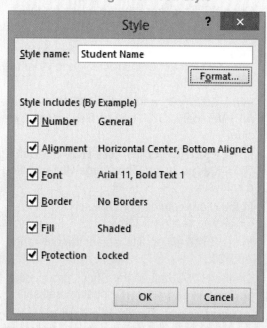

Merging Cell Styles

- When you create a new cell style, you can use it only in the workbook where you created it.

- If you need to use cell styles you created in other workbooks, you can copy or merge the cell styles from the other workbooks into your current workbook.

- You can also copy or merge cell styles from other Excel templates into a current Excel template.

- The Undo command cannot reverse the effects of a cell style merge. Be sure you want to copy over all of the cell styles from the source workbook to the destination workbook.

- If the workbook into which you merge cell styles has style names that match the style names of the source workbook, the new cell styles can override the existing ones.

- You may want to delete unwanted cell styles from the source workbook before you merge styles.

- You can access the Merge Styles command at the bottom of the Cell Styles gallery in the Styles group on the HOME tab of the Ribbon.

Try It!   Merging Cell Styles

1 In the **E52TryA_xx** file, on the HOME tab, in the Styles group, click Cell Styles 📝 to view the custom cell style you created in the previous Try It.

2 Open **E52TryB** from the data files for this lesson.

3 Save the file as **E52TryB_xx** in the location where your teacher instructs you to store the files for this lesson.

4 In the **E52TryB_xx** file, click VIEW > Arrange All > Vertical > OK. The two files display side by side.

5 In the **E52TryB_xx** file, click HOME > Cell Styles 📝 > Merge Styles. The Merge Styles dialog box displays.

6 In the Merge styles from box, click **E52TryA_xx.xlsx** > OK.

7 In the **E52TryB_xx** file, select the cell range A6:B20.

8 On the HOME tab, in the Styles group, click Cell Styles 📝, and click your custom cell style.

  ✓ *Depending on the width of your screen, you may need to click the Styles dialog box launcher* ⌕ *to display the cell styles.*

9 Save the **E52TryB_xx** file, and close it.

10 Save the **E52TryA_xx** file, and leave it open to use in the next Try It.

Merging cell styles

Customizing a Table Style

■ You can convert a list of data in Excel into a **table** using the Format as Table button 📝 on the HOME tab.

■ You can select an overall table format and other formatting settings on the TABLE TOOLS DESIGN tab.

■ Use one of Excel's existing table formats or create a custom table style that will appear in the Table Style gallery. You can then apply that table style to any other table.

■ When you create a new table style, you can set the new table style as the default table Quick Style to be used in that workbook.

■ Using the New Table Quick Style dialog box, you can format the following table elements:

  ● Whole Table: Applies a formatting choice to the entire table.

  ● First Column Stripe: Applies a formatting choice to the first column in the table as well as each alternating column.

  ● Second Column Stripe: Applies a formatting choice to the second column in the table as well as each alternating column.

  ● First Row Stripe: Applies a formatting choice to the first row in the table as well as each alternating row.

  ● Second Row Stripe: Applies a formatting choice to the second row in the table as well as each alternating row.

  ● Last Column: Applies a formatting choice to the last column in a table. The last column usually contains totals.

  ● First Column: Applies a formatting choice to the first column in a table. The first column usually contains headings.

  ● Header Row: Applies a formatting choice to the header row in a table.

- Total Row: Applies a formatting choice to the final totals row in a table.
- First Header Cell: Applies a formatting choice to the first cell in the header row. This cell often contains no data.
- Last Header Cell: Applies a formatting choice to the final cell in the header row in a table.
- First Total Cell: Applies a formatting choice to the first cell in the total row. This cell often contains the heading "Total".

- Last Total Cell: Applies a formatting choice to the final cell in the total row. This cell often holds an overall total number.

- A new table style only consists of the formatting you apply as you create the table style. It will not automatically use any direct cell formatting you may have applied or use new cell styles you have created.

Try It! Creating a New Table Style

1 In the **E52Try_xx** file, clear the cell formatting from the cell range A2:H2.

   a. Select the cell range A2:H2.

   b. On the HOME tab, click Clear *Clear* > Clear Formats.

2 Select the cell range A2:H7, and format it as a table.

   a. On the HOME tab, click Format as Table.

   b. Select Table Style Light 1.

   c. Verify that the data range shown in the Format As Table dialog box reflects the cell range A2:H7.

   ✓ Excel will automatically insert absolute references. Recall that you learned about absolute references in Excel, Lesson 8.

   d. Verify that the My table has headers check box is selected, and click OK.

   e. On the TABLE TOOLS DESIGN tab, select the following options in the Table Style Options group: Header Row, Total Row, Last Column. Deselect any other options.

   ✓ If your custom cell style is applied to cell A8 when you have added the Total row, click in cell A8 and then Clear > Clear Formats to remove the cell style.

3 Click HOME > Format as Table > New Table Style. The New Table Style dialog box displays.

4 In the Name box, type your name.

5 In the Table Element box, click Header Row > Format. The Format Cells dialog box displays.

6 Click the Fill tab, and under Background Color click Black.

7 Click the Font tab, and in the Font style list, click Bold.

8 On the Font tab, click the Color drop-down arrow, click White, Background 1, and click OK.

9 In the Table Element box, click Total Row > Format.

10 On the Font tab, in the Font style list, click Bold.

11 Click the Border tab, in the Style box click the double line option (last option in the second column), and under Presets click Outline.

12 Click the Fill tab, click the brighter blue in the theme colors (fifth option in the first row), and click OK.

13 In the Table Element box, scroll down, click Last Total Cell > Format.

14 Click the Fill tab, on the Standard colors palette click Orange, and click OK.

15 In the Table Element box, scroll up, click Whole Table > Format.

16 Click the Border tab, click the Color drop-down arrow, click Blue-Gray, Text 2, Lighter 40%, under Presets click Inside, and click OK.

17 Click OK to apply the changes and close the New Table Style dialog box.

18 Click inside the table, click TABLE TOOLS DESIGN, and in the Table Styles gallery click your custom table style.

   ✓ Depending on the width of your screen, you may need to click the Quick Styles button to display the table styles.

19 Save and close the file, and exit Excel.

(continued)

Try It!   **Creating a New Table Style** (continued)

Creating a table Quick Style

New Table Style	?	×

Name: Student Name

Table Element:

Whole Table
First Column Stripe
Second Column Stripe
First Row Stripe
Second Row Stripe
Last Column
First Column
Header Row
Total Row

Preview

Format   Clear

Element Formatting:

InsideVertical, InsideHorizontal Borders

☐ Set as default table style for this document

OK   Cancel

Lesson 52—Practice

The worksheet you designed to track accessories sold each day at your PhotoTown store has proven very helpful, and the corporate headquarters may adopt it throughout the company. In this project, you will create a custom theme that follows the company publication standards.

DIRECTIONS

1. Start Excel, if necessary, and open **E52Practice** from the data files for this lesson.
2. Save the file as **E52PracticeA_xx** in the location where your teacher instructs you to store the files for this lesson.
3. Add a header that has your name at the left, the date code in the center, and the page number code at the right, and change back to **Normal** view.
4. Click **PAGE LAYOUT** > **Colors** ■ > **Customize Colors**.
5. Click the **Accent 5** button and select **More Colors**.

6. Set Red to **224**, Green to **183**, and Blue to **119** and click **OK**.
7. Click the **Accent 6** button, and click **More Colors**.
8. Change Red to **160**, Green to **113**, and Blue to **255**, and click **OK**.
9. In the Name box, type **PhotoTown**, and click **Save** to save the new color set.
10. Select the cell range A6:C6.
11. Click **HOME** > **Fill Color** 🎨- > **Gold, Accent 4, Lighter 40%**.
12. Click **HOME** > **Font Color** **A** > **Blue, Accent 1, Darker 25%**.

13. Click **PAGE LAYOUT** > Fonts A > **Customize Fonts**.

14. Click the Heading font drop-down arrow, and click **Arial Rounded MT Bold**.

15. Click the Body font drop-down arrow, and click **Baskerville Old Face**.

16. In the Name box, type **PhotoTown**, and click **Save** to save the new font set.

17. Select cell range **A6:C6**, press and hold CTRL , and click cell **A2**.

18. Click **HOME** > Font > Arial Rounded MT Bold.

19. Click **PAGE LAYOUT** > Themes [Aa] > **Save Current Theme**.

20. Save the theme as **E52PracticeB_xx** in the location where your teacher instructs you to store the files for this lesson.

21. **With your teacher's permission**, print the worksheet. It should look similar to Figure 52-1.

22. Save and close the file, and exit Excel.

Figure 52-1

PhotoTown

Photo products sold on 7/22

Employee	Product	No. Sold
Jairo Campos	T-shirts	2
Kere Freed	Photo books	1
Taneel Black	Photo books	2
Jairo Campos	Mugs	4
Jairo Campos	T-shirts	1
Akira Ota	Greeting cards	100
Akira Ota	3-D photos	
Kere Freed	Greeting cards	150
Taneel Black	Photo books	2

Total receipts   214.75

Lesson 52—Apply

PhotoTown corporate headquarters is looking to adopt the worksheet you designed throughout the company. In this project, you will create a custom table style that follows the company publication standards. You will also create a custom cell style and merge the style into another worksheet.

DIRECTIONS

1. Start Excel, if necessary, and open **E52ApplyA** from the data files for this lesson.

2. Save the file as **E52ApplyA_xx** in the location where your teacher instructs you to store the files for this lesson.

3. Add a header that has your name at the left, the date code in the center, and the page number code at the right, and change back to **Normal** view.

4. Click HOME > **Format as Table** 📄 > **New Table Style**.

5. In the Name box, type your name.

6. Apply the following formatting to the different table elements:

   a. Whole Table: On the **Border** tab, click **Inside** and **Outline**. On the **Font** tab, select **Bold** font style and **Blue, Accent 1** font color.

   b. Header Row: On the **Fill** tab, click the **orange** color in the **Theme** colors area (sixth color from the left). On the **Font** tab, click **Bold** and the **Blue, Accent 5** font color.

   c. Total Row: On the **Fill** tab, click the **red** color in the **Standard** colors area (second color from the left). On the **Border** tab, click a **thick line** style, and click **Outline**.

   d. Second Row Stripe: On the **Fill** tab, click the **light gray** color in the **Theme** colors area (third color from the left).

   e. Last Column: On the **Fill** tab, click the **blue-gray** color in the **Theme** colors area (fourth color from the left). On the **Font** tab, click **Bold**.

7. Select the cell range **A5:E14**, and format this range as a table with your new table style.

8. Click TABLE TOOLS DESIGN, verify that the **Header Row** and **Banded Rows** options are checked, and click to select the **Total Row** and **Last Column** check boxes.

9. Create a new cell style:

   a. Click the cell range **A1:B1**.

   b. Format the cell with a **Black, Text 1** fill color, **White, Background 1** font color, and a **28 pt** font size.

   c. On the TABLE TOOLS DESIGN tab, click **Cell Styles** 📄 > **New Cell Style**.

   ✓ *Depending on the width of your screen, you may need to click the Styles dialog box launcher* 🔳 *to display the cell styles.*

   d. Name the cell style **PhotoTown Title**, and click **OK**.

10. Save the E52ApplyA_xx file. It should look similar to Figure 52-2 on the next page.

11. Open **E52ApplyB** from the data files for this lesson.

12. Save the file as **E52ApplyB_xx** in the location where your teacher instructs you to store the files for this lesson.

13. Add a header that has your name at the left, the date code in the center, and the page number code at the right, and change back to **Normal** view.

14. Arrange the files so you can view them side by side, vertically.

15. In the **E52ApplyB_xx** file, merge the custom cell style you created in the **E52ApplyA_xx** file.

   a. In the **E52ApplyB_xx** file, click HOME > **Cell Styles** 📄 > **Merge Styles**.

   b. In the **Merge styles from** box, click **E52ApplyA_xx.xlsx** > **OK**.

16. In the **E52ApplyB_xx** file, apply the **PhotoTown Title** cell style to the cell range **A1:B1**.

17. Save the **E52ApplyB_xx** file. It should look similar to Figure 52-3 on the next page.

18. **With your teacher's permission**, print both worksheets.

19. Save and close both files, and exit Excel.

Figure 52-2

PhotoTown

Photo products sold on 7/22

Employee ▼	Product ▼	No. Sold ▼	Cost per Item ▼	Total Sales ▼
Akira Ota	T-shirts	2	10	20
Kere Freed	Photo books	1	6.25	6.25
Taneel Black	Photo books	2	6.25	12.5
Jairo Campos	Mugs	4	4	16
Jairo Campos	T-shirts	1	10	10
Akira Ota	Greeting cards	100	0.55	55
Akira Ota	3-D photos	3	2.25	6.75
Kere Freed	Greeting cards	150	0.55	82.5
Jairo Campos	Photo books	2	6.25	12.5
Total				221.5

Figure 52-3

PhotoTown

Photo products sold on 7/23

Employee ▼	Product ▼	No. Sold ▼	Cost per Item ▼	Total Sales ▼
Akira Ota	T-shirts	5	10	50
Kere Freed	Photo books	6	6.25	37.5
Taneel Black	Photo books	8	6.25	50
Jairo Campos	Mugs	0	4	0
Jairo Campos	T-shirts	2	10	20
Akira Ota	Greeting cards	80	0.55	44
Akira Ota	3-D photos	3	2.25	6.75
Kere Freed	Greeting cards	75	0.55	41.25
Jairo Campos	Photo books	2	6.25	12.5
Total				262

Lesson 53

Customizing Data Entry

➤ What You Will Learn

Entering Labels on Multiple Lines
Entering Fractions and Mixed Numbers
Using Form Controls

WORDS TO KNOW

ActiveX
Reusable software
components developed
by Microsoft.

Form
A document used to
collect and organize
information.

Format
To apply attributes to
cell data to change
the appearance of the
worksheet.

Form controls
Tools used to create
forms.

Line break
A code inserted into text
that forces it to display on
two different lines.

Software Skills   Excel offers a variety of ways to customize data entry. When entering labels, especially long ones, you may want to display them on more than one line so the column will not need to be as wide. Entering fractions requires a special technique so they display properly. You can create a form by inserting form controls on a worksheet to make data entry even easier.

What You Can Do

Entering Labels on Multiple Lines

■   If you have long column labels, you can adjust the column width to fit them.

■   This doesn't always look pleasing, however, especially when the column label is much longer than the data in the column.

• For example, the two columns shown here are much larger than their data:

Unit Number   Total Annual Sales
2                       $125,365.97

■   One of the easiest ways to fix this problem is to enter the column label with **line breaks**.

■   Entering line breaks between words in a cell enables you to place several lines of text in the same cell, like this next example:

	Total
Unit	Annual
Number	Sales
2	$125,365.97

■   The height of the row adjusts automatically to accommodate the multiple-line column label.

■   You can also use the Wrap Text command in the Alignment group of the HOME tab to wrap multiple lines of text within a cell.

Try It!   Entering Labels on Multiple Lines

1 Start Excel, and open **E53Try** from the data files for this lesson.

2 Save the file as **E53Try_xx** in the location where your teacher instructs you to store the files for this lesson.

3 Click cell C11, and type **Cases**.

4 Press ALT + ENTER to insert a line break, and type **Ordered**.

5 In cell D11, type **Price per Case**.

6 In cell E11, type **Product Total Sales**.

7 Click cell D11, and on the HOME tab, click Wrap Text 📑.

8 With cell D11 still selected, on the HOME tab, click Format Painter 🖌, and click cell E11.

9 Click cell D11, in the formula bar, place the insertion point after Price, press ALT + ENTER, and press ENTER.

10 Save the changes to the file, and leave it open to use in the next Try It.

Enter a line break within a cell

Sales Tracker				
Date:	9/21/2014			
Customer:	3829992			
Salesperson:	Greg Bimmel	▼		
		Cases Ordered	Price per Case	Product Total Sales
Chew Toys, asst.		3/4	$ 18.75	$ 14.06
Med. Bonie		1/2	$ 53.00	$ 26.50
Leash		1 1/8	$ 190.00	$ 213.75
Puppy Food		5 1/2	$ 24.50	$ 134.75
			Grand Total	$ 389.06

Entering Fractions and Mixed Numbers

- If you type the value 1/3 into a cell with a General number format, Excel formats it as a date (in this case, January 3).

- To enter a fraction, you must precede it with a zero (0) and a space, which tells Excel that the data is a number. For example, to enter 1/3, type 0 1/3.

- When Excel recognizes the data as a fraction, it applies the Fraction number format to the cell.

- A fraction appears as a decimal value in the Formula bar. The fraction 1/3 appears as 0.333333333333333 in the Formula bar.

- When entering a mixed number (a number and a fraction), simply type it. For example, type 4, a space, and the fraction 1/2 to result in 4 1/2.

- You can **format** existing data to look like fractions using the Format Cells command.

Try It!   Entering Fractions and Mixed Numbers

1 In the **E53Try_xx** file, click cell C12 and type **0**, press SPACEBAR, type **3/4**, and press ENTER .

2 In cell C13, type **0 1/2**, and press ENTER

3 In cell C14, type **1 1/8**, and press ENTER .

4 In cell C15 type **5 1/2**, and press ENTER .

5 Save the changes to the file, and leave it open to use in the next Try It.

Entering fractions and mixed numbers

	Cases Ordered	Price per Case	Product Total Sales	
Date:	9/21/2014			
Customer:	3829992			
Salesperson:	Alice Harper			
Chew Toys, asst.	3/4	$ 18.75	$ 14.06	
Med. Bonie	1/2	$ 53.00	$ 26.50	
Leash	1 1/8	$ 190.00	$ 213.75	
Puppy Food	5 1/2	$ 24.50	$ 134.75	
		Grand Total	$ 389.06	

Using Form Controls

■ You can insert **form controls** in a worksheet to create a **form** for collecting information that can be stored and analyzed.

■ For example, a human resources department might use a form to collect and store employee information.

■ Use the commands in the Controls group on the DEVELOPER tab of the Ribbon to insert form controls.

  ✓ *Recall that the DEVELOPER tab does not display by default; you must use the Excel Options to make it available.*

■ Available form controls include the following:

  • Button: Performs an action, such as a running macro.

  • Combo box: Also known as a drop-down list box. You can type an entry or choose one item from the list.

  • Check box: Turns a value on or off. A check box can be selected (turned on), cleared (turned off), or mixed (allow multiple selection).

  • Spin button: Increases or decreases a value, such as a number increment, time, or date. You can also type a value directly into the cell.

  • List box: Displays a list of one or more text items from which a user can choose.

  • Option button: Allows a single choice in a set of mutually exclusive choices. An option button can be selected (turned on), cleared (turned off), or mixed (allow multiple selection). An option button is also referred to as a radio button.

  • Group box: Groups related controls into a rectangle and can include a label.

  • Label: Descriptive text (such as titles, captions, pictures) or brief instructions.

  • Scroll bar: Scrolls through a range of values.

■ Some form controls are disabled by default. You can enable them by changing the **ActiveX** Settings in the Trust Center Settings on the Trust Center tab in the Excel Options; however, this may allow potentially dangerous controls to run on your computer.

  ✓ *If you need additional controls or more flexibility than form controls allow, you can insert ActiveX controls using the commands in the Controls group on the DEVELOPER tab of the Ribbon.*

■ Consider the form layout and the order of the form controls when inserting form controls.

■ The insertion point moves from control to control based on the order in which controls are inserted in the document, not based on the order in which the controls are arranged.

Try It! **Using Form Controls**

1 In the **E53Try_xx** file, click cell C9, and on the HOME tab, in the Editing group, click Clear 🧹 Clear▾ > Clear All.

2 Click FILE > Options > Customize Ribbon.

3 Under Customize the Ribbon, click to select the Developer check box, and click OK. The DEVELOPER tab displays on the Ribbon.

4 Click DEVELOPER.

5 In the Controls group, click Insert 🧰 Insert, and click the Combo Box form control button 📑.

6 Position the insertion point at the top edge of cell C9.

  ✓ *The insertion pointer changes to a crosshair symbol* +.

7 Click and drag the crosshair insertion pointer across the cell range C9:D9, and release the mouse button.

8 Click the New Sheet button ⊕ to create a new sheet.

9 On Sheet1, click cell A1, type **Alice Harper**, and press ENTER.

10 Click cell A2, type **Greg Bimmel**, and press ENTER.

11 Click cell A3, type **Lucinda Diego**, and press ENTER.

12 Click the Sales Tracker tab, right-click the list box form control, and click Format Control. The Format Control dialog box displays.

13 On the Control tab, click in the Input range text box, click Sheet2, and select the cell range A1:A3.

14 Click OK.

15 Click the combo box drop-down arrow, and click Greg Bimmel.

16 Save and close the file, and exit Excel.

Form controls on the DEVELOPER tab

Pete's Pets

214 North Place Street, Cumberland, OH 43732

Sales Tracker

Date:	9/21/2014			
Customer:	3829992			
Salesperson:	Greg Bimmel	▼		
	Alice Harper			
	Greg Bimmel		**Product**	
	Lucinda Diego			
	Ordered	**per Case**	**Total Sales**	
Chew Toys, asst.	3/4	$ 18.75	$ 14.06	
Med. Bonie	1/2	$ 53.00	$ 26.50	
Leash	1 1/8	$ 190.00	$ 213.75	
Puppy Food	5 1/2	$ 24.50	$ 134.75	
		Grand Total	$ 389.06	

Lesson 53—Practice

As assistant manager for a local PhotoTown store, you have been asked to create a weekly payroll tracker. In this project, you will use line breaks and text wrapping to make the worksheet visually appealing and easy to read.

DIRECTIONS

1. Start Excel, if necessary, and open **E53Practice** from the data files for this lesson.

2. Save the file as **E53Practice_xx** in the location where your teacher instructs you to store the files for this lesson.

3. Add a header that has your name at the left, the date code in the center, and the page number code at the right, and change back to **Normal** view.

4. In cell **E6**, type **Hourly**, press `ALT` + `ENTER`, type **Rate**, and press `ENTER`.

5. In cell **D6**, type **Regular Weekly Hours**, and press `ENTER`.

6. In cell **C6**, type **Full or Part Time**, and press `ENTER`.

7. Select the cell range **C6:E6**, and on the HOME tab, click **Center** ≡.

8. Select cell **C6** > **Wrap Text** 🗟.

9. On the HOME tab, click **Format Painter** 🖌, and click cell **D6**.

10. Select cell **C6**, and click in the formula bar. Move the insertion point to just before the **P**, press `ALT`, and press `ENTER`.

11. Click cell **G24**, type **Weekly Payroll** and press `ENTER`.

12. Click cell **G24** > **Align Right** ≡.

13. **With your teacher's permission**, print the worksheet. It should look similar to Figure 53-1.

14. Save and close the file, and exit Excel.

Figure 53-1

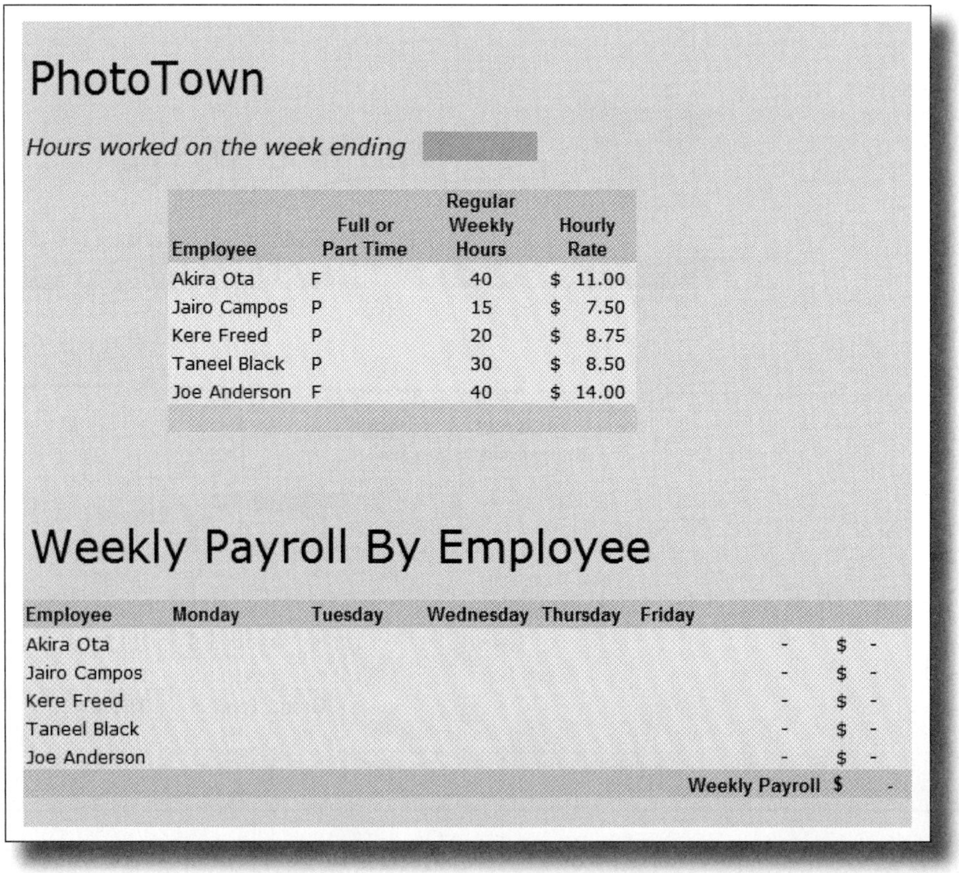

Lesson 53—Apply

As assistant manager for a local PhotoTown store, you have created a weekly payroll tracker. In this project, you will calculate the total weekly hours worked for each clerk and insert a form control.

DIRECTIONS

1. Start Excel, if necessary, open **E53Apply** from the data files for this lesson.

2. Save the file as **E53Apply_xx** in the location where your teacher instructs you to store the files for this lesson.

3. Add a header that has your name at the left, the date code in the center, and the page number code at the right, and change back to **Normal** view.

4. In cell **G18**, type **Total Hours This Week**, and press `ENTER`.

5. In cell **H18**, type **Weekly Income**, and press `ENTER`.

6. Select cells **G18:H18** > **Wrap Text**.

7. Change the column width for column G to **11**, and adjust the row height for row 18.

8. In cell **D4**, enter the fraction **8/15**, and press `ENTER`. Notice that Excel autmatically interprets the fraction as a date.

9. Enter the following hours for the employees:

Employee	Day	Hours
Kere Freed	Monday	3/4
Taneel Black	Tuesday	4 1/2
Taneel Black	Thursday	5 1/2
Joe Anderson	Thursday	6 1/2

   ✓ *When entering the Monday hours, remember to type a zero followed by a space before typing the fraction.*

10. Click cell **G4** > DEVELOPER > Insert .

11. Click the Check Box form control button ☑.

12. Position the insertion point at the top edge of cell G4, drag the crosshair insertion pointer across the cell range G4:H4, and release the mouse button

14. Right-click the check box form control > **Edit Text**.

15. Replace the existing text label with **Approved by manager**, right-click the check box form control > **Exit Edit Text**.

16. Click outside of the form control, and click the check box of the form control.

19. **With your teacher's permission**, print the worksheet. It should look similar to Figure 53-2 on the next page.

20. Save and close the file, and exit Excel.

Figure 53-2

PhotoTown

Hours worked on the week ending   15-Aug   ☑ Approved by manager

Employee	Full or Part Time	Regular Weekly Hours	Hourly Rate
Akira Ota	F	40	$ 11.00
Jairo Campos	P	15	$ 7.50
Kere Freed	P	20	$ 8.75
Taneel Black	P	30	$ 8.50
Joe Anderson	F	40	$ 14.00

Weekly Payroll By Employee

Employee	Monday	Tuesday	Wednesday	Thursday	Friday	Total Hours This Week	Weekly Income
Akira Ota	8	8	8	8	8	40	$ 440.00
Jairo Campos	3		3		3	9	$ 67.50
Kere Freed	3/4		5	5		11	$ 94.06
Taneel Black	5	4 1/2	5	5 1/2	5	25	$ 212.50
Joe Anderson	5	5	6	6 1/2	8	31	$ 427.00
					Weekly Payroll		$ 1,241.06

Lesson 54

Formatting and Replacing Data Using Functions

➤ What You Will Learn

Formatting Text with Functions
Replacing Text with Functions

Software Skills   Using a series of simple text functions, such as PROPER, UPPER, and LOWER, you can quickly change text that has been entered incorrectly. For example, with the UPPER function, you can change the text in a cell to all uppercase. You can use the SUBSTITUTE and REPLACE functions to update existing data (such as department names, cost codes, or dates).

WORDS TO KNOW

Case
The use of capital (uppercase) and small letters (lowercase) in text.

What You Can Do

Formatting Text with Functions

- If you enter your own text into a worksheet, chances are that you entered it with the correct **case**. For example, every sentence probably begins with a capital letter.

- If you're using text from another source, however, it may or may not be properly capitalized. Excel provides some functions that might be able to solve such a problem:

  - PROPER (*text*)—Capitalizes the first letter at the beginning of each word, plus any letters that follow any character that is not a letter, such as a number or a punctuation mark.

  - UPPER (*text*)—Changes all letters to uppercase.

  - LOWER (*text*)—Changes all letters to lowercase.

Try It!   **Formatting Text Using the PROPER Function**

1 Start Excel, and open **E54Try** from the data files for this lesson.

2 Save the file as **E54Try_xx** in the location where your teacher instructs you to store the files for this lesson.

3 Click cell C33.

4 Click FORMULAS > Text ⬛.

5 Click PROPER. The Function Arguments dialog box displays.

6 In the Text box, type **C12** (the source data).

7 Click OK.

8 Save the changes to the file, and leave it open to use in the next Try It.

The Text function in the Functions Library

FILE	HOME	INSERT	PAGE LAYOUT	FORMULAS	DATA	REVIEW

Insert Function | AutoSum | Recently Used | Financial | Logical | Text | Date & Time | Lookup & Reference | Math & Trig | More Functions

C33

	A	B			D
10	Jennifer	Flynn	9876 Wilshire A	BAHTTEXT	INDIANAPOLIS
11	Eram	Hassan	8123 Maple Ave	CHAR	INDIANAPOLIS
12	Betty	High	7543 newport b	CLEAN	INDIANAPOLIS
13	Ashley	Kay	8738 Log Run Dr	CODE	FISHERS
14	Chu	Lee	5821 Wilshire A	CONCATENATE	INDIANAPOLIS
15	Wu	Lee	6467 Riverside	DOLLAR	FISHERS
16	Martha	Luck	4131 Brown Roa	EXACT	INDIANAPOLIS
17	Chu Gi	Nguyen	8794 Dean Road	FIND	INDIANAPOLIS
18	Julie	Powell	5466 North Pen	FIXED	CARMEL
19	Bonnie	Sferruzzi	21 Adams Way	LEFT	CARMEL
20	Antonia	WHITNEY	2414 Hidden Va	LEN	Carmel
21				LOWER	
22				MID	
23				NUMBERVALUE	
24				PROPER	
25				REPLACE	
				REPT	
26	First Name	Last Name	Address	RIGHT	City
27	Barbara	Adamson	7770 Dean Road	SEARCH	INDIANAPOLIS
28	Carlos	Altare	4125 Fairlinks A	SUBSTITUTE	
29	Jan	Borough	7556 Hilltop Wa	T	INDIANAPOLIS
30	Mary Jane	Brink	704 Fairway Dri		INDIANAPOLIS
31	Jennifer	Flynn	9876 Wilshire A	TEXT	INDIANAPOLIS
32	Eram	Hassan	8123 Maple Ave	TRIM	INDIANAPOLIS
33	Betty	High		UNICHAR	INDIANAPOLIS
34	Ashley	Kay	8738 Log Run Dr	UNICODE	Fishers
35	Chu	Lee	5821 Wilshire A	UPPER	INDIANAPOLIS
36	Wu	Lee	6467 Riverside		Fishers
37	Martha	Luck	4131 Brown Roa	VALUE	INDIANAPOLIS
38	Chu Gi	Nguyen	8794 Dean Road	fx Insert Function...	INDIANAPOLIS
39	Julie	Powell	5466 North Pennsylvania street		CARMEL

Try It!   Formatting Text Using the UPPER Function

1 In the **E54Try_xx** file, select cell D28.

2 Click FORMULAS > Text A.

3 Click UPPER.

4 In the Text box, type **D7** (the source data).

5 Click OK.

6 Save the changes to the file, and leave it open to use in the next Try It.

The Function Arguments dialog box

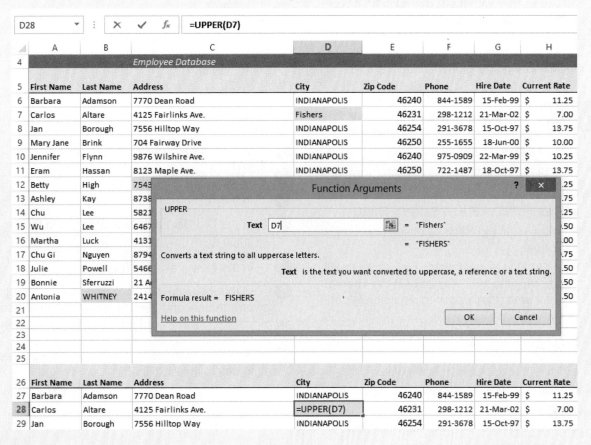

Try It!   Formatting Text Using the LOWER Function

1 In the **E54Try_xx** file, select cell B41.

2 Click FORMULAS > Text A.

3 Click LOWER.

4 In the Text box, type **B20** (the source data).

5 Click OK.

6 Save the changes to the file, and leave it open to use in the next Try It.

Replacing Text with Functions

- Sometimes, all an old worksheet needs in order to be useful again is an update.

- One way in which you can update data (such as department names, cost codes, or dates) is to substitute good text for the outdated text.

  - SUBSTITUTE (*text, old_text, new_text, instance_num*)—Replaces *old_text* with *new_text* in the cell you specify with the text argument. If you specify a particular *instance* of *old_text*, such as instance 3, then SUBSTITUTE replaces only that specific instance—the third instance—of *old_text* and not all of them.

- REPLACE (*old_text, start_num, num_chars, new_text*)—Replaces *old_text* with *new_text*, beginning at the position (*start_num*) you specify. The argument *num_chars* tells Excel how many characters to replace. This allows you to replace 4 characters with only 2 if you want.

Try It!   **Changing Text Using the SUBSTITUTE Function**

1 In the **E54Try_xx** file, click cell E7.

2 Use advanced find options to locate a shaded cell without any data:

   a. Click HOME > Find & Select > Find.

   b. In the Find and Replace dialog box, click Format.

   c. In the Find Format dialog box, click the Fill tab, click the light gray color in the Theme color area (third option in the first row), and click OK.

   d. Click Options, and in the Search box, select By Columns.

   e. Verify that the Look in box is Values.

   f. Click to select the Match entire cell contents check box, and click Find Next.

   g. Close the Find and Replace dialog box.

3 In cell K27, click FORMULAS > Text Ⓐ.

4 Click SUBSTITUTE.

5 In the Text box, type **K6** (the source data).

6 In the Old_Text box, type **2** (the item being substituted).

7 In the New_Text box, type **6**.

8 In the Instance_num box, type **2** (indicating that only the second 2 in the cell will be changed).

9 Click OK.

10 Save the changes to the file, and leave it open to use in the next Try It.

The Function Arguments dialog box for the SUSTITUTE function

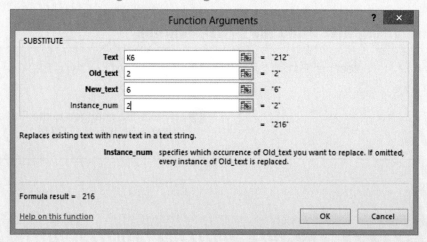

Try It!   **Changing Text Using the REPLACE Function**

1. In the **E54Try_xx** file, select cell Q27.

2. Click FORMULAS > Text [A].

3. Click REPLACE.

4. In the Old Text box, type **P27** (the source data).

5. In the Start_num box, type **4** (to indicate that the change should begin at the fourth digit from the left).

6. In the Num_chars box, type **2** (to indicate that 2 digits should be changed).

7. In the New_text box, type **50** (indicating that the Adjusted Rate should end in .50).

8. Click OK.

9. Save and close the file, and exit Excel.

Lesson 54—Practice

As the new Human Resources Manager for PhotoTown, you've been getting familiar with various worksheets. You notice that the Payroll worksheet needs to be updated with new department numbers. In this project, you will correct the text using Excel's SUBSTITUTE text function to avoid retyping the data.

DIRECTIONS

1. Start Excel, if necessary, and open **E54Practice** from the data files for this lesson.

2. Save the file as **E54Practice_xx** in the location where your teacher instructs you to store the files for this lesson.

3. Insert a new column between columns E and F:

   a. Click the column header for column **F**.

   b. Right-click, and click **Insert**.

4. Click cell **E7**, click at the beginning of the formula bar, type **Old** and a space, and press [ENTER].

5. Click cell **F7**, type **New Department Number**, aand press [ENTER].

6. Use the SUBSTITUTE text function to change all of the department numbers beginning with a 6 to begin with a 9 instead:

   a. With cell **F8** selected, click **FORMULAS** > **Text** [A] > **SUBSTITUTE**.

   b. In the Text box, type **E8**.

   c. In the Old_text box, type **6**.

   d. In the New_text box, type **9**.

   e. In the Instance_num box, type **1** and click **OK**.

7. Copy the formula down the cell range **F9:F37**:

   a. In cell F8, click **HOME** > **Copy** 📋.

   b. Select the cell range **F9:F37**.

   c. On the **HOME** tab, click the **Paste** drop-down arrow > **Formulas** 𝑓ₓ.

8. Click **INSERT** > **Header & Footer** 📄 > **Header** 📄 > **Prepared by UserName Today's Date, Page 1**.

9. In PAGE LAYOUT view, in the header, replace the username with your name.

10. **With your teacher's permission**, print the worksheet. It should look similar to Figure 54-1 on the next page.

11. Save and close the file, and exit Excel.

Figure 54-1

PhotoTown Employee Listing
Miller Rd
Unit #2166

Employee ID Number	Title	First Name	Last Name	Old Department Number	New Department Number	Department Name	Rate	Soc Sec No.
63778	Mr.	Carlos	Altare	610412pr	910412pr	processing	$6.30	504-12-3131
71335	Mr.	Taneed	Black	218975am	218975am	asst. manager	$7.00	775-15-1315
31524	Mrs.	Jan	Borough	611748qc	911748qc	quality control	$6.50	727-25-6981
18946	Mr.	Shakur	Brown	482178ca	482178ca	cashier	$7.00	505-43-9587
22415	Mr.	Jairo	Campos	614522in	914522in	inker	$7.20	110-56-2897
20965	Mrs.	Rafiquil	Damir	611748qc	911748qc	quality control	$6.15	102-33-5656
64121	Mrs.	Diana	Dogwood	618796so	918796so	special orders	$6.20	821-55-3262
30388	Mrs.	Lucy	Fan	610412pr	910412pr	processing	$6.55	334-25-6959
44185	Mrs.	Jennifer	Flynn	482178ca	482178ca	cashier	$7.00	221-32-9585
32152	Ms.	Katerina	Flynn	271858kc	271858kc	kiosk control	$7.10	107-45-9111
31885	Ms.	Kere	Freed	610412pr	910412pr	processing	$7.10	222-15-9484
33785	Mr.	Eram	Hassan	271858kc	271858kc	kiosk control	$6.85	203-25-6984
55648	Mr.	Tyrell	Johnson	218975am	218975am	asst. manager	$6.50	468-25-9684
60219	Ms.	Verna	Latinz	611748qc	911748qc	quality control	$6.30	705-85-6352
28645	Mr.	Wu	Lee	618796so	918796so	special orders	$7.00	255-41-9784
67415	Mr.	Shamir	Lewis	610412pr	910412pr	processing	$7.10	112-42-7897
27995	Mrs.	Maria	Navarro	610412pr	910412pr	processing	$6.30	302-42-8465
32151	Mr.	Tony	Navarro	271858kc	271858kc	kiosk control	$6.35	401-78-9855
28499	Mr.	Chu Gi	Nguyen	611748qc	911748qc	quality control	$6.85	823-55-6487
17564	Mr.	Juan	Nuniez	614522in	914522in	inker	$7.00	208-65-4932
14558	Mr.	Akira	Ota	611748qc	911748qc	quality control	$7.25	285-68-9853
31022	Mrs.	Meghan	Ryan	610412pr	910412pr	processing	$7.00	421-85-6452
41885	Mrs.	Kate	Scott	482178ca	482178ca	cashier	$6.85	489-55-4862
25448	Mr.	Jyoti	Shaw	611748qc	911748qc	quality control	$6.50	389-24-6567
23151	Ms.	Jewel	Vidito	611748qc	911748qc	quality control	$6.55	885-63-7158
37785	Mrs.	Corrine	Walters	618796so	918796so	special orders	$6.65	622-34-8891
58945	Mrs.	Antonia	Whitney	271858kc	271858kc	kiosk control	$6.75	312-86-7141
57445	Mr.	Shale	Wilson	482178ca	482178ca	cashier	$7.00	375-86-3425
36684	Mrs.	Shiree	Wilson	482178ca	482178ca	cashier	$7.10	415-65-6658
55412	Mrs.	Su	Yamaguchi	610412pr	910412pr	processing	$6.30	324-75-8021

Lesson 54—Apply

You are the new Human Resources Manager for PhotoTown, and you've been working with various worksheets. It's been brought to your attention that the Payroll worksheet has several text-related problems. In this project, you will correct the text using Excel's text functions.

DIRECTIONS

1. Start Excel, if necessary, and open **E54Apply** from the data files for this lesson,

2. Save the file as **E54Apply_xx** in the location where your teacher instructs you to store the files for this lesson.

3. Add a header that has your name at the left, the date code in the center, and the page number code at the right, and change back to **Normal** view.

4. Insert a new column between columns F and G:
   a. Click the column header for column **G**.
   b. Right-click, and click **Insert**.

5. Use the UPPER text function to capitalize the letters at the end of each new department number:
   a. Click cell **G8** > **FORMULAS** > **Text** > **UPPER**.
   b. In the Text box, type **F8**, and click **OK**.
   c. Drag the fill handle down to copy this formula down the cell range **G9:G37**.

6. Copy the text in cell F7 to G7:
   a. Click cell **F7**.
   b. Drag the fill handle to **G7**.

7. Insert a new column between columns H and I:
   a. Click the column header for column **I**.
   b. Right-click, and click **Insert**.

8. Use the PROPER text function to capitalize the department names using title case in column H:
   a. Click cell **I8** > **FORMULAS** > **Text** > **PROPER**.
   b. In the Text box, type **H8**, and click **OK**.
   c. Drag the fill handle down to copy this formula down the cell range **I9:I37**.

9. Copy the text in cell H7 to I7 using the fill handle method in step 6.

10. Hide columns F and H:
    a. Click the **F** column header, press and hold CTRL, and click the **H** column header.
    b. Right-click, and click **Hide**.

11. **With your teacher's permission**, print the worksheet. It should look similar to Figure 54-2 on the next page.

12. Save and close the file, and exit Excel.

Figure 54-2

PhotoTown Employee Listing
Miller Rd
Unit #2166

Employee ID Number	Title	First Name	Last Name	Old Department Number	New Department Number	Department Name	Rate	Soc Sec No.
63778	Mr.	Carlos	Altare	610412pr	910412PR	Processing	$6.30	504-12-3131
71335	Mr.	Taneed	Black	218975am	218975AM	Asst. Manager	$7.00	775-15-1315
31524	Mrs.	Jan	Borough	611748qc	911748QC	Quality Control	$6.50	727-25-6981
18946	Mr.	Shakur	Brown	482178ca	482178CA	Cashier	$7.00	505-43-9587
22415	Mr.	Jairo	Campos	614522in	914522IN	Inker	$7.20	110-56-2897
20965	Mrs.	Rafiquil	Damir	611748qc	911748QC	Quality Control	$6.15	102-33-5656
64121	Mrs.	Diana	Dogwood	618796so	918796SO	Special Orders	$6.20	821-55-3262
30388	Mrs.	Lucy	Fan	610412pr	910412PR	Processing	$6.55	334-25-6959
44185	Mrs.	Jennifer	Flynn	482178ca	482178CA	Cashier	$7.00	221-32-9585
32152	Ms.	Katerina	Flynn	271858kc	271858KC	Kiosk Control	$7.10	107-45-9111
31885	Ms.	Kere	Freed	610412pr	910412PR	Processing	$7.10	222-15-9484
33785	Mr.	Eram	Hassan	271858kc	271858KC	Kiosk Control	$6.85	203-25-6984
55648	Mr.	Tyrell	Johnson	218975am	218975AM	Asst. Manager	$6.50	468-25-9684
60219	Ms.	Verna	Latinz	611748qc	911748QC	Quality Control	$6.30	705-85-6352
28645	Mr.	Wu	Lee	618796so	918796SO	Special Orders	$7.00	255-41-9784
67415	Mr.	Shamir	Lewis	610412pr	910412PR	Processing	$7.10	112-42-7897
27995	Mrs.	Maria	Navarro	610412pr	910412PR	Processing	$6.30	302-42-8465
32151	Mr.	Tony	Navarro	271858kc	271858KC	Kiosk Control	$6.35	401-78-9855
28499	Mr.	Chu Gi	Nguyen	611748qc	911748QC	Quality Control	$6.85	823-55-6487
17564	Mr.	Juan	Nuniez	614522in	914522IN	Inker	$7.00	208-65-4932
14558	Mr.	Akira	Ota	611748qc	911748QC	Quality Control	$7.25	285-68-9853
31022	Mrs.	Meghan	Ryan	610412pr	910412PR	Processing	$7.00	421-85-6452
41885	Mrs.	Kate	Scott	482178ca	482178CA	Cashier	$6.85	489-55-4862
25448	Mr.	Jyoti	Shaw	611748qc	911748QC	Quality Control	$6.50	389-24-6567
23151	Ms.	Jewel	Vidito	611748qc	911748QC	Quality Control	$6.55	885-63-7158
37785	Mrs.	Corrine	Walters	618796so	918796SO	Special Orders	$6.65	622-34-8891
58945	Mrs.	Antonia	Whitney	271858kc	271858KC	Kiosk Control	$6.75	312-86-7141
57445	Mr.	Shale	Wilson	482178ca	482178CA	Cashier	$7.00	375-86-3425
36684	Mrs.	Shiree	Wilson	482178ca	482178CA	Cashier	$7.10	415-65-6658
55412	Mrs.	Su	Yamaguchi	610412pr	910412PR	Processing	$6.30	324-75-8021

Lesson 55

Working with Subtotals

➤ What You Will Learn

Using Go To and Go To Special
Creating Subtotals
Creating Nested Subtotals
Hiding or Displaying Details
Removing Subtotals
Manually Outlining and Adding Subtotals

Software Skills   You can use the Go To command to instantly jump to any cell in a worksheet. With the Subtotals feature, you can create automatic totals within the records of a database to help you perform more complex analyses. For example, if the database contains sales records for various stores, you can create totals for each store or each salesperson. Use the Subtotals feature to total numeric data instantly without having to insert rows, create formulas, or copy data.

What You Can Do

Using Go To and Go To Special

■ Go To is a feature that allows you to tell Excel the exact address of the cell that you want to be the current active cell.

■ Using Go To changes the location of the active cell.

■ If your goal is not to locate data, but to find particular kinds of cells quickly and select them, then you need a different kind of Find command—Go To Special.

■ Using Go To Special, you can locate cells that contain the following:
- Comments
- Constants
- Formulas
- Row differences, Column differences
- Precedents, Dependents
- Blanks
- Conditional formats
- Data validation

- You can also locate the following:
  - Cells in the current region
  - Cells in the current array
  - Objects
  - The last cell with data
  - Visible (non-hidden) cells

- Some of the Go To commands are accessible from the Find & Select menu on the HOME tab; others are in the Go To Special dialog box.

  ✓ *If you want to select a group of related cells using Go To, click the Special button in the Go To dialog box; then choose the type of cells you want to select and click OK*

Try It!   **Using Go To and Go To Special**

① Start Excel, and open **E55Try** from the data files for this lesson.

② Save the file as **E55Try_xx** in the location where your teacher instructs you to store the files for this lesson.

③ On the HOME tab, click Find & Select 🔍 > Go To. The Go To dialog box displays.

④ In the Reference text box, type **A1**.

⑤ Click OK.

⑥ On the HOME tab, click Find & Select 🔍 > Go To Special.

⑦ Click to select the Formulas option, and click OK.

⑧ Save the changes to the file, and leave it open to use in the next Try It.

The Go To Special dialog box

Creating Subtotals

- You can use the Subtotal feature to insert subtotals between similar rows in an Excel list without having to create custom **functions**.

  ✓ *You learned about the SUBTOTAL function and creating a subtotal in Lesson 11.*

  - Instead of entering DSUM formulas to total a field for particular rows, you can use the Subtotal feature. For example, you can subtotal a sales list to compute the amount sold by each salesperson on a given day.

  - You can also use the Subtotal feature to insert other **database functions**, such as DCOUNT and DAVERAGE.

    ✓ *You will learn more about using database functions in Lesson 71.*

- Recall that the Subtotal feature:
  - Calculates subtotals for all rows that contain the same entry in one column.
  - Inserts the totals in a row just below that group of data.
  - Calculates a grand total.
  - Inserts a label for each group totaled/subtotaled.
  - Displays the outline controls.

- For the Subtotal feature to work, all records containing values that contribute to that subtotal (or other calculation) must be sorted together.
  - Before applying the subtotal feature, sort the list so that all records that are to be calculated together, are grouped together. This way, for example, all of the "Sacramento" entries will be in a group.

- Excel inserts a subtotal line whenever it detects a change in the value of the chosen field—for instance, a change from "Sacramento" to "San Francisco."

- Also, if the subtotal line is to show the average pledge amount for all callers to the Sacramento office, then each pledge must contain "Sacramento" in one column—preferably one with a meaningful field name, such as "Office."

■ When you click the Subtotal button on the DATA tab, a dialog box displays from which you can make several choices:

- *At each change in*—Select the field name by which you want to total.

- *Use function*—Select a database function.

- *Add subtotal to*—Select one or more fields to use with the database function you selected.

- *Replace current subtotals*—Select this option to create a new subtotal within a database, removing any current subtotals. Deselect this option to retain current subtotals.

- *Page break between groups*—Places each subtotaled group on its own page.

- *Summary below data*—Inserts the subtotals/grand total below each group, rather than above it.

- *Remove All*—Removes all subtotals.

■ Subtotals act just like any other formula; if you change the data, the total will recalculate automatically.

■ You can use the Subtotal feature on a filtered list.

- The totals are calculated based only on the displayed data.

  ✓ *You learned about filtering a list in Lesson 32.*

■ You cannot use the Subtotals feature on an Excel table. You must first convert the table to a list, and then use the Subtotals feature.

Try It!   **Creating Subtotals**

1 In the **E55Try_xx** file, sort the list before you add subtotals:

     a. Select the cell range A5:G29.

     b. On the HOME tab, click Sort & Filter.

     c. Click Sort A to Z.

2 Click DATA > Subtotal.

3 In the At each change in drop-down list, click Item Type, if necessary.

     ✓ *A new subtotal will be calculated at each change within the column you choose here.*

4 In the Use function box, click Sum, if necessary.

5 In the Add Subtotal to box, click to select the Items Sold and Value Sold check boxes. Deselect all other check boxes.

6 Verify that Summary below data is checked.

7 If desired, you can choose the Replace current subtotals option.

8 Click OK.

9 Save the changes to the file, and leave it open to use in the next Try It.

Creating Nested Subtotals

■ You can create subtotals within subtotals (nested subtotals).

■ To create nested subtotals, sort the list by both of the fields you wish to total.

   ✓ *You need to subtotal the list before you can create a nested subtotal.*

Try It!   **Creating Nested Subtotals**

① In the **E55Try_xx** file, select the cell range A5:G37, if necessary.

② Click DATA > Subtotal ⊞.

③ Click the At each change in box drop-down arrow, and click Description.

④ Verify that the Use function box is still Sum

⑤ Verify that the Add subtotal to options of Items Sold and Value Sold are checked.

⑥ Verify that Summary below data is checked.

⑦ Click to deselect the Replace current subtotals check box.

⑧ Click OK.

⑨ Save the changes to the file, and leave it open to use in the next Try It.

Nested subtotals

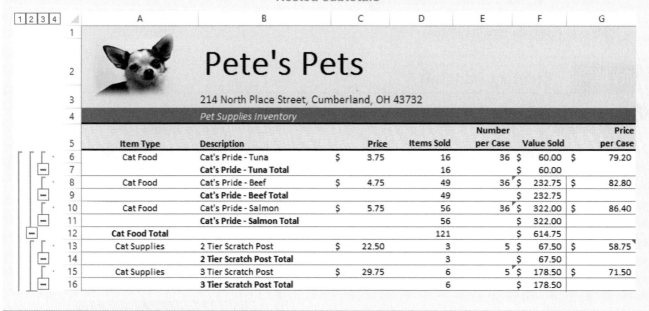

1 2 3 4		A	B	C	D	E	F	G
	1							
	2		**Pete's Pets**					
	3		214 North Place Street, Cumberland, OH 43732					
	4		*Pet Supplies Inventory*					
	5	**Item Type**	**Description**	**Price**	**Items Sold**	**Number per Case**	**Value Sold**	**Price per Case**
	6	Cat Food	Cat's Pride - Tuna	$ 3.75	16	36	$ 60.00	$ 79.20
	7		**Cat's Pride - Tuna Total**		16		$ 60.00	
	8	Cat Food	Cat's Pride - Beef	$ 4.75	49	36	$ 232.75	$ 82.80
	9		**Cat's Pride - Beef Total**		49		$ 232.75	
	10	Cat Food	Cat's Pride - Salmon	$ 5.75	56	36	$ 322.00	$ 86.40
	11		**Cat's Pride - Salmon Total**		56		$ 322.00	
	12	**Cat Food Total**			121		$ 614.75	
	13	Cat Supplies	2 Tier Scratch Post	$ 22.50	3	5	$ 67.50	$ 58.75
	14		**2 Tier Scratch Post Total**		3		$ 67.50	
	15	Cat Supplies	3 Tier Scratch Post	$ 29.75	6	5	$ 178.50	$ 71.50
	16		**3 Tier Scratch Post Total**		6		$ 178.50	

Hiding or Displaying Details

- The Subtotal feature displays the outline controls around the worksheet frame.
- With the outline controls, you can hide or display the records within any given group.
  - For example, you could hide the details of each salesperson's individual sales, and show only his or her subtotal.
  - You could also show details for some salespeople while hiding the details for others.

- The first subtotal added to a worksheet subdivides it into *three* levels of data.
  - The highest detail number always represents the view with *all* the data.
  - Detail level 1 always represents grand totals only.
  - Intermediate detail levels represent summaries of detail levels.
- Each subtotal added to a worksheet that already contains subtotals adds one detail level.

Try It!	Hiding or Displaying Details

1 In the **E55Try_xx** file, select cell C12.

2 On the DATA tab, click Hide Detail ⌐̲. Notice that all the rows in the Cat Food type are hidden.

3 In the outline control area, click the plus sign ⊞ to the left of row 12.

4 Click the 1 outline level button ①to hide the entire list.

5 Click the 3 outline level button ③ to show the subtotals.

6 On the DATA tab, click Show Detail ⁺̲ to show the entire list.

7 Save the changes to the file, and leave it open to use in the next Try It.

Removing Subtotals

- You can remove the subtotals from a list by clicking the Remove All button in the Subtotal dialog box.
- You can also remove subtotals by creating new subtotals that replace old ones.

- If you just created the subtotals and you don't like the results, click the Undo button on the Quick Access Toolbar to remove the subtotals, and then start over.

Try It!	Removing Subtotals

1 In the **E55Try_xx** file, click anywhere in the list.

2 On the DATA tab, click Subtotal ▦.

3 Click Remove All.

4 Save the changes to the file, and leave it open to use in the next Try It.

Manually Outlining and Adding Subtotals

- Even with the Subtotal feature, you might still want to manually outline (group) a list.
  - For example, you might use the Group feature to manually group particular rows together.
- You can use the Group feature to create a list that contains totals for multiple fields in the same row.

- You can also use the Group feature to manually group columns together, in a situation where your data is arranged mainly in rows (rather than mainly in columns).
- Use the Group feature on an Excel table to add subtotals and outlining controls to the table.

Try It!   **Manually Outlining and Adding Subtotals**

① In the **E55Try_xx** file, right-click the heading for row 13, and click Insert.

② Select the cell range A6:G12.

③ On the DATA tab, click Group 📇.

④ Verify that the Rows option is selected, and click OK.

⑤ Click HOME > AutoSum Σ.

⑥ Click DATA > Ungroup 📇.

⑦ Verify that the Rows option is selected, and click OK.

⑧ Save and close the file, and close Excel.

Lesson 55—Practice

The August usage statistics for Giant Frog Supermarkets' leased network space have been added to Intellidata's ongoing usage logs. With so much new data to keep track of, the workbook now needs to be reorganized so managers can view meaningful summaries of the data. In this project, you will use the Go To feature to locate data and add subtotals to make the data easier to analyze.

DIRECTIONS

1. Start Excel, if necessary, and open **E55Practice** from the data files for this lesson.

2. Save the file as **E55Practice_xx** in the location where your teacher instructs you to store the files for this lesson.

3. Group the sheets. Add a footer that has your name at the left, the date code in the center, and the page number code at the right, and change back to **Normal** view. Ungroup the sheets.

4. Click the **Forecasts** worksheet.

5. On the HOME tab, click **Find & Select** 🔍 > **Go To**.

6. In the Reference box, type **G74**, and click **OK**.

7. On the HOME tab, click **Find & Select** 🔍 > **Go To Special**.

8. Select **Comments**, if necessary, and click **OK**.

9. Click **REVIEW** > **Edit Comment** 📝 to read the comment.

10. Click cell **D38** to close the comment.

11. On the REVIEW tab, click **Delete Comment** 🗑, and type **1974** in cell **D38**.

12. Click the **Usage statistics 0804** worksheet tab.

13. In the Usage statistics 0804 worksheet, create subtotals for each Sunday that begins a measurement period:
    a. Select the cell range **A5:G140**.
    b. Click **DATA** > **Subtotal** 📇.
    c. Verify that the **At each change in** list is **Date**.
    d. Verify that the **Use function** list is **Sum**.
    e. In the **Add subtotal to** list, click to select the **Avg. Bandwidth**, **Data In**, and **Data Out** check boxes. Verify that the **Transactions** check box is selected.

f. Click to deselect the **Replace current subtotals** check box, if necessary.

g. Click to deselect the **Page break between groups** check box, if necessary.

h. Verify that the **Summary below data** check box is selected.

i. Click **OK**. Notice that there are now three levels of detail. Level 3 shows all the data; level 2 shows just the subtotals for each week; and level 1 shows only the grand totals.

14. Adjust column widths as necessary.

15. Click the 2 outline level button ☐2 to view all the subtotals.

16. Select the cell range **A1:G150**, click **PAGE LAYOUT > Print Area** 🖨 **> Set Print Area**.

17. **With your teacher's permission**, print the worksheet. It should look similar to Figure 55-1.

18. Save and close the file, and exit Excel.

Figure 55-1

Intellidata
Hosting · Management · Warehousing

Usage statistics

Giant Frog Supermarkets - District # 0855

Period of 4 July - 4 September 2014

Date	Department	Region	Kb/sec Avg. Bandwidth	Mb Data In	Mb Data Out	Transactions
7/4/2014 Total			1404.9	23093	133364	579502
7/11/2014 Total			1339.5	22300	125960	555785
7/18/2014 Total			1377.7	23944	129681	566206
7/25/2014 Total			1464.4	25935	139778	586438
8/1/2014 Total			1439.5	24978	142019	578358
8/8/2014 Total			1400.8	23830	139363	572934
8/15/2014 Total			1406.2	24204	139935	487461
8/22/2014 Total			1410.9	27659	149379	577563
8/29/2014 Total			1433.6	28952	158298	605427
Grand Total			12677.5	224895	1257777	5109674

Lesson 55—Apply

You are a manager for Intellidata, an information technology management company. You have been working on the ongoing usage worksheets that track the leased network space data for Giant Frog Supermarkets. You now need to tabulate the data so that other managers can view meaningful summaries of the data. In this project, you will create nested subtotals to make the data easier to analyze.

DIRECTIONS

1. Start Excel, if necessary, and open **E55Apply** from the data files for this lesson.

2. Save the file as **E55Apply_xx** in the location where your teacher instructs you to store the files for this lesson.

3. Group the sheets. Add a footer that has your name at the left, the date code in the center, and the page number code at the right, and change back to **Normal** view. Ungroup the sheets.

4. On the **Usage statistics 0804** worksheet, calculate the average bandwidth for each department:

    a. Select the cell range **A5:G150**, and click **DATA > Subtotal** ▦.

    b. In the **At each change in** list, click to select **Department**.

    c. In the **Use function** list, click to select **Average**.

    d. In the **Add subtotal to** list, click to select **Avg. Bandwidth**, if necessary. Click to deselect **Data In**, **Data Out**, and **Transactions**.

    e. Click to deselect the **Replace current subtotals** check box if necessary, and click **OK**.

    ✓ *There are now four levels of detail. Level 1 is the grand total (plus the "grand average" bandwidth). Level 2 summarizes each week, and level 3 summarizes each department. Level 4 contains the complete data.*

5. Create subtotals for each department:

    a. With the cell range still selected, click **Subtotal** ▦.

    b. Verify that the **At each change in** list is **Department**.

    c. In the **Use function** list, click **Sum**.

    d. In the **Add subtotal to** list, verify that **Avg. Bandwidth** is selected. Click to select **Data In**, **Data Out**, and **Transactions**, and click **OK**.

    ✓ *There are now five levels of detail.*

6. Click outline level button ③ to display only the department averages, weekly totals, and grand totals. **With your teacher's permission**, select the print setting option to Fit Sheet on One Page, and print the worksheet.

7. Display the detail rows for the Accounting department for the week of August 22. **With your teacher's permission**, select the print setting option to Fit Sheet on One Page, and print the worksheet.

8. Click outline level button ② to display just weekly totals.

9. Expand the outline to show all of the department averages for the week of August 29.

10. Expand the outline to show the Point of sale department's detail for the week of August 29, as shown in Figure 55-2 on the next page.

11. Manually add a new group:

    a. Insert a new row above row **236**.

    b. In cell **C236**, type **POS North and South Total**.

    c. Apply bold and right alignment formatting to cell **C236**.

    d. In cell **D236**, insert a formula that totals the average bandwidths for **Point of sale North** and **Point of sale South**.

    e. Select rows **234** to **236**, click **DATA > Group** to group the three rows.

    ✓ *There are now six levels of detail.*

12. **With your teacher's permission**, print the worksheet. It should look similar to Figure 55-3.

13. Save and close the file, and exit Excel.

Figure 55-2

Intellidata
Hosting · Management · Warehousing

Usage statistics
Giant Frog Supermarkets - District # 0855
Period of 4 July - 4 September 2014

	Date	Department	Region	Avg. Bandwidth (Kb/sec)	Data In (Mb)	Data Out (Mb)	Transactions
31	7/4/2014 Total			1404.9	23093	133364	579502
57	7/11/2014 Total			1339.5	22300	125960	555785
83	7/18/2014 Total			1377.7	23944	129681	566206
109	7/25/2014 Total			1464.4	25935	139778	586438
135	8/1/2014 Total			1439.5	24978	142019	578358
161	8/8/2014 Total			1400.8	23830	139363	572934
187	8/15/2014 Total			1406.2	24204	139935	487461
213	8/22/2014 Total			1410.9	27659	149379	577563
218		Merchandising Average		51.9			
223		Purchasing Average		82.8			
228		Distribution Average		17.66666667			
233		Accounting Average		171.0333333			
234	8/29/2014	Point of sale	North	203.3	6115	28024	89135
235	8/29/2014	Point of sale	South	155.8	1732	15331	62357
236	8/29/2014	Point of sale	Central	104.3	1900	15367	62654
237		Point of sale Total		463.4	9747	58722	214146
238		Point of sale Average		154.4666667			
239	8/29/2014 Total			1433.6	28952	158298	605427
240		Grand Total					
241		Grand Average		93.90740741			
242	Grand Total			12677.5	224895	1257777	5109674

Figure 55-3

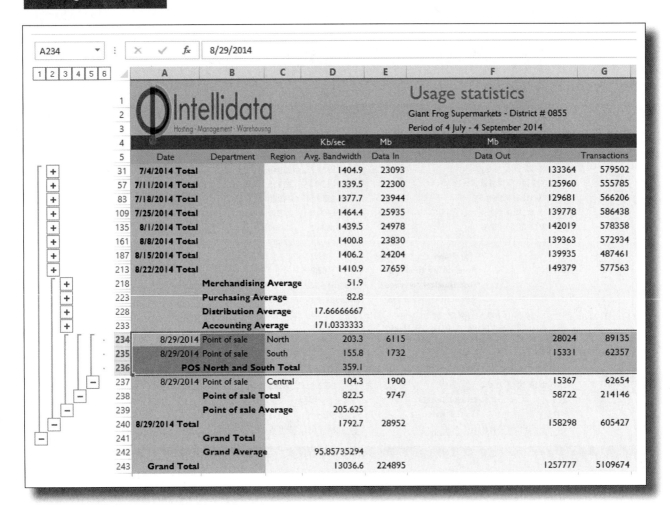

	A	B	C	D	E	F	G
A234				8/29/2014			

	Date	Department	Region	Avg. Bandwidth	Data In	Data Out	Transactions
				Kb/sec	Mb	Mb	
31	7/4/2014 Total			1404.9	23093	133364	579502
57	7/11/2014 Total			1339.5	22300	125960	555785
83	7/18/2014 Total			1377.7	23944	129681	566206
109	7/25/2014 Total			1464.4	25935	139778	586438
135	8/1/2014 Total			1439.5	24978	142019	578358
161	8/8/2014 Total			1400.8	23830	139363	572934
187	8/15/2014 Total			1406.2	24204	139935	487461
213	8/22/2014 Total			1410.9	27659	149379	577563
218		Merchandising Average		51.9			
223		Purchasing Average		82.8			
228		Distribution Average		17.66666667			
233		Accounting Average		171.0333333			
234	8/29/2014	Point of sale	North	203.3	6115	28024	89135
235	8/29/2014	Point of sale	South	155.8	1732	15331	62357
236		POS North and South Total		359.1			
237	8/29/2014	Point of sale	Central	104.3	1900	15367	62654
238		Point of sale Total		822.5	9747	58722	214146
239		Point of sale Average		205.625			
240	8/29/2014 Total			1792.7	28952	158298	605427
241		Grand Total					
242		Grand Average		95.85735294			
243	Grand Total			13036.6	224895	1257777	5109674

Intellidata
Hosting · Management · Warehousing

Usage statistics
Giant Frog Supermarkets - District # 0855
Period of 4 July - 4 September 2014

End-of-Chapter Activities

➤ Excel Chapter 6—Critical Thinking

Payroll Calculations

You are the corporate payroll clerk at PhotoTown, and you've been calculating payroll checks manually ever since you were hired a month ago. Now that you're familiar with Excel, you want to use the features you have learned to complete this weekly task more easily.

DIRECTIONS

1. Start Excel, if necessary, and open **ECT06** from the data files for this chapter.

2. Save the file as **ECT06_xx** in the location where your teacher instructs you to store the files for this chapter.

3. Type the following column labels on two lines:
   a. In cell **A7**, type **Check Number**.
   b. In cell **B7**, type **Employee ID Number**.
   c. In cell **E7**, type **Hours Worked**.
   d. Adjust the column widths as needed.

4. Separate the **Name** column into **First Name** and **Last Name**:
   a. Insert a column to the right of column D.
   b. Select the cell range **D8:D37**, click **DATA > Text to Columns**.
   c. Click the **Delimited** file type option, if necessary.
   d. Click the **Space** Delimiter option, and deselect the **Tab** Delimiter option.
   e. Format both columns as text, and set the Destination to cell **$D$8**.
   f. In cell **D7**, type **First Name**, and in cell **E7**, type **Last Name**.

5. Enter the hours everyone has worked as mixed fractions, as shown in Illustration A.

6. Use **Go To** to locate the cell that displays the total cost of the payroll this week:
   a. Click **HOME > Find & Select > Go To**.
   b. Choose **PayrollTotal** from the list, and click **OK** to select cell **L41**.

7. Enter today's date in cell **H3**, and apply the Short Date format.

8. In the cell range **J2:L2**, insert a group box form control.
   a. Click **DEVELOPER > Insert > Group Box (Form Control)**.
   b. Draw the group box form control over the cell range **J2:L6**.
   c. Edit the text label to be **Featured Employee**.

9. In the group box form control, in the cell **K3**, insert a label form control.
   a. On the **DEVELOPER** tab, click **Insert > Label (Form Control)**.
   b. Draw the label box form control over cell **K3**.
   c. Edit the text label to be **Kere Freed**.

10. Format the cells with the coloring shown in Illustration 6A on the next page.
    a. Fill all cells in the worksheet with the **Gold, Accent 4, Lighter 60%** color.
    b. Fill rows 1–6 with the **Gold, Accent 4, Lighter 40%** color.
    c. Select the cell range **A7:L7**, and use the Cell Styles gallery to apply the **Accent 5** style.

11. Create two custom views:
    a. Save the current settings as a custom view called **Full View**.
    b. Hide columns C–G, and create a view named **Payroll Checks**.
    c. **With your teacher's permission**, print the worksheet.

12. View the worksheet using the **Full View** custom view.

13. Click **INSERT** > **Header & Footer**, type your name, and change back to **Normal** view.

14. Set the print area for the cell range **A1:L41**, and adjust the page breaks.

15. **With your teacher's permission**, print the worksheet in **Full View** in landscape orientation. It should look similar to Illustration 6A.

16. Save and close the file, and exit Excel.

Illustration 6A

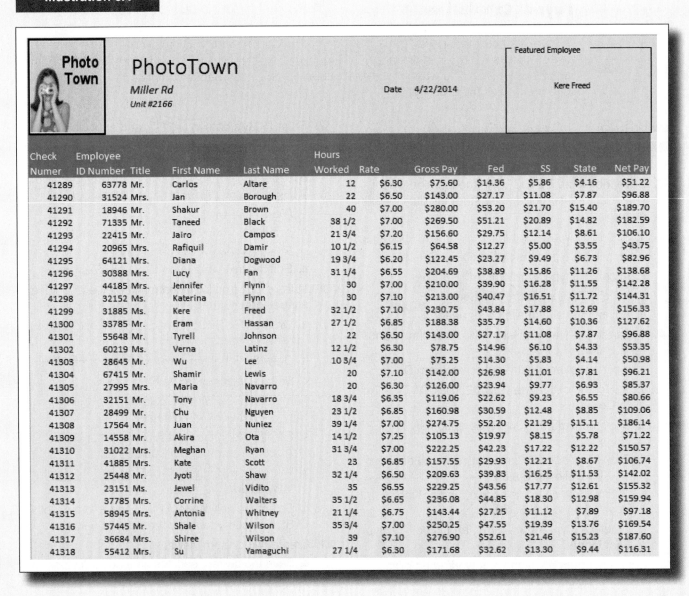

Check Numer	Employee ID Number	Title	First Name	Last Name	Hours Worked	Rate	Gross Pay	Fed	SS	State	Net Pay
41289	63778	Mr.	Carlos	Altare	12	$6.30	$75.60	$14.36	$5.86	$4.16	$51.22
41290	31524	Mrs.	Jan	Borough	22	$6.50	$143.00	$27.17	$11.08	$7.87	$96.88
41291	18946	Mr.	Shakur	Brown	40	$7.00	$280.00	$53.20	$21.70	$15.40	$189.70
41292	71335	Mr.	Taneed	Black	38 1/2	$7.00	$269.50	$51.21	$20.89	$14.82	$182.59
41293	22415	Mr.	Jairo	Campos	21 3/4	$7.20	$156.60	$29.75	$12.14	$8.61	$106.10
41294	20965	Mrs.	Rafiquil	Damir	10 1/2	$6.15	$64.58	$12.27	$5.00	$3.55	$43.75
41295	64121	Mrs.	Diana	Dogwood	19 3/4	$6.20	$122.45	$23.27	$9.49	$6.73	$82.96
41296	30388	Mrs.	Lucy	Fan	31 1/4	$6.55	$204.69	$38.89	$15.86	$11.26	$138.68
41297	44185	Mrs.	Jennifer	Flynn	30	$7.00	$210.00	$39.90	$16.28	$11.55	$142.28
41298	32152	Ms.	Katerina	Flynn	30	$7.10	$213.00	$40.47	$16.51	$11.72	$144.31
41299	31885	Ms.	Kere	Freed	32 1/2	$7.10	$230.75	$43.84	$17.88	$12.69	$156.33
41300	33785	Mr.	Eram	Hassan	27 1/2	$6.85	$188.38	$35.79	$14.60	$10.36	$127.62
41301	55648	Mr.	Tyrell	Johnson	22	$6.50	$143.00	$27.17	$11.08	$7.87	$96.88
41302	60219	Ms.	Verna	Latinz	12 1/2	$6.30	$78.75	$14.96	$6.10	$4.33	$53.35
41303	28645	Mr.	Wu	Lee	10 3/4	$7.00	$75.25	$14.30	$5.83	$4.14	$50.98
41304	67415	Mr.	Shamir	Lewis	20	$7.10	$142.00	$26.98	$11.01	$7.81	$96.21
41305	27995	Mrs.	Maria	Navarro	20	$6.30	$126.00	$23.94	$9.77	$6.93	$85.37
41306	32151	Mr.	Tony	Navarro	18 3/4	$6.35	$119.06	$22.62	$9.23	$6.55	$80.66
41307	28499	Mr.	Chu	Nguyen	23 1/2	$6.85	$160.98	$30.59	$12.48	$8.85	$109.06
41308	17564	Mr.	Juan	Nuniez	39 1/4	$7.00	$274.75	$52.20	$21.29	$15.11	$186.14
41309	14558	Mr.	Akira	Ota	14 1/2	$7.25	$105.13	$19.97	$8.15	$5.78	$71.22
41310	31022	Mrs.	Meghan	Ryan	31 3/4	$7.00	$222.25	$42.23	$17.22	$12.22	$150.57
41311	41885	Mrs.	Kate	Scott	23	$6.85	$157.55	$29.93	$12.21	$8.67	$106.74
41312	25448	Mr.	Jyoti	Shaw	32 1/4	$6.50	$209.63	$39.83	$16.25	$11.53	$142.02
41313	23151	Ms.	Jewel	Vidito	35	$6.55	$229.25	$43.56	$17.77	$12.61	$155.32
41314	37785	Mrs.	Corrine	Walters	35 1/2	$6.65	$236.08	$44.85	$18.30	$12.98	$159.94
41315	58945	Mrs.	Antonia	Whitney	21 1/4	$6.75	$143.44	$27.25	$11.12	$7.89	$97.18
41316	57445	Mr.	Shale	Wilson	35 3/4	$7.00	$250.25	$47.55	$19.39	$13.76	$169.54
41317	36684	Mrs.	Shiree	Wilson	39	$7.10	$276.90	$52.61	$21.46	$15.23	$187.60
41318	55412	Mrs.	Su	Yamaguchi	27 1/4	$6.30	$171.68	$32.62	$13.30	$9.44	$116.31

PhotoTown

Miller Rd

Unit #2166

Date 4/22/2014

Featured Employee

Kere Freed

➤ Excel Chapter 6—Portfolio Builder

Women and Children First

In American History, your class is studying the Titanic. Questions have been raised as to whether the rule of the sea, "women and children first," was followed. You and your classmates hope to analyze the data and come up with an analysis of who was most likely to survive.

DIRECTIONS

1. Start Excel, if necessary, and open **EPB06** from the data files for this chapter.

2. Save the file as **EPB06_xx** in the location where your teacher instructs you to store the files for this chapter.

3. Add a header that has your name at the left, the date code in the center, and the page number code at the right, and change back to **Normal** view.

4. The first thing you notice is that the data is not as readable as it might be. Use **Find & Replace** to replace the numbers with the text: **Yes** and **No**:

   a. Select the cell range **C6:C1318**, and on the HOME tab, click **Find & Select** 🔍 > **Replace**.

   b. Replace **1** with **Yes**, and **0** with **No**.

   c. Close the Find and Replace dialog box.

5. Next, sort the database into two groups—those who survived and those who did not:

   a. Select the cell range **A5:K1318**, and click **DATA** > **Filter** ▼.

   b. On the DATA tab, click **Sort** ⬇, and create a custom sort on the values of the following:

Survived?	Z to A
Class	A to Z
Sex	Z to A
Age	Smallest to largest

6. Add subtotals that count the survivors (or non-survivors):

   a. Create an initial subtotal based on count of the records based on **Survived?**. Add a page break between groups.

   b. Create a nested subtotal that calculates the average age based on **Class**. Do not add a page break between groups.

   c. Add another nested subtotal that counts the number of survivors (or non-survivors) by sex.

7. Use the outline controls to display only the totals, and adjust the column widths as needed to display data. **With your teacher's permission**, set the print area, and print the worksheet in landscape orientation on one page.

8. Redisplay all data and remove the subtotals.

9. Set up criteria ranges to do some further analysis on the survivors, as shown in Illustration 6B. In order to determine how many children survived, you will need to separate children from the total male and female survivors.

   a. First, create a criteria range that identifies all male survivors who are 18 or younger. Do not apply this criteria range, or any of the others you create.

   b. Next, create a second criteria range that identifies all male survivors.

   c. Repeat steps 9a and 9b to create criteria ranges for females 18 or younger and all females.

   d. Next, create a criteria range that identifies all survivors 18 or younger.

10. Insert the labels shown in Illustration 6B on the next page to identify Total, % of Survivors, % of Total, Male survivors, Female survivors, and Child survivors.

11. You can use the criteria ranges you have already set up as an argument in the **DCOUNT** function to calculate total survivors. To determine the numbers of male and female survivors, subtract males and females who are 18 or younger from the total male and female survivors. Proceed as follows:

   a. In the Total cell for male survivors, type =DCOUNT($A$5:$K$1318,$A$5, and select the total male survivor criteria range. Type) to end this portion of the formula. To subtract the male children from the total number of male survivors, type a minus sign (-), insert the **DCOUNT** function again, and use the same arguments except use the criteria range for the males <=18. If you have set up criteria ranges as shown in Illustration 6B, your formula for male survivors would be: =DCOUNT($A$5:$K$1318,$A$5,N7:X8)-DCOUNT($A$5:$K$1318,$A$5,N5:X6).

   b. Repeat this process to identify the adult female survivors.

   c. Use the same function and arguments to count the child survivors. (You do not have to do any subtracting for the child survivors, so **DCOUNT** is used only once in the cell.)

12. Total the number of all survivors in the cell beneath the Child survivors total.

13. Create criteria ranges and formulas similar to those for the survivors to calculate the total non-survivors, as shown in Illustration 6B. Total the non-survivors as you did for the survivors.

14. Now you are ready to perform the final calculations for percentages of survivors and non-survivors:

   a. In the **% of Survivors** cell for male survivors, divide the number of male survivors by the total of all survivors. Format the result as a percent with two decimal places. Copy the formula for the female and child survivors.

   b. Use the same procedure to calculate the percentage of non-survivors for male, female, and child.

   c. To calculate what percent of the total number of passengers were male survivors, divide the total male survivors by the sum of the total survivors and total non-survivors. Format the result as a percent with two decimal places. Copy the formula for female and child survivors.

   d. Use the same procedure to show the percentages of non-survivors for male, female, and child.

15. Adjust the column widths as needed.

16. Set the cell range **N5:X41** as the print area, and adjust the page breaks.

17. **With your teacher's permission**, print the print area.

18. Save and close the file, and exit Excel.

Illustration 6B

Passenger data (columns H–K)

#	Room	Ticket #	Boat	Sex
5	Room	Ticket #	Boat	Sex
6			4	female
7	B-5	24160 L221	2	female
8	B-18	111361 L57 19s 7d	4	female
9			9	female
10			3	female
11			8	female
12		17608 L262 7s 6d	4	female
13			6	female
14			8	female
15		17754 L224 10s 6d	4	female
16	B-49		7	female
17	C-125	17582 L153 9s 3d	3	female
18			5	female
19				female
20			5	female
21	D-?	13502 L77	10	female
22		17608 L262 7s 6d	4	female
23			6	female
24			5	female
25			7	female
26			5	female
27			7	female
28			10	female
29			6	female
30			7	female
31			10	female
32			7	female
33	C-87		4	female
34			3	female
35			6	female
36			8	female
37			10	female
38	B-5	24160 L221	2	female
39	C-7		8	female
40			5	female
41			6	female
42	C-7		8	female

Advanced filter criteria ranges (columns N–X)

#	Order	Class	Survived?	Name	Age	Embarked	Destination	Room	Ticket #	Boat	Sex
5	Order	Class	Survived?	Name	Age	Embarked	Destination	Room	Ticket #	Boat	Sex
6			Yes		<=18						male
7	Order	Class	Survived?	Name	Age	Embarked	Destination	Room	Ticket #	Boat	Sex
8			Yes								male
9	Order	Class	Survived?	Name	Age	Embarked	Destination	Room	Ticket #	Boat	Sex
10			Yes		<=18						female
11	Order	Class	Survived?	Name	Age	Embarked	Destination	Room	Ticket #	Boat	Sex
12			Yes								female
14	Order	Class	Survived?	Name	Age	Embarked	Destination	Room	Ticket #	Boat	Sex
15			Yes		<=18						
25	Order	Class	Survived?	Name	Age	Embarked	Destination	Room	Ticket #	Boat	Sex
26			No		<=18						male
27	Order	Class	Survived?	Name	Age	Embarked	Destination	Room	Ticket #	Boat	Sex
28			No								male
29	Order	Class	Survived?	Name	Age	Embarked	Destination	Room	Ticket #	Boat	Sex
30			No		<=18						female
31	Order	Class	Survived?	Name	Age	Embarked	Destination	Room	Ticket #	Boat	Sex
32			No								female
34	Order	Class	Survived?	Name	Age	Embarked	Destination	Room	Ticket #	Boat	Sex
35			No		<=18						

Survivor summary

	Total	% of Survivors	% of Total
Male survivors	119	26.50%	9.06%
Female survivors	267	59.47%	20.34%
Child survivors	63	14.03%	4.80%
	449		

Non-survivor summary

	Total	% of Non-Survivors	% of Total
Male non-survivors	678	78.47%	51.64%
Female non-survivors	142	16.44%	10.81%
Child non-survivors	44	5.09%	3.35%
	864		

Creating Charts, Shapes, and Templates

Lesson 56

Formatting Chart Elements

> ## ➤ What You Will Learn

Changing Chart Elements
Setting Data Label Options
Setting Data Table Options
Formatting a Data Series

WORDS TO KNOW

Categories
For most charts, a category is information in a worksheet row. If you select multiple rows of data for a chart, you'll create multiple categories, and these categories will be listed along the x-axis.

Data series
For most charts, a data series is the information in a worksheet column. If you select multiple columns of data for a chart, you'll create multiple data series. Each data series is then represented by its own color bar, line, or column.

Data table
This optional table looks like a small worksheet, and displays the data used to create the chart.

Legend key
Symbol in a legend that identifies the color or pattern of a data series in a chart.

Plot area
The area that holds the data points on a chart.

Software Skills   A chart presents complex numerical data in a graphical format. Because a chart tells its story visually, you must make the most of the way your chart looks. There are many ways in which you can enhance a chart; for example, you can add color or pattern to the chart background, and format the value and category axes so that the numbers are easier to understand.

What You Can Do

Changing Chart Elements

- A chart may include some or all of the parts shown in Figure 56-1 on the next page.
- You can format various chart elements such as the data labels, data table, plot area, legend, chart title, axis titles, and the data series.
- As you move your mouse pointer over a chart, the name of the chart element appears in the ScreenTip.
- You can select specific chart elements for formatting from the Current Selection group of the CHART TOOLS LAYOUT tab.
- A chart title describes the purpose of the chart. You can change the font, color, and size of the chart title as with any other text.
- The **plot area** of a chart is the element that holds the data points on a chart. You can change the plot area of the chart by modifying the border color or style, or applying a shadow or pattern to the background. You can also apply 3-D formatting effects to the plot area if a chart has a background.

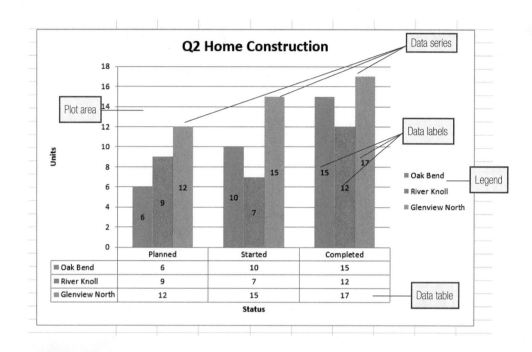

Figure 56-1

Try It! Changing Chart Elements

1 Start Excel, and open **E56Try** from the data files for this lesson.

2 Save the file as **E56Try_xx** in the location where your teacher instructs you to store the files for this lesson.

3 Click the Country Antiques Q3 Sales Chart tab, if necessary.

4 Click CHART TOOLS DESIGN > Add Chart Element ⅰ > Chart Title > Above Chart.

5 Type **Third Quarter Sales,** and press ENTER .

6 Move the mouse pointer over the chart, and click when you see the ScreenTip for Plot Area.

7 With the plot area selected, click CHART TOOLS FORMAT, and, in the Current Selection group, click Format Selection 🎇 to display the Format Plot Area task pane.

8 Click FILL > Gradient fill.

9 Click the Effects button ⬠ > 3-D FORMAT > Top bevel > Circle.

10 Click Bottom bevel > Circle.

11 In the Lighting group, in the Angle box, type **60**.

12 Close the Format Plot Area task pane.

13 Save the changes to the file, and leave it open to use in the next Try It.

The Format Plot Area task pane

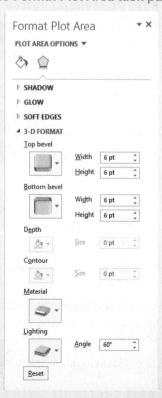

Setting Data Label Options

- As shown in Figure 56-2, you can add data labels to a chart by choosing where you want the labels placed:
  - Centered on the data point(s)
  - Inside the end of the data point(s)
  - Inside the base of the data point(s)
  - Outside the end of the data point(s)

  ✓ *Data labels should be legible and not overlap.*

- You can choose exactly what to display in the data label, such as the:
  - Data series name
  - **Category** name
  - Data value and/or percentage
  - **Legend key**

  ✓ *For charts with multiple series, you have to format the data labels for each series independently.*

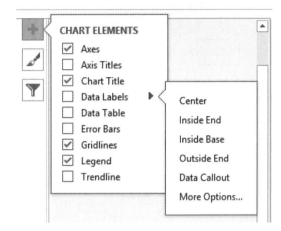

Figure 56-2

| Try It! | **Setting Data Label Options** |

1. In the **E56Try_xx** file, select the chart on the Country Antiques Q3 Sales Chart tab, if necessary.

2. Click the CHART ELEMENTS shortcut button ⊞, point to Data Labels, click the Data Labels arrow that appears on the right ▶, and click Inside Base.

3. Observe the data labels. By default, Excel uses the data value as the data label. In this instance, the dollar values overlap, making them illegible.

4. In the CHART ELEMENTS shortcut menu, click Data Labels to unselect it and clear the labels.

5. In the CHART ELEMENTS shortcut menu, point to Data Labels, click the Data Labels arrow ▶ > Center. All of the data labels are centered within the data points.

6. Click one of the August data labels to select all of the August data labels.

7. Point to Data Labels, click the arrow ▶, and click More Options to display the Format Data Labels task pane.

8. In the Label Position group, click Inside End.

9. Click one of the September data labels to select all of the September data labels.

Data label options

(continued)

Try It!   **Setting Data Label Options** *(continued)*

⑩ In the Label Contains group, click Series Name.

⑪ In the Label Contains group, click Legend key.

⑫ Notice that the gray legend key and the name September appear beside the data value in the data label.

⑬ Click to unselect Series Name, click to unselect Legend key, click Inside End, and close the Format Data Labels task pane.

⑭ Save the changes to the file, and leave it open to use in the next Try It.

Setting Data Table Options

- You can add a data table to the bottom of a chart.

- The **data table** looks like a small worksheet, and it lists the data used to create the chart.

- Adding a data table to a chart allows a viewer to easily understand the values plotted on the chart.

- Data tables have only a few basic options beyond normal formatting such as the fill and border colors.

- You can add a border around the cells in the data table—horizontally, vertically, or around the table's outline.

- You can choose whether or not to display the legend keys as part of the table.

- Data table formatting options, such as fill and shadow, are applied to the data inside the cells of the table, not to the table itself.

Try It!   **Setting Data Table Options**

① In the **E56Try_xx** file, click the chart on the Country Antiques Q3 Sales Chart tab to select it.

② Click the CHART ELEMENTS shortcut button ➕ > Data Table. A data table appears below the chart with the legend key displayed next to the data series name.

③ Click the CHART ELEMENTS shortcut button ➕, point to Data Table, click the Data Table arrow ▶, and click More Options.

④ In the Format Data Table task pane, click Fill & Line ◇ > FILL > Solid fill.

⑤ In the FILL group, click Fill Color 🎨 ▾, and click Orange from the Standard Colors group.

⑥ In the FILL group, click No fill, and close the Format Data Table task pane.

⑦ Save the changes to the file, and leave it open to use in the next Try It.

The Format Data Table task pane

Format Data Table   ▾ ✕

TABLE OPTIONS ▾ | TEXT OPTIONS

◇ ⬠ ⏹

◢ DATA TABLE OPTIONS

Table Borders

☑ Horizontal

☑ Vertical

☑ Outline

☑ Show legend keys

Formatting a Data Series

- When you create a chart, Excel automatically assigns a color to each **data series** in the chart.
- That color appears as the bars of a column chart, the slices of a pie chart, and the legend key.
  - You may want to change the color of a particular data series to coordinate with your other business documents.
  - Even if you're printing the chart in black and white, you may want to change the color of a data series to better distinguish it from other colors in the chart that translate to a similar gray tone.

- In certain chart types, such as bar and column charts, you can adjust the amount of space between each series in a group or between each category by changing the Series Options.
- In line charts, you can change the type and look of the markers used to plot each data point.
- In pie charts, you can change the position of the first slice within the pie, and the amount of separation between the remaining slices.

Try It!   **Formatting a Data Series**

1. In the **E56Try_xx** file, click the chart on the Country Antiques Q3 Sales Chart tab to select it, if necessary.

2. Click CHART TOOLS FORMAT, in the Current Selection group click the Chart Elements drop-down box Chart Area , and click Series "July".

3. In the Current Selection group, click Format Selection 🏷 to display the Format Data Series task pane.

4. In the Series Overlap box, type **-30%**.

5. In the Gap Width box, type **30%**, and close the Format Data Series task pane.

6. Save and close the file, and exit Excel.

Lesson 56—Practice

You're keeping the books for Special Events, the premiere party planners in your local area, and you've been asked to produce a couple of different sales charts based on last month's sales figures. The owner will choose one to use in a presentation for her bank so the stakes are high. In this project, you will format a sales chart.

DIRECTIONS

1. Start Excel, if necessary, and open **E56Practice** from the data files for this lesson.
2. Save the file as **E56Practice_xx** in the location where your teacher instructs you to store the files for this lesson.
3. For the **Chart-July Party Sales** worksheet, add a custom header that has your name at the left, the date code in the center, and the page number code at the right.

   ✓ *Recall that you learned about inserting a custom header in Lesson 44.*

4. Click the **Chart-July Party Sales** tab, and click the chart on the **Chart-July Party Sales** to select it, if necessary.
5. Click the **CHART ELEMENTS** shortcut button + > **Data Table**.
6. Hover the pointer over Data Table, click the arrow ▶ > **With Legend Keys**.
7. In the CHART ELEMENTS shortcut menu, hover the pointer over Chart Title, click the **Chart Title** arrow ▶ > **Centered Overlay**.
8. Type **July Party Sales**, and press ENTER.

9. Click **CHART TOOLS FORMAT** and, in the **Chart Elements** drop-down menu, click **Plot Area**.

10. In the CHART TOOLS FORMAT tab, in the Shape Styles group, click the **Shape Fill** drop-down arrow ⧆ Shape Fill ▾ > **Gradient** > **Linear Diagonal – Top Right to Bottom Left** in the Light group.

11. Click **CHART TOOLS FORMAT**, and, in the **Chart Elements** drop-down menu, click **Series "private"**.

12. In the **CHART ELEMENTS** shortcut menu, click **Data Labels** > **Outside End**.

13. With the series still selected, click **Format Selection** in the Current Selection group to display the Format Data Series task pane.

14. In the Series Overlap text box, type **-25%**.

15. In the Gap Width text box, type **200%**.

16. **With your teacher's permission**, print the chart. Your chart should look like Figure 56-3.

17. Save and close the file, and exit Excel.

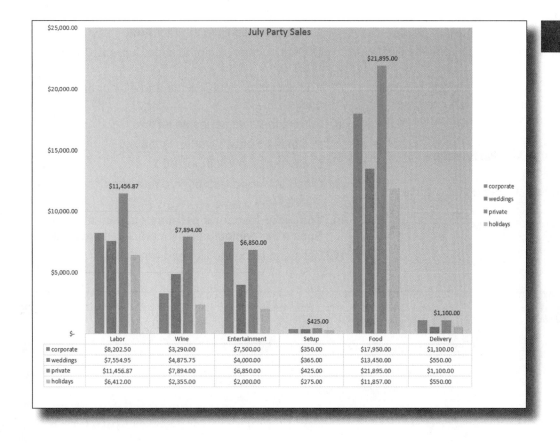

Figure 56-3

	Labor	Wine	Entertainment	Setup	Food	Delivery
corporate	$8,202.50	$3,290.00	$7,500.00	$350.00	$17,950.00	$1,100.00
weddings	$7,554.95	$4,875.75	$4,000.00	$365.00	$13,450.00	$550.00
private	$11,456.87	$7,894.00	$6,850.00	$425.00	$21,895.00	$1,100.00
holidays	$6,412.00	$2,355.00	$2,000.00	$275.00	$11,857.00	$550.00

Lesson 56—Apply

You work in the accounting department for Special Events, the premiere party planners in your local area. You are preparing different sales charts based on last month's sales figures for the owner to use in a presentation for her bank. In this project, you will format another sales chart using the skills you learned in this lesson.

DIRECTIONS

1. Start Excel, if necessary, and open **E56Apply** from the data files for this lesson.

2. Save the file as **E56Apply_xx** in the location where your teacher instructs you to store the files for this lesson.

3. For the **July Party Sales** worksheet, add a custom header that has your name at the left, the date code in the center, and the page number code at the right.

4. Select the chart on the **July Party Sales** worksheet, if necessary.

5. Add a chart title, **July Party Sales**, above the chart.

6. Format the chart elements as follows:
   a. Add a data table and show the legend keys in the table.
   b. Apply a solid fill to the Plot Area.
   c. Change the fill color to **Blue, Accent 1, Lighter 80%**.

7. Add data labels outside the end of your data points.

8. Format the data series as follows:
   a. Set the Series Overlap to **-10%**.
   b. Set the Gap Width to **200%**.

9. Close any open task panes. Your chart should look Figure 56-4.

10. **With your teacher's permission**, print the chart. Submit the printout or file for grading as required.

11. Save and close the file, and exit Excel.

Figure 56-4

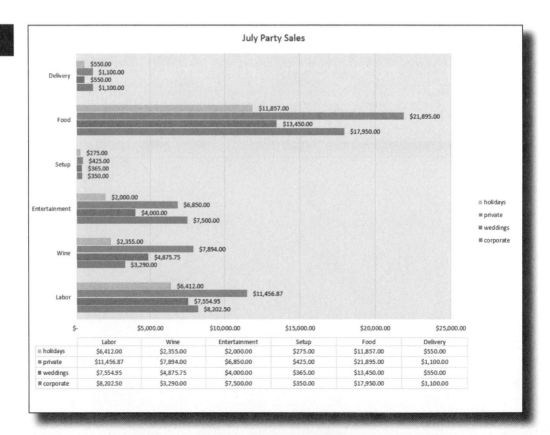

Lesson 57

Formatting the Value Axis

➤ What You Will Learn

Creating a Stock Chart
Modifying the Value Axis
Formatting Data Markers
Formatting a Legend
Adding a Secondary Value Axis to a Chart

Software Skills   Because Excel is used every day by thousands of investors—many of whom invest as a profession—it has to be capable of producing charts specifically tailored to the needs and expectations of those users. A stock chart is no ordinary graphical rendering, since it often has to show several related values (such as opening and closing values) on a single chart.

What You Can Do

Creating a Stock Chart

- Charting stock data requires a special type of chart designed to handle standard stock information.
- Excel offers four different kinds of stock charts:
  - High-Low-Close
  - Open-High-Low-Close
  - Volume-High-Low-Close
  - Volume-Open-High-Low-Close
- Each chart handles a different set of data taken from this standard set of stock information:
  - Volume: the number of shares of a particular stock traded during the market day.
  - Open: the value of the stock at the time when the market opened for the day.
  - High: the highest value at which the stock was traded that day.
  - Low: the lowest value at which the stock was traded that day.
  - Close: the value of the stock when the market closed for the day.

WORDS TO KNOW

Data marker
The symbol that appears on a stock chart to mark a specific data point.

Legend
An optional part of the chart, the legend displays a description of each data series included in the chart.

Value axis
The vertical scale of a chart on which the values from each category are plotted, sometimes called the Y axis.

- To create a stock chart, you must enter the data in columns or rows in the order specified by the type of stock chart you want.

  ✓ *For example, if you select the Open-High-Low-Close chart, you must enter the data in four columns (or rows) in that order: open, high, low, close.*

- For row (or column) labels, you can use the stock symbol or name if you are going to track more than one type of stock, or you can use the date if you're tracking one stock's trading pattern over several days.

- A stock chart is also ideal for charting certain kinds of scientific data, such as temperature changes throughout the day.

Try It!   **Creating a Stock Chart**

① Start Excel, and open **E57Try** from the data files for this lesson.

② Save the file as **E57Try_xx** in the location where your teacher instructs you to store the files for this lesson.

③ On the table worksheet, select the range A5:F258.

④ Create a Volume-Open-High-Low-Close stock chart on a new worksheet:

    a. Click the INSERT tab, and click the Charts dialog box launcher ⌐ to display the Insert Chart dialog box.

    b. Click the All Charts tab > Stock > Volume-Open-High-Low-Close > OK.

    c. On the CHART TOOLS DESIGN tab, in the Location group, click Move Chart 🔲 to open the Move Chart dialog box.

    d. Click New sheet, and type **Stock Chart** in the box.

    e. Click OK to move the chart to its own worksheet page.

⑤ Add the title **Midwest Pharmaceutical Stock Tracking** above the chart.

⑥ Save the changes to the file, and leave it open to use in the next Try It.

The Volume-Open-High-Low-Close stock chart

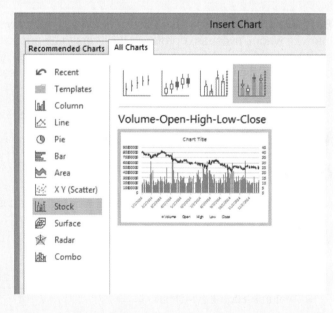

Modifying the Value Axis

- The vertical, or **value axis**, provides a scale for the values of the data for most chart types.

  ✓ *For bar charts, the horizontal and vertical axes are reversed.*

- You can change the font, size, color, attributes, alignment, and placement of text or numbers along the axis.

- You can add axis titles from the CHART ELEMENTS shortcut menu.

  - You can also add axis titles from the Add Chart Element button on the CHART TOOLS DESIGN tab.

- To control whether an axis should be displayed, select an axis, and click the Format Selection button from the Current Selection group on the CHART TOOLS DESIGN tab.

  - In addition, you can adjust the scale used along either axis so that the numbers are easy to read.

Try It!   Modifying the Value Axis

1 In the **E57Try_xx** file, select the chart on the Stock Chart tab, if necessary.

2 Click the CHART ELEMENTS shortcut button ⊞ > Axis Titles.

3 On the CHART TOOLS FORMAT tab, in the Current Selection group, click the Chart Elements drop-down arrow Chart Area , click Vertical (Value) Axis Title, type **Volume (in millions)**, and press ENTER .

4 On the CHART TOOLS FORMAT tab, in the Current Selection group, click the Chart Elements drop-down arrow, click Secondary Vertical (Value) Axis Title, type **Value**, and press ENTER .

5 Click the Chart Elements drop-down arrow > Vertical (Value) Axis > Format Selection 🏷.

6 In the Format Axis task pane, in the AXIS OPTIONS group, under Bounds, type **10000000** in the Minimum text box, and press ENTER .

7 In the Format Axis task pane, in the AXIS OPTIONS group, click the Display units drop-down arrow > Millions.

8 In the Format Axis task pane, click NUMBER to display the number options.

9 In the Category list box click Number, in the Decimal places box type **0**, and press ENTER .

> ✓ Because the stock exchange is not operating every day of the year, there are points along the horizontal axis with no data because Excel assumes that all dates should be included in the axis, not just the dates in your data table. You will need to modify the horizontal axis.

10 On the CHART TOOLS FORMAT tab, in the Current Selection group, click the Chart Elements drop-down arrow, click Horizontal (Category) Axis. Notice that the task pane displays the selected axis options.

11 In the Format Axis task pane, in the AXIS OPTIONS group, under Axis Type, click Text axis.

12 Click the Chart Elements drop-down arrow > Secondary Vertical (Value) Axis.

13 In the Format Axis task pane, click NUMBER, and in the Category list box click Currency to convert the stock values.

14 In the AXIS OPTIONS group, under Bounds, type **20.0** in the Minimum text box, press ENTER and close the Format Axis task pane.

15 Save the changes to the file, and leave it open to use in the next Try It.

The Format Axis task pane

Format Axis ▾ ✕

AXIS OPTIONS ▾ | TEXT OPTIONS

◇ ⬠ ▦ 📊

▲ AXIS OPTIONS

Bounds

Minimum	20.0	Reset
Maximum	45.0	Auto

Units

Major	5.0	Auto
Minor	1.0	Auto

Horizontal axis crosses

◉ Automatic
○ Axis value   20.0
○ Maximum axis value

Display units   None   ▾

☐ Show display units label on chart

☐ Logarithmic scale Base 10

☐ Values in reverse order

▷ TICK MARKS

▷ LABELS

▷ NUMBER

Formatting Data Markers

- When you create a stock chart, Excel uses a series of standard **data markers** for the open, close, high-low, volume, close up, and close down values.

- Some of these markers may be too small, too dark, or too light to appear clearly on a printout.

- To improve the appearance of your chart, you may want to adjust the data markers used by Excel.

- You can select a series to change, and select from the Marker Options in the Format Data Series task pane.

- You can change the fill color, size, shape, outline color, and outline style of each data marker used in a stock chart.

  ✓ *You can also change the data markers used in line, xy (scatter), and radar charts.*

- You can choose to hide the data markers by selecting None in the Marker Options area of the Format Data Series task pane.

Try It!   **Formatting Data Markers**

1. In the **E57Try_xx** file, select the chart on the Stock Chart tab, if necessary.

2. On the CHART TOOLS FORMAT tab, in the Current Selection group, click the Chart Elements drop-down arrow, click Series "High," and click Format Selection.

3. In the Format Data Series task pane, click Fill & Line ◇ > MARKER > MARKER OPTIONS > Built-in.

4. In the Type drop-down list, choose the triangle, and in the Size box enter **4**.

5. Click FILL > Solid fill.

6. Click the Color button, and in the Standard Colors palette click Light Green.

   ✓ *The light green triangle data marker has been added to the legend.*

7. Click the Chart Elements drop-down arrow > Series "Low" > Format Selection.

8. In the Format Data Series task pane, click Fill & Line ◇ > MARKER > MARKER OPTIONS > Built-in.

9. In the Type drop-down list, choose the circle, and in the Size box enter **3**.

10. Click FILL > Solid fill.

11. Click the Color button, in the Standard Colors palette click Red, and close the Format Data Series task pane.

    ✓ *The red circle data marker has been added to the legend.*

12. Save the changes to the file, and leave it open to use in the next Try It.

Formatting data markers

Format Data Series   ▾ ✕

SERIES OPTIONS ▾

◇ ⬠ ili

∿ LINE | ∿ MARKER

▲ MARKER OPTIONS

○ Automatic
○ None
● Built-in

Type ▵ ▾

Size 4 ↕

▷ FILL

▷ BORDER

Formatting a Legend

- Though a **legend** is automatically displayed when you create a chart, you can choose where you want to place it.
- You can place the legend at the top, left, bottom, or right of the chart. You can also choose to overlap the legend over the chart.

- You can access the Format Legend task pane by clicking More Options in the CHART ELEMENTS shortcut menu.
- You can change the fill color, size, border color, and outline style of a legend.

Try It!   Formatting a Legend

1. In the **E57Try_xx** file, select the chart on the Stock Chart tab, if necessary.
2. Click the CHART ELEMENTS shortcut button + > Legend to hide the legend.
3. Click the CHART ELEMENTS shortcut button + > Legend arrow ▶ > Top.
4. Click to select the legend, and on the CHART TOOLS FORMAT tab click Format Selection.
5. In the Format Legend task pane, click to unselect the Show the legend without overlapping the chart option.

6. Click Fill & Line.
7. Under FILL, click the Color button, and in the Theme Colors palette click Blue, Accent 1, Lighter 80%.
8. Under BORDER, click Solid line.
9. Under BORDER, click the Color button, in the Theme Colors palette click Black, Text 1, and close the Format Legend task pane.
10. Save the changes to the file, and leave it open to use in the next Try It.

Adding a Secondary Value Axis to a Chart

- To track two related but different values, use two value axes in the chart.
- The value axes appear on opposite sides of the chart.
- For example, Excel uses two value axes for a stock chart that includes both the volume of stock trading and the value of the stock.

- One axis plots the stock's trading volume.
- The other axis plots the stock's value at open, close, high, and low points in the day.
- Secondary value axes are most common on stock charts and will appear automatically when Excel determines that two value axes are needed, but you can manually add a secondary axis to other types of charts as well.

Try It!   Adding a Secondary Value Axis to a Chart

1. In the **E57Try_xx** file, select the YTD Average Table tab.
2. On the CHART TOOLS DESIGN tab, click Select Data.
3. In the Select Data Source dialog box, under Legend Entries (Series), click the Add button to add a series.

4. In the Edit Series dialog box, click the Collapse Dialog button for Series name, click the YTD Table worksheet tab, click cell E5, and click the Restore Dialog button.
5. In the Edit Series dialog box, click the Collapse Dialog button for Series values, click the YTD Table worksheet tab if necessary, select the range E6:E258, and click the Restore Dialog button.

(continued)

Try It!   **Adding a Secondary Value Axis to a Chart** (continued)

6 In the Edit Series dialog box, click OK.

7 Click OK to close the Select Data Source dialog box.

8 Right-click the orange line > Format Data Series.

9 In the Format Data Series task pane, under SERIES OPTIONS, click Secondary Axis.

10 On the CHART TOOLS FORMAT tab, in the Current Selection group, click the Chart Elements drop-down arrow, click Secondary Vertical (Value) Axis, and click Format Selection 🐾.

11 In the Format Axis task pane, in the AXIS OPTIONS group, under Bounds, type **100.00** in the Maximum text box, press [ENTER] , and close the Format Axis task pane.

12 Save and close the file, and exit Excel.

Lesson 57—Practice

You work in the Communications department of Midwest Pharmaceutical, and the annual shareholders' meeting is scheduled for next week. Your job is to create and format a stock chart for the CFO's presentation. You want to add axis labels, axis titles, and data markers to the stock chart using your new Excel skills.

DIRECTIONS

1. Start Excel, if necessary, and open **E57Practice** from the data files for this lesson.

2. Save the file as **E57Practice_xx** in the location where your teacher instructs you to store the files for this lesson.

3. Select the range **A3:E66**.

4. Create a **Volume-High-Low-Close** stock chart on its own worksheet tab:
   a. Click **INSERT > Charts** dialog box launcher 🗗 .
   b. Click the **All Charts** tab > **Stock** > **Volume-High-Low-Close** > **OK**.
   c. Click **Chart Tools Design** > **Move Chart** 📊 to open the Move Chart dialog box.
   d. Click **New sheet**, and in the New sheet text box type **Q1 Stock Chart**.
   e. Click **OK** to move the chart to its own worksheet page.

5. Click the chart title to select it, type **Midwest Pharmaceutical First Quarter Stock**, and press [ENTER] .

6. Click the **CHART ELEMENTS** shortcut button ⊕, click the **Axis Titles** arrow ▶, and click to select the **Primary Vertical** and **Secondary Vertical** check boxes.

7. On the CHART TOOLS FORMAT tab, in the Current Selection group, click the **Chart Elements** drop-down arrow [Chart Area ▾], click **Vertical (Value) Axis Title**, type **Volume (in millions)**, and press [ENTER] .

8. On the CHART TOOLS FORMAT tab, in the Current Selection group, click the **Chart Elements** drop-down arrow, click **Secondary Vertical (Value) Axis Title**, type **Stock Price (USD)**, and press [ENTER] .

9. Click to select the primary vertical axis (the vertical axis on the left), and click **Format Selection** 🐾 .

10. In the Format Axis task pane, in the AXIS OPTIONS group, in the Display units box, click **Millions**.

11. In the Minimum group text box, type **12500000**, and press [ENTER] .

12. Click to unselect the **Show display units label on chart** check box.

   ✓ *If you notice that the Minimum axis value does not change to 12,500,000, type 1.25E7 in the Minimum text box.*

13. Click to select the horizontal axis, and in the AXIS OPTIONS group, click **Text axis**.

14. Click **Size & Properties** 🔠, and in the Text direction list click **Rotate all text 270°**.

15. Click to select the secondary vertical axis (the vertical axis on the right), and click **Axis Options** 📊.

16. Click **NUMBER**, and in the Category list click **Currency** to convert the stock values.

17. Under AXIS OPTIONS, in the Minimum text box, type **25.0**.

18. Click the **CHART ELEMENTS** shortcut button ➕ > **Axis Titles** arrow ▶ > **Primary Horizontal** to unselect it.

19. Close the Format Axis task pane.

20. Add a custom header that has your name at the left, the date code in the center, and the page number code at the right.

21. **With your teacher's permission**, print the chart. The chart should look like Figure 57-1.

22. Save and close the file, and exit Excel.

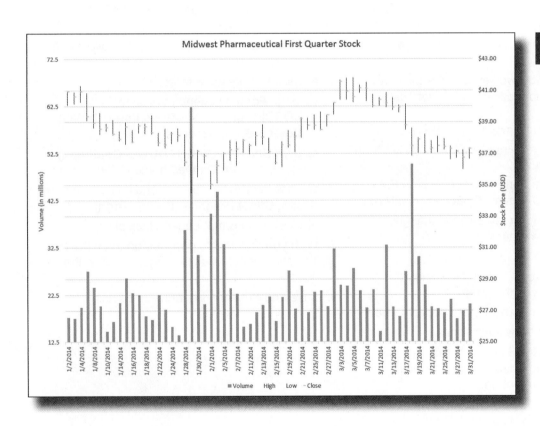

Figure 57-1

Lesson 57—Apply

You are preparing for the annual shareholders' meeting for Midwest Pharmaceutical. You have created a stock chart for the CFO's presentation, and now you want to format it so the data is clear and legible. You want to add and format data markers so that the shareholders will be able to easily see the performance of the stock.

DIRECTIONS

1. Start Excel, if necessary, and open **E57Apply** from the data files for this lesson

2. Save the file as **E57Apply_xx** in the location where your teacher instructs you to store the files for this lesson.

3. Add a custom header that has your name at the left, the date code in the center, and the page number code at the right

4. On the **Q1 Stock Chart** worksheet, click the chart to select it, and add formatting to the "High" data series.

   a. Click **CHART TOOLS FORMAT > Chart Elements** drop-down arrow > **Series "High" > Format Selection**.

   b. In the Format Data Series task pane, click **Fill & Line > MARKER > Marker Options > Built-in**.

   c. In the **Type** drop-down list, click the triangle, and in the Size box enter **4**.

   d. Click **FILL > Solid fill**.

   e. Click the **Color** button, and in the Standard Colors palette click **Light Green**.

   f. Click **BORDER**, if necessary, and click **No line**.

5. Add formatting to the "Low" data series.

   a. On the CHART TOOLS FORMAT tab, click the Chart Elements drop-down arrow > **Series "Low" > Format Selection**.

   b. In the Format Data Series task pane, in the MARKER OPTIONS group, click **Built-in**.

   c. In the Type drop-down list, click the circle, and in the Size box enter **3**.

   d. Click **FILL > Solid fill**.

   e. Click the **Color** button, and in the Standard Colors palette click **Red**.

6. Add formatting to the "Volume" data series.

   a. On the CHART TOOLS FORMAT tab, click the **Chart Elements** drop-down arrow > **Series "Volume" > Format Selection**.

   b. Click **FILL**, if necessary > **Solid fill**.

   c. Click the **Color** button, and in the Theme Colors palette click **Gold, Accent 4**.

7. Add formatting to the legend at the bottom of the chart.

   a. Click the legend to select it.

   b. In the Format Legend task pane, in the BORDER group, click **Solid line > Outline Color > Gold, Accent 4**.

   c. Click **Effects ⬠ > SHADOW > Color** button > **Gold, Accent 4** in the Theme Colors palette.

   d. Click the **Presets** button, and in the Outer group click **Offset Diagonal Bottom Right**.

   e. Close the Format Legend task pane.

8. **With your teacher's permission**, print the chart. The chart should look like Figure 57-2 on the next page.

9. Save and close the file, and exit Excel.

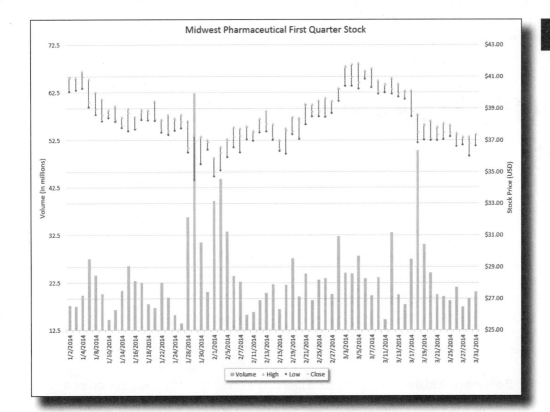

Figure 57-2

Lesson 58

Creating Stacked Area Charts

➤ **What You Will Learn**

Creating a Stacked Area Chart
Formatting the Chart Floor and Chart Walls
Displaying Chart Gridlines
Applying a Chart Layout and Chart Styles

WORDS TO KNOW

Chart floor
The horizontal floor below the data on a 3-D chart.

Chart wall
The vertical wall behind the data on a 3-D chart.

Gridlines
In the worksheet, gridlines are the light gray outline that surrounds each cell. In charts, gridlines are the lines that appear on a chart, extending from the value or category axes.

Stacked area chart
A special type of area chart in which the values for each data series are stacked on one another, creating one large area.

Software Skills   Whether you're creating a chart for a big presentation or a printed report, you want that chart to look as good as possible. Using a 3-D chart adds a high-tech look to an otherwise ordinary presentation of the facts. As with other chart elements, basic formatting can enhance the look of your chart. You also may want to display or hide gridlines to make the values on the axes easier to read.

What You Can Do

Creating a Stacked Area Chart

■ In a **stacked area chart**, the values in each data series are stacked on top of each other, creating a larger area.

   ● Whereas a line chart would show the relative positions of multiple series compared to one another, a stacked area chart shows their cumulative position.

   ● Each entry is stacked on top of the previous one, forming a peak that represents the sum of all series' entries together.

■ Use a stacked area chart to emphasize the difference in values between two data series, while also illustrating the total of the two.

   ✓ *A stacked area chart can be used to track the relative contribution of each item in the data series to the cumulative total.*

■ In a 100% stacked area chart, for each category, all of the series combine to consume the entire height of the chart.

■ Both stacked area and 100% stacked area charts come in 2-D and 3-D versions.

Try It!   Creating a Stacked Area Chart

1 Start Excel, and open **E58Try** from the data files for this lesson.

2 Save the file as **E58Try_xx** in the location where your teacher instructs you to store the files for this lesson.

3 Select the range A9:G18.

4 Click INSERT > Insert Area Chart 📊 > 3-D Stacked Area from the gallery.

5 On the CHART TOOLS DESIGN tab, in the Location group, click Move Chart 📊, and move the chart to a New sheet titled **Patient Care Chart**.

6 Click the Chart Title, and type **Patient Care Chart**.

7 Save the changes to the file, and leave it open to use in the next Try It.

Formatting the Chart Floor and Chart Walls

■ Three-dimensional charts include a **chart wall**, which forms the side and back of the chart, and the **chart floor**, which forms the bottom of the chart.

   ✓ Because 3-D pie charts are not plotted on vertical and horizontal axes, they do not include chart walls and a floor.

■ You can apply standard formatting options, such as fill color, borders, shadows, and glows to the chart walls and floors.

■ Select the element from the Chart Elements drop-down box, click Format Selection, and use the task pane to format the floor or wall.

Try It!   Formatting the Chart Floor and Chart Walls

1 In the **E58Try_xx** file, select the chart on the Patient Care Chart tab, if necessary.

2 On the CHART TOOLS FORMAT tab, in the Current Selection group, click the Chart Elements drop-down arrow `Chart Area` > Walls > Format Selection 🖌.

3 In the Format Walls task pane, click FILL > Gradient fill > Preset gradients > Bottom Spotlight - Accent 1.

4 On the CHART TOOLS FORMAT tab, in the Current Selection group, click the Chart Elements drop-down arrow, and click Floor.

5 In the Format Floor task pane, under FILL, click Solid fill.

6 Click the Color button, and in the Theme Colors palette click Blue, Accent 1.

7 Close the Format Floor task pane.

8 Save the changes to the file, and leave it open to use in the next Try It.

(continued)

Try It!　**Formatting the Chart Floor and Chart Walls** (continued)

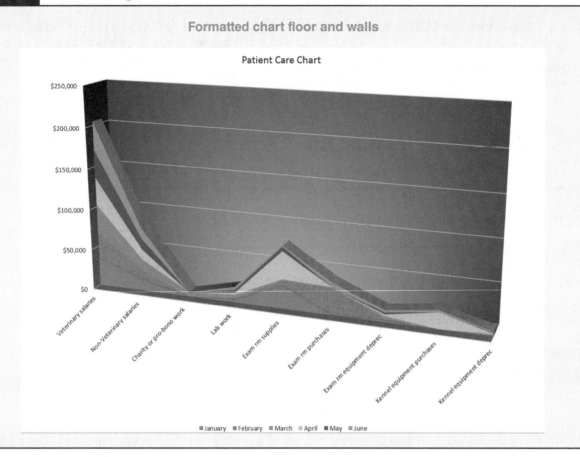

Formatted chart floor and walls

Displaying Chart Gridlines

- On Excel charts, **gridlines** can help guide the eye along a given axis.
- You can access the gridlines options from the CHART ELEMENTS shortcut menu.

- You can increase the number of major gridlines by changing the point at which the gridlines recur.
- You can also display minor gridlines, which fall between major gridlines.

Try It!　**Displaying Chart Gridlines**

1　In the **E58Try_xx** file, select the chart on the Patient Care Chart tab, if necessary.

2　Click the CHART ELEMENTS shortcut button [+], point to Gridlines, click the Gridlines arrow ▶ > Primary Major Vertical.

3　Save the changes to the file, and leave it open to use in the next Try It.

Applying a Chart Layout and Chart Styles

- When you create a chart, Excel adds a legend and assigns default colors to each series in the chart.

- You can manually adjust the colors and placements of many items on a chart.

- Excel includes two built-in formatting features: Chart Styles and Chart Layout. These features work together to help you quickly format charts.

- You can apply a built-in chart style from the Chart Styles gallery on the CHART TOOLS DESIGN tab.
  - These styles include several grayscale, monotone, and multi-colored options, and even 3-D formatting.

- You can use the Change Colors button in the Charts Styles group of the CHART TOOLS DESIGN tab to apply different color schemes.

- You can use the Quick Layout button in the Chart Layouts group of the CHART TOOLS DESIGN tab to format the placement of chart elements such as the legend, chart title, and the data labels.

  ✓ *The number of chart layout options available depends on the type of chart you are formatting.*

- Once these formatting features have been applied, you can still manually adjust any chart element.

Try It!   **Applying a Chart Layout and Chart Styles**

1. In the **E58Try_xx** file, select the chart on the Patient Care Chart tab, if necessary.

2. Click CHART TOOLS DESIGN > Quick Layout ▦ > Layout 2.

3. On the CHART TOOLS DESIGN tab, in the Chart Styles gallery, click Style 8.

   ✓ *If you are working on a smaller screen, you can click the Quick Layouts button to access the Chart Styles gallery.*

4. Click the chart title, type **Wood Hills Patient Care Expenses**, and press [ENTER].

5. Click the HOME tab, and click the Increase Font Size button A˙ twice to increase the font size of the chart title to 20 points.

6. On the HOME tab, click the Font Color drop-down arrow, and in the Theme Colors palette click Orange, Accent 2.

7. Click CHART TOOLS DESIGN > Switch Row/ Column ▦.

8. Click the CHART ELEMENTS shortcut button ➕, point to Axes, click the Axes arrow ▶, and click More Options.

9. In the Format Axis task pane, in the AXIS OPTIONS group, under Axis position, click the Categories in reverse order check box to select it.

10. On the CHART TOOLS FORMAT tab, in the Current Selection group, click the Chart Elements drop-down arrow > Walls.

11. In the Format Walls task pane, click Fill & Line ◇, and in the FILL group click Gradient fill.

12. On the CHART TOOLS FORMAT tab, in the Current Selection group, click the Chart Elements drop-down arrow > Floor.

13. In the Format Floor task pane, in the FILL group, click Solid fill.

14. Click the Color button, in the Theme Colors palette click Blue, Accent 1, Lighter 40%, and close the Format Floor task pane.

15. Save and close the file, and exit Excel.

(continued)

Try It!   **Applying a Chart Layout and Chart Styles** *(continued)*

Final stacked chart

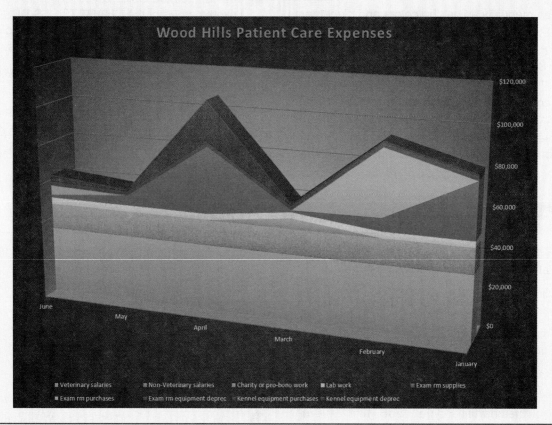

Lesson 58—Practice

You've just been hired by Premiere Formatting. The company hires recent graduates with expertise in Excel to help local businesses with their spreadsheet requirements. Your first assignment is to produce a stacked area chart for Midwest Pharmaceutical. You need to create and format a chart to show a breakdown of the company's first quarter expenses.

DIRECTIONS

1. Start Excel, if necessary, and open **E58Practice** from the data files for this lesson.

2. Save the file as **E58Practice_xx** in the location where your teacher instructs you to store the files for this lesson.

3. Select the range **A3:E10**.

4. Click **INSERT > Insert Area Chart** ▲▼ **> 3-D Stacked Area** from the gallery.

5. On the CHART TOOLS DESIGN tab, in the Location group, click **Move Chart** ▥.

6. In the Move Chart dialog box, click **New sheet**, in the New sheet text box type **Budget Chart**, and click **OK**.

7. On the CHART TOOLS DESIGN tab, click **Quick Layout** ▦ **> Layout 5** to position the chart elements.

8. Click the chart title to select it, type **First Quarter Budget**, and press [ENTER].

9. Click **HOME > Font Color** drop-down arrow ▲▼.

10. In the Theme Colors palette, click **Blue, Accent 1, Darker 50%**.

11. On the HOME tab, click **Increase Font Size** A̅ three times to increase the font size of the chart title to **20 points**.

12. Add a custom header that has your name at the left, the date code in the center, and the page number code at the right.

13. **With your teacher's permission**, print the chart. The chart should look like Figure 58-1.

14. Save and close the file, and exit Excel.

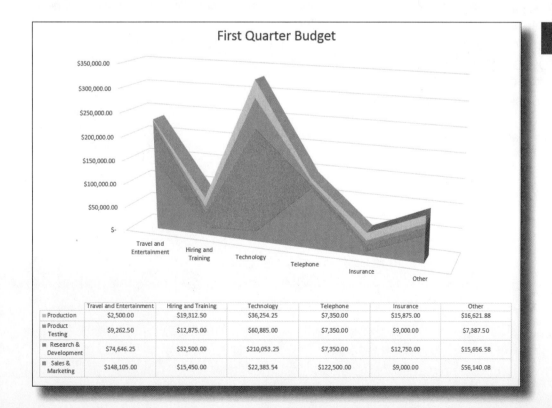

Figure 58-1

First Quarter Budget

	Travel and Entertainment	Hiring and Training	Technology	Telephone	Insurance	Other
Production	$2,500.00	$19,312.50	$36,254.25	$7,350.00	$15,875.00	$16,621.88
Product Testing	$9,262.50	$12,875.00	$60,885.00	$7,350.00	$9,000.00	$7,387.50
Research & Development	$74,646.25	$32,500.00	$210,053.25	$7,350.00	$12,750.00	$15,656.58
Sales & Marketing	$148,105.00	$15,450.00	$22,383.54	$122,500.00	$9,000.00	$56,140.08

Lesson 58—Apply

You work for Premiere Formatting, and one of your first assignments is to produce stacked area charts for Midwest Pharmaceutical. The company shareholders want to see a breakdown of its first quarter expenses. In this project, you will format a 3-D budget chart by applying a chart style, formatting the chart walls and floor, and adding gridlines.

DIRECTIONS

1. Start Excel, if necessary, and open **E58Apply** from the data files for this lesson.

2. Save the file as **E58Apply_xx** in the location where your teacher instructs you to store the files for this lesson.

3. Add a custom header that has your name at the left, the date code in the center, and the page number code at the right.

4. On the CHART TOOLS DESIGN tab, click **More** ▾ to open the Chart Styles gallery, and click **Style 7**.

5. Format the chart walls of the budget chart.
   a. Click **CHART TOOLS FORMAT** > Chart Elements drop-down arrow `Chart Area ▾` > **Walls** > **Format Selection** 🗇 .
   b. In the Format Walls task pane, click **FILL** > **Solid fill** > **Color**.
   c. In the Theme Colors palette, click **Green, Accent 6, Lighter 40%**.

6. Format the chart floor of the budget chart.
   a. On the CHART TOOLS FORMAT tab, click the **Chart Elements** drop-down arrow > **Floor**.
   b. In the Format Floor task pane, click **FILL** > **Solid fill** > **Color**.
   c. In the Theme Colors palette, click **Green, Accent 6, Darker 25%**.

7. Click the **CHART ELEMENTS** shortcut button ➕ , point to Gridlines, click the Gridlines arrow ▶ > **Primary Minor Vertical Gridlines**.

8. Format the data table of the budget chart.
   a. On the CHART TOOLS FORMAT tab, click the **Chart Elements** drop-down arrow > **Data Table**.
   b. In the Format Data Table task pane, click **BORDER** > **Solid line** > **Color**.
   c. In the Theme Colors palette, click **Green, Accent 6, Darker 25%**.

9. Format the horizontal axis.
   a. On the CHART TOOLS FORMAT tab, click the **Chart Elements** drop-down arrow > **Horizontal (Category) Axis**.
   b. On the HOME tab, click **Decrease Font Size** A˅ to decrease the font size to **8 points**.

10. **With your teacher's permission**, print the chart. Your chart should look like Figure 58-2 on the next page.

11. Save and close the file, and exit Excel.

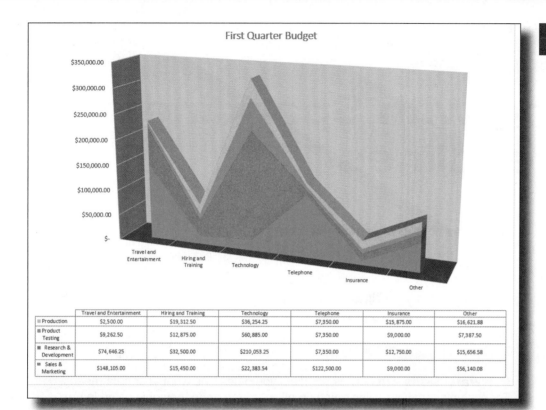

Figure 58-2

	Travel and Entertainment	Hiring and Training	Technology	Telephone	Insurance	Other
Production	$2,500.00	$19,312.50	$36,254.25	$7,350.00	$15,875.00	$16,621.88
Product Testing	$9,262.50	$12,875.00	$60,885.00	$7,350.00	$9,000.00	$7,387.50
Research & Development	$74,646.25	$32,500.00	$210,053.25	$7,350.00	$12,750.00	$15,656.58
Sales & Marketing	$148,105.00	$15,450.00	$22,383.54	$122,500.00	$9,000.00	$56,140.08

Lesson 59

Working with Sparklines and Trendlines

➤ What You Will Learn

Inserting a Line, Column, or Win/Loss Sparkline
Formatting a Sparkline
Inserting a Trendline
Using a Trendline to Predict

WORDS TO KNOW

Sparkline
Tiny charts within a
worksheet cell that
represent trends in
a series of values.

Trendline
A line that helps
determine the trend, or
moving average, of your
existing data.

Software Skills   Trendlines can help you determine what your data means. For example, are your sales going up all year long or do they only go up in the summer? On a worksheet, a sparkline can save you the effort of creating a chart at all because it is like adding a mini chart right in your worksheet.

What You Can Do

Inserting a Line, Column, or Win/Loss Sparkline

- **Sparklines** are like mini charts placed in the worksheet itself.
- Sparklines can show trends in data, or highlight maximum and minimum values.
- Excel will automatically update the sparkline as your data changes.
- Charts are objects that sit on top of the worksheet and can be moved independent of the data. Sparklines appear as a cell background. You can add descriptive text on top of the sparkline.
- Excel includes three distinct sparkline types:
  - Line 📈: tracks the data using a solid line.
  - Column 📊: tracks the data using vertical bars.
  - Win/Loss 📊: tracks the positive (win) or negative (loss) change in the data.
    - ✓ *A data value equal to zero is treated as a gap in the Win/Loss sparkline.*
- You can delete a sparkline by selecting Clear Selected Sparklines from the Sparklines group in the shortcut menu when you right-click a sparkline.

| Try It! | **Inserting a Line, Column, or Win/Loss Sparkline** |

1 Start Excel, and open **E59TryA** from the data files for this lesson.

2 Save the file as **E59TryA_xx** in the location where your teacher instructs you to store the files for this lesson.

3 Click to select the cell H9, and click the INSERT tab.

4 In the Sparklines group, click Line 〰.

5 Select the cell range E9:G9 to fill the Data Range box in the Create Sparklines dialog box, and click OK.

6 Expand the width of column H.

✓ *The sparkline will expand to fill the column width.*

7 Drag the AutoFill Handle ⌐ of cell H9 down to H14 to add a sparkline to the remaining cells.

8 Save the changes to the file, and leave it open to use in the next Try It.

Sparklines in place on the worksheet

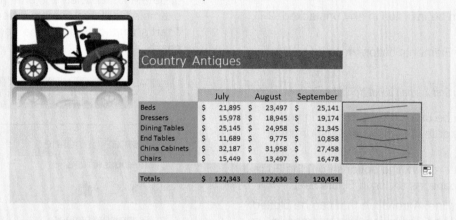

Country Antiques	July	August	September	
Beds	$ 21,895	$ 23,497	$ 25,141	
Dressers	$ 15,978	$ 18,945	$ 19,174	
Dining Tables	$ 25,145	$ 24,958	$ 21,345	
End Tables	$ 11,689	$ 9,775	$ 10,858	
China Cabinets	$ 32,187	$ 31,958	$ 27,458	
Chairs	$ 15,449	$ 13,497	$ 16,478	
Totals	$ 122,343	$ 122,630	$ 120,454	

Formatting a Sparkline

■ When a sparkline is inserted, the SPARKLINE TOOLS DESIGN tab is automatically displayed on the Ribbon.

- Use the Sparkline Color button ⬚ Sparkline Color ▾ to format the color of a sparkline's line.

- Use the Marker Color button ⬚ Marker Color ▾ to format the color of the data markers on a sparkline.

- Use the Style gallery to choose one of the style formats for a sparkline.

■ You can also determine which data points, such as the high point, low, first, last, or negative values, to highlight on a sparkline.

Try It!   Formatting a Sparkline

1 In the **E59TryA_xx** file, select the cell range H9:H14, and click the SPARKLINE TOOLS DESIGN tab, if necessary.

2 In the Show group, click High Point to add a data marker at the highest point of each sparkline.

3 Click the Sparkline Color drop-down arrow ☒ Sparkline Color ▾ , and in the Standard colors palette click Light Blue.

4 In the Style gallery, click the More button ▾ , and select Sparkline Style Accent 2, Lighter 40%.

5 Save the changes to the file, and leave it open to use in the next Try It.

Inserting a Trendline

■ **Trendlines** can be inserted in any unstacked, 2-D, non-pie chart.

■ Use the Chart Elements button ⊞ to insert a trendline.

   ✓ *Recall that you first learned about trendlines in Lesson 37.*

■ Trendlines can be used to show trends in your recorded data, or to suggest a forecast of future data.

■ Excel provides six trendline options from the Format Trendline task pane, as shown in Figure 59-1.

   ● Linear trendline: A trendline that can be plotted in a straight line, indicating that the trend is increasing or decreasing at a steady rate.

   ● Logarithmic trendline: A trendline that can be plotted in a gentle curve, indicating that the trend increases sharply and then levels out over time.

   ● Polynomial trendline: A trendline that curves following data that fluctuates in highs and lows over time.

   ● Power trendline: A trendline that curves upward, indicating that the trend is increasingly moving up.

   ● Exponential trendline: A trendline that is a gentle curve downward, indicating that the values rise or fall at constantly increasing rates.

   ● Moving average trendline: A trendline that smoothes out fluctuations over time; it determines the average of a specified number of values at each point on the line.

■ Excel uses chart animation to automatically update a chart when you change your data. For example, when you create a trendline, Excel's chart animation will add the trendline to your chart.

Figure 59-1

Try It! **Inserting a Trendline**

1 In the **E59TryA_xx** file, select cells D8:G14.

2 Click the INSERT tab > Insert Column Chart ▮▮ ▾ > Clustered Column Chart in the 2-D Column group.

3 Drag the chart below the worksheet data.

4 Click the CHART ELEMENTS button + > Trendline.

5 In the Add Trendline dialog box, click September > OK.

6 Click the trendline to select it, right-click, and click Format Trendline.

7 In the Format Trendline task pane, in the TRENDLINE OPTIONS group, click Polynomial.

8 Close the Format Trendline task pane.

9 Save and close the file.

10 Leave Excel open.

Using a Trendline to Predict

■ You can use trendlines to chart the trends of a set of data and to project into the future based on the slope of the curve.

■ Trendlines can deal with any data over time. Income and expense reports are a good example of this type of data.

Try It! **Projecting Income and Expenses with Trendlines**

1 Start Excel, and open **E59TryB** from the data files for this lesson.

2 Save the file as **E59TryB_xx** in the location where your teacher instructs you to store the files for this lesson.

3 Select the data range C2:D38.

4 Click INSERT > Insert Line Chart ⋙ ▾ .

5 Under 2-D, click Line. A line chart displays showing the trend.

6 Click the CHART ELEMENTS button +, hover over Trendline, click the Trendline arrow ▸, and click Linear Forecast.

7 In the Add Trendline dialog box, click Income > OK.

8 In the CHART ELEMENTS shortcut menu, hover over Trendline, click the Trendline arrow ▸, and click Linear Forecast.

9 In the Add Trendline dialog box, click Expense > OK.

10 Save and close the file, and exit Excel.

Income and expense trendlines

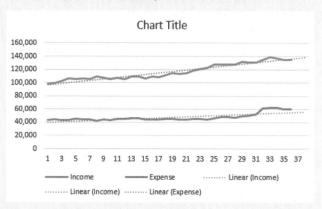

Lesson 59—Practice

As the manager of PhotoTown, you are concerned that sales have fallen off lately. You decide to track each individual's gross sales for a week and try to identify a trend. In this project, you will insert a trendline. In addition, you think the employees should be selling more T-shirts than they are, so you decide to track their sales and talk to anyone you feel is underperforming.

DIRECTIONS

1. Start Excel, if necessary, and open **E59Practice** from the data files for this lesson.
2. Save the file as **E59Practice_xx** in the location where your teacher instructs you to store the files for this lesson.
3. Click the **Daily Sales** worksheet tab.
4. Create a scatter chart for employee sales.
   a. Select the cells **A4:G8**.
   b. Click **INSERT > Insert Scatter (X, Y) or Bubble Chart** .
   c. In the Scatter group, click **Scatter**.
5. Move the new chart to its own tab.
   a. Click the chart to select it.
   b. On the CHART TOOLS DESIGN tab, in the Location group, click **Move Chart**.
   c. In the New sheet box, type **Employee Sales Chart**, and click **OK**.
6. Click the **Chart Elements** button ⊞, hover the pointer over **Trendline**, click the Trendline arrow ▶ > **Linear Forecast**.
7. In the Add Trendline dialog box, select the first employee, **Akira Ota**, and click **OK**.

8. Repeat steps 6 and 7 for each of the other three employees.
9. Highlight the data series that is trending upward.
   a. Click the **CHART TOOLS FORMAT** tab, click the **Chart Elements** box Chart Area ▾ , **Series "Taneel Black" Trendline 1**.
   b. On the CHART TOOLS FORMAT tab, click the **More** button ▾ to display the Shape Styles gallery.
   c. Click **Intense Line – Accent 6** from the gallery.
10. Add a chart title.
    a. On the chart, click the chart title to select it.
    b. Type **PhotoTown Daily Sales by Employee**, and press ENTER .
11. For all worksheets, add a header that has your name at the left, the date code in the center, and the page number code at the right, and change back to **Normal** view.
12. **With your teacher's permission**, print the chart. Your chart should look like Figure 59-2 on the next page.
13. Save and close the file, and exit Excel

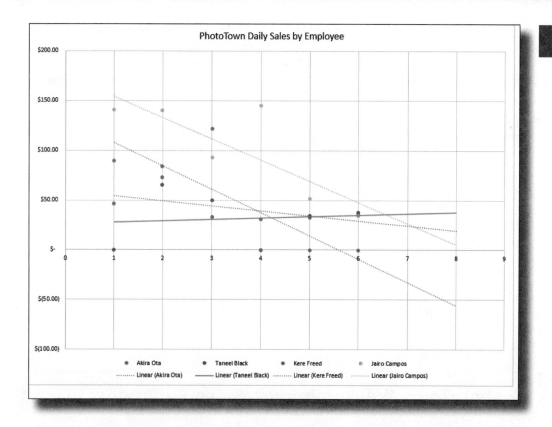

Figure 59-2

Lesson 59—Apply

You are the manager of PhotoTown, and you think the employees should be selling more T-shirts than they are. Because you are concerned that sales have fallen off, you decide to track each individual's gross sales for a week to identify a trend. You need this data so that you can talk to anyone you feel is underperforming. In this project, you will insert a sparkline to track the employees' sales.

DIRECTIONS

1. Start Excel, if necessary, and open **E59Apply** from the data files for this lesson.

2. Save the file as **E59Apply_xx** in the location where your teacher instructs you to store the files for this lesson.

3. Click the **Sales by Product** worksheet tab.

4. Add sparklines to the T-shirt sales.

   a. Click cell **J5** to select it.

   b. Click **INSERT** > **Line** 📈 in the Sparklines group.

   c. Select cells **B5:G5** to fill the Data Range box of the Create Sparklines dialog box, and click **OK**.

   d. Drag the AutoFill Handle down to cell **J8**.

5. With the cells still selected, on the SPARKLINE TOOLS DESIGN tab, in the Group group, click **Ungroup**.
6. Format the sparklines based on performance.
   a. Click cell **J5** to select it.
   b. On the SPARKLINE TOOLS DESIGN tab, click the **Sparkline Color** drop-down arrow Sparkline Color, and in the Standard Colors palette click **Red**.
   c. Click cell **J6** to select it.
   d. On the SPARKLINE TOOLS DESIGN tab, click the **Sparkline Color** drop-down arrow Sparkline Color, and in the Standard Colors palette click **Green**.
   e. Select the cell range **J7:J8**.
   f. Click the **Sparkline Color** drop-down arrow Sparkline Color, and in the Standard Colors palette click **Yellow**.
7. Select cells **J5:J8**, and in the Show group click **High Point** to add a data marker at the point of each employee's highest sales.
8. **With your teacher's permission**, print the **Sales by Product** worksheet. Your worksheet should look like Figure 59-3.
9. Save and close the file, and exit Excel.

Figure 59-3

PhotoTown Weekly Product Sales By Product

T-shirts

Employee	Monday	Tuesday	Wednesday	Thursday	Friday	Saturday	Price	Receipts	Tracking
Akira Ota	2	4	0	1	2	1	$ 10.00	$ 100.00	
Taneel Black	0	1	2	0	1	2	$ 10.00	$ 60.00	
Kere Freed	4	2	3	0	0	0	$ 10.00	$ 90.00	
Jairo Campos	5	10	3	4	2	1	$ 10.00	$ 250.00	
							Total Receipts	$ 500.00	

Photo books

Employee	Monday	Tuesday	Wednesday	Thursday	Friday	Saturday	Price	Receipts	Tracking
Akira Ota	1	1	1	1	1	2	$ 6.25	$ 43.75	
Taneel Black	0	5	1	0	2	1	$ 6.25	$ 56.25	
Kere Freed	1	2	2	0	0	0	$ 6.25	$ 31.25	
Jairo Campos	5	1	3	5	2	1	$ 6.25	$ 106.25	
							Total Receipts	$ 237.50	

Lesson 60

Drawing and Positioning Shapes

➤ What You Will Learn

Drawing Shapes
Resizing, Grouping, Aligning, and Arranging Shapes

Software Skills   After putting all that hard work into designing and entering data for a worksheet, of course you want it to look its best. You already know how to add formatting, color, and borders to a worksheet to enhance its appeal. To make your worksheet stand out from all the rest, you may need to do something "unexpected," such as adding your own art. You can insert predesigned shapes (such as stars or arrows) or combine them to create your own designs.

What You Can Do

Drawing Shapes

- You can use the Shapes button in the Illustration group of the INSERT tab to create many **shapes**.

  ✓ *Depending on the size of your screen, you may need to click the Illustrations button to access the Shapes button.*

- You can add lines, rectangles, arrows, equation shapes, stars and banners, and callouts as shown in Figure 60-1, on the next page, to highlight important information in your worksheet.
- You can add a text box or a callout—a shape in which you can type your own text.
- A text box or callout, like other shapes, can be placed anywhere on the worksheet.
- The Shapes button presents you with a palette of shapes sorted by category that makes it easy for you to select the shape you want to insert.
- To insert a shape, select the shape, and drag in a cell to create it—no actual drawing skills are needed.
- After inserting a shape, you can format it as needed.

WORDS TO KNOW

Adjustment handle
A yellow diamond-shaped handle that appears with some objects. You can drag this handle to manipulate the shape of the object, such as the width of a wide arrow, or the tip of a callout pointer.

Group
Objects can be grouped together so they can act as a single object. Grouping makes it easier to move or resize a drawing that consists of several objects.

Order
The position of an object with respect to other objects that are layered or in a stack.

Shape
A predesigned object (such as a banner or star) that can be drawn with a single dragging motion.

Sizing handles
Small white circles that appear around the perimeter of the active drawing object. You can resize an object by dragging one of these handles.

Stack
A group of drawing objects layered on top of one another, possibly partially overlapping. Use the Order command to change the position of a selected object within the stack.

- When you insert a shape, the DRAWING TOOLS FORMAT tab displays.
- You can insert more shapes from the Shapes gallery in the Insert Shapes group.

Figure 60-1

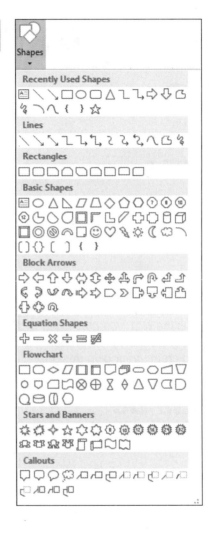

Try It!   **Drawing Shapes**

1 Start Excel, and open **E60Try** from the data files for this lesson.

2 Save the file as **E60Try_xx** in the location where your teacher instructs you to store the files for this lesson.

3 Select the P&L sheet, if necessary.

4 Click INSERT > Shapes ✏.

5 In the Rectangles group, click Rounded Rectangle (second item from the left).

6 Click and hold at the upper-left corner of cell F6, drag downward to the lower-right corner of cell J9, and release the pointer.

✓ *All shapes will appear using a default style and color.*

7 On the DRAWING TOOLS FORMAT tab, in the Insert Shapes group, click the More button ⊤.

8 In the Rectangles group, click Rectangle.

9 Click and hold at the upper-left corner of cell G14, drag downward to the lower-right corner of cell I16, and release the pointer.

10 Save the changes to the file, and leave it open to use in the next Try It.

Resizing, Grouping, Aligning, and Arranging Shapes

- A shape can also be resized, moved, and copied, like any other object, such as clip art.
    - To resize an object, drag one of the **sizing handles**.
    - To manipulate the shape of an object, drag the **adjustment handle** if one is available with that particular object.
- You can move shapes so that they partially cover other shapes.
    - To move a shape, drag it.
    - To move a shape more precisely, use Snap to Grid. When you drag a shape, it snaps automatically to the closest gridline or half-gridline.
    - The Snap to Shape command is similar, but it snaps a shape to the edge of a nearby shape when you drag the first shape close enough.

- Shapes can be aligned in relation to each other automatically.
    - For example, you might align objects so that their top edges line up.
    - Shapes can be aligned along their left, right, top, or bottom edges.
    - Shapes can also be aligned horizontally through their middles.
- When needed, you can change the **order** of objects that are layered (in a **stack**) so that a particular object appears on top of or behind another object.
- Click an object to select it.
    - Sometimes, selecting one object in a stack is difficult because the objects overlap and even obscure other objects below them in the stack.
    - The Selection task pane makes it easy to select a specific object because all the objects on a worksheet appear in a list. Click an object in the task pane to select it.
    - The Selection task pane also makes it easy to rearrange objects in the stack.
- You can **group** two or more objects together so they act as one object.

Try It!   **Resizing, Grouping, Aligning, and Arranging Shapes**

1. In the **E60Try_xx** file, on the P&L tab, click the rounded rectangle, and drag it into place fitting the area between cells F14 and J17.

2. Select the rectangle and drag it inside the rounded rectangle, as shown in the figure.

3. To draw a third shape, on the DRAWING TOOLS FORMAT tab, in the Insert Shapes group, click the More button ⬇.

4. In the Block Arrows group, click Right Arrow, and click anywhere in the worksheet to insert the shape.

5. Move and resize the right arrow shape to fit inside the rounded rectangle, as shown in the figure.
    a. Drag the arrow inside the rounded rectangle.
    b. Drag the center-top sizing handle and the center-bottm sizing handle to stretch the arrow's height to fit just inside the top and bottom border of the rounded rectangle.

6. Click the PAGE LAYOUT tab, and in the Arrange group click Selection Pane 🔖 to display the Selection task pane.

7. Press and hold CTRL, and click the Right Arrow, Rectangle, and Rounded Rectangle shape names.

8. On the DRAWING TOOLS FORMAT tab, in the Arrange group, click Align ⤴ > Align Middle.

9. With the shapes still selected, on the DRAWING TOOLS FORMAT tab, in the Arrange group, click Group ⊡, and in the drop-down menu click Group.

10. Close the Selection task pane.

11. Save and close the file, and exit Excel.

(continued)

Try It!　**Resizing, Grouping, Aligning, and Arranging Shapes** *(continued)*

Arranging shapes

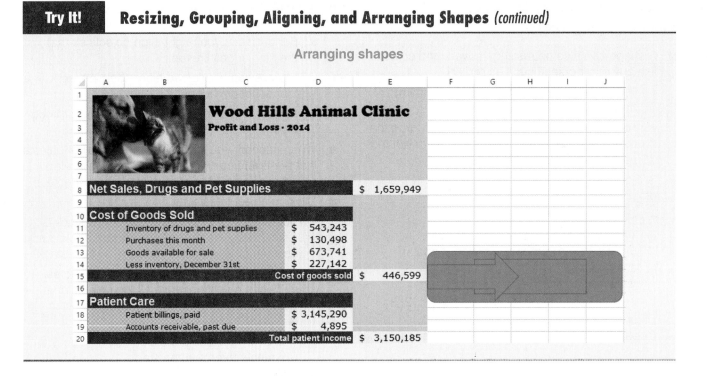

Lesson 60—Practice

You're the accountant at Sydney Crenshaw Realty, and you need to compile a year-to-date spreadsheet showing the total sales and commissions paid. You want to add your company logo. In this project, you will insert, format, arrange, and group shapes to create the company logo.

DIRECTIONS

1. Start Excel, if necessary, and open **E60Practice** from the data files for this lesson.

2. Save the file as **E60Practice_xx** in the location where your teacher instructs you to store the files for this lesson.

3. Add a header that has your name at the left, the date code in the center, and the page number code at the right.

4. Click **PAGE LAYOUT** > **Themes** > **Retrospect**.

5. Click **INSERT** > **Shapes** ✎ > **Rectangle** from the Rectangles group.

6. Click and hold at the upper-left corner of cell **B2**, and drag downward and to the right to form a rectangle about the height of the title text.

7. Resize the new rectangle.

   a. On the DRAWING TOOLS FORMAT tab, in the Size group, in the Shape Height box, type **.28**.

   b. On the DRAWING TOOLS FORMAT tab, in the Size group, in the Shape Width box, type **.48**.

8. On the DRAWING TOOLS FORMAT tab, in the Insert Shapes group, click the More button ⬇, and in the Basic Shapes group, click **Isosceles Triangle** to add a second shape in cell **B1** about the size of the previously inserted rectangle.

9. Resize the new triangle.

   a. On the DRAWING TOOLS FORMAT tab, in the Size group, in the Shape Height box, type **.22**.

   b. On the DRAWING TOOLS FORMAT tab, in the Size group, in the Shape Width box, type **.48**.

10. Drag the triangle over the top of the rectangle to form the shape of a house.

11. Arrange the house shape.

   a. Press and hold `CTRL`, click the triangle shape, and click the rectangle shape.

   b. Click **DRAWING TOOLS FORMAT > Align** 🔲 > **Align Center**.

   c. On the DRAWING TOOLS FORMAT tab, click **Group** 🔲 > **Group**.

   d. Drag the right edge of the "house" even with the right edge of column B.

   e. Align the top edge of the house to just below the column header, as shown in Figure 60-2.

12. Save and close the file, and exit Excel.

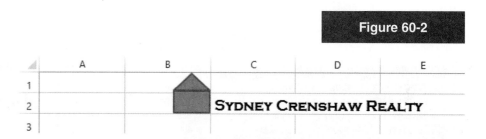

Figure 60-2

Lesson 60—Apply

As the accountant at Sydney Crenshaw Realty, you have created a year-to-date spreadsheet showing the total sales and commissions paid. You now want to call attention to some record sales figures. In this project, you will add shapes and format them with color and effects to highlight data in the worksheet.

DIRECTIONS

1. Start Excel, if necessary, and open **E60Apply** from the data files for this lesson.

2. Save the file as **E60Apply_xx** in the location where your teacher instructs you to store the files for this lesson.

3. Add a header that has your name at the left, the date code in the center, and the page number code at the right.

4. Insert a brace that visually groups the data from the month of May:

   a. Click **INSERT > Shapes** ▽ > **Right Brace** (the last shape in the Basic Shapes group).

   b. Click and hold at the upper-left corner of cell **G21**, and drag downward to the lower-left corner of cell **G23**.

5. Insert an arrow that points to the brace you just inserted:

   a. On the INSERT tab, click **Shapes** ▽ > **Left Arrow** (the second arrow in the Block Arrows group).

   b. Click at the upper-left corner of cell **H21**, and drag downward to the lower-right corner of cell **I23**.

6. Align the brace and arrow together.

   a. Drag the arrow closer to the right brace, press and hold `CTRL`, and select both the left arrow and the right brace.

   b. On the DRAWING TOOLS FORMAT tab, click **Align** 🔲 > **Align Middle**.

   c. With both shapes still selected, click **Group** 🔲 > **Group**.

7. Select the **12-Point Star** from the Stars and Banners group.

8. Click at the upper-left corner of the **F1** cell and drag downward to the lower-right corner of the **F3** cell.

9. With the shape still selected, change the shape height to **.76**, and change the shape width to **.93**.

10. **With your teacher's permission**, print the worksheet. Your worksheet should look like Figure 60-3.

11. Save and close the file, and exit Excel.

Figure 60-3

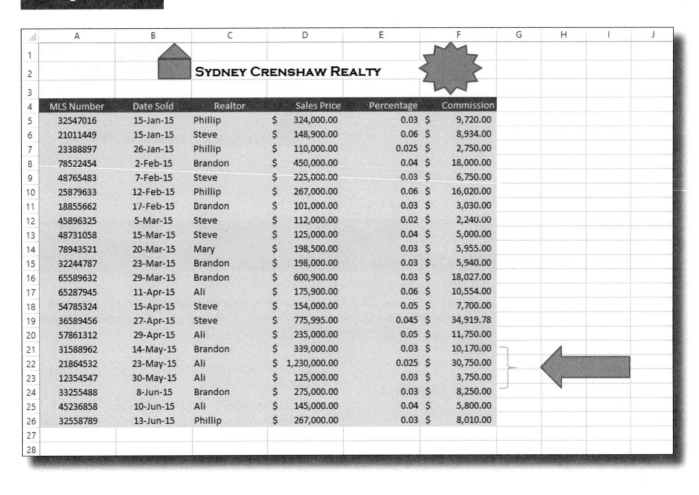

	A	B	C	D	E	F	G	H	I	J
1										
2			SYDNEY CRENSHAW REALTY							
3										
4	MLS Number	Date Sold	Realtor	Sales Price	Percentage	Commission				
5	32547016	15-Jan-15	Phillip	$ 324,000.00	0.03	$ 9,720.00				
6	21011449	15-Jan-15	Steve	$ 148,900.00	0.06	$ 8,934.00				
7	23388897	26-Jan-15	Phillip	$ 110,000.00	0.025	$ 2,750.00				
8	78522454	2-Feb-15	Brandon	$ 450,000.00	0.04	$ 18,000.00				
9	48765483	7-Feb-15	Steve	$ 225,000.00	0.03	$ 6,750.00				
10	25879633	12-Feb-15	Phillip	$ 267,000.00	0.06	$ 16,020.00				
11	18855662	17-Feb-15	Brandon	$ 101,000.00	0.03	$ 3,030.00				
12	45896325	5-Mar-15	Steve	$ 112,000.00	0.02	$ 2,240.00				
13	48731058	15-Mar-15	Steve	$ 125,000.00	0.04	$ 5,000.00				
14	78943521	20-Mar-15	Mary	$ 198,500.00	0.03	$ 5,955.00				
15	32244787	23-Mar-15	Brandon	$ 198,000.00	0.03	$ 5,940.00				
16	65589632	29-Mar-15	Brandon	$ 600,900.00	0.03	$ 18,027.00				
17	65287945	11-Apr-15	Ali	$ 175,900.00	0.06	$ 10,554.00				
18	54785324	15-Apr-15	Steve	$ 154,000.00	0.05	$ 7,700.00				
19	36589456	27-Apr-15	Steve	$ 775,995.00	0.045	$ 34,919.78				
20	57861312	29-Apr-15	Ali	$ 235,000.00	0.05	$ 11,750.00				
21	31588962	14-May-15	Brandon	$ 339,000.00	0.03	$ 10,170.00				
22	21864532	23-May-15	Ali	$ 1,230,000.00	0.025	$ 30,750.00				
23	12354547	30-May-15	Ali	$ 125,000.00	0.03	$ 3,750.00				
24	33255488	8-Jun-15	Brandon	$ 275,000.00	0.03	$ 8,250.00				
25	45236858	10-Jun-15	Ali	$ 145,000.00	0.04	$ 5,800.00				
26	32558789	13-Jun-15	Phillip	$ 267,000.00	0.03	$ 8,010.00				
27										
28										

Lesson 61

Formatting Shapes

➤ What You Will Learn

Formatting Shapes
Adding Shape Effects

Software Skills   When shapes such as rectangles, block arrows, and banners are added to a worksheet, they originally appear in the default style—a shape with a blue outline filled with the Accent 1 color. You can change both the color and the outline style of any shape. You can also create custom colors. You can also add special effects such as shadows and soft edges.

What You Can Do

Formatting Shapes

- When a shape is selected, the DRAWING TOOLS FORMAT tab automatically appears on the Ribbon in anticipation of your need to edit it.
- Since all new shapes appear in the default style, you might want to change:
  - Shape Styles: A set of formats that include the outline color and style, edge effects, and fill.
  - Shape Fill: The color, picture, gradient, or texture that fills a shape.

    ✓ *A line shape cannot be filled. A line's color is determined by the Shape Outline settings.*

  - Shape Outline: The color, weight, and style of the border that outlines a shape.

    ✓ *You can change the color, weight, and style of a line. You can also add arrows at one or both ends.*

  - Shape Effects: Complex formats applied with a single click.
- When changing any color on a shape, either the fill or the outline, you can use the Colors dialog box to create a custom color, and even to add transparency if desired.

Try It!   Formatting Shapes

1 Start Excel, and open **E61Try** from the data files for this lesson.

2 Save the file as **E61Try_xx** in the location where your teacher instructs you to store the files for this lesson.

3 Click the P&L worksheet tab > PAGE LAYOUT > Selection Pane 🔍.

4 In the Selection task pane, click Rectangle > DRAWING TOOLS FORMAT.

5 In the Shape Styles group, click the Shape Fill drop-down arrow ⬠ Shape Fill ▾ , and in the Theme Colors palette click Orange, Accent 2, Lighter 60%.

6 Click the Shape Outline drop-down arrow ⬠ Shape Outline ▾ , and in the Standard Colors palette click Dark Red.

7 In the Selection task pane, click Right Arrow.

8 Click the Shape Fill drop-down arrow ⬠ Shape Fill ▾ > Gradient > More Gradients.

9 In the FILL group, click Gradient fill.

10 In the Format Shape task pane, click Preset gradients ▦ ▾ > Bottom Spotlight, Accent 4.

11 In the Type list, click Linear.

12 In the Direction list, click Linear Diagonal - Top Left to Bottom Right (the first option).

13 Click LINE > Outline color ⬠ ▾ > Gold, Accent 4, Darker 25%.

14 In the Selection task pane, click Rounded Rectangle.

15 On the DRAWING TOOLS FORMAT tab, click the Shape Styles More button ▾ > Moderate Effect - Orange Accent 2.

16 Close the Selection and Format Shape task panes.

17 Save the changes to the file, and leave it open to use in the next Try It.

The Selection and Format Shape task panes

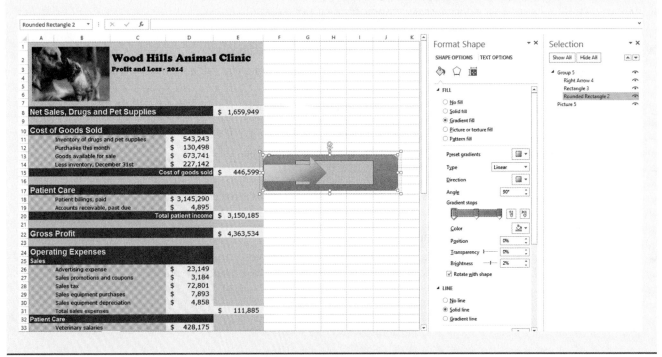

Adding Shape Effects

- Shape **effects** that you can apply to a selected shape include:
  - Shadows
  - Reflections
  - Glows
  - Soft edges
  - Beveled edges
  - 3-D rotations

- Each shape effect style comes with options that allow you to customize the effect to get the look you want.
- The Preset category on the Shape Effects drop-down menu displays a set of common effects, with the options already pre-selected for you.
- Choose one of the Preset effects to change the look of a selected shape.

Try It!   **Adding Shape Effects**

1 In the **E61Try_xx** file, on the P&L tab, click PAGE LAYOUT > Selection Pane 🔲.

2 In the Selection task pane, click Rectangle > DRAWING TOOLS FORMAT.

3 In the Shape Styles group, click Shape Effects 🔲 > Glow > Gold, 8 pt glow, Accent color 4.

4 In the Selection task pane, click Rounded Rectangle and click the DRAWING TOOLS FORMAT tab, if necessary.

5 On the DRAWING TOOLS FORMAT tab, in the Shape Styles group, click Shape Effects 🔲 > Reflection > Tight Reflection, 4 pt offset.

6 Close the Selection task pane.

7 Save and close the file, and exit Excel.

Lesson 61—Practice

As the accountant for Sydney Crenshaw Realty, you've already created a spreadsheet to track year-to-date sales and commissions with some basic shapes. Now you'd like to format the shapes with some color and dimension.

DIRECTIONS

1. Start Excel, if necessary, and open **E61Practice** from the data files for this lesson.

2. Save the file as **E61Practice_xx** in the location where your teacher instructs you to store the files for this lesson.

3. Add a header that has your name at the left, the date code in the center, and the page number code at the right

4. Click **PAGE LAYOUT** > **Selection Pane** 🗐.

5. In the Selection task pane, click **Isosceles Triangle**.

6. Click **DRAWING TOOLS FORMAT**, and click the Shape Styles **More** button to open the gallery.

7. Click **Moderate Effect - Orange, Accent 2**.

8. In the Selection task pane, click **Rectangle**.

9. On the DRAWING TOOLS FORMAT tab, click the Shape Styles **More** button to open the gallery.

10. Click **Moderate Effect - Brown, Accent 3**.

11. On the DRAWING TOOLS FORMAT tab, in the Shape Styles group, click **Shape Effects** 🗐 > **Reflection**.

12. In the Reflection Variations group, click **Tight Reflection, touching**.

13. Close the Selection task pane.

14. **With your teacher's permission**, print the worksheet. Your worksheet should look like Figure 61-1.

15. Save and close the file, and exit Excel.

Figure 61-1

	A	B	C	D	E	F	G	H	I
1									
2			SYDNEY CRENSHAW REALTY						
3									
4	MLS Number	Date Sold	Realtor	Sales Price	Percentage	Commission			
5	32547016	15-Jan-15	Phillip	$ 324,000.00	0.03	$ 9,720.00			
6	21011449	15-Jan-15	Steve	$ 148,900.00	0.06	$ 8,934.00			
7	23388897	26-Jan-15	Phillip	$ 110,000.00	0.025	$ 2,750.00			
8	78522454	2-Feb-15	Brandon	$ 450,000.00	0.04	$ 18,000.00			
9	48765483	7-Feb-15	Steve	$ 225,000.00	0.03	$ 6,750.00			
10	25879633	12-Feb-15	Phillip	$ 267,000.00	0.06	$ 16,020.00			
11	18855662	17-Feb-15	Brandon	$ 101,000.00	0.03	$ 3,030.00			
12	45896325	5-Mar-15	Steve	$ 112,000.00	0.02	$ 2,240.00			
13	48731058	15-Mar-15	Steve	$ 125,000.00	0.04	$ 5,000.00			
14	78943521	20-Mar-15	Mary	$ 198,500.00	0.03	$ 5,955.00			
15	32244787	23-Mar-15	Brandon	$ 198,000.00	0.03	$ 5,940.00			
16	65589632	29-Mar-15	Brandon	$ 600,900.00	0.03	$ 18,027.00			
17	65287945	11-Apr-15	Ali	$ 175,900.00	0.06	$ 10,554.00			
18	54785324	15-Apr-15	Steve	$ 154,000.00	0.05	$ 7,700.00			
19	36589456	27-Apr-15	Steve	$ 775,995.00	0.045	$ 34,919.78			
20	57861312	29-Apr-15	Ali	$ 235,000.00	0.05	$ 11,750.00			
21	31588962	14-May-15	Brandon	$ 339,000.00	0.03	$ 10,170.00			
22	21864532	23-May-15	Ali	$ 1,230,000.00	0.025	$ 30,750.00			
23	12354547	30-May-15	Ali	$ 125,000.00	0.03	$ 3,750.00			
24	33255488	8-Jun-15	Brandon	$ 275,000.00	0.03	$ 8,250.00			
25	45236858	10-Jun-15	Ali	$ 145,000.00	0.04	$ 5,800.00			
26	32558789	13-Jun-15	Phillip	$ 267,000.00	0.03	$ 8,010.00			
27									
28									
29									

Lesson 61—Apply

You are working with a spreadsheet of year-to-date sales and commissions for Sydney Crenshaw Realty. You've been enhancing the spreadsheet with basic shapes and formatting. Now you want to format the shapes with color and effects to draw attention to certain data.

DIRECTIONS

1. Start Excel, if necessary, and open **E61Apply** from the data files for this lesson.

2. Save the file as **E61Apply_xx** in the location where your teacher instructs you to store the files for this lesson.

3. Add a header that has your name at the left, the date code in the center, and the page number code at the right

4. Click **PAGE LAYOUT** > **Selection Pane** 🔲.

5. In the Selection task pane, click the Group that includes the Left Arrow and the Right Brace.

6. On the DRAWING TOOLS FORMAT tab, click the Shape Styles **More** button to open the gallery, and click **Intense Effect - Orange, Accent 2**.

7. In the Selection pane, select the Right Brace.

8. On the DRAWING TOOLS FORMAT tab, click the Shape Styles **More** button to open the gallery, and click **Subtle Line - Accent 3**.

9. In the Selection task pane, click the **12-Point Star**.

10. On the DRAWING TOOLS FORMAT tab, click the Shape Styles **More** button to open the gallery, and click **Moderate Effect - Tan, Accent 5**.

11. With the shape still selected, click **Shape Effects** > **Shadow** > **Offset Diagonal Top Left** (the third item in the third row of the Outer group).

12. Close the Selection task pane.

13. **With your teacher's permission**, print the worksheet. Your worksheet should look like Figure 61-2.

14. Save and close the file, and exit Excel.

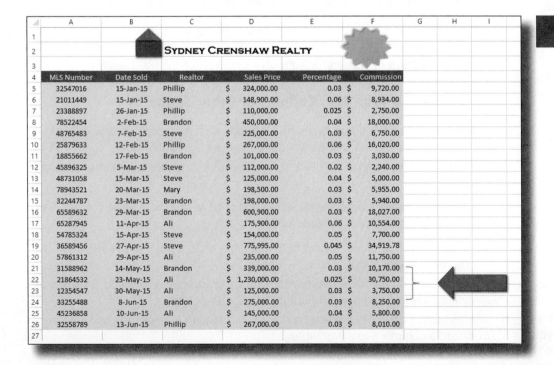

Figure 61-2

Lesson 62

Enhancing Shapes with Text and Effects

➤ **What You Will Learn**

Adding Text to a Text Box, Callout, or Other Shape
Adding 3-D Effects
Rotating Shapes
Inserting a Screen Capture

WORDS TO KNOW

Callout
Text that's placed in a special AutoShape balloon. A callout, like a text box, "floats" over the cells in a worksheet—so you can position a callout wherever you like.

Extension point
The yellow diamond handle that indicates the position where a callout can be resized or extended.

Rotation handle
A white rotation symbol that appears just over the top of most objects when they are selected. Use this handle to rotate the object manually.

Screenshot
A screenshot is a picture of all or part of an open window, such as another application or a Web page.

Text box
A small rectangle that "floats" over the cells in a worksheet, into which you can add text. A text box can be placed anywhere you want.

Software Skills   If you need to place text in some spot within the worksheet that doesn't correspond to a specific cell, you can "float" the text over the cells by creating a text box or by adding a callout. A text box or callout can be placed anywhere in the worksheet, regardless of the cell gridlines. You can add text to any shape. Add 3-D effects or rotation to shapes to really make them stand out. You can use the screen capture feature to take a picture of any open application or Web page.

What You Can Do

Adding Text to a Text Box, Callout, or Other Shape

- A **callout** is basically a **text box** with a shape, such as a cartoon balloon, with an extension that points to the information you wish to write about.
  - When a callout shape is selected, a yellow diamond indicates the **extension point**.
    - ✓ *On other shapes, this yellow diamond handle is called an adjustment handle, because it lets you adjust the outline of the shape itself.*
  - Drag this yellow extension point to make the callout point precisely to the data you wish to talk about.
  - Text boxes do not have these extensions, but you can easily add an arrow or line shape to a text box to accomplish the same thing.
- You can use a callout like a text box, to draw attention to important information, or to add a comment to a worksheet.

- You can add text to any shape.

  ✓ *If the shape already contains text, the text you type will be added to the end of the existing text. You can replace text by first selecting it, and then typing new text.*

- The border of a selected shape changes to indicate whether you're editing the object itself (solid border) or the text in the object (dashed border).

  - To move, resize, copy, or delete the object, the border must be solid.
  - To edit or add text in a text box or shape, the border must be dashed.

Try It! **Adding Text to a Text Box, Callout, or Other Shape**

1 Start Excel, and open **E62TryA** from the data files for this lesson.

2 Save the file as **E62TryA_xx** in the location where your teacher instructs you to store the files for this lesson.

3 Click the P&L worksheet tab > PAGE LAYOUT > Selection Pane 🔲.

4 In the Selection task pane, click Rectangle, and type **This cost is down because of better inventory management.**

5 Select the text in the shape, and click HOME.

6 Click Font Color **A ˅** , and in the Standard Colors palette click Dark Red.

7 With the text still selected, click te Decrease Font **A˅** four times to change the font size to 8 points.

8 In the Alignment group, click Center ≡ .

9 With the rectangle still selected, right-click the rectangle, and in the shortcut menu click Format Text Effects.

10 In the Format Shape task pane, under TEXT OPTIONS, click Textbox 🄰. In the Left Margin box type **.5**, and in the Top margin box type **.1**.

11 Create a callout:

   a. Click INSERT > Shapes and choose Rectangular Callout from the Callouts group.

   b. Draw a callout in the area of F34:I36.

   c. Type **Next year's purchases should be much lower than this.**

   d. Select the text you typed in step 11c, click HOME, and click Decrease Font **A˅** three times to change the font size to 9.

   e. In the Alignment group, click Center ≡ , and close the Format Shape task pane.

   f. Click the border of the callout shape.

   ✓ *Clicking the border allows you to change the format of the whole text box, not just the text.*

   g. Click DRAWING TOOLS FORMAT, click the Shape Styles More button ▾ ,and click Intense Effect - Orange, Accent 2.

12 Click and hold the yellow extension point, and drag it until the callout tip points to cell D38.

13 Close the Selection and Format Shapes task panes.

14 Save the changes to the file, and leave it open to use in the next Try It.

Formatting the text options of a shape

Format Shape	▾ ✕
SHAPE OPTIONS	**TEXT OPTIONS**

🄰 🄰 🄰

◢ **TEXT BOX**

Vertical alignment	Top ▾
Text direction	Horizontal ▾

☐ Resize shape to fit text
☐ Allow text to overflow shape

Left margin	
Right margin	0.1"
Top margin	
Bottom margin	0.05"

☑ Wrap text in shape

Columns...

Adding 3-D Effects

- When you add 3-D effects to an object, that object appears to have depth.
- You can add 3-D effects to any object, even grouped objects.
- To select a 3-D rotation style, use the Shape Effects button in the Shape Styles group on the DRAWING TOOLS FORMAT tab.
  - If you choose 3-D Rotation Options, the Format Shape task pane displays where you can customize the settings.
  - You can set the exact degree of rotation and other options such as whether you want the text in the shape (if any) to be rotated with the shape.
  - Objects are rotated along three axes—X (horizontal), Y (vertical), and Z (depth dimension).
- In the Format Shape task pane, shown in Figure 62-1, you can adjust the format of a 3-D shape, by selecting the depth, surface texture, and other options.
  - You can adjust the style of the edge of your 3-D shape. You can also change the color and contour of this third dimension.
  - Use the Material feature to select a surface texture—such as the apparent material used.
  - You can change how the surface is lit (both the color of the light and the angle at which it shines on the 3-D object).

Figure 62-1

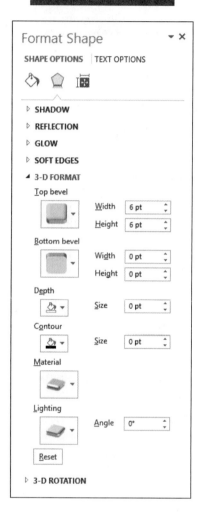

Try It!   **Adding 3-D Effects**

1 In the **E62TryA_xx** file, click the P&L tab, if necessary.

2 Click the callout shape to select it.

3 On the DRAWING TOOLS FORMAT, click Shape Effects ◔, click Bevel, and in the Bevel group click Circle.

4 On the DRAWING TOOLS FORMAT, click Shape Effects ◔, click 3-D Rotation, and in the Oblique group click Oblique Top Right.

5 Save the changes to the file, and leave it open to use in the next Try It.

Rotating Shapes

- A shape can be rotated around an invisible pin holding its center in place on the worksheet.
  - Use the Rotate button on the DRAWING TOOLS FORMAT tab to rotate a shape to the left or the right by 90 degrees.

- You can rotate a shape by a custom amount.
- Shapes can be manually rotated, using the **rotation handle**.

- A shape can also be flipped vertically (turning it completely upside down), or flipped horizontally (turning it backward to face the opposite direction).

Try It!   **Rotating Shapes**

1 In the **E62TryA_xx** file, click the P&L tab, if necessary.

2 Click the callout shape to select it, if necessary.

3 Click and hold the rotation handle, and drag the pointer to the right to change the rotation amount of the shape so that the angle matches the figure.

4 Click and hold the yellow extension point, and drag it until the callout tip points to cell D38.

5 Save the changes to the file, and leave it open to use in the next Try It.

Manually rotating a shape

30	Sales equipment depreciation	$	4,858
31	Total sales expenses		$ 111,885
32	**Patient Care**		
33	Veterinary salaries	$	428,175
34	Non-Veterinary salaries	$	158,410
35	Charity or pro-bono work	$	11,219
36	Lab work	$	41,876
37	Examination room supplies	$	178,145
38	Examination room equipment purchases	$	41,189
39	Examination room equipment depreciation	$	29,141
40	Kennel equipment purchases	$	13,789

Inserting a Screen Capture

- You can add a picture of any open application or Web page to your Excel worksheet.
- **Screenshots** are helpful for capturing information that will change or expire.
- Only open windows that have not been minimized to the taskbar can be captured with this tool.

- Available screenshots appear as thumbnails on the Available Windows gallery. Selecting one of the thumbnails will insert the picture of that window in your file.
- Choose Screen Clipping to insert a part of a window, such as a logo, a set of instructions, or a dialog box.
- When you click Screen Clipping, the entire screen becomes temporarily whited out. Use the mouse to outline the part of the screen that you want to capture.

Try It!   Inserting a Screen Capture

1 In the **E62TryA_xx** file, select the P&L tab, if necessary.

2 Open **E62TryB.jpg** from the data files for this lesson.

✓ Use File Explorer to open the folder containing your data files. Double-click on the **E62TryB.jpg** file to open it in your image viewer.

3 Minimize all open windows except Excel and your image viewer, and reposition the Excel window and the image viewer so that you can see the P&L worksheet and the image.

4 In Excel, click INSERT, and in the Illustrations group click Screenshot 📷 to view your Available Windows gallery.

5 Click Screen Clipping, click and hold at the upper left corner of the image, and drag the pointer over the picture in your image viewer to select only the picture.

✓ Screen Clipping whites out your screen. Dragging the mouse over the desired area of the screen restores the color to that area and highlights the portion of your screen that will be inserted into Excel.

6 Once the screen clipping has been added to your worksheet, drag the picture to the open area of your spreadsheet between the two text boxes.

✓ You may need to scroll down to view the screen clipping.

7 With the screen clipping still selected, click PICTURE TOOLS FORMAT > Picture Border drop-down arrow.

8 Click Automatic to add a border around your screenshot.

9 Save and close the file, and exit Excel.

Using screen clipping

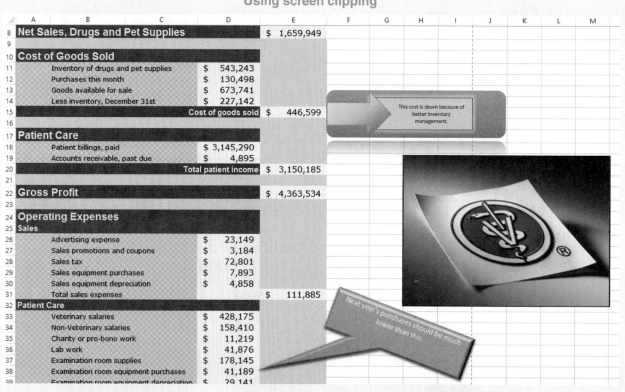

Lesson 62—Practice

The year-to-date sales and commission report that you've been working on for Sydney Crenshaw Realty is coming along nicely, but you think that adding some additional text or callouts might make the information you are tracking easier to understand. In this project, you will add text to shapes, format the shapes, and insert a callout.

DIRECTIONS

1. Start Excel, if necessary, and open **E62Practice** from the data files for this lesson.
2. Save the file as **E62Practice_xx** in the location where your teacher instructs you to store the files for this lesson.
3. Add a header that has your name at the left, the date code in the center, and the page number code at the right.
4. Add text to the tan star shape:
   a. Right-click the star > **Edit Text**.
   b. Type **Rated #1**.
   c. Select the text **Rated #1**.
   d. On the HOME tab click **Middle Align** ≡ > **Center** ≡.
5. Change the text margins in the tan star shape:
   a. Right-click the star > **Format Shape**.
   b. In the Format Shape task pane, click **TEXT OPTIONS** > **Textbox** 🗛.

c. In the Left margin box, type **0**.
d. In the Right margin box, type **0**.
e. In the Top margin box, type **0**.
f. In the Bottom margin box, type **0**.
g. Close the Format Shape task pane.

6. Add text to the red arrow shape:
   a. Click the red arrow, and click it again to select it in the group.
   b. Right-click the arrow > **Edit Text**.
   c. Type **Best Month**.
7. Insert a callout to bring attention to the highest commission figure.
   a. Click **INSERT** > **Shapes** 🗗 > **Rectangular Callout**.
   b. Draw a callout in the area of **H16:I18**.
8. **With your teacher's permission**, print the worksheet.
9. Save and close the file, and exit Excel.

Lesson 62—Apply

You have been working on the year-to-date sales and commission report for Sydney Crenshaw Realty. You want to format the shapes within the report with effects and a picture to call attention to certain data. In this project, you will use effects to format shapes and insert a screen capture to enhance the report.

DIRECTIONS

1. Start Excel, if necessary, and open **E62Apply** from the data files for this lesson.
2. Save the file as **E62Apply_xx** in the location where your teacher instructs you to store the files for this lesson.

3. Add a header that has your name at the left, the date code in the center, and the page number code at the right.
4. Add the **Preset 4** 3-D effect to the star shape.
5. Add the following text to the callout shape: **Largest commission ever paid by our firm.** Set the font size to **11**, if necessary.

6. Format the shape as follows:

   a. Shape height **0.93"**.

   b. Shape width **1.31"**.

   c. Apply the **Colored Fill - Green, Accent 6** style to the shape.

   d. Apply the **Orange, Accent 2** color to the shape outline.

7. Apply the **Circle** bevel shape effect.

8. Rotate the callout so that it looks similar to Figure 62-2.

9. Position the callout's yellow extension point on the line between F19 and G19 to indicate the larger commission figure.

10. Click **PAGE LAYOUT**, and in the Sheet Options group, under Gridlines, click to unselect the **View** check box to view the worksheet without gridlines.

11. **With your teacher's permission**, print the worksheet.

12. Save and close the file, and exit Excel.

Figure 62-2

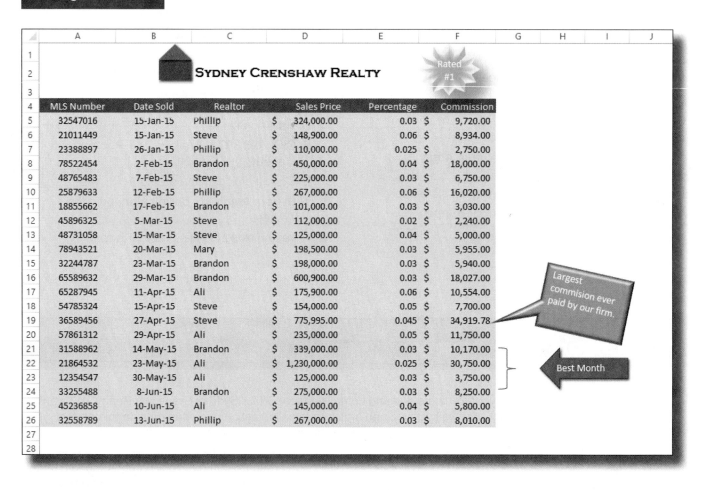

Lesson 63

Working with Templates

➤ What You Will Learn

Adding a Watermark or Other Graphics
Formatting the Worksheet Background
Creating a Workbook Template
Creating a Chart Template

Software Skills To make a worksheet look more professional, you might want to customize the standard templates Excel provides by choosing company-style fonts and colors, adding a watermark, or applying a custom worksheet background.

Excel comes with built-in templates you can use to apply consistent formatting to your worksheets. You can create a custom workbook template to personalize your workbooks and ensure a consistent and professional look. An easy way to create a custom workbook template is to modify an existing template. You can also create a chart template to apply formatting to a new or existing chart.

What You Can Do

Adding a Watermark or Other Graphics

■ You can re-create the look of a **watermark** by placing the graphic behind your Excel data.

- You can add the watermark graphic to either the header or footer of every page.

- This graphic begins within either the header or footer area, and, depending on its size, extends into the data area to act as a watermark.

- After inserting the graphic, you can adjust the size so that it fills the page.

- You can also adjust the inserted graphic's brightness and contrast in order to make the worksheet data, which appears on top of the watermark, easier to read.

■ Watermarks appear only on the worksheet on which they were added, and not every worksheet within a workbook.

Try It!   Adding a Watermark or Other Graphics

1. Start Excel, and open **E63TryA** from the data files for this lesson.

2. Save the file as **E63TryA_xx** in the location where your teacher instructs you to store the files for this lesson.

3. Click the July 22 tab, if necessary

4. Click INSERT > Header & Footer 📄.

5. Click in the middle section of the header, and in the HEADER & FOOTER TOOLS DESIGN tab, in the Header & Footer Elements group, click Picture 🖻.

   ✓ *A watermark picture can be added in any of the three header sections depending on your desire to add other header elements to your page.*

6. In the Insert Pictures window, in the From a file group, click Browse.

7. Select **E63TryB.jpg** from the data files for this lesson, and click Insert.

   ✓ *In Page Layout view, an inserted picture appears as a picture code in the header or footer.*

8. On the HEADER & FOOTER TOOLS DESIGN tab, in the Header & Footer Elements group, click Format Picture 🖻.

9. In the Format Picture dialog box, on the Size tab, in the Scale group, in the Height box, type **75**.

10. Click the Picture tab, and in the Image control group, in the Brightness box, type **60**.

11. On the Picture tab, in the Image control group, in the Contrast box, type **20**, and click OK.

12. Click outside of the header to view the inserted picture.

13. Save the changes to the file, and leave it open to use in the next Try It.

The HEADER & FOOTER TOOLS DESIGN tab

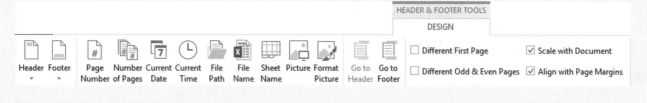

Formatting the Worksheet Background

- You can add a graphic to the background of the worksheet, behind the data.
- Unlike a watermark, a background image is used for on-screen display purposes only, and does not print.
  - You might want to add a worksheet background graphic to enhance a worksheet you know will only be used in onscreen presentations.
  - Because you won't be able to adjust the brightness or contrast of your image after it's inserted, for the best effect, be sure to use a graphic that's very light in color, so that your data can still be read.

    ✓ *After inserting a graphic for use as a worksheet background, if you have trouble reading your data, you can apply a fill color to just the data cells so that the data can be more easily read.*

- The background isn't included when you create a Web page from the worksheet, unless you create the Web page from the whole workbook.
- The Show group on the VIEW tab includes a number of options to alter the version of the worksheet you see.
  - Headings: Removes the row and column headings.
  - Gridlines: Removes the cell gridlines.
  - Ruler: Removes the horizontal and vertical rulers.
  - Formula Bar: Removes the formula bar that appears under the Ribbon.

    ✓ *The options on this tab affect only the onscreen view of the worksheet and do not affect how the file prints.*

Try It! Formatting the Worksheet Background

1 In the **E63TryA_xx** file, click the July 23 tab to select it.

2 Click PAGE LAYOUT, and in the Page Setup group click Background 🖼.

3 In the Insert Pictures window, in the From a file group, click Browse.

4 Select **E63TryB.jpg** from the data files for this lesson, and click Insert.

✓ *The background image cannot be sized or recolored. A small image will be tiled to fill the background.*

5 Select the cell range A5:C16, and click HOME.

6 Click Fill Color 🅰 ▾, and in the Theme Colors palette click Gold, Accent 4, Lighter 60%.

7 Click PAGE LAYOUT > Delete Background 🖼 to remove the background image.

8 Save the changes to the file, and leave it open to use in the next Try It.

The Page Setup group

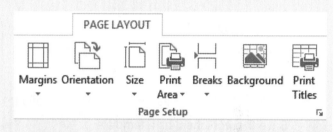

Creating a Workbook Template

- If you create workbooks with a lot of similar elements—a company name and logo, similar column and row labels, and so on—create one workbook and save it as a **template**.

  - You can create a new workbook based on any existing workbook without creating a template from it first.

  - However, if you often base new workbooks on a particular workbook, you can save time by creating a template.

  - For example, with a template, you won't have to delete the data from the copied workbook before you can enter new data.

- With a template, you can quickly create new workbooks that contain the same elements.

- By default, templates are saved in the Templates folder in the following file path: C:\Users\Username\My Documents\Custom Office Templates

  ✓ *Based on your computer's configuration, your file path may be different than the one given here.*

- Use the PERSONAL tab on Word's New start screen in the Backstage view to access the custom templates in your personal template gallery.

- You can create a subfolder in the Templates folder; that subfolder will appear as a folder on the PERSONAL tab in the Backstage view.

- You can edit and modify templates that you create as well as any existing templates.

  - When saving a template, you can save it as read-only to prevent any accidental changes.

    ✓ *Template files have .xltx file name extensions. Macro-enabled template files have .xltm file extensions.*

- You can delete a template by using File Explorer to browse to the folder with the file, right-clicking the file, and selecting Delete.

| Try It! | **Creating a Workbook Template** |

1 In the **E63TryA_xx** file, double-click the July 22 tab, and type **Products Sold**.

2 Modify the worksheet in the following ways:

   a. Edit cell B4 to remove the date.

   b. Switch to Sheet3, select the cell range A2:C21, and click HOME > Copy.

   c. Switch to the Products Sold sheet, select cell A7, and click Paste.

   d. Click cell E4 to select it, and on the HOME tab, in the Font group, click Borders 🔲 ▾ > Bottom border.

   e. Click VIEW, and deselect the Gridlines option.

3 Save the worksheet as a template:

   a. Click FILE > Save As > Browse.

   b. In the Save As dialog box, click the Save as type list > Excel Template.

   c. Click the New folder button, name the new folder **Class**, and click Open.

   d. In the File name box, type **E63TryC_xx**, and click Save.

   e. Close the template.

4 Create a new workbook using the new template:

   a. Click FILE > New.

   b. On the New tab in the Backstage view, click the PERSONAL tab, and click the Class folder.

   c. Click the **E63TryC_xx** template, and click OK.

5 In cell E4 type **July 24**.

6 In cell C7 type **10**, in cell C12 type **5**, in cell C17 type **4**, and in cell C22 type **2**.

7 Save the file as **E63TryD_xx** in the location where your teacher instructs you to store the files for this lesson.

8 Save and close the file, and exit Excel.

A custom template in a Templates subfolder

| Try It! | **Deleting a Workbook Template** |

1 Start File Explorer, and browse to the file path C:\Users\Username\My Documents\Custom Office Templates.

   ✓ *Your file path may be different than the one given here; check with your teacher for the correct file path.*

2 Click the Class folder > Open.

3 Right-click the **E63TryC_xx** template file > Delete. Click Yes to confirm the deletion, if necessary.

4 Click the back button to view the Class folder.

5 Right-click the Class folder > Delete. Click Yes to confirm the deletion, if necessary.

6 Close File Explorer.

Creating a Chart Template

- You can create a chart template from a chart that you have customized.
- Right-click the chart, and use the Save as Template command.
- A chart template is saved as a .crtx file.

- By default, Excel stores custom chart templates in the following file path: C:\Users\Username\ My Documents\Custom Office Templates.

  ✓ *Based on your computer's configuration, your file path may be different than the one given here.*

- You can delete a custom chart template by using the Manage Templates feature in the Insert Chart dialog box.

Try It!   **Creating a Chart Template**

---

1 Start Excel, and open the **E63TryE** file from the data files for this lesson.

2 Save the file as **E63TryE_xx** in the location where your teacher instructs you to store the files for this lesson.

3 On the Patient Care Chart chart sheet, click the chart to select it, and right-click.

4 In the shortcut menu, click Save as Template.

5 In the File name box, type **E63TryE**. Notice that Chart Template Files is already selected in the Save as type list.

6 Click Save.

7 Save the changes to the file, and leave it open to use in the next Try It.

The Save Chart Template dialog box

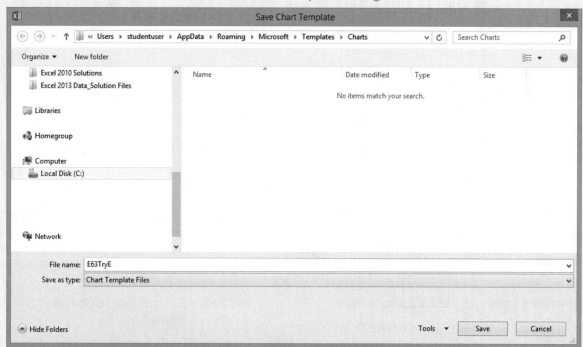

Try It!   Creating a Chart from a Custom Chart Template

1 In the **E63TryE_xx** file, click the Patient care breakdown tab.

2 Select the cell range B9:F18.

3 Click INSERT > Charts dialog box launcher ⌐ .

4 In the Insert Chart dialog box, click the All Charts tab > Templates.

5 Click the **E63TryE** chart template > OK.

6 Move the chart to below the data.

7 Save the changes to the file, and leave it open to use in the next Try It.

A custom chart template

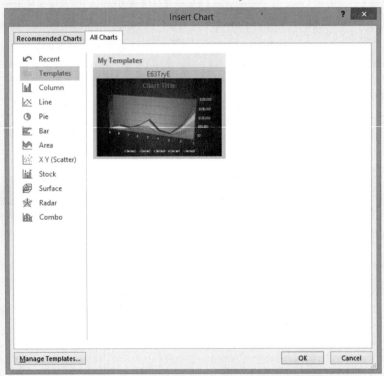

Try It!   Deleting a Custom Chart Template

1 In the **E63TryE_xx** file, on the Patient care breakdown tab, click INSERT, if necessary.

2 Click the Charts dialog box launcher ⌐ .

3 In the Insert Chart dialog box, click the All Charts tab > Templates > Manage Templates
   Manage Templates... .

4 In the Charts Explorer window, right-click **E63TryE** > Delete. Click Yes to confirm the deletion, if necessary.

5 Close the Charts Explorer window, and click the Close button to close the Insert Chart dialog box.

6 Save and close the file, and exit Excel.

Lesson 63—Practice

The worksheet you designed to track sales each day at Pete's Pets has proven very helpful, and the corporate headquarters may adopt it throughout the company. Before you send it off for their review, you want to add some professional formatting touches. In this project, you will add a background picture and a watermark.

DIRECTIONS

1. Start Excel, if necessary, and open **E63PracticeA** from the data files for this lesson.

2. Save the file as **E63PracticeA_xx** in the location where your teacher instructs you to store the files for this lesson.

3. Add a background picture:
   a. Click **PAGE LAYOUT** > **Background** 📷.
   b. In the Insert Pictures window, in the From a file group, click **Browse**.
   c. Select **E63PracticeB.jpg** from the data files for this lesson, and click **Insert**.

4. Apply the **Orange, Accent 2, Lighter 60%** color fill to the cell range **E15:L20**.

5. Add borders to the column labels:
   a. Select the range **E15:L15**, if necessary.
   b. Click **HOME** > **Border**.
   c. Select **Top and Double Bottom Border**.

6. Click **VIEW** > **Gridlines** to hide the gridlines. Your worksheet should look like Figure 63-1 on the next page.

7. Add a watermark:
   a. Click the **Watermark** worksheet tab.
   b. Click **INSERT** > **Header & Footer** 📄.
   c. Click in the middle section of the header, and on the HEADER & FOOTER TOOLS DESIGN tab, click **Picture** 📷.

d. In the Insert Pictures window, in the From a file group, click **Browse**.

e. Select **E63PracticeB.jpg** from the data files for this lesson, and click **Insert**.

f. On the HEADER & FOOTER TOOLS DESIGN tab, click **Format Picture** 📷.

g. In the Format Picture dialog box, check that the **Lock aspect ratio** check box is selected.

h. Set the Scale Height to **75%**. (The Scale Width will automatically change to 75%.)

i. Click the **Picture** tab, and set the Brightness to **75%**.

j. Set the Contrast to **25%**, and click **OK**.

8. Click outside of the header > **VIEW** > **Gridlines** to hide gridlines.

9. Select the range **E15:L20**.

10. Click **HOME** > **Fill Color** > **Gold, Accent 4, Lighter 60%**. Your worksheet should look like Figure 63-2 on the next page.

11. For all worksheets, add a footer that has your name at the left, the date code in the center, and the page number code at the right.

12. **With your teacher's permission**, print the **Watermark** worksheet.

13. Save and close the file, and exit Excel.

Figure 63-1

Figure 63-2

Lesson 63—Apply

You are the sales manager at Pete's Pets. Corporate headquarters has asked you to create a template from the worksheet you designed to track daily sales. You want to modify the existing worksheet to make it more usable as a template. In this project, you will create a custom workbook template from an existing worksheet. You will also create a custom chart template.

DIRECTIONS

1. Start Excel, if necessary, and open **E63ApplyA** from the data files for this lesson.

2. Save the file as **E63ApplyA_xx** in the location where your teacher instructs you to store the files for this lesson.

3. Click the **Watermark** worksheet tab.

4. Select the range **F16:K20**, and press ⌈DEL⌋.

5. Save the changes to the **E63ApplyA_xx** file.

6. Create a template from the workbook:
   a. Click **FILE** > **Save As**.
   b. In the Save As dialog box, click the **Save as type** list > **Excel Template**.
   c. Save the template in the location where your teacher instructs you to store the files for this lesson.
   d. Name the template file **E63ApplyB_xx**.

7. Click the **Background** worksheet tab.

8. Create a 3-D clustered column chart on its own sheet tab:
   a. Select the cell range **E15:K20**.
   b. Click **INSERT** > **Insert Column Chart** ⅰⅰ ▾ > **3-D Clustered Column Chart**.
   c. Move the chart to a new sheet titled **Daily Sales Chart**.

9. Customize the formatting on the chart:
   a. Add a chart title: **Daily Sales**.
   b. On the CHART TOOLS DESIGN tab, click **Change Colors** > **Color 3**.

10. Save the changes to the **E63ApplyB_xx** template file.

11. Create a chart template:
   a. Click the chart to select it, and right-click.
   b. Click **Save as Template**.
   c. In the File name box, type **E63ApplyC**.
   d. Click **Save**.

12. Save the changes to the **E63ApplyB_xx** template file.

13. Delete the **E63ApplyC** chart template:
   a. Click **INSERT** > **Charts** dialog box launcher ⌐.
   b. In the Insert Chart dialog box, click the **All Charts** tab > **Templates** > **Manage Templates** Manage Templates…
   c. Right-click **E63ApplyC** > **Delete**. Click **Yes** to confirm the deletion, if necessary.
   d. Close the Charts Explorer window, and click the **Close** button to close the Insert Chart dialog box.

14. Add a custom footer that has your name at the left, the date code in the center, and the page number code at the right.

15. **With your teacher's permission**, print the **Daily Sales Chart** worksheet. Your worksheet should look like Figure 63-3 on the next page.

16. Save and close the file, and exit Excel.

Figure 63-3

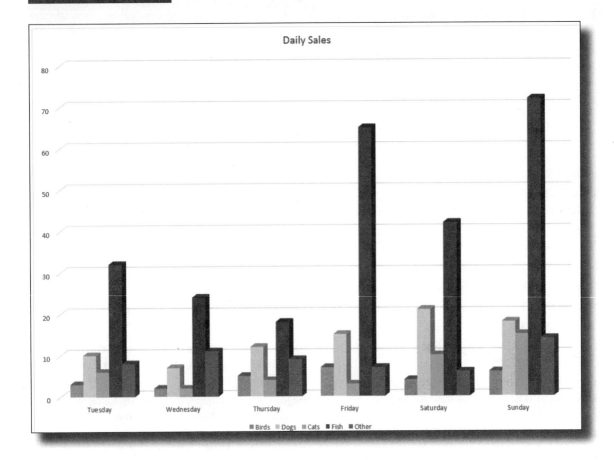

End-of-Chapter Activities

➤ Excel Chapter 7—Critical Thinking

Cash Flow Projection

You are the founder of a public relations firm called Jones PR. You are looking for additional capital from angel investors and other local seed capital sources, and you need to make presentations to investors soon.

One important set of data you need to present is a Cash Flow Projection. The cash flow projection will forecast your company's future performance based on data you have captured from past performance. You need to embellish the raw data you'll present with charts that show comparisons and trends. You also want to save the workbook as a custom template to use in the future.

DIRECTIONS

1. Start Excel, if necessary, and open **ECT07A** from the data files for this chapter.

2. Save the file as **ECT07A_xx** in the location where your teacher instructs you to store the files for this chapter.

3. Apply the **Integral** theme and the **Calibri** font set to the worksheet.

4. Enter **16000** in cell **B4**. Notice that previously applied formatting rules make the entries in cells B7:C7 turn red.

5. Select the range **A12:N12**, and insert a **Line with Markers** chart.

   a. Move the chart to its own sheet called **Comparison**.

   b. Return to the **Cash Flow** worksheet, and select and copy the cell range **A38:N38**.

   c. Return to the **Comparison** worksheet, and paste the copied data into the chart.

   d. With the chart selected, click **CHART TOOLS DESIGN** > **Quick Layout** > **Layout 1**.

   e. Add **Receipts vs. Cash Out** as the chart title.

   f. Edit the chart series so that the ranges **C12:N12** and **C38:N38** on the **Cash Flow** worksheet are charted.

      ✓ *Right-click the chart area, click Select Data, and edit the chart data range.*

   g. Specify the range **C6:N6** on the **Cash Flow** worksheet for the X axis labels.

   h. Edit the series name entries in the legend.

   i. Delete the vertical axis title. The finished chart should look like Illustration 7A on the next page.

6. Return to the **Cash Flow** worksheet, select the range **A38:N38**, and insert a **Scatter** chart.

   a. Move the chart to its own sheet called **Trend**.

   b. Edit the chart series so that the cell range **C38:N38** on the **Cash Flow** worksheet is charted.

   c. Specify the cell range **C6:N6** on the **Cash Flow** worksheet for the X axis labels, making sure that cell **A38** on the **Cash Flow** worksheet is specified as the series name.

   d. Change the chart title to **Cash Out Trend**.

   e. Format the data labels to display on the right of the data points on the chart.

   f. Add a linear trendline to the chart to show the trend for cash out over time.

   g. Display the legend on the right side of the chart. The finished chart should look like Illustration 7B on the next page.

7. Add a custom header to the **Cash Flow** worksheet that has your name at the left, the date code in the center, and the page number code at the right.

8. Close any open task panes.

9. Save the changes to the **ECT07A_xx** workbook.

10. Save the **ECT07A_xx** workbook as an Excel template named **ECT07B_xx** in the location where your teacher instructs you to store the files for this chapter.

11. With your teacher's permission, print the **Comparison** and **Trend** chart worksheets.

12. Save and close the **ECT07B_xx** file, and exit Excel.

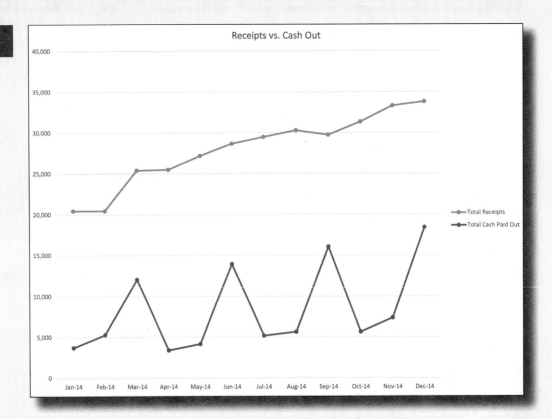

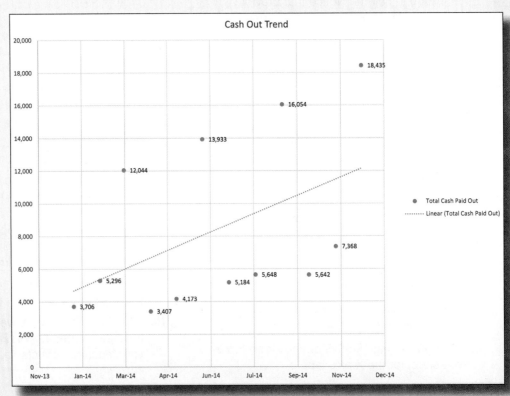

➤ Excel Chapter 7—Portfolio Builder

Daily Sales Report

As assistant sales manager for Country Crazy Antiques, you've been asked to put together a collection of reports to present to the owner. You need to create a template for tracking a day's worth of sales.

The warehouse manager has also asked you to embellish the inventory report with shapes and text effects to help call attention to the pertinent information before the next meeting.

DIRECTIONS

1. Start Excel, if necessary, and open **EPB07A** from the data files for this chapter.

2. Save the file as **EPB07A_xx** in the location where your teacher instructs you to store the files for this chapter.

3. Add a custom header that has your name at the left, the date code in the center, and the page number code at the right.

4. The existing worksheet has all the necessary columns and totals, but you need to add formatting.

    a. Add the **Green, Accent 6, Lighter 80%** fill to the cell range A1:O50.

    b. Select rows 1–4, and fill with **Gold, Accent 4, Lighter 60%**.

    c. Select cell E2, and apply the **Consolas** font, size **20**, in bold.

    d. Select the cell range **B8:K8**, and apply the **Gold, Accent 4, Lighter 80%** fill.

    e. Use the Format Painter to apply the B8:K8 formatting to the cell range **B9:K33**.

    f. Select the cell range **B7:K7**, and fill with **Green, Accent 6, Darker 25%**. Increase the font size, then add a border of your choice.

5. Adjust the column widths if necessary, and save the file. The completed worksheet should look similar to Illustration 7C on the next page.

6. Create a template from the workbook, and save the file as **EPB07B_xx** in the location where your teacher instructs you to store the files for this chapter. Close the file.

7. Open **EPB07C** from the data files for this project.

8. Save the file as **EPB07C_xx** in the location where your teacher instructs you to store the files for this chapter.

9. Add a custom header that has your name at the left, the date code in the center, and the page number code at the right.

10. Create a logo for the Country Crazy Antiques store using various shapes:

    a. In the area below the table, create at least four objects, such as squares, rectangles, ovals, or any other shape of your choice.

    b. Combine the objects, overlapping at least one object, to form a pleasing logo.

11. Open the Selection task pane, and use it to select and group the individual shapes you used to create a logo for Country Crazy Antiques.

12. Apply various fill, outline, and shape effect styles to create a logo you feel represents the business.

13. Move the finished logo to the area at the left of the Country Crazy Antiques title, and resize as necessary to fit within the cell range A1:A6, as shown in Illustration 7D.

14. Insert a banner from the Stars and Banners group under the Country Crazy Antiques title in rows 4 and 5.

15. Add the text **Inventory as of 6/10/14** to the banner you created, and format the text as you like.

16. Select the banner, and format it with the **Subtle Effect - Green, Accent 6** shape style.

17. Insert a **Rounded Rectangular Callout** from the callouts group.

18. Add the following text to the callout: **End table sale was held 6/1–6/3**, and format the text as you like.

19. Apply the **Subtle Effect - Green, Accent 6** shape style.

20. Apply the **Preset 2** shape effect.

21. Resize the callout as necessary, and rotate it as shown in Illustration 7D on the next page.

22. Apply the **Gold, Accent 4, Lighter 40%** shape fill.
23. Adjust the column widths if necessary.

24. **With your teacher's permission**, print the worksheet.
25. Close the workbook, saving all changes, and exit Excel.

Illustration 7C

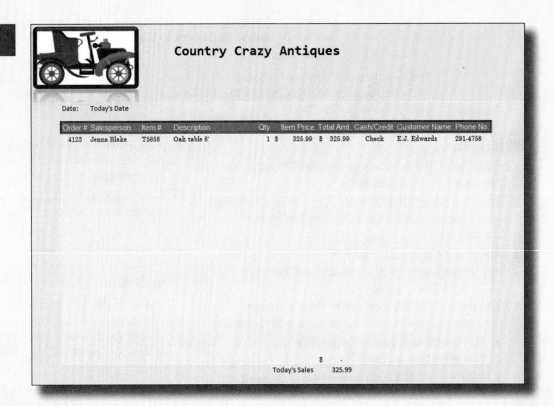

Illustration 7D

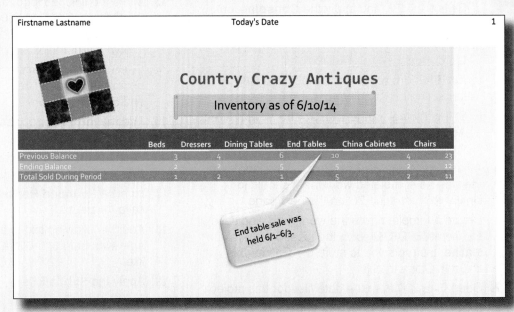

Chapter 8

Creating Macros and Using Data Analysis Tools

Lesson 64

Recording a Macro

➤ **What You Will Learn**

Adding the DEVELOPER Tab to the Ribbon
Setting the Macro Security Level
Setting Trusted Locations
Saving a Workbook That Contains Macros
Recording a Macro
Running a Macro
Editing a Macro
Copying Macros Between Workbooks

Software Skills   You can automate the performance of a sequence of tasks in Excel by creating a macro. This automation reduces the time it takes to repeat the tasks, and increases accuracy.

What You Can Do

Adding the DEVELOPER Tab to the Ribbon

■ The **DEVELOPER tab** on the Ribbon contains useful commands for creating and running **macros**. The default setting is for Excel to not display the DEVELOPER tab.

   ✓ *You do not have to enable the DEVELOPER tab in order to record a macro because there are other ways to start a macro recording, such as the New Macro button on the status bar. However, having the DEVELOPER tab available makes the process of running and managing macros easier.*

WORDS TO KNOW

Absolute recording
A macro recording in which the cells being acted upon are referenced absolutely, so the references do not change depending on the active cell position when the macro begins running. Absolute is the default setting.

DEVELOPER tab
An optional Ribbon tab that contains commands of use to advanced users, such as commands for creating and managing macros.

Macro
A series of recorded actions that can be replayed when needed. The recorded actions are carried out automatically for the user.

Macro security
A macro setting that enables or disables macros when the workbook is opened by a person other than the person who created the file. The default security setting is to disable macros.

  Adding the DEVELOPER Tab to the Ribbon

1 Start Excel, and open a new, blank worksheet.

2 Click FILE > Options.

3 Click Customize Ribbon.

4 In the Customize the Ribbon list (on the right side of the dialog box), place a check mark next to Developer.

✓ *Note: The check mark may already be there if another student has already added this to the Ribbon.*

5 Click OK to close the Excel Options dialog box. Notice the DEVELOPER tab appears to the right of the VIEW tab.

6 Leave Excel open for the next Try It.

Setting the Macro Security Level

■ To minimize the risk of a macro virus or other malware threat contained in a macro, Excel includes the **macro security** feature. Its default setting is to disable all macros and display a notification option when working with a file that contains macros.

■ Set the protection and security levels to the level of restriction or openness according to your comfort level, or according to the policy established by the IT department where you work. You may set the security level to one of four choices:

- Disable all macros without notification
- Disable all macros with notification
- Disable all macros except digitally signed macros
- Enable all macros

■ The settings on the computer you are using may be different than the default settings that are assumed for these directions. It is always advisable to check the settings and make any necessary changes.

■ You can access the macro security levels using the Macro Security button in the Code group of the DEVELOPER tab.

■ Use the Macro Security button to display the Macro Settings tab of the Trust Center dialog box.

Module
A container for VBA code.

Relative recording
A macro recording in which the cells being acted upon depend on the active cell position when the macro begins running.

Trusted location
A folder designated as a trusted location for Excel files that contain macros. Any file placed in this trusted location folder will open without the dialog box and with the macros enabled.

Visual Basic for Applications (VBA)
A version of the Visual Basic programming language designed for use within Microsoft Office applications. Macros are stored and edited using this language.

.xlsm
The file extension of an Excel 2007–2013 file that contains a macro.

  Setting the Macro Security Level

1 In Excel, click Macro Security ⚠ to open the Trust Center and show the current macro security setting.

2 Verify that the setting is: Disable all macros with notification.

✓ *With this setting, a worksheet with a macro will be disabled and a warning window will display to allow you to enable the macro if you trust the source of the workbook.*

3 Click OK to close the dialog box.

4 Leave Excel open to use in the next Try It.

(continued)

Try It! **Setting the Macro Security Level** *(continued)*

Macro security settings

Trust Center	?	×

Trusted Publishers

Trusted Locations

Trusted Documents

Trusted App Catalogs

Add-ins

ActiveX Settings

Macro Settings

Protected View

Message Bar

External Content

File Block Settings

Privacy Options

Macro Settings

○ Disable all macros without notification

◉ Disable all macros with notification

○ Disable all macros except digitally signed macros

○ Enable all macros (not recommended; potentially dangerous code can run)

Developer Macro Settings

☐ Trust access to the VBA project object model

Setting Trusted Locations

■ In most of the Office applications (including Excel), you can define **trusted locations**. These are specific folders that you mark as safe, so that whenever you open a file from one of those locations, all of the usual safety precautions don't apply.

■ For example, if you place an Excel file that contains macros in a trusted location, when you open that file, the security setting from the previous section doesn't restrict your ability to run macros.

Try It!   **Setting Trusted Locations**

① Click FILE > Options to display the Excel Options dialog box.

② Click Trust Center.

③ Click Trust Center Settings [Trust Center Settings...] to display the Trust Center dialog box.

④ Click Trusted Locations.

⑤ Click Add new location.

⑥ In the Microsoft Office Trusted Location dialog box, click Browse.

⑦ Navigate to the folder where the data files for this class are stored, and click OK.

⑧ Click the Subfolders of this location are also trusted check box.

⑨ Click OK. The trusted location is included.

⑩ In the Trust Center dialog box, with the user location path you added still selected, click Remove. The trusted location is removed.

⑪ Click OK to close the Trust Center dialog box.

⑫ Click OK to close the Excel Options dialog box.

⑬ Close the blank workbook without saving changes, and leave Excel open to use in the next Try It.

Saving a Workbook That Contains Macros

- The default file extension for Excel 2013 is. xlsx. This file format cannot contain macros, by design, to avoid potential malware threats associated with macros.

- A workbook must be saved in **.xlsm** format in order to enable it to store macros.

  ✓ *When you save a file in .xlsm format, it does not overwrite the original file in .xlsx format.*

Try It!   **Saving a Workbook That Contains Macros**

1. Open **E64TryA** from the data files for this lesson.
2. Click FILE > Save As.
3. Navigate to the location where your teacher instructs you to store the files for this lesson.
4. In the Save As dialog box, click the Save as type drop-down list > Excel Macro-Enabled Workbook.
5. In the File name box, change the file name to **E64TryA_xx**.
6. Click Save.
7. Leave the **E64TryA_xx** file open to use in the next Try It.

Recording a Macro

- The Macro Recorder records every action you take, and stores them in a macro that you can later play back to reproduce the steps.

  ✓ *Recording a macro requires planning and some practice. It is not uncommon to have to record a macro several times because errors were made in the recording process. If you make a mistake, delete the macro and record a new one.*

- By default, Excel records the actual addresses of the cells you affect when recording. For example, if the active cell happens to be cell D2 when you begin recording a macro that makes the active cell bold, the macro will always make cell D2 bold, regardless of the position of the active cell when you run that macro. This is called **absolute recording**, and it is the default behavior.

- If you go with the default setting of absolute recording, the macro begins recording your actions based on the cell that is active. When you create the macro, select the desired cell before you click Record.

- The alternative is **relative recording**, which performs the recorded action on whatever cell or range is selected before running the macro.

- On the DEVELOPER tab, click Use Relative References or Use Absolute References to switch between absolute and relative recording.

- You can name a macro to make it easier to reference; however, you cannot use spaces in a macro name.

Try It!   **Recording a Macro**

1. In the **E64TryA_xx** file, click cell B2, and click the DEVELOPER tab.
2. Click Record Macro 🖹.

   OR

   Click the Record Macro button 🖩 on the status bar.
3. In the Record Macro dialog box, in the Macro name text box, type **TopSales**.

   ✓ *The macro name cannot have spaces.*
4. In the Shortcut key text box, type **t**.

   ✓ *This will be your shortcut key used to run the macro. If you choose a shortcut key that Excel already has assigned to another action, the macro will override the other action in this workbook.*

(continued)

Try It!   **Recording a Macro** *(continued)*

5 In the Description text box, type **Date, sales by Z-A order, top seller**.

Define the macro before recording it

6 Click OK. The recording begins.

7 Without re-clicking in cell B2, but with the cell still selected, type **=NOW()**, and press `ENTER`.

✓ *This will place the current date and time in this cell each time the file is opened. Notice that this cell has a date format applied to it so that only the date displays.*

8 Select cells A5:B9.

9 Click DATA > Sort 🔲.

10 In the Sort dialog box, open the Sort by drop-down list and click Column B.

11 Click OK.

12 Click cell B3, type =, click cell A9, and press `ENTER`.

✓ *This will place the top sales person's name in cell B3 when the macro is run.*

13 Click DEVELOPER > Stop Recording ▪ Stop Recording .

OR

Click the Stop Record Macro button ☐ on the status bar.

14 Save the changes to the file, and leave it open to use in the next Try It.

Running a Macro

▪ To run a macro, you can use the Macros command on the DEVELOPER tab to open a Macro dialog box from which you can select the macro you want.

▪ You can also use the shortcut key combination you defined when you created the macro.

▪ You can also assign a macro to the Quick Access Toolbar or the Ribbon, and then run it from its button.

Try It!   **Running a Macro**

1 In the **E64TryA_xx** file, select the cell range A5:B9, and click DATA > Sort A to Z ↓ to re-sort the list by name, so you can test the macro.

2 Click cell B2 and press `CTRL` + `T`. The macro runs.

3 Click cell E2 and press `CTRL` + `T` again. The macro runs again.

✓ *This time the macro places =NOW() in cell E2. It does that because you did not click B2 after beginning the macro recording but before typing =NOW(). You recorded a relative reference macro that begins running at the active cell. We'll fix that later in the lesson, when you learn about editing a macro in VBA. Notice that the references to A5:B9 still work, though, because they are absolute references by default.*

(continued)

Try It!   **Running a Macro** *(continued)*

④ Widen column E so that the content of cell E2 is visible.

⑤ Select cell E2, and press ⌈DEL⌉ .

⑥ Click cell B5, and type **5000**.

⑦ Click cell B2.

⑧ Click DEVELOPER > Macros ▣ to display the Macro dialog box.

✓ *The Macro dialog box provides an alternate way of running a macro. You must use this method for macros for which there is no shortcut key combination or button.*

⑨ Click the TopSales macro, and click Run to run the macro again.

⑩ Save the changes to the file, and leave it open to use in the next Try It.

Try It!   **Adding a Macro to the Quick Access Toolbar**

① In the **E64TryA_xx** file, click FILE > Options.

② Click Quick Access Toolbar.

③ Open the Choose commands from drop-down list, and click Macros.

④ Click TopSales.

⑤ Click Add.

⑥ Click OK. A button for the macro now appears on the Quick Access Toolbar.

⑦ Click cell B7, and type **100**.

⑧ Click cell B2.

⑨ On the Quick Access Toolbar, click the TopSales macro button ▪▪. The macro re-runs and re-sorts the list with the new value.

⑩ Save the changes to the file, and leave it open to use in the next Try It.

Editing a Macro

■ If you make a mistake during recording, you can delete the macro, or you can edit the macro in **Visual Basic for Applications (VBA)**.

■ Editing the macro requires a basic understanding of VBA, which you may not have yet. However, many of the commands are simple to figure out by their names, so that you can identify unwanted parts of the macro to delete or correct typos.

Try It!   **Editing a Macro**

① In the **E64TryA_xx** file, click DEVELOPER > Macros ▣ to open the Macro dialog box.

② Click TopSales, and click Edit. Visual Basic for Applications opens, showing the macro code.

③ Click to place the insertion point at the beginning of the text: **ActiveCell.FormulaR1C1 = "=NOW()"**.

④ Type **Range("B2").Select**, and press ⌈ENTER⌉ .

✓ *Adding this line of code selects cell B2 as the first action in the macro.*

⑤ Click FILE > Close and Return to Microsoft Excel.

⑥ Save the changes to the file, and leave it open to use in the next Try It.

Try It!   Deleting a Macro

1. In the **E64TryA_xx** file, click DEVELOPER > Macros 📑 to open the Macro dialog box.

2. Click TopSales, and click Delete.

3. Click Yes to confirm.

4. Right-click the macro button you placed on the Quick Access Toolbar earlier, and click Remove from Quick Access Toolbar.

5. Close the workbook without saving your changes to it so that macro is still in the saved copy.

6. Leave Excel open to use in the next Try It.

Copying Macros Between Workbooks

- Macro code is stored in a **module** within the file.

- You can access VBA modules in the Microsoft Visual Basic for Applications window from the Visual Basic button on the DEVELOPER tab.

- You can open a module like a file and edit its content.

- Each time you create a new macro in the worksheet, Excel adds it to the Modules folder of the Visual Basic project with the name Module1, Module2, etc.

- You can copy a module to another macro-enabled Excel workbook to make the macros in the module available for use in that workbook.

  ✓ *When you copy a macro from one workbook to another, Excel does not copy its shortcut key. You will need to reassign the shortcut key by editing the macro.*

- You can edit or delete individual macros in a workbook by using the Organizer.

Try It!   Copying Macros Between Workbooks

1. In Excel, open **E64TryA_xx** from the location where your teacher instructs you to store the files for this lesson.

2. In the SECURITY WARNING bar, click Enable Content to enable the macro.

3. Create a new, blank workbook.

4. Click FILE > Save As.

5. Navigate to the location where your teacher instructs you to store the files for this lesson.

6. In the Save As dialog box, in the File name box, type **E64TryB_xx**.

7. Click the Save as type drop-down list > Excel Macro-Enabled Workbook.

8. Click Save.

9. In the **E64TryB _xx** file, click DEVELOPER > Visual Basic 📝.

10. In the Microsoft Visual Basic for Applications window, on the Standard shortcut menu, click Project Explorer 📝. Notice that Module1 of the E64TryA_xx.xlsm file is highlighted in the Project - VBAProject pane.

(continued)

Try It!   **Copying Macros Between Workbooks** *(continued)*

⑪ Click and hold Module1, and drag it on top of the VBAProject(E64TryB_xx.xlsm) project. The macro is copied in a Modules folder.

⑫ Under VBAProject(E64TryB_xx.xlsm), click the plus sign next to the Modules folder to open it and view the macro.

⑬ Close the Microsoft Visual Basic for Applications window.

⑭ Save and close the **E64TryA_xx** and **E64TryB_xx** files, and exit Excel.

Copying a macros module to another workbook

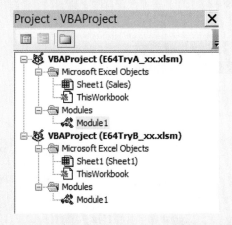

Lesson 64—Practice

The Membership Chairperson for the Small Business Professional Organization is tracking attendance for the organization's quarterly meeting. She has asked you to create a worksheet to show the RSVP replies and to track who said they would come to the meeting but did not show up. In this project, you will create a macro that shows the members who said they would attend, but who did not actually attend the meeting.

DIRECTIONS

1. Start Excel, if necessary, and open **E64Practice** from the data files for this lesson.
2. Click **FILE > Save As**.
3. Navigate to the location where your teacher instructs you to store the files for this lesson.
4. In the File name box, type **E64Practice_xx**.
5. Click the **Save as type** drop-down list > **Excel Macro-Enabled Workbook**.
6. Click **Save**.
7. Add a header with your full name on the left, and today's date on the right. Return to **Normal** view.
8. Select the range **A2:G62**.
9. Click **INSERT > Table** 🗔.
10. In the Create Table dialog box, verify that the cell range is **A2:G62**, verify that the **My table has headers** check box is selected, and click **OK**.
11. Click cell **A2** to make this the active cell.

12. Click **DEVELOPER > Record Macro** 🗔 to display the Record Macro dialog box.
13. In the Macro Name text box, type **MeetingAttendance**. Do not put a space in the macro name.
14. In the Shortcut key box, type **t**.

   ✓ *If you receive a message telling you a macro is already assigned to that key, choose another key.*

15. In the Description box, type **People who said they would attend, but did not**.
16. In the Store macro in box, verify that This Workbook is selected, and click **OK**.
17. Click the down arrow on cell **E2**, click to clear the **No** check box, and click **OK**.

   ✓ *This shows all the people who said they would attend the meeting.*

18. Click the down arrow on cell **F2**, click to clear the **Yes** check box, and click **OK**.

   ✓ *This shows who said they would attend, but did not attend the meeting.*

19. Click **DEVELOPER > Stop Recording**

   ■ Stop Recording .

20. Click **DATA > Clear** ▼ to remove the filters.

21. Click **A2**.

22. Press CTRL + T to run the macro.

23. **With your teacher's permission,** print the worksheet. Your worksheet should look like the one shown in Figure 64-1.

24. Save and close the file, and exit Excel.

Figure 64-1

Firstname Lastname						Today's Date

Small Business Professional Organization

Spring Networking Meeting

Last Name ▼	First Name ▼	RSVP Received ▼	Reminder ▼	RSVP Response ▼	Attended ▼
Chang	Joshua	yes		Yes	No
Copp	Seth	No	Yes	Yes	No
Devereaux	Domique	yes		Yes	No
Huang	Griffin	No	Yes	Yes	No
Klein	Nathaniel	yes		Yes	No
Nishiba	Arielle	No	Yes	Yes	No
Reisman	Sophia	yes		Yes	No

Lesson 64—Apply

You are a member of the Small Business Professional Organization. The Membership Chairperson has asked you to create a chart comparing the revenue from the sales of products and services over a period of six months. Since the Membership Chairperson has asked you to do this in the past, you want to record a macro to create the chart.

DIRECTIONS

1. Start Excel, if necessary, and open **E64ApplyA** from the data files for this lesson. Notice that this file is already in a macro-enabled file format.

2. Save the file as **E64ApplyA_xx** in the location where your teacher instructs you to store the files for this lesson.

3. For all worksheets, add a header that has your name at the left, the date code in the center, and the page number code at the right, and change back to **Normal** view.

4. Prepare to record a macro that creates a chart comparing the revenue from the sales of products and services over a period of six months:

Macro name: **Sales**

Shortcut key: **Ctrl+s**

Store macro in: **This Workbook**

Description: **Sales and services revenue chart**

   ✓ *If you receive a message saying a macro is already assigned to the shortcut key, choose another key.*

5. Perform the following actions as the macro recorder records them:

    a. On the Sales tab, select the cell range **A2:C8**.

    b. Click **INSERT** > **Insert Column Chart** ▮▮▾ > **3-D Clustered Column** (the first option in the 3-D Column group).

    c. Click **CHART TOOLS DESIGN**, and in the Chart Styles group click **Style 4**.

6. End the recording.

7. Delete the chart from the workbook, and run the macro to re-create the chart.

8. Edit the macro in the VBA Editor to change the style applied to the chart to **Style 3**:

    a. Click **DEVELOPER** > **Macros** 📇 .

    b. In the Macros dialog box, click the **Macros in** drop-down arrow, and click **This Workbook**.

    c. Click **Edit**.

    d. In the E64Apply_xx.xlsm - Module1 (Code) window, change the ActiveChart.Chartstyle to **288**.

    e. Save the macro project.

    f. Close the VBA window.

9. Delete the chart from the workbook, and run the macro to re-create the chart.

10. Reposition the chart so that the upper-left corner of the chart is at the upper-left corner of cell C10.

11. **With your teacher's permission,** print the **Sales** worksheet. Your chart should look like the one shown in Figure 64-2.

12. Copy the macro to a blank workbook:

    a. Create a new, blank workbook.

    b. Save the file as a Macro-Enabled Workbook named **E64ApplyB_xx** in the location where your teacher instructs you to store the files for this lesson.

    c. In the **E64ApplyB_xx** file, click **DEVELOPER** > **Visual Basic** 📇 .

    d. In the Microsoft Visual Basic for Applications window, on the Standard shortcut menu, click **Project Explorer** ❧ to view the Project - VBAProject pane, if necessary.

    e. Under VBAProject(E64ApplyA_xx.xlsm), click the plus sign next to the Modules folder to open it and view the Module1 macro.

    f. Click and hold **Module1**, and drag it on top of the VBAProject(E64ApplyB_xx.xlsm) project.

    g. Under VBAProject(E64ApplyB _xx.xlsm), click the plus sign next to the Modules folder to open it and view the macro.

13. Close the Microsoft Visual Basic for Applications window.

14. Save and close the **E64ApplyA_xx** and **E64ApplyB_xx** files, and exit Excel.

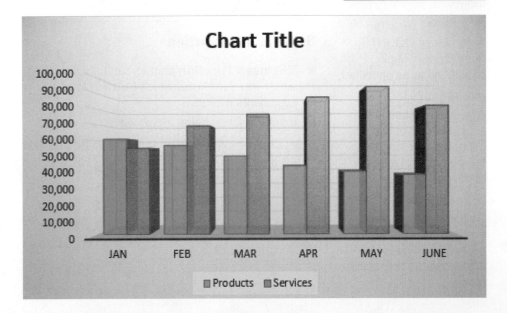

Figure 64-2

Lesson 65

Using Functions

➤ What You Will Learn

Using Insert Function
Creating an IF Function
Creating SUMIF, COUNTIF, and AVERAGEIF Functions
Creating SUMIFS, COUNTIFS, and AVERAGEIFS Functions
Using the TODAY Function and the NOW Function
Using the TRANSPOSE Function

WORDS TO KNOW

Array
An orderly arrangement
of numbers.

AVERAGEIF function
A function that averages
the values in a range that
meet a certain condition.

AVERAGEIFS function
A version of AVERAGEIF
that allows multiple
conditions to be specified.

COUNTIF function
A function that uses
a criteria to count the
number of items in a
range.

COUNTIFS function
A version of COUNTIF
that allows multiple
conditions to be specified.

IF function
A logical function that
executes one of two
actions depending on
the outcome of a yes/no
question.

Insert Function
An Excel feature that
prompts the user for the
required and optional
arguments for a specified
function.

Software Skills　Excel includes logical functions that enable you to set up
conditions where a calculation is performed only if the conditions are met, such as
IF, SUMIF, COUNTIF, and AVERAGEIF. Such functions are somewhat more complex
to set up than other functions, so you may prefer to construct them using Insert
Function, a built-in utility in Excel that prompts you for the necessary arguments. You
can use functions to automate the insertion of data in your worksheet, such as using
the TODAY and NOW functions to add today's date. You can also use functions to
reposition data, such as using the TRANSPOSE function to switch the position of
row and column data.

What You Can Do

Using Insert Function

- The **Insert Function** feature can help you construct functions in cases where
  either you don't know which function to use or you don't remember what
  arguments it takes.
- Insert Function helps in two ways:
  - It allows you to look up functions based on what they do.
  - It prompts you for the arguments needed for the chosen function.

Try It!　**Inserting a Function**

① Start Excel, and open **E65Try** from the data files for this lesson.

② Save the file as **E65Try_xx** in the location where your teacher has instructed you to save your work.

③ On the IF worksheet tab, click cell A13, and type **Total**.

④ Click cell B13, and click the Insert Function *fx* button on the formula bar to open the Insert Function dialog box.

The Insert Function button

Insert Function button

⑤ In the Search for a Function box, type **add**, and click Go.

　✓ *We already know that we want the SUM function in this case; step 5 is just for practice.*

⑥ In the list of functions that appears, click SUM, and read the description of it at the bottom of the dialog box.

⑦ Click OK to open the Function Arguments dialog box with text boxes for each of the arguments.

　✓ *The SUM function has only one required argument. Labels for required arguments are bold.*

⑧ Confirm that the Number1 argument displays B5:B12.

　✓ *If Excel guesses at the range incorrectly, you can manually correct it, or you can select the range yourself. You can click the Collapse Dialog Box button to the right of the argument to get the dialog box out of the way, select the desired range, and then click the Expand Dialog Box button or press Enter to bring the dialog box back to full view.*

⑨ Click OK to display the formula result in the cell.

⑩ Save the changes to the file, and leave it open to use in the next Try It.

Logical function
A function that evaluates a yes/no condition and then takes an action based on the result.

NOW function
A function that displays the current date and time on a worksheet or calculates a value based on the current date and time.

SUMIF function
A function that sums the values in a range that meet a certain condition.

SUMIFS function
A version of SUMIF that allows multiple conditions to be specified.

TODAY function
A function that obtains the current date from the computer.

TRANSPOSE function
A function that copies data located in a row into a column or copies data located in a column into a row.

Arguments for the SUM function

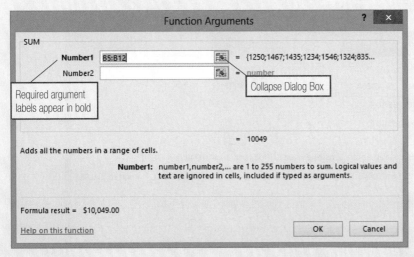

Creating an IF Function

- **Logical functions** enable you to set up yes/no questions, and then perform one action or another based on the answer

- **IF** is the simplest of the logical functions. It has three arguments:
  - The logical condition
  - What to do if it is true
  - What to do if it is false

- For example, suppose that if cell A1 contains 100, you want cell B1 to show "Perfect Score"; otherwise, B1 should show "Thanks for Playing." To achieve this, you would place the following function in B1:

  =IF(A1=100,"Perfect Score","Thanks for Playing")

- Enclose text strings in quotation marks, and use commas to separate the arguments.

- You can use Insert Function to enter the arguments instead of typing them manually.

- Like most other functions, you can use the IF function in conjunction with other functions, such as AND or OR.

- For example, suppose you want to find out who sold item number 15634 for $150 in a range of sales data where column A contains the name of the salesperson, column B contains the item number, and column C contains the cost of the item. To achieve this, you would use the following function:

  =IF(AND(C1=150)B1=15634,A1)

Try It!	**Creating an IF Function**

1 In the **E65Try_xx** file, on the IF worksheet tab, click cell C5.

2 Click Insert Function.

3 Click the Or select a category list > Logical.

4 In the Select a function list, click IF.

5 Click OK to open the Function Arguments dialog box.

6 In the Logical test box, type **B5>=1000**.

7 In the Value_if_true box, type **B5*0.05**.

8 In the Value_if_false box, type **B5*0.02**.

9 Click OK to place the function in cell C5.

10 Copy the function from cell C5 to the range C6:C12.

✓ *Use any copy method you like. You can drag the fill handle, or use the Copy and Paste commands.*

11 Save the changes to the file, and leave it open to use in the next Try It.

Arguments for the IF function

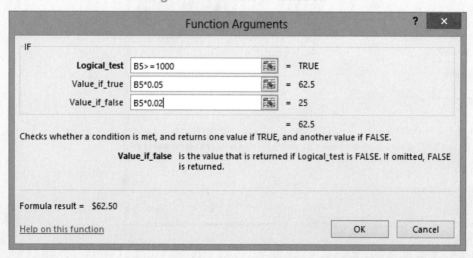

Creating SUMIF, COUNTIF, and AVERAGEIF Functions

- The **SUMIF**, **COUNTIF**, and **AVERAGEIF** functions combine the IF function with either SUM, COUNT, or AVERAGE. The SUM, COUNT, or AVERAGE operation is performed upon cells within the specified range that meet a certain logical condition.

- The syntax is:

  =SUMIF(range,criteria,sum_range)

- In some cases the range to evaluate (*range*) and the range to calculate (*sum_range*) are the same. In that case, you can omit the *sum_range* argument.

- To specify that a criterion not be a certain value, precede the value with <>. For example, to exclude records where the value is 500, you would use <>500 as the criterion.

- COUNTIF and AVERAGEIF work the same way as SUMIF, with the same types of arguments.

Try It!　　**Creating a SUMIF Function**

① In the **E65Try_xx** file, click the SUMIF worksheet tab.

② Click cell B15 > Insert Function.

③ Type **SUMIF**, and click Go.

④ Click SUMIF in the list of functions, if necessary, and click OK.

⑤ In the Range box, type **D4:D13**.

⑥ In the Criteria box, type **Yes**.

  ✓ *Quotation marks around the criteria are required, even if the criteria are numeric. Insert Function automatically puts quotation marks around the criteria for you.*

⑦ In the Sum Range box, type **C4:C13**.

⑧ Click OK. The result ($802.00) appears in cell B15.

⑨ Save the changes to the file, and leave it open to use in the next Try It.

Enter the arguments for the SUMIF function

Function Arguments	?	×

SUMIF

Range	D4:D13	🔢	= {"No";"Yes";"No";"No";"Yes";"Yes";"No";"
Criteria	"Yes"	🔢	= "Yes"
Sum_range	C4:C13	🔢	= {978;159;399;205;249;40;178;354;246;3

= 802

Adds the cells specified by a given condition or criteria.

　　　　　Sum_range are the actual cells to sum. If omitted, the cells in range are used.

Formula result =　$802.00

Help on this function   OK   Cancel

Creating SUMIFS, COUNTIFS, and AVERAGEIFS Functions

- The **SUMIFS**, **COUNTIFS**, and **AVERAGEIFS** functions are the same as SUMIF, COUNTIF, and AVERAGEIF except that they allow multiple criteria.

- For the function to be evaluated as true, all the criteria must be met.

Try It!   **Creating an AVERAGEIFS Function**

① In the **E65Try_xx** file, on the SUMIF worksheet tab, click cell A16, and type **Avg Due for Dog Items**.

② Click cell B16 > Insert Function.

③ Type **AVERAGEIFS**, and click Go > OK.

④ In the Average_range box, type **C4:C13**.

⑤ In the Criteria_range1 box, type **D4:D13**.

⑥ In the Criteria1 box, type **No**.

⑦ In the Criteria_range2 box, type **E4:E13**.

⑧ In the Criteria2 box, type **Dog**.

⑨ Click OK. The function appears in the cell.

⑩ Save the changes to the file, and leave it open for the next Try It.

Arguments for the AVERAGEIFS function

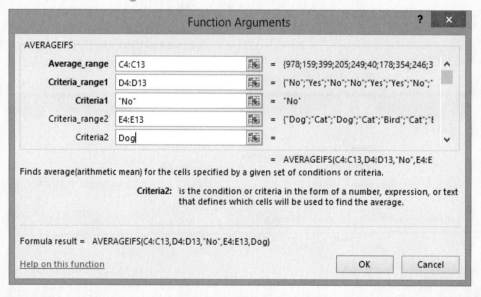

Using the TODAY Function and the NOW Function

- You can use the **TODAY function** to add today's date to a worksheet cell.

- Excel stores dates as sequential serial numbers so that they can be used in calculations using January 1, 1900 as serial number 1. For example, January 1, 2015 is serial number 42005 because it is 42,005 days after January 1, 1900.

- The TODAY function obtains the serial number of the date from your computer, and formats it as a date.

- The syntax for the TODAY function is: **=TODAY ()**

- The **NOW function** displays the current date and time on a worksheet. It can also be used to calculate a value based on the current date and time. Each time the worksheet is opened, the value is updated.

- The syntax for the NOW function is: **=NOW ()**

Try It!   **Using the TODAY Function and the NOW Function**

1   In the **E65Try_xx** file, on the SUMIF worksheet, click cell C1.

2   Type **=TODAY()**.

3   Press ENTER to display the formula result in the cell.

4   Click cell D1, and type **=NOW()**.

5   Press ENTER to display the formula result in the cell. (Adjust the column width as necessary.)

6   Save the changes to the file, and leave it open to use in the next Try It.

The TODAY function

| C1 | ▼ | : | × | ✓ | fx | =TODAY() |

	A	B	C
1	**Sales and Payments**		5/17/2013
2			

Using the TRANSPOSE Function

- The **TRANSPOSE function** is one of Excel's Lookup & Reference functions.

- You can use the TRANSPOSE function to switch the position of rows and columns.

  ✓ *TRANSPOSE does not work with data in a table. First convert the table to text, and then TRANSPOSE.*

- The TRANSPOSE function requires an **array** argument.

- The syntax for the TRANSPOSE function is:

  { = TRANSPOSE (Array)}

  ✓ *The curly braces—{ }— around the function indicate that the function is an array function.*

- Use the first row of the array as the first column of the new array, the second row of the array as the second column of the new array, and so on.

- You must enter the TRANSPOSE function as an array formula in a range that has the same number of rows and columns, respectively, as the source range has columns and rows.

  - For example, to transpose a cell range of two columns and five rows, you must indicate a cell range of five rows and two columns in the worksheet.

  - You can transpose a cell range to a range of blank cells, as long as there are enough blank cells to contain the data that will be transposed.

- You must indicate the array or range of cells on a worksheet that you want to transpose before using the Insert Function button.

Try It!   **Using the TRANSPOSE Function**

1   In the **E65Try_xx** file, on the SUMIF worksheet, select the cell range H3:R7.

2   Click FORMULAS > Lookup & Reference 🔍 > TRANSPOSE to display the Function Arguments dialog box.

3   In the Array box, type **A3:E13**.

    OR

    Click the collapse dialog button, select the **A3:E13** cell range, and click the expand dialog button.

4   Press CTRL , SHIFT , and ENTER at the same time to insert the TRANSPOSE array formula into the cell range H3:R7.

    ✓ *If you click OK instead of using the Control, Shift, and Enter key combination, the formula will return an error value.*

5   Adjust the column widths.

6   Save and close the file, and exit Excel.

Lesson 65—Practice

Your boss at Wood Hills Animal Clinic has asked you to modify the monthly sales report and create an analysis of sales based on several factors such as animal type (cat versus dog, for example) and purpose (ear infection versus flea control, for example). In this project, you will insert functions to aid in the analysis of the data.

DIRECTIONS

1. Start Excel, if necessary, and open **E65Practice** from the data files for this lesson.
2. Save the file as **E65Practice_xx** in the location where your teacher instructs you to store the files for this lesson.
3. Add a header that has your name at the left, the date code in the center, and the page number code at the right, and change back to **Normal** view.
4. Click cell D99, and type the formula **=SUM(K8:K94)** to compute the total sales revenues.
5. Use Insert Function to create a formula in cell D100 to sum the sales from dog products:
   a. Click cell **D100**.
   b. On the formula bar, click **Insert Function** _fx_ to open the Insert Function dialog box.
   c. In the Search for a function box, type **SUMIF > Go > OK**.
   d. In the Function Arguments dialog box, for the Range argument, type **C8:C94**.
   e. In the Criteria argument, type **"Dog"**.

   ✓ Typing the quotation marks is optional; if you do not type them, Excel will add them for you automatically.

   f. In the Sum_range argument, type **K8:K94**.
   g. Click **OK**.
6. Use the process in step 5 to sum the sales of cat products in cell D101.

   ✓ The function to be placed in cell D101 is identical to the one in cell D100 except it uses Cat rather than Dog in the criteria argument.

7. Use Insert Function to create a formula in cell D103 to sum the sales from flea products:
   a. Click cell **D103**.
   b. On the formula bar, click **Insert Function** _fx_.
   c. Click **SUMIF > OK**.

   d. In the Function Arguments dialog box, for the Range argument, type **B8:B94**.
   e. In the Criteria argument, type **"Flea"**.
   f. In the Sum_range argument, type **K8:K94**.
   g. Click **OK**.
8. Use the process in step 7 to insert SUMIF functions in cells **D104** and **D105**. For cell D104, use **"Flea and Tick"** as the critieria argument. For cell D105, use **"Heartworm"** as the criteria argument.
9. Complete the functions for cells **D108:D114** using the same methods as in steps 5–8 except use **AVERAGE** and **AVERAGEIF** functions.

   ✓ Notice that cell D108 is the average sales and D112 is the average sales of flea products.

10. In cell **D106**, type =D99-SUM(D103:D105).
11. In cell **D115**, enter an **AVERAGEIFS** function that averages the values that are not Flea, Flea and Tick, or Heartworm:
    a. Click cell **D115**.
    b. On the formula bar, click **Insert Function** _fx_.
    c. Type **AVERAGEIFS > Go > OK**.
    d. In the Average_range argument, type **K8:K94**.
    e. In the Criteria_range1 argument, type **B8:B94**.
    f. In the Criteria1 argument, type **"<>Flea"**.

    ✓ Make sure you put the <> inside the quotation marks.

    g. In the Criteria_range2 argument, type **B8:B94**.
    h. In the Criteria2 argument, type **"<>Flea and Tick"**.
    i. In the Criteria_range3 argument, type **B8:B94**.
    j. In the Criteria3 argument, type **"<>Heartworm"**.
    k. Click **OK**.
12. Use a function to insert today's date in cell E98:
    a. Click cell **E98**.
    b. Type **=TODAY()**.
    c. Press [ENTER].

13. **With your teacher's permission**, print the cell range **A98:E117**. Your worksheet should look like the one shown in Figure 65-1.

14. Save and close the file, and exit Excel.

Sales Analysis	5/27/2013
Total Sales	$263,465.96
Sales of dog only products	$157,691.75
Sales of cat only products	$24,091.11
Sales of flea products	$18,630.10
Sales of flea and tick products	$1,748.85
Sales of heartworm products	$70,944.70
Other sales	$172,142.31
Average Sales	$3,028.34
Average sales of dog only products	$3,583.90
Average sales of cat only products	$1,853.16
Average sales of flea products	$1,693.65
Average sales of flea and tick products	$874.43
Average sales of heartworm products	$7,094.47
Average of other sales	$2,689.72

Lesson 65—Apply

You work in the sales department of Pete's Pets. Your manager has asked you to create an analysis of the store's sales based on several factors such as animal type and salesperson. Your manager also wants you to find out who sold a particular item. In this project, you will insert functions and transpose data to aid in the analysis of the sales report.

DIRECTIONS

1. Start Excel, if necessary, and open **E65Apply** from the data files for this lesson.

2. Save the file as **E65Apply_xx** in the location where your teacher instructs you to store the files for this lesson.

3. Add a header that has your name at the left, the date code in the center, and the page number code at the right, and change back to **Normal** view.

4. In cell **D54**, use the **COUNTIF** function to compute the number of **Cats** sold.

5. In cell **D55**, use the **COUNTIF** function to compute the number of **Fish** sold.

6. In cell **D62**, use the **SUMIF** function to compute the total sales for **Alice Harper**.

7. In cell **D63**, use the **SUMIF** function to compute the total sales for **Bob Cook**.

8. In cell **E62**, use the **AVERAGEIF** function to compute the average sale for **Alice Harper**.

9. In cell **E63**, use the **AVERAGEIF** function to compute the average sale for **Bob Cook**.

10. In cell **D66**, use **SUMIFS** to compute the total fish sales for **Alice Harper**.

11. In cell **D67**, use **SUMIFS** to compute the total fish sales for **Bob Cook**.

12. In cell **E66**, use **SUMIFS** to compute the total accessory sales for **Alice Harper**.

13. In cell **E67**, use **SUMIFS** to compute the total accessory sales for **Bob Cook**.

14. In cell **D70**, use **AVERAGEIFS** to calculate the average fish sale for **Alice Harper**.

15. In cell **D71**, use **AVERAGEIFS** to calculate the average fish sale for **Bob Cook**.

16. In cell **E70**, use **AVERAGEIFS** to calculate the average accessory sale for **Alice Harper**.

17. In cell **E71**, use **AVERAGEIFS** to calculate the average accessory sale for **Bob Cook**.

18. In cell **E52**, use the **TODAY** function to insert today's date.

19. In cells **H61:J63**, use the **TRANSPOSE** function to transpose the rows and columns of the cell range C61:E63.

20. In cell **J65**, use the **VLOOKUP** function to find out who sold item 51478.

    ✓ *You learned about LOOKUP functions in Excel Lesson 35.*

    a. Click cell **H65**.

    b. Type **Who sold item 51478?**

c. Click cell **J65**.

d. In the Lookup_value argument, type **51478**.

e. In the Table_array argument, type **B10:G49**.

f. In the Col_index_num argument, type **4**.

g. Click **OK**.

21. In cell **J67**, use the **HLOOKUP** function to find out what item was sold for $27.65.

    a. Click cell **H67**.

    b. Type **What item # sold for $27.65?**

    c. Click cell **J67**.

    d. In the Lookup_value argument, type **"Item #"**.

    e. In the Table_array argument, type **B9:G49**.

    f. In the Row_index_num argument, type **20**.

    ✓ *Notice that the row index number is the row number in the table, not the worksheet.*

    g. In the Range_lookup argument, type **FALSE**.

    ✓ *Use FALSE to find the exact match.*

    h. Click **OK**.

21. Apply **Accounting Format** with two decimal places to all the functions you created.

22. Adjust the column widths as needed.

23. **With your teacher's permission**, print cells **B52:K71**. Your worksheet should look like the one shown in Figure 65-2.

24. Save and close the file, and exit Excel.

Figure 65-2

Sales Recap				6/25/2013					
Dogs sold		3							
Cats sold		2							
Fish sold		9							
Pet sales	$	1,696.37							
Feed sales	$	200.71							
Accessories	$	464.16							
Salesperson	Total Sales		Average Sales			Salesperson	Alice Harper	Bob Cook	
Alice Harper	$	1,059.37	$	48.15		Total Sales	$ 1,059.37	$ 1,301.87	
Bob Cook	$	1,301.87	$	72.33		Average Sales	$ 48.15	$ 72.33	
			Total Accessories						
Salesperson	Total Fish Sales		Sales				Who sold item 51478?	Alice Harper	
Alice Harper	$	135.15	$	297.96					
Bob Cook	$	17.22	$	166.20			What item # sold for $27.65?	48681	
			Average Accessories						
Salesperson	Average Fish Sales		Sales						
Alice Harper	$	22.53	$	27.09					
Bob Cook	$	5.74	$	18.47					

Lesson 66

Working with Absolute References and Using Financial Functions

➤ What You Will Learn

Using Absolute, Relative, and Mixed References
Enabling Iterative Calculations
Using Financial Functions

WORDS TO KNOW

Absolute reference
A cell reference that remains fixed when copied to another cell.

Circular reference
When a formula in Excel refers to the cell that contains the formula, either directly or indirectly.

FV
The Future Value function. Calculates the future value of an investment when given the rate, the number of periods, and the payment amount.

Iterative calculation
A repeated calculation

Mixed reference
A cell reference in which the row is absolute and the column is relative, or vice-versa.

Software Skills   Usually when you create a function, the cell references are relative. When you copy the function to another cell, the cell references change in relation to the new location. Sometimes, though, you may not want the cell reference to change. In cases like that, you need an absolute reference. Excel enables you to create relative, absolute, or mixed references as needed. Absolute references come in handy when you are creating functions that calculate interest rates, payments, loan periods, and other financial information.

What You Can Do

Using Absolute, Relative, and Mixed References

- When you create a formula and then copy or move the formula, a **relative reference** changes to reflect the new position.

- For example, in Figure 66-1 on the next page, cell D3 contains the formula =B3+C3. If you copy that formula to cell D4, it will automatically change to =B4+C4. It increments the row number by one because the copy is being placed one row below the original.

- Cell references are relative by default in Excel; you do not need to do anything special to create a relative cell reference.

- An **absolute reference** to a cell locks the cell's reference when the formula is moved or copied. Absolute references are created by placing a dollar sign ($) before both the row and the column of the cell reference, like this: $B$3.

NPER
The Number of Periods function. Calculates the number of payments on a loan when given the rate, payment amount, and present value.

PMT
The Payment function. Calculates a payment when given the rate, number of periods, and present value.

PV
The Present Value function. Calculates the present value of an investment when given rate, number of periods, and payment amount.

Relative reference
A cell reference that changes when copied to another cell. The default setting.

Figure 66-1

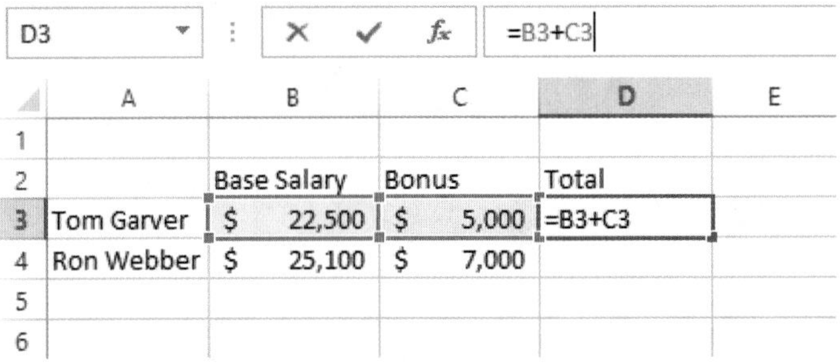

- For example, in Figure 66-2, in cell C5, the following formula appears: =B5+$B$1. If you copy that formula to cell C6, the reference to B5 will change because it is relative, but the reference to B1 will not because it is absolute. The resulting formula in cell C6 will be =B6+$B$1.

Figure 66-2

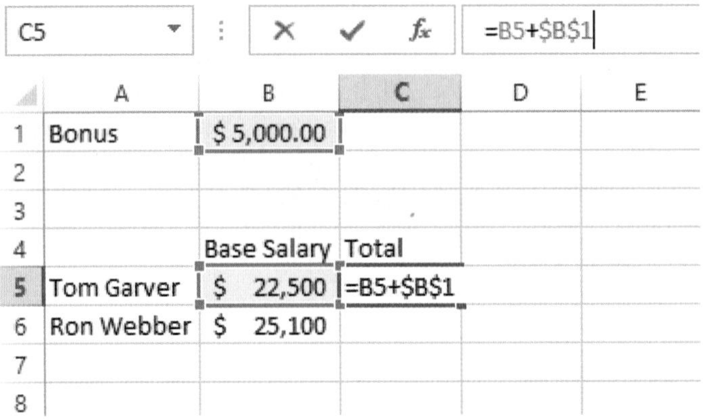

- A **mixed reference** is one in which only one dimension is absolute. For example, $B1 locks the column but not the row, and B$1 locks the row but not the column.
- To create absolute or mixed references, you can manually type the dollar signs into the formulas in the appropriate places.
- You can also toggle a cell reference among all the possible combinations of absolute, relative, and mixed by pressing F4 when the insertion point is within the cell reference.

Try It!   Using Absolute References

1. Start Excel, and open **E66Try** from the data files for this lesson.

2. Save the file as **E66Try_xx** in the location where your teacher instructs you to store the files for this lesson.

3. On the Taxes worksheet, click cell H3, type =G3*$A$18, and press ENTER .

4. Click cell H3, and press CTRL + C to copy the formula to the Clipboard.

5. Select the cell range H4:H15, and press CTRL + V to paste the formula into those cells.

6. Browse the contents of several of the pasted cells to confirm that the reference to A18 remained absolute.

7. Save the changes to the file, and leave it open to use in the next Try It.

The reference to the Total is relative; the reference to the Tax rate is absolute

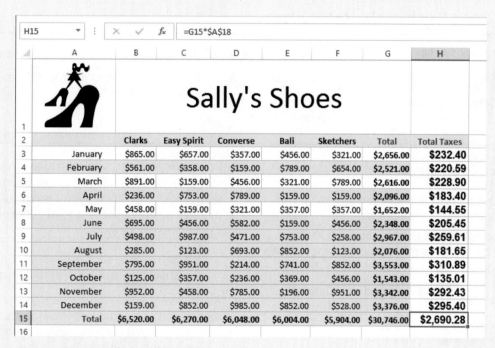

	A	B	C	D	E	F	G	H
2		Clarks	Easy Spirit	Converse	Bali	Sketchers	Total	Total Taxes
3	January	$865.00	$657.00	$357.00	$456.00	$321.00	$2,656.00	$232.40
4	February	$561.00	$358.00	$159.00	$789.00	$654.00	$2,521.00	$220.59
5	March	$891.00	$159.00	$456.00	$321.00	$789.00	$2,616.00	$228.90
6	April	$236.00	$753.00	$789.00	$159.00	$159.00	$2,096.00	$183.40
7	May	$458.00	$159.00	$321.00	$357.00	$357.00	$1,652.00	$144.55
8	June	$695.00	$456.00	$582.00	$159.00	$456.00	$2,348.00	$205.45
9	July	$498.00	$987.00	$471.00	$753.00	$258.00	$2,967.00	$259.61
10	August	$285.00	$123.00	$693.00	$852.00	$123.00	$2,076.00	$181.65
11	September	$795.00	$951.00	$214.00	$741.00	$852.00	$3,553.00	$310.89
12	October	$125.00	$357.00	$236.00	$369.00	$456.00	$1,543.00	$135.01
13	November	$952.00	$458.00	$785.00	$196.00	$951.00	$3,342.00	$292.43
14	December	$159.00	$852.00	$985.00	$852.00	$528.00	$3,376.00	$295.40
15	Total	$6,520.00	$6,270.00	$6,048.00	$6,004.00	$5,904.00	$30,746.00	$2,690.28
16								

H15 — =G15*$A$18

Sally's Shoes

Try It!   Using Mixed References

1. In the **E66Try_xx** file, click the Area worksheet tab.

2. In cell C5, type =$B5*C$4, and press ENTER .

3. Click cell C5, and drag the fill handle down to fill the cell range C6:C9 with the formula.

4. Click in any filled cell, and look at the formula bar. Notice that the relative references changed, and that the absolute references remained the same.

5. Copy the formula from cell C5 into the remainder of the range (through cell F9).

6. Save the changes to the file, and leave it open to use in the next Try It.

Enabling Iterative Calculations

- Before you work with financial functions that may have a **circular reference**, it is helpful to enable **iterative calculations**. This means that you will be able to work with a formula that refers to a cell that contains that formula.

- You can access the Calculation options in the Formulas tab of the Excel Options settings.

- You can control the maximum number of iterations that Excel performs.

- You can also control the amount of acceptable change, or precision, that you need before Excel finishes the calculation.

- Be careful when setting calculation options because they will apply to all open workbooks.

- When you save a workbook, Excel saves the calculation setting that was applied when the workbook was open.

- When you open workbooks, Excel will apply the calculation settings of the first workbook you open.

- For example, if you first open workbook A (which had iteration disabled when it was last saved) and then open Workbook B (with iteration enabled when it was last saved), Excel will keep iteration disabled.

Try It! **Enabling Iterative Calculations**

1. In the **E66Try_xx** file, click FILE > Options.
2. In the Excel Options dialog box, click Formulas.
3. In the Calculations options group, click Enable iterative calculation to select the check box.
4. Click OK to close the Excel Options dialog box.
5. Save the changes to the file, and leave it open to use in the next Try It.

Using Financial Functions

- Excel includes a set of financial functions that can calculate variables in a loan or investment equation.

- They are considered a set because each function solves for a particular variable, and the other pieces of information are arguments within that function.

Function	Purpose	Required Arguments	Optional Arguments
PMT	Calculates a loan payment	RATE, NPER, PV,	FV, TYPE
RATE	Calculates a loan rate	NPER, PMT, PV	FV, TYPE, GUESS
NPER	Calculates the number of periods in a loan	RATE, PMT, PV	FV, TYPE
PV	Calculates the present value (beginning balance)	RATE, NPER, PMT	FV, TYPE
FV	Calculates the future value (ending balance)	RATE, NPER, PMT	PV, TYPE

- For example, if you know the loan length (60 months), the loan rate (5.9% per year), and the loan amount ($20,000), you can calculate your monthly payment with the PMT function:

=PMT(.059/12,60,20000)

✓ Note that you divide the interest rate by 12 because the interest rate is per year, and a payment is made monthly.

- Alternatively, suppose you want to know how much money you can afford to borrow at 7% interest for 60 months if you can pay $250 a month:

=PV(0.07/12,60,250)

- To find out how much an investment made now will be worth later, such as buying a savings bond, use the FV function. For example, suppose you buy a $10,000 savings bond that pays 5% interest, is compounded monthly, and matures in 20 years:

=FV(0.05/12,20*12,0,10000)

✓ The third argument (PMT) is 0 because you don't make any payments after the initial investment of $10,000.

- In actual usage, you would probably want to put those values into cells, and then reference the cells in the functions rather than hard-coding the actual numbers in. That way, you could change the variables and see different results without modifying the functions themselves.

Try It! — Using Financial Functions

1 In the **E66Try_xx** file, click the Functions worksheet tab.

2 In cell B3, type **60,000**.

3 In cell B4, type **.065**.

4 In cell B5, type **1**.

5 In cell B6, type **60**.

6 In cell B8, type **=PMT(B4/12,-B6,B3)**.

✓ Notice the – preceding B6; this is to make the value negative, so the result in B8 will be positive.

7 In cell B12, type **=PV(B13/12,B15,-B17)**.

✓ B17 is referred to as a negative so the formula result will be positive. The same is true for B26 in step 8.

8 In cell B32, type **=FV(B31,B28*B29,,-B26)**.

✓ Notice that there are two commas in a row in this function because the PMT argument is blank.

9 Save and close the file, and exit Excel.

Lesson 66—Practice

The manager at Sally's Shoes wants to analyze the potential revenue from various sales scenarios per month. She knows that women want to purchase shoes for a lower price, but a few people want the high-end style and are willing to pay the price for a unique designer shoe. Should the manager focus on more customers purchasing lower priced shoes, or on fewer customers purchasing higher priced shoes? You have been tasked with creating a worksheet to analyze the potential revenue from these scenarios. In this project, you will use references and formulas to calculate the data.

DIRECTIONS

1. Start Excel, if necessary, and open **E66Practice** from the data files for this lesson.

2. Save the file as **E66Practice_xx** in the location where your teacher instructs you to store the files for this lesson.

3. Add a custom header that has your name at the left, the date code in the center, and the page number code at the right.

4. Click **FILE** > **Options** > **Formulas**, and click the **Enable iterative calculations** check box to select it, if necessary.

5. In cell **C5**, type **=$B5*C$4**.

6. Use the Fill feature to fill in the rest of the sales data, down to cell **F9**.

7. Select cells **A3:F9**, and press CTRL + C to copy.

8. Click in cell **A13**, and press CTRL + V to paste.

9. Change the values in cells **C14:F14** to **35**, **50**, **75**, and **100**, from left to right.

10. Edit the formula in cell **C15** to **=$B15*C$14**.

11. Copy the formula from cell **C15** into the rest of the sales data, replacing the previous values in each cell.

12. **With your teacher's permission**, print the worksheet. Your worksheet should look like the one shown in Figure 66-3.

13. Save and close the file, and exit Excel.

Figure 66-3

	A	B	C	D	E	F	G
1				Sally's Shoes			
2							
3				Price Points			
4			$45	$65	$85	$125	
5	Number of Sales	50	2,250.00	3,250.00	4,250.00	6,250.00	
6		75	3,375.00	4,875.00	6,375.00	9,375.00	
7		100	4,500.00	6,500.00	8,500.00	12,500.00	
8		125	5,625.00	8,125.00	10,625.00	15,625.00	
9		150	6,750.00	9,750.00	12,750.00	18,750.00	
10							
11							
12							
13				Price Points			
14			$35	$50	$75	$100	
15	Number of Sales	50	1,750.00	2,500.00	3,750.00	5,000.00	
16		75	2,625.00	3,750.00	5,625.00	7,500.00	
17		100	3,500.00	5,000.00	7,500.00	10,000.00	
18		125	4,375.00	6,250.00	9,375.00	12,500.00	
19		150	5,250.00	7,500.00	11,250.00	15,000.00	
20							
21							

Lesson 66—Apply

You are helping the manager at Sally's Shoes analyze the potential revenue from various sales scenarios per month. Sales have been very high so far this year and the manager is considering expanding the business. In this project, you will use financial functions to analyze loan scenarios for expanding the business.

DIRECTIONS

1. Start Excel, if necessary, and open **E66Apply** from the data files for this lesson.

2. Save the file as **E66Apply_xx** in the location where your teacher instructs you to store the files for this lesson.

3. Add a custom header that has your name at the left, the date code in the center, and the page number code at the right.

4. Click **FILE** > **Options** > **Formulas**, and click the **Enable iterative calculations** check box to select it, if necessary.

5. In the Payment Calculation grid, calculate what the payment would be on a four-year loan of **$30,000** with a monthly interest rate of **5.25%**. Fill the numbers for the calculation into cells **B4:B6**, and reference those cells in a function in cell **B7**.

   ✓ *Make the reference to the present value negative, so that the amount in cell B7 is positive.*

6. In the Present Value Calculation grid, calculate the present value of a loan with **$800** in monthly payments at **4.35%** interest rate for **360** months.

   ✓ *Make the reference to the payment amount negative, so that the amount in cell B11 is positive.*

7. In the Compound Interest Calculation grid, calculate the future value (FV) of an investment of **$4,000** with a **3.25%** interest rate, compounded monthly, for **5** years.

  ✓ *Make the reference to the present value amount negative, so that the amount in cell B23 is positive.*

  ✓ *The periodic interest rate is the annual interest rate (B19) divided by the number of compounding periods per year (B20).*

8. With your teacher's permission, print the worksheet. Your worksheet should look like the one shown in Figure 66-4.

9. Save and close the file, and exit Excel.

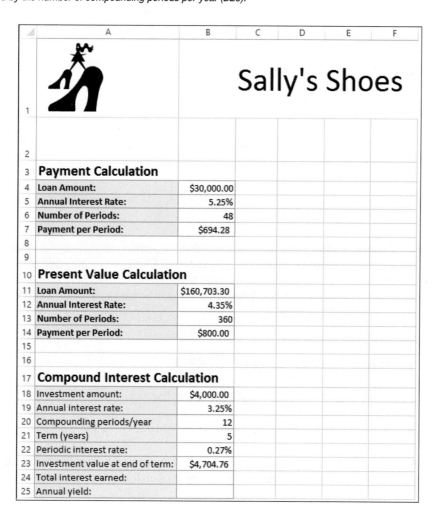

Figure 66-4

Sally's Shoes

	A	B
3	**Payment Calculation**	
4	Loan Amount:	$30,000.00
5	Annual Interest Rate:	5.25%
6	Number of Periods:	48
7	Payment per Period:	$694.28
8		
9		
10	**Present Value Calculation**	
11	Loan Amount:	$160,703.30
12	Annual Interest Rate:	4.35%
13	Number of Periods:	360
14	Payment per Period:	$800.00
15		
16		
17	**Compound Interest Calculation**	
18	Investment amount:	$4,000.00
19	Annual interest rate:	3.25%
20	Compounding periods/year	12
21	Term (years)	5
22	Periodic interest rate:	0.27%
23	Investment value at end of term:	$4,704.76
24	Total interest earned:	
25	Annual yield:	

Lesson 67

Creating and Interpreting Financial Statements

➤ What You Will Learn

Loading the Analysis ToolPak Add-On
Calculating a Moving Average
Calculating Growth Based on a Moving Average
Charting the Break-Even Point with a Line Chart
Using Goal Seek

WORDS TO KNOW

Break-even point
The number of units, or individual items, you must sell to begin making a profit, given your fixed costs for the unit, cost per unit, and revenue per unit.

Goal Seek
A method of performing what-if analysis in which the result (the goal) is known, but the value of a single dependent variable is unknown.

Moving average
A sequence of averages computed from parts of a data series. In a chart, a moving average corrects for the fluctuations in data, showing the pattern or trend more clearly.

Variable
An input value that changes depending on the desired outcome.

What-if analysis
Excel's term for a series of tools that perform calculations involving one or more variables.

Software Skills   Excel contains more financial capabilities than just simple loan and investment calculation. You can use Excel to create and analyze financial statements and scenarios that include moving averages, growth calculations, and income and expense projections. You can use Excel tools, such as Goal Seek, to perform what-if analysis.

What You Can Do

Loading the Analysis ToolPak Add-On

- To use Excel's analysis features, you need the Analysis ToolPak, which is not loaded by default.
- If you are working on a PC in a lab that is regularly used for computer classes, the Analysis ToolPak may have already been loaded by a previous student.

Try It!   **Determining Whether the Analysis ToolPak Add-On Is Loaded**

1 Start Excel, and open **E67Try** from the data files for this lesson.

2 Save the file as **E67Try_xx** in the location where your teacher instructs you to store the files for this lesson.

3 Click the DATA tab.

4 Look for a Data Analysis command. If you don't see one, the Analysis Toolpak is not loaded.

Try It!   **Loading the Analysis ToolPak Add-On**

1 In Excel, click FILE > Options.

2 Click Add-Ins.

3 At the bottom of the dialog box, confirm that Manage is set to Excel Add-ins, and click Go.

4 In the Add-Ins dialog box, click the Analysis ToolPak check box to select it.

5 Click OK.

6 On the DATA tab, confirm that there is now an Analysis group with a Data Analysis command.

7 Leave Excel open to use in the next Try It.

Calculating a Moving Average

- A **moving average** is considered more accurate than a simple average of a set of numbers in predicting future trends. A moving average is used with data that represents changes over time to smooth out short-term fluctuations and highlight the long-term trends.

- To calculate a moving average, start with a subset of the data (for example, items 1–20 in a 100-item list) and calculate their average. That average becomes the first data point. Then you calculate the average of items 2–21 on the list, and that average becomes the second data point. You progress through the entire list until you have a complete set of data points.

- Calculating a moving average would be very labor-intensive by hand, so it makes sense to use a program like Excel to do the calculations.

- Excel's Moving Average data analysis tool makes the process easy. You can specify how many numbers to use in the averaging calculation.

Try It!   **Calculating a Moving Average**

1 In the **E67Try_xx** file, click the Moving Average worksheet tab, if necessary.

   ✓ *This data represents the share price of mutual funds for a month.*

2 On the DATA tab, in the Analysis group, click Data Analysis ▥ to open the Data Analysis dialog box.

3 In the Analysis Tools list, click Moving Average > OK.

4 In the Moving Average dialog box, in the Input Range box, type **A2:A31**.

   ✓ *You can also click the Collapse Dialog Box button next to Input Range, and select the desired range.*

(continued)

Try It! Calculating a Moving Average *(continued)*

5 In the Interval box, type **5**. This tells Excel how many numbers to average for one output.

6 In the Output Range box, type **B2:B31**.

 ✓ *You can also click the Collapse Dialog Box button next to Output Range, and select the desired range.*

7 Click the Chart Output check box to select it.

8 Click OK. A line chart is generated from the raw data and the moving average data.

9 Click in the chart area to select it, and drag a corner to make the chart larger.

10 To see how the moving average works, click cell B8. In the formulat bar, the formula =AVERAGE(A4:A8) shows that the average is of the data in cells A4, A5, A6, A7, and A8.

11 Save the changes to the file, and leave it open to use in the next Try It.

Enter the specifications for the moving average calculation

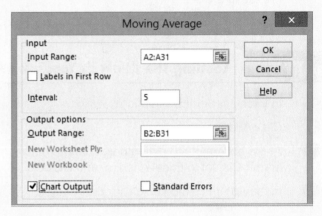

Calculating Growth Based on a Moving Average

- When you have historical data, it is possible to predict what might happen in the future. You can use the GROWTH function to analyze a pattern of data from the past and create a new pattern of data for the future.

- The GROWTH function creates a statistical prediction for the future that can be used to compare actual data with what you predicted.

 ✓ *It is best to base the predictions you create with the GROWTH function on stable and reliable known data.*

- The GROWTH function arguments are [known-y], [known-x], [new known-x].
  - Known-x is the known original data.
  - Known-y is the past output based on the known-x values.
  - New known-x is the known new data.
- Given that information, the GROWTH function will predict the future output based on the new known-x values.

Try It! Calculating Growth Based on a Moving Average

1 In the **E67Try_xx** file, click the Growth worksheet tab.

2 Examine the data in the worksheet and note the following:

- The data in column A represents days of the month. The cell range A2:A16 is the first half of the month (the known-x), and the cell range A19:A33 is the second half of the month (the new known-x).

- The data in the cell range B2:B16 is moving average data for the first half of the month (the known-y).

- The GROWTH function will be used to predict the moving averages to be placed in the cell range B19:B33.

3 Click cell B19, and type =GROWTH(.

4 For the first argument, drag across cells B2:B6 to select that range, and type a comma (,) to separate the arguments.

Try It! **Calculating Growth Based on a Moving Average** *(continued)*

5 For the second argument, drag across the cell range A2:A6, and type a comma (,) to separate the arguments.

6 For the third argument, drag across the cell range A19:A23. This represents 5 days that will be used to predict future growth.

7 Press [ENTER] to complete the function. The final function in cell B19 should be =GROWTH(B2:B6,A2:A6,A19:A23).

8 Copy the formula in cell B19 into the cell range B20:B33.

✓ *Notice that starting at cell B30 an error message displays, #VALUE!. That's because the GROWTH formula in cell B30 refers to data in cell A34, and there is no data in cell A34.*

9 Select the cell range B30:B33, and press [DEL] to clear the content of those cells.

✓ *Based on the mutual fund's moving average growth experienced from the first of the month to the fifteenth of the month, you can predict that by the end of the month the mutual fund will be at the value shown in cell B29.*

10 Save the changes to the file, and leave it open to use in the next Try It.

Charting the Break-Even Point with a Line Chart

■ You can enter your known costs and your projected income from sales to calculate when your revenue will exceed your costs, the **break-even point**.

■ You can create a break-even line chart based on known expenses and projected income.

■ This calculation can help you analyze finances to know how much you need to sell in order to make a profit, as well as how much more you need to sell in order to make a pre-determined profit amount.

Try It!   **Charting the Break-Even Point with a Line Chart**

1 In the **E67Try_xx** file, click the Break-Even worksheet tab.

2 In cell B1, type **100**.

3 In cell B2, type **1**.

4 In cell B3, type **6**.

5 In cell B6, type =A6*$B$2+$B$1.

✓ *Notice the absolute references to cells B1 and B2.*

6 Copy the formula in cell B6 to cells B7:B30. Cell B30 should show $125.00.

7 In cell C6, type =A6*$B$3.

8 Copy the formula in cell C6 to cells C7:C30. Cell C30 should show $150.00.

9 In cell D6, type =C6-B6.

10 Copy the formula in cell D6 to cells D7:D30. Cell D30 should show $25.00.

11 Select the cell range B5:D30, and click INSERT > Insert Line Chart ⋏ ⋎ > Stacked Line (the second chart in the 2-D section).

✓ *The point where the Profit and Revenue lines cross is the break-even point.*

12 Click the chart to select it, and drag it closer to the data.

13 Save the changes to the file, and leave it open to use in the next Try It.

Using Goal Seek

- You can use **Goal Seek** to perform **what-if analysis** when you know the result (the goal), but not the value of one of the input **variables** (the variables that create the result).

- For example, you could use Goal Seek to determine the exact amount you need to borrow at 8.25% interest to keep the payment at $1,000 per month.

- Access the Goal Seek analysis tool from the What-If Analysis button in the Data Tools group on the DATA tab.

- When you input the known variables into the Goal Seek Status dialog box, the tool will show whether it found a solution and, if so, the solution. It will also change the values on the worksheet.

Try It!   Using Goal Seek to Perform What-If Analysis

1. In the **E67Try_xx** file, click the Goal Seek tab.

2. Click **DATA** > **What-If Analysis** > **Goal Seek**.

3. In the Goal Seek dialog box, in the Set cell box, type **B8**. This is the location of the input variable you know, payment per period.

4. In the To value box, type **750**. This is the value of the input variable you know; you want to pay $750 per month.

5. In the By changing cell box, type **B3**.

6. Click OK. Goal Seek finds a solution for the loan amount you need to borrow.

7. In the Goal Seek Status dialog box, click OK to accept the solution.

8. Save and close the file, and exit Excel

Entering variables in Goal Seek

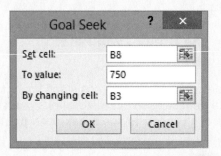

Lesson 67—Practice

The owner of Best Movies Theater has asked you to analyze the attendance of his theater. He wants you to create a report to show actual and forecasted attendance. In this project, you will use Excel functions to calculate a moving average of the attendance of the theater.

DIRECTIONS

1. Start Excel, if necessary, and open **E67Practice** from the data files for this lesson.

2. Save the file as **E67Practice_xx** in the location where your teacher instructs you to store the files for this lesson.

3. Add a header that has your name at the left, the date code in the center, and the page number code at the right, and change back to **Normal** view.

4. Check that the Data Analysis command is on the DATA tab, and enable the Analysis ToolPak, if necessary:

   a. Click **FILE** > **Options** > **Add-Ins**.

   b. Confirm that Manage is set to **Excel Add-ins**, and click **Go**.

   c. In the Add-Ins dialog box, click the **Analysis ToolPak** check box to select it, and click **OK**.

5. Select **DATA** > **Data Analysis** to open the Data Analysis dialog box.

6. Click **Moving Average** > **OK**.
7. In the Input box, type **A2:A31**.
8. In the Interval box, type **7**.
9. In the Output box, type **B2:B31**.
10. Click the **Chart Output** check box, if necessary.
11. Click **OK**.

12. Drag the lower-right corner of the chart frame to enlarge the chart so it is more readable.

   ✓ *You can delete the function from cells B2:B7 when finished; they show an #N/A error rather than a value. This is expected.*

13. **With your teacher's permission,** print the chart. Your chart should look like the one shown in Figure 67-1.
14. Save and close the file, and exit Excel.

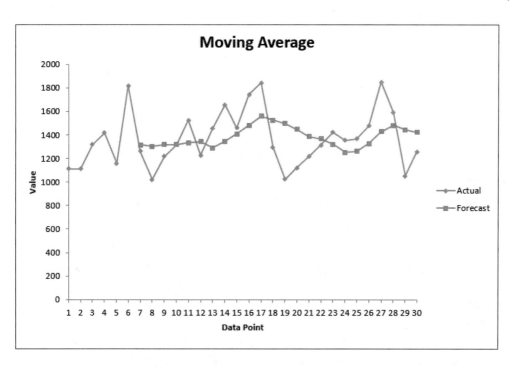

Figure 67-1

Lesson 67—Apply

You are creating financial statements for the owner of several small businesses so that he can make decisions about a side seasonal business. The owner is considering expanding the business and wants you to provide the total loan amount that he can apply for given a set monthly payment. In this project, you will use Excel functions to show growth based on a moving average and show the break-even point for the business. You will also use Goal Seek to find the total loan amount for which the owner can apply.

DIRECTIONS

1. Start Excel, if necessary, and open **E67Apply** from the data files for this lesson.
2. Save the file as **E67Apply_xx** in the location where your teacher instructs you to store the files for this lesson.

3. For all worksheets, add a header that has your name at the left, the date code in the center, and the page number code at the right, and change back to **Normal** view.
4. Check that the Data Analysis command is on the DATA tab, and enable the Analysis ToolPak, if necessary.

5. On the **Moving Average** worksheet tab, redo the moving average calculations in column B to change the interval from **7** data points to **5** data points, and create a line chart showing the moving average.

    ✓ *You can delete the function from cells B3:B6 when finished; they show an #N/A error rather than a value. This is expected.*

6. On the **Growth** worksheet tab, in the cell range **B19:B33**, use the **GROWTH** function to use 5 days to predict future growth based on the moving averages in the cell range **B2:B16**.

    ✓ *You can delete the function from B30:B33 when finished; they show a #VALUE error rather than a value. This is expected.*

7. On the **Break-Even** worksheet tab, fill in the **Cost**, **Revenue**, and **Profit** columns (the cell range **B6:D105**) with formulas that include absolute references to cells **B1, B2**, and **B3**.

8. Create a **Stacked Line** chart from the cell range **B5:D105** showing the break-even point.

9. On the **Goal Seek** worksheet tab, use the Goal Seek feature to find the loan amount of a monthly payment of **$250** for 5 years at an interest rate of 8.50%.

10. **With your teacher's permission**, print the charts from the **Moving Average** and **Break-Even** worksheets. Your charts should look like the ones shown in Figure 67-2.

11. Save and close the file, and exit Excel.

Figure 67-2

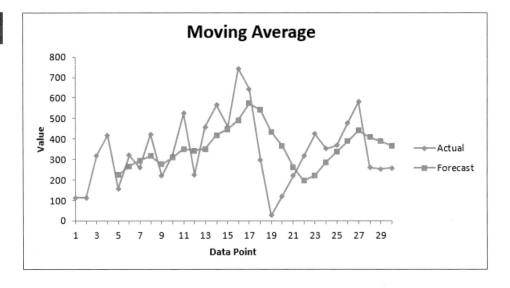

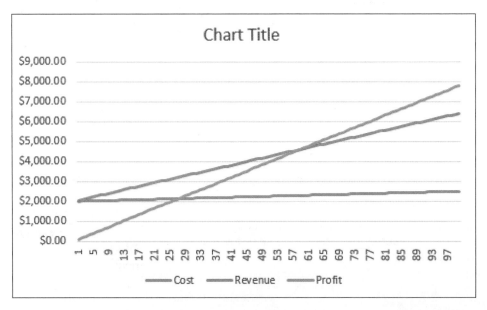

Lesson 68

Creating Scenarios and Naming Ranges

➤ What You Will Learn

Creating a Scenario Using the Scenario Manager
Naming a Range
Creating a Scenario Summary

Software Skills   With scenarios, you can create and save several versions of
a worksheet based on "what-if" data. For example, you can create a best case,
probable case, and worst case scenario for your company's annual sales. After you
create your scenarios, you can use Scenario Manager to print the various versions
of your data quickly.

What You Can Do

Creating a Scenario Using the Scenario Manager

- **Scenarios** help you see possible outcomes of an unpredictable future.
- You can create and save versions of your worksheet data based on changing
  variables.
- With the **Scenario Manager** in Excel, you can plug in the most likely values for
  several possible situations, and save the scenarios with the resulting worksheet
  data.
- Access the Scenario Manager from the What-If Analysis button in the Data Tools
  group on the DATA tab.
- You can print and compare scenarios, save them, and switch between them.
- When you switch to a particular scenario, Excel plugs the saved values into the
  appropriate cells in your worksheet that represent variables and then adjusts
  formula results as needed.

Try It!   Creating a Scenario Using the Scenario Manager

1 Start Excel, and open **E68Try** from the data files for this lesson.

2 Save the file as **E68Try_xx** in the location where your teacher instructs you to store the files for this lesson.

3 Examine the formulas in cells B9:D13 to see how the bike cost data was determined.

✓ *Notice that named ranges have been defined for cells B2 and B3, and the names are used in the formulas in the cell range B9:D9.*

4 Click DATA > What-If Analysis 🔲❓ > Scenario Manager.

5 Click Add to display the Add Scenario dialog box.

6 In the Scenario name text box, type **Worst Case**.

7 In the Changing cells box, type **B2:B3**.

8 In the Comment section, type **Worst case scenario**, replacing the default comment.

✓ *These are the cells where you will change the input data that causes the scenario to change the value in the results cells. If the hourly rate goes up, then the cost of modifying the bikes goes up.*

9 Click OK to display the Scenario Values dialog box with the current contents of cells B2 and B3.

10 In the 1: Hourly_labor_cost field, type **58**.

11 In the 2: Material_and_supplies_cost field, type **75**.

12 Click OK to display the Scenario Manager dialog box.

13 Click Show to see the results of the change.

✓ *Notice the negative profit.*

14 Add two more scenarios the same way, viewing each scenario's result after creating it:

■ Add a Most Likely Case in which the Hourly_labor_cost is 45 and the Material_and_supplies cost is 57.

■ Add a Best Case scenario in which the Hourly_labor_cost is 37 and the Material_and_supplies cost is 52.

15 Click Close to close the Scenario Manager dialog box.

16 Save the changes to the file, and leave it open to use in the next Try It.

Specifying the scenario's name and
the cells that will change

Specifying the scenario values to use in
the cells that will change

Naming a Range

- It is sometimes helpful to give ranges descriptive names.
- A range can be a single cell or multiple cells.
- When a range has a name, you can use the name in formulas and functions in place of the row-and-column cell references.

- You can manually name each range by typing in the Name box on the formula bar, or you can use the naming tools on the FORMULAS tab.
- For example, to name cells based on the labels in adjacent cells, you can use Create from Selection.

Try It!   **Naming Ranges**

1. In the **E68Try_xx** file, select cell B13.

2. On the far-left end of the formula bar, click in the Name box, type **Beach_cruzer_profit**, and press ENTER.

   ✓ *You can use the sizing tool on the formula bar to view the entire name of the range.*

   Name the selected range

   The Name box   The Sizing tool

3. Click cell C13, click in the Name box, type **Off_road_profit**, and press ENTER.

4. Click cell D13 click in the Name box, type **Iron_man_profit**, and press ENTER.

5. Select the cell range A15:B15.

6. Click FORMULAS > Create from Selection ▥.

7. Select the Left Column check box, if necessary, and click OK to assign the name Total_Profit to cell B15.

8. Save the changes to the file, and leave it open to use in the next Try It.

Creating a Scenario Summary

- If you have created many scenarios on many different sheets, the best way to view the multiple results is to create a summary sheet of all your scenarios.

- You can create a scenario summary as a worksheet or as a PivotTable.

Try It!   **Creating a Scenario Summary**

1. In the **E68Try_xx** file, click DATA > What-If Analysis ▦ > Scenario Manager to display the Scenario Manager dialog box.

2. Click Summary to display the Scenario Summary dialog box.

3. In the Result cells box, type **B13,C13,D13,B15**.

Create the scenario summary

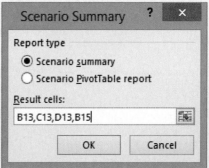

(continued)

Try It!   Creating a Scenario Summary (continued)

4 Click OK.

✓ *A comparison summary chart appears on a new tab.
You can view each scenario and analyze the numbers to
help you decide what business decisions to make. Your
summary report may look like this example.*

5 Save and close the file, and exit Excel.

Scenario Summary

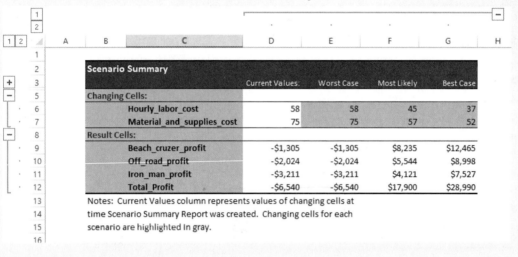

Scenario Summary		Current Values:	Worst Case	Most Likely	Best Case
Changing Cells:					
Hourly_labor_cost		58	58	45	37
Material_and_supplies_cost		75	75	57	52
Result Cells:					
Beach_cruzer_profit		-$1,305	-$1,305	$8,235	$12,465
Off_road_profit		-$2,024	-$2,024	$5,544	$8,998
Iron_man_profit		-$3,211	-$3,211	$4,121	$7,527
Total_Profit		-$6,540	-$6,540	$17,900	$28,990

Notes: Current Values column represents values of changing cells at
time Scenario Summary Report was created. Changing cells for each
scenario are highlighted In gray.

Lesson 68—Practice

You are the owner of a theater company called The Back Street Players. Your customers have been complaining of the high ticket prices. You are considering changing the ticket prices for an upcoming show. You want to use Excel to compare the ticket price scenarios to help you compare the profit and make your decision. In this project, you will define named ranges and use them to create scenarios.

DIRECTIONS

1. Start Excel, if necessary, and open **E68Practice** from the data files for this lesson.

2. Save the file as **E68Practice_xx** in the location where your teacher instructs you to store the files for this lesson.

3. Add a header that has your name at the left, the date code in the center, and the page number code at the right, and change back to **Normal** view.

4. On the **Glass Menagerie** worksheet, select the cell range **B6:C11**, and click **FORMULAS > Create from Selection** 🖳.

5. Check that the **Left Column** check box is selected, and click **OK**. Names are assigned to cells C6:C11.

6. Select range **F6:G7**, and click **FORMULAS > Create from Selection** 🖳.

7. Check that the **Left Column** check box is selected, and click **OK**.

8. Click **DATA > What-If Analysis** 🔢 **> Scenario Manager**.

9. Click **Add**.

10. In the Add Scenario dialog box, in the Scenario Name box, type **Scenario 1**.

11. In the Changing cells text box, type **C6:C11,E5,G6:G7**.

12. Click **OK**. If you see a warning that at least one of the changing cells has a formula in it, click **OK**.

13. In the Scenario Values dialog box, click **OK** to accept the existing values as the scenario values.

14. Click **Add** to start a new scenario.

15. In the Scenario Name box, type **Scenario 2**.

16. Click **OK**. If you see a warning that at least one of the changing cells has a formula in it, click **OK**.

17. In the Scenario Values dialog box, change the value of 5: Ticket_Price to **$9.00**, and click **OK**.

18. Click **Show** to show Scenario 2.

19. Click **Close** to close the Scenario Manager dialog box.

20. **With your teacher's permission**, print the selection **A2:H15**. Your worksheet should look like the one shown in Figure 68-1.

21. Save and close the file, and exit Excel.

Figure 68-1

	A	B	C	D	E	F	G	H	I
1									
2		The Back Street Players Presents							
3		*The Glass Menagerie*							
4									
5					*If the play is 85% sold out:*				
6		Costumes	$ 682.15		Tickets Sold		1207		
7		Scenery	$ 957.15		Ticket Price	$	9.00		
8		Theater Rental	$ 1,500.00		Revenue	$	10,863.00		
9		Electrician	$ 225.00						
10		Royalty fee	$ 1,350.00		Expenses	$	9,663.00		
11		Playbills	$ 4,948.70		Profit	$	1,200.00		
12									
13									
14		No. of Playbills Printed	1207						
15		Cost each to print	$ 4.10						
16									

Lesson 68—Apply

You are the owner of Breakaway Bike Shop, and you are raising your labor charges in January. A customer of Breakaway Bike Shop is in a dilemma about some bike work he would like to have done. Some work is needed right away, while other parts that are showing wear could conceivably be put off until after the winter holidays. The customer needs help deciding among several scenarios—doing some of the work now and putting off the rest indefinitely, doing all of the work now, or waiting until after the winter holidays to do the work. In this project, you will use scenarios to create the reports he needs to compare the costs and make his decision.

DIRECTIONS

1. Start Excel, if necessary, and open **E68Apply** from the data files for this lesson.

2. Save the file as **E68Apply_xx** in the location where your teacher instructs you to store the files for this lesson.

3. Create a scenario called **Minimum Replacements** in which the values in the following ranges are saved as they currently appear:
   - B26:F26
   - B28:F28
   - B37:F38
   - G3

4. Create another scenario called **Recommended Replacements** in which these values change.
   - B26   RPL
   - C26   2
   - D26   Aurens BR321
   - E26   1
   - F26   39.25
   - B28   RPL
   - C28   2
   - D28   Aurens BI321
   - E28   .10
   - F28   4.95
   - B37   RPL
   - C37   1

   - D37   Road Warrior 18F
   - E37   .15
   - F37   25.75
   - B38   RPL
   - C38   1
   - D38   Road Warrior 18R
   - E38   .25
   - F38   28.95

   ✓ Leave the value in G3 as it currently appears.

5. Create another scenario called **All Work After January** that is identical to the Recommended Replacements scenario from step 4 except that the value of cell **G3** changes to **50.00**.

   ✓ The simplest way to accomplish this is to first display the changed values in the worksheet. Use the Scenario Manager to display the values associated with the Recommended Replacements scenario. Then create the new scenario, and the only value you have to edit is G3.

6. Create a summary report with **G3** as the result cell.

7. For all worksheets, add a custom header that has your name at the left, the date code in the center, and the page number code at the right, and change back to **Normal** view.

8. **With your teacher's permission**, print the **Scenario Summary** worksheet. Your worksheet should look like the one shown in Figure 68-2 on the next page.

9. Save and close the file, and exit Excel.

Figure 68-2

		Current Values:	Minimum Replacements	Recommended Replacements	All Work After January
Scenario Summary					
Changing Cells:					
$B$26	RPL		N/A	RPL	RPL
$C$26		2			2	2
$D$26	Aurens BR321			Aurens BR321	Aurens BR321
$E$26		1.00			1.00	1.00
$F$26		$39.25			$39.25	$39.25
$B$28	RPL		N/A	RPL	RPL
$C$28		2			2	2
$D$28	Aurens BI321			Aurens BI321	Aurens BI321
$E$28		0.10			0.10	0.10
$F$28		$4.95			$4.95	$4.95
$B$37	RPL		OK	RPL	RPL
$C$37		1			1	1
$D$37	Road Warrior 18F			Road Warrior 18F	Road Warrior 18F
$E$37		0.15			0.15	0.15
$F$37		$25.75			$25.75	$25.75
$B$38	RPL		RPL	RPL	RPL
$C$38		1	1	1	1
$D$38	Road Warrior 18R			Road Warrior 18R	Road Warrior 18R
$E$38		0.25			0.25	0.25
$F$38		$28.95			$28.95	$28.95
$G$3		$40.00	$40.00	$40.00	$50.00
Result Cells:					
$G$3		$40.00	$40.00	$40.00	$50.00

Notes: Current Values column represents values of changing cells at
time Scenario Summary Report was created. Changing cells for each
scenario are highlighted in gray.

Lesson 69

Finding and Fixing Errors in Formulas

> ## ➤ **What You Will Learn**
>
> Using Formula Error Checking
> Understanding Error Messages
> Showing Formulas
> Evaluating Individual Formulas
> Using the Watch Window
> Tracing Precedents and Dependents

WORDS TO KNOW

Dependents
Formulas whose results depend on the value in a cell.

Evaluate
To view the intermediate results step-by-step, as Excel solves a formula.

Error Checking
An information button on a cell. Error Checking options can contain information about an error in the cell contents.

Precedent
A cell referenced in a formula.

Watch Window
A floating window that allows you to watch the results of formulas change as you change data.

Software Skills   If you have a problem with formulas in a large or complex worksheet, working through each formula to locate the values in the cells it references and to verify that everything is all right can be a tedious, complex job unless you use Excel's error and formula auditing features.

What You Can Do

Using Formula Error Checking

- When background error checking is enabled in Excel, a small triangle in the upper-left corner of a cell indicates a possible error. When you select the cell, an **Error Checking** button appears. Click the Error Checking button to see a message explaining what the potential error is. See Figure 69-1 on the next page.

  ✓ *If errors do not appear in Error Checking options, the feature may not be enabled. Click FILE > Options > Formulas, and select the Enable background error checking check box.*

- Excel checks for the following errors:
  - Formulas that result in an error value, such as #DIV/0.
  - Formulas containing a text date entered using a two-digit year, such as =YEAR("02/20/27"), because it is not clear which century is being referenced.
  - Numbers stored as text rather than actual numbers, because this can cause sorting and other errors.
  - Formulas that are inconsistent with formulas in surrounding cells.

- For example, if Excel notices the pattern =SUM(A2:A10), =SUM(B2:B10) in two adjacent cells, and then sees the formula =SUM(C2:C4) in another adjacent cell, it will flag it as a possible mistake because it doesn't fit the pattern of the other formulas.
- Formulas that omit adjacent cells, as in Figure 69-1.
- An unprotected formula, if worksheet protection is enabled.

    ✓ *If you turn on worksheet protection, all cells are protected against changes by default. You can selectively unprotect the cells you want to allow others to enter data into. However, if you unprotect a cell with a formula, Excel will see that as a possible error, because it's unusual that you would want someone else to change your formulas.*

- A formula that refers to empty cells.
- Invalid data entered into a cell.
- An inconsistent formula in a calculated table column.

■ When you find an error in a formula, one way in which you might need to correct it is to change the cell(s) that the formula references. For example, you might need to change the formula =SUM(D2:D10) so that it reads =SUM(D2:D12).

■ When you click a cell with a formula, and then click in the formula bar, the cells referenced by the formula are outlined with colored borders. You can drag these colored borders and drop them on different cells, in order to change the cells used in the formula. You can also resize a colored border to make the formula reference more or fewer cells in that range.

Understanding Error Messages

■ The following is a list of some error messages you might get if you enter data or formulas incorrectly:

- **####** The cell contains an entry that's wider than the cell can display. In most cases, you can just widen the column to correct the problem.
- **#VALUE!** The wrong type of data was used in a formula. Possible causes are entering text when a formula requires a number or logical value, or entering a range in a formula or function that requires a single value.
- **#DIV/0!** A formula is attempting to divide a value by zero. For example, if the value in cell B5 in the formula =A5/B5 is zero, or if cell B5 is empty, the result will be the #DIV/0! error.
- **#NAME?** Excel doesn't recognize text in the formula. Possible causes include a misspelling or using a nonexistent range name, using a label in a formula if the Accept labels in formulas option is turned off, or omitting a colon (:) in a range reference.

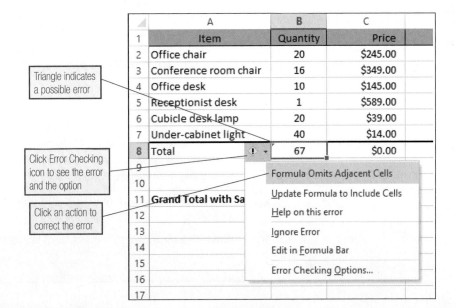

Triangle indicates a possible error

Click Error Checking icon to see the error and the option

Click an action to correct the error

Figure 69-1

- **#N/A** No value is available to the formula or function. Possible causes include omitting a required argument in a formula or function or entering an invalid argument in a formula or function.
- **#REF!** A cell reference is invalid. Possible causes include deleting cells referred to by formulas.
- **#NUM** Indicates a problem with a number in a formula or function. Possible causes include using a nonnumeric argument in a function that requires a numeric argument, or entering a formula that produces a number too large or too small for Excel to represent.
- **#NULL!** The formula contains incorrect operators or cell references using ranges in formulas. For example, if you left the comma out of the following formula, a #NULL! error would occur: SUM(A1:A6,C1:C6).

- A circular reference is a special kind of error that's caused when a formula references itself. For example, if you're adding the values of a group of cells and include the cell that contains the formula, you are creating an endless loop, which generates a circular reference error.
- When a circular reference occurs, an error message appears, followed by a Help screen filled with tips to help you correct the error.
- Until you correct a circular reference, the status bar displays the words "CIRCULAR REFERENCES" and if the worksheet with the error is displayed, the address of the cell(s) with the Circular Reference error appears after "CIRCULAR REFERENCES" in the status bar.
- You can also locate any cell(s) that contain circular references by using the Circular References option on the Error Checking button on the FORMULAS tab.

Try It!   Correcting Formula Errors

1 Start Excel, and open **E69Try** from the data files for this lesson. If you see a circular reference warning, click OK.

2 Save the file as **E69Try_xx** in the location where your teacher instructs you to store the files for this lesson.

3 On the Office Items worksheet, click cell B8. An Error Checking shortcut button appears to the left.

4 Click the Error Checking shortcut button ◈.

5 Click Update Formula to Include Cells.

6 Click FORMULAS > Error Checking ◈. The Error Checking dialog box displays to point out the error in C8.

7 Click Copy Formula from Left.

8 Click OK to confirm that error checking is complete.

9 Apply the Accounting Format to cell C8.

10 Use Format Painter to copy the formatting from C8 to D8.

11 Click the Sales Tax worksheet tab.

12 Click cell B12 > Error Checking shortcut button ◈.

13 Click Convert XX to 20XX.

14 Examine the formulas in column D to figure out why there is such a large value in cell D3 and zero values in the cell range D4:D7.

✓ *The formula for calculating tax is correct in cell D2. However, the formula was filled down with relative references instead of absolute references. Every row needs to reference the sales tax rate in cell B11. Fix this by making cells D2:D7 have an absolute reference to B11.*

15 Change the formula in cell D2 to **=B2*C2*$B$11**.

✓ *Instead of retyping the formula in cell D2, you could click in the B11 reference in the formula bar, and press F4 to cycle through the relative/absolute reference combinations until you arrive at $B$11.*

16 Copy the formula in cell D2 to the cell range D3:D7.

17 Save the changes to the file, and leave it open to use in the next Try It.

Showing Formulas

■ Sometimes it can be helpful to view the actual formulas in the cells, rather than the formula results. To do this, you can either press `CTRL` + `` ` `` (the accent mark above the Tab key, not an apostrophe) or you can click FORMULAS > Show Formulas. Repeat the command to switch back to viewing the worksheet normally.

Try It!   Showing Formulas

1 In the **E69Try_xx** file, click FORMULAS > Show Formulas 🗺 to display the formulas.

2 Click Show Formulas 🗺 again to toggle the feature off.

3 Save the changes to the file, and leave it open to use in the next Try It.

Evaluating Individual Formulas

■ When a formula has multiple calculations in it, it can be helpful to **evaluate** each part of the formula step by step.

■ You can access the Evaluate Formula command in the Formula Auditing group on the FORMULAS tab.

Try It!   Evaluating a Formula

1 In the **E69Try_xx** file, click the Sales Tax worksheet tab, if necessary.

2 Click cell E2.

3 Click FORMULAS > Evaluate Formula ⓐ. The Evaluate Formula dialog box opens, showing the following:

(**B2***C2)+D2

4 Click Evaluate. The value of the first reference appears in italic, and the second reference is underlined:

(20***C2**)+D2

5 Click Evaluate. The value of the second reference appears in italic, and the portion of the formula that is in parentheses is underlined:

(*20*245*)+D2

6 Click Evaluate. The portion of the formula in parentheses is calculated:

(***4900***)+D2

7 Click Evaluate. The parentheses are removed and D2 becomes underlined:

4900+**D2**

8 Click Evaluate. The value of D2 appears:

4900+416.5

9 Click Evaluate. The final result of the formula appears:

$5,316.50

10 Click Close.

11 Save the changes to the file, and leave it open to use in the next Try It.

Using the Watch Window

- Using the **Watch Window**, you can watch the results of your formulas change as you change other data, even if that formula is located in a cell that's out of view, on another worksheet, or located in another open workbook.

- You can watch multiple cells and their formulas.
- Access the Watch Window command in the Formula Auditing group on the FORMULAS tab.

Try It!   Using the Watch Window

1. In the **E69Try_xx** file, on the FORMULAS tab, click Watch Window 🖼.

2. Click Add Watch.

3. On the Sales Tax worksheet, select cell E3. An absolute reference to that cell appears in the Add Watch dialog box.

4. Click Add. The cell reference appears in the Watch Window.

5. Change the value in cell B3 to **20**, and press `ENTER` . Notice that the result for E3 changes in the Watch Window.

6. Change the value in cell B3 back to **16**.

7. Click the **E69Try_xx** watch item in the Watch Window to select it.

8. Click Delete Watch to remove the watch.

9. Close the Watch Window.

10. Save the changes to the file, and leave it open to use in the next Try It.

Tracing Precedents and Dependents

- With the Trace Precedents button, you can trace a formula's **precedents**—cells referred to by the formula. This can help you find and fix errors that have to do with wrong cell references.

- If you are concerned about changing the value in a cell, you can trace its **dependents** with the Trace Dependents button. A dependent is a cell whose value depends on the value in another cell.
- When you trace precedents or dependents, arrows point to the related cells.

Try It!   Tracing Precedents and Dependents

1. In the **E69Try_xx** file, click the Office Items worksheet tab.

2. Click cell D2.

3. On the FORMULAS tab, in the Formula Auditing group, click Trace Precedents 🔷. A line appears from cells B2 through D2 with blue dots in each field that contributes to the value in D2.

4. Click Remove Arrows 🔍.

5. Click cell D5 > Trace Precedents 🔷. Lines appear that show cell D5's precedents.

6. Click Trace Dependents 🔷. A line appears that shows cell D5's dependents.

7. Click Remove Arrows 🔍.

8. Save and close the file, and exit Excel.

Lesson 69—Practice

It looks like the sale of your old building and the purchase of a new headquarters for the Wood Hills Animal Clinic is going to go through. Before you can get final approval for your loan, however, you must prepare a balance sheet and a profit and loss statement. You've been working on the profit and loss statement, and there's just something wrong with the numbers. Your hope is that Excel's powerful formula auditing tools can help you sort out the problem.

DIRECTIONS

1. Start Excel, if necessary, and open **E69Practice** from the data files for this lesson. Click OK if the file opens with a warning notice about a circular error.

2. Save the file as **E69Practice_xx** in the location where your teacher instructs you to store the files for this lesson.

3. For all worksheets, add a header that has your name at the left, the date code in the center, and the page number code at the right, and change back to **Normal** view.

4. Look over the data on both worksheet tabs to see areas where there might be errors in formulas because data is missing or data doesn't look as expected.

   ✓ *Notice that when you are on the Balance Sheet worksheet, the status bar shows there is a circular reference, but no cell reference is given. Move to the P&L worksheet. Notice that the status bar now shows there is a circular reference in cell E57.*

5. In the **P&L** worksheet, click cell **E57**. The formula in this cell is =SUM(E32,E43,E56,E57).

6. Edit this circular reference error by removing **E57** from the formula. The new formula should read =SUM(E32,E43,E56).

   ✓ *Be sure to remove the last comma. If not, you will receive an error message.*

7. Click cell **E64**, and view the formula in the formula bar.

   ✓ *Cell E64 should have a calculation in it to show the earnings per share of common stock. The formula to calculate earnings per share of common stock is to divide net income by common stock shares outstanding. However, the current formula in cell E64 references E62, a blank cell.*

8. Edit this reference error by changing E62 in the formula to **E61**.

9. **With your teacher's permission**, print both worksheets.

10. Save and close the file, and exit Excel.

Lesson 69—Apply

You are the owner of Old Southern Furniture. You want to use Excel to create formulas to calculate the commission, bonuses, and earnings for each of your salespeople. Then, you want to use Excel's formula auditing tools to help ensure that your formulas are accurate and valid.

DIRECTIONS

1. Start Excel, if necessary, and open **E69Apply** from, the data files for this lesson.

2. Save the file as **E69Apply_xx** in the location where your teacher instructs you to store the files for this lesson.

3. Add a header that has your name at the left, the date code in the center, and the page number code at the right, and change back to **Normal** view.

4. Create formulas that calculate the commission and bonuses for each salesperson.

   a. In cell **C13**, create a formula that multiplies cell **B13** by an absolute reference to cell **B9**.

   b. Copy the formula from cell **C13** to the cell range **C14:C24**.

   c. In cell **D13**, use an **IF** function to show the value of cell **B10** if the value of cell **B13** is greater than **$40,000,** and otherwise to show **$0**. Refer to B10 with an absolute reference.

   d. Copy the formula from cell **D13** to the cell range **D14:D24**.

   e. Use **Format Painter** to copy the formatting from cell **C13** to the cell range **D13:D24**.

5. Create formulas that calculate the total earnings, which is the total of commissions and bonuses.

   a. In cell **E13**, use a **SUM** function to add to the cell range **B13:D13**.

   b. Copy the function from cell **E13** to the cell range **E14:E24**.

6. Click any cell in the **Comm.** column, and trace the precedents. Remove the arrows.

7. Click any cell in the **Bonus** column, and trace the precedents. Remove the arrows.

8. Click any cell in the **Total Earnings** column, and trace the precedents. Remove the arrows.

9. In cell **B9**, type **0.06**, and in cell **B10**, type **$200**. Apply the **Percentage** format, zero decimal places, to cell **B9**.

10. Click cell **B9** and trace its dependents. Remove the arrows.

11. Click cell **B10** and trace its dependents. Remove the arrows.

12. Click any cell in the **Sales** column, and trace its dependents. Remove the arrows.

13. Evaluate a formula in column B.

14. Show the formulas in all cells. Adjust column widths as necessary so that all formulas are fully visible and the worksheet fits on a single page across.

15. **With your teacher's permission**, print the cell range **A9:E24** with the formulas showing. Your worksheet should look like the one shown in Figure 69-2 on the next page.

16. Return to viewing formula results in the cells, and readjust column widths as needed.

17. Save and close the file, and exit Excel.

Figure 69-2

	A	B	C	D	E
1					
2					
3					
4					
5		Old Southern Fur			
6		Biweekly Earnings Review			
7		41640			
8					
9	Commission Rate	0.06			
10	Bonus on sales over $40K	200			
11					
12	Salesperson	Sales	Comm.	Bonus	Total Earnings
13	Carl Jackson	44202	=B13*$B$9	=IF(B13>40000,$B$10,0)	=SUM(B13:D13)
14	Ni Li Yung	41524	=B14*$B$9	=IF(B14>40000,$B$10,0)	=SUM(B14:D14)
15	Tom Wilson	43574	=B15*$B$9	=IF(B15>40000,$B$10,0)	=SUM(B15:D15)
16	Jill Palmer	39612	=B16*$B$9	=IF(B16>40000,$B$10,0)	=SUM(B16:D16)
17	Rita Nuez	39061	=B17*$B$9	=IF(B17>40000,$B$10,0)	=SUM(B17:D17)
18	Maureen Baker	38893	=B18*$B$9	=IF(B18>40000,$B$10,0)	=SUM(B18:D18)
19	Kim Cheng	31120	=B19*$B$9	=IF(B19>40000,$B$10,0)	=SUM(B19:D19)
20	Lloyd Hamilton	41922	=B20*$B$9	=IF(B20>40000,$B$10,0)	=SUM(B20:D20)
21	Ed Fulton	45609	=B21*$B$9	=IF(B21>40000,$B$10,0)	=SUM(B21:D21)
22	Maria Alvarez	30952	=B22*$B$9	=IF(B22>40000,$B$10,0)	=SUM(B22:D22)
23	Katie Wilson	31472	=B23*$B$9	=IF(B23>40000,$B$10,0)	=SUM(B23:D23)
24	Tim Brown	44783	=B24*$B$9	=IF(B24>40000,$B$10,0)	=SUM(B24:D24)
25					
26					

End-of-Chapter Activities

➤ Excel Chapter 8—Critical Thinking

Analyzing a Business Opportunity

You are interested in purchasing a business, and you want to analyze the financial numbers of the business from the past two years to see if it is a profitable, growing company. You will analyze the raw data that the current owner has provided to make sure the business would be a good investment.

If you do purchase the business, you will need to get a small business loan. You are considering two different loans, each with different terms. You will use what you know about financial functions to determine which loan is a better deal.

DIRECTIONS

1. Start Excel, if necessary, and open **ECT08** from the data files for this chapter.

2. Save the file as **ECT08_xx** in the location where your teacher instructs you to store the files for this chapter.

3. On the **Expenses** worksheet, in cell **G5**, create a **SUMIF** function that sums the values from **D5:D124** where "Facility Rental" appears in column C.

4. Enter the appropriate **SUMIF** functions in columns **G** and **I** that summarize the data in the ways described by the labels in columns **F** and **H**. Illustration 8A shows the totals that should appear in the cells when the functions are correctly created.

   ✓ If you apply absolute references to all the cells in the function in G5, it makes it easier to copy and paste the function into other cells and then modify the copies to meet the new criteria. For example, you can copy the function into G6 and change Facility Rental to Loan Payment.

5. On the **Summary** tab, examine the **SUMIFS** functions in cells **C5** and **D5**.

   ✓ Notice that in both functions, the date Jan-13 is being referenced as a general number: 40179. To determine the numeric equivalent of a date, temporarily set the cell's number format to General.

6. Using C5 and D5 as examples, complete the rest of the functions for the cell range **C6:D28**.

   ✓ Because the cell references are absolute, you can copy and paste the functions from cells C5 and D5 into the remaining cells, and then edit each copy.

   ✓ You may want to set all the dates in column A temporarily to General format to make it easier to see what numbers to use for the dates. Don't forget to set them back to the custom Date format of MMM-YY when you are finished.

   ✓ Another shortcut: after completing column C's functions, copy them to column D, and use Find and Replace to replace all instances of "Fixed" with "Variable."

7. Copy the formula from cell **E5** to the cell range **E6:E28**.

8. Create a line chart from the values in column **E**, using the dates in column **A** as labels. Display the legend.

9. Add an exponential trend line to the chart.

10. Place the chart on its own sheet in the workbook. Name the sheet **Net Profit**.

    ✓ To place the chart on its own sheet, right-click the chart border and click Move Chart.

11. On the **Loans** sheet, use the **PMT** function to calculate the monthly payments on two different loans, both for **$2 million**:

    Loan 1: **6% APR for 60 months**
    Loan 2: **5% APR for 48 months**

12. On the **Loans** worksheet, in cell **B10**, create a formula that evaluates whether the amount in cell B9 is less than the smallest value in column **E** of the **Summary** worksheet (hint: use the =MIN function). If it is less, display **OK**. If it is not less, display **No**. Copy the formula to cell **C10**, changing any cell references as needed.

13. Create a scenario for the current values on the **Loans** sheet, with cell **B4** as the changing cell. Name the scenario **2 Million Loan**.

14. Create another scenario in which the loan amount is $2,500,000. Name it **2.5 Million Loan**. Show the **2.5 Million Loan** scenario, then show the **2 Million Loan** scenario.

15. For all worksheets, add a header that has your name at the left, the date code in the center, and the page number code at the right, and change back to **Normal** view.

16. **With your teacher's permission**, print the **Loans** worksheet and the **Net Profit** chart.

17. Save and close the file, and exit Excel.

Illustration 8A

2-Year Total of Expenses		2-Year Total Expenses by Type	
Facility Rental	$19,200	Fixed	$48,000
Loan Payment	$28,800	Variable	$6,268,911
Materials	$5,567,857		
Payroll	$694,826	**2013 Expenses by Type**	
Utilities	$6,228	Fixed	$24,000
		Variable	$2,642,102
2013 Expenses			
Facility Rental	$9,600	**2014 Expenses by Type**	
Loan Payment	$14,400	Fixed	$24,000
Materials	$2,344,531	Variable	$3,626,809
Payroll	$294,522		
Utilities	$3,049		
2014 Expenses			
Facility Rental	$9,600		
Loan Payment	$14,400		
Materials	$3,223,326		
Payroll	$400,304		
Utilities	$3,179		

➤ Excel Chapter 8—Portfolio Builder

Projecting Business Scenarios

The purchase of the business seems to be a good decision. However, the net profit per month seems to fluctuate quite a bit, making it difficult to predict how much money you can safely borrow to purchase the business. You can be more confident by calculating a moving average of the monthly profits, and by setting up several scenarios with varying degrees of optimism, ranging from worst case to best case.

DIRECTIONS

1. Start Excel, if necessary, and open **EPB08** from the data files for this chapter.

2. Save the file as **EPB08_xx** in the location where your teacher instructs you to store the files for this chapter.

3. On the **Summary** worksheet, in the **F** column, create a 5-interval moving average of the values in the **E** column, and chart the output.

   ✓ *Enable the Analysis Toolpak Add-On, if necessary.*

4. Move the chart to its own sheet. Name the sheet **Profit Moving Average**.

5. On the **Summary** sheet, in the cell range **B29:B40**, use the **GROWTH** function to predict the future monthly gross revenues for 2015. Use the cell ranges for 2014 only in the **GROWTH** function arguments.

6. Copy the formula from cell **E28** to the cell range **E29:E40**.

7. In cell **C29**, enter **$1,500**. Copy that value to the cell range **C30:C40**.

8. In cell **D29**, enter **$370,000**. Copy that value to the cell range **D30:D40**.

9. Use **Format Painter** to copy the formatting from cell **B29** to the cell range **C29:E40**.

10. Type **$1,500** in cell **I29**. Enter **$200,000** in cell **I30**.

11. In cell **C29**, enter a formula that provides an absolute reference to **I29**.

12. In cell **D29**, enter a formula that provides an absolute reference to **I30**.

13. Copy the formulas from the cell range **C29:D29** to the cell range **C30:D40**.

14. Create a scenario called **Best Case** that allows **I29** and **I30** to change, and uses the current values of those cells.

15. Create another scenario called **Most Likely** that sets cell **I29** to **$1750** and cell **I30** to **$300,000**.

16. Create another scenario called **Worst Case** that sets cell **I29** to **$2000** and cell **I30** to **$400,000**.

17. Show the **Most Likely** scenario.

18. For all worksheets, add a header that has your name at the left, the date code in the center, and the page number code at the right, and change back to **Normal** view.

19. **With your instructor's permission**, print the range **A29:E40** on the **Summary** worksheet, and print the **Profit Moving Average** chart.

20. Save and close the file, and exit Excel.

Chapter 9

(Courtesy Goodluz/Shutterstock)

Importing and Analyzing Database Data

Lesson 70

Importing Data into Excel

➤ What You Will Learn

Importing Data from an Access Database
Importing Data from a Web Page
Importing Data from a Text File
Importing Data from an XML File

WORDS TO KNOW

Database
An organized collection of data. Database data is commonly organized by rows (records) and columns (fields).

Datasheet
In Access, a spreadsheet-like view of a table.

Delimited
Separated. A delimited text file, for example, uses consistent characters such as a tab or comma to separate data into columns.

Software Skills　You may want to use Excel to manipulate data that originates in other programs. Excel can import data from many sources, including Access, text files, Web pages, and XML files.

What You Can Do

Importing Data from an Access Database

■ You can import the data from an Access **database** table into Excel and then use the features of Excel to format the data, add calculations, create charts, and so on, to help you analyze the data in a meaningful way.

■ Access databases store data in **tables**.

■ A table is most commonly viewed in a **datasheet**, which is very much like an Excel worksheet. Each row in a datasheet represents a **record**, and each column represents a **field**. See Figure 70-1.

■ Once you import data from Access, you cannot use the undo command to undo the import. If you don't like the results, close the file without saving the changes.

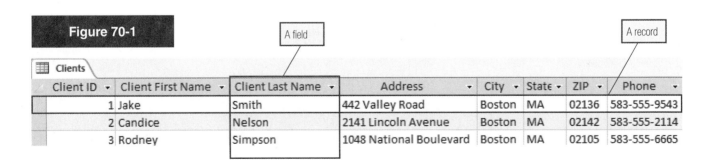

Figure 70-1

A field

A record

Clients							
Client ID ▾	Client First Name ▾	Client Last Name ▾	Address ▾	City ▾	State ▾	ZIP ▾	Phone ▾
1	Jake	Smith	442 Valley Road	Boston	MA	02136	583-555-9543
2	Candice	Nelson	2141 Lincoln Avenue	Boston	MA	02142	583-555-2114
3	Rodney	Simpson	1048 National Boulevard	Boston	MA	02105	583-555-6665

Try It!   **Importing Data from an Access Database**

❶ Start Excel, and open **E70TryA.xlsx** from the data files for this lesson.

❷ Save the file as **E70TryA_xx** in the location where your teacher instructs you to store the files for this lesson.

   ✓ The file has no data in it; however, notice that the tabs are named Access, Web, Text, and XML.

❸ Click cell A2. This is the location where you want to import the data.

❹ Click DATA > Get External Data > From Access ⬚. The Select Data Source dialog box opens.

   ✓ If the Excel window is wide enough, From Access appears as its own button, and you do not have to click Get External Data to see it.

❺ Navigate to the data files for this lesson, and click **E70TryB.accdb**.

The Import Data dialog box

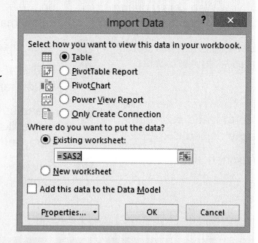

❻ Click Open to display the Import Data dialog box.

❼ Click OK to accept the default settings in the dialog box and =$A$2 as the start of the import range. Excel imports the data and formats it as a table.

❽ Save the changes to the file, and leave it open to use in the next Try It.

Delimiter character
In a delimited text file, the character that is used to separate columns. Tabs and commas are the most common.

Field
A single column in a database.

Markup language
A set of codes inserted into a text file to indicate the formatting and purpose of each block of text. HTML and XML are both markup languages.

Record
A single row in a database.

Table
In Access, a container for database records.

XML
Stands for EXtensible Markup Language. It is a markup language similar to HTML, but designed for use with databases rather than Web sites. XML is widely used for a variety of data storage and retrieval applications.

Importing Data from a Web Page

■ In Excel 2013, you can download data from Web pages with a few clicks. This process works best when the data being imported is already in a tabular format.

Try It!   **Importing Data from a Web Page**

❶ In the **E70TryA_xx** file, click the Web worksheet tab.

❷ Click cell A2. This is the location where you want to import the data.

❸ Open a Web browser, and navigate to **http://www.global-view.com/forex-trading-tools/chartpts.html**.

   ✓ If the URL provided is no longer available, explore other pages that include currency exchange tables that could be imported into Excel.

❹ On the main page, under Printer-Friendly Tables, click the USD hyperlink.

   ✓ USD stands for U.S. Dollars.

❺ In the Address bar in the Web browser, select the URL of the page, and press CTRL + C to copy it.

❻ Close the browser window.

(continued)

Try It!   Importing Data from a Web Page *(continued)*

7   Switch to Excel, and click DATA > Get External Data > From Web 📇. A New Web Query dialog box opens, with your default Web page showing.

> ✓ *If the Excel window is wide enough, From Web appears as its own button, and you do not have to click Get External Data to see it.*

8   In the Address bar of the New Web Query dialog box, click to select the current address, and press CTRL + V to paste the copied URL.

9   Click Go. The currency exchange page appears in the dialog box.

10   Click the yellow arrow to the left of the table's upper-left corner. The arrow turns to a green check mark and the table is selected.

11   Click Import. The Import Data dialog box opens.

12   Click OK to accept =$A$2 as the start of the import range. The data is imported.

13   Clean up the worksheet and format as you would like. For example, format cell A2 as a date, and adjust the column widths.

14   Save the changes to the file, and leave it open to use in the next Try It.

Selecting the table from which you want to import in the New Web Query dialog box

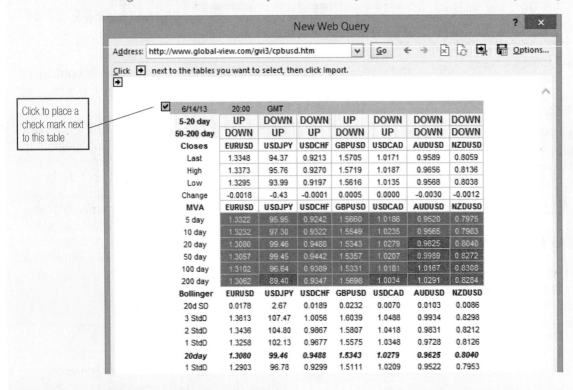

Importing Data from a Text File

- Plain text files can store **delimited** data by using a consistent **delimiter character**. For example, columns may be separated by either tabs or commas; rows are typically separated by paragraph breaks.

- Delimited text files typically have a .txt or .csv extension. CSV stands for comma-separated values.

Try It!   **Importing Data from a Text File**

1 In the **E70TryA_xx** file, click the Text worksheet tab.

2 Click cell A2. This is the location where you want to import the data.

3 Click DATA > Get External Data > From Text 📄. The Import Text File dialog box opens.

4 Navigate to and select **E70TryC.txt** file, and click Import. The Text Import Wizard runs.

5 Click Next to accept Delimited as the file type.

6 Click Next to accept Tab as the delimiter character.

7 On the Step 3 of 3 screen, click the second column heading (the dates), and click the Date option button.

8 Click Finish to complete the import. The Import Data dialog box opens.

9 Click OK to accept the entry range of =$A$2. The data is imported.

10 Save the changes to the file, and leave it open to use in the next Try It.

Importing Data from an XML File

- **XML** is a relative of HTML. Like HTML, it uses bracketed codes to indicate the formatting and function of each piece of data that the file contains. This is called a **markup language**.

- There may be times when data is in an XML file and you would like to analyze the data using the power of Excel. XML pages are typically viewed via a browser.

- There are two ways to import an XML file. You can use From Other Sources 📄 on the DATA tab, or you can click the DEVELOPER tab, and in the XML group, click Import 📄.

Try It!   **Importing Data from an XML File**

1 In the **E70TryA_xx** file, click the XML worksheet tab.

2 Click cell A2. This is the location where you want to import the data.

3 Select DATA > Get External Data > From Other Sources 📄.

4 Click From XML Data Import to open the Select Data Source dialog box.

5 Navigate to the data files for this lesson, and click **E70TryD.xml**.

6 Click Open.

7 In the confirmation box, click OK to confirm that Excel will create a schema for the data being imported.

8 In the Import Data dialog box, click OK to accept the location of $A$2. The data is imported.

9 Save and close the file, and exit Excel.

Lesson 70—Practice

A real estate broker at World Services Real Estate is working for a family from Europe interested in purchasing a second residence in the United States. As the broker's assistant, you have been asked to provide a worksheet with information about the consumer price index in the United States. In this project, you will import data from the Web on exchange rates that will help the real estate agent provide information for the family.

DIRECTIONS

1. Start Excel, if necessary, and open **E70Practice** from the data files for this lesson.

2. Save the file as **E70Practice_xx** in the location where your teacher instructs you to store the files for this lesson.

3. Add a header that has your name at the left, the date code in the center, and the page number code at the right, and change back to **Normal** view.

4. Open a browser, and go to **http://www.bls.gov/ news.release/cpi.t01.htm**, the Consumer Price Index Web page. Select the URL, and press `CTRL` + `C` to copy it to the Clipboard.

   ✓ If the URL provided is no longer available, explore other pages at www.bls.gov to find data that could be important to a real estate agent, and that can be imported into Excel.

5. Identify a table that contains consumer price index data.

6. Switch to Excel, and click **DATA** > **Get External Data** > **From Web**.

7. In the Address box of the New Web Query dialog box, press `CTRL` + `V` to paste the address copied in step 4. Alternatively, you can type **http://www.bls. gov/news.release/cpi.t01.htm** (or the address of another page you found on that site that contains appropriate data). Click **Go**.

8. If a Script Error dialog box appears, click **Yes** to continue running scripts on the page.

9. (Optional) Drag the border of the New Web Query dialog box to enlarge the window so you can see more of the page.

10. Click the yellow arrow to the left of the main table to select it. It changes to a green check mark.

11. Click **Import**. If a Script Error dialog box appears, click **Yes** to continue running scripts on the page

12. in the Import Data dialog box, in the Existing worksheet box, type =$A$2. The data appears in the worksheet.

13. Clean up and format the data where the data did not import perfectly. Refer to the Web page to see how it was formatted.

14. Save and close the file, and exit Excel.

Lesson 70—Apply

A real estate broker at World Services Real Estate was asked to prepare real estate data for a family from Europe interested in purchasing a second residence in the United States. In this project, you will create one workbook with several worksheets of data from various sources to help this client make a decision as to where to buy. You will also provide them with information about the consumer price index in the United States.

DIRECTIONS

1. Start Excel, if necessary, and open **E70ApplyA** from the data files for this lesson.

2. Save the file as **E70ApplyA_xx** in the location where your teacher instructs you to store the files for this lesson.

3. Add a header on all worksheets that has your name at the left, the date code in the center, and the page number code at the right, and change back to **Normal** view.

4. On the **Real Estate** worksheet, import the data as a table from the Access database file **E70ApplyB.accdb**, starting in cell A3.

   ✓ That database contains only one table, so you are not prompted to choose which table the data is coming from.

5. Format the list prices with the **Accounting** format, with no decimal places. Adjust the list price column width.

6. Sort the data by the highest list price to the lowest list price. Look at the common characteristics of the houses at the top of the list.

7. Copy the entire table to the **Bedrooms** tab, and sort the data based on the number of bedrooms, from most to fewest. Adjust the column widths, as necessary.

8. **With your teacher's permission,** print only the first page of the **Bedrooms** worksheet.

9. Save and close the file, and exit Excel.

Lesson 71

Working with Excel Tables

➤ **What You Will Learn**

Converting Ranges to Tables
Showing a Totals Row in a Table
Viewing Two Tables Side-by-Side
Applying Icon Sets

WORDS TO KNOW

Banded columns
Alternating colors in
columns in a table.

Banded rows
Alternating colors in rows
in a table.

Filter
To reduce the number of
records displayed on the
screen by applying one or
more criteria.

Icon Sets
Icons that are placed in a
cell based on the value of
the cell.

Table
In Excel, a range of cells
in a datasheet that have
been grouped together
into a single unit for
formatting and data
analysis.

Software Skills   You can create a table in Excel to sort, filter, and analyze data.
A worksheet can have multiple tables, and placing tables side by side is a good
way to compare data quickly. Putting the two tables on one worksheet, rather than
on separate worksheets, lets the user filter and compare data on a single sheet.
Icons can be placed in cells to visually represent criteria of the data in the cell. For
example, colored dots can represent a high value, medium value, or low value.

What You Can Do

Converting Ranges to Tables

- Worksheet ranges can be turned into **tables** for easy analysis. A table can easily
  be sorted and **filtered** via the drop-down lists associated with each column
  heading.

- A table also offers visually pleasing formatting with **banded rows** or **banded
  columns**. The alternating lighter and darker colors make it easy to follow data
  across a row, or down a column, increasing the accuracy of your work. See
  Figure 71-1 on the next page.

- Banding is added by default when you create a table out of a data range that
  does not have previously existing fill applied to it. The worksheets in the Try It
  exercises in this lesson already have background fill, so you will not see banding
  applied when you create the tables.

- To add or remove banding, use the Banded Rows command on the TABLE
  TOOLS DESIGN tab.

- Multiple ranges in a worksheet can be converted into separate tables.

  ✓ *When inserting two tables on the same worksheet, there must be at least one row or one column
    between the data ranges in order for Excel to know that the data will be treated as two tables.*

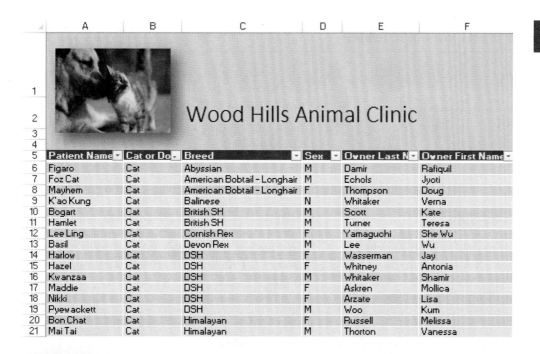

Figure 71-1

Try It!   Converting Ranges to Tables

1 Start Excel, and open **E71Try** from the data files for this lesson.

2 Save the file as **E71Try_xx** in the location where your teacher instructs you to store the files for this lesson.

3 Click the July 22 worksheet tab to select it, if necessary.

4 Select the cell range A6:D23.

5 Click INSERT > Table.

6 Click OK to accept the =$A$6:$D$23 range. The range is converted into a table.

7 Select the cell range A29:D46.

8 Click INSERT > Table.

9 Click OK to accept the =$A$29:$D$46 range.

10 Save the changes to the file, and leave it open to use in the next Try It.

Showing a Totals Row in a Table

- Using a Totals row provides a way of summarizing data in the table without having to create formulas or functions for each column. It is one of the many benefits of analyzing data in tabular form in Excel.

Try It!   **Showing a Totals Row in a Table**

1 In the **E71Try_xx** file, on the July 22 tab, click cell A23.

2 Right-click cell A23 and on the shortcut menu that appears, click Table > Totals Row. A totals row appears in the table.

3 Click cell A47.

4 Right-click cell A47 and on the shortcut menu that appears, click Table > Totals Row. A totals row appears in the table.

5 Save the changes to the file, and leave it open to use in the next Try It.

Viewing Two Tables Side-by-Side

■ Excel provides an easy way to view two tables side-by-side in separate windows. They can be in the same worksheet, or on different worksheets in the same workbook, or even in different workbooks.

✓ When you view the same workbook in more than one window at once, the window names have numbers appended to them in the title bar. For example, E71Try.xlsx becomes E71Try.xlsx:1 and E71Try.xlsx:2 when viewed side by side.

Try It!   **Viewing Two Tables Side-by-Side by Moving a Table**

1 In the **E71Try_xx** file, on the July 22 tab, select the cell range A30:D48.

2 Position the mouse pointer over the table border, so the pointer turns into a 4-headed arrow.

3 Drag the table up and to the right so that the upper-left corner is in cell F6, and release the mouse button.

4 Adjust the column widths as needed.

5 In the table on the left, click the drop-drop-down arrow at the top of the Product column.

6 Click the Select All check box to deselect it, click the Greeting Cards check box, and click OK.

   ✓ Notice that the left table is sorted on greeting cards, and the right table displays the data that happens to be in the same rows.

7 Click the filter arrow at the top of the Product column again to reopen the menu.

8 Click the Select All check box to select it, and click OK. The filter is removed.

9 Select the cell range F6:I24.

10 Using the same process as in steps 2–3, move the selected table back to its original position, in cells A30:D48.

11 Use the Format Painter to format the fill color of the cell range F24:I24 to match the rest of the filled cells.

12 Save the changes to the file, and leave it open to use in the next Try It.

Side-by-side tables, filtered, in one worksheet

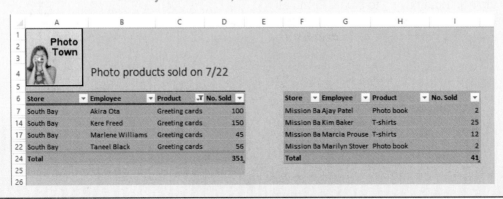

Try It!   **Viewing Two Tables Side-by-Side by Opening an Additional Window**

1 In the **E71Try_xx** file, click VIEW > New Window 🖻.

  ✓ *This creates a new window for the active workbook. It may not be evident that there is a new window until they are viewed side by side.*

2 Click VIEW > View Side by Side 🗗. Both window panes become visible, stacked one on top of the other.

  ✓ *If more than two windows are open, Excel opens a dialog box to have you select the windows you wish to compare.*

3 Click VIEW > Arrange All 🗐. The Arrange Windows dialog box opens.

4 Click Vertical > OK. The windows appear vertically tiled.

5 Click VIEW > Synchronous Scrolling 🗐 to toggle the feature off.

  ✓ *The Synchronous Scrolling button is a toggle button. Clicking it again turns on the synchronous scrolling. Whether you have it turned on or off depends on what you need to do while viewing the worksheets side by side.*

6 In the window on the left, scroll the worksheet so that cell A1 is in the upper-left corner.

7 In the window on the right, scroll the worksheet so that cell A25 is in the upper-left corner.

8 Click VIEW > Synchronous Scrolling to toggle that feature on again.

9 Drag the scroll bar in either window down to scroll the tables a few rows. Notice that both tables scroll together.

10 Click VIEW > Synchronous Scrolling to toggle that feature off.

11 In the table in the left window, click the drop-down arrow at the top of the Product column. A menu opens.

12 Click Select All to deselect it, and click Greeting Cards > OK.

13 Click the arrow at the top of the Product column again to reopen the menu.

14 Click Select All to select it, and click OK. The filter is removed.

15 In the right window, click the July 23 tab. Now two different sheets are displayed side-by-side.

16 Close the window on the right. The workbook itself remains open.

17 Maximize the remaining window if it does not automatically maximize.

18 Save the changes to the file, and leave it open to use in the next Try It.

Applying Icon Sets

■ You can use **icon sets** to display a visual image in each cell, depending on the data in the cell.

■ Icons are placed in cells based on a percentile. The icons are in sets of 3, 4, or 5. The number in the set determines the number of percentile groups that Excel divides the data into. For example, if you choose an icon set of 3, the data is divided into three percentile groups.

■ You can edit the default meanings of the icons.

■ Icons can be applied to a cell range or a table of data. If icons are applied to a cell range, rather than a table, the range must be named.

  ✓ *You learned how to set up named ranges in Lesson 68.*

Try It!　Applying Icon Sets

1 In the **E71Try_xx** file, click the Comparison worksheet tab.

　✓ *This worksheet contains two tables comparing the sales of both stores on two days.*

2 Click cell F8, type **=E8–D8**, and press `ENTER`. The formula is automatically filled into the rest of the table in column F.

3 Select the cell range F8:F27.

4 On the HOME tab, in the Styles group, click Conditional Formatting 📊 > Icon Sets.

5 In the Directional group, click 3 Arrows (Colored) to apply the arrows to the cell range.

6 Save the changes to the file, and leave it open to use in the next Try It.

Try It!　Editing the Icon Definitions

1 In the **E71Try_xx** file, on the Comparison worksheet, select the cell range F8:F27.

2 On the HOME tab, in the Styles group, click Conditional Formatting 📊 > Manage Rules.

3 Click the Icon Set rule, and click Edit Rule. The Edit Formatting Rule dialog box opens.

4 Next to the green up-pointing arrow icon, click the Type drop-down list, and click Number. In the Value box, type **10**.

5 Next to the yellow side-pointing arrow icon, click the Type drop-down list, and click Number. In the Value box, type **0** if it does not already appear there.

6 Click OK to close the Edit Formatting Rule dialog box.

7 Click OK to close the Conditional Formatting Rules Manager dialog box and apply the changed rule to the cells.

8 Save and close the file, and exit Excel.

Setting formatting rules for icons

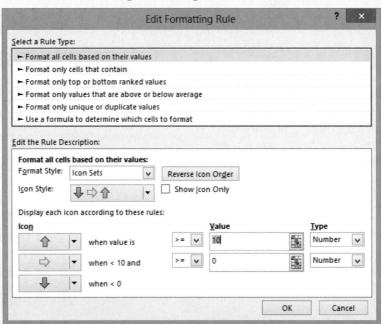

Lesson 71—Practice

Rural Estates Real Estate has asked you to analyze differences among some of the properties the company has for sale. You will convert some of their raw data to a table and use icon sets with this table. You will also sort and filter the data to glean meaningful information from it.

DIRECTIONS

1. Start Excel, if necessary, and open **E71Practice** from the data files for this lesson.
2. Save the file as **E71Practice_xx** in the location where your teacher instructs you to store the files for this lesson.
3. Add a header that has your name at the left, the date code in the center, and the page number code at the right, and change back to **Normal** view.
4. On the **Report 1** worksheet, select the cell range **A1:L121**.
5. Click **INSERT** > **Table** ▦ > **OK** to accept the proposed data range.
6. Filter to show only properties with three or more bathrooms:
   a. Click the drop-down arrow on the **Baths** field.
   b. Click **Select All** to deselect all.
   c. Click the **3**, **3.5**, **4**, and **5** check boxes, and click **OK**.
7. Sort in Descending order by List Price:
   a. Click the drop-down arrow on the **List Price** field.
   b. Click **Sort Largest to Smallest**.
8. Select column **H**.
9. Click **HOME** > **Conditional Formatting** > **Icon Sets** > **3 Flags**.
10. Filter to show only green-flagged entries:
    a. Click the drop-down arrow on the **SqFt** field.
    b. Point to **Filter by Color**, and click the **green flag** icon.
11. Adjust the column widths as needed so that no entries are truncated and there is no wasted space.
12. Click **PAGE LAYOUT** > **Orientation** > **Landscape**.
13. Click **PAGE LAYOUT** > **Margins** > **Narrow**. All the fields should now fit on one page of a printout.
14. **With your teacher's permission,** print the worksheet. Your worksheet should look like the one shown in Figure 71-2.
15. Save and close the file, and exit Excel.

Figure 71-2

	A	B	C	D	E	F	G	H	I	J	K	L
1	Agent	Date Listed	Area	Community	List Price	Bedrooms	Baths	SqFt	Type	Pool	Spa	HOA Fees
6	Jeffery	8/28/2015	Coastal	Arandale	$1,200,500	5	5	4,696	Single Family	TRUE	TRUE	FALSE
7	Garcia	4/3/2014	Coastal	Mira Mesa	$799,000	6	5	4,800	Single Family	TRUE	TRUE	FALSE
8	McDonald	5/6/2014	Inland	Hadley	$625,000	6	4	3,950	Single Family	TRUE	TRUE	FALSE
10	Hood	6/3/2014	East County	Escondido	$574,900	5	4	4,700	Single Family	TRUE	TRUE	FALSE
31	Hood	7/14/2014	Coastal	Marysville	$374,900	4	3	3,927	Single Family	FALSE	TRUE	FALSE
42	Carter	8/31/2014	East County	Bonita	$365,000	5	3	3,938	Single Family	TRUE	TRUE	FALSE
49	Langston	7/21/2014	Coastal	Mira Mesa	$349,000	4	3	3,930	Single Family	TRUE	FALSE	FALSE

Lesson 71—Apply

You work in the sales department for Rural Estates Real Estate. Your manager has asked you to analyze differences among some of the properties the company has for sale. In this project, you will sort and filter the data in the tables based on your manager's criteria. You will also use icon sets and edit the icon formatting rules to make it easier to interpret the data.

DIRECTIONS

1. Start Excel, if necessary, and open **E71Apply** from the data files for this lesson.

2. Save the file as **E71Apply_xx** in the location where your teacher instructs you to store the files for this lesson.

3. Click the **Summary** worksheet tab, add a header that has your name at the left, the date code in the center, and the page number code at the right, and change back to **Normal** view.

4. Click the **Report 1** worksheet tab, sort the table by **SqFt** from largest to smallest and filter to show only Coastal, Single Family dwellings that have a pool and that do not have HOA fees.

5. In the **List Price** column, apply the **3 Traffic Lights (Unrimmed)** icon set.

6. Modify the definitions on the icon set to reverse the icon order, so that the lower-priced properties show the green circles. Adjust the width of the **List Price** column, if necessary.

7. On the **Summary** worksheet, in cell **A1**, type **Best Single-Family Values**, and format it as **Bold** and **14-point**.

8. Copy the cell range **A1:L1** from the **Report 1** worksheet to the cell range **A2:L2** on the **Summary** worksheet.

9. Copy the cells from the **Report 1** worksheet that show a green circle to the **Summary** worksheet, starting in cell **A3**. Adjust the column widths, as needed.

   ✓ *The icon colors change to reflect the new table of data. The rule for the icon set now compares the prices in the cell range E3:E8.*

10. On the **Summary** worksheet, in cell **A10**, type **Best Condo and Duplex Values**.

11. Use Format Painter to copy the formatting from cell **A1** to cell **A10**.

12. Copy and paste the content of row 2 into row 11.

13. On the **Report 1** worksheet, clear all filters, and re-filter to show only Coastal dwellings that are *not* Single Family.

14. Sort the table by **SqFt**, with largest values first.

15. Clear the icon set from the **List Price** column.

16. In the List Price column, apply the **3 flags** icon set.

17. Reverse the order of the icon set, so the cheapest properties show green flags.

18. Edit the icon set rule as follows:

    Red flag: when value is **>=50%**

    Yellow flag: when **<50 and >=20%**

    Green flag: when **<20**

19. Filter the table to show only green-flag properties.

20. Copy the green-flag properties to the **Summary** worksheet, starting in cell **A12**. Adjust the column widths, as needed.

21. Change the page orientation to **Landscape**.

22. **With your teacher's permission,** print the **Summary** worksheet. Your worksheet should look like the one shown in Figure 71-3 on the next page.

23. Save and close the file, and exit Excel.

Figure 71-3

	A	B	C	D	E	F	G	H	I	J	K	L
1	**Best Single-Family Values**											
2	Agent	Date Listed	Area	Community	List Price	Bedrooms	Baths	SqFt	Type	Pool	Spa	HOA Fees
3	Langston	7/21/2014	Coastal	Mira Mesa	$349,000	4	3	3,930	Single Family	TRUE	FALSE	FALSE
4	Conners	6/30/2015	Coastal	Mira Mesa	$229,500	6	3	2,700	Single Family	TRUE	TRUE	FALSE
5	Barnes	3/13/2014	Coastal	Arandale	$264,900	3	2.5	2,495	Single Family	TRUE	TRUE	FALSE
6	Carter	4/6/2014	Coastal	Mono Lake	$309,900	5	3	2,447	Single Family	TRUE	TRUE	FALSE
7	Hamilton	2/23/2014	Coastal	Bend	$425,900	5	3	2,414	Single Family	TRUE	TRUE	FALSE
8	Garcia	8/2/2014	Coastal	Linda Vista	$359,900	3	2	2,198	Single Family	TRUE	FALSE	FALSE
9												
10	**Best Condo and Duplex Values**											
11	Agent	Date Listed	Area	Community	List Price	Bedrooms	Baths	SqFt	Type	Pool	Spa	HOA Fees
12	Langston	8/22/2014	Coastal	Arandale	$264,900	3	2.5	2,062	Condo	FALSE	TRUE	TRUE
13	Barnes	9/26/2014	Coastal	Marysville	$239,900	4	3	2,041	Condo	FALSE	TRUE	TRUE
14	Conners	5/26/2014	Coastal	Linda Vista	$229,900	4	3	2,041	Condo	FALSE	TRUE	TRUE
15	Carter	4/14/2014	Coastal	Mira Mesa	$259,900	3	3	1,734	Condo	FALSE	TRUE	TRUE
16	Carter	6/17/2014	Coastal	Mono Lake	$235,990	3	2	1,656	Condo	TRUE	TRUE	TRUE
17	Garcia	7/28/2015	Coastal	Bend	$215,000	3	2.5	1,640	Condo	TRUE	TRUE	TRUE
18	Jeffery	4/21/2014	Coastal	Marysville	$238,000	3	2.5	1,590	Condo	FALSE	TRUE	TRUE

Lesson 72

Using Advanced Filters, Slicers, and Database Functions

Argument
A parameter for a function. Database functions include three arguments: the database (or list) range, a field from the list, and the criteria you want to use to qualify the function.

Criteria range
The area of the worksheet that contains the fields to evaluate against the criteria you specify.

Database range
The worksheet range that includes the field names in the top row and the database records in subsequent rows.

Extract
To copy records that match specified criteria to another place in the worksheet.

Slicer
An Excel filtering component that contains a set of buttons to enable you to quickly filter data.

➤ What You Will Learn

Using Advanced Filters
Working with Slicers
Using Database Functions

Software Skills   When you search for data in a long list of records, you can use Excel's filtering features to display only the records that match criteria you specify. Filtering is just one way to work with data from a database. Excel includes a variety of functions that are designed specifically for working with database data. These functions enable you to perform common arithmetic operations such as averaging, summing, and counting on data that meets criteria you specify. Database functions are in some ways similar to the logical (IF) functions you learned about in Chapter 8, but they are designed specifically for acting upon database data.

What You Can Do

Using Advanced Filters

- With an advanced filter you can filter records in a list in one of two ways:
  - You can hide records that do not match the criteria you specify—in much the same way as with a regular filter.
  - You can **extract** records to another place in the worksheet.
- Although an advanced filter can hide records just like a regular filter, it's different in many ways.
  - An advanced filter allows you to enter more complex criteria than a regular filter.
  - Instead of selecting criteria from a drop-down list, you enter it in a special area in the workbook—or even a worksheet by itself—set aside for that purpose.

- In the marked cells of this criteria range, you enter the items you want to match from the list, or expressions that describe the type of comparison you wish to make.

- You then open a dialog box in which you specify the range where the list or table is contained, the range containing the criteria, and the range to which you want records copied/extracted (if applicable).

- If you want to compare the values of two fields as part of the filter, create a formula that performs the comparison (beginning with an equals sign) and place it in a cell that has a blank cell directly above it. Then select the blank cell and the cell containing the formula as the criteria range.

- For the comparison operation, refer to the cells in the first data row of the table. Excel will assume that you want to calculate the entire table based on that same pattern.

- Here are some more examples. Each of them assumes that you are evaluating data in a table where the first data row is 7, and that you are using cells M1:M2 (some empty cells away from the main table) as the criteria range. Cell M1 is left blank, and cell M2 contains the value shown in this table.

To find	Place this in cell M2
Records where column F is less than column G	=F7<G7
Records where column F does not equal column G	=F7<>G7
Records where column F is blank	=F7=""
Records where column F equals column G	=F7=G7

Try It!	**Using an Advanced Filter to Extract Records**

1   Start Excel, and open **E72TryA** from the data files for this lesson.

2   Save the file as **E72TryA_xx** in the location where your teacher instructs you to store the files for this lesson.

3   On the Criteria worksheet, create a criterion that includes racers who placed third or better in their qualifying heats:

   a. Click the Criteria worksheet tab.

   b. Click cell E2, type <=3, and press ⏎ .

4   Apply an advanced filter that finds the matching racers from the July Race worksheet and places it in a blank area of the worksheet:

   a. Click the July Race worksheet tab.

   b. Click DATA > Advanced 🏷 to open the Advanced Filter dialog box.

   c. In the List range box, type $A$8:$H$44.

   d. In the Criteria range box, click the Collapse Dialog Box button 📇 to collapse the dialog box.

   e. Click the Criteria worksheet tab.

   f. Select the cell range A1:H2, and press ⏎ to return to the dialog box.

   g. In the Advanced Filter dialog box, under Action, click Copy to another location. The Copy to box becomes available.

   h. Click in the Copy to box, and click cell J8 on the July Race tab.

   i. Click OK to apply the filter. The matching records appear in range J8:Q33.

   j. Adjust the column widths as needed for columns J through Q.

5   Save the changes to the file, and leave it open to use in the next Try It.

The Advanced Filter dialog box

Try It!   Using an Advanced Filter to Filter In-Place

1 In the **E72TryA_xx** file, click the Criteria worksheet, click cell E2, and press `DEL` to clear the previous criterion.

2 Click cell D2, type **<=12:01:00 AM**, and press `ENTER`.

  ✓ *Excel stores all time values as relative to a point on the clock. So an elapsed time of one minute is stored as "12:01 AM," or one minute of elapsed time past midnight—which is Excel's "zero hour."*

3 Apply an advanced filter that finds the matching racers from the June Race worksheet and filters the data in-place:

  a. Click the June Race worksheet tab.

  b. On the DATA tab, click Advanced to open the Advanced Filter dialog.

  c. In the List range box, type $A$8:$H$44.

  d. In the Criteria range box, click the Collapse Dialog Box button to collapse the dialog box.

  e. Click the Criteria worksheet tab.

  f. Select the cell range A1:H2, and press `ENTER`.

  g. Click OK. The list is filtered on the June Race worksheet to show only the matching records.

4 Save and close the file, and leave Excel open for the next Try It.

Try It!   Using an Advanced Filter with a Comparison Operator

1 Open **E72TryB** from the data files for this lesson.

2 Save the file as **E72TryB_xx** in the location where your teacher instructs you to store the files for this lesson.

3 Click the Criteria worksheet tab, click A2, type **=H7<E7*3**, and press `ENTER`. The formula result appears as FALSE. This is normal.

  ✓ *This formula checks to see whether the Items Remaining is less than 3 times the Items Per Case. It appears at the moment to refer to cells on the Criteria worksheet tab, but when it is used for the advanced filter's criteria, it will refer to the table on the August Sales worksheet. The fact that it evaluates to FALSE at the moment is irrelevant.*

4 Click the August Sales worksheet tab.

5 Click DATA > Advanced to open the Advanced Filter dialog.

6 In the List range box, type $A$6:$K$93.

7 In the Criteria range box, click the Collapse Dialog Box button.

8 Click the Criteria worksheet tab, select the cell range A1:A2, and press `ENTER` to return to the dialog box.

9 Click OK. The filter is applied, and eight records appear.

10 Save the changes to the file, and leave it open to use in the next Try It.

Working with Slicers

- You can use **slicers** to easily view and select the criteria on which you want to filter your data.

- Insert a slicer using the Slicer button ▤ in the Filters group on the INSERT tab.

- The fields are displayed as column names in the Insert Slicers dialog box. A slicer will be displayed for every field that you select.

- After you create a slicer, it appears on the worksheet alongside the table.

- If you insert more than one slicer, the slicers display in layers.

- You can move slicers within the worksheet to view them more easily.

- Select the item(s) in the slicer on which you want to filter the data.

- To select more than one item in a slicer, hold down the Control key `CTRL` , and click the items on which you want to filter.

- To remove a filter in the slicer, click the Clear Filter button ▧ on the slicer.

- You can change the slicer settings or apply slicer styles from the SLICER TOOLS OPTIONS tab.

- To delete a slicer, click on a slicer to select it, and press `DEL` . You can also right-click a slicer, and click Remove "Name of slicer."

  ✓ *When you delete a slicer, the filter(s) applied to your data are not removed.*

- You can also use slicers to group records so you can analyze the filtered set of data.

Try It! Inserting Multiple Slicers

1 In the **E72TryB_xx** file, on the August Sales worksheet tab, click any cell in the table.

2 Click INSERT > Slicer ▤ to display the Insert Slicers dialog box.

3 Click the Drug check box, click the To treat check box, and click OK.

4 Click and drag the To Treat slicer so that its upper-left corner is in the upper-left corner of cell O6.

5 Click and drag the Drug slicer so that its upper-left corner is in the upper-left corner of cell M6.

6 In the Drug slicer, scroll down and click Revolution. The table displays the data for the selected drug. Notice that the To treat slicer automatically filters to show the criteria (in this case, Cat, Dog, and Puppy or Kitten) which apply to the Drug criteria (Revolution) that you selected as the filter.

7 In the To Treat slicer, click Dog. The table displays the data for the selected drug and the selected animal it can treat.

8 Click the Drug slicer, and scroll down to view the Revolution criteria. Notice that it is still selected.

9 Save the changes to the file, and leave it open to use in the next Try It.

The Insert Slicer dialog box

Insert Slicers	?	✕

☑ Drug
☐ For use on
☑ To treat
☐ No. of Cases
☐ Items per Case
☐ Loose Items
☐ Items on Hand
☐ Items Remaining
☐ No. Sold
☐ Item Price
☐ Total Sales

OK   Cancel

Try It!   **Applying Styles to Slicers**

① In the **E72TryB_xx** file, on the August Sales worksheet tab, click the Drug slicer.

② Click the SLICER TOOLS OPTIONS tab.

③ In the Slicer Styles gallery, click Slicer Style Light 2.

④ Click the To treat slicer.

⑤ In the Slicer Styles gallery, click Slicer Style Light 4.

⑥ Save the changes to the file, and leave it open to use in the next Try It.

Styles applied to slicers

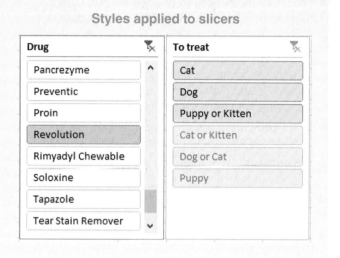

Try It!   **Clearing a Slicer Filter**

① In the **E72TryB_xx** file, on the August Sales worksheet tab, click the To treat slicer.

② On the To treat slicer, click the Clear Filter button . The filter clears and resets to the filtered criteria for Revolution.

③ Click the Drug slicer, and scroll down to view the Revolution criteria.

④ Press and hold the Control key , and click Soloxine. Notice that the table displays the filtered data, and the To treat slicer displays the filtered criteria.

⑤ On the Drug slicer, click the Clear Filter button . The two filters in the Drug slicer are cleared. Notice that the To treat slicer is also cleared because its criteria depend on the Drug criteria.

⑥ Save the changes to the file, and leave it open to use in the next Try It.

Try It!   Deleting a Slicer

1 In the **E72TryB_xx** file, on the August Sales worksheet tab, click the Drug slicer.

2 In the Drug slicer, scroll down if necessary, and click Revolution. The table displays the filtered data.

3 Right-click the To treat slicer, and click Remove "To treat."

4 Click the Drug slicer, and press [DEL]. Notice that the table remains filtered on the item you selected in the slicer.

5 Save and close the file, and leave Excel open for the next Try It.

Using Database Functions

- Excel provides several functions specifically designed to be used with a table. (A table is, essentially, a simple database.)

- With one of these functions, you can perform a calculation on records in your table or list that meet particular criteria. You enter the criteria you want to use in the database function by typing the criteria in the worksheet, just as you do with advanced filters.

- In a database function, a field is the name of the column to be used in the function.

- All database functions have three **arguments**:
  - The **database range** is the range in the table or list that includes all the records and the field name row.
  - The **field** is the name of the column you wish to use in the function. Instead of the field name, you can also specify a number that represents the field's database column (not the worksheet column).
  - The **criteria range** is the range that contains the criteria.

- Each database function follows this syntax: **=functionname(database range, field, criteria range)**

- The available database functions are:

DAVERAGE	Averages the values in a column of a list or database that match conditions you specify.
DCOUNT	Counts the cells that contain numbers in a column of a list or database that match conditions you specify.
DCOUNTA	Counts nonblank cells in a column or row.
DGET	Extracts a single value from a column of a list or database that matches conditions you specify.
DSUM	Adds the numbers in a column of a list or database that match conditions you specify.

Try It!   Using Database Functions

1 Open **E72TryC** from the data files for this lesson.

2 Save the file as **E72TryC_xx** in the location where your teacher instructs you to store the files for this lesson.

3 On the August Sales worksheet, select the cell range A6:K93.

4 Click FORMULAS > Define Name ⊑ to display the New Name dialog box.

(continued)

Try It!   **Using Database Functions** *(continued)*

5   In the Name box, type **Sales_August**, and click OK.

Naming the data range

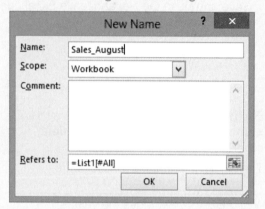

6   Click the Aug Sales Analysis worksheet tab.

7   Click cell C3, and click the Insert Function button *fx* on the formula bar.

8   In the Search for a function box, type **DMAX**, and click Go.

9   In the Select a function box, click DMAX > OK to open the Function Arguments dialog box.

10   In the Database box, type **Sales_August**.

✓ *Sales_August is a range name that refers to A6:K93.*

11   In the Field box, type **"Total Sales"**.

✓ *Total Sales is the column name being referenced in the table.*

12   In the Criteria box, type **Sales_August**.

✓ *Normally you would enter a criteria range here, but in this case we want to include data from the entire data range.*

13   Click OK. The result of the function appears in the cell (33707.45).

14   Click cell N3, type **=C3**, and press ENTER .

15   Click cell B3, type **=DGET(Sales_August,"Drug",N2:N3)**, and press ENTER . This formula searches the database range for a match to the value in the criteria range. Adjust the column width as needed to make the result fit.

16   Click cell E6, and type **Flea***.

✓ *The asterisk is a wildcard.*

17   Click cell C6, type **=DMAX(Sales_August,"Total Sales",E5:E6)**, and press ENTER . This finds the maximum total sales value matching the criteria.

18   Click cell N6, and type **=C6**, and press ENTER .

19   Copy the formula from cell B3 to cell B6. Because the formula in cell B3 uses relative references, its cell references change to refer to rows 5 and 6: =DGET(Sales_August,"Drug",N5:N6).

✓ *This formula searches the database range for a match to the value in the criteria range.*

20   Click cell C9, type **=DAVERAGE(Sales_August,"Items on Hand",Sales_August)**, and press ENTER .

✓ *This formula provides the average of the Items on Hand field.*

21   Save and close the file, and exit Excel.

A database function

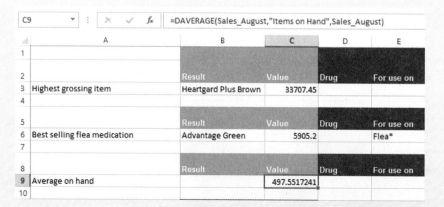

Lesson 72—Practice

The owner of Pete's Pets has asked you to help her extract data from the company's databases. The owner wants to use the data to create and process wholesale orders. You will use Excel to examine the company's current database and use advanced filtering, slicers, and database functions to provide the information the owner needs.

DIRECTIONS

1. Start Excel, if necessary, and open **E72Practice** from the data files for this lesson.

2. Save the file as **E72Practice_xx** in the location where your teacher instructs you to store the files for this lesson.

3. For all worksheets, add a header that has your name at the left, the date code in the center, and the page number code at the right, and change back to **Normal** view.

4. Use an advanced filter to create separate (extracted) list of items that need to be reordered:

   ✓ *An item should be reordered if its current inventory is at or below the reorder level.*

   a. On the **Inventory** worksheet, in cell **H2**, type =D6<=E6.

   b. Select the cell range **A5:H32**.

   c. Click **DATA** > **Advanced** ▼ to open the Advanced Filter dialog box. The List range is already filled in.

   d. Click in the Criteria range box, type =$H$1:$H$2.

   e. Click **Copy to another location**.

   f. In the Copy to box, type **J5**.

   g. Click **OK** to apply the filter and extract the records.

5. Select cell **H2**, and press DEL.

6. Move the filtered records to the **Order Form** worksheet:

   a. Select the range **J5:Q20**.

   b. Press CTRL + X.

   c. Click the **Order Form** worksheet tab.

   d. Click cell **A5**.

   e. Press CTRL + V.

7. Adjust the column widths so that all data is displayed.

8. On the **Order Form** worksheet, in cell I5, type **On Order**.

9. Enter the following values in each cell in the ranges:

   I6:I9: **2**

   I10:I12: **4**

   I13:I17: **2**

   I18:I20: **10**

10. In cell **J5**, type **Cost**.

11. In cell **J6**, type =H6*I6.

12. Copy the formula from cell **J6** to the range **J7:J20**.

13. Use the Format Painter to copy the formatting from cell **H6** to the cell range **J6:J20**.

14. In cell **I22**, type **Total**.

15. In cell **J22**, type =SUM(J6:J20).

16. Click **PAGE LAYOUT** > **Orientation** > **Landscape**. Your worksheet should look like the one shown in Figure 72-1 on the next page.

17. On the **Inventory** worksheet, convert the data range to a table, and insert a slicer that filters all flavors of Cat's Pride cat food.

    a. Click the **Inventory** worksheet tab.

    b. Select the cell range **A5:H32**.

    c. Click **INSERT** > **Table** > **OK**.

    d. Click **INSERT** > **Slicer** > **Description** > **OK**.

    e. In the Description slicer, press and hold CTRL, and click **Cat's Pride - Beef**, **Cat's Pride - Salmon**, and **Cat's Pride - Tuna**.

18. Move the Description slicer to below the filtered table. Your worksheet should look like the one shown in Figure 72-2 on the next page.

19. **With your teacher's permission,** print the worksheets.

20. Save and close the file, and exit Excel.

Figure 72-1

	A	B	C	D	E	F	G	H	I	J
1										
2										
3										
4										
5	Product #	Description	Price	Current Inventory	Reorder When	Number per Case	My Cost	Price per Case	On Order	Cost
6	24813	Lg. Collar - Red	$17.50	4	4	12	$ 5.25	$ 63.00	2	$ 126.00
7	24814	Lg. Collar - Black	$17.50	4	4	12	$ 5.25	$ 63.00	2	$ 126.00
8	24815	Lg. Collar - Blue	$17.50	4	4	12	$ 5.25	$ 63.00	2	$ 126.00
9	24816	Lg. Collar - Green	$17.50	4	4	12	$ 5.25	$ 63.00	2	$ 126.00
10	34897	Sm. Bonie	$2.00	22	25	100	$ 0.50	$ 50.00	4	$ 200.00
11	34898	Med. Bonie	$2.75	18	25	100	$ 0.53	$ 53.00	4	$ 212.00
12	34899	Lg. Bonie	$3.50	6	25	100	$ 0.64	$ 64.00	4	$ 256.00
13	44212	Sm. Training Leash	$13.75	9	10	25	$ 7.60	$ 190.00	2	$ 380.00
14	44213	Lg. Training Leash	$15.25	6	10	25	$ 9.80	$ 245.00	2	$ 490.00
15	55123	2 Tier Scratch Post	$22.50	3	5	5	$11.75	$ 58.75	2	$ 117.50
16	34897	Chew Toys, asst.	$3.25	27	30	25	$ 0.75	$ 18.75	2	$ 37.50
17	77898	Med. Cedar Chip Bed	$23.50	4	5	5	$14.80	$ 74.00	2	$ 148.00
18	83122	Gourmet Delight - Turkey	$2.25	27	30	14	$ 1.80	$ 25.20	10	$ 252.00
19	83123	Gourmet Delight - Chicken	$2.25	24	30	14	$ 1.90	$ 26.60	10	$ 266.00
20	83144	Cat's Pride - Tuna	$3.75	16	18	36	$ 2.20	$ 79.20	10	$ 792.00
21										
22										Total	$3,655.00
23										

Figure 72-2

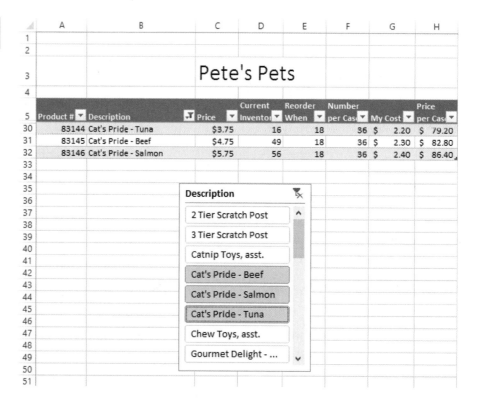

Lesson 72—Apply

You are the sales manager for Kat's Catering and you want to use database data to create a vendor report. In addition, one of your vendors, Emily's Herbs, has misplaced their sales order. The vendor knows how many cases were ordered, but doesn't have a description of the item. In this project, you will use Excel to examine the company's current database and use advanced filtering and database functions to create a vendor report. You will also use slicers to filter the data to answer the vendor's question.

DIRECTIONS

1. Start Excel, if necessary, and open **E72Apply** from the data files for this lesson.

2. Save the file as **E72Apply_xx** in the location where your teacher instructs you to store the files for this lesson.

3. For all worksheets, add a header that has your name at the left, the date code in the center, and the page number code at the right, and change back to **Normal** view.

4. On the **Supplies totals** worksheet, in cell **B6**, type **=DSUM(Order,"Cases Ordered",B4:B5)**, and press ENTER.

   ✓ *This finds the number of cases ordered for the vendor name shown in cell B5. Notice that the Supplies list table has a defined name of "Order."*

5. In cell **B7**, create a **=DAVERAGE** function that calculates the average cost per case for the vendor name shown in cell B5.

6. In cell **B8**, create a **=DSUM** function that calculates the total weight of the order for the vendor name shown in cell **B5**.

7. In cell **B9**, create a **=DSUM** function that calculates the total cost of the order for the vendor name shown in cell **B5**.

8. In cell **B10**, calculate the shipping charge, which is $20 for every 50 pounds of weight in the order.

9. In cell **B11**, calculate the total order cost, which is the order cost plus the shipping charge.

10. Copy the cell range **B6:B11** to the cell range **C6:G11**.

11. Set the worksheet's orientation to **Landscape** and the margins to **Narrow**.

12. Adjust the column widths so that the worksheet will fit on one page. Your worksheet should look like the one shown in Figure 72-3 on the next page.

13. On the **Supplies list** worksheet, insert slicers to find the name of the product for which Emily's Herbs ordered 7 cases.

    ✓ *Hint: Filter on the criteria Description, Vendor, and Cases Ordered.*

    a. Click the **Supplies list** worksheet tab.

    b. Select the cell range **A7:G35**.

    c. Click **INSERT** > **Slicer** 📊 > **Description**.

    d. In the Description slicer, press and hold CTRL, and click **Description**, **Vendor**, and **Cases Ordered**.

    e. In the Cases Ordered slicer, click **7**.

    f. In the Vendor slicer, click **Emily's Herbs**.

14. Move the slicers below the filtered table.

15. Adjust the column widths so that the worksheet will fit on one page. Your worksheet should look like the one shown in Figure 72-4 on the next page.

16. **With your teacher's permission,** print the worksheets.

17. Save and close the file, and exit Excel.

Figure 72-3

	A	B	C	D	E	F	G
1							
2							
3							
4		Vendor	Vendor	Vendor	Vendor	Vendor	Vendor
5		Clarksville Food Supply	JC Foods	Emily's Herbs	Town Bakery	Mike's Meat Supply	Clarksville Fishery
6	No. of cases ordered	40	61	25	30	27	22
7	Average cost per case	$ 16.45	$ 15.74	$ 16.19	$ 22.73	$ 35.25	$ 37.63
8	Total weight	597	707	96	396	1350	660
9	Cost of order	$ 729.25	$ 939.55	$ 417.65	$ 676.90	$ 934.25	$ 844.25
10	Shipping charge	$ 238.80	$ 282.80	$ 38.30	$ 158.40	$ 540.00	$ 264.00
11	Total cost	$ 968.05	$ 1,222.35	$ 455.95	$ 835.30	$ 1,474.25	$ 1,108.25
12							

Figure 72-4

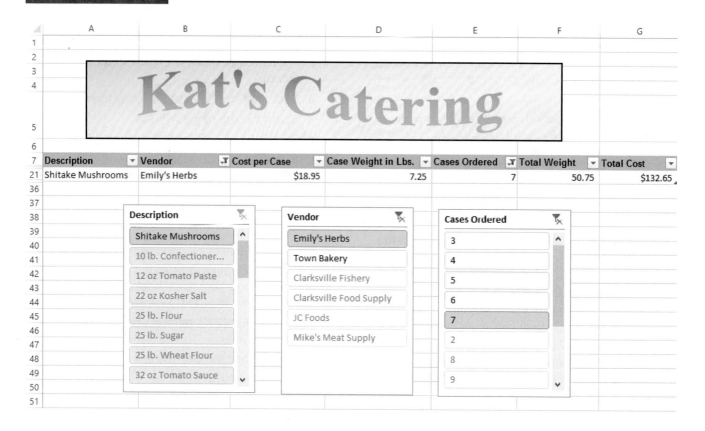

Lesson 73

Using Flash Fill and Data Consolidation

➤ What You Will Learn

Working with Flash Fill
Consolidating Data
Working with Consolidated Data

Software Skills   Data that is formatted and organized is easier to work with and analyze. Excel's Flash Fill feature can help you format and organize data. For example, you can combine first, middle, and last names from separate columns into one column. Excel's data consolidation feature allows you to consolidate the data from similar worksheets into a single worksheet. For example, you may have a workbook that contains separate worksheets for three months' worth of sales. After consolidation, you have a single worksheet that contains the totals for the three-month period.

What You Can Do

Working with Flash Fill

- The **Flash Fill** feature in Excel can recognize the pattern in the text and change the organization or format of the text for the series.
- You can use Flash Fill to reformat names that have been typed in lowercase to uppercase or change the format of phone numbers to include parentheses for the area code.
- You can use Flash Fill to split data into more than one column or combine data from multiple columns into one column.
- Flash Fill works best when the data labels are consistent. For example, all names have middle initials or all addresses use the same type of postal codes.
- If the data labels are not consistent, Flash Fill may not always format or separate the data elements correctly.
- You can use Flash Fill with data ranges or tables.

Try It!   **Using Flash Fill to Combine Data Elements**

1. Start Excel, and open **E73TryA** from the data files for this lesson.

2. Save the file as **E73TryA_xx** in the location where your teacher instructs you to store the files for this lesson.

3. On the June Race worksheet tab, click the column C heading.

4. On the HOME tab, in the Cells group, click Insert ⊞.

5. Click cell C8, and type **Racer Full Name**, and press [ENTER].

6. In cell C9, type **Carl Allan**, and press [ENTER].

7. In cell C10, type **Martin**. Notice that the Flash Fill suggestions fill the rest of the column.

8. Press [ENTER]. Flash Fill places the suggestions in the column, and the Flash Fill options button appears to the right of the first filled cell.

9. Click the Flash Fill Options button 📋 > Accept suggestions.

10. Save the changes to the file, and leave it open to use in the next Try It.

The Flash Fill Options button

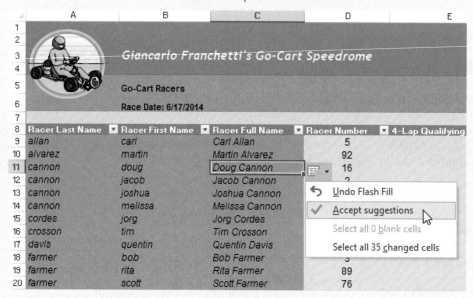

Try It!   **Using Flash Fill to Separate Data Elements**

1. In the **E73TryA_xx** file, click the July Race worksheet tab.

2. Click cell B9, type **Carl**, and press [ENTER].

3. In cell B10, type **Martin**, and press [ENTER]. Flash Fill completes the column with first name data.

4. Click cell C9, type **Allan**, and press [ENTER].

5. In cell C10, type **Alvarez**, and press [ENTER]. Flash Fill completes the column with last name data.

6. Save and close the file. Leave Excel open to use in the next Try It.

Consolidating Data

- With Excel's Consolidate feature, you can consolidate data from separate ranges into a single worksheet.

- You can also consolidate data using 3-D formulas.

- The data can come from the same worksheet, separate worksheets, and even separate workbooks.

- You can consolidate identically structured databases. This is called **consolidation by position**. When you consolidate data by position, you're telling Excel to consolidate the data in the exact same cells on several worksheets.

- You can consolidate data from differently structured databases. This is called **consolidation by category**. When you consolidate data by category, you're telling Excel to consolidate data based on the row and column labels you're using.

  ✓ *The following Try It uses consolidation by category because the worksheets being consolidated have different data ranges.*

Try It!   **Consolidating Data**

1. Create a new blank workbook.

2. Save the workbook as **E73TryB_xx** in the location where your teacher instructs you to store the files for this lesson.

3. Open the **E73TryC**, **E73TryD**, and **E73TryE** files from the data files for this lesson, and browse the contents of each.

   ✓ *Notice that each one contains product numbers in the A column, but different part numbers appear, and in different orders, in each one. This inconsistency makes consolidation by category appropriate for this job.*

4. In the **E73TryB_xx** file, click DATA > Consolidate ▤ to open the Consolidate dialog box.

5. Verify that the Function setting is Sum.

6. In the Reference box, click the Collapse Dialog Box button ▣, switch to **E73TryC**, select the cell range A1:D10, and press [ENTER].

7. In the Consolidate dialog box, click Add.

8. In the Reference box, select the cell range reference, and click [DEL] to clear the reference.

9. Click the Collapse Dialog Box button ▣, switch to **E73TryD**, select the cell range A1:D12, and press [ENTER] to return to the dialog box.

10. In the Consolidate dialog box, click Add.

11. Repeat steps 8–10 to add references to the cell range A1:D11 in **E73TryE**.

12. In the Consolidate dialog box, under Use labels in, click the Top row and Left column check boxes to select them.

   ✓ *If you do not mark these check boxes, Excel considers this a consolidation by position, so in this case it is important to mark them.*

13. Click the Create links to source data check box to select it.

14. Click OK. The consolidated data appears.

15. Save the changes to the **E73TryB_xx** file, and leave it open to use in the next Try It.

16. Close the **E73TryC**, **E73TryD**, and **E73TryE** files without saving changes.

The Consolidate dialog box

Consolidate	?	✕

Function:
Sum ▾

Reference:
[E73TryE.xlsx]Sheet1!$A$1:$D$11   ▤   Browse...

All references:
[E73TryC.xlsx]Sheet1!$A$1:$D$10
[E73TryD.xlsx]Sheet1!$A$1:$D$12
[E73TryE.xlsx]Sheet1!$A$1:$D$11

Add

Delete

Use labels in
☑ Top row
☑ Left column   ☑ Create links to source data

OK   Close

Working with Consolidated Data

- After consolidating data, the results appear in Excel in a special format, containing buttons along the left side for collapsing and expanding the view of the results. See Figure 73-1.

- Click a plus sign to expand a category; click a minus sign to collapse it.

Figure 73-1

	A	B	C	D	E
1			Jan	Feb	Mar
2		E73Trye	3,453	3,478	3,301
3	A-407		3,453	3,478	3,301
4		E73Tryc	1,082	1,095	1,022
5		E73Tryd	5,000	5,600	5,441
6		E73Trye	3,000	3,246	3,224
7	A-401		9,082	9,941	9,687
8		E73Tryc	1,189	1,325	1,246
9		E73Tryd	5,354	5,211	5,526
10	A-403		6,543	6,536	6,772
13	A-404		6,748	6,360	6,428
15	A-409		1,174	1,116	1,140
17	A-412		1,398	1,218	1,567

Try It!   Working with Consolidated Data

1. In the **E73TryB_xx** file, double-click the divider between the columns A and B headers to widen column A.

2. Click the plus sign next to product number A-407 to expand that list.

3. Double-click the divider between the columns B and C headers to widen column B.

4. Click the plus sign next to product number A-401 to expand that list.

   ✓ Notice that the product number appears at the bottom of the list of expanded records for it, not at the top. For example, row 7, where A-401 appears, contains a summary of the contents of rows 4–6.

5. Select columns A:E.

6. Click DATA > Sort A to Z. The list is sorted by column A (the product numbers).

   ✓ You might notice the green triangles in the corners of some cells, indicating a possible error. These are not really errors, though; Excel has marked them as errors incorrectly. If you expand more records, you will notice that the rows that have the error indicators on them are the rows for product numbers that appeared in only one of the worksheets that were consolidated.

   ✓ The column labels in B through E were moved to the bottom of the list during the sort in step 6. Now you need to move them back to their normal positions.

7. Select row 1, and click HOME > Insert.

8. Select the cell range C53:E53, and press CTRL + X to cut them to the Clipboard.

9. Click cell C1, and press CTRL + V to paste the column labels.

10. Save and close the file, and exit Excel.

Lesson 73—Practice

It's the end of the quarter, and it's time to draw some conclusions about product sales for Holy Habañero, which sells its hot sauces through nine different sales channels. Since the details for each month are stored on separate worksheets, you've decided to use the Consolidate command to bring the data together.

DIRECTIONS

1. Start Excel, if necessary, and open **E73Practice** from the data files for this lesson.

2. Save the file as **E73Practice_xx** in the location where your teacher instructs you to store the files for this lesson.

3. Make a copy of the **March** worksheet to use as a template for the consolidated figures:

   a. Right-click the **March** worksheet tab.

   b. Click **Move or Copy**.

   c. In the Before sheet list, click **(move to end)**.

   d. Click the **Create a copy** check box.

   e. Click **OK**. A **March (2)** worksheet appears.

   f. Double-click the **March (2)** worksheet tab, type **Totals**, and press [ENTER] .

4. On the **Totals** worksheet, select the cell range **B8:I16**, and press [DEL] to clear the cells.

5. Select the cell range **B19:I27**, and press [DEL] to clear the cells.

6. Click cell B3, edit the text in to read **Quarterly Sales Breakdown**, and press [ENTER] .

7. Click cell B4, edit the text to read **Q1 2014 Totals**, and press [ENTER] .

8. On the **Totals** worksheet, total the Unit sales for the last three months:

   a. Click **B8**.

   b. Click **DATA > Consolidate** .

   c. Choose **Sum** from the Function list, if necessary.

   d. Click in the **Reference** box, click the **Collapse Dialog Box** button , click the **January** worksheet tab, select the cell range **B8:I16**, and press [ENTER] .

   e. In the Consolidate dialog box, click **Add**.

   f. In the Reference box, select the cell range reference, and press [DEL] to clear the reference.

   g. Click the **Collapse Dialog Box** button , click the **February** worksheet tab, select the cell range **B8:I16**, and press [ENTER] .

h. Repeat steps f–g to add the same range on the **March** worksheet.

i. Click the **Create links to source data** check box to select it.

   ✓ *Do not mark the Top row or Left column check box.*

j. Click **OK**. The summarized data appears.

   ✓ *Excel inserts hidden rows that contain links to the selected data. To view hidden rows, click the plus sign next to any row.*

9. Test the automatic updating process by changing cell **H12** in the **January** worksheet to **960**.

   ✓ *Cell J27 in the Totals worksheet should change from 13,339 to 13,371.*

10. Consolidate the data for Gross sales (B19:I27) on the **Totals** worksheet:

   a. On the **Totals** worksheet, click **B46**.

   b. Click **DATA > Consolidate** .

   c. Choose **Sum** from the Function list, if necessary.

   d. On the All References list, click the entry for the **January** worksheet, and click **Delete**.

   e. Click the entry for the **February** worksheet, and click **Delete**.

   f. Click the entry for the **March** worksheet, and click **Delete**.

   g. Click in the **Reference** box, click the **Collapse Dialog Box** button , click the **January** worksheet tab, select the cell range **B19:I27**, and press [ENTER] .

   h. In the Consolidate dialog box, click **Add**.

   i. In the Reference box, select the cell range reference, and press [DEL] to clear the reference.

   j. Click the **Collapse Dialog Box** button , click the **February** worksheet tab, select the cell range **B19:I27**, and press [ENTER] .

   k. In the Consolidate dialog box, click **Add**.

   l. Repeat steps i–k to add the same range on the **March** worksheet.

m. Click the **Create links to source data** check box to select it, if necessary.

    ✓ *Do not mark the Top row or Left column check box.*

n. Click **OK**. The summarized data appears.

11. Widen **column J** to accommodate the widest entry, if necessary.

12. For all worksheets, add a header that has your name at the left, the date code in the center, and the page number code at the right, and change back to **Normal** view.

13. **With your teacher's permission,** print the **Totals** worksheet. Your worksheet should look like the one shown in Figure 73-2.

14. Save and close the file, and exit Excel.

Figure 73-2

Quarterly Sales Breakdown
Q1 2014 Totals

	Retail				Wholesale				Total
Unit sales	Direct mail catalog	Fundraising catalog	Online	Trade exhibits	Non-profit resellers	For-profit retailers (unit)	For-profit retailers (bulk)	Restaurants (bulk)	
Belly of the Beast	249	182	305	356	323	647	1,632	1,488	5,182
Magma Core	339	173	110	581	295	418	1,760	1,648	5,324
Typhoon Warning	278	155	579	971	891	1,721	3,328	2,528	10,451
Uranium 235	1,564	1,885	1,985	2,744	602	2,474	3,808	3,536	18,598
Szechuan Singe	1,067	1,164	1,240	1,575	1,623	2,142	2,816	1,744	13,371
Wasabi Fusion	282	450	783	1,362	1,983	2,442	3,936	2,736	13,974
Sorrento Serrano	236	350	477	233	447	1,073	1,088	272	4,176
Yucatan Bomb	255	224	270	186	228	1,334	1,472	384	4,353
Toast Jammer	185	379	113	143	336	831	-	-	1,987

	Direct mail catalog	Fundraising catalog	Online	Trade exhibits	Non-profit resellers	For-profit retailers (unit)	For-profit retailers (bulk)	Restaurants (bulk)	
Gross sales									
Belly of the Beast	$ 1,730.55	$ 1,264.90	$ 2,424.75	$ 2,830.20	$ 1,130.50	$ 3,073.25	$ 6,936.00	$ 5,952.00	$ 25,342.15
Magma Core	$ 2,356.05	$ 1,202.35	$ 874.50	$ 4,618.95	$ 1,032.50	$ 1,985.50	$ 7,480.00	$ 6,592.00	$ 26,141.85
Typhoon Warning	$ 1,932.10	$ 1,077.25	$ 4,603.05	$ 7,719.45	$ 3,118.50	$ 8,174.75	$14,144.00	$10,112.00	$ 50,881.10
Uranium 235	$10,869.80	$13,100.75	$15,780.75	$21,814.80	$ 2,107.00	$11,751.50	$16,184.00	$14,144.00	$ 105,752.60
Szechuan Singe	$ 9,549.65	$10,417.80	$12,338.00	$15,671.25	$ 7,709.25	$11,245.50	$14,784.00	$ 8,720.00	$ 90,435.45
Wasabi Fusion	$ 2,523.90	$ 4,027.50	$ 7,790.85	$13,551.90	$ 9,419.25	$12,820.50	$20,664.00	$13,680.00	$ 84,477.90
Sorrento Serrano	$ 2,112.20	$ 3,132.50	$ 4,746.15	$ 2,318.35	$ 2,123.25	$ 5,633.25	$ 5,712.00	$ 1,360.00	$ 27,137.70
Yucatan Bomb	$ 1,517.25	$ 1,332.80	$ 1,876.50	$ 1,292.70	$ 672.60	$ 4,335.50	$ 5,520.00	$ 1,152.00	$ 17,699.35
Toast Jammer	$ 1,100.75	$ 2,255.05	$ 785.35	$ 993.85	$ 991.20	$ 2,700.75	$ -	$ -	$ 8,826.95

        $ 436,695.05

        Taxes paid $ 8,753.95

        Sales after taxes **$ 427,941.10**

Lesson 73—Apply

You are the sales manager of the Brown Street store of the Fulton Appliances chain of stores. The second week of August sales have ended, and you want to provide headquarters with a summary of the week's sales. You want to combine the data from each of the day's sales. You also notice that the names in the spreadsheet are not capitalized, and you need to correct this.

DIRECTIONS

1. Start Excel, if necessary, and open **E73Apply** from the data files for this lesson.

2. Save the file as **E73Apply_xx** in the location where your teacher instructs you to store the files for this lesson.

3. For all worksheets, add a header that has your name at the left, the date code in the center, and the page number code at the right, and change back to **Normal** view.

4. Use Flash Fill to uppercase the names of the salespeople:

   a. Select the cell range **B10:B13**, and press `CTRL` + `C` to copy it.

   b. Click cell **L10**, and press `CTRL` + `V` to paste it in the cell range **L:10:L13**.

   c. Click cell **M10**, type **Jack Smithe**, and press `ENTER`.

   d. In cell M11, type **Joe**, and press `ENTER`.

   e. Select the cell range **M10:M13**, and press `CTRL` + `C` to copy it.

   f. Click cell **B10**, and press `CTRL` + `V` to paste it in the cell range **B10:B13**.

   g. Copy and paste the cell range **B10:B13** to the rest of the cell ranges with names of salespeople.

   h. Select the cell range **L10:M13**, and press `DEL`.

5. Using consolidation by category, insert the **Sum** function to summarize the sales data from the **August Week 2** worksheet into a single table on the **Summary** worksheet in the cell range **C10:J13**. Include the total sales and the commission amounts, or manually re-create them after doing the consolidation by copying the functions from the **August Week 2** worksheet into the appropriate cells on the **Summary** worksheet.

6. Using consolidation by category, insert the **Average** function to average the sales data from the **August Week 2** worksheet into a single table on the **Summary** worksheet in the cell range **C20:H23**. Do not include total sales or commissions (columns I and J).

7. Format the cells containing the averages with the **Number** format, and show one decimal place.

8. Adjust the column widths as necessary, and format the worksheet as you like.

9. **With your teacher's permission,** print the **Summary** worksheet. Your worksheet should look like the one shown in Figure 73-3 on the next page.

10. Save and close the file, and exit Excel.

Figure 73-3

	A	B	C	D	E	F	G	H	I	J
1										
2		JJ Fulton Appliances								
3										
4		Brown Street Store								
5		Summary of Sales, Week of August 12th								
6										
7										
8										
9	Totals for the Week	Salesperson	Dishwasher	Oven	Refrigerator	Television	Washer	Dryer	Total Sales	Commission
10		Jack Smithe	9	8	9	7	8	7	$ 28,006.47	$ 2,030.47
11		Joe Cooper	7	3	6	9	5	6	$ 22,195.22	$ 1,609.15
12		Sally Peters	3	6	9	16	6	4	$ 30,684.64	$ 2,224.64
13		Peter Carter	7	4	3	13	2	2	$ 20,325.26	$ 1,473.58
14										
15										
16										
17										
18										
19	Averages for the Week	Salesperson	Dishwasher	Oven	Refrigerator	Television	Washer	Dryer		
20		Jack Smithe	1.8	1.6	1.5	2.3	1.6	1.8		
21		Joe Cooper	1.8	1.5	2.0	1.8	1.7	1.2		
22		Sally Peters	1.0	1.2	2.3	2.7	1.5	1.3		
23		Peter Carter	1.4	1.3	1.0	2.2	1.0	1.0		

Lesson 74

Linking Workbooks

➤ What You Will Learn

Linking Workbooks
Modifying a Linked Workbook

Software Skills   In Excel, you can link to data created in another Microsoft program, such as Word or PowerPoint. When you change the Excel data, the data in the source file will update automatically. For example, if you link Excel data to a Word document and then change that data, the changes are automatically updated within the Word document.

WORDS TO KNOW

Link
A reference to data stored in another file. When that data is changed, the data is updated in the destination file automatically.

What You Can Do

Linking Workbooks

- You can create a **link** between files to create a connection between the data in the files.

- In a linked file, if you change the data in the source file, the data in the destination file changes.

- You can change the link to update manually instead of automatically.

- You can perform other maintenance tasks with the links in your destination file, such as breaking a link and retaining local formatting changes whenever a link is updated.

- Typically, all Microsoft programs support linking, so you can apply the same process to link Excel data in programs other than those of Microsoft Office.

Try It!   **Linking a Workbook to a PowerPoint Presentation**

1 Start Excel, and open the **E74TryA** file from the data files for this lesson.

2 Save the file as **E74TryA_xx** in the location where your teacher instructs you to store the files for this lesson.

3 Start PowerPoint, and open the **E74TryB** file from the data files for this lesson.

4 Save the file as **E74TryB_xx** in the location where your teacher instructs you to store the files for this lesson.

✓ *For the purposes of this lesson, it is helpful to have the linked files in the same folder. You can link files that are in different file locations, but the files need to stay in their original locations for the files to stay linked.*

5 In the **E74TryA_xx** Excel file, click the January worksheet tab.

6 Select the cell range A6:J16, and on the HOME tab, click Copy.

7 Switch to the **E74TryB_xx** PowerPoint presentation, and on the HOME tab, click the Paste drop-down arrow **Paste** > Paste Special.

8 In the Paste Special dialog box, click Paste link.

9 In the As list, click Microsoft Excel Worksheet Object.

10 Click OK. The linked Excel data is placed on the slide.

11 Resize the linked Excel data, and reposition it on the slide as shown in the graphic.

12 Close the **E74TryA_xx** file without saving changes, and exit Excel.

13 Save the changes to the **E74TryB_xx** file, and leave it open to use in the next Try It.

Linked data from an Excel workbook

			Retail				Wholesale			Total
Unit sales		Direct mail catalog	Fundraising catalog	Online	Trade exhibits	Non-profit resellers	For-profit resellers (unit)	For-profit resellers (bulk)	Restaurants (bulk)	
	Belly of the Beast	98	65	105	112	132	240	672	640	2,064
	Magma Core	105	50	31	194	98	169	704	736	2,087
	Typhoon Warning	91	46	350	332	291	594	1,440	1,280	4,424
	Uranium 235	515	614	625	904	234	1,021	1,472	1,664	7,049
	Szechuan Singe	348	393	404	520	594	912	960	832	4,963
	Wasabi Fusion	94	150	261	454	661	814	1,312	912	4,658
	Sorrento Serrano	79	104	162	74	192	513	480	144	1,748
	Yucatan Bomb	84	68	87	63	87	632	672	176	1,869
	Toast Jammer	61	145	32	45	94	367	-	-	744

Modifying a Linked Workbook

- You can update data linked to an Excel workbook without having the Excel source file open.

- For example, if you have linked Excel data in a Word document (the destination file), you can open that Word document and double-click the data. Excel automatically starts and opens the linked workbook so you can make changes.

- After you make changes and save them, the changes are automatically updated through the link to the source file.

- If the destination file is not currently open when you make changes in the Excel source file, the changes will be updated when the destination file is opened later.

- Because Excel uses the file path as its location, if the source file is moved from the location where it was originally linked to the destination file, you will need to update the link.

Try It!　　**Modifying a Linked Workbook**

1 In the **E74TryB_xx** file, double-click the linked Excel data. Excel opens the **E74TryA_xx** file with the linked data selected.

　　✓ *If a security warning appears, click Enable Content.*

2 Arrange the Excel and PowerPoint windows side by side.

3 In the **E74TryA_xx** file, click cell D10, type **350**, and press ᴇɴᴛᴇʀ .

4 In the **E74TryB_xx** file, notice the change reflected in the PowerPoint presentation.

5 Save the changes to the **E74TryA_xx** file, and exit Excel.

6 Save the changes to the **E74TryB_xx** file, and close it. Leave PowerPoint open to use in the next Try It.

Try It!　　**Manually Updating a Link**

1 In PowerPoint, open the **E74TryB_xx** file from the location where your teacher instructs you to store the files for this lesson.

2 In the security notice dialog box, click Cancel.

3 Click the linked Excel data to select it.

4 Right-click the Excel data, and click Update Link.

5 Save and close the file, and exit PowerPoint.

Manually updating linked data

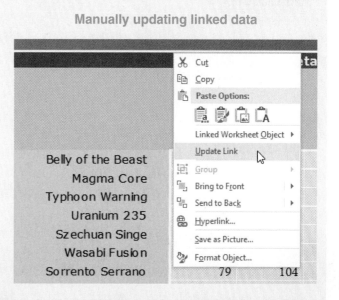

Lesson 74—Practice

You are the sales manager for Holy Habañero, which sells hot sauces through nine different sales channels. The owner of the company has asked you create a PowerPoint presentation for the total gross sales figures from the first quarter of the year. You want to create a link to the Excel workbook so that you know the data can be updated if it changes in the future.

DIRECTIONS

1. Start Excel, if necessary, and open **E74PracticeA** from the data files for this lesson.

2. Save the file as **E74PracticeA_xx** in the location where your teacher instructs you to store the files for this lesson.

3. Start PowerPoint, and open the **E74PracticeB** file from the data files for this lesson.

4. Save the file as **E74PracticeB_xx** in the location where your teacher instructs you to store the files for this lesson.

   ✓ *For the purposes of this project, it is helpful to have the linked files in the same folder.*

5. In the **E74PracticeB_xx** file, click in the **Created by:** text box, and type your name.

6. Switch to the **E74PracticeA_xx** file, and click the **Totals** worksheet tab

7. Select the cell range **A45:J84**, and on the HOME tab, click **Copy** 📋.

8. Switch to the **E74PracticeB_xx** file, and on the HOME tab, click the **Paste** drop-down arrow ^{Paste} > **Paste Special**.

9. In the Paste Special dialog box, click **Paste link**.

10. In the As list, click **Microsoft Excel Worksheet Object**.

11. Click **OK** to place the linked Excel data on the slide.

12. Resize the linked object. Your worksheet should look like the one shown in Figure 74-1 on the next page.

13. Close the **E74PracticeA_xx** file without saving changes, and exit Excel.

14. **With your teacher's permission,** print the **E74PracticeB_xx** presentation.

15. Save and close the **E74PracticeB_xx** file, and exit PowerPoint.

Figure 74-1

 **Total Gross Sales Breakdown**

Created by:
Firstname
Lastname

Gross sales	Direct mail catalog	Fundraising catalog	Online	Trade exhibits	Non-profit resellers	For-profit retailers (unit)	For-profit retailers (bulk)	Restaurants (bulk)	
Belly of the Beast	$ 1,730.55	$ 1,264.90	$ 2,424.75	$ 2,830.20	$ 1,130.50	$ 3,073.25	$ 6,936.00	$ 5,952.00	$ 25,342.15
Magma Core	$ 2,356.05	$ 1,202.35	$ 874.50	$ 4,618.95	$ 1,032.50	$ 1,985.50	$ 7,480.00	$ 6,592.00	$ 26,141.85
Typhoon Warning	$ 1,932.10	$ 1,077.25	$ 4,603.05	$ 7,719.45	$ 3,118.50	$ 8,174.75	$14,144.00	$10,112.00	$ 50,881.10
Uranium 235	$10,869.80	$13,100.75	$15,780.75	$21,814.80	$ 2,107.00	$11,751.50	$16,184.00	$14,144.00	$ 105,752.60
Szechuan Singe	$ 9,549.65	$10,417.80	$12,338.00	$15,671.25	$ 7,709.25	$11,245.50	$14,784.00	$ 8,720.00	$ 90,435.45
Wasabi Fusion	$ 2,523.90	$ 4,027.50	$ 7,790.85	$13,551.90	$ 9,419.25	$12,820.50	$20,664.00	$13,680.00	$ 84,477.90
Sorrento Serrano	$ 2,112.20	$ 3,132.50	$ 4,746.15	$ 2,318.35	$ 2,123.25	$ 5,633.25	$ 5,712.00	$ 1,360.00	$ 27,137.70
Yucatan Bomb	$ 1,517.25	$ 1,332.80	$ 1,876.50	$ 1,292.70	$ 672.60	$ 4,335.50	$ 5,520.00	$ 1,152.00	$ 17,699.35
Toast Jammer	$ 1,100.75	$ 2,255.05	$ 785.35	$ 993.85	$ 991.20	$ 2,700.75	$ -	$ -	$ 8,826.95
									$ 436,695.05
								Taxes paid	$ 8,753.95
								Sales after taxes	**$ 427,941.10**

Lesson 74—Apply

As the sales manager for Holy Habañero, you have been concerned about the unit sales in your inventory. You created several Excel worksheets to show the unit sales for the first three months of the year. The corporate office has asked to review your figures, so you need to prepare a PowerPoint presentation and link Excel data to the presentation. In this project, you will link an Excel workbook to a PowerPoint presentation, update the data, and manually update the link.

DIRECTIONS

1. Start Excel, if necessary, and open **E74ApplyA** from the data files for this lesson.

2. Save the file as **E74Apply_xx** in the location where your teacher instructs you to store the files for this lesson.

3. Start PowerPoint, and open the **E74ApplyB** file from the data files for this lesson.

4. Save the file as **E74ApplyB_xx** in the location where your teacher instructs you to store the files for this lesson

   ✓ *For the purposes of this project, it is helpful to have the linked files in the same folder.*

5. In the **E74 Apply B_xx** file, click in the **Created by:** text box, and type your name.

6. In the PowerPoint file, insert a link to the total unit sales data from the Excel worksheet:

   a. Switch to the **E74ApplyA_xx** file, and click the **Totals** worksheet tab

   b. Select the cell range **A6:J44**, and on the HOME tab, click **Copy** 📋 .

   c. Switch to the **E74ApplyB_xx** file, and on the HOME tab, click the **Paste** drop-down arrow ᴾᵃˢᵗᵉ > **Paste Special**.

   d. In the Paste Special dialog box, click **Paste link**.

   e. In the As list, click **Microsoft Excel Worksheet Object**.

   f. Click **OK** to place the linked Excel data on the slide.

   g. Resize the linked object, and reposition it on the slide.

7. Close the **E74ApplyA_xx** file without saving changes, and exit Excel.

8. Save the **E74ApplyB_xx** file.

9. Edit the unit sales data in Excel:

   a. Double-click the linked Excel data. Excel opens the **E74ApplyA_xx** file with the linked data selected.

   b. Change the Online value for Magma Core to **185**.

   c. Change the Direct mail catalog value for Toast Jammer to **250**.

   d. Save the **E74ApplyA_xx** Excel file, and exit Excel.

10. In the PowerPoint file, check that the data has been updated.

11. Spell check the presentation.

12. **With your teacher's permission,** print the **E74ApplyB_xx** presentation. Your worksheet should look like the one shown in Figure 74-2 on the next page.

13. Save and close the **E74ApplyB_xx** file, and exit PowerPoint.

Figure 74-2

Total Unit Sales—1st Qtr

Created by:
Firstname
Lastname

Unit sales	Retail				Wholesale				Total
	Direct mail catalog	Fundraising catalog	Online	Trade exhibits	Non-profit resellers	For-profit retailers (unit)	For-profit retailers (bulk)	Restaurants (bulk)	
Belly of the Beast	249	182	305	356	323	647	1,632	1,488	5,182
Magma Core	339	173	185	581	295	418	1,760	1,648	5,399
Typhoon Warning	278	155	579	971	891	1,721	3,328	2,528	10,451
Uranium 235	1,564	1,885	1,985	2,744	602	2,474	3,808	3,536	18,598
Szechuan Singe	1,067	1,164	1,240	1,575	1,623	2,142	2,816	1,744	13,371
Wasabi Fusion	282	450	783	1,362	1,983	2,442	3,936	2,736	13,974
Sorrento Serrano	236	350	477	233	447	1,073	1,088	272	4,176
Yucatan Bomb	255	224	270	186	228	1,334	1,472	384	4,353
Toast Jammer	250	379	113	143	336	831	-	-	2,052

Lesson 75

Using PivotTables

➤ What You Will Learn

Working with PivotTables
Working with PivotTable Fields
Sorting PivotTable Fields
Formatting a PivotTable

Software Skills   PivotTables can help you analyze complex data in a variety of ways. For example, you can use a PivotTable to summarize a database with employee data and filter or group the data by name, region, address, or salary. With the PivotTable, you can display information for each employee, or you can rearrange the table to display employees by region. You can use a data model, such as the Excel Data Model, to build a relational data source. With a Data Model-based PivotTable, you can analyze the details of your data.

What You Can Do

Working with PivotTables

- You can more easily summarize and analyze data with a **PivotTable** than you can with a regular table.

  ✓ *You first learned about PivotTables in Lesson 36.*

- For example, you can use a PivotTable to summarize a **database** with many tables and filter to the exact data elements that you want.

- You can create your own PivotTable, or you can use the recommended PivotTables that Excel provides from the Tables group on the INSERT tab or the TABLES tab of the Quick Analysis Tool.

- The source data for your PivotTable can be a data range or table in an Excel workbook, or it can be data that is stored outside of Excel, such as a Microsoft Access or Microsoft SQL Server database, or in an Online Analytical Processing (OLAP) cube file.

- When you create a PivotTable from an external data source, you link the data to that source.

- A **Data Model** is a feature in Excel 2013 that integrates data from multiple tables to build a relational **data source** inside an Excel workbook. You can use the data model to create and manage the relationships among your data.

- You can choose to add the data to the Excel Data Model when you create a PivotTable.

  ✓ *You will learn more about the Excel Data Model in Lesson 77.*

- As with a regular Excel table, you can insert a slicer or a timeline for a PivotTable.

- If you are using Windows XP, you can publish a PivotTable report, or an external data range from a Microsoft Query, as a PivotTable list on an interactive Web page.

- If you are using Windows 8, you can publish a PivotTable in an Excel workbook as a Web page.

Try It! **Creating a PivotTable from Excel Worksheet Data**

❶ Start Excel, and open **E75TryA** from the data files for this lesson.

❷ Save the file as **E75TryA_xx** in the location where your teacher instructs you to store the files for this lesson.

❸ On the August Sales worksheet, click anywhere in the data range.

❹ Click INSERT > PivotTable 🗗 to display the Create PivotTable dialog box.

❺ Click OK to accept the default placement of the PivotTable on a new worksheet.

❻ Double-click on the new worksheet tab, type **Pet Drug Sales**, and press ENTER .

❼ Save the changes to the file, and leave it open to use in the next Try It.

Try It! **Creating a PivotTable from an Access Database**

❶ Start Access, and open the **E75TryB** file from the data files for this lesson.

❷ Save the file as **E75TryB_xx** in the location where your teacher instructs you to store the files for this lesson.

  ✓ *It is helpful to have linked files in the same folder.*

❸ Close the **E75TryB_xx** file.

❹ In the **E75TryA_xx** file, click the Access worksheet tab.

❺ Click cell A1.

❻ Click INSERT > PivotTable 🗗 to display the Create PivotTable dialog box.

❼ Under Choose the data that you want to analyze, click Use an external data source > Choose Connection. Excel displays the connections that are available.

❽ In the Existing Connections dialog box, click E75TryB_xx RealEstate > Open.

  ✓ *If you do not see the appropriate connection, you can browse to the location where your teacher instructs you to store the files for this lesson.*

❾ In the Create PivotTable dialog box, check that the Existing Worksheet Location is Access!$A$1.

❿ Click the Add this data to the Data Model check box to select it.

⓫ Click OK.

⓬ Save the changes to the file, and leave it open to use in the next Try It.

Creating a PivotTable from an external data source

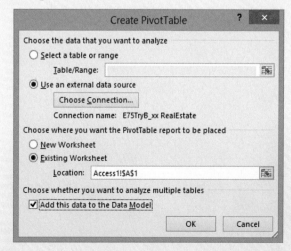

Working with PivotTable Fields

- When you create a blank PivotTable, you need to add **fields** to it to show the summarized data.

- When you insert a recommended PivotTable, you can modify the PivotTable fields in the PivotTable Fields task pane.

- To display the PivotTable Fields task pane, use the Field List button in the Show group on the PIVOTTABLE TOOLS ANALYZE tab.

- In Excel 2013, the Field List in the PivotTable Fields task pane displays the tables in the Excel Data Model.

- The PivotTable Fields task pane displays the Field Section stacked on top of the Areas Section, by default.

- You can click the Tools button ⚙▾ to change the view of the Field Sections and the Areas Section.

- You can drag fields into the four areas of the Areas Section to rearrange the fields.

  - FILTERS: Area fields shown as a **report filter** above the PivotTable. These fields can drill down into the data to show only the items relating to a particular category.

  - COLUMNS: Area fields shown as Column Labels at the top of the PivotTable. These are typically fields that categorize the data, for example, by date, time, or item.

  - ROWS: Area fields shown as Row Labels on the left side of the PivotTable. These are typically text fields that describe the data.

  - VALUES: Area fields that summarize numeric values in the PivotTable, for example, a sum calculating the total sales.

- You can click the drop-down arrow of an area field to access more options. For example, you can change a field in the VALUES area to calculate on an average instead of a sum by choosing Value Field Settings and selecting Average from the Value Field Settings dialog box.

- To remove a field from a PivotTable, deselect the field's check box in the Field List. You can also click the field's down-arrow in the Area Section and click Remove Field, or you can drag it out of the Area Section.

Try It! **Adding PivotTable Fields**

1 In the **E75TryA_xx** file, click the Pet Drug Sales worksheet tab, and click in the PivotTable box to display the PivotTable Fields task pane.

2 Drag the Drug field into the ROWS area.

3 Drag the For use on field into the FILTERS area.

4 Drag the To treat field into the COLUMNS area.

5 Drag the Total Sales field into the VALUES area.

6 Save the changes to the file, and leave it open to use in the next Try It.

(continued)

Try It! | **Adding PivotTable Fields** *(continued)*

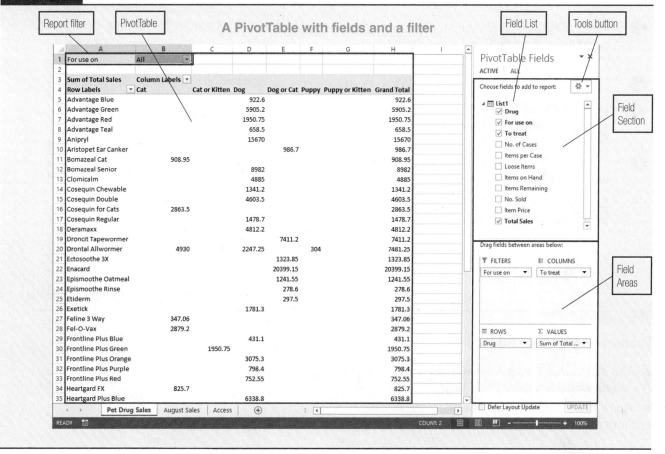

A PivotTable with fields and a filter

Sorting PivotTable Fields

- You can sort PivotTable data so that it's easier to find the items you want to analyze.

- You can sort in alphabetical order or on values, such as from highest to lowest or oldest to newest.

- For the best sort results, be sure that your data doesn't have extra spaces at the front of the data elements.

- Sorting PivotTable data has some limitations.
  - You can't sort case-sensitive text entries.
  - You can't sort data by a format, such as cell or font color, or by conditional formatting indicators, such as icon sets.

- To sort, click the AutoSort drop-drop-down arrow to the left of the field label.

- You can set custom sort options by clicking More Sort Options from the AutoSort menu.

Try It! | **Sorting PivotTable Fields**

1 In the **E75TryA_xx** file, on the Pet Drug Sales worksheet, and click the Row Labels drop-down arrow.

2 Click Sort Z to A ↓. The PivotTable is sorted by drug names in reverse alphabetical order.

3 Click the Row Labels drop-down arrow > Sort A to Z ↓. The PivotTable is sorted by drug names in alphabetical order.

4 Save the changes to the file, and leave it open to use in the next Try It.

Try It!   **Creating a Custom Sort for PivotTable Fields**

1   In the **E75TryA_xx** file, on the Pet Drug Sales worksheet, click the Row Labels drop-down arrow.

2   Click More Sort Options.

3   Under Sort options, click the Ascending (A to Z) by drop-down arrow, and click Sum of Total Sales.

4   Click OK. The PivotTable is sorted by the values of the total sales in ascending order.

5   Save the changes to the file, and leave it open to use in the next Try It.

The custom sort dialog box

Formatting a PivotTable

- You can format a PivotTable with a PivotTable style, as you would a regular Excel table.
- Apply PivotTable style options, such as banded rows or columns, to make it easier to read the data.

Try It!   **Formatting a PivotTable**

1   In the **E75TryA_xx** file, on the Pet Drug Sales worksheet, click in the PivotTable.

2   Click PIVOTTABLE TOOLS DESIGN.

3   Click the PivotTable Styles More button ⏷.

4   In the Dark group, click Pivot Style Dark 2.

5   On the PIVOTTABLE TOOLS DESIGN tab, in the PivotTable Style Options group, click the Banded Rows and Banded Columns check boxes to select them.

6   Save and close the file, and exit Excel.

Lesson 75—Practice

You work in the sales department of Best Sales Real Estate. Your manager has asked you to create a spreadsheet showing the total sales by each salesperson broken out by the areas and communities where the properties were sold. Your manager also wants the spreadsheet to show only single family homes from the Coastal and East County areas. In this project, you will create a PivotTable from the Excel data and filter it so that your manager can easily analyze the data.

DIRECTIONS

1. Start Excel, if necessary, and open **E75Practice** from the data files for this lesson.

2. Save the file as **E75Practice_xx** in the location where your teacher instructs you to store the files for this lesson.

3. Create a PivotTable from the cell range **A1:L121**, and place it on a new worksheet:
   a. On the **Report 1** worksheet, click in the table.
   b. Click **INSERT > PivotTable** 📄.
   c. Click the **Add this data to the Data Model** check box to select it.
   d. Click **OK**.

4. Double-click the **Sheet1** tab, type **Single Family**, and press ENTER .

5. In the PivotTable, show the total sales of each salesperson by area and community:
   a. On the **Single Family** worksheet, click the PivotTable.
   b. Drag the **Agent** field into the **ROWS** area.
   c. Drag the **Area** field into the **COLUMNS** area.
   d. Drag the **Community** field into the **COLUMNS** area.
   e. Drag the **List Price** field into the **VALUES** area.
      ✓ Notice that the PivotTable does not include the icon sets from the data table.
   f. Drag the **Type** field into the **FILTERS** area.

6. Filter the PivotTable to display only Single Family homes.
   a. On the **Single Family** worksheet, click cell **B1**, and click the **All** drop-down arrow.
   b. Click the **All** plus sign to expand the list.
   c. Click **Single Family**.
   d. Click **OK**.

7. Filter the PivotTable to display only Coastal and East County area properties:
   a. On the **Single Family** worksheet, click cell **B3**, and click the **Column Labels** drop-down arrow.
   b. Click to deselect the **Inland** check box.
   c. Click **OK**.

8. Format the cell range **B6:V20** with the **Accounting** format and no decimals.

9. Close the PivotTable Fields task pane.

10. Select the cell range **A1:V20**, and click **VIEW > Zoom to Selection**.

11. Adjust the column widths as needed. Your worksheet should look like the one shown in Figure 75-1 on the next page.

12. For all worksheets, add a header that has your name at the left, the date code in the center, and the page number code at the right, and change back to **Normal** view.

13. **With your teacher's permission,** print the **Single Family** worksheet in **Landscape** orientation with the scaling set to **Fit Sheet on One Page**.

14. Save and close the file, and exit Excel.

Figure 75-1

Type | Single Family

Sum of List Price | Column Labels

Row Labels	Arandale	Bellevue	Bend	Linda Vista	Marysville	Mira Mesa	Mono Lake	Coastal Total	Bonita	Corona	East Lake	Escondido	Rockville	Santa Fe	Temecula	Tulare	Westood	Westwood	Zion	East County Total	Grand Total
Barnes	264,900	355,000		345,000				964,900						208,750						208,750	1,173,650
Carter							309,900	309,900	365,000	339,900	225,000				297,500	269,900		317,500		1,814,800	2,124,700
Conners			229,900			229,500		459,400	229,900											229,900	689,300
Garcia				359,900		799,000		1,158,900								229,500				229,500	1,388,400
Hamilton			425,900					425,900			304,900									304,900	730,800
Hood					374,900	389,000	369,900	1,133,800	249,000	249,900		574,900								1,073,800	2,207,600
Jeffery	1,550,400						248,500	1,798,900		338,876				247,500						586,376	2,385,276
Kennedy					379,000			379,000				208,750								208,750	587,750
Lam									229,500			480,990				205,000	239,900			1,155,390	1,155,390
Langston			359,000			349,000		708,000	685,000				245,000		225,911				325,000	1,480,911	2,188,911
McDonald	398,000							398,000													398,000
Severson					379,900		406,900	786,800					205,500		349,000					554,500	1,341,300
Smith			389,500			339,900		729,400													729,400
Tyson									289,000				204,900					225,911		719,811	719,811
Grand Total	2,213,300	355,000	1,404,300	704,900	1,133,800	2,106,400	1,335,200	9,252,900	2,047,400	928,676	529,900	1,264,640	655,400	456,250	872,411	704,400	239,900	543,411	325,000	8,567,388	17,820,288

Lesson 75—Apply

As sales manager of Best Sales Real Estate, you have created a spreadsheet showing the total sales by each salesperson broken out by the areas and communities where the properties were sold. The regional manager has asked you to show him the average list price of each salesperson from one report, as well as the average list price by area from another report. He also wants to see the prices sorted from highest to lowest. In this project, you will modify the data of an existing PivotTable and create a second PivotTable. You will also sort and format the data for both PivotTables.

DIRECTIONS

1. Start Excel, if necessary, and open **E75Apply** from the data files for this lesson.

2. Save the file as **E75Apply_xx** in the location where your teacher instructs you to store the files for this lesson.

3. For all worksheets, add a header that has your name at the left, the date code in the center, and the page number code at the right, and change back to **Normal** view

4. Modify the PivotTable to show the average list price of each salesperson:

    a. On the **PivotTables** worksheet, click **PIVOTTABLE TOOLS ANALYZE > Field List** to display the PivotTable Fields task pane.

    b. Click to deselect the **Area**, **Community**, and **Type** check boxes.

    c. In the **VALUES** area, click the **Sum of List Price** drop-down arrow > **Value Field Settings**.

    d. In the Value Field Settings dialog box, on the Summarize Values By tab, click **Average > OK**.

5. In cell **A2**, label the PivotTable **Report 1 PivotTable**. Apply **Bold** to the text, and increase the font size to **14 point**.

6. In cell **A20**, create the label **Report 2 PivotTable**. Apply **Bold** to the text, and increase the font size to **14 point**.

7. Create a PivotTable from the **Report 2** worksheet, and place it on the PivotTables worksheet starting at cell **A21**:

    a. Click the **Report 2** worksheet tab, and click in the table.

    b. Click **INSERT > PivotTable**.

    c. In the Create PivotTable dialog box, click the **Existing Worksheet** option to select it.

    d. In the Location box, click the **Collapse Dialog Box** button, click the **PivotTables** worksheet tab, click cell **A21**, and press ENTER to return to the dialog box.

    e. Click the **Add this data to the Data Model** check box to select it.

    f. Click **OK**.

8. In the **Report 2 PivotTable**, show the average list price of each area:

   a. Drag the **Area** field to the **ROWS** area.

   b. Drag the **List Price** field to the **VALUES** area.

   c. In the **VALUES** area, click the **Sum of List Price** drop-down arrow > **Value Field Settings**.

   d. In the Value Field Settings dialog box, on the Summarize Values By tab, click **Average** > **OK**.

9. Format the average list prices of both PivotTables with the **Accounting** format.

10. Sort the average list price of the **Report 1 PivotTable** from highest to lowest:

    a. In the **Report 1 PivotTable**, click the **Row Labels** drop-down arrow.

    b. Click **More Sort Options**.

    c. Under Sort Options, click the **Descending (Z to A) by** option.

    d. Click the **Descending (Z to A) by** list > **Average of List Price**.

    e. Click **OK**.

11. Sort the average list price of the **Report 2 PivotTable** from highest to lowest using the same process as in step 10.

12. Format the **Report 1 PivotTable** with the PivotTable Style Dark 3 style:

    a. Click in the **Report 1 PivotTable**.

    b. Click **PIVOTTABLE TOOLS DESIGN**.

    c. Click the PivotTable Styles **More** button ⯆ > **Pivot Style Dark 3**.

13. Format the **Report 2 PivotTable** with the **Pivot Style Dark 5** style using the same process as in step 12.

14. Close the PivotTable Fields task pane.

15. **With your teacher's permission,** print the **PivotTables** worksheet. Your worksheet should look like the one shown in Figure 75-2.

16. Save and close the file, and exit Excel.

Figure 75-2

	A	B
1		
2	**Report 1 PivotTable**	
3	Row Labels ⯆	Average of List Price
4	Jeffery	$ 398,972.00
5	Garcia	$ 351,315.71
6	Hood	$ 349,400.00
7	McDonald	$ 345,383.33
8	Smith	$ 317,741.67
9	Hamilton	$ 301,101.83
10	Severson	$ 296,182.77
11	Langston	$ 295,550.92
12	Tyson	$ 295,535.17
13	Barnes	$ 293,925.00
14	Kennedy	$ 290,950.00
15	Conners	$ 282,950.00
16	Carter	$ 282,349.29
17	Lam	$ 260,959.00
18	**Grand Total**	$ 308,614.79
19		
20	**Report 2 PivotTable**	
21	Row Labels ⯆	Average of List Price
22	Coastal	$ 363,166.41
23	Inland	$ 293,109.93
24	East County	$ 271,850.93
25	**Grand Total**	$ 308,614.79

Lesson 76

Using PivotCharts

➤ What You Will Learn

Creating a PivotChart from a PivotTable
Creating a PivotChart from an External Data Source
Working with PivotChart Fields
Formatting a PivotChart

Software Skills　PivotCharts can help you summarize and visualize large amounts of data. A PivotChart shows data series, categories, and chart axes in the same way as a standard chart; however, a PivotChart also has interactive filtering controls right on the chart so you can quickly analyze a subset of your data. For example, you can use a PivotChart to summarize a database with many tables and filter to show only the exact data elements that you want.

What You Can Do

Creating a PivotChart from a PivotTable

■ You can more easily summarize and analyze data with a **PivotChart** than you can with a regular chart.

✓ You first learned about PivotCharts in Lesson 36.

■ You can create your own PivotChart, or you can use the recommended PivotCharts that Excel provides.

■ Use the Recommended Charts command in the Charts group on the INSERT tab to insert a recommended PivotChart. Excel indicates a PivotChart with a PivotTable icon in the upper-right corner of the recommended chart.

■ When you insert a recommended PivotChart, Excel will automatically create a **coupled** PivotTable as well.

■ You can also create a **decoupled** PivotChart from Excel worksheet data without first creating a PivotTable.

Try It!   **Creating a Coupled PivotChart**

① Start Excel, and open the **E76TryA** file from the data files for this lesson.

② Save the file as **E76TryA_xx** in the location where your teacher instructs you to store the files for this lesson.

③ On the Nov Sales worksheet, click in the table.

④ Click INSERT > Recommended Charts ▮⊹ to display the Insert Chart dialog box.

⑤ On the Recommended Charts tab, click the Sum of Cost by Product Type chart (the second chart from the top).

⑥ Click OK. The PivotChart is inserted on a new worksheet.

⑦ Drag the PivotChart so that its upper-left corner is at the edge of cell E12.

⑧ Double-click the Sheet1 worksheet tab, type **Excel PivotChart**, and press ENTER .

⑨ Save the changes to the file, and leave it open to use in the next Try It.

Inserting a Recommended PivotChart

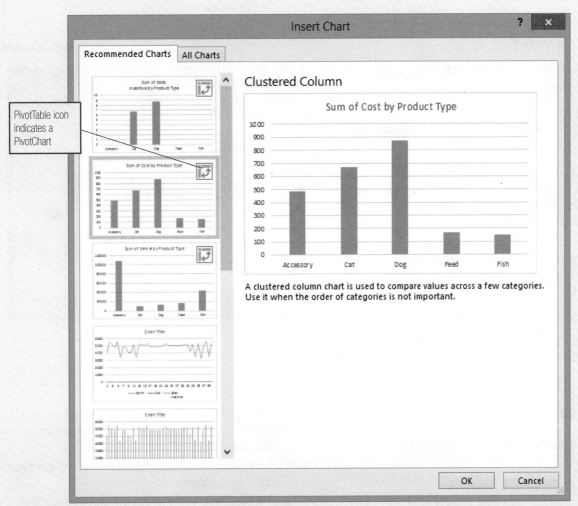

Creating a PivotChart from an External Data Source

- The source data for your PivotChart can be a data range or table in an Excel workbook, a PivotTable, or data that is stored outside of Excel, such as data from a Microsoft Access database.
- When you create a PivotChart from an external data source, you link the data to that source.
- You can use the data connections that Excel finds for you, or you can browse to a specific data connection.
- An Excel Data Model is automatically created when you create a recommended PivotChart.

Try It! Creating a PivotChart from an Access Database

1. Start Access, and open the **E76TryB** file from the data files for this lesson. Enable content if necessary.
2. Save the file as **E76TryB_xx** in the location where your teacher instructs you to store the files for this lesson.

   ✓ *It is helpful to have linked files in the same folder.*
3. Close the **E76TryB_xx** file.
4. In the **E76TryA_xx** file, click the Access worksheet tab.
5. Click cell A1.
6. Click INSERT > PivotChart to display the Create PivotChart dialog box.
7. Under Choose the data that you want to analyze, click Use an external data source > Choose Connection. Excel displays the connections that are available.
8. In the Existing Connections dialog box, click E76Try_xx RealEstate > Open.

   ✓ *If you do not see the appropriate connection, you can browse to the location where your teacher instructs you to store the files for this lesson.*
9. In the Create PivotTable dialog box, check that the Existing Worksheet Location is Access!$A$1.
10. Click OK. A PivotTable and a PivotChart are inserted on the worksheet.
11. Drag the PivotChart so that its upper-left corner is at the edge of cell F5.
12. Save the changes to the file, and leave it open to use in the next Try It.

Creating a PivotChart from an external data source

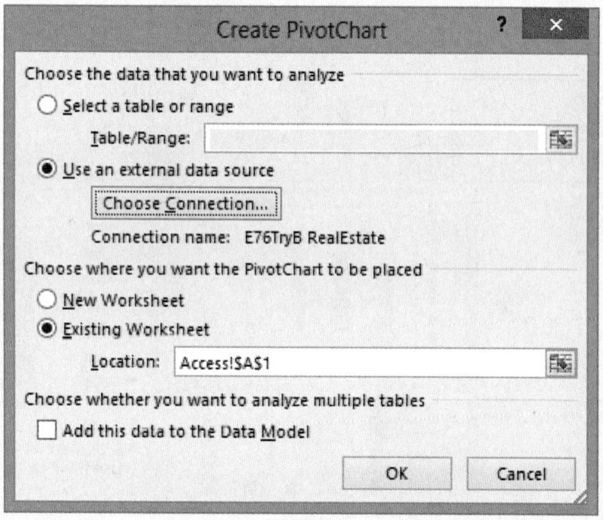

Working with PivotChart Fields

- You can customize a PivotChart with the commands on the PIVOTCHART TOOLS ANALYZE, DESIGN, and FORMAT tabs.
- When you create a PivotChart, you need to add fields to it to show your data.
- You can modify the PivotChart fields in the PivotChart Fields task pane, which is similar to the PivotTable Fields task pane.
- To display the PivotChart Fields task pane, use the Field List button in the Show/Hide group on the PIVOTCHART TOOLS ANALYZE tab.
- You can drag fields into the four areas of the Areas Section to rearrange the fields.
  - FILTERS: Area fields shown as a report filter above the PivotChart. These fields can drill down into the data to show only the items relating to a particular category.

- LEGEND (SERIES): Area fields shown as the legend labels of the PivotChart. These fields are also shown as Column Labels at the top of the PivotTable.
- AXIS (CATEGORIES): Area fields shown as the horizontal (category) axis, or the x-axis, of the PivotChart. These fields are also shown as Row Labels at the top of the PivotTable.
- VALUES: Area fields shown as the vertical (value) axis, or the y-axis, of the PivotChart, for example, the prices of homes.

■ You can click the drop-down arrow of an area field to access more options. For example, you can change a field in the VALUES area to calculate an average instead of a sum by choosing Value Field Settings and selecting Average from the Value Field Settings dialog box.

■ To remove a field from a PivotChart, deselect the field's check box in the Field List. You can also click the field's down-arrow in the Area Section and click Remove Field, or you can drag it out of the Area Section.

■ You can filter and sort the data in a PivotChart the same way you filter and sort data in a PivotTable. Select the items you want to display from the drop-down buttons on the chart.

Try It! Adding PivotChart Fields

❶ In the **E76TryA_xx** file, on the Access worksheet tab, click the PivotChart box to display the PivotChart Fields task pane.

❷ Drag the Area field into the FILTERS area.

❸ Drag the Sold field into the LEGEND (SERIES) area.

❹ Drag the Agent field into the AXIS (CATEGORIES) area.

❺ Drag the List Price field into the VALUES area.

❻ Save the changes to the file, and leave it open to use in the next Try It.

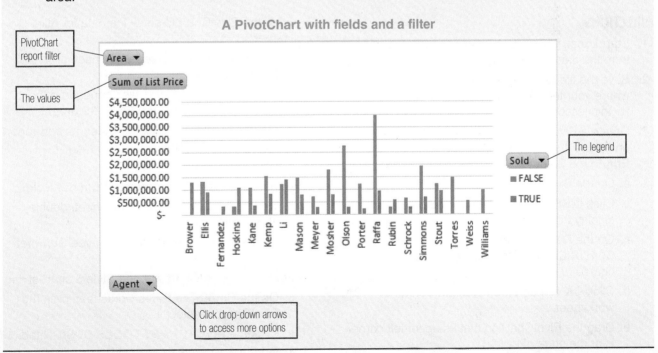

A PivotChart with fields and a filter

Formatting a PivotChart

■ You can format a PivotChart as you would a regular Excel chart.

■ Apply PivotChart style, color, and layout options from the PIVOTCHART TOOLS DESIGN tab.

■ You can also access style and color options from the Chart Styles shortcut button that appears to the right of the PivotChart.

Try It!   **Formatting a PivotChart**

1 In the **E76TryA_xx** file, on the Access worksheet, click the PivotChart.

2 Click the PIVOTCHART TOOLS DESIGN tab.

3 In the Chart Styles group, click the PivotChart Styles More button ⬇.

4 Click Style 7.

5 Apply the Accounting format to the cell range B5:D25.

6 Close the PivotTable Fields task pane.

7 Save and close the file, and exit Excel.

Lesson 76—Practice

You are the owner of Pete's Pets, a local pet store. Your store has just finished its summer sale, and you want to know how one of your employees performed. You want to chart the data by product type and filter the total sales by salesperson. In this project, you will create a PivotChart from the Excel data and filter it. You will also format the chart so that it can be included in the employee's performance review.

DIRECTIONS

1. Start Excel, if necessary, and open **E76Practice** from the data files for this lesson.

2. Save the file as **E76Practice_xx** in the location where your teacher instructs you to store the files for this lesson.

3. Create a PivotChart from the cell range **B9:G49**, and place it on a new worksheet named **Employee Sales**:
   a. On the **Sales Data** worksheet, click in the table.
   b. Click **INSERT > Recommended Charts** 📊 to display the Insert Chart dialog box.
   c. On the Recommended Charts tab, click the **Sum of Cost by Product Type** chart (the first chart).
   d. Click **OK** to insert the PivotChart on a new worksheet.
   e. Drag the PivotChart so that its upper-left corner is at the edge of cell **D12**.
   f. Rename the worksheet **Employee Sales**.

4. Filter the PivotChart to show the data for Alice Harper:
   a. On the **Employee Sales** worksheet, click the PivotChart to select it.
   b. In the PivotChart Fields task pane, drag the **Salesperson** field to the **FILTERS** area.
   c. On the PivotChart, click the **Salesperson** report filter drop-down arrow.
   d. Click **Alice Harper > OK**.

5. Rename the chart to **Employee Summer Sales**:
   a. On the **Employee Sales** worksheet, double-click the PivotChart title.
   b. Replace the title text with **Employee Summer Sales**.

6. Format the PivotChart with the Style 5 chart style:
   a. On the **Employee Sales** worksheet, click the PivotChart to select it.
   b. Click the **PIVOTCHART TOOLS DESIGN** tab.
   c. In the Chart Styles group, click the PivotChart Styles **More** button ⬇.
   d. Click **Style 5**.

7. Apply the **Accounting** format to the PivotTable cell range **B4:B8**.

8. Close the PivotTable Fields task pane.

9. For all worksheets, add a header that has your name at the left, the date code in the center, and the page number code at the right, and change back to **Normal** view.

10. Change the page orientation to **Landscape**.

11. **With your teacher's permission,** print the **Employee Sales** worksheet. Your worksheet should look like the one shown in Figure 76-1.

12. Save and close the file, and exit Excel.

Figure 76-1

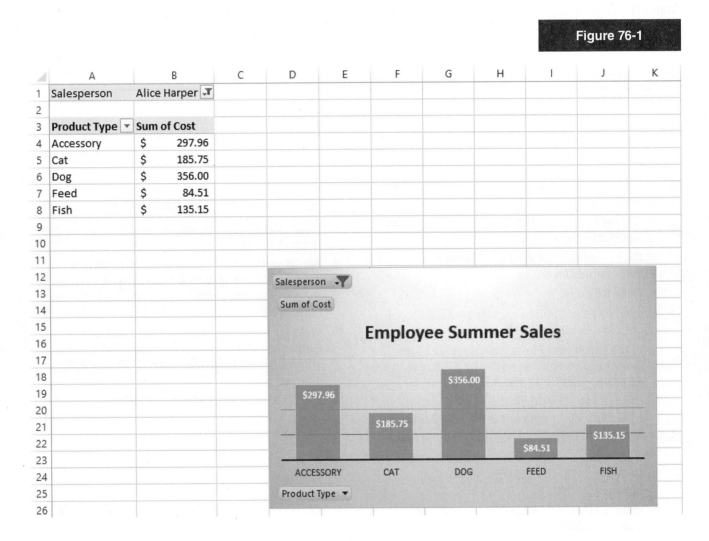

Lesson 76—Apply

As the owner of Pete's Pets, a local pet store, you plan to give one of your two employees a raise. Your store has just finished its summer sale, and you want to know which of your salespeople had the best sales for each of your products and overall. You created a PivotChart to show one of your employee's sales data, and you now want to modify the chart so that it shows the product sales for each salesperson. In this project, you will modify a PivotChart and filter the data so that you can easily compare your employee's summer sales. You will also format the charts.

DIRECTIONS

1. Start Excel, if necessary, and open **E76Apply** from the data files for this lesson.

2. Save the file as **E76Apply_xx** in the location where your teacher instructs you to store the files for this lesson.

3. Modify the report filter to show the data for both salespeople:

    a. On the **Employee Sales** worksheet, click the PivotChart to select it.

    b. On the PivotChart, click the **Salesperson** report filter drop-down arrow.

    c. Click **All > OK**.

4. Modify the PivotChart to show the total sales for each salesperson filtered by product type:

    a. In the PivotChart Fields task pane, drag the **Salesperson** field from the FILTERS area to the **LEGEND (SERIES)** area.

    b. Drag the **Product Type** field from the AXIS (CATEGORIES) area to the **FILTERS** area.

5. Format the PivotChart to include a legend and data labels:

    a. Click the **CHART ELEMENTS** shortcut button ⊞.

    b. In the CHART ELEMENTS shortcut menu, click the **Legend** check box to select it.

    c. In the CHART ELEMENTS shortcut menu, click the **Data Labels** check box to select it.

6. Format the PivotChart with the Style 6 chart style:

    a. On the **Employee Sales** worksheet, click the PivotChart to select it.

    b. Click the **PIVOTCHART TOOLS DESIGN** tab.

    c. In the Chart Styles group, click the PivotChart Styles **More** button ⊡.

    d. Click **Style 6**.

7. Close the PivotTable Fields task pane.

8. Move and resize the chart so that it fits in the cell range B10:H24.

9. For all worksheets, add a header that has your name at the left, the date code in the center, and the page number code at the right, and change back to **Normal** view.

10. **With your teacher's permission,** print the **Employee Sales** worksheet. Your worksheet should look like the one shown in Figure 76-2 on the next page.

11. Save and close the file, and exit Excel.

Figure 76-2

	A	B	C	D	E	F	G	H
1	Product Type	(All) ▾						
2								
3		Salesperson ▾						
4		Alice Harper	Bob Cook					
5	Sum of Cost	$ 1,059.37	$1,301.87					
6								
7								
8								
9								
10								
11								
12								
13								
14								
15								
16								
17								
18								
19								
20								
21								
22								
23								
24								

Product Type ▾

Sum of Cost

Employee Summer Sales

$1,400.00
$1,200.00
$1,000.00
$800.00
$600.00
$400.00
$200.00
$-

$1,059.37

$1,301.87

Total

Salesperson ▾
■ Alice Harper
■ Bob Cook

Lesson 77

Using PowerPivot and Power View

> ### ➤ What You Will Learn

> Using PowerPivot to Manage Data
> Creating a Power View Report
> Working with Power View Fields
> Formatting a Power View Report

WORDS TO KNOW

PowerPivot
An Excel add-in that can create and modify the Excel data model.

Power View
A feature in Excel that presents data in an interactive report format.

Software Skills   Excel provides two powerful data analysis features to work with and present your data. You can use PowerPivot to work directly with a data model and make changes to the data. For example, you can add tables to the data model and create relationships among them. Once the data is prepared, you can use Power View to create an interactive report. With Power View, you can choose the layout and format of the data, present different sets of data, and filter data within the Power View sheet itself.

What You Can Do

Using PowerPivot to Manage Data

- **PowerPivot** is a feature in Excel that comes with Office 2013 Professional Plus and Office 365 Professional Plus.

  ✓ *You first learned about PowerPivot in Lesson 38.*

- In Excel 2013, the Data Model engine is directly integrated, meaning that you can modify and manage the data in the data model because the data model resides within Excel itself.

  ✓ *In previous versions of Excel, the data model was separate.*

- You must first activate the PowerPivot Add-in before you can use PowerPivot. Enable the PowerPivot Add-in from the Excel Options on the FILE tab.

  ✓ *The Microsoft Office PowerPivot for Excel 2013 add-in is a COM Add-in.*

- You must open a PowerPivot-enabled worksheet from within Excel.

- With PowerPivot, you can add tables to the Excel Data Model, as well as modify and delete them.

- To access the Excel Data Model, use the Manage button in the Data Model group on the POWERPIVOT tab.

- Tables are organized into individual tabbed pages in the PowerPivot window.

- If the tables are named, the table names appear as the names of the tabs.

- When you add table data to the Excel Data Model, you can use PowerPivot to create a relationship between two tables or among multiple tables.

- You can add a table only once within the Excel Data Model.

- Use PowerPivot to add data from a data range or table in an Excel workbook, or from data that is stored outside of Excel, such as data from a Microsoft Access database.

- You can interact with your data in the PowerPivot window like you can in an Excel worksheet. For example, you can sort the data in the PowerPivot window, and it will sort in the Excel worksheet.

Try It!   **Adding PowerPivot to the Ribbon**

1 Start Excel, create a blank workbook, and click FILE > Options.

2 In the Excel Options dialog box, click Add-Ins.

3 In the Manage drop-down box, select COM Add-ins > Go.

4 In the COM Add-Ins dialog box, click the Microsoft Office PowerPivot for Excel 2013 check box.

5 Click OK. The POWERPIVOT tab appears on the Ribbon.

Try It!   **Using PowerPivot to Manage Data**

1 In Excel, click FILE > Open, and open **E77TryA** from the data files for this lesson.

   ✓ *You must first enable the PowerPivot add-in in the Excel Options, then you can open a PowerPivot worksheet from within Excel. Do not use File Explorer to open a PowerPivot worksheet.*

2 Save the file as **E77TryA_xx** in the location where your teacher instructs you to store the files for this lesson.

3 On the Men's Inventory worksheet, click in the PivotTable in the cell range A25:C30.

4 Click POWERPIVOT > Manage 📊 to display the PowerPivot for Excel window. Notice that the Men table is already in the Excel Data Model.

5 In the table, in the Category column, click the Category drop-down arrow > Sort A to Z ↓. The data is sorted in the PowerPivot window and the Excel worksheet.

6 Close the PowerPivot for Excel window.

7 Save the changes to the file, and leave it open to use in the next Try It.

Try It!   Adding Data to the Excel Data Model

1 In the **E77TryA_xx** file, click the Women's Inventory worksheet tab, and click in the table in the cell range A8:L14.

2 On the POWERPIVOT tab, click Add to Data Model. The Women data table is added to the Excel Data Model.

3 Close the PowerPivot for Excel window.

4 In the Excel worksheet, click the Teen's Inventory worksheet tab, and click cell A9.

5 Click INSERT > PivotTable.

6 In the Create PivotTable dialog box, under Choose where you want the PivotTable report to be placed, click Existing Worksheet.

7 In the Location box, type **A20**.

8 Click the Add this data to the Data Model check box > OK.

9 Click POWERPIVOT > Manage to display the PowerPivot for Excel window.

10 In the PowerPivot for Excel window, click the Range tab. Notice that the cell range data has been added to the Excel Data Model.

11 Close the PowerPivot for Excel window.

12 Save the changes to the file, and leave it open to use in the next Try It.

Cell range data in the Excel Data Model

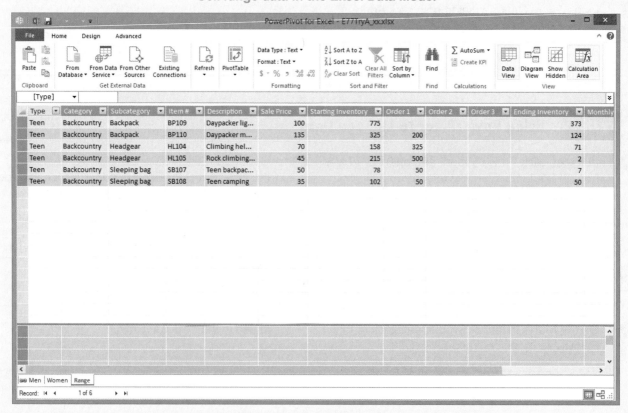

Creating a Power View Report

- **Power View** is a feature in Excel that comes with Office 2013 Professional Plus and Office 365 Professional Plus.

  ✓ You first learned about Power View in Excel Lesson 38.

- You can use Power View sheets to present and further analyze your data in an interactive report.
- Power View requires Silverlight, a free plug-in from Microsoft.
- You can enable the Power View add-in the first time you insert a Power View report. To insert a Power View report, use the Power View button on the INSERT tab.
- If you don't have Silverlight installed, click Install Silverlight, follow the installation steps, and in Excel click Reload.

  ✓ If the Power View Field List displays the message Power View needs data to work with, select the range of cells containing your data, and click Power View on the INSERT tab.

- You can choose to create a new Power View sheet, or add the data to an existing Power View sheet.
- The source data for your Power View sheet can be a data range or table in an Excel workbook, a PivotTable, or data that is stored outside of Excel, such as data from a Microsoft Access database.
- When you add a Power View sheet from data that is not already in the Excel Data Model, Excel automatically adds the data to the Excel Data Model.
- If you insert a Power View sheet by mistake, you can immediately delete the Power View sheet and Excel will automatically delete the data from the Excel Data Model.

  ✓ If the data existed in the Excel Data Model before you added the Power View sheet, the data will remain in place.

  ✓ Use PowerPivot to view the current data in the Excel Data Model.

Try It! Creating a Power View Report

1. In the **E77TryA_xx** file, click the Teen's Inventory worksheet tab, and select the cell range A8:L14.
2. Click INSERT > Power View 📊.
3. If necessary, click Install Silverlight, follow the installation steps, and in Excel click Reload.

  ✓ If the Power View Field List displays the message Power View needs data to work with, select the range of cells containing your data, and click Power View on the INSERT tab.

4. Click in the title box, and type **Teen Inventory**.
5. Save the changes to the file, and leave it open to use in the next Try It.

A Power View sheet

Click here to add a title

Type	Category	Subcategory	Item #	Description	Sale Price
Teen	Backcountry	Backpack	BP109	Daypacker light, teen	100
Teen	Backcountry	Backpack	BP110	Daypacker morningstar, teen	135
Teen	Backcountry	Headgear	HL104	Climbing helmet, teen	70
Teen	Backcountry	Headgear	HL105	Rock climbing helmet, teen	45
Teen	Backcountry	Sleeping bag	SB107	Teen backpacker	50
Teen	Backcountry	Sleeping bag	SB108	Teen camping	35
Total					**435**

Working with Power View Fields

- You can customize a Power View sheet with the commands on the POWER VIEW tab and its contextual tabs on the Ribbon. For example, the DESIGN tab will appear on the Ribbon next to the POWER VIEW tab when you select a data item, and the TEXT tab will appear when you select the title box.

- The POWER VIEW tab has many of the commands found in other tabs on the Ribbon. For example, the POWER VIEW tab has its own Copy, Paste, and Undo commands.

- You can add objects, such as a table or chart, to a Power View sheet.

- You can add and modify the fields of the object in the Power View Fields task pane.

- To display the Power View Fields task pane, use the Field List button in the View group on the POWER VIEW tab.

- Drag fields into the two areas in the Areas Section to rearrange the fields.

  - TILE BY: This area acts as a report filter above the Power View chart or table. Fields in this area can drill down into the data to show only the items relating to a particular category.

  - FIELDS: This area contains the data fields. You can reorder the fields in this area.

- You can filter the data by adding fields to the Filters area on the right side of the Power View sheet.

- To remove a field from the Area Section, deselect the field's check box in the Field List. You can also click the field's down-arrow in the Area Section and click Remove Field, or you can drag it out of the Area Section.

- You can click the drop-down arrow of an area field to access more options. For example, you can choose to show the count of an item.

Try It!   **Adding and Removing Power View Fields**

1 In the **E77TryA_xx** file, on the Power View1 worksheet tab, click in the table to select it.

2 In the Power View Fields task pane, click the Category, Item#, Sale Price, and Type check boxes to deselect them.

3 Click the Ending Inventory and Starting Inventory check boxes to select them.

4 In the FIELDS area, click and hold the Starting Inventory field, and drag it above the Ending Inventory field.

5 Save the changes to the file, and leave it open to use in the next Try It.

The Power View Fields task pane

Power View Fields   ✕
ACTIVE | ALL

▲ Range
  ☐ Category
  ☑ Description   → Fields List
  ☑ Σ Ending Inventory
  ☐ Item #   → Fields Area
  ☐ Σ Monthly Revenue
  ☐ Σ Order 1
  ☐ Order 2
  ☐ Order 3
  ☐ Σ Sale Price
  ☑ Σ Starting Inventory
  ☑ Subcategory
  ☐ Type

Drag fields between areas below: → Areas Section
TILE BY

[   ]

FIELDS
  Subcategory   ▼
  Description   ▼
  Σ Starting Inventory   ▼
  Σ Ending Inventory   ▼

Formatting a Power View Report

- You can use the Power View commands to visualize and present your data in a variety of ways.
- You can change the visualization of a Power View object without having to re-create the object. For example, you can choose to visualize the data as a table, a chart, or a map.
- Use the commands in the Switch Visualization group of the DESIGN tab.

- You can format a Power View sheet with a theme, background, and font set.
- The options in the Themes group on the POWER VIEW tab apply to the whole Power View sheet.
- You can enhance your Power View sheet with a background image.
- You can adjust the position and transparency of a background image to make it look like a watermark.

Try It!   Formatting a Power View Report

1 In the **E77TryA_xx** file, on the Power View1 worksheet, click the first Backpack data element.

2 Click the DESIGN tab.

3 In the Switch Visualization group, click Table ⊞ > Matrix. The table changes to a matrix with totals.

    ✓ *Resize the table so that all data can be seen, if necessary.*

4 Click the POWER VIEW tab.

5 In the Background Image group, click Set Image ▨ > Set Image.

6 Browse to the data files for this lesson, click the **E77TryB** file, and click Open.

7 In the Background Image group, click Image Position ▨ > Stretch.

8 Close the Filter area.

9 Close the Power View Fields task pane.

10 Save and close the file, and exit Excel.

Lesson 77—Practice

You work in the sales office of Sydney Crenshaw Realty, a national chain of real estate brokers. You have an Excel spreadsheet of sales data for your local real estate office. You want to create a Power View report to show the commissions of the realtors to analyze which realtors are earning the most commissions.

DIRECTIONS

1. Start Excel, if necessary, and open **E77Practice** from the data files for this lesson.
2. Save the file as **E77Practice_xx** in the location where your teacher instructs you to store the files for this lesson.
3. Add the POWERPIVOT tab to the Ribbon, if necessary:
   a. Click **FILE** > **Options** > **Add-Ins**.
   b. In the Manage drop-down box, select **COM Add-ins** > **Go**.

   c. In the COM Add-Ins dialog box, click the **Microsoft Office PowerPivot for Excel 2013** check box.
   d. Click **OK**.
4. Add the data to the Excel Data Model:
   a. On the **Year-to-Date Sales** worksheet, select the cell range **A4:F26**.
   b. Click **POWERPIVOT** > **Add to Data Model** 📊.
   c. In the Create Table dialog box, click the **My table has headers** check box, and click **OK**.
   d. Close the PowerPivot for Excel window.

5. Create a Power View report with a Stacked Column chart of the commission earned by each realtor:

   a. With the cell range **A4:F26** selected, click **INSERT** > **Power View** 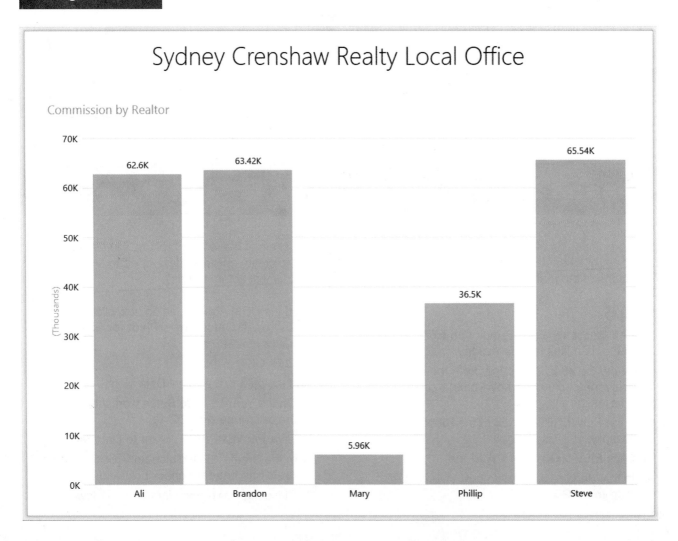.

      ✓ *If necessary, Install Silverlight, and in Excel click Reload. If the Power View Field List displays the message Power View needs data to work with, select the range of cells containing your data, and click Power View on the INSERT tab.*

   b. Click in the title box, and type **Sydney Crenshaw Realty Local Office**.

   c. Click a data element in the table to select the table.

   d. In the Power View Fields task pane, click the **Date Sold**, **MLS Number**, **Percentage**, and **Sales Price** check boxes to deselect them.

   e. Click **DESIGN** > **Column Chart** > **Stacked Column**.

   f. Resize the Power View object by dragging the lower-right corner down until it fills the sheet.

   g. Click **LAYOUT** > **Data Labels** > **Show**.

6. Change the name of the Power View sheet tab to **Commissions**.

7. Close the Filter area.

8. Close the Power View Fields task pane.

9. **With your teacher's permission,** print the **Commissions** sheet, and write your name on it. Your worksheet should look like the one shown in Figure 77-1.

10. Save and close the file, and exit Excel.

Figure 77-1

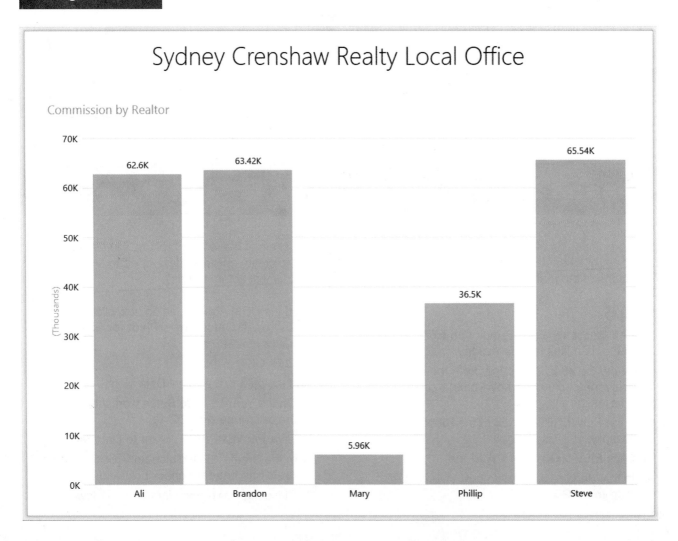

Lesson 77—Apply

You are the owner of Pete's Pets, a local pet store, and your store has completed its sales for the month of November. You want to know what type of animal was sold in each of the cats, dogs, and fish categories, and which salesperson sold them. You would like to create and format a Power View report to show at the next employee meeting.

DIRECTIONS

1. Start Excel, if necessary, and open **E77ApplyA** from the data files for this lesson.

2. Save the file as **E77ApplyA_xx** in the location where your teacher instructs you to store the files for this lesson.

3. Add the POWERPIVOT tab to the Ribbon, if necessary:
   a. Click **FILE** > **Options** > **Add-Ins**.
   b. In the Manage drop-down box, select **COM Add-ins** > **Go**.
   c. In the COM Add-Ins dialog box, click the **Microsoft Office PowerPivot for Excel 2013** check box.
   d. Click **OK**.

4. Add the data to the Excel Data Model:
   a. On the **Nov Sales** worksheet, click in the table.
   b. Click **POWERPIVOT** > **Add to Data Model** 📊.
   c. Close the PowerPivot for Excel window.

5. Create a Power View report named **November Pet Sales** with a table of the product descriptions, salesperson's name, and cost:
   a. On the **Nov Sales** worksheet, click in the table.
   b. Click **INSERT** > **Power View** 📊.

   ✓ If necessary, install Silverlight, and in Excel click Reload. If the Power View Field List displays the message Power View needs data to work with, select the range of cells containing your data, and click Power View on the INSERT tab.

   c. Click in the title box, and type **November Pet Sales**.
   d. Click a data element in the table to select the table.
   e. In the Power View Fields task pane, click the **Item #**, **Product Type**, and **Sales Incentive** check boxes to deselect them.
   f. Resize the Power View object by dragging the lower-right corner down until it fills the sheet.

6. Filter the Power View report on cats, dogs, and fish:
   a. Click a data element in the table to select the table.
   b. In the Power View Fields task pane, drag the **Product Type** field to the **Filters** area.
   c. In the Product Type filter list, click the **Cat**, **Dog**, and **Fish** check boxes to select them.
   d. Close the Filter area.

7. Tile the Power View report on cats, dogs, and fish, and format the tiles to display at the bottom of the report:
   a. Click a data element in the table to select the table.
   b. In the Power View Fields task pane, drag the **Product Type** field to the **TILE BY** area.
   c. Click the **Dog** tile.
   d. On the DESIGN tab, in the Tiles group, click **Tile Type** > **Tile Flow**.

8. Apply the **Currency** format to the cost data:
   a. Click a cost data element in the table.
   b. On the DESIGN tab, in the Number group, click **Number** drop-down arrow > **Currency**.

9. Add a background image to the Power View report:
   a. Click the **POWER VIEW** tab.
   b. In the Background Image group, click **Set Image** 🖼 > **Set Image**.
   c. Browse to the data files for this lesson, click the **E77ApplyB** file, and click **Open**.

10. Close the Power View Fields task pane.

11. **With your teacher's permission,** print the **Power View1** sheet, and write your name on it. Your worksheet should look like the one shown in Figure 77-2 on the next page.

12. Save and close the file, and exit Excel.

Figure 77-2

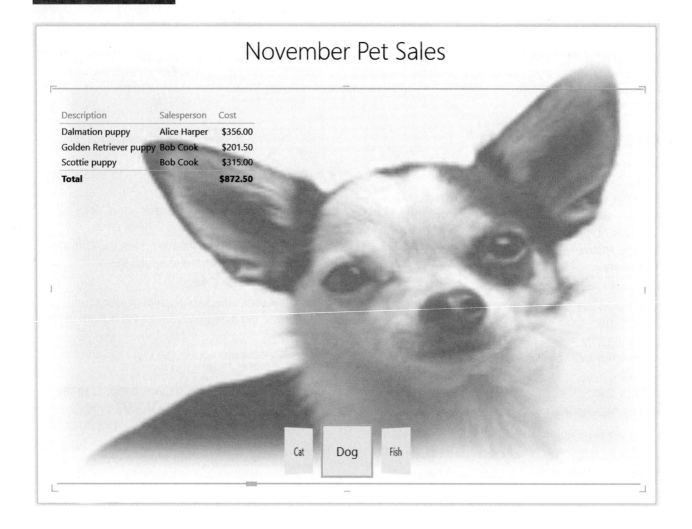

November Pet Sales

Description	Salesperson	Cost
Dalmation puppy	Alice Harper	$356.00
Golden Retriever puppy	Bob Cook	$201.50
Scottie puppy	Bob Cook	$315.00
Total		**$872.50**

Cat   Dog   Fish

End-of-Chapter Activities

➤ Excel Chapter 9—Critical Thinking

Chamber of Commerce Presentation

At the Center City Chamber of Commerce, you have been asked to gather, analyze, and present some information at a business meeting with guests who may be interested in relocating their businesses to Center City. You will present information to them about local real estate, schools, and existing businesses that will help them make up their minds. You will convey meaningful information in a concise and attractive format, using the skills you learned in this chapter.

DIRECTIONS

1. Start Excel, if necessary, and create a new blank workbook. Save the workbook as **ECT09A_xx** in the location where your teacher instructs you to store the files for this chapter.

2. Insert two new worksheets, and rename the worksheet tabs to match the categories of data you will be presenting: **Real Estate**, **Schools**, and **Local Businesses**.

3. Copy the real estate data from **ECT09B** workbook into the **ECT09A_xx** workbook on the **Real Estate** worksheet.

   ✓ *One way to perform step 3 is to copy the entire worksheet. This method has the advantage of retaining all the content and formatting. Right-click the tab of the sheet to be copied and click Move or Copy. In the Move or Copy dialog box, select your new workbook as the Move To value, and click the Create a Copy check box to select it. Then delete the Real Estate tab you created in step 2, and rename the imported worksheet's tab Real Estate.*

4. Create a new worksheet named **Real Estate Summary**. Place it immediately after the **Real Estate** worksheet.

5. On the **Real Estate Summary** worksheet, for each area, create a PivotTable of the areas and their communities, and provide an average price of the homes for sale in each community. Use any method you like. Format the prices with the **Accounting** format.

6. On the **Real Estate Summary** worksheet, create a PivotChart showing the average list price of the homes for sale in each community. Format the PivotChart with **Style 6**. Resize the chart so that all data is legible.

7. On the **Real Estate** worksheet, filter the data to exclude homes with fewer than two bedrooms, and add icon sets to the bedrooms and bathrooms. Determine the most appropriate icon set to use to visually indicate the number of bedrooms and bathrooms in the homes.

8. On the **Schools** worksheet, import the school district SAT score data from the **ECT09C** XML file. Allow Excel to create a schema based on the XML source data. In the imported school data, delete the **avgsqft** and **avgsaleprice** columns. Format the school data by renaming the headings. Sort the data alphabetically by school district name.

9. On the **Schools** worksheet, show the high schools with the highest SAT scores in a separate table below the original table.

   ✓ *One way is to copy the table and use a slicer to filter the highest score.*

10. Save the **ECT09A_xx** file, and leave it open for later use.

11. Open the **ECT09D** file from the data files for this project, and save it as **ECT09D_xx** in the location where your teacher instructs you to store the files for this project.

12. Complete the **Sales Summary** worksheet by consolidating the data from each of the month worksheets. Create a link to the source data. Move the label from cell J6 into cell **J7**.

13. On the **Sales Summary** worksheet, convert the cell range A7:I17 to a table, and then add a **Totals** row to it. Use the drop-down arrow in the Totals row label to show averages for each area, and change the row's label to **Average**.

   ✓ *Hint: Every cell has to have a numeric value for the function to calculate properly.*

14. On the **Sales Summary** worksheet, format the cell range **B8:J18** with the **Accounting** format. Make the font usage consistent by using Format Painter to copy the font settings from cell **B8** to the cell range **H8:J17**. Adjust the column widths as needed.

15. Save and close the **ECT09D_xx** file.

16. In the **ECT09A_xx** workbook, on the **Local Businesses** worksheet, import the data from the **Sales Summary** worksheet in the **ECT09D_xx** workbook.

17. For all worksheets, add a header that has your name at the left, the date code in the center, and the page number code at the right, and change back to **Normal** view.

18. **With your teacher's permission,** print the **ECT09A_xx** workbook.

19. Save and close the file, and exit Excel.

➤ Excel Chapter 9—Portfolio Builder

Basketball Team Data

To promote attendance at professional team sports competitions in the state, the Indiana Visitors Bureau has asked you to collect data about the most recent season's win/loss records of the professional basketball teams based in Indiana. You will collect statistics on the Indiana Pacers (men's basketball) and the Indiana Fever (women's basketball) and present it in an attractively formatted Excel workbook.

DIRECTIONS

1. Start Excel, if necessary, and create a new blank workbook. Save the workbook as **EPB09_xx** in the location where your teacher instructs you to store the files for this chapter.

2. Insert two new worksheets, and rename the worksheet tabs as follows: **Summary**, **Pacers**, and **Fever**.

3. Search the Web to collect data about each team's wins and losses for the last full season played, and place it on that team's worksheet in the workbook. For each game played, include at least the date, the opponent, and the final score, with each team's score in a separate column.

   ✓ *If both scores are in a single column, use the Text to Columns feature on the DATA tab to split the scores into separate columns.*

4. On each worksheet, if there is already a column that indicates whether it was a win or a loss, delete that column. Then create (or re-create) the Win/Loss column to use an IF function that determines whether the score of the Pacers/Fever was higher than the score of the opponent. If the Pacers'/Fever's score was higher, "**WIN**" should appear in the Win/Loss column. If not, "**LOSS**" should appear there.

5. Convert each team's statistics list into a table.

6. Format the two worksheets attractively and as consistently as possible, given that you may have collected different statistics on each team.

7. On the **Summary** worksheet, summarize the data from the other sheets, providing as many meaningful statistics as you can extrapolate from the data you gathered.

8. On the **Summary** worksheet, use Conditional Formatting to set the team's name in **green** font if it had more wins than losses, or in **red** font if it had more losses than wins.

9. In each of the tables, add a **point difference** column, and calculate its value as the team's final score in the game minus the opponent's final score. The number in this column will be **positive** if the team won, and **negative** if they lost.

10. On the **Summary** worksheet, include **Average Point Difference** as one of the statistics you provide.

11. On each of the team worksheets, create a **Moving Average of Point Difference** column, and calculate a **6-interval moving average** for the point difference. Create a chart for each team, and place the chart on the **Summary** sheet, next to each team's other statistics. Label, size, and format each chart so it is easily understandable.

✓ *Illustration 9A shows one possible Summary worksheet design.*

12. For all worksheets, add a header that has your name at the left, the date code in the center, and the page number code at the right, and change back to **Normal** view.

13. **With your teacher's permission,** print the **Summary** worksheet.

14. Save and close the file, and exit Excel.

Illustration 9A

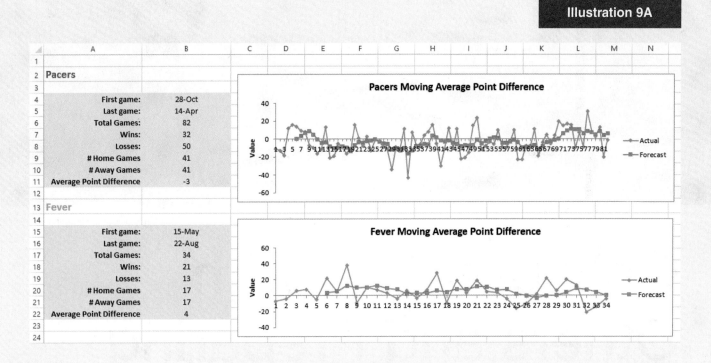

Collaborating with Others and Preparing a Final Workbook for Distribution

Lesson 78

Tracking Changes

➤ What You Will Learn

Creating and Modifying a Shared Workbook
Tracking Changes in a Shared Workbook
Managing Comments in a Shared Workbook
Merging Changes
Removing Workbook Sharing

WORDS TO KNOW

Change history
A listing of all changes made in a workbook. You can view the change history in the workbook or on its own worksheet.

Comment
A note attached to a worksheet cell for reference.

Track Changes
A process that keeps track of all changes made to a workbook each time you save it.

Shared workbook
An Excel workbook that you are using collaboratively with other users. When you turn on track changes, the workbook becomes a shared workbook automatically.

Software Skills   When you are working on a large worksheet or a major project, you may need to work with other members of your team to complete all the parts of the worksheet that need to be completed. Collaborating successfully in Excel 2013 means that you need to be able to create and edit your own sections, add comments to the worksheet, see what changes others are making, merge many changes into one worksheet, and turn off sharing when you no longer need it.

What You Can Do

Creating and Modifying a Shared Workbook

- Sharing a workbook enables you to allow other authors to make changes in the file.

- You can turn a regular workbook into a **shared workbook** by using the Share Workbook command in the Changes group on the REVIEW tab.

- You can restrict the editing of the workbook by removing users from the Share Workbook dialog box.

- On the Advanced tab of the Share Workbook dialog box, you can set sharing options to specify how long changes are kept, when the changes in the file are updated, and how any conflicting changes will be resolved.

- You can tell Excel whether you want to update the file automatically as people work on it or update the file when it is saved.

- You can choose whether you want to see everyone's changes in the file or see only other users' changes.

- If your worksheet contains a table, you will be prompted to convert the table to a range before sharing the file.

■ You can save a shared workbook to a network location or your Windows Live SkyDrive account so that others can work with the file.

■ You can tell Excel whether you want to be prompted to decide about changes that are in conflict or whether you want the saved changes to be the ones that are preserved in the file.

Try It!   **Sharing a Workbook**

1 Start Excel, and open **E78TryA** from the data files for this lesson.

2 Save the file as **E78TryA_xx** in the location where your teacher instructs you to store the files for this lesson.

3 Click REVIEW > Share Workbook 🖼.

4 Click the Allow changes by more than one user at the same time check box.

5 Click OK.

6 If prompted, click OK to save the workbook.

7 Save the changes to the file, and leave it open to use in the next Try It.

Sharing a workbook

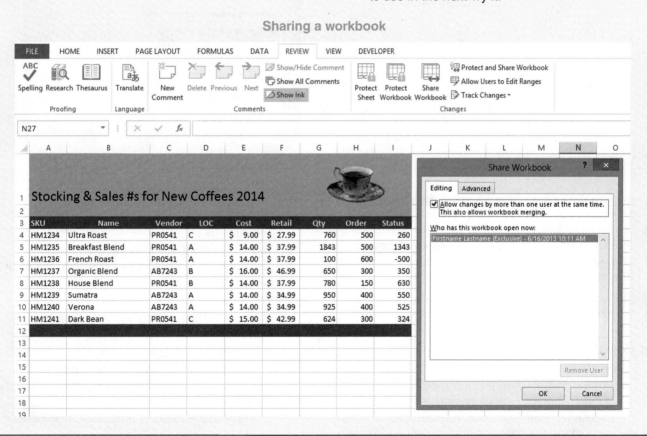

| Try It! | **Setting Sharing Options** |

1 In the **E78TryA_xx** file, click REVIEW > Share Workbook 🖳.

2 In the Share Workbook dialog box, click the Advanced tab.

3 Review the Advanced share settings.

4 Under Update changes, click Automatically every.

5 Click OK.

6 Save the changes to the file, and leave it open to use in the next Try It.

Setting sharing options

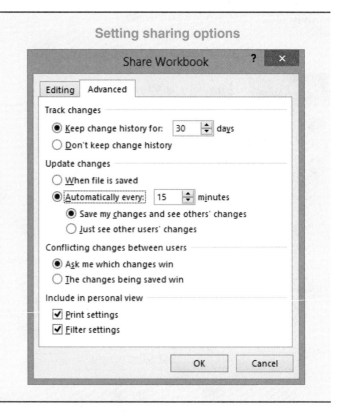

Tracking Changes in a Shared Workbook

- Excel 2013 makes it easy for you to track the changes that are made in a shared workbook so that you can choose whether to keep, reject, or edit the changes.

- To turn on tracking, use the **Track Changes** command in the Changes group on the REVIEW tab.

- Use the Highlight Changes command to set the tracking options.

  - The Highlight Changes dialog box enables you to make choices about the way changes are tracked in your workbook. You can choose when and where the changes are highlighted. You can also decide whether you want the changes to be highlighted on the sheet or listed on a new worksheet.

  - You can specify when changes are saved in the Highlight Changes dialog box: Since I last saved, All, Not yet reviewed, or Since date.

- You can choose whose changes you want to review: Everyone, Everyone but Me, or you (as indicated by your username or initials).

- You can specify where to track changes on a worksheet, for example, within a specific cell or a cell range.

- When you select the Highlight changes on screen check box, any changes on the worksheet appear in bordered cells with a flag in the upper-left corner.

- When you click List changes on a new sheet and All is selected in the When setting, a History worksheet is added to the workbook listing all changes made by date, time, user, and location.

  ✓ *The History worksheet is only available until you save the workbook.*

- When you are ready to accept or reject changes, you can choose to do so based on when changes were made, who made the changes, and where the changes are located.

Try It!   Turning on Tracking

1 In the **E78TryA_xx** file, click REVIEW > Track Changes 📝.

2 Click Highlight Changes.

3 Click the Track changes while editing check box, if necessary.

4 Click the When check box > When drop-down arrow > All.

5 Click the Who check box > Who drop-down arrow > Everyone, if necessary.

6 Click the Highlight changes on screen check box, if necessary.

7 Click OK, and click OK to confirm that no changes were found.

8 Click cell G4, and change the value to **820**. Notice the flag in the upper-left corner of the cell.

9 Click cell H4, and change the value to **550**.

10 Save the changes to the file, and leave it open to use in the next Try It.

Try It!   Displaying Change History

1 In the **E78TryA_xx** file, click cell G9, and change the value to **925**.

2 Click cell H9, and change the value to **450**.

3 Save the workbook.

4 On the REVIEW tab, click Track Changes > Highlight Changes.

5 Click List changes on a new sheet.

6 Click OK.

7 Review the History worksheet.

8 Save the changes to the file, and leave it open to use in the next Try It.

The change history

	A	B	C	D	E	F	G	H	I	J	K
1	Action Number ▾	Date ▾	Time ▾	Who ▾	Change ▾	Sheet ▾	Range ▾	New Value ▾	Old Value ▾	Action Type ▾	Losing Action ▾
2	1	6/16/2013	9:59 AM	Cat Skintik	Cell Change	Sheet1	G4	820	760		
3	2	6/16/2013	9:59 AM	Cat Skintik	Cell Change	Sheet1	H4	550	500		
4	3	6/16/2013	10:01 AM	Cat Skintik	Cell Change	Sheet1	G9	925	950		
5	4	6/16/2013	10:01 AM	Cat Skintik	Cell Change	Sheet1	H9	450	400		
6											
7	The history ends with the changes saved on 6/16/2013 at 10:01 AM.										

Highlight Changes dialog box:

☑ Track changes while editing. This also shares your workbook.

Highlight which changes
☑ When: All
☑ Who: Everyone
☐ Where:

☑ Highlight changes on screen
☑ List changes on a new sheet

[OK] [Cancel]

Managing Comments in a Shared Workbook

- Using **comments** in a shared workbook is the same as doing so in an unshared workbook.
- Use the commands in the Comments group on the REVIEW tab of the Ribbon.
- A red triangle appears in the upper-right corner of any cell with an attached comment.

- You can edit the contents of a comment that has been previously inserted.
- Use the Previous and Next commands to navigate among the comments.
- You can choose to show or hide a single comment, or you can show all comments.
- You can delete a single comment, or you can delete all comments in a worksheet.

Try It!   Creating and Editing Comments

1. In the **E78TryA_xx** file, click cell I6.

2. On the REVIEW tab, click New Comment ⬚.

3. In the comment box, type **Order more immediately**.

4. Click cell A1.

5. On the REVIEW tab, in the Comments group, click Next ⬚ to display the comment.

6. On the REVIEW tab, in the Comments group, click Edit Comment ⬚.

7. In the comment, replace the text *Order more immediately* with the text **This has been ordered**.

8. Click outside of the comment.

9. On the REVIEW tab, in the Comments group, click Show All Comments ⬚.

10. Save the changes to the file, and leave it open to use in the next Try It.

Editing a comment

Qty	Order	Status
820	550	270
1843	500	1343
100	600	-500
650	300	350
780	150	630
925	450	475
925	400	525
624	300	324

Firstname Lastname:
This has been ordered

Merging Changes

- When you share a workbook and want to compare the changes you and your colleagues have made before combining those changes into one worksheet, you can use the Compare and Merge Workbooks command.
- You can only merge changes that have been made on the same shared workbook, and the workbook must be shared before the Compare and Merge Workbooks command becomes available.

- You can manage workbook versions by selecting which workbooks to merge.
- By default, the Compare and Merge Workbooks command isn't available on the Ribbon; you need to add it to the Quick Access Toolbar.
- You can merge the workbook data by selecting the file with changed values in the Select Files to Merge Into Current Workbook dialog box.

  ✓ *You can open and merge multiple copies of the same workbook by pressing and holding Ctrl while clicking files in the Select Files to Merge Into Current Workbook dialog box.*

Try It!   **Adding the Compare and Merge Workbooks Command to the QAT**

1 In the **E78TryA_xx** file, click FILE > Options > Quick Access Toolbar in the left pane.

2 In the Choose commands from list, click All Commands.

3 Scroll down the list, and click Compare and Merge Workbooks > Add.

4 Click OK.

5 Save and close the file. Leave Excel open to use in the next Try It.

Try It!   **Merging Workbook Data**

1 Open the **E78TryB** file from the data files for this lesson.

2 Save the file as **E78TryB_xx** in the location where your teacher instructs you to store the files for this lesson.

3 Click REVIEW > Share Workbook 🖥.

4 Click the Allow changes by more than one user at the same time check box.

5 Click OK > OK.

6 Save the file as **E78TryC_xx** in the location where your teacher instructs you to store the files for this lesson.

7 In cell G7, change the value to **400**.

8 Save and close the **E78TryC_xx** file.

9 Open the **E78TryB_xx** file again.

10 On the Quick Access Toolbar, click Compare and Merge Workbooks ⊙.

11 In the Select Files to Merge Into Current Workbook dialog box, browse to the location where your teacher instructs you to store the files for this lesson to, and click **E78TryC_xx**.

12 Click OK. The new file data is merged with the current file, and the value you changed is flagged on the worksheet.

13 Save the changes to the **E78TryB_xx** file, and leave it open to use in the next Try It.

Removing Workbook Sharing

■ When you are ready to stop sharing the workbook, you can turn the sharing workbook feature off by using the Share Workbook command in the Changes group on the REVIEW tab.

■ You can remove other users by clicking the names of colleagues in the Who Has This Workbook Open Now list of the Share Workbook dialog box and clicking Remove User.

■ Click to remove the check mark in the Allow changes by more than one user at the same time check box.

✓ *You need to remove workbook protection before sharing or unsharing a workbook. Click Unprotect Shared Workbook in the Changes group of the REVIEW tab to remove protection.*

Try It! **Removing Workbook Sharing**

1 In the **E78TryA_xx** file, click REVIEW > Share Workbook 🖳.

2 In the Share Workbook dialog box, click Allow changes by more than one user at the same time to unselect the check box.

3 Click OK.

4 Click Yes if prompted about the effects the change will have on other users.

5 Save and close the workbook, and exit Excel.

The Share Workbook dialog box

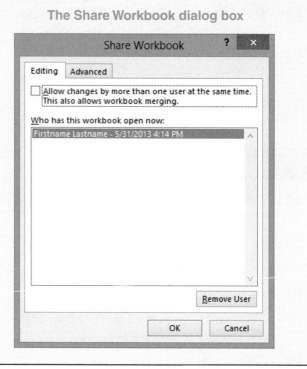

Lesson 78—Practice

You and several friends have decided to go in together to start a great new coffee shop in Portland, Oregon, called Grounds for Thought. You are preparing an expense report worksheet for you and your friends to access and edit. You want to track the changes in the worksheet and update the worksheet with your expenses. You also want to share the workbook. In this project, you will track the changes within the worksheet and view the history of those changes.

DIRECTIONS

1. Start Excel, if necessary, and open **E78Practice** from the data files for this lesson.

2. Save the file as **E78Practice_xx** in the location where your teacher instructs you to store the files for this lesson.

3. Click **REVIEW** > **Share Workbook** > **Allow changes** check box.

4. Click **OK** twice.

5. On the REVIEW tab, click **Track Changes** 📝 > **Highlight Changes**.

6. Click the **When** arrow, if necessary, and click **All**.

7. Click the **Who** arrow, and click **Everyone**.

8. Click the **List changes on a new sheet** check box.

9. Click **OK** twice.

10. Enter the following values:

    D11: Santa Fe

    E11: 375.00

    F11: 50.00

    G11: 25.00

    H11: 75.00

    J11: 100.00

    K11: 100.00

11. Save the workbook.

12. Adjust the column widths, as needed.
13. On the REVIEW tab, click **Track Changes** ⟩ >
    Highlight Changes.
14. Click **List changes on a new sheet** > **OK** to see
    the **History** worksheet.
15. Turn off sharing by clicking **Share Workbook** >
    **Allow changes by more than one user at the
    same time** check box to deselect it > **OK**.
16. Click **Yes** if prompted about the effects the change
    will have on other users.

17. Add a header that has your name at the left, the
    date code in the center, and the page number
    code at the right, and change back to **Normal**
    view.
18. **With your teacher's permission,** print the
    worksheet. Your worksheet should look like the one
    shown in Figure 78-1.
19. Save and close the file, and exit Excel.

Figure 78-1

	Date	Account	Description		Hotel	Transport	Fuel	Meals	Phone	Entertainment	Misc		Total	

Expense Report

						STATEMENT							
PURPOSE:						NUMBER:				PAY PERIOD:		From	
												To	
EMPLOYEE INFORMATION:													
	Name					Position				SSN			
	Department					Manager				Employee ID			
Date	Account	Description		Hotel	Transport	Fuel	Meals	Phone	Entertainment	Misc		Total	
		Santa Fe		$ 375.00	$ 50.00	$ 25.00	$ 75.00		$ 100.00	$ 100.00	$ -	
Total				$ 375.00	$ 50.00	$ 25.00	$ 75.00	$ -	$ 100.00	$ 100.00	$ -	
										Subtotal	$ -	
										Cash Advances		
APPROVED:					NOTES:					Total	$ -	

Lesson 78—Apply

You and your friends are excited to start your new coffee shop, Grounds for Thought. You are preparing an inventory worksheet and want to apply sharing and track changes. When you last took inventory of the coffee, you noticed that one of the coffees had been overstocked. You want to insert a comment into the worksheet to let your partners know not to order more of that particular coffee.

DIRECTIONS

1. Start Excel, if necessary, and open **E78ApplyA** from the data files for this lesson.

2. Save the file as **E78ApplyA_xx** in the location where your teacher instructs you to store the files for this lesson.

3. Set up the workbook for sharing:

   a. Click **REVIEW** > **Share Workbook** > **Allow changes** check box.

   b. Click **OK** twice.

4. Turn on tracking:

   a. On the REVIEW tab, click **Track Changes** ⯈ > **Highlight Changes**.

   b. Click the **When** arrow, if necessary, and click **All**.

   c. Click the **Who** arrow, and click **Everyone**.

   d. Click **OK** twice.

5. Save the **E78ApplyA_xx** file.

6. Now save the file as **E78ApplyB_xx** in the location where your teacher instructs you to store the files for this lesson.

7. Make several changes to the values.

8. In cell I5, insert the comment **Do not order any more**.

9. Save and close the **E78ApplyB_xx** workbook.

10. Merge the **E78ApplyA_xx** and **E78ApplyB_xx** workbooks:

    a. Reopen the **E78ApplyA_xx** file.

    b. On the Quick Access Toolbar, click the **Compare and Merge Workbooks** button ◉.

    c. In the Select Files to Merge Into Current Workbook dialog box, navigate to **E78ApplyB_xx**, and click **OK**.

11. Save the workbook.

12. Turn off sharing:

    a. Click **REVIEW** > **Share Workbook** > **Allow changes** check box to deselect it.

    b. Click **OK** , and click **Yes**.

13. Add a header that has your name at the left, the date code in the center, and the page number code at the right, and change back to **Normal** view.

14. Change the page layout orientation to **Landscape**.

15. **With your teacher's permission,** print the **E78ApplyA_xx** workbook. Your workbook should look similar to the one shown in Figure 78-2 on the next page.

16. Save and close the file, and exit Excel.

Figure 78-2

	A	B	C	D	E	F	G	H	I	J	K	L
1	\multicolumn{9}{l}{Stocking & Sales #s for New Coffees 2014}				
2												
3	SKU	Name	Vendor	LOC	Cost	Retail	Qty	Order	Status			
4	HM1234	Ultra Roast	PR0541	C	$ 9.00	$ 27.99	800	500	300			
5	HM1235	Breakfast Blend	PR0541	A	$ 14.00	$ 37.99	2100	500	1600			
6	HM1236	French Roast	PR0541	A	$ 14.00	$ 37.99	750	600	150			
7	HM1237	Organic Blend	AB7243	B	$ 16.00	$ 46.99	800	750	50			
8	HM1238	House Blend	PR0541	B	$ 14.00	$ 37.99	600	150	450			
9	HM1239	Sumatra	AB7243	A	$ 14.00	$ 34.99	545	300	245			
10	HM1240	Verona	AB7243	A	$ 14.00	$ 34.99	256	400	-144			
11	HM1241	Dark Bean	PR0541	C	$ 15.00	$ 42.99	744	200	544			
12												
13												

Firstname Lastname:
Do not order any more

Lesson 79

Ensuring Data Integrity

➤ **What You Will Learn**

Turning Off AutoComplete
Controlling Data Entry with Data Validation
Circling Invalid Data
Copying Validation Rules
Removing Duplicate Data
Controlling Recalculation

WORDS TO KNOW

Input message
A message that appears when a user clicks in a cell providing information on how to enter valid data.

Paste Special
A variation of the Paste command that allows you to copy part of the data relating to a cell—in this case, the validity rules associated with that cell—and not the data in the cell itself.

Recalculation
The process of computing formulas and displaying the results as values in the cells that contain the formulas.

Validation
A process that enables you to maintain the accuracy of the database by specifying acceptable entries for a particular field.

Software Skills   When working with worksheet data, it is all too easy to enter incorrect information. This is especially true when several people maintain a database. Since the accuracy of your data is often critical—especially if the data tells you what to charge for a product or what to pay someone—controlling the validity of the data is paramount. Anything you can do to control data entry and identify errors will contribute to the quality of your work.

What You Can Do

Turning Off AutoComplete

- Excel's AutoComplete feature can complicate data entry in an Excel worksheet, because AutoComplete can alter the case of an entry or complete an entry in a manner the user doesn't intend.

- For example, if a previous entry in the field is Westlane and the user is entering only West, AutoComplete will nonetheless fill in Westlane.

Try It!   **Turning Off AutoComplete**

1 Start Excel, and open **E79Try** from the data files for this lesson.

2 Save the file as **E79Try_xx** in the location where your teacher instructs you to store the files for this lesson.

3 Click FILE > Options > Advanced.

4 Under Editing options, click the Enable AutoComplete for cell values check box to deselect it.

5 Click OK

6 Save the changes to the file, and leave it open to use in the next Try It.

Controlling Data Entry with Data Validation

■ With data **validation**, you can control the accuracy of the data entered into a worksheet.

■ By specifying the type of entries that are acceptable, you can prevent invalid data from being entered. For example, you could create a list of valid department numbers, and prevent someone from entering a department number that wasn't on the list.

■ You can set other rules as well, such as whole numbers only; numbers less than or greater than some value; or data of a specific length, such as five characters only.

■ After entering the criteria for what constitutes a valid entry, you can also specify a particular error message to appear when an incorrect entry is typed.

■ In addition, you can create an **input message** that displays when a user clicks a cell to help that user enter the right type of data.

■ The types of validation criteria that are possible are:

  ● Any value
  ● Whole number
  ● Decimal
  ● List
  ● Date
  ● Time
  ● Text length—limits the number of characters that can be entered
  ● Custom—requires the use of logical formulas

    ✓ *With the Custom option, you can enter a formula that compares the entry value with a value in another column. For example, you could set up a rule that if the Rented column contains the word Yes, then the Number of Occupants field must have a value greater than zero.*

■ If you restrict entries to a specified list, a down-arrow button appears when the cell is selected. Clicking the button displays a drop-down list of the acceptable entries, from which you can select.

  ✓ *Entries in a restricted list are case-sensitive. If the list specifies Yes and the user instead types yes, for example, Excel will reject the entry. Whenever possible, use lowercase letters for list entries to prevent case-sensitivity problems and speed up data entry.*

■ Data validation is designed to check against data entered directly into cells in the worksheet. Data validation doesn't apply if the cell entry is the result of:

  ● Data copied there using the fill handle.
  ● Data pasted or moved from another location.
  ● Data that is the result of a formula.

Try It!   **Setting Up a Simple Data Validation Rule**

1 In the **E79Try_xx** file, on the Office Items worksheet, select the cell range C4:C15.

2 Click DATA > Data Validation 🖉 to open the Data Validation dialog box.

3 On the Settings tab, click the Allow drop-down arrow, and click Whole number.

4 Click the Data drop-down arrow, and click greater than.

5 Click in the Minimum text box, and type **0**.

6 Click the Error Alert tab, click in the Error message text box, and type **Positive whole numbers only**.

7 Click OK.

8 Click cell C11, type **0**, and press ENTER . The error message appears.

9 Click Cancel to close the error message box.

✓ *Clicking Cancel removes the number you entered from cell C11. If you were to click Retry, the number would remain in the cell, highlighted black, and the cell active, waiting for you to retry your entry.*

10 Save the changes to the file, and leave it open to use in the next Try It.

A validation rule that allows positive whole numbers only

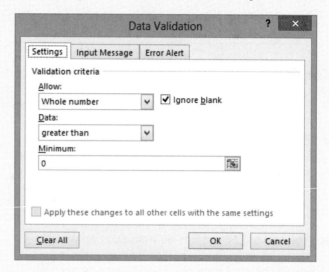

Try It!   **Setting Up Custom Validation**

1 In the **E79Try_xx** file, on the Office Items worksheet, select the cell range A4:A15.

2 Click DATA > Data Validation 🖉 to open the Data Validation dialog box.

3 On the Settings tab, click the Allow drop-down arrow, and click Custom.

4 Click in the Formula text box, and type **=ISTEXT(A4)**.

✓ *This formula refers to the first cell in the range; the validation formulas for the other cells in the range will be for those cells because Excel considers this a relative reference.*

5 Click the Input Message tab, click in the Title box, and type **Item Name**.

6 Click in the Input message box, and type **Enter only the item name from the catalog**.

7 Click the Error Alert tab, click the Style drop-down arrow, and click Stop, if necessary.

8 Click in the Title text box, and type **Verify Item Name**.

9 Click in the Error message text box, and type **The item name must be text only**.

10 Click OK to close the dialog box. Notice the message that appears.

(continued)

Try It! Setting Up Custom Validation *(continued)*

The Input Message tab

11 Click each of the cells in the range A5:A15. Notice the message appears for them too.

12 Click cell B4. No message appears because there is no validation set up for that cell.

13 Click cell A12, type **12345**, and press ENTER. An error message appears.

14 Click Cancel to clear the error message.

15 Save the changes to the file, and leave it open to use in the next Try It.

Try It! Turning Off Notification of Errors

1 In the **E79Try_xx** file, click cell A4.

2 On the DATA tab, click Data Validation to open the Data Validation dialog box.

3 Click the Input Message tab, and click the Show input message when cell is selected check box to deselect it.

4 Click the Error Alert tab, and click the Show error alert after invalid data is entered check box to deselect it.

5 Click the Settings tab, click the Apply these changes to all other cells with the same settings check box.

6 Click OK.

7 Click A12, type **12345**, and press ENTER. No warning appears.

8 Save the changes to the file, and leave it open to use in the next Try It.

Circling Invalid Data

■ Even with data validation rules in effect, sometimes invalid data can still be recorded. Data entered by copying and pasting, by using the fill handle, or as the result of a formula all bypass Excel's validation rules, for example.

■ With the Circle Invalid Data command, data that violates specified validation rules is identified quickly with a red circle.

■ As you correct the data, the circle in that cell automatically disappears.

■ You can remove any remaining circles (for errors you want to ignore) with the Clear Validation Circles command.

Try It!   Circling Invalid Data

1 In the **E79Try_xx** file, on the DATA tab, click the click Data Validation drop-down arrow Data Validation > Circle Invalid Data. Cell A12 shows a red circle, indicating the validation rule is violated.

2 Click cell A12, and press DEL . The red circle remains.

3 With cell A12 still selected, type **Product**, and press ENTER . The red circle goes away.

4 Click cell A12, and press DEL .

5 Save the changes to the file, and leave it open to use in the next Try It.

Try It!   Turning On Notification of Errors

1 In the **E79Try_xx** file, select the cell range A4:A15.

2 On the DATA tab, click Data Validation to open the Data Validation dialog box.

3 Click the Error Alert tab, and click the Show error alert after invalid data is entered check box to select it.

4 Click OK.

5 Save the changes to the file, and leave it open to use in the next Try It.

Copying Validation Rules

■ You can copy validation rules between cells using the Clipboard. This enables you to reuse a rule without having to re-create it from scratch.

■ To copy a validation rule, use the **Paste Special** feature of the Clipboard. This enables you to specify what aspect of the copied range you want to paste.

Try It!   Copying Validation Rules

1 In the **E79Try_xx** file, on the Office Items worksheet, select the cell range A4:A11.

2 Press CTRL + C to copy.

3 Click the Sales Tax worksheet tab.

4 On the Sales Tax worksheet, select the cell range A4:A11.

5 Click CTRL + V to paste. (The two lists are identical, so it's okay to overwrite the content.) The content is copied, and so is the validation rule.

6 Click the Office Items worksheet tab, click cell C4, and press CTRL + C to copy the cell.

7 Click the Sales Tax worksheet tab, and select the cell range B4:B14.

8 Click HOME > Paste drop-down arrow Paste > Paste Special.

9 In the Paste Special dialog box, under Paste, click Validation.

10 Click OK. Only the validation rule is copied.

11 Save the changes to the file, and leave it open to use in the next Try It.

Removing Duplicate Data

- Another type of invalid data that might be entered into a worksheet is a duplicate entry.

- Sometimes, duplicates are valid. For example, if two people happen to make $18.45 an hour, that might be perfectly normal. However, if the worksheet contains a database, such as a list of employees or customers, duplicates may indicate an error.

- To remove duplicate entries from a range, use the Remove Duplicates command. When you remove duplicate entries this way, Excel identifies what it considers duplicates, and automatically removes them for you.

  ✓ *You cannot remove duplicates from data that is outlined or subtotaled. To remove duplicates, remove the outlining/subtotaling.*

| Try It! | **Removing Duplicate Data** |

1 In the **E79Try_xx** file, click the Office Items worksheet tab.

2 Click DATA > Remove Duplicates to open the Remove Duplicates dialog box.

3 Under Columns, click to deselect all the check boxes except Catalog Item Number.

4 Click OK.

5 Click OK to the message that a duplicate has been removed.

6 Save the changes to the file, and leave it open to use in the next Try It.

The Remove Duplicates dialog box

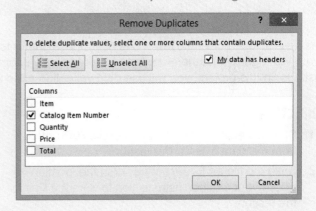

Controlling Recalculation

- **Recalculation** options allow you to control the way that Excel recalculates formulas.

- By default, Excel 2013 recalculates a worksheet as soon as you make a change to a formula or an element, such as a name, on which your formulas depend.

- If the worksheet is very large and contains tables whose formulas depend on several values, recalculation of those formulas can take a bit of time.

- When you recalculate a worksheet, the pointer changes to an hourglass, and the word "Recalculation" followed by the number of cells left to be recalculated appears on the left side of the formula bar.

- You can manually control when Excel calculates your worksheet.

- Use the commands in the Calculate group on the FORMULAS tab of the Ribbon.

- When manual recalculation is turned on and you make a change in a value, formula, or name, the "Calculate" message displays on the status bar.

- When you want Excel to recalculate a worksheet that has been set to manually calculate, use the Calculate Now command.

Try It! Changing Calculation Options

1 In the **E79Try_xx** file, on the Office Items worksheet, click FORMULAS.

2 Click Calculation Options ▦ > Manual.

3 Click cell C7, type **7**, and press ENTER . Notice that the total in cell E7 did not recalculate.

4 Click Calculate Now ▦ . The formulas calculate.

5 Click Calculation Options ▦ > Automatic.

6 Save and close the file, and exit Excel.

Lesson 79—Practice

As an employee of PhotoTown, one of your assignments is to make the photo product order form easier to use. Your manager wants the order form to contain only information that matches up with the inventory and product listings. In this project, you will use data validation rules and turn on manual recalculation of formulas.

DIRECTIONS

1. Start Excel, if necessary, and open **E79Practice** from the data files for this lesson.

2. Save the file as **E79Practice_xx** in the location where your teacher instructs you to store the files for this lesson.

3. For all worksheets, add a header that has your name at the left, the date code in the center, and the page number code at the right, and change back to **Normal** view.

4. On the **Order Form** worksheet, test the list-based order form:

   a. Click cell **B12**.

   b. Type **PZ101**, and press TAB . The Description field shows Photo puzzle, and the Size, Color, and Price per Item are filled in.

   c. Click cell **G12**, type **1**, and press ENTER .

5. Add a validation rule for the Item # field that permits only valid item numbers:

   a. Select the cell range **B12:B28**.

   b. Click **DATA** > **Data Validation** ▧ .

   c. Click the **Settings** tab, click the **Allow** drop-down arrow > **List**.

   d. Click the **Collapse Dialog** button ▦ next to the Source box.

   e. Click the **Product Listing** worksheet tab.

   f. Select the cell range **A9:A68**, and press ENTER to return to the dialog box.

   g. Click **OK** to create the rule.

6. Click cell **B13**, click the drop-down arrow that appears to the right, scroll down, and click **GC075**. The information about the product is filled in.

7. Click **FORMULAS** > **Calculation Options** ▦ > **Manual**.

8. Click cell **C13**, and look at the formula in the formula bar to see how the worksheet is constructed.

   ✓ An IF function evaluates B13 and then looks up data from the Product Listing sheet with VLOOKUP.

9. Click cell **G13**, type **2**, and press ENTER .

10. On the FORMULAS tab, click **Calculate Now** ▦ to calculate the formula.

11. Click **FORMULAS** > **Calculation Options** ▦ > **Automatic**.

12. **With your teacher's permission,** print the **Order Form** worksheet using **Fit Sheet on One Page**.

13. Save and close the file, and exit Excel.

Lesson 79—Apply

You are working with PhotoTown's photo product order form. Your manager wants you to add data validation messages to make the form easier for the customer to use. He wants the empty order rows to be removed whenever an order contains only a few items. You also need to limit the greeting card text box to a certain number of characters to match the character limit of the database. In this project, you will set data validation rules for the orders and use remove duplicates to remove the extra rows.

DIRECTIONS

1. Start Excel, if necessary, and open **E79Apply** from the data files for this lesson.

2. Save the file as **E79Apply_xx** in the location where your teacher instructs you to store the files for this lesson.

3. For all worksheets, add a header that has your name at the left, the date code in the center, and the page number code at the right, and change back to **Normal** view.

4. On the **Order Form** worksheet, add a validation rule for the Qty field (cell range **G12:G28**) that permits only whole positive numbers and shows a Stop type error message that explains the rule when it is violated.

5. Test the validation rule and make any corrections needed.

6. Add a validation rule for the Greeting card text box (merged cell **G35**) that permits a maximum of 180 characters. Set an input message of **Enter up to 180 characters**. If the rule is violated, an error message should appear: **Please enter a message of no more than 180 characters**.

7. To test the validation rule, attempt to enter the following text into cell **G35**. (Use ⌗ALT⌗ + ⌗ENTER⌗ to insert line breaks.) Press ⌗ENTER⌗ when finished.

   Wheaten's Glenn Apple Orchard
   First Annual Harvest Festival
   September 12th to 28th
   10:00 A.M. to 6:00 P.M.

   Hay rides, apple picking, cider
   tasting, corn maze, and more!
   Take NC-7 to R.R. 12, west 10 miles.

8. When the error message appears, click Retry, and edit the entry to fewer than 180 characters:

   Wheaten's Glenn Apple Orchard
   Harvest Festival
   Sept. 12th to 28th
   10 A.M. to 6 P.M.

   Hay rides, apple picking, cider
   tasting, corn maze, and more!
   NC-7 to R.R. 12, west 10m.

9. Click cell **G35** > HOME > **Top Align** ≡.

10. Use **Remove Duplicates** to remove any duplicate items in rows **B12:I28**.

    ✓ *This has the effect of removing all of the blank rows from the order form except one. However, it does not completely delete the rows; it only deletes their content and formatting.*

11. Select the unformatted rows (rows 16–28), and click **HOME** > **Delete** ✗. Your worksheet should look like the one shown in Figure 79-1 on the next page.

12. **With your teacher's permission,** print the **Order Form** worksheet using **Fit Sheet on One Page**.

13. Save and close the file, and exit Excel.

Figure 79-1

	A	B	C	D	E	F	G	H	I	J	K
1											
2	**PhotoTown**										
3											
4		Customer Photo Product Order Form									
5		Date		6/1/2013							
6											
7											
8	**Customer Name**										
9	**Address**				City		**State**		Zip		
10											
11		Item #	Description		Size		Color	Qty	Price per Item	Total	
12		PZ101	Photo puzzle		4" x 6"		65 piece	1	15	$ 15.00	
13		GC075	Photo card featuring a favorite 4" x 6" p		75 cards and envelopes		White	2	18	$ 36.00	
14		BL104	Mini football with favorite photo		N/A		N/A	1	25	$ 25.00	
15											
16								Total items ordered		4	
17								Subtotal		$ 76.00	
18								Tax		$ 4.56	
19								Grand total		$ 80.56	
20		**Special Instructions**									
21		*If you're ordering greeting cards, please select greeting to use*						Greeting card text (optional charge)			
22			We're married!			Baby's first birthday		Wheaten's Glenn Apple Orchard			
23			Our wedding day			Thank you!		Harvest Festival			
24			Look here's here (baby)			Many thanks		Sept. 12th to 28th			
25			Just arrived (baby)			Sending you lots of love		10 A.M. to 6 P.M.			
26			The newest edition (baby)			Merry Christmas and a Happy New Year		Hay rides, apple picking, cider			
27			Our family just got bigger (baby)			Greetings from our home to yours		tasting, corn maze, and more!			
28			Graduation day			Peace on earth		NC-7 to R.R. 12, west 10m.			
29			Announcing graduation			Happy holidays					
30			Look who's a year older!			Happy holidays from our family					
31			Peace, Pax, Paz			Happy holidays from all of us					
32			Lots of love from our family			Season's greetings					
33			Happy Hanukkah			Peace					
34			Shalom (dove)			Feliz navidad					
35			Shalom (night)			Feliz navidad y prospero ano					
36			Happy new year			We've moved!					
37											
38											
39											
40		Have you enclosed your photos or photo disc in the attached envelope?									
41											

Lesson 80

Protecting Data

➤ What You Will Learn

Locking and Unlocking Cells in a Worksheet
Protecting a Range
Protecting a Worksheet
Protecting a Workbook

Software Skills   If you design worksheets for others to use, or if you share a lot of workbooks, you may wish to protect certain areas of a worksheet from changes. You can protect any cell you want to prevent it from accepting new data or changes. You can also protect an entire worksheet or workbook so that others may only view its contents and not make changes.

What You Can Do

Locking and Unlocking Cells in a Worksheet

- To prevent changes to selected cells or ranges in a worksheet, you can **protect** the worksheet.
    - All cells in an Excel worksheet are **locked** by default.
    - When you turn on worksheet protection, the locked cells cannot be changed.
    - To allow changes in certain cells or ranges, unlock just those cells before protecting the worksheet.
    - If you **unlock** a cell that contains a formula, an Error Options button appears to remind you that you might not want to allow other people to change your formulas.

        ✓ *You can choose to ignore these errors when they appear, or tell Excel to lock the cell again.*

- If necessary, you can **unprotect** a protected worksheet so that you can change the data in locked cells.
- You can protect charts and other objects in a worksheet by using this same process.

WORDS TO KNOW

Lock
Cells that, if the worksheet is later protected, cannot be changed.

Protect
To prevent changes to locked or protected areas or objects.

Unlock
To enable changes in particular cells of a worksheet you want to later protect.

Unprotect
To remove protection from a worksheet or workbook.

Workbook structure
Excel 2013 enables you to preserve the structure of your workbook so that others cannot change the basic setup of the file. For example, preserving the structure ensures that others won't be able to add or remove worksheets.

- If someone tries to make a change to a protected cell, a message indicates that the cell is protected and considered read-only.

- You can use TAB to move between the unlocked cells of a protected worksheet.

- You can set the tab order of your worksheet by using locked and unlocked cells. For example, when you have both locked and unlocked cells in a protected worksheet, you can only tab into the unlocked cells.

- The tab order goes from left to right in the first row, then left to right in the second row, and so on. You can change the tab order by changing which cells are locked or unlocked.

- However, if ranges were locked using the Allow Users to Edit Ranges dialog box as explained in the next section, the Tab key does not work.

- Users can copy the data in a locked cell, but they can't move or delete it.

- Data can't be copied to a part of the worksheet that's protected.

Try It!   **Locking and Unlocking Cells in a Worksheet**

1 Start Excel, and open **E80Try** from the data files for this lesson.

2 Save the file as **E80Try_xx** in the location where your teacher instructs you to store the files for this lesson.

3 On the Order Form worksheet, lock the areas of the worksheet that customers will use to enter data:

  a. Select the cell range B8:B9.

  b. On the HOME tab, click Format [icon] > Lock Cell.

  c. Lock the following cells in the same manner: E9, G9, I9, B12:B28, G12:G28, B35:B49, D35:D49, B53, and G36.

4 Save the changes to the file, and leave it open to use in the next Try It.

The Lock Cells command

Protecting a Range

- When you unlock cells to allow changes, you can tell Excel to allow changes from anyone, or just selected individuals.

- To unlock cells for everyone, remove the Lock Cell protection format.

- To allow changes to selected individuals, use the Allow Users to Edit Ranges dialog box, shown in Figure 80-1 on the next page.

- When protecting ranges within a worksheet, you can tell Excel to create a workbook with the details of the permissions you've granted—the range addresses and passwords you've specified.

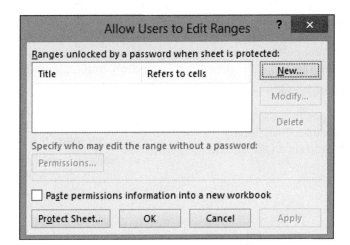

Figure 80-1

Try It! **Protecting a Range**

1 In the **E80Try_xx** file, click the Product Listing worksheet tab.

2 In the Name box, click the drop-down arrow, and click the range name Products, as shown in the figure below.

The Name box

3 Click REVIEW > Allow Users to Edit Ranges 🗐.

4 In the Allow Users to Edit Ranges dialog box, click New.

5 In the New Range dialog box, in the Title box, type **Product Listing**.

6 In the Range Password box, type **supersecret**, and click OK.

7 In the Confirm Password dialog box, type **supersecret**, and click OK.

8 In the Allow Users to Edit Ranges dialog box, click Protect Sheet.

9 In the Password to unprotect sheet box, type **supersecret**.

10 Check the Select locked cells, Select unlocked cells, Insert rows, and Sort check boxes to select them, and click OK.

11 Confirm the password, and click OK again.

12 Save the changes to the file, and leave it open to use in the next Try It.

The New Range dialog box

New Range

Title:
Product Listing

Refers to cells:
='Product Listing'!$A$9:$E$68

Range password:
●●●●●●●●●●●

Permissions...   OK   Cancel

Protecting a Worksheet

- Even if you activate worksheet protection, the cells you have unlocked are not protected.

  ✓ *Changes can still be made to those cells.*

- You can also prevent changes to objects, such as clip art or shapes, hyperlinks, PivotTables, and scenarios, which are stored variations of a worksheet.

- Use the options in the Protect Sheet dialog box to prevent certain actions, such as formatting, inserting columns and rows, deleting columns and rows, sorting, and filtering.

- You can password-protect the sheet so that no one can unprotect the worksheet accidentally.

  - If you forget the password, you will not be able to unprotect the worksheet later on.
  - However, you can copy the data to another, unprotected worksheet, to start over.
  - Passwords are case sensitive.

Try It! Protecting a Worksheet

1. In the **E80Try_xx** file, click the Order Form worksheet tab.
2. Click REVIEW > Protect Sheet 🔒.
3. In the Password to unprotect sheet box, type **mysecret**.
4. Under Allow all users of this worksheet to, click to deselect all check boxes except the Select unlocked cells checkbox, and click OK.
5. In the Confirm Password dialog box, type **mysecret**, and click OK.
6. Save the changes to the file, and leave it open to use in the next Try It.

Protect Sheet dialog box

Protecting a Workbook

- You can protect an entire workbook against certain kinds of changes.
- By protecting the **workbook structure**, you can prevent worksheets from being added, moved, hidden, unhidden, renamed, or deleted.
- You can also prevent a workbook's window from being resized or repositioned.

- You can add a password from the Protect Structure and Windows dialog box. A password will prevent users from changing the protection level of a workbook.
- If you want to share a workbook with others, and track the changes they make, you can still protect the workbook so that they can't erase the change history.

| Try It! | **Protecting a Workbook** |

1 In the **E80Try_xx** file, on the Order Form worksheet, on the REVIEW tab, click Protect Workbook ▦.

2 In the Protect Structure and Windows dialog box, click Structure, if necessary.

3 In the Password box, type **secret**, and click OK.

4 In the Confirm Password dialog box, type **secret**, and click OK.

5 Save and close the file, and exit Excel.

Lesson 80—Practice

You are the payroll manager for Marcus Furniture and you've just created the monthly earnings report used for generating commission checks. You need to have the data checked before the checks can be issued, but you want to ensure that no one can change the data in the file without notifying you. You want to protect certain areas of the worksheet, while still allowing you full access later.

DIRECTIONS

1. Start Excel, if necessary, and open **E80Practice** from the data files for this lesson.

2. Save the file as **E80Practice_xx** in the location where your teacher instructs you to store the files for this lesson.

3. On the **Feb Earnings** worksheet, unlock the areas into which data may be typed:

   a. Click the **Feb Earnings** worksheet tab, and select the cell range **D9:D23**.

   b. Click **HOME > Format** ▦ **> Lock Cell**.

   c. Repeat step b to unlock cell **A5**.

4. Protect the **Feb Earnings** worksheet so that only you can make changes:

   a. Click **REVIEW > Protect Sheet** ▦.

   b. In the Password to unprotect sheet box, type **protection**.

   c. In the **Allow all users of this worksheet to** section, verify that the **Select unlocked cells option** is the only check box checked, and click OK.

   d. In the Confirm Password dialog box, type **protection**, and click **OK**.

5. Test the worksheet protection:

   a. Click cell **D9**, type **5000**, and press ⏎.

   b. Click cell **A9**, and try to change the name. This cell should be locked and protected.

6. Save and close the file, and exit Excel.

Lesson 80—Apply

As the payroll manager for Marcus Furniture, you have created the monthly earnings report used for generating commission checks. You protected certain areas of the worksheet, and now you need to make some changes.

DIRECTIONS

1. Start Excel, if necessary, and open **E80Apply** from the data files for this lesson.

2. Save the file as **E80Apply_xx** in the location where your teacher instructs you to store the files for this lesson.

3. On the **Feb Earnings** worksheet, unprotect the worksheet.
   a. Click **REVIEW > Unprotect Sheet** 🔲.
   b. In the Password box, type **protection**, and click **OK**.

4. Edit the worksheet.
   a. Click cell **C11**, and type **$850**.
   b. Click cell **B17**, and type **Mary Williams**.
   c. Click cell **C17**, type **$750**, and press ENTER.

5. Protect the worksheet again; do not set a password.

6. Type the sales amounts in column D that are shown in Figure 80-2 on the next page.

7. Copy the **Feb Earnings** worksheet, place it before the **Comm-Bonus** worksheet, and name it **Mar Earnings**.

8. Change the text in cell **A5** to **March Earnings Report**.

9. Try to make an entry in any cell in the table other than in the Sales column to see if the cells are still locked.

10. Make an entry in the **Sales** column to see if the cells are unlocked, and delete all the entries in the Sales column.

11. For all worksheets, add a header that has your name at the left, the date code in the center, and the page number code at the right, and change back to **Normal** view.

12. **With your teacher's permission**, print the **Feb Earnings** worksheet.

13. Save and close the file, and exit Excel.

Figure 80-2

	A	B	C	D	E	F	G	H
1								
2								
3				**Marcus Furniture**				
4								
5				February Earnings Report				
6								
7			BASE		COMM.	COMM.		TOTAL
8		ASSOCIATE	SALARY	SALES	RATE	AMT.	BONUS	EARNINGS
9		Bob Walraven	$1,000.00	$14,978.00	11%	$1,647.58	$450.00	$3,097.58
10		Mike Davis	$1,000.00	$10,254.00	8%	$820.32	$300.00	$2,120.32
11		Bill Mergenthal	$850.00	$7,521.00	5%	$376.05	$0.00	$1,226.05
12		Pete Sanger	$850.00	$9,874.00	7%	$691.18	$250.00	$1,791.18
13		Dorothy Bishop	$750.00	$6,023.00	4%	$240.92	$0.00	$990.92
14		Mary La Rue	$1,100.00	$13,458.00	11%	$1,480.38	$450.00	$3,030.38
15		Ernest Dedmon	$1,000.00	$9,141.00	7%	$639.87	$250.00	$1,889.87
16		Karen Frisch	$750.00	$10,394.00	8%	$831.52	$300.00	$1,881.52
17		Mary Williams	$750.00	$7,889.00	5%	$394.45	$0.00	$1,144.45
18		Mike McCutcheon	$750.00	$6,574.00	4%	$262.96	$0.00	$1,012.96
19		Lorna Myers	$900.00	$10,974.00	8%	$877.92	$300.00	$2,077.92
20		James Neely	$950.00	$14,958.00	11%	$1,645.38	$450.00	$3,045.38
21		Scott Gratten	$850.00	$13,425.00	11%	$1,476.75	$450.00	$2,776.75
22		Betty Miller	$925.00	$10,957.00	8%	$876.56	$300.00	$2,101.56
23		Fillard Willmore	$1,000.00	$14,958.00	11%	$1,645.38	$450.00	$3,095.38

Lesson 81

Securing a Workbook

➤ What You Will Learn

Using Document Inspector
Encrypting a Workbook
Identifying Workbooks Using Keywords

Software Skills   As you prepare a workbook to share with others, it's important to know how to secure the file in various ways. Excel 2013 enables you to inspect your workbook for hidden properties or personal information you might not want to share. You can also encrypt your workbook and assign a password. You can add tags to the file to help you find it easily later when you search for it.

What You Can Do

Using Document Inspector

- The **Document Inspector** in Excel 2013 enables you to check the workbook for information that you don't want to share with others.
- The tool evaluates the workbook for hidden properties or personal information you might not want to share.
- By default, all the check boxes in the Document Inspector are selected. Use the Remove All command to remove any information you don't want to include in the presentation, and then use Reinspect to reinspect the document.

Try It! Using Document Inspector

1 Start Excel, and open **E81Try** from the data files for this lesson.

2 Save the file as **E81Try_xx** in the location where your teacher instructs you to store the files for this lesson.

3 Click FILE.

4 In the Backstage view, on the Info tab, click Check for Issues ⊘.

5 Click Inspect Document > Inspect. Review the inspection results.

6 Click Close to close the Document Inspector.

7 Click the Back button ⊙ to exit the Backstage view.

8 Save the changes to the file, and leave it open to use in the next Try It.

The Document Inspector inspection results

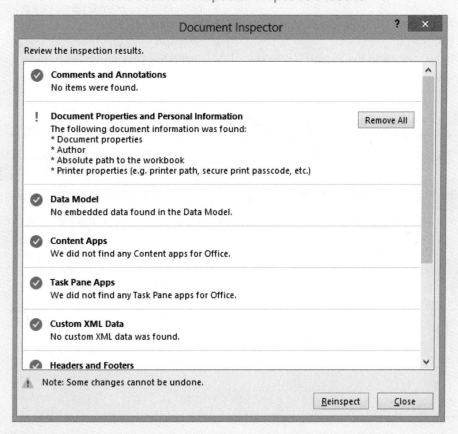

Encrypting a Workbook

■ Encrypting a workbook protects the workbook and enables you to assign a password so that others can open the file only if they have the necessary password.

■ Excel will prompt you to enter and then re-enter the password.

■ Keep the password in a safe place because Excel does not store a copy of the password in a way that you can retrieve it if you forget it later.

■ You can remove password **encryption** by displaying the Encrypt Document dialog box, clearing the entry in the Password box, and clicking OK.

Try It!   **Encrypting with a Password**

1 In the **E81Try_xx** file, click FILE.

2 In the Backstage view, on the Info tab, click Protect Workbook 🔒.

3 Click Encrypt with Password.

4 In the Encrypt Document dialog box, in the Password box, type **newpres34**, and click OK.

5 In the Confirm Password dialog box, in the Reenter password box, type **newpres34**.

6 Click OK.

7 Save the changes to the file, and leave it open to use in the next Try It.

Identifying Workbooks Using Keywords

■ You can add keywords to help you identify the workbook in a search.

■ Enter tags for the workbook in the Properties area of the Info tab of the Backstage view.

■ To enter multiple keywords or key phrases, separate the keywords or key phrases with commas.

■ You can remove keywords and other **metadata** using the Document Properties panel.

Try It!   **Adding Keywords to a Workbook**

1 In the **E81Try_xx** file, click FILE.

2 In the Backstage view, on the right side of the Info tab, click the Properties button.

3 Click Show Document Panel.

4 In the Document Properties panel, in the Keywords box, type **gardening, budget**.

5 Close the Document Properties panel.

6 Save and close the file, and exit Excel.

The Document Properties panel

ℹ Document Properties ▼			Location:	C:\Users\studentuser\Documents\E81Try_xx.xlsx		✳ Required field ✕
Author:	Title:	Subject:		Keywords:	Category:	
Firstname Lastname				gardening, budget		
Status:						
Comments:						

Lesson 81—Practice

You are working on a workbook for two clients. You will inspect the workbook for issues, apply passwords, and add keywords to the workbook properties.

DIRECTIONS

1. Start Excel, if necessary, and open **E81Practice** from the data files for this lesson.
2. Save the file as **E81Practice_xx** in the location where your teacher instructs you to store the files for this lesson.
3. Click **FILE**.
4. In the Backstage view, on the Info tab, click **Check for Issues** 🔍 > **Inspect Document**.
5. In the Document Inspector, click **Inspect**.
6. Review the results, and click **Close** to close the Document Inspector.
7. In the Backstage view, on the Info tab, click **Protect Workbook** 🔒 > **Encrypt with Password**.
8. In the Encrypt Document dialog box, in the Password box, type **pass123#**, and click **OK**.

9. In the Confirm Password dialog box, in the Reenter password box, type **pass123#**, and click **OK**.
10. In the Backstage view, on the Info tab, click **Properties** > **Show Document Panel**.
11. In the Document Properties panel, in the Keywords box, type **inventory, reorders**.
12. Close the Document Properties panel.
13. Save the file.
14. Click **FILE**. The Info tab of the Backstage view should look like the one shown in Figure 81-1.
15. Click the Back button 🔙 to exit the Backstage view.
16. Save and close the file, and exit Excel.

Figure 81-1

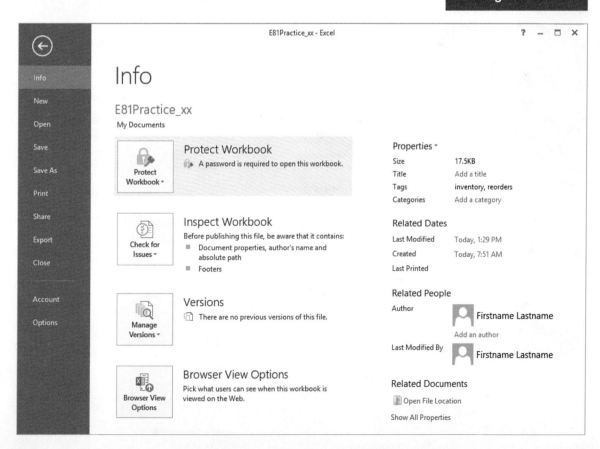

Lesson 81—Apply

You are working on worksheets for two clients. You will inspect the worksheets for issues, apply passwords, and protect the worksheets. You will also add keywords to the properties.

DIRECTIONS

1. Start Excel, if necessary, and open **E81Apply** from the data files for this lesson.
2. Save the file as **E81Apply_xx** in the location where your teacher instructs you to store the files for this lesson.
3. Run the Document Inspector, and remove any found information.

4. Add the password **marketing456&** to the workbook.
5. Add the keywords **marketing, yearly budget** to the workbook, and close the Document Properties panel. Your workbook should look like the one shown in Figure 81-2.
6. Save and close the file, and exit Excel.

Figure 81-2

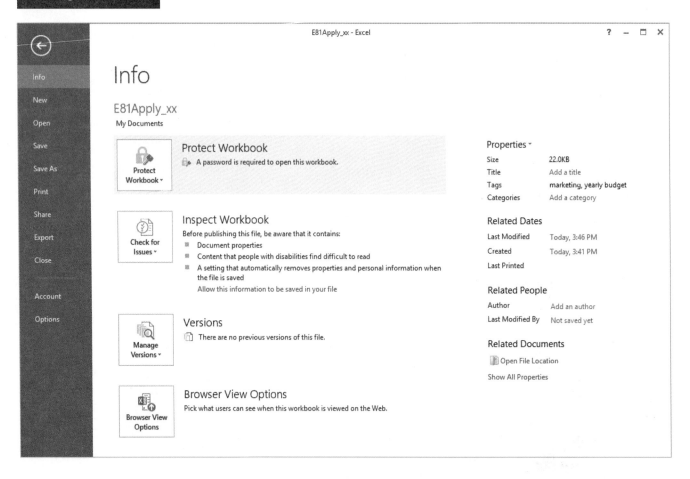

Lesson 82

Finalizing a Workbook

➤ What You Will Learn

Adding a Digital Signature
Checking for Accessibility Issues
Marking a Workbook As Final
Managing Versions

Software Skills   Especially when you're working with sensitive financial data, you need some way of letting others know a workbook they review is authentically from you. You can digitally sign the workbook to let your colleagues know that they are working with an approved version of the file. Excel 2013 offers features to make workbooks easier for users with disabilities to use. You can check the accessibility of your workbook and correct a workbook for possible issues. When you are finished with your workbook, you can mark it as final to show that no further changes should be made to the file. Use Excel's Manage Versions feature to search for an auto-saved version of a file you have not yet manually saved.

What You Can Do

Adding a Digital Signature

■ You can apply a **digital signature** to a worksheet or a workbook to indicate that the information is authentically from you.

■ To sign the worksheet or workbook with a digital signature, you need a digital ID. You can obtain a digital ID from a Microsoft Partner.

✓ *Follow your instructor's instruction on how—or whether—to use digital signatures with Microsoft Excel.*

■ You can add a digital signature line to a worksheet by using the Signature Line command in the Text group on the INSERT tab.

■ To sign a digital signature line, right-click the digital signature line and click Sign.

■ You can assign a digital signature to a workbook by clicking FILE, and using the Protect Workbook command on the Info tab in the Backstage view.

■ When you add a digital signature, you can enter a purpose or instructions to the signer.

■ A digital signature remains valid as long as the workbook is not changed.

■ If you change the workbook at a later time, you will need to sign the file again to make the signature valid.

WORDS TO KNOW

Accessibility
The ability to make documents easier for people with disabilities to use.

Accessibility Checker
A feature in Excel that checks for and displays issues in a document that might be challenging for a user with a disability.

Alternative text (alt text)
Text that appears when you move the mouse pointer over a picture or object.

Digital Signature
An electronic signature that is stored with the workbook to let others know the file is authentic or meets a standard that is important to the group.

Try It! Adding a Digital Signature Line to a Worksheet

1. Start Excel, and open **E82Try** from the data files for this lesson.

2. Save the file as **E82Try_xx** in the location where your teacher instructs you to store the files for this lesson.

3. Click cell F16.

4. Click INSERT > Signature Line 🖊.

5. In the Signature Setup dialog box, click in the Suggested signer box, and type your name.

6. Click OK. A digital signature line appears.

7. Save the changes to the file, and leave it open to use in the next Try It.

The Signature Setup dialog box

Signature Setup

Suggested signer (for example, John Doe):
Firstname Lastname

Suggested signer's title (for example, Manager):

Suggested signer's e-mail address:

Instructions to the signer:
Before signing this document, verify that the content you are signing is correct.

☐ Allow the signer to add comments in the Sign dialog
☑ Show sign date in signature line

OK   Cancel

Try It! Adding a Digital Signature

1. In the **E82Try_xx** file, click FILE.

2. In the Backstage view, on the Info tab, click Protect Workbook 🔒 > Add a Digital Signature.

   ✓ Follow your instructor's instruction on how—or whether—to use digital signatures with Microsoft Excel.

3. If so instructed, in the Get a Digital ID dialog box, click No.

4. In the worksheet, right-click the digital signature line, and click Sign.

5. If so instructed, in the Get a Digital ID dialog box, click No.

6. Save the changes to the file, and leave it open to use in the next Try It.

Checking for Accessibility Issues

- You can use **accessibility** features in Excel 2013 to make workbooks more accessible to users with disabilities.

- Use the **Accessibility Checker** to check and correct a workbook for possible issues that might make it hard for a user with a disability to read or interpret the content.

- Access the Accessibility Checker from the Check for Issues button on the Info tab on the FILE tab in the Backstage view.

- **Alternative text**, or **alt text**, is an accessibility feature that helps people who use screen readers to understand the content of a picture in a workbook.

   ✓ Alt text may not work with touch-screen or mobile devices.

- When making a workbook accessible, you should include alt text for objects such as pictures, embedded objects, charts, and tables.

- When you use a screen reader to view a workbook, or save it to a file format such as HTML, alt text appears in most browsers when the picture doesn't display.

   ✓ You may have to adjust the computer's browser settings to display alt text.

- You can add alt text from the Size & Properties button on the Format Picture task pane.

Try It! Using the Accessibility Checker

1. In the **E82Try_xx** file, click FILE.

2. In the Backstage view, on the Info tab, click Check for Issues 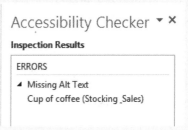 > Check Accessibility. Notice the Missing Alt Text error.

3. Save the changes to the file, and leave it open to use in the next Try It.

The Accessibility Checker task pane

> Accessibility Checker ▾ ✕
>
> **Inspection Results**
>
> ERRORS
>
> ◢ Missing Alt Text
>   Cup of coffee (Stocking _Sales)

Try It! Adding Alternative Text (Alt Text)

1. In the **E82Try_xx** file, right-click the picture of the cup of coffee, and click Size & Properties to display the Size & Properties group of the Format Picture task pane.

2. Click ALT TEXT.

3. Click in the Title box, and type **Cup of coffee**.

4. Click in the Description box, and type **A picture of the best coffee from Grounds for Thought**. The Accessibility Checker Inspection Results now finds no accessibility issues.

5. Close the Format Picture and Accessibility Checker task panes.

6. Save the changes to the file, and leave it open to use in the next Try It.

The ALT TEXT group of the Format Picture task pane

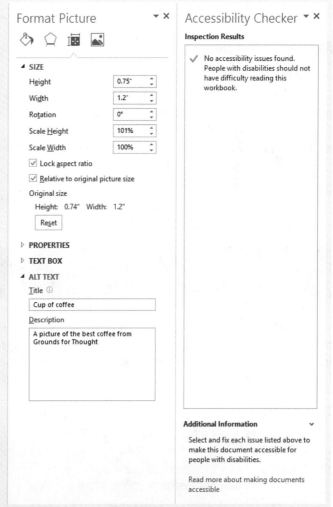

Marking a Workbook As Final

■ When you mark your workbook as final, colleagues who view the workbook see that it is marked as read-only so no further changes can be made.

■ The message bar at the top of the Excel window lets users know that the file has been marked as final.

■ For many general purposes, this level of protection may be fine, but users can click Edit Anyway in the message bar to continue to edit the file.

■ Users can save the workbook under another name and edit the file as desired.

■ If you need stronger security for the workbook, add a password or restrict editing privileges before sharing the file.

■ When a file is marked as final, the Marked As Final icon appears in the status bar.

■ When you add a digital signature to a file, the file is automatically marked as final.

■ Before you can mark a file as final, you must turn off workbook sharing.

Try It!   Marking a Workbook As Final

❶ In the **E82Try_xx** file, click FILE > Protect Workbook 🖫.

❷ Click Mark as Final.

❸ Click OK.

❹ In the information message box, click OK.

❺ Close the file, and exit Excel.

Managing Versions

■ Excel automatically saves your workbooks to a temporary folder while you are working on them.

■ If you forget to save your changes, or if Excel crashes, you can restore the file using AutoRecover.

■ If you don't see the file in the AutoRecover list, or if you're looking for an auto-saved version of a file that has no previously saved versions, you can use the Manage Versions feature to search for the file.

■ Access the Manage Versions command from the Info tab of the FILE tab.

■ You can recover unsaved workbooks from the default location of the UnsavedFiles folder.

■ You can also use the Manage Versions command to delete all unsaved workbooks.

Lesson 82—Practice

You work for the Grounds for Thought Coffee Company, and you need to enhance the company's expense report form. This form will allow employees to get reimbursed by the company. You want to add two digital signature lines to the worksheet, one for the employee and one for the manager. You also want to check for any accessibility issues and correct them.

DIRECTIONS

1. Start Excel, if necessary, and open **E82Practice** from the data files for this lesson.

2. Save the file as **E82Practice_xx** in the location where your teacher instructs you to store the files for this lesson.

3. Add a header that has your name at the left, the date code in the center, and the page number code at the right, and change back to **Normal** view.

4. Add a digital signature for an employee signature in cell C20:

   a. Click cell **C20**.

   b. Click **INSERT > Signature Line** 📝.

   c. In the Signature Setup dialog box, click in the **Suggested signer** box, and type **Employee Signature**.

   d. Click **OK**.

5. Add a digital signature for a manager in cell F20 using the process in step 4.

6. Check the workbook for accessibility issues:

   a. Click **FILE**.

   b. In the Backstage view, on the Info tab, click **Check for Issues** 🗐 **> Check Accessibility**.

7. Ignore the Merged Cells errors, and correct the missing alt text error:

   a. Right-click the picture of the cup of coffee, and click **Size & Properties**.

   b. Click **ALT TEXT**.

   c. Click in the **Title** box, and type **Cup of coffee**.

   d. Click in the **Description** box, and type **A picture of a cup of French Roast coffee**.

8. Close the Format Picture and Accessibility Checker task panes.

9. Change the page layout orientation to **Landscape**.

10. **With your teacher's permission,** print the worksheet. Your workbook should look like the one shown in Figure 82-1.

11. Save and close the file, and exit Excel.

Figure 82-1

	A	B	C	D	E	F	G	H	I	J	K	L
1	Expense Report											
2												
3												
4	PURPOSE:				STATEMENT NUMBER:							
5												
6	EMPLOYEE INFORMATION:											
7		Name				Position						
8		Department				Manager			Employee ID			
9												
10	Date	Account	Description		Hotel	Transport	Fuel	Meals	Phone	Entertainment	Misc	Total
11												
12	Total				$ -	$ -	$ -	$ -	$ -	$ -	$ -	$ -
13										Subtotal	$ -	
14										Cash Advances		
15		NOTES:								Total	$ -	
16												
17												
18												
19												
20												
21												
22												
23			X			X						
24			Employee Signature			Manager Signature						
25												

Lesson 82—Apply

You have just traveled to a coffee convention for the Grounds for Thought Coffee Company. You now need to complete an expense report to get reimbursed by the company for your travel expenses. You want to complete the worksheet, check for and correct any accessibility issues, and mark the workbook as final before submitting it to your manager.

DIRECTIONS

1. Start Excel, if necessary, and open **E82Apply** from the data files for this lesson.

2. Save the file as **E82Apply_xx** in the location where your teacher instructs you to store the files for this lesson.

3. In cell **C7**, type your name.

4. In cell **A11**, type today's date.

5. Add a digital signature to the Employee Signature line.

   a. Right-click the **Employee Signature line**.

   b. Click **Sign**.

   c. Follow your instructor's instruction on how to sign with a digital signature.

6. Check the workbook for accessibility issues. Ignore the Merged Cells errors.

7. Mark the workbook as final:

   a. Click **FILE** > **Protect Workbook** 🖫.

   b. Click **Mark as Final**.

   c. Click **OK**.

   d. In the information message box, click **OK**.

8. Close any open task panes.

9. Close the file, and exit Excel.

Lesson 83

Sharing a Workbook

➤ What You Will Learn

Setting Precise Margins for Printing
Uploading a Workbook to Windows Live SkyDrive

Software Skills   After you finish working with workbook content and adding a digital signature, you may be ready to share your file with others. Excel 2013 makes it easy to send a worksheet to colleagues. You can make some last-minute choices about the margins for printing the worksheet information and, if you like, you can post the workbook on Windows Live SkyDrive so that you can access and modify it using the Excel 2013 Web App.

What You Can Do

Setting Precise Margins for Printing

- Excel 2013 offers a number of ways to control what you want to print.
- You can set a print area by highlighting the range you want to print and clicking Print Area in the PAGE LAYOUT tab. Use the Set Print Area command to let the program know you want to print the highlighted range.
- You can enter precise measurements for the margins by setting print options:
  - Click FILE to display the Backstage view, and click Print. Click the Margins arrow toward the bottom of the center column, and click Custom Margins.
  - Enter the values you want to set for each of the page areas: header, right margin, footer, bottom margin, left margin, and top margin.
  - If you want to center the content horizontally or vertically (or both), click the check boxes in the Center on page area of the Page Setup dialog box.

WORDS TO KNOW

Windows Live SkyDrive
A free Microsoft offering that is part of Windows Live, enabling you to post and share documents in a Web-based library. You can also use Windows Live SkyDrive with the Excel Web App to co-author workbooks.

Excel Web App
The online version of Excel 2013 that you can access through Windows Live SkyDrive or SharePoint Workspace 2013.

Try It!   Setting Precise Margins for Printing

1 Start Excel, and open **E83Try** from the data files for this lesson.

2 Save the file as **E83Try_xx** in the location where your teacher instructs you to store the files for this lesson.

3 Click FILE > Print.

4 Click Normal Margins ⬚ > Custom Margins.

5 In the Page Setup dialog box, set the Top margin to 1.0, the Bottom margin to 1.25, and the Left and Right margins to 1.2.

6 Under Center on page, click to select the Horizontally check box.

7 Click OK.

8 Save the changes to the file, and leave it open to use in the next Try It.

Setting precise margins

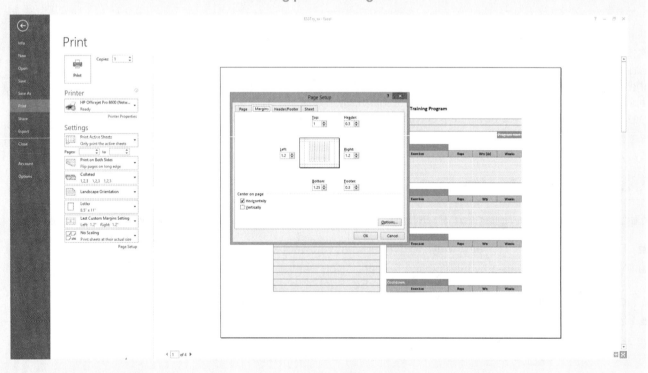

Uploading a Workbook to Windows Live SkyDrive

■ Excel 2013 offers you the ability to save a workbook to your **Windows Live SkyDrive** account so that you can work on it from any point you have Web access.

■ If you don't have a Windows Live SkyDrive account, Excel 2013 will prompt you to create one when you choose Save To Cloud on the Share tab in the Backstage view.

■ After you save the workbook file to your Windows Live SkyDrive account, you can access the file using the **Excel Web App**.

■ Once you have Web access, you can log in to your Windows Live account.

■ You can use the Excel Web App to open, review, and edit your workbook online.

■ When you open a workbook in the Excel Web App, the workbook opens in the Edit in Browser view and automatically displays the Ribbon with the tools you need to review, edit, and save the file.

■ You can choose to open the workbook in Excel instead of working in it in the Excel Web App.

■ Your changes to a file in Excel Web App are automatically saved.

Try It!   Uploading a Workbook to Windows Live SkyDrive

1 In the **E83Try_xx** file, click FILE > Save As.

2 Click SkyDrive ☁.

3 If you don't have a Windows Live SkyDrive account, click Sign up.

✓ *Your instructor will let you know if you should sign up for an account.*

OR

If you already have an account, click Sign In, enter your Windows Live ID e-mail address and password, and click OK.

4 Click your SkyDrive ☁.

5 Click the folder in which you want to save the file.

✓ *Your instructor will let you know which account and folder to use to store the file.*

6 In the Save As dialog box, in the File name box, type **E83Try_webapp_xx**.

7 Click Save.

8 Close the workbook, and close Excel.

Try It!   Working in the Excel Web App

1 Open your Web browser, and go to **https://skydrive.live.com**.

2 Log in with your Windows Live ID.

3 Click the folder in which you saved the workbook file.

4 Click the workbook to display it in the Microsoft Excel Web App window. The Excel Web App automatically displays the Ribbon with the tools you need to review, edit, and save the file.

5 In the Excel Web App, on the Info & Schedule worksheet tab, click cell E4 and type **Jonas Smith**.

6 Click cell E5, and type your name.

7 In the Excel Web app, click the OPEN IN EXCEL tab.

8 Click Yes to confirm that you want to open the file. The workbook opens in Excel.

9 Click cell J6, and type today's date.

10 Save the Excel file, and close Excel.

11 In the browser window, click **E83Try_webapp_xx**, and view the changes.

12 Review the workbook in the browser.

13 In the Microsoft Excel Web App window, click FILE > Exit.

14 Close the browser to sign out of SkyDrive.

(continued)

Working in the Excel Web App

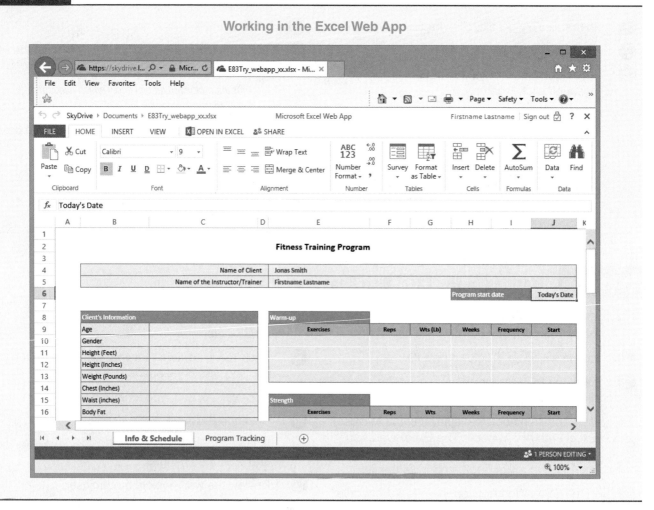

Lesson 83—Practice

You and two of your colleagues are collaborating on a research project that requires you to gather field data from a variety of sites around the United States. During the course of your research, you will need to be able to share your workbook with each other online. You want to change the margins of the data tables so that you can print your results to be included in the final research workbook.

DIRECTIONS

1. Start Excel, if necessary, and open **E83Practice** from the data files for this lesson.

2. Save the file as **E83Practice_xx** in the location where your teacher instructs you to store the files for this lesson.

3. Click **FILE > Print**.

4. Click **Normal Margins** ⬚ **> Custom Margins**.

5. In the Page Setup dialog box, set the **Top** margin to **0.5**, the **Bottom** margin to **0.5**, and the **Left** and **Right** margins to **1.0**.

6. Click **OK**.

7. Click **No Scaling** > **Fit Sheet on One Page**.

8. Click Save.

9. Save the file to the SkyDrive:

   ✓ *Your instructor will let you know if you should sign up for an account.*

   a. Click **FILE** > **Save As**.

   b. If you already have an account, click **Sign In**, enter your Windows Live ID e-mail address and password, and click **OK**.

   c. Click your **SkyDrive** ☁️ , if necessary, and click the folder in which you want to save the file.

   ✓ *Your instructor will let you know which account and folder to use to store the file.*

   d. In the Save As dialog box, in the File name box, type **E83Practice_webapp_xx**.

   e. Click **Save**.

10. Close the workbook in Excel.

11. Open your Web browser, and go to **https://skydrive.live.com**.

12. Log in with your Windows Live ID.

13. Click the folder where you saved the workbook, and click the **E83Practice_webapp_xx** workbook to display it in the Excel Web App.

14. Edit the file in your browser by changing the dates in the Survey 1 column to the current date. Your file should look like the one shown in Figure 83-1.

15. Click **FILE** > **Exit**.

16. Close the browser to sign out of SkyDrive.

Figure 83-1

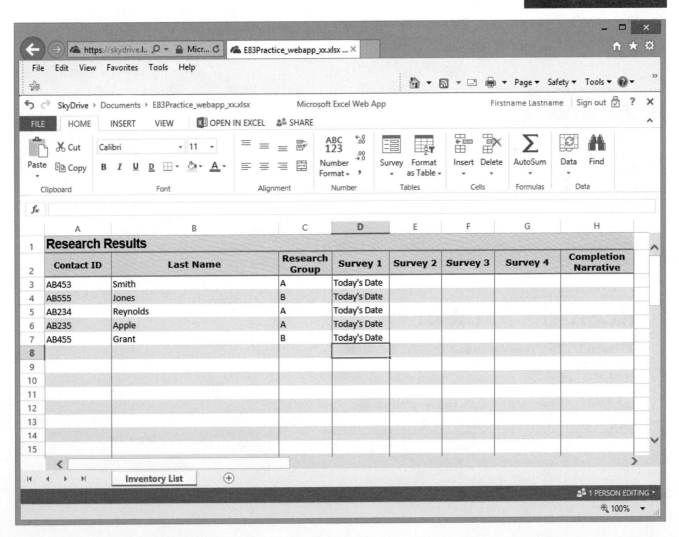

Lesson 83—Apply

You are collaborating on a research project with several other people. You need to gather field data from a variety of sites around the United States. During the course of your research, you want to share your workbook online and set custom print margins so that the full report can be printed.

DIRECTIONS

1. Start Excel, if necessary, and open **E83Apply** from the data files for this lesson.

2. Save the file as **E83Apply_xx** in the location where your teacher instructs you to store the files for this lesson.

3. Set the print margins for the worksheet so that the content is centered **vertically** and **horizontally** on the page and the margins are **0.75** all the way around.

4. Save the file to your SkyDrive account as **E83Apply_webapp_xx**, close the Excel workbook, and close Excel.

5. Open your Web browser, and go to **https://skydrive.live.com**.

6. Log in with your Windows Live ID.

7. Click the SkyDrive folder where you saved the workbook file.

8. Click the **E83Apply_webapp_xx** workbook to display it in the Excel Web App.

9. In the Excel Web App, enter the following data in the cell range A6:D7 as shown in Figure 83-2:

AB235	Apple	A	10/1/2014
AB455	Grant	B	9/30/2014

10. Click **FILE > Exit**.

11. Close the browser to sign out of SkyDrive.

Figure 83-2

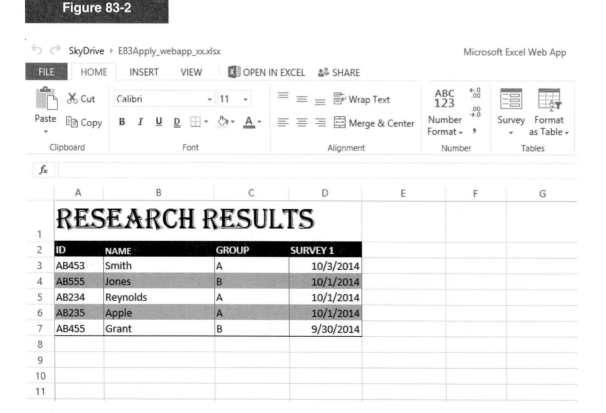

End-of-Chapter Activities

➤ Excel Chapter 10—Critical Thinking

Assessing Educational Outcomes

Your school has been working hard to raise test scores in Math and Science, and one of the projects your teachers have undertaken this year involves doing a series of assessments that track a series of results in Math and Science classes.

You have been given a workbook that someone else created, so you want to check the workbook for data integrity and accessibility. Because a variety of teachers will be adding values to the worksheet, you need to set up the file for track changes and sharing. You also want to use data validation rules to circle the failing scores and make them easier to identify. You will encrypt the file and save it to a Windows Live SkyDrive account so all teachers can access the file from home as well as school.

DIRECTIONS

1. Start Excel, if necessary, and open **ECT10** from the data files for this chapter.

2. Save the file as **ECT10_xx** in the location where your teacher has instructed you to save files for this chapter.

3. Inspect the workbook for issues. Do not remove any of the document properties or personal information.

4. Check and correct any accessibility issues.

5. Click **REVIEW**, and turn on the sharing feature.

6. Set Track Changes to highlight all changes that are introduced. In the **When** box, select **All**.

7. Make changes to the values in column E.

8. Save the file, and use Highlight Changes to display the change history on a new sheet.

9. View the change history.

10. Remove sharing from the workbook.

11. In cell I22, add a digital signature line, and in the suggested signer box, type **Approver for assessment scores**.

12. For all cells with scores, add data validation for a **whole number** that is **greater than or equal to 25**. Circle the invalid data of failing percentages.

13. Save the file, and then save the file to your Windows Live SkyDrive account as **ECT10_webapp_xx**. Close the Excel workbook, and close Excel.

14. Open your Web browser, and go to **https://skydrive.live.com**.

   ✓ *Check with your instructor before you access the Web. Depending on the security settings for your computer lab, you may be limited in the types of sites you can access and use.*

15. Log in to your Windows Live SkyDrive account, and open the workbook.

16. Click OK to remove the data validation and digital signature objects from the file.

17. Edit the file in the browser by making changes to the values, and save the file. Your file should look similar to Illustration 10A on the next page.

18. **With your teacher's permission,** print the workbook, and write your name and today's date on the printout.

19. Close the browser to sign out of SkyDrive.

Illustration 10A

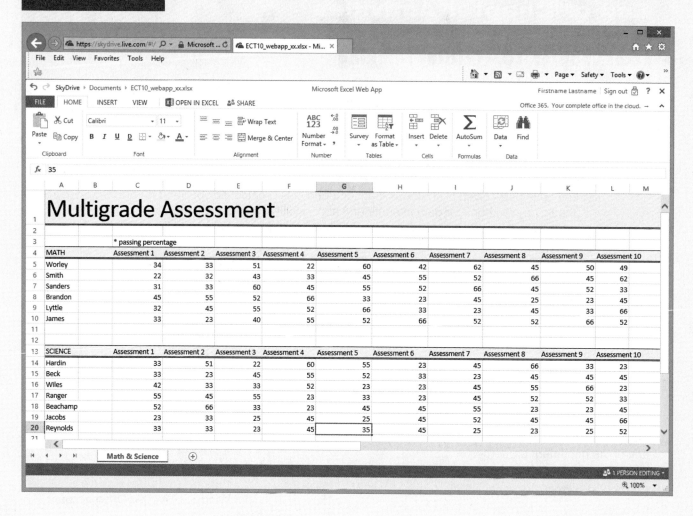

➤ Excel Chapter 10—Portfolio Builder

Budgeting a Movie

You've been working with a local video producer to help him put together a treatment for a new film he wants to produce. It's been a fun project, and now some major industry investors are interested in finding out more about the production.

The producer has asked you to create a draft of the budget that you, he, and the director will fine-tune together. You need to create the worksheet, share the file, password protect the worksheet, and save it to Windows Live SkyDrive so that each of you can access the file from any point you have Web access.

DIRECTIONS

1. Start Excel, if necessary, and open **EPB10** from the data files for this chapter.

2. Save the file as **EPB10_xx** in the location where your teacher has instructed you to save files for this chapter.

3. Set up the workbook for sharing.

4. Set the tracking options so all changes are recorded.

5. Enter dollar values in the cell range **E16:21** and the cell range **G16:21**.

6. Save the workbook, and display the change history.

7. On **Sheet1**, set the print margins to **0.5** all around, and center the content on the page.

8. Remove sharing from the workbook.

9. Protect the workbook structure. Do not use a password.

10. Mark the file as final.

11. Edit the file to remove the worksheet protection features.

12. Save the file to Windows Live SkyDrive as **EPB10_webapp_xx**. Close the Excel workbook, and close Excel.

13. Open the file in the Excel Web App, and edit the workbook in the browser window.

14. **With your teacher's permission,** print the workbook, and write your name and today's date on the printout.

15. Close the browser to sign out of SkyDrive.

Index